# David Sang, Graham Jones, Richard Woodside and Gurinder Chadha

## Cambridge International AS and A Level

# Physics
## Coursebook

**Completely Cambridge -Cambridge resources for Cambridge qualifications**

Cambridge University Press works closely with University of Cambridge International Examinations (CIE) as parts of the University of Cambridge.
We enable thousands of students to pass their CIE exams by providing comprehensive, high-quality, endorsed resources.

To find out more about University of Cambridge International Examinations
visit www.cie.org.uk

To find out more about Cambridge University Press
visit www.cambridge.org/cie

## CAMBRIDGE
### UNIVERSITY PRESS

CAMBRIDGE UNIVERSITY PRESS
Cambridge, New York, Melbourne, Madrid, Cape Town,
Singapore, São Paulo, Delhi, Mexico City

Cambridge University Press
The Edinburgh Building, Cambridge CB2 8RU, UK

www.cambridge.org
Information on this title: www.cambridge.org/9780521183086

First published 2010
7th printing 2013

Printed in India by Replika Press Pvt. Ltd

*A catalogue record for this publication is available from the British Library*

ISBN 978-0-521-18308-6 Paperback with CD-ROM for Windows and Mac

# Contents

| | |
|---|---|
| Introduction | vii |
| Acknowledgements | viii |

## 1 Kinematics – describing motion — 1

| | |
|---|---|
| Speed | 1 |
| Distance and displacement, scalar and vector | 4 |
| Speed and velocity | 5 |
| Displacement–time graphs | 7 |
| Combining displacements | 9 |
| Combining velocities | 10 |

## 2 Accelerated motion — 15

| | |
|---|---|
| The meaning of acceleration | 15 |
| Calculating acceleration | 15 |
| Units of acceleration | 16 |
| Deducing acceleration | 17 |
| Deducing displacement | 18 |
| Measuring velocity and acceleration | 19 |
| Determining velocity and acceleration in the laboratory | 19 |
| The equations of motion | 21 |
| Deriving the equations of motion | 24 |
| Uniform and non-uniform acceleration | 25 |
| Acceleration caused by gravity | 26 |
| Determining $g$ | 27 |
| Motion in two dimensions – projectiles | 30 |
| Understanding projectiles | 32 |

## 3 Dynamics – explaining motion — 40

| | |
|---|---|
| Calculating the acceleration | 40 |
| Understanding SI units | 42 |
| The pull of gravity | 44 |
| Mass and inertia | 46 |
| Top speed | 47 |
| Moving through fluids | 49 |
| Identifying forces | 50 |
| Newton's third law of motion | 53 |

## 4 Forces – vectors and moments — 57

| | |
|---|---|
| Combining forces | 57 |
| Components of vectors | 59 |
| Centre of gravity | 62 |
| The turning effect of a force | 63 |
| The torque of a couple | 67 |

## 5 Work, energy and power — 73

| | |
|---|---|
| Doing work, transferring energy | 74 |
| Gravitational potential energy | 78 |
| Kinetic energy | 79 |
| g.p.e.–k.e. transformations | 80 |
| Down, up, down – energy changes | 81 |
| Energy transfers | 82 |
| Power | 85 |

## 6 Momentum — 92

| | |
|---|---|
| The idea of momentum | 92 |
| Modelling collisions | 93 |
| Understanding collisions | 95 |
| Explosions and crash landings | 98 |
| Momentum and Newton's laws | 100 |
| Understanding motion | 100 |

## 7 Matter — 107

| | |
|---|---|
| Macroscopic properties of matter | 107 |
| The kinetic model | 110 |
| Explaining pressure | 112 |
| Changes of state | 113 |

## 8 Deforming solids — 119

| | |
|---|---|
| Compressive and tensile forces | 119 |
| Stretching materials | 121 |
| Describing deformation | 124 |
| Strength of a material | 125 |
| Elastic potential energy | 126 |

## 9 Electric fields — 132

| | |
|---|---|
| Attraction and repulsion | 132 |
| Investigating electric fields | 134 |
| Electric field strength | 136 |
| Force on a charge | 138 |

## 10 Electric current, potential difference and resistance    144

Circuit symbols and diagrams    144
Electric current    145
The meaning of voltage    148
Electrical resistance    149
Electrical power    151

## 11 Kirchhoff's laws    157

Kirchhoff's first law    157
Kirchhoff's second law    159
Applying Kirchhoff's laws    160
Resistor combinations    162
Ammeters and voltmeters    165

## 12 Resistance and resistivity    171

The $I$–$V$ characteristic for a
   metallic conductor    172
Ohm's law    173
Resistance and temperature    174
Resistivity    177

## 13 Practical circuits    183

Internal resistance    184
Potential dividers    186
Potentiometer circuits    189

## 14 Waves    195

Describing waves    195
Longitudinal and transverse waves    198
Wave energy    199
Intensity    199
Wave speed    200
Electromagnetic waves    202
Electromagnetic radiation    203
Orders of magnitude    203
The nature of electromagnetic waves    204
Polarisation    204

## 15 Superposition of waves    212

The principle of superposition of waves    212
Diffraction of waves    213
Interference    216
The Young double-slit experiment    220
Diffraction gratings    223

## 16 Stationary waves    231

From moving to stationary    231
Nodes and antinodes    232
Formation of stationary waves    232
Observing stationary waves    233
Determining the wavelength
   and speed of sound    237
Eliminating errors    238

## 17 Radioactivity    242

Looking inside the atom    242
Alpha-particle scattering and
   the nucleus    242
A simple model of the atom    245
Nucleons and electrons    246
Discovering radioactivity    249
Radiation from radioactive substances    249
Properties of ionising radiation    251
Randomness and decay    254

## 18 Circular motion    258

Describing circular motion    258
Angles in radians    259
Steady speed, changing velocity    260
Angular velocity    261
Centripetal forces    262
Calculating acceleration and force    264
The origins of centripetal forces    266

## 19 Gravitational fields 272

| | |
|---|---|
| Representing a gravitational field | 273 |
| Gravitational field strength $g$ | 275 |
| Energy in a gravitational field | 277 |
| Gravitational potential | 277 |
| Orbiting under gravity | 278 |
| The orbital period | 279 |
| Orbiting the Earth | 280 |

## 20 Oscillations 287

| | |
|---|---|
| Free and forced oscillations | 287 |
| Observing oscillations | 288 |
| Describing oscillations | 289 |
| Simple harmonic motion | 291 |
| Graphical representations of s.h.m. | 292 |
| Frequency and angular frequency | 294 |
| Equations of s.h.m. | 295 |
| Energy changes in s.h.m. | 299 |
| Damped oscillations | 300 |
| Resonance | 302 |

## 21 Thermal physics 312

| | |
|---|---|
| Changes of state | 312 |
| Energy changes | 313 |
| Internal energy | 315 |
| The meaning of temperature | 317 |
| Thermometers | 318 |
| Calculating energy changes | 320 |

## 22 Ideal gases 330

| | |
|---|---|
| Molecules in a gas | 330 |
| Measuring gases | 331 |
| Boyle's law | 332 |
| Changing temperature | 333 |
| Ideal gas equation | 334 |
| Modelling gases – the kinetic model | 336 |
| Temperature and molecular kinetic energy | 338 |

## 23 Coulomb's law 343

| | |
|---|---|
| Electric fields | 343 |
| Coulomb's law | 343 |
| Electric field strength for a radial field | 345 |
| Electric potential | 346 |
| Comparing gravitational and electric fields | 350 |

## 24 Capacitance 356

| | |
|---|---|
| Capacitors in use | 356 |
| Energy stored in a capacitor | 358 |
| Capacitors in parallel | 361 |
| Capacitors in series | 362 |
| Comparing capacitors and resistors | 363 |
| Capacitor networks | 364 |

## 25 Magnetic fields and electromagnetism 371

| | |
|---|---|
| Producing and representing magnetic fields | 371 |
| Magnetic force | 374 |
| Magnetic flux density | 375 |
| Measuring magnetic flux density | 376 |
| Currents crossing fields | 378 |
| Forces between currents | 380 |
| Relating SI units | 381 |

## 26 Charged particles 387

| | |
|---|---|
| Observing the force | 387 |
| Orbiting charges | 389 |
| Electric and magnetic fields | 391 |
| Discovering the electron | 393 |

## 27 Electromagnetic induction 399

| | |
|---|---|
| Observing induction | 399 |
| Explaining electromagnetic induction | 400 |
| Faraday's law of electromagnetic induction | 405 |

Lenz's law 407
Using induction: eddy currents, generators and transformers 410

## 28 Alternating currents 416

Sinusoidal current 416
Alternating voltages 417
Measurements using a cathode-ray oscilloscope 418
Power and a.c. 419
Why use a.c. for electricity supply? 421
Transformers 422
Rectification 424

## 29 Quantum physics 431

Modelling with particles and waves 431
Particulate nature of light 433
The photoelectric effect 437
Line spectra 440
Explaining the origin of line spectra 441
Photon energies 443
Isolated atoms 444
The nature of light – waves or particles? 444
Electron waves 444
The nature of the electron – wave or particle? 448

## 30 Nuclear physics 454

Mass and energy 454
Energy released in radioactive decay 457
Binding energy and stability 458
The mathematics of radioactive decay 460
Decay graphs and equations 462
Decay constant and half-life 464

## 31 Direct sensing 469

Sensor components 469
The operational amplifier (op-amp) 473
Negative feedback 477

The inverting amplifier 478
The non-inverting amplifier 479
Output devices 480

## 32 Medical imaging 487

The nature and production of X-rays 487
X-ray attenuation 490
Improving X-ray images 491
Computerised axial tomography 494
Using ultrasound in medicine 498
Echo sounding 500
Ultrasound scanning 502
Magnetic resonance imaging 504

## 33 Communications systems 512

Radio waves 512
Analogue and digital signals 517
Channels of communication 520
Comparison of different channels 523

## Appendices 534

A1 Practical skills at AS level 534

A2 Further practical skills 546

B Physical quantities and units 554
C Data, formulae and relationships 555
D The Periodic Table 557

## Answers to Test yourself questions 558

## Glossary 585

## Index 595

This book covers the entire syllabus of CIE Physics for A and AS level. It is in three parts:

- Chapters 1–17: the AS level content, covered in the first year of the course;
- Chapters 18–33: the remaining A level content, including Applications of Physics, covered in the second year of the course;
- Appendices: practical skills, and useful data and formulae.

The main task of a textbook like this is to explain the various concepts of physics which you need to understand and to provide you with questions which will help you to test your understanding and prepare for the examinations. You will find that each chapter has the same structure.

- At the start there are objectives, mapping out the content of the chapter.
- The main text explains ideas and outlines the evidence which supports them.
- Worked examples show how to tackle particular types of problems.
- 'Test yourself' questions allow you to check your understanding as you go along.
- At the end, there is a detailed summary which links back to the objectives at the start.
- Finally, at the end of each chapter there are questions of two sorts: general questions which relate to the material covered in the whole chapter, and exam-style questions which will give you practice at tackling the sort of structured questions which appear in exams.

When tackling questions, it is a good idea to make a first attempt without referring to the textbook or to your notes. This will help to reveal any gaps in your understanding. By sorting out any problems at an early stage you will progress faster as the course continues.

The CD-ROM which accompanies this book includes a worksheet for each chapter with more questions. The later questions on each worksheet are designed to provide more of a challenge for able students.

In this book, the maths has been kept to the minimum required by the CIE Physics AS and A level syllabus. If you are also studying mathematics, you may find that more advanced techniques such as calculus will help you with many aspects of physics.

Studying physics can be a stimulating and worthwhile experience. It is an international subject; no single country has a monopoly on the development of the ideas. Discovering how men and women from many countries have contributed to our knowledge and well-being can be a rewarding exercise. We hope that this book will help you to succeed in examinations but also that it will stimulate your curiosity and fire your imagination. Today's students become the next generation of physicists and engineers, and we hope that you will learn from the past to take physics to ever greater heights.

# Acknowledgements

We would like to thank the following for permission to reproduce images:

Cover, Omikron / SPL

Figure 1.1, Edward Kinsman / Photo Researchers, Inc.; 1.2, Yves Herman / Reuters / Corbis; 1.3, © Dominic Burke / Alamy; 1.13a, Robert Harding Picture Library / Alamy; 2.1, Time & Life Pictures / Getty Images; 2.7, David Scharf; 2.12, Lockheed Martin Astronautics; 2.22, Michel Pissotte / Action Plus; 2.27, Professor Harold Egerton / SPL; 3.1, Getty Images; 3.6, Blickwinkel / Schmidbauer / Alamy; 3.7, Keith Kent / SPL; 3.9, Richard Francis / Action Plus; 3.11, Jamie Squire / Staff / Getty; 3.12, Mira / Alamy; 4.1, Phil Cole / Staff / Getty; 4.9, Andrew Lambert / SPL; 4.14, AFP / Getty; 4.16, Corbis Premium RS / Alamy; 5.1, George Steinmetz; 5.2, Popperfoto; 5.3, Mike Clarke / Getty; 5.12, Images Colour Library; 5.15, Bob Martin / Allsport; 5.16, SPL; 5.19, AustraliaLK; 6.1, TRL Ltd. / SPL; 6.2, arabianEye; 6.3, Andrew Lambert; 6.4, Andrew Lambert; 6.7, Motoring Picture Library / Alamy; 6.12, SPL; 6.14, SPL; 7.1, Andrew Dunn; 8.1, Stacy Walsh Rosenstock / Alamy; 8.17, Alex Wong / Getty; 9.1, Kent Wood / SPL; 9.4, Sheila Terry / SPL; 9.6, Andrew Lambert / SPL; 9.14, Andrew Lambert / SPL; 10.1, Adam Hart-Davis / SPL; 10.2, Adam Hart-Davis / SPL; 10.3, Adam Hart-Davis / SPL; 10.4, Adam Hart-Davis / SPL; 10.11, Andrew Lambert; 10.13, Leslie Garland Picture Library ; 10.14, Maxamillian Stock LTD / SPL; 11.1, TEK Image / SPL; 11.2, CC Studio / SPL; 11.19, Andrew Lambert; 11.23, Andrew Lambert / SPL; 12.1, Takeshi Takahara / SPL ; 12.4, imagebroker / Alamy; 12.5, Richard Megna / Fundamental Photos / SPL; 13.1a, SPL; 13.1b, Sheila Terry; 13.10, Andrew Lambert; 14.1, Jim Reed Photography / SPL; 14.2, SPL; 14.4, Hermann Eisenbeiss / SPL; 14.6, sciencephotos / Alamy; 14.10, Tom Pietrasik / Corbis; 14.11, © Popperfoto / Reuters; 14.12, Chris Pearsall / Alamy; 14.13, Dr Morley Read / SPL; 14.14, Physics Today Collection / American Institute of Physics / SPL; 14.20, Michael Brooke; 14.21, Peter Aprahamian / Sharples Stress Engineers Ltd / SPL; 15.1, Pascal Goetgheluck / SPL; 15.2, ImageState / Alamy; 15.7, ImageState / Alamy; 15.9, © superclic / Alamy; 15.14, © Bruce Coleman Inc. / Alamy; 15.21, © Phototake Inc. / Alamy; 15.24, Photography by Ward; 16.1a, Alex Bartel / SPL; 16.1b, Bettmann / CORBIS; 16.2, Tim Ridley; 16.7, Andrew Lambert; 16.13, hipp stenoglepsis / Ian Sanders / Alamy; 17.1, Karen Kasmauski; 17.2, University Of Cambridge, Cavendish Laboratory; 17.8, Stocktrek Images, Inc. / Alamy; 17.9, Jean-Loup Charmet / SPL; 17.14, N Feather / SPL; 17.17, Leslie Garland Picture Library / Alamy; 17.18, Andrew Lambert / SPL; 18.1, Dinodia Images / Alamy; 18.12, Marvin Dembinsky Photo Associates; 18.16, Action plus sports images; 19.1, Ken Fisher; 19.10, © NASA Images / Alamy; 20.1, iStock; 20.2, Andrew Lambert; 20.3, Andrew Lambert / SPL; 20.14, Gurinder Chadha; 20.29, Robin MacDougall; 20.31, Andrew Lambert / SPL; 20.33, David Leah / SPL; 20.35, Simon Fraser; 21.1, Tony Camacho / SPL; 21.6, Martyn F. Chillmaid / SPL; 21.12, Andrew Lambert / SPL; 22.1, Patrick Dumas / Eurelios / SPL; 22.2, David Mack / SPL; 23.1, Health Protection Agency / SPL; 24.1, David Hay Jones / SPL; 24.2, Andrew Lambert / SPL; 25.1, Alex Bartel / SPL; 25.12, Martyn F. Chillmaid / SPL; 26.1, Omikron / SPL; 26.2, Andrew Lambert / SPL; 26.8, Andrew Lambert / SPL; 26.12, SPL; 27.1, Sean Gallup / Getty Images; 27.15, Bill Longchore / SPL; 28.1, Tom Bonaventure; 28.3, Adam Gault / SPL; 28.7, Andrew Lambert Photography / SPL; 28.10, Chris Knapton / SPL; 28.13, Greenshoots Communications / Alamy; 20.28, Andrew Lambert / SPL; 20.30, Andrew Lambert / SPL; 29.1, © PHOTOTAKE Inc. / Alamy; 29.2, © STphotography / Alamy; 29.3, Paul Broadbent / Alamy; 29.5, Volker Steger / SPL; 29.12, Department of Physics Imperial College / SPL; 29.13, Department of Physics Imperial College / SPL; 29.14, Department of Physics Imperial College / SPL; 29.19, SPL; 29.20, SPL; 29.21, Professor Dr Hannes Lichte, Technische Universitat, Dresden; 29.23, Dr David Wexler, coloured by Dr Jeremy Burgess / SPL; 29.24, Dr Tim Evans / SPL; 30.1, US Navy / SPL; 31.1, Ria Novosti; 31.9, Cristian Nitu; 31.10, sciencephotos / Alamy; 31.21, Simon Belcher; 32.1, Mauro Fermariello / SPL; 32.3, AJ Hop Photo / Hop Americain / SPL; 32.8, Edward Kinsman / SPL; 32.14, Zephyr / SPL; 32.15, GustoImages / SPL; 32.17, Michelle Del Guercio / SPL; 32.20, Scott Camazine / SPL; 32.21, medicimage; 32.25, GustoImages / SPL; 32.28, Professor AT Elliott, Department of Clinical Physics and Bioengineering, Glasgow University; 32.29, Geoff Tomkinson / SPL; 32.35, Alfred Pasieka / SPL; 32.36, Sovereign, ISM / SPL; 33.1, SPL; 33.2, S. Hammid; 33.13, iStock; 33.14, iStock; 33.15, iStock; 33.17, Peter Ryan / SPL; 33.19, Eyebyte / Alamy.

SPL = Science Photo Library

The author and publishers are grateful for the permissions granted to reproduce materials in either the original or adapted form. While every effort has been made, it has not always been possible to identify the sources of all the materials used, or to trace all copyright holders. If any omissions are brought to our notice, we will be happy to include the appropriate acknowledgements on reprinting.

# 1 Kinematics – describing motion

## Objectives

After studying this chapter, you should be able to:

- [ ] define displacement, speed and velocity
- [ ] draw and interpret displacement–time graphs
- [ ] describe laboratory methods for determining speed
- [ ] use vector addition to add two or more vectors

## Describing movement

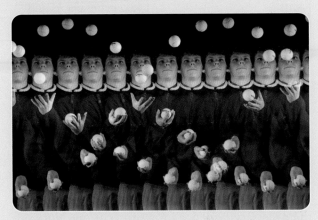

**Figure 1.1** This boy is juggling three balls. A stroboscopic lamp flashes at regular intervals; the camera is moved to one side at a steady rate to show separate images of the boy.

Our eyes are good at detecting movement. We notice even quite small movements out of the corners of our eyes. It's important for us to be able to judge movement – think about crossing the road, cycling or driving, or catching a ball.

Figure 1.1 shows a way in which movement can be recorded on a photograph. This is a stroboscopic photograph of a boy juggling three balls. As he juggles, a bright lamp flashes several times a second so that the camera records the positions of the balls at equal intervals of time.

If we knew the time between flashes, we could measure the photograph and calculate the speed of a ball as it moves through the air.

## Speed

We can calculate the average speed of something moving if we know the distance it moves and the time it takes:

$$\text{average speed} = \frac{\text{distance}}{\text{time}}$$

In symbols, this is written as: $v = \dfrac{x}{t}$

where $v$ is the average speed and $x$ is the distance travelled in time $t$. The photograph (Figure 1.2) shows Ethiopia's Kenenisa Bekele posing next to the score board after breaking the world record in a men's 10 000 metres race. The time on the clock in the photograph enables us to work out his average speed.

If the object is moving at a constant speed, this equation will give us its speed during the time taken. If its speed is changing, then the equation gives us its **average speed**. Average speed is calculated over a period of time.

**Figure 1.2** Ethiopia's Kenenisa Bekele set a new world record for the 10 000 metres race in 2005.

If you look at the speedometer in a car, it doesn't tell you the car's average speed; rather, it tells you its speed at the instant when you look at it. This is the car's **instantaneous speed**.

## Test yourself

1 Look at Figure **1.2**. The runner ran 10 000 m, and the clock shows the total time taken. Calculate his average speed during the race.

## Units

In the Système Internationale d'Unités (the SI system), distance is measured in metres (m) and time in seconds (s). Therefore, speed is in metres per second. This is written as $m\,s^{-1}$ (or as m/s). Here, $s^{-1}$ is the same as 1/s, or 'per second'.

There are many other units used for speed. The choice of unit depends on the situation. You would probably give the speed of a snail in different units from the speed of a racing car. Table **1.1** includes some alternative units of speed.

Note that in many calculations it is necessary to work in SI units ($m\,s^{-1}$).

| | |
|---|---|
| $m\,s^{-1}$ | metres per second |
| $cm\,s^{-1}$ | centimetres per second |
| $km\,s^{-1}$ | kilometres per second |
| $km\,h^{-1}$ or km/h | kilometres per hour |
| mph | miles per hour |

**Table 1.1** Units of speed.

## Drive slower, live longer

Modern cars are designed to travel at high speeds – they can easily exceed national speed limits. However, road safety experts are sure that driving at lower speeds increases safety and saves the lives of drivers, passengers and pedestrians in the event of a collision. The police must identify speeding motorists. They have several ways of doing this.

On some roads, white squares are painted at intervals on the road surface. By timing a car between two of these markers, the police can determine whether the driver is speeding. Speed cameras can measure the speed of a passing car. The camera shown in Figure **1.3** is of the type known as a 'Gatso'. The camera is usually mounted in a yellow box, and the road has characteristic markings painted on it.

The camera sends out a radar beam (radio waves) and detects the radio waves reflected by a car. The frequency of the waves is changed according to the instantaneous speed of the car. If the car is travelling above the speed limit, two photographs are taken of the car. These reveal how far the car has moved in the time interval between the photographs, and these can provide the necessary evidence for a prosecution. Note that the radar 'gun' data is not itself sufficient; the device may be confused by multiple reflections of the radio waves, or when two vehicles are passing at the same time.

Note also that the radar gun provides a value of the vehicle's instantaneous speed, but the photographs give the average speed.

**Figure 1.3** A typical 'Gatso' speed camera (named after its inventor, Maurice Gatsonides). The box contains a radar speed gun which triggers a camera when it detects a speeding vehicle.

# Determining speed

You can find the speed of something moving by
measuring the time it takes to travel between two fixed
points. For example, some motorways have emergency
telephones every 2000 m. Using a stopwatch you
can time a car over this distance. Note that this can
only tell you the car's average speed between the two
points. You cannot tell whether it was increasing its
speed, slowing down, or moving at a constant speed.

## Laboratory measurements of speed

Here are some different ways to measure the speed of
a trolley in the laboratory as it travels along a straight
line. They can be adapted to measure the speed of
other moving objects, such as a glider on an air track,
or a falling mass.

## Using two light gates

The leading edge of the card in Figure 1.4 breaks
the light beam as it passes the first light gate. This

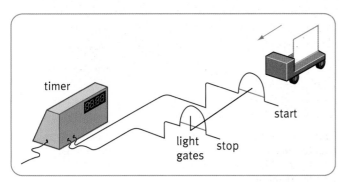

Figure 1.4 Using two light gates to find the average speed of
a trolley.

starts the timer. The timer stops when the front of
the card breaks the second beam. The trolley's speed
is calculated from the time interval and the distance
between the light gates.

## Using one light gate

The timer in Figure 1.5 starts when the leading edge
of the card breaks the light beam. It stops when the
trailing edge passes through. In this case, the time
shown is the time taken for the trolley to travel a
distance equal to the length of the card. The computer
software can calculate the speed directly by dividing
the distance by the time taken.

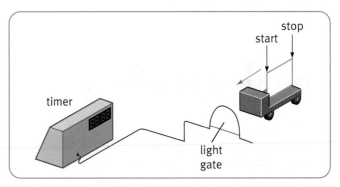

Figure 1.5 Using a single light gate to find the average speed of
a trolley.

## Using a ticker-timer

The ticker-timer (Figure 1.6) marks dots on the tape
at regular intervals, usually $\frac{1}{50}$ s (i.e. 0.02 s). (This
is because it works with alternating current, and in
most countries the frequency of the alternating mains

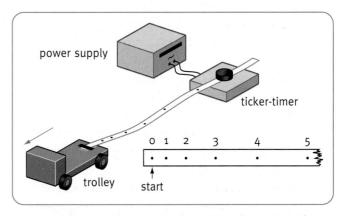

Figure 1.6 Using a ticker-timer to investigate the motion of
a trolley.

is 50 Hz.) The pattern of dots acts as a record of the trolley's movement.

Start by inspecting the tape. This will give you a description of the trolley's movement. Identify the start of the tape. Then look at the spacing of the dots:

• even spacing – constant speed
• increasing spacing – increasing speed.

Now you can make some measurements. Measure the distance of every fifth dot from the **start** of the tape. This will give you the trolley's distance at intervals of 0.1 s. Put the measurements in a table. Now you can draw a distance–time graph.

### Using a motion sensor

The motion sensor (Figure 1.7) transmits regular pulses of ultrasound at the trolley. It detects the reflected waves and determines the time they took for the trip to the trolley and back. From this, the computer can deduce the distance to the trolley from the motion sensor. It can generate a distance–time graph. You can determine the speed of the trolley from this graph.

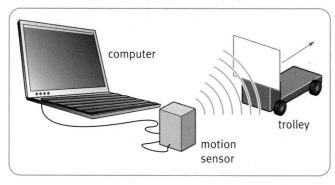

**Figure 1.7** Using a motion sensor to investigate the motion of a trolley.

### Choosing the best method

Each of these methods for finding the speed of a trolley has its merits. In choosing a method, you might think about the following points.

• Does the method give an average value of speed or can it be used to give the speed of the trolley at different points along its journey?
• How precisely does the method measure time – to the nearest millisecond?
• How simple and convenient is the method to set up in the laboratory?

4 A trolley with a 5.0 cm long card passed through a single light gate. The time recorded by a digital timer was 0.40 s. What was the average speed of the trolley in m s⁻¹?

5 Figure **1.8** shows two ticker-tapes. Describe the motion of the trolleys which produced them.

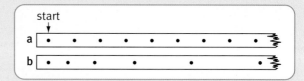

**Figure 1.8** Ticker-tapes; for Test yourself Q **5**.

6 Four methods for determining the speed of a moving trolley have been described. Each could be adapted to investigate the motion of a falling mass. Choose two methods which you think would be suitable, and write a paragraph for each to say how you would adapt it for this purpose.

# Distance and displacement, scalar and vector

In physics, we are often concerned with the distance moved by an object in a particular direction. This is called its **displacement**. Figure **1.9** illustrates the difference between distance and displacement. It shows the route followed by walkers as they went from town A to town C. Their winding route took them through town B, so that they covered a total distance of 15 km. However, their displacement was much less than this. Their finishing position was just 10 km from where they started. To give a complete statement of their displacement, we need to give both distance and direction:

displacement = 10 km 30° E of N

Displacement is an example of a **vector quantity**. A vector quantity has both magnitude (size) and direction. Distance, on the other hand, is a **scalar quantity**. Scalar quantities have magnitude only.

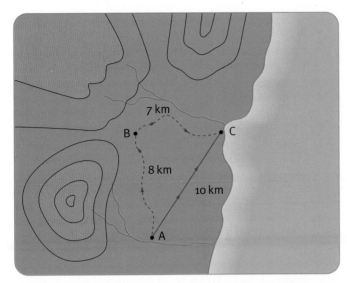

**Figure 1.9** If you go on a long walk, the distance you travel will be greater than your displacement. In this example, the walkers travel a distance of 15 km, but their displacement is only 10 km, because this is the distance from the start to the finish of their walk.

| Quantity | Symbol for quantity | Symbol for unit |
|---|---|---|
| distance | $d$ | m |
| displacement | $s, x$ | m |
| time | $t$ | s |
| speed, velocity | $v$ | $m\,s^{-1}$ |

**Table 1.2** Standard symbols and units. (Take care not to confuse italic *s* for displacement with s for seconds. Notice also that *v* is used for both speed and velocity.)

> ### *Test yourself*
>
> 7  Which of these gives speed, velocity, distance or displacement? (Look back at the definitions of these quantities.)
>    **a** The ship sailed south-west for 200 miles.
>    **b** I averaged 7 mph during the marathon.
>    **c** The snail crawled at $2\,mm\,s^{-1}$ along the straight edge of a bench.
>    **d** The sales representative's round trip was 420 km.

# Speed and velocity

It is often important to know both the speed of an object and the direction in which it is moving. Speed and direction are combined in another quantity, called **velocity**. The velocity of an object can be thought of as its speed in a particular direction. So, like displacement, velocity is a **vector** quantity. Speed is the corresponding scalar quantity, because it does not have a direction. So, to give the velocity of something, we have to state the direction in which it is moving. For example, an aircraft flies with a velocity of $300\,m\,s^{-1}$ due north. Since velocity is a vector quantity, it is defined in terms of displacement:

$$\text{velocity} = \frac{\text{change in displacement}}{\text{time taken}}$$

Alternatively, we can say that velocity is the rate of change of an object's displacement. From now on, you need to be clear about the distinction between velocity and speed, and between displacement and distance. Table **1.2** shows the standard symbols and units for these quantities.

## Speed and velocity calculations

We can write the equation for velocity in symbols:

$$v = \frac{s}{t}$$

$$v = \frac{\Delta s}{\Delta t}$$

The word equation for velocity is:

$$\text{velocity} = \frac{\text{change in displacement}}{\text{time taken}}$$

Note that we are using $\Delta s$ to mean 'change in displacement *s*'. The symbol $\Delta$, Greek letter delta, means 'change in'. It does not represent a quantity (in the way that *s* does); it is simply a convenient way of representing a change in a quantity. Another way to write $\Delta s$ would be $s_2 - s_1$, but this is more time-consuming and less clear.

The equation for velocity, $v = \frac{\Delta s}{\Delta t}$, can be rearranged as follows, depending on which quantity we want to determine:

$$\text{change in displacement } \Delta s = v \times \Delta t$$

change in time $\Delta t = \dfrac{\Delta s}{v}$

Note that each of these equations is balanced in terms of units. For example, consider the equation for displacement. The units on the right-hand side are $m\,s^{-1} \times s$, which simplifies to m, the correct unit for displacement.

Note also that we can, of course, use the same equations to find speed and distance, that is:

speed $v = \dfrac{d}{t}$

distance $d = v \times t$

time $t = \dfrac{d}{v}$

## Worked examples

1   A car is travelling at $15\,m\,s^{-1}$. How far will it travel in 1 hour?

**Step 1** It is helpful to start by writing down what you know and what you want to know:

$v = 15\,m\,s^{-1}$
$t = 1\,h = 3600\,s$
$d = ?$

**Step 2** Choose the appropriate version of the equation and substitute in the values. Remember to include the units:

$d = v \times t$
$\quad = 15 \times 3600$
$\quad = 5.4 \times 10^4\,m$
$\quad = 54\,km$

The car will travel 54 km in 1 hour.

2   The Earth orbits the Sun at a distance of 150 000 000 km. How long does it take light from the Sun to reach the Earth? (Speed of light in space $= 3.0 \times 10^8\,m\,s^{-1}$.)

continued ⋯⟶

**Step 1** Start by writing what you know. Take care with units; it is best to work in m and s. You need to be able to express numbers in scientific notation (using powers of 10) and to work with these on your calculator.

$v = 3.0 \times 10^8\,m\,s^{-1}$
$x = 150\,000\,000\,km$
$\quad = 150\,000\,000\,000\,m$
$\quad = 1.5 \times 10^{11}\,m$

**Step 2** Substitute the values in the equation for time:

$t = \dfrac{x}{v} = \dfrac{1.5 \times 10^{11}}{3.0 \times 10^8} = 500\,s$

Light takes 500 s (about 8.3 minutes) to travel from the Sun to the Earth.

In examinations, many candidates lose marks because of problems with calculators. Always use your own calculator. To calculate the time $t$, you press the buttons in the following sequence:

[1.5] [EXP] [11] [÷] [3] [EXP] [8]

or

[1.5] [×10ⁿ] [11] [÷] [3] [×10ⁿ] [8]

## Making the most of units

In Worked example 1 and Worked example 2, units have been omitted in intermediate steps in the calculations. However, at times it can be helpful to include units as this can be a way of checking that you have used the correct equation; for example, that you have not divided one quantity by another when you should have multiplied them. The units of an equation must be balanced, just as the numerical values on each side of the equation must be equal.

If you take care with units, you should be able to carry out calculations in non-SI units, such as kilometres per hour, without having to convert to metres and seconds.

For example, how far does a spacecraft travelling at $40\,000\,\text{km}\,\text{h}^{-1}$ travel in one day? Since there are 24 hours in one day, we have:

$$\text{distance travelled} = 40\,000\,\text{km}\,\text{h}^{-1} \times 24\,\text{h}$$
$$= 960\,000\,\text{km}$$

## Test yourself

8   A submarine uses sonar to measure the depth of water below it. Reflected sound waves are detected 0.40 s after they are transmitted. How deep is the water? (Speed of sound in water = $1500\,\text{m}\,\text{s}^{-1}$.)

9   The Earth takes one year to orbit the Sun at a distance of $1.5 \times 10^{11}$ m. Calculate its speed. Explain why this is its average speed and not its velocity.

# Displacement–time graphs

We can represent the changing position of a moving object by drawing a displacement–time graph. The gradient (slope) of the graph is equal to its velocity (Figure 1.10). The steeper the slope, the greater the velocity. A graph like this can also tell us if an object is moving forwards or backwards. If the gradient is negative, the object's velocity is negative – it is moving backwards.

## Test yourself

10  The displacement–time sketch graph in Figure 1.11 represents the journey of a bus. What does the graph tell you about the journey?

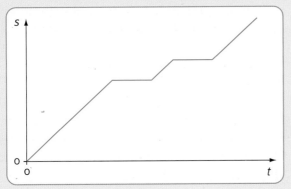

**Figure 1.11** For Test yourself Q 10.

*continued ⋯⋖*

11  Sketch a displacement–time graph to show your motion for the following event. You are walking at a constant speed across a field after jumping off a gate. Suddenly you see a bull and stop. Your friend says there's no danger, so you walk on at a reduced constant speed. The bull bellows, and you run back to the gate. Explain how each section of the walk relates to a section of your graph.

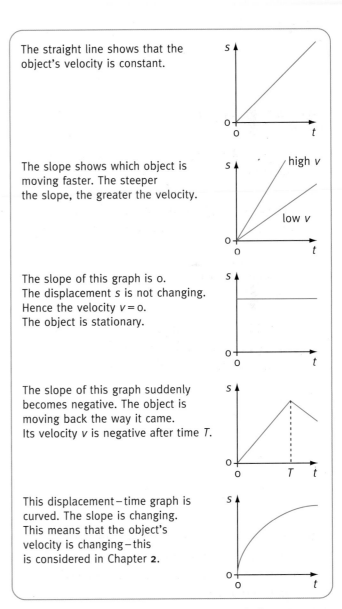

The straight line shows that the object's velocity is constant.

The slope shows which object is moving faster. The steeper the slope, the greater the velocity.

The slope of this graph is 0. The displacement s is not changing. Hence the velocity v = 0. The object is stationary.

The slope of this graph suddenly becomes negative. The object is moving back the way it came. Its velocity v is negative after time T.

This displacement–time graph is curved. The slope is changing. This means that the object's velocity is changing – this is considered in Chapter 2.

**Figure 1.10** The slope of a displacement–time (s–t) graph tells us how fast an object is moving.

## Deducing velocity from a displacement–time graph

A toy car moves along a straight track. Its displacement at different times is shown in Table 1.3. This data can be used to draw a displacement–time graph from which we can deduce the car's velocity.

| Displacement / m | 1.0 | 3.0 | 5.0 | 7.0 | 7.0 | 7.0 |
|---|---|---|---|---|---|---|
| Time / s | 0.0 | 1.0 | 2.0 | 3.0 | 4.0 | 5.0 |

Table 1.3 Displacement (*s*) and time (*t*) data for a toy car.

It is useful to look at the data first, to see the pattern of the car's movement. In this case, the displacement increases steadily at first, but after 3.0 s it becomes constant. In other words, initially the car is moving at a steady velocity, but then it stops.

Now we can plot the displacement–time graph (Figure 1.12).

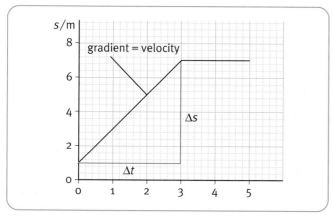

Figure 1.12 Displacement–time graph for a toy car; data as shown in Table 1.3.

We want to work out the velocity of the car over the first 3.0 seconds. We can do this by working out the gradient of the graph, because:

velocity = gradient of displacement–time graph

We draw a right-angled triangle as shown. To find the car's velocity, we divide the change in displacement by the change in time. These are given by the two sides of the triangle labelled $\Delta s$ and $\Delta t$.

$$\text{velocity } v = \frac{\text{change in displacement}}{\text{change in time}}$$

$$= \frac{\Delta s}{\Delta t}$$

$$= \frac{(7.0 - 1.0)}{(3.0 - 0)} = \frac{6.0}{3.0} = 2.0 \, \text{m s}^{-1}$$

If you are used to finding the gradient of a graph, you may be able to reduce the number of steps in this calculation.

## Test yourself

12 Table 1.4 shows the displacement of a racing car at different times as it travels along a straight track during a speed trial.
   a Determine the car's velocity.
   b Draw a displacement–time graph and use it to find the car's velocity.

| Displacement / m | 0 | 85 | 170 | 255 | 340 |
|---|---|---|---|---|---|
| Time / s | 0 | 1.0 | 2.0 | 3.0 | 4.0 |

Table 1.4 Displacement (*s*) and time (*t*) data for Test yourself Q 12.

13 A veteran car travels due south. The distance it travels at hourly intervals is shown in Table 1.5.
   a Draw a distance–time graph to represent the car's journey.
   b From the graph, deduce the car's speed in km h$^{-1}$ during the first three hours of the journey.
   c What is the car's average speed in km h$^{-1}$ during the whole journey?

| Time / h | Distance / km |
|---|---|
| 0 | 0 |
| 1 | 23 |
| 2 | 46 |
| 3 | 69 |
| 4 | 84 |

Table 1.5 Data for Test yourself Q 13.

# Combining displacements

The walkers shown in Figure **1.13** are crossing difficult ground. They navigate from one prominent point to the next, travelling in a series of straight lines. From the map, they can work out the distance that they travel and their displacement from their starting point.

distance travelled = 25 km

(Lay thread along route on map; measure thread against map scale.)

displacement = 15 km north-east

(Join starting and finishing points with straight line; measure line against scale.)

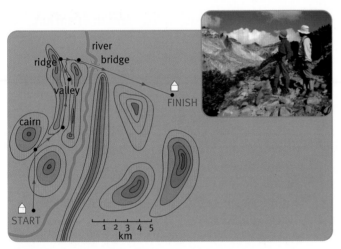

**Figure 1.13** In rough terrain, walkers head straight for a prominent landmark.

A map is a scale drawing. You can find your displacement by measuring the map. But how can you *calculate* your displacement? You need to use ideas from geometry and trigonometry. Worked examples **3** and **4** show how.

This process of adding two displacements together (or two or more of any type of vector) is known as **vector addition**. When two or more vectors are added together, their combined effect is known as the **resultant** of the vectors.

## Worked examples

**3** A spider runs along two sides of a table (Figure **1.14**). Calculate its final displacement.

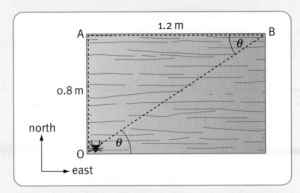

**Figure 1.14** The spider runs a distance of 2.0 m, but what is its displacement?

**Step 1** Because the two sections of the spider's run (OA and AB) are at right angles, we can **add** the two displacements using Pythagoras's theorem:

$$OB^2 = OA^2 + AB^2$$
$$= 0.8^2 + 1.2^2 = 2.08$$
$$OB = \sqrt{2.08} = 1.44\,\text{m} \approx 1.4\,\text{m}$$

**Step 2** Displacement is a vector. We have found the **magnitude** of this vector, but now we have to find its direction. The angle $\theta$ is given by:

$$\tan \theta = \frac{\text{opp}}{\text{adj}} = \frac{0.8}{1.2}$$

$$= 0.667$$

$$\theta = \tan^{-1}(0.667)$$
$$= 33.7° \approx 34°$$

So the spider's displacement is 1.4 m at an angle of 34° north of east.

**4** An aircraft flies 30 km due east and then 50 km north-east (Figure **1.15**). Calculate the final displacement of the aircraft.

*continued ⋯➔*

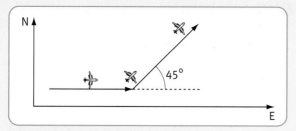

**Figure 1.15** What is the aircraft's final displacement?

Here, the two displacements are not at 90° to one another, so we can't use Pythagoras's theorem. We can solve this problem by making a scale drawing, and measuring the final displacement. (However, you could solve the same problem using trigonometry.)

**Step 1** Choose a suitable scale. Your diagram should be reasonably large; in this case, a scale of 1 cm to represent 5 km is reasonable.

**Step 2** Draw a line to represent the first vector. North is at the top of the page. The line is 6 cm long, towards the east (right).

**Step 3** Draw a line to represent the second vector, starting at the end of the first vector. The line is 10 cm long, and at an angle of 45° (Figure 1.16).

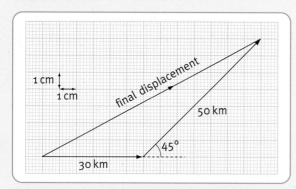

**Figure 1.16** Scale drawing for Worked example 4. Using graph paper can help you to show the vectors in the correct directions.

**Step 4** To find the final displacement, join the start to the finish. You have created a

continued ···▷

**vector triangle**. Measure this displacement vector, and use the scale to convert back to kilometres:

length of vector = 14.8 cm

final displacement = 14.8 × 5 = 74 km

**Step 5** Measure the angle of the final displacement vector:

angle = 28° N of E

Therefore the aircraft's final displacement is 74 km at 28° north of east.

## Test yourself

14 You walk 3.0 km due north, and then 4.0 km due east.
   a Calculate the total distance in km you have travelled.
   b Make a scale drawing of your walk, and use it to find your final displacement. Remember to give both the magnitude and the direction.
   c Check your answer to part **b** by calculating your displacement.

15 A student walks 8.0 km south-east and then 12 km due west.
   a Draw a vector diagram showing the route. Use your diagram to find the total displacement. Remember to give the scale on your diagram and to give the direction as well as the magnitude of your answer.
   b Calculate the resultant displacement. Show your working clearly.

# Combining velocities

Velocity is a vector quantity and so two velocities can be combined by vector addition in the same way that we have seen for two or more displacements.

Imagine that you are attempting to swim across a river. You want to swim directly across to the opposite bank, but the current moves you sideways at the same time as you are swimming forwards. The outcome is that you will end up on the opposite bank, but downstream of your intended landing point. In effect, you have two velocities:

• the velocity due to your swimming, which is directed straight across the river;
• the velocity due to the current, which is directed downstream, at right angles to your swimming velocity.

These combine to give a **resultant** (or net) velocity, which will be diagonally downstream. In order to swim directly across the river, you would have to aim upstream. Then your resultant velocity could be directly across the river.

## Worked example

5 An aircraft is flying due north with a velocity of 200 m s⁻¹. A side wind of velocity 50 m s⁻¹ is blowing due east. What is the aircraft's resultant velocity (give the magnitude and direction)?

Here, the two velocities are at 90°. A sketch diagram and Pythagoras's theorem will suffice to solve the problem.

**Step 1** Draw a sketch of the situation – this is shown in Figure 1.17a.

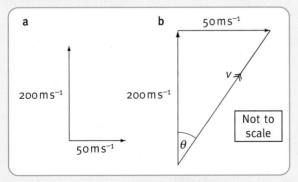

**Figure 1.17** Finding the resultant of two velocities – for Worked example 5.

*continued* ⋯⇢

**Step 2** Now sketch a vector triangle. Remember that the second vector starts where the first one ends. This is shown in Figure 1.17b.

**Step 3** Join the start and end points to complete the triangle.

**Step 4** Calculate the magnitude of the resultant vector $v$ (the hypotenuse of the right-angled triangle).

$$v^2 = 200^2 + 50^2 = 40\,000 + 2500 = 42\,500$$

$$v = \sqrt{42\,500} = 206 \text{ m s}^{-1}$$

**Step 5** Calculate the angle $\theta$:

$$\tan \theta = \frac{50}{200}$$

$$= 0.25$$

$$\theta = \tan^{-1} 0.25 = 14°$$

So the aircraft's resultant velocity is 206 m s⁻¹ at 14° east of north.

## Test yourself

16 A swimmer can swim at 2.0 m s⁻¹ in still water. She aims to swim directly across a river which is flowing at 0.80 m s⁻¹. Calculate her resultant velocity. (You must give both the magnitude and the direction.)

17 A stone is thrown from a cliff and strikes the surface of the sea with a vertical velocity of 18 m s⁻¹ and a horizontal velocity $v$. The resultant of these two velocities is 25 m s⁻¹.
 a Draw a vector diagram showing the two velocities and the resultant.
 b Use your diagram to find the value of $v$.
 c Use your diagram to find the angle between the stone and the vertical as it strikes the water.

# End-of-chapter questions

1   A car travels one complete lap around a circular track at a constant speed of $120\,\text{km}\,\text{h}^{-1}$.
    a   If one lap takes 2.0 minutes, show that the length of the track is 4.0 km.
    b   Explain why values for the **average speed** and **average velocity** are different.
    c   Determine the magnitude of the displacement of the car in a time of 1.0 minute.
    (The circumference of a circle $= 2\pi R$ where $R$ is the radius of the circle.)

2   A boat leaves point A and travels in a straight line to point B (Figure **1.18**). The journey takes 60 s.

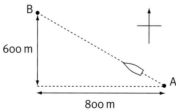

**Figure 1.18**  For End-of-chapter Q **2**.

Calculate:
a   the distance travelled by the boat
b   the total displacement of the boat
c   the average velocity of the boat.
Remember that each vector quantity must be given a direction as well as a magnitude.

**3** A boat travels at $2.0\,\mathrm{m\,s^{-1}}$ east towards a port, $2.2\,\mathrm{km}$ away. When the boat reaches the port, the passengers travel in a car due north for 15 minutes at $60\,\mathrm{km\,h^{-1}}$.

Calculate:
**a** the total distance travelled
**b** the total displacement
**c** the total time taken
**d** the average speed in $\mathrm{m\,s^{-1}}$
**e** the magnitude of the average velocity.

**4** A river flows from west to east with a constant velocity of $1.0\,\mathrm{m\,s^{-1}}$. A boat leaves the south bank heading due north at $2.40\,\mathrm{m\,s^{-1}}$. Find the resultant velocity of the boat.

## Exam-style questions

**1** **a** Define **displacement**. [1]
   **b** Use the definition of displacement to explain how it is possible for an athlete to run round a track yet have no displacement. [2]

**2** A girl is riding a bicycle at a constant velocity of $3.0\,\mathrm{m\,s^{-1}}$ along a straight road. At time $t=0$, she passes a boy sitting on a stationary bicycle. At time $t=0$, the boy sets off to catch up with the girl. His velocity increases from time $t=0$ until $t=5.0\,\mathrm{s}$ when he has covered a distance of $10\,\mathrm{m}$. He then continues at a constant velocity of $4.0\,\mathrm{m\,s^{-1}}$.
   **a** Draw the displacement–time graph for the girl from $t=0$ to $12\,\mathrm{s}$. [1]
   **b** On the same graph axes, draw the displacement–time graph for the boy. [2]
   **c** Using your graph, determine the value of $t$ when the boy catches up with the girl. [1]

**3** A student drops a small black sphere alongside a vertical scale marked in centimetres. A number of flash photographs of the sphere are taken at $0.1\,\mathrm{s}$ intervals, as shown in the diagram. The first photograph is taken with the sphere at the top at time $t=0$.

**a** Explain how the diagram shows that the sphere reaches a constant speed. [2]
**b** Determine the constant speed reached by the sphere. [2]
**c** Determine the distance that the sphere has fallen when $t = 0.8\,\mathrm{s}$. [2]

**4 a** State **one** difference between a scalar quantity and a vector quantity and give an example of each. [3]
**b** A plane has an air speed of $500\,\mathrm{km\,h^{-1}}$ due north. A wind blows at $100\,\mathrm{km\,h^{-1}}$ from east to west. Draw a vector diagram to calculate the resultant velocity of the plane. Give the direction of travel of the plane with respect to north. [4]
**c** The plane flies for 15 minutes. Calculate the displacement of the plane in this time. [1]

**5** A small aircraft for one person is used on a short horizontal flight. On its journey from A to B, the resultant velocity of the aircraft is $15\,\mathrm{m\,s^{-1}}$ in a direction 60° east of north and the wind velocity is $7.5\,\mathrm{m\,s^{-1}}$ due north.

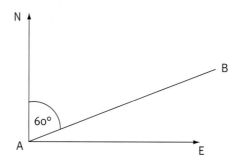

**a** Show that for the aircraft to travel from A to B it should be pointed due east. [2]
**b** After flying 5 km from A to B, the aircraft returns along the same path from B to A with a resultant velocity of $13.5\,\mathrm{m\,s^{-1}}$.
Assuming that the time spent at B is negligible, calculate the average speed for the complete journey from A to B and back to A. [3]

# 2 Accelerated motion

## Objectives

After studying this chapter, you should be able to:

☐ define acceleration

☐ draw and interpret velocity–time graphs

☐ derive and use the equations of uniformly accelerated motion

☐ describe a method for determining the acceleration due to gravity, $g$

☐ explain projectile motion

## Quick off the mark

Figure 2.1 The cheetah is the world's fastest land animal. Its acceleration is impressive, too.

The cheetah has a maximum speed of over $30\,\mathrm{m\,s^{-1}}$ ($108\,\mathrm{km/h}$). From a standing start a cheetah can reach $20\,\mathrm{m\,s^{-1}}$ in just three or four strides, taking only two seconds.

A car cannot increase its speed as rapidly but on a long straight road it can easily travel faster than a cheetah.

## The meaning of acceleration

In everyday language, the term **accelerating** means 'speeding up'. Anything whose speed is increasing is accelerating. Anything whose speed is decreasing is decelerating.

To be more precise in our definition of acceleration, we should think of it as **changing velocity**. Any object whose speed is changing or which is changing its **direction** has **acceleration**. Because acceleration is linked to velocity in this way, it follows that it is a **vector** quantity.

Some examples of objects accelerating are shown in Figure 2.2.

## Calculating acceleration

The acceleration of something indicates the rate at which its velocity is changing. Language can get awkward here. Looking at the sprinter in Figure 2.3, we might say, 'The sprinter accelerates **faster** than the car'. However, 'faster' really means 'greater speed'. It is better to say, 'The sprinter has a greater acceleration than the car'.

Acceleration is defined as follows:

> acceleration = rate of change of velocity
>
> $$\text{average acceleration} = \frac{\text{change in velocity}}{\text{time taken}}$$

So to calculate acceleration $a$, we need to know two quantities – the change in velocity $\Delta v$ and the time taken $\Delta t$:

$$a = \frac{\Delta v}{\Delta t}$$

Sometimes this equation is written differently. We write $u$ for the **initial velocity**, and $v$ for the **final velocity** (because $u$ comes before $v$ in the alphabet). The moving object accelerates from $u$ to $v$ in a time $t$ (this is the same as the time represented by $\Delta t$ above). Then the acceleration is given by the equation:

$$a = \frac{v - u}{t}$$

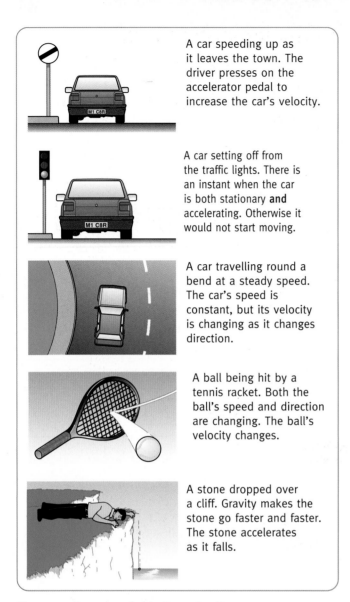

Figure 2.2 Examples of objects accelerating.

A car speeding up as it leaves the town. The driver presses on the accelerator pedal to increase the car's velocity.

A car setting off from the traffic lights. There is an instant when the car is both stationary **and** accelerating. Otherwise it would not start moving.

A car travelling round a bend at a steady speed. The car's speed is constant, but its velocity is changing as it changes direction.

A ball being hit by a tennis racket. Both the ball's speed and direction are changing. The ball's velocity changes.

A stone dropped over a cliff. Gravity makes the stone go faster and faster. The stone accelerates as it falls.

You must learn the definition of acceleration. It can be put in words or symbols. If you use symbols you must state what those symbols mean.

# Units of acceleration

The unit of acceleration is m s$^{-2}$ (metres per second squared). The sprinter might have an acceleration of 5 m s$^{-2}$; her velocity increases by 5 m s$^{-1}$ every second. You could express acceleration in other units. For example, an advertisement might claim that a car accelerates from 0 to 60 miles per hour (mph) in 10 s. Its acceleration would then be 6 mph s$^{-1}$ (6 miles per hour per second). However, mixing together hours and seconds is not a good idea, and so acceleration is almost always given in the standard SI unit of m s$^{-2}$.

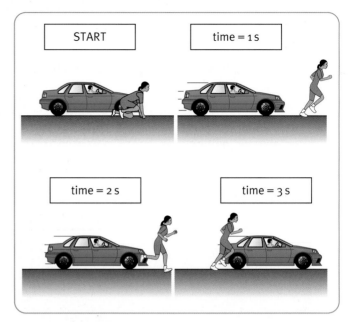

Figure 2.3 The sprinter has a greater acceleration than the car, but her top speed is less.

## Worked examples

1 Leaving a bus stop, the bus reaches a velocity of 8.0 m s$^{-1}$ after 10 s. Calculate the acceleration of the bus.

**Step 1** Note that the bus's initial velocity is 0 m s$^{-1}$. Therefore:

change in velocity $\Delta v = (8.0 - 0)$ m s$^{-1}$

time taken $\Delta t = 10$ s

**Step 2** Substitute these values in the equation for acceleration:

$$\text{acceleration} \quad a = \frac{\Delta v}{\Delta t} = \frac{8.0}{10}$$

$$= 0.80 \text{ m s}^{-2}$$

2 A sprinter starting from rest has an acceleration of 5.0 m s$^{-2}$ during the first 2.0 s of a race. Calculate her velocity after 2.0 s.

**Step 1** Rearranging the equation $a = \frac{v - u}{t}$ gives:

$v = u + at$

*continued* ···▷

**Step 2** Substituting the values and calculating gives:

$$v = 0 + (5.0 \times 2.0) = 10\,\text{m s}^{-1}$$

3  A train slows down from $60\,\text{m s}^{-1}$ to $20\,\text{m s}^{-1}$ in 50 s. Calculate the magnitude of the deceleration of the train.

**Step 1** Write what you know:

$$u = 60\,\text{m s}^{-1} \qquad v = 20\,\text{m s}^{-1} \qquad t = 50\,\text{s}$$

**Step 2** Take care! Here the train's final velocity is less than its initial velocity. To ensure that we arrive at the correct answer, we will use the alternative form of the equation to calculate $a$.

$$a = \frac{v - u}{t}$$

$$= \frac{20 - 60}{50} = \frac{-40}{50} = -0.80\,\text{m s}^{-2}$$

The minus sign (negative acceleration) indicates that the train is slowing down. It is decelerating. The magnitude of the deceleration is $0.80\,\text{m s}^{-2}$.

## Test yourself

1  A car accelerates from a standing start and reaches a velocity of $18\,\text{m s}^{-1}$ after 6.0 s. Calculate its acceleration.

2  A car driver brakes gently. Her car slows down from $23\,\text{m s}^{-1}$ to $11\,\text{m s}^{-1}$ in 20 s. Calculate the magnitude (size) of her deceleration. (Note that, because she is slowing down, her acceleration is negative.)

3  A stone is dropped from the top of a cliff. Its acceleration is $9.81\,\text{m s}^{-2}$. How fast is it moving:
   **a** after 1 s
   **b** after 3 s?

# Deducing acceleration

The gradient of a velocity–time graph tells us whether the object's velocity has been changing at a high rate or a low rate, or not at all (Figure 2.4). We can deduce the value of the acceleration from the gradient of the graph:

acceleration = gradient of velocity–time graph

The graph (Figure 2.5) shows how the velocity of a cyclist changed during the start of a sprint race. We can find his acceleration during the first section of the graph (where the line is straight) using the triangle as shown.

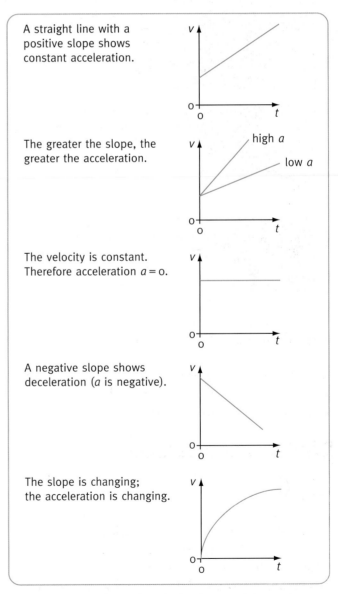

Figure 2.4 The gradient of a velocity–time graph is equal to acceleration.

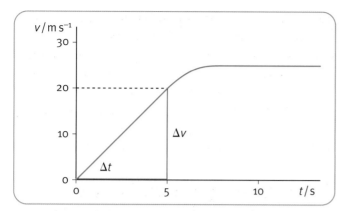

**Figure 2.5** Deducing acceleration from a velocity–time graph.

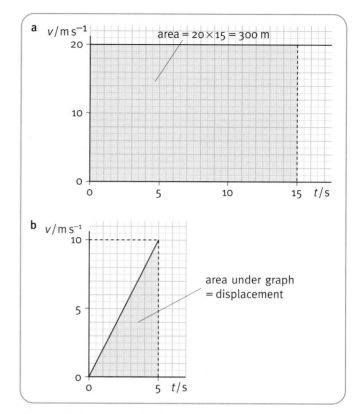

**Figure 2.6** The area under the velocity–time graph is equal to the displacement of the object.

The change in velocity $\Delta v$ is given by the vertical side of the triangle. The time taken $\Delta t$ is given by the horizontal side.

$$\text{acceleration} = \frac{\text{change in velocity}}{\text{time taken}}$$

$$= \frac{20 - 0}{5}$$

$$= 4.0 \, \text{m s}^{-2}$$

A more complex example where the velocity–time graph is curved is shown on page **25**.

# Deducing displacement

We can also find the displacement of a moving object from its velocity–time graph. This is given by the area under the graph:

displacement = area under velocity–time graph

It is easy to see why this is the case for an object moving at a constant velocity. The displacement is simply velocity × time, which is the area of the shaded rectangle (Figure **2.6a**).

For changing velocity, again the area under the graph gives displacement (Figure **2.6b**). The area of each square of the graph represents a distance travelled: in this case, $1 \, \text{m s}^{-1} \times 1 \, \text{s}$, or 1 m. So, for this simple case in which the area is a triangle, we have:

$$\text{displacement} = \tfrac{1}{2} \text{base} \times \text{height}$$

$$= \tfrac{1}{2} \times 5.0 \times 10 = 25 \, \text{m}$$

It is easy to confuse displacement–time graphs and velocity–time graphs. Check by looking at the quantity marked on the vertical axis.

For more complex graphs, you may have to use other techniques such as counting squares to deduce the area, but this is still equal to the displacement.

(Take care when counting squares: it is easiest when the sides of the squares stand for one unit. Check the axes, as the sides may represent 2 units, or 5 units, or some other number.)

## Test yourself

4 A lorry driver is travelling at the speed limit on a motorway. Ahead, he sees hazard lights and gradually slows down. He sees that an accident has occurred, and brakes suddenly to a halt. Sketch a velocity–time graph to represent the motion of this lorry.

*continued* ⋯⟩

**5** Table **2.1** shows how the velocity of a motorcyclist changed during a speed trial along a straight road.

  **a** Draw a velocity–time graph for this motion.
  **b** From the table, deduce the motorcyclist's acceleration during the first 10 s.
  **c** Check your answer by finding the gradient of the graph during the first 10 s.
  **d** Determine the motorcyclist's acceleration during the last 15 s.
  **e** Use the graph to find the total distance travelled during the speed trial.

| Velocity/$ms^{-1}$ | 0 | 15 | 30 | 30 | 20 | 10 | 0 |
|---|---|---|---|---|---|---|---|
| Time/s | 0 | 5 | 10 | 15 | 20 | 25 | 30 |

**Table 2.1** Data for a motorcyclist.

# Measuring velocity and acceleration

In a car crash, the occupants of the car may undergo a very rapid deceleration. This can cause them serious injury, but can be avoided if an air-bag is inflated within a fraction of a second. Figure **2.7** shows the tiny accelerometer at the heart of the system, which detects large accelerations and decelerations.

The acceleration sensor consists of two rows of interlocking teeth. In the event of a crash, these move

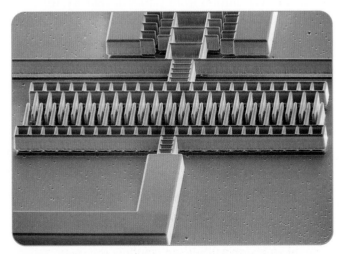

**Figure 2.7** A micro-mechanical acceleration sensor is used to detect sudden accelerations and decelerations as a vehicle travels along the road. This electron microscope image shows the device magnified about 1000 times.

relative to one another, and this generates a voltage which triggers the release of the air-bag.

At the top of the photograph, you can see a second sensor which detects sideways accelerations. This is important in the case of a side impact.

These sensors can also be used to detect when a car swerves or skids, perhaps on an icy road. In this case, they activate the car's stability-control systems.

# Determining velocity and acceleration in the laboratory

In Chapter 1, we looked at ways of finding the velocity of a trolley moving in a straight line. These involved measuring distance and time, and deducing velocity. Now we will see how these techniques can be extended to find the acceleration of a trolley.

## One light gate

The computer records the time for the first 'interrupt' section of the card to pass through the light beam of the light gate (Figure **2.8**). Given the length of the interrupt, it can work out the trolley's initial velocity $u$. This is repeated for the second interrupt to give final velocity $v$. The computer also records the time interval $t_3 - t_1$ between these two velocity measurements. Now it can calculate the acceleration $a$ as shown below.

$$u = \frac{l_1}{t_2 - t_1} \qquad (l_1 = \text{length of first section of the interrupt card})$$

and

$$v = \frac{l_2}{t_4 - t_3} \qquad (l_2 = \text{length of second section of the interrupt card})$$

Therefore:

$$a = \frac{\text{change in velocity}}{\text{time taken}}$$

$$= \frac{v - u}{t_3 - t_1}$$

Sometimes two light gates are used with a card of length $l$. The computer can still record the times as shown above and calculate the acceleration in the same way, with $l_1 = l_2 = l$.

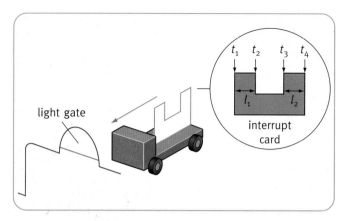

Figure 2.8 Determining acceleration using a single light gate.

| Section of tape | Time at start / s | Time interval / s | Length of section / cm | Velocity / m s⁻¹ |
|---|---|---|---|---|
| 1 | 0.0 | 0.10 | 5.2 | 0.52 |
| 2 | 0.10 | 0.10 | 9.8 | 0.98 |
| 3 | 0.20 | 0.10 | 14.5 | 1.45 |

Table 2.2 Data for Figure 2.10.

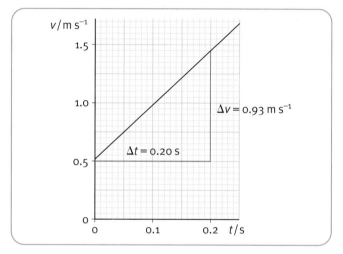

Figure 2.10 Deducing acceleration from measurements of a ticker-tape.

## Using a ticker-timer

The practical arrangement is the same as for measuring velocity. Now we have to think about how to interpret the tape produced by an accelerating trolley (Figure 2.9).

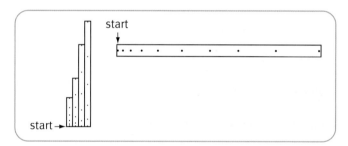

Figure 2.9 Ticker-tape for an accelerating trolley.

The tape is divided into sections, as before, every five dots. Remember that the time interval between adjacent dots is 0.02 s. Each section has five gaps and represents 0.10 s.

You can get a picture of the trolley's motion by placing the sections of tape side-by-side. This is in effect a velocity–time graph.

The length of each section gives the trolley's displacement in 0.10 s, from which the average velocity during this time can be found. This can be repeated for each section of the tape, and a velocity–time graph drawn. The gradient of this graph is equal to the acceleration. Table 2.2 and Figure 2.10 show some typical results.

The acceleration is calculated to be:

$$a = \frac{\Delta v}{\Delta t}$$

$$= \frac{0.93}{0.20} \approx 4.7 \text{ m s}^{-2}$$

## Using a motion sensor

The computer software which handles the data provided by the motion sensor can calculate the acceleration of a trolley. However, because it deduces velocity from measurements of position, and then calculates acceleration from values of velocity, its precision is relatively poor.

## Test yourself

6 Sketch a section of ticker-tape for a trolley which travels at a steady velocity and which then decelerates.

7 Figure 2.11 shows the dimensions of an interrupt card, together with the times recorded as it passed through a light gate. Use these measurements to calculate the acceleration of the card. (Follow the steps outlined on page 19.)

*continued ···⟩*

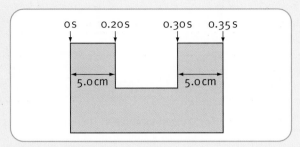

**Figure 2.11** For Test yourself Q 7.

8 Two adjacent five-dot sections of a ticker-tape measure 10 cm and 16 cm, respectively. The interval between dots is 0.02 s. Deduce the acceleration of the trolley which produced the tape.

# The equations of motion

As a space rocket rises from the ground, its velocity steadily increases. It is accelerating (Figure 2.12).

Eventually it will reach a speed of several kilometres per second. Any astronauts aboard find themselves pushed back into their seats while the rocket is accelerating.

The engineers who planned the mission must be able to calculate how fast the rocket will be travelling and where it will be at any point in its journey. They have sophisticated computers to do this, using more elaborate versions of the equations given below.

There is a set of equations which allows us to calculate the quantities involved when an object is moving with a constant acceleration. The quantities we are concerned with are:

$s$    displacement

$u$    initial velocity

$v$    final velocity

$a$    acceleration

$t$    time taken

**Figure 2.12** A rocket accelerates as it lifts off from the ground.

Here are the four **equations of motion**.

equation 1:  $v = u + at$

equation 2:  $s = \dfrac{(u + v)}{2} \times t$

equation 3:  $s = ut + \frac{1}{2}at^2$

equation 4:  $v^2 = u^2 + 2as$

Take care when you use these equations. They can only be used:

• for motion in a straight line
• for an object with constant acceleration.

To get a feel for how to use these equations, we will consider some worked examples. In each example, we will follow the same procedure.

**Step 1** We write down the quantities which we know, and the quantity we want to find.

**Step 2** Then we choose the equation which links these quantities, and substitute in the values.

**Step 3** Finally, we calculate the unknown quantity.

We will look at where these equations come from in the next section.

## Worked examples

4 The rocket shown in Figure 2.12 lifts off from rest with an acceleration of $20 \, \mathrm{m\,s^{-2}}$. Calculate its velocity after $50 \, \mathrm{s}$.

**Step 1** What we know:
$$u = 0 \, \mathrm{m\,s^{-1}}$$
$$a = 20 \, \mathrm{m\,s^{-2}}$$
$$t = 50 \, \mathrm{s}$$

and what we want to know: $v = ?$

**Step 2** The equation linking $u$, $a$, $t$ and $v$ is equation 1:

$$v = u + at$$

Substituting gives:

$$v = 0 + (20 \times 50)$$

**Step 3** Calculation then gives:

$$v = 1000 \, \mathrm{m\,s^{-1}}$$

So the rocket will be travelling at $1000 \, \mathrm{m\,s^{-1}}$ after $50 \, \mathrm{s}$. This makes sense, since its velocity increases by $20 \, \mathrm{m\,s^{-1}}$ every second, for $50 \, \mathrm{s}$.

You could use the same equation to work out how long the rocket would take to reach a velocity of $2000 \, \mathrm{m\,s^{-1}}$, or the acceleration it must have to reach a speed of $1000 \, \mathrm{m\,s^{-1}}$ in $40 \, \mathrm{s}$, and so on.

5 The car shown in Figure 2.13 is travelling along a straight road at $8.0 \, \mathrm{m\,s^{-1}}$. It accelerates at $1.0 \, \mathrm{m\,s^{-2}}$ for a distance of $18 \, \mathrm{m}$. How fast is it then travelling?

*continued ⋯⟶*

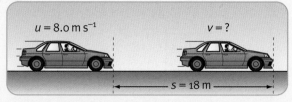

$u = 8.0 \, \mathrm{m\,s^{-1}}$     $v = ?$

$s = 18 \, \mathrm{m}$

**Figure 2.13** For Worked example 5. This car accelerates for a short distance as it travels along the road.

In this case, we will have to use a different equation, because we know the distance during which the car accelerates, not the time.

**Step 1** What we know:
$$u = 8.0 \, \mathrm{m\,s^{-1}}$$
$$a = 1.0 \, \mathrm{m\,s^{-2}}$$
$$s = 18 \, \mathrm{m}$$

and what we want to know: $v = ?$

**Step 2** The equation we need is equation 4:

$$v^2 = u^2 + 2as$$

Substituting gives:

$$v^2 = 8.0^2 + (2 \times 1.0 \times 18)$$

**Step 3** Calculation then gives:

$$v^2 = 64 + 36 = 100 \, \mathrm{m^2\,s^{-2}}$$

$$v = 10 \, \mathrm{m\,s^{-1}}$$

So the car will be travelling at $10 \, \mathrm{m\,s^{-1}}$ when it stops accelerating.

(You may find it easier to carry out these calculations without including the units of quantities when you substitute in the equation. However, including the units can help to ensure that you end up with the correct units for the final answer.)

6 A train (Figure 2.14) travelling at $20 \, \mathrm{m\,s^{-1}}$ accelerates at $0.50 \, \mathrm{m\,s^{-2}}$ for $30 \, \mathrm{s}$. Calculate the distance travelled by the train in this time.

*continued ⋯⟶*

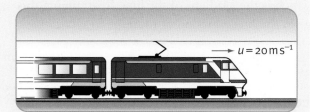

**Figure 2.14** For Worked example **6**. This train accelerates for 30 s.

**Step 1** What we know:

$$u = 20 \text{ m s}^{-1}$$
$$t = 30 \text{ s}$$
$$a = 0.50 \text{ m s}^{-2}$$

and what we want to know: $s = ?$

**Step 2** The equation we need is equation 3:

$$s = ut + \tfrac{1}{2}at^2$$

Substituting gives:

$$s = (20 \times 30) + \tfrac{1}{2} \times 0.5 \times (30)^2$$

**Step 3** Calculation then gives:

$$s = 600 + 225 = 825 \text{ m}$$

So the train will travel 825 m while it is accelerating.

7 The cyclist in Figure **2.15** is travelling at 15 m s$^{-1}$. She brakes so that she doesn't collide with the wall. Calculate the magnitude of her deceleration.

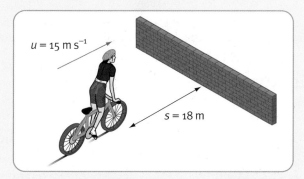

**Figure 2.15** For Worked example **7**. The cyclist brakes to stop herself colliding with the wall.

*continued* ···>

This example shows that it is sometimes necessary to rearrange an equation, to make the unknown quantity its subject. It is easiest to do this before substituting in the values.

**Step 1** What we know:

$$u = 15 \text{ m s}^{-1}$$
$$v = 0 \text{ m s}^{-1}$$
$$s = 18 \text{ m}$$

and what we want to know: $a = ?$

**Step 2** The equation we need is equation 4:

$$v^2 = u^2 + 2as$$

Rearranging gives:

$$a = \frac{v^2 - u^2}{2s}$$

$$a = \frac{0^2 - 15^2}{2 \times 18} = \frac{-225}{36}$$

**Step 3** Calculation then gives:

$$a = -6.25 \text{ m s}^{-2} \approx -6.3 \text{ m s}^{-2}$$

So the cyclist will have to brake hard to achieve a deceleration of magnitude 6.3 m s$^{-2}$. The minus sign shows that her acceleration is negative, i.e. a deceleration.

## Test yourself

9 A car is initially stationary. It has a constant acceleration of 2.0 m s$^{-2}$.
   a Calculate the velocity of the car after 10 s.
   b Calculate the distance travelled by the car at the end of 10 s.
   c Calculate the time taken by the car to reach a velocity of 24 m s$^{-1}$.

*continued* ···>

**10** A train accelerates steadily from $4.0 \, \text{m s}^{-1}$ to $20 \, \text{m s}^{-1}$ in $100 \, \text{s}$.
  **a** Calculate the acceleration of the train.
  **b** From its initial and final velocities, calculate the average velocity of the train.
  **c** Calculate the distance travelled by the train in this time of $100 \, \text{s}$.

**11** A car is moving at $8.0 \, \text{m s}^{-1}$. The driver makes it accelerate at $1.0 \, \text{m s}^{-2}$ for a distance of $18 \, \text{m}$. What is the final velocity of the car?

# Deriving the equations of motion

On the previous pages, we have seen how to make use of the equations of motion. But where do these equations come from? They arise from the definitions of velocity and acceleration.

We can find the first two equations from the velocity–time graph shown in Figure **2.16**. The graph represents the motion of an object. Its initial velocity is $u$. After time $t$, its final velocity is $v$.

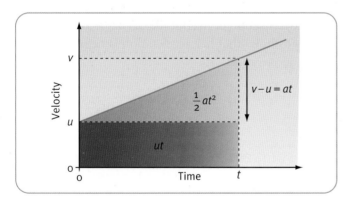

**Figure 2.16** This graph shows the variation of velocity of an object with time. The object has constant acceleration.

## Equation 1

The graph of Figure **2.16** is a straight line, therefore the object's acceleration $a$ is constant. The gradient (slope) of the line is equal to acceleration.

The acceleration is defined as:

$$a = \frac{(v - u)}{t}$$

which is the gradient of the line. Rearranging this gives the first equation of motion:

$$v = u + at \qquad \text{(equation 1)}$$

## Equation 2

Displacement is given by the area under the velocity–time graph. Figure **2.17** shows that the object's average velocity is half-way between $u$ and $v$. So the object's average velocity, calculated by averaging its initial and final velocities, is given by:

$$\frac{(u + v)}{2}$$

The object's displacement is the shaded area in Figure **2.17**. This is a rectangle, and so we have:

displacement = average velocity × time taken

and hence:

$$s = \frac{(u + v)}{2} \times t \qquad \text{(equation 2)}$$

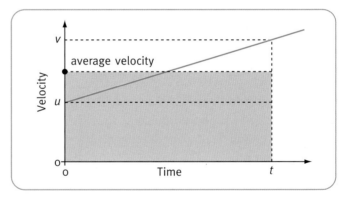

**Figure 2.17** The average velocity is half-way between $u$ and $v$.

## Equation 3

From equations 1 and 2, we can derive equation 3:

$$v = u + at \qquad \text{(equation 1)}$$

$$s = \frac{(u + v)}{2} \times t \qquad \text{(equation 2)}$$

Substituting $v$ from equation 1 gives:

$$s = \left( \frac{u + u + at}{2} \right) \times t$$

$$= \frac{2ut}{2} + \frac{at^2}{2}$$

So

$$s = ut + \frac{1}{2}at^2 \qquad \text{(equation 3)}$$

Looking at Figure **2.16**, you can see that the two terms on the right of the equation correspond to the areas of the rectangle and the triangle which make up the area under the graph. Of course, this is the same area as the rectangle in Figure **2.17**.

## Equation 4

Equation 4 is also derived from equations 1 and 2.

$$v = u + at \qquad \text{(equation 1)}$$

$$s = \frac{(u + v)}{2} \times t \qquad \text{(equation 2)}$$

Substituting for time $t$ from equation 1 gives:

$$s = \frac{(u + v)}{2} \times \frac{(v - u)}{a}$$

Rearranging this gives:

$$2as = (u + v)(v - u)$$
$$= v^2 - u^2$$

Or simply:

$$v^2 = u^2 + 2as \qquad \text{(equation 4)}$$

## Investigating road traffic accidents

The police frequently have to investigate road traffic accidents. They make use of many aspects of physics, including the equations of motion. The next two questions will help you to apply what you have learned to situations where police investigators have used evidence from skid marks on the road.

### Test yourself

**12** Trials on the surface of a new road show that, when a car skids to a halt, its acceleration is $-7.0\,\text{m s}^{-2}$. Estimate the skid-to-stop distance of a car travelling at the speed limit of $30\,\text{m s}^{-1}$ (approx. $110\,\text{km h}^{-1}$ or $70\,\text{mph}$).

**13** At the scene of an accident on a country road, police find skid marks stretching for $50\,\text{m}$. Tests on the road surface show that a skidding car decelerates at $6.5\,\text{m s}^{-2}$. Was the car which skidded exceeding the speed limit of $25\,\text{m s}^{-1}$ ($90\,\text{km h}^{-1}$) on this road?

# Uniform and non-uniform acceleration

It is important to note that the equations of motion only apply to an object which is moving with a constant acceleration. If the acceleration $a$ was changing, you wouldn't know what value to put in the equations. Constant acceleration is often referred to as uniform acceleration.

The velocity–time graph in Figure **2.18** shows **non-uniform** acceleration. It is not a straight line; its gradient is changing (in this case, decreasing).

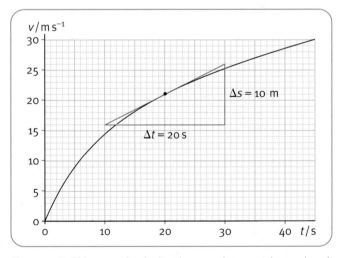

**Figure 2.18** This curved velocity–time graph cannot be analysed using the equations of motion.

The acceleration at any instant in time is given by the gradient of the velocity–time graph. The triangle in Figure **2.18** shows how to find the acceleration at $t = 20$ seconds.

- At the time of interest, mark a point on the graph.
- Draw a **tangent** to the curve at that point.
- Make a large right-angled triangle, and use it to find the gradient.

You can find the change in displacement of the body as it accelerates by determining the area under the velocity–time graph.

To find the displacement of the object in Figure **2.18** between $t = 0$ and $20\,\text{s}$, the most straightforward, but lengthy, method is just to count the number of small squares.

In this case up to $t = 20\,\text{s}$, there are about 250 small squares. This is tedious to count but you can save yourself a lot of time by drawing a line from the origin to the point at $20\,\text{s}$. The area of the triangle is easy to find (200 small squares) and then you only have to count the number of small squares between the line you have drawn and the curve on the graph (about 50 squares).

In this case each square is $1\,\text{m s}^{-1}$ on the $y$-axis by $1\,\text{s}$ on the $x$-axis, so the area of each square is $1 \times 1 = 1\,\text{m}$ and the displacement is $250\,\text{m}$. In other cases note carefully the value of each side of the square you have chosen.

## Test yourself

**14** The graph in Figure **2.19** represents the motion of an object moving with varying acceleration. Lay your ruler on the diagram so that it is tangential to the graph at point P.
  **a** What are the values of time and velocity at this point?
  **b** Estimate the object's acceleration at this point.

continued ⋯⟩

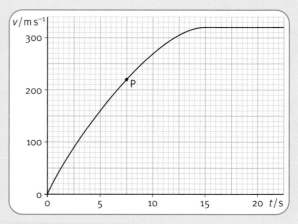

**Figure 2.19** For Test yourself Q **14**.

**15** The velocity–time graph (Figure **2.20**) represents the motion of a car along a straight road for a period of $30\,\text{s}$.
  **a** Describe the motion of the car.
  **b** From the graph, determine the car's initial and final velocities over the time of $30\,\text{s}$.
  **c** Determine the acceleration of the car.
  **d** By calculating the area under the graph, determine the displacement of the car.
  **e** Check your answer to part **d** by calculating the car's displacement using $s = ut + \frac{1}{2}at^2$.

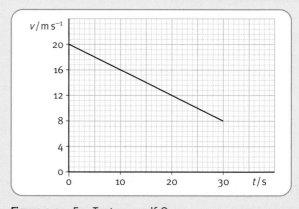

**Figure 2.20** For Test yourself Q **15**.

# Acceleration caused by gravity

If you drop a ball or stone, it falls to the ground. Figure **2.21**, based on a multiflash photograph, shows the ball at equal intervals of time. You can see that the ball's velocity increases as it falls because the spaces between the images of the ball increase steadily. The ball is accelerating.

Figure 2.21 This diagram of a falling ball, based on a multiflash photo, clearly shows that the ball's velocity increases as it falls.

A multiflash photograph is useful to demonstrate that the ball accelerates as it falls. Usually, objects fall too quickly for our eyes to be able to observe them speeding up. It is easy to imagine that the ball moves quickly as soon as you let it go, and falls at a steady speed to the ground. Figure 2.21 shows that this is not the case.

If we measure the acceleration of a freely falling object on the surface of the Earth, we find a value of about $9.81\,\mathrm{m\,s^{-2}}$. This is known as the **acceleration of free fall**, and is given the symbol $g$:

acceleration of free fall, $g = 9.81\,\mathrm{m\,s^{-2}}$

The value of $g$ depends on where you are on the Earth's surface, but for examination purposes we take $g = 9.81\,\mathrm{m\,s^{-2}}$.

If we drop an object, its initial velocity $u = 0$. How far will it fall in time $t$? Substituting in $s = ut + \frac{1}{2}at^2$ gives displacement $s$:

$$s = \frac{1}{2} \times 9.81 \times t^2$$
$$= 4.9 \times t^2$$

Hence, by timing a falling object, we can determine $g$.

*Test yourself*

**16** If you drop a stone from the edge of a cliff, its initial velocity $u = 0$, and it falls with acceleration $g = 9.81\,\mathrm{m\,s^{-2}}$. You can calculate the distance $s$ it falls in a given time $t$ using an equation of motion.
  **a** Copy and complete Table **2.3**, which shows how $s$ depends on $t$.
  **b** Draw a graph of $s$ against $t$.
  **c** Use your graph to find the distance fallen by the stone in 2.5 s.
  **d** Use your graph to find how long it will take the stone to fall to the bottom of a cliff 40 m high. Check your answer using the equations of motion.

| Time / s | 0 | 1.0 | 2.0 | 3.0 | 4.0 |
|---|---|---|---|---|---|
| Displacement / m | 0 | 4.9 | | | |

Table 2.3 Time ($t$) and displacement ($s$) data for Test yourself Q **16**.

**17** An egg falls off a table. The floor is 0.8 m from the table-top.
  **a** Calculate the time taken to reach the ground.
  **b** Calculate the velocity of impact with the ground.

# Determining $g$

One way to measure the acceleration of free fall $g$ would be to try bungee-jumping (Figure **2.22**). You

Figure 2.22 A bungee-jumper falls with initial acceleration $g$.

would need to carry a stopwatch, and measure the time between jumping from the platform and the moment when the elastic rope begins to slow your fall. If you knew the length of the unstretched rope, you could calculate $g$.

There are easier methods for finding $g$ which can be used in the laboratory. We will look at three of these and compare them.

## Method 1: Using an electronic timer

In this method, a steel ball-bearing is held by an electromagnet (Figure 2.23). When the current to the magnet is switched off, the ball begins to fall and an electronic timer starts. The ball falls through a trapdoor, and this breaks a circuit to stop the timer. This tells us the time taken for the ball to fall from rest through the distance $h$ between the bottom of the ball and the trapdoor.

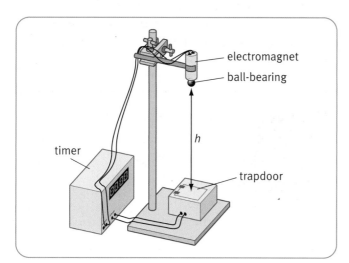

**Figure 2.23** The timer records the time for the ball to fall through the distance $h$.

Here is how we can use one of the equations of motion to find $g$:

displacement $s = h$
time taken $= t$
initial velocity $u = 0$
acceleration $a = g$

Substituting in $s = ut + \frac{1}{2}at^2$ gives:

$$h = \frac{1}{2}gt^2$$

and for any values of $h$ and $t$ we can calculate a value for $g$.

A more satisfactory procedure is to take measurements of $t$ for several different values of $h$. The height of the ball bearing above the trapdoor is varied systematically, and the time of fall measured several times to calculate an average for each height. Table 2.4 and Figure 2.24 show some typical results. We can deduce $g$ from the gradient of the graph of $h$ against $t^2$.

| $h$/m | $t$/s | $t^2$/s$^2$ |
|---|---|---|
| 0.27 | 0.25 | 0.063 |
| 0.39 | 0.30 | 0.090 |
| 0.56 | 0.36 | 0.130 |
| 0.70 | 0.41 | 0.168 |
| 0.90 | 0.46 | 0.212 |

**Table 2.4** Data for Figure 2.24. These are mean values.

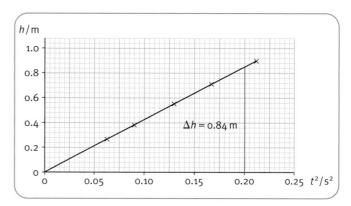

**Figure 2.24** The acceleration of free fall can be determined from the gradient.

The equation for a straight line through the origin is:

$$y = mx$$

In our experiment we have:

$$\underset{(y)}{h} = \underset{(m)}{\left(\tfrac{1}{2}g\right)} \underset{(x)}{t^2}$$

The gradient of the straight line of a graph of $h$ against $t^2$ is equal to $\frac{g}{2}$. Therefore:

$$\text{gradient} = \frac{g}{2} = \frac{0.84}{0.20} = 4.2$$

$$g = 4.2 \times 2 = 8.4\,\text{m s}^{-2}$$

## Sources of uncertainty

The electromagnet may retain some magnetism when it is switched off, and this may tend to slow the ball's fall. Consequently, the time $t$ recorded by the timer may be longer than if the ball were to fall completely freely. From $h = \frac{1}{2}gt^2$, it follows that, if $t$ is too great, the experimental value of $g$ will be too small. This is an example of a **systematic error** – all the results are systematically distorted so that they are too great (or too small) as a consequence of the experimental design.

Measuring the height $h$ is awkward. You can probably only find the value of $h$ to within ±1 mm at best. So there is a **random error** in the value of $h$, and this will result in a slight scatter of the points on the graph, and a degree of uncertainty in the final value of $g$. For more about errors, see Appendix **A1**.

## Method 2: Using a ticker-timer

Figure **2.25** shows a weight falling. As it falls, it pulls a tape through a ticker-timer. The spacing of the dots on the tape increases steadily, showing that the weight is accelerating. You can analyse the tape to find the acceleration, as discussed on page **20**.

This is not a very satisfactory method of measuring $g$. The main problem arises from friction between the tape and the ticker-timer. This slows the fall of the weight and so its acceleration is less than $g$. (This is another example of a systematic error.)

The effect of friction is less of a problem for a large weight, which falls more freely. If measurements are made for increasing weights, the value of acceleration gets closer and closer to the true value of $g$.

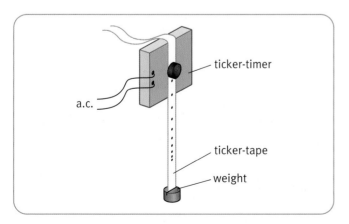

**Figure 2.25** A falling weight pulls a tape through a ticker-timer.

## Method 3: Using a light gate

Figure **2.26** shows how a weight can be attached to a card 'interrupt'. The card is designed to break the light beam twice as the weight falls. The computer can then calculate the velocity of the weight twice as it falls, and hence find its acceleration.

initial velocity $u = \dfrac{x}{t_2 - t_1}$

final velocity $v = \dfrac{x}{t_4 - t_3}$

Therefore:

acceleration $a = \dfrac{v - u}{t_3 - t_1}$

The weight can be dropped from different heights above the light gate. This allows you to find out whether its acceleration is the same at different points in its fall. This is an advantage over Method 1, which can only measure the acceleration from a stationary start.

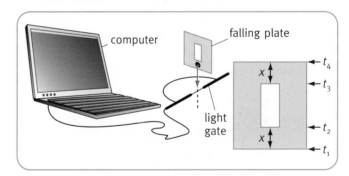

**Figure 2.26** The weight accelerates as it falls. The upper section of the card falls more quickly through the light gate.

### Worked example

8  To get a rough value for $g$, a student dropped a stone from the top of a cliff. A second student timed the stone's fall using a stopwatch. Here are their results:

estimated height of cliff = 30 m

time of fall = 2.6 s

Use the results to estimate a value for $g$.

*continued* ⋯▸

**Step 1** Calculate the average speed of the stone:

average speed of stone during fall

$$= \frac{30}{2.6} = 11.5 \, \text{m s}^{-1}$$

**Step 2** Find the values of $v$ and $u$:

final speed $v = 2 \times 11.5 \, \text{m s}^{-1} = 23.0 \, \text{m s}^{-1}$

initial speed $u = 0 \, \text{m s}^{-1}$

**Step 3** Substitute these values into the equation for acceleration:

$$a = \frac{v - u}{t} = \frac{23.0}{2.6} = 8.8 \, \text{m s}^{-2}$$

Note that you can reach the same result more directly using $s = ut + \frac{1}{2}at^2$, but you may find it easier to follow what is going on using the method given here. We should briefly consider why the answer is less than the expected value of $g = 9.81 \, \text{m s}^{-2}$. It might be that the cliff was higher than the student's estimate. The timer may not have been accurate in switching the stopwatch on and off. There will have been air resistance which slowed the stone's fall.

---

### Test yourself

**18** A steel ball falls from rest through a height of 2.10 m. An electronic timer records a time of 0.67 s for the fall.
  **a** Calculate the average acceleration of the ball as it falls.
  **b** Suggest reasons why the answer is not exactly 9.81 m s$^{-2}$.

**19** In an experiment to determine the acceleration due to gravity, a ball was timed electronically as it fell from rest through a height $h$. The times $t$ shown in Table 2.5 were obtained.
  **a** Plot a graph of $h$ against $t^2$.
  **b** From the graph, determine the acceleration of free fall, $g$.
  **c** Comment on your answer.

*continued* ⋯⇥

| Height / m | 0.70 | 1.03 | 1.25 | 1.60 | 1.99 |
|---|---|---|---|---|---|
| Time / s | 0.99 | 1.13 | 1.28 | 1.42 | 1.60 |

**Table 2.5** Height ($h$) and time ($t$) data for Test yourself Q **19**.

**20** In Chapter **1**, we looked at how to use a motion sensor to measure the speed and position of a moving object. Suggest how a motion sensor could be used to determine $g$.

# Motion in two dimensions – projectiles
## A curved trajectory

A multiflash photograph can reveal details of the path, or trajectory, of a projectile. Figure **2.27** shows the trajectories of a projectile – a bouncing ball. Once the ball has left the child's hand and is moving through the air, the only force acting on it is its weight.

**Figure 2.27** A bouncing ball is an example of a projectile. This multiflash photograph shows details of its motion which would escape the eye of an observer.

The ball has been thrown at an angle to the horizontal. It speeds up as it falls – you can see that the images of the ball become farther and farther apart. At the same time, it moves steadily to the right. You can see this from the even spacing of the images across the picture. The ball's path has a mathematical shape known as a **parabola**. After it bounces, the ball is moving more slowly. It slows down, or decelerates, as it rises – the images get closer and closer together.

We interpret this picture as follows. The vertical motion of the ball is affected by the force of gravity, that is, its weight. When it rises it has a vertical deceleration of magnitude $g$, which slows it down, and when it falls it has an acceleration of $g$, which speeds it up. The ball's horizontal motion is unaffected by gravity. In the absence of air resistance, the ball has a constant velocity in the horizontal direction. We can treat the ball's vertical and horizontal motions separately, because they are independent of one another.

## Components of a vector

In order to understand how to treat the velocity in the vertical and horizontal directions separately we start by considering a constant velocity.

If an aeroplane has a constant velocity $v$ at an angle $\theta$ as shown in Figure 2.28, then we say that this velocity has two effects or **components**, $v_N$ in a northerly direction and $v_E$ in an easterly direction. These two components of velocity add up to make the actual velocity $v$.

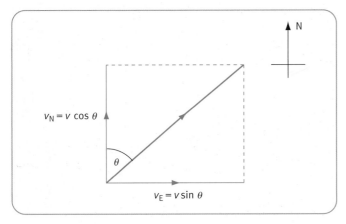

Figure 2.28 Components of a velocity. The component due north, $v_N = v \cos \theta$ and the component due east $v_E = v \sin \theta$.

This process of taking a velocity and determining its effect along another direction is known as **resolving** the velocity along a different direction. In effect splitting the velocity into two components at right angles is the reverse of adding together two vectors – it is splitting one vector into two vectors along convenient directions.

To find the component of any vector (e.g. displacement, velocity, acceleration) in a particular direction, we can use the following strategy.

**Step 1** Find the angle $\theta$ between the vector and the direction of interest.

**Step 2** Multiply the vector by the cosine of the angle $\theta$.

So the component of an object's velocity $v$ at angle $\theta$ to $v$ is equal to $v \cos \theta$ (Figure 2.28).

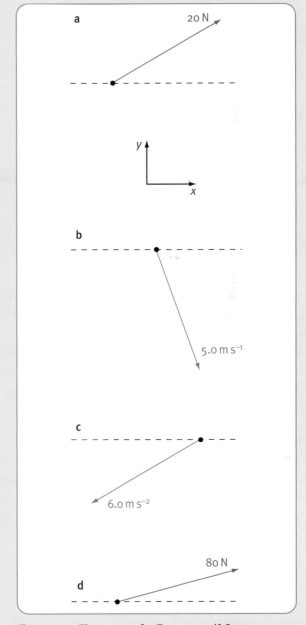

Figure 2.29 The vectors for Test yourself Q 21.

# Understanding projectiles

We will first consider the simple case of a projectile thrown straight up in the air, so that it moves vertically. Then we will look at projectiles which move horizontally and vertically at the same time.

## Up and down

A stone is thrown upwards with an initial velocity of $20\,\mathrm{m\,s^{-1}}$. Figure **2.30** shows the situation.

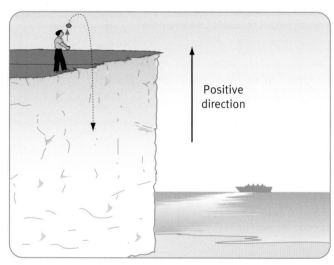

**Figure 2.30** Standing at the edge of the cliff, you throw a stone vertically upwards. The height of the cliff is 25 m.

It is important to use a consistent sign convention here. We will take upwards as positive, and downwards as negative. So the stone's initial velocity is positive, but its acceleration $g$ is negative. We can solve various problems about the stone's motion by using the equations of motion.

### How high?

How high will the stone rise above ground level of the cliff?

As the stone rises upwards, it moves more and more slowly – it decelerates, because of the force of gravity. At its highest point, the stone's velocity is zero. So the quantities we know are:

| | | |
|---|---|---|
| initial velocity | $= u$ | $= 20\,\mathrm{m\,s^{-1}}$ |
| final velocity | $= v$ | $= 0\,\mathrm{m\,s^{-1}}$ |
| acceleration | $= a$ | $= -9.81\,\mathrm{m\,s^{-2}}$ |
| displacement | $= s$ | $= ?$ |

The relevant equation of motion is $v^2 = u^2 + 2as$. Substituting values gives:

$$0^2 = 20^2 + 2 \times (-9.81) \times s$$

$$0 = 400 - 19.62s$$

$$s = \frac{400}{19.62} = 20.4\,\mathrm{m} \approx 20\,\mathrm{m}$$

The stone rises 20 m upwards, before it starts to fall again.

### How long?

How long will it take from leaving your hand for the stone to fall back to the clifftop?

When the stone returns to the point from which it was thrown, its displacement $s$ is zero. So:

$$s = 0 \quad u = 20\,\mathrm{m\,s^{-1}} \quad a = -9.81\,\mathrm{m\,s^{-2}} \quad t = ?$$

Substituting in $s = ut + \frac{1}{2}at^2$ gives:

$$0 = 20t \times \frac{1}{2}(-9.81) \times t^2$$
$$= 20t - 4.905t^2 = (20 - 4.905t) \times t$$

There are two possible solutions to this:

- $t = 0\,\mathrm{s}$, i.e. the stone had zero displacement at the instant it was thrown
- $t = 4.1\,\mathrm{s}$, i.e. the stone returned to zero displacement after 4.1 s, which is the answer we are interested in.

### Falling further

The height of the cliff is 25 m. How long will it take the stone to reach the foot of the cliff?

This is similar to the last example, but now the stone's final displacement is 25 m below its starting point. By our sign convention, this is a negative displacement, and $s = -25\,\mathrm{m}$.

## Test yourself

**22** In the example above (Falling further), calculate the time it will take for the stone to reach the foot of the cliff.

*continued ⋯⋗*

**23** A ball is fired upwards with an initial velocity of 30 m s$^{-1}$. Table **2.6** shows how the ball's velocity changes. (Take $g = 9.81$ m s$^{-2}$.)
  **a** Copy and complete the table.
  **b** Draw a graph to represent the data.
  **c** Use your graph to deduce how long the ball took to reach its highest point.

| Velocity / m s$^{-1}$ | 30 | 20.19 | | | | |
|---|---|---|---|---|---|---|
| Time / s | 0 | 1.0 | 2.0 | 3.0 | 4.0 | 5.0 |

**Table 2.6** For Test yourself Q **23**.

## Vertical and horizontal at the same time

Here is an example to illustrate what happens when an object travels vertically and horizontally at the same time.

In a toy, a ball-bearing is fired horizontally from a point 0.4 m above the ground. Its initial velocity is 2.5 m s$^{-1}$. Its position at equal intervals of time have been calculated and are shown in Table **2.7**. These results are also shown in Figure **2.31**. Study the table and the graph. You should notice the following.

- The horizontal distance increases steadily. This is because the ball's horizontal motion is unaffected by the force of gravity. It travels at a steady velocity horizontally.
- The vertical distances do not show the same pattern. The ball is accelerating downwards. (These figures have been calculated using $g = 9.81$ m s$^{-2}$.)

| Time / s | Horizontal distance / m | Vertical distance / m |
|---|---|---|
| 0.00 | 0.00 | 0.000 |
| 0.04 | 0.10 | 0.008 |
| 0.08 | 0.20 | 0.031 |
| 0.12 | 0.30 | 0.071 |
| 0.16 | 0.40 | 0.126 |
| 0.20 | 0.50 | 0.196 |
| 0.24 | 0.60 | 0.283 |
| 0.28 | 0.70 | 0.385 |

**Table 2.7** Data for the example of a moving ball, as shown in Figure **2.31**.

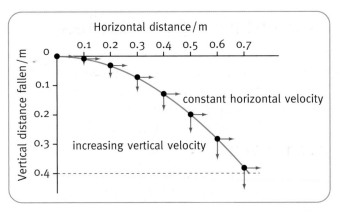

**Figure 2.31** This sketch shows the path of the ball projected horizontally. The arrows represent the horizontal and vertical components of its velocity.

You can calculate the distance $s$ fallen using the equation of motion $s = ut + \frac{1}{2}at^2$. (The initial vertical velocity $u = 0$.)

The horizontal distance is calculated using:

horizontal distance $= 2.5 \times t$

The vertical distance is calculated using:

vertical distance $= \frac{1}{2} \times 9.81 \times t^2$

## Worked examples

**9** A stone is thrown horizontally with a velocity of 12 m s$^{-1}$ from the top of a vertical cliff.

Calculate how long the stone takes to reach the ground 40 m below and how far the stone lands from the base of the cliff.

**Step 1** Consider the ball's vertical motion. It has zero initial speed vertically and travels 40 m with acceleration 9.81 m s$^{-2}$ in the same direction.

$$s = ut + \frac{1}{2}at^2$$

$$40 = 0 + \frac{1}{2} \times 9.81 \times t^2$$

Thus $t = 2.86$ s.

**Step 2** Consider the ball's horizontal motion. The ball travels with a constant horizontal

*continued* ⋯➤

velocity, $12\,\mathrm{m\,s^{-1}}$, as long as there is no air resistance.

distance travelled $= u \times t = 12 \times 2.86 = 34.3\,\mathrm{m}$

> You may find it easier to summarise the information like this:
>
> vertically $s = 40$   $u = 0$   $a = 9.81$   $t = ?$   $v = ?$
> horizontally $u = 12$   $v = 12$   $a = 0$   $t = ?$   $s = ?$

**10** A ball is thrown with an initial velocity of $20\,\mathrm{m\,s^{-1}}$ at an angle of 30° to the horizontal (Figure 2.32). Calculate the horizontal distance travelled by the ball (its **range**).

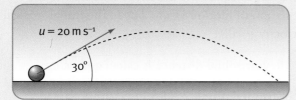

**Figure 2.32** Where will the ball land?

**Step 1** Split the ball's initial velocity into horizontal and vertical components:

initial velocity $= u = 20\,\mathrm{m\,s^{-1}}$

horizontal component of initial velocity
$= u \cos\theta = 20 \times \cos 30° = 17.3\,\mathrm{m\,s^{-1}}$

vertical component of initial velocity
$= u \sin\theta = 20 \times \sin 30° = 10\,\mathrm{m\,s^{-1}}$

**Step 2** Consider the ball's vertical motion. How long will it take to return to the ground? In other words, when will its displacement return to zero?

$u = 10\,\mathrm{m\,s^{-1}}$   $a = -9.81\,\mathrm{m\,s^{-2}}$   $s = 0$   $t = ?$

Using $s = ut + \frac{1}{2}at^2$, we have:

$0 = 10t - 4.905t^2$

This gives $t = 0\,\mathrm{s}$ or $t = 2.04\,\mathrm{s}$. So the ball is in the air for $2.04\,\mathrm{s}$.

*continued* ⋯▸

**Step 3** Consider the ball's horizontal motion. How far will it travel horizontally in the 2.04 s before it lands? This is simple to calculate, since it moves with a constant horizontal velocity of $17.3\,\mathrm{m\,s^{-1}}$.

horizontal displacement $s = 17.3 \times 2.04$
$= 35.3\,\mathrm{m}$

Hence the horizontal distance travelled by the ball (its range) is about 35 m.

## Test yourself

**24** A stone is thrown horizontally from the top of a vertical cliff and lands 4.0 s later at a distance 12.0 m from the base of the cliff. Ignore air resistance.
  **a** Calculate the horizontal speed of the stone.
  **b** Calculate the height of the cliff.

**25** A stone is thrown with a velocity of $8\,\mathrm{m\,s^{-1}}$ into the air at an angle of 40° to the horizontal.
  **a** Calculate the vertical component of the velocity.
  **b** State the value of the vertical component of the velocity when the stone reaches its highest point. Ignore air resistance.
  **c** Use your answers to **a** and **b** to calculate the time the stone takes to reach it highest point.
  **d** Calculate the horizontal component of the velocity.
  **e** Use your answers to **c** and **d** to find the horizontal distance travelled by the stone while climbing to its highest point.

**26** The range of a projectile is the horizontal distance it travels before it reaches the ground. The greatest range is achieved if the projectile is thrown at 45° to the horizontal.
  A ball is thrown with an initial velocity of $40\,\mathrm{m\,s^{-1}}$. Calculate its greatest possible range when air resistance is considered to be negligible.

# Summary

☐ Acceleration is equal to the rate of change of velocity.

☐ Acceleration is a vector quantity.

☐ The gradient of a velocity–time graph is equal to acceleration: $a = \dfrac{\Delta v}{\Delta t}$

☐ The area under a velocity–time graph is equal to displacement (or distance travelled).

☐ The equations of motion (for constant acceleration in a straight line) are:

$$v = u + at$$

$$s = \frac{(u + v)}{2} \times t$$

$$s = ut + \tfrac{1}{2}at^2$$

$$v^2 = u^2 + 2as$$

☐ Vectors such as forces can be resolved into components. Components at right angles to one another can be treated independently of one another. For a velocity $v$ at an angle $\theta$ to the $x$-direction, the components are:

  $x$-direction: $v\cos\theta$

  $y$-direction: $v\sin\theta$

☐ For projectiles, the horizontal and vertical components of velocity can be treated independently. In the absence of air resistance, the horizontal component of velocity is constant while the vertical component of velocity downwards increases at a rate of $9.81\,\text{m}\,\text{s}^{-2}$.

# End-of-chapter questions

1   A motorway designer can assume that cars approaching a motorway enter a slip road with a velocity of $10\,\text{m}\,\text{s}^{-1}$ and reach a velocity of $30\,\text{m}\,\text{s}^{-1}$ before joining the motorway. Calculate the minimum length for the slip road, assuming that vehicles have an acceleration of $4.0\,\text{m}\,\text{s}^{-2}$.

2   A train travels at $50\,\text{m}\,\text{s}^{-1}$ when the driver applies the brakes and gives the train a constant deceleration of magnitude $0.50\,\text{m}\,\text{s}^{-2}$ for $100\,\text{s}$. Describe what happens to the train. Calculate the distance travelled by the train in $100\,\text{s}$.

3   A boy stands on a cliff edge and throws a stone vertically upwards at time $t = 0$. The stone leaves his hand at $20\,\text{m}\,\text{s}^{-1}$. Take the acceleration of the ball as $9.8\,\text{m}\,\text{s}^{-2}$.
    a   Show that the equation for the displacement of the ball is

$$s = 20t - 4.9t^2$$

    b   What is the height of the stone $2.0\,\text{s}$ after release and $6.0\,\text{s}$ after release?
    c   When does the stone return to the level of the boy's hand? Assume the boy's hand does not move vertically after the ball is released.

4    The graph in Figure **2.33** shows the variation of velocity with time of two cars A and B, which
     are travelling in the same direction over a period of time of 40 s. Car A, travelling at a constant
     velocity of $40\,\mathrm{m\,s^{-1}}$, overtakes car B at time $t = 0$. In order to catch up with car A, car B immediately
     accelerates uniformly for 20 s to reach a constant velocity of $50\,\mathrm{m\,s^{-1}}$. Calculate:
     **a**   how far A travels during the first 20 s
     **b**   the acceleration and distance of travel of B during the first 20 s
     **c**   the additional time taken for B to catch up with A
     **d**   the distance each car will have then travelled since $t = 0$.

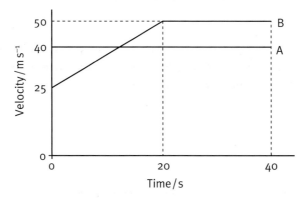

**Figure 2.33**  Speed–time graphs for two cars, A and B. For
End-of-chapter Q **3**.

5    An athlete competing in the long jump leaves the ground with a velocity of $5.6\,\mathrm{m\,s^{-1}}$ at an angle of
     30° to the horizontal.
     **a**   Determine the vertical component of the velocity and use this value to find the time between
            leaving the ground and landing.
     **b**   Determine the horizontal component of the velocity and use this value to find the horizontal
            distance travelled.

# Exam-style questions

1    The diagram shows an arrangement used to measure the acceleration of a metal plate as it
     falls vertically.

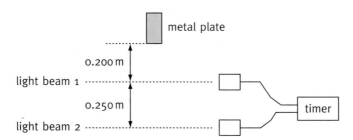

The metal plate is released from rest and falls a distance of 0.200 m before breaking light beam 1. It then falls a further 0.250 m before breaking light beam 2.

**a** Calculate the time taken for the plate to fall 0.200 m from rest. (You may assume that the metal plate falls with an acceleration equal to the acceleration of free fall.) [2]

**b** The timer measures the speed of the metal plate as it falls through each light beam. The speed as it falls through light beam 1 is $1.92\,\mathrm{m\,s^{-1}}$ and the speed as it falls through light beam 2 is $2.91\,\mathrm{m\,s^{-1}}$.

  **i** Calculate the acceleration of the plate between the two light beams. [2]

  **ii** State and explain **one** reason why the acceleration of the plate is not equal to the acceleration of free fall. [2]

**2** The diagram shows the velocity–time graph for a vertically bouncing ball. The ball is released at A and strikes the ground at B. The ball leaves the ground at D and reaches its maximum height at E. The effects of air resistance can be neglected.

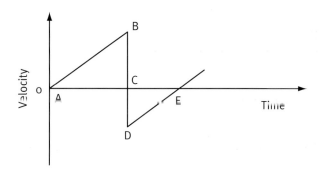

**a** State:

  **i** why the velocity at D is negative [1]

  **ii** why the gradient of the line AB is the same as the gradient of line DE [1]

  **iii** what is represented by the area between the line AB and the time axis [1]

  **iv** why the area of triangle ABC is greater than the area of triangle CDE. [1]

**b** The ball is dropped from rest from an initial height of 1.2 m. After hitting the ground the ball rebounds to a height of 0.80 m. The ball is in contact with the ground between B and D for a time of 0.16 s.

Using the acceleration of free fall, calculate:

  **i** the speed of the ball immediately before hitting the ground [2]

  **ii** the speed of the ball immediately after hitting the ground [2]

  **iii** the acceleration of the ball while it is in contact with the ground. State the direction of this acceleration. [3]

3   A student measures the speed $v$ of a trolley as it moves down a slope. The variation of $v$ with time $t$ is shown on the graph.

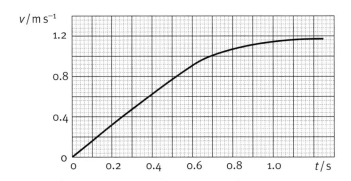

a  Use the graph to find the acceleration of the trolley when $t = 0.7\,\text{s}$.   [2]
b  State how the acceleration of the trolley varies between $t = 0$ and $t = 1.0\,\text{s}$. Explain your answer by reference to the graph.   [3]
c  Determine the distance travelled by the trolley between $t = 0.6$ and $t = 0.8\,\text{s}$.   [3]
d  The student obtained the readings for $v$ using a motion sensor. The readings may have random errors and systematic errors. Explain how these two types of error affect the velocity–time graph.   [2]

4   A car driver is travelling at speed $v$ on a straight road. He comes over the top of a hill to find a fallen tree on the road ahead. He immediately brakes hard but travels a distance of 60 m at speed $v$ before the brakes are applied. The skid marks left on the road by the wheels of the car are of length 140 m. The police investigate whether the driver was speeding and establish that the car decelerates at $2.0\,\text{m s}^{-2}$ during the skid.

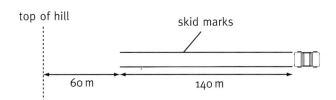

a  Determine the initial speed $v$ of the car before the brakes are applied.   [2]
b  Determine the time taken between the driver coming over the top of the hill and applying the brakes. Suggest whether this shows whether the driver was alert to the danger.   [2]
c  The speed limit on the road is 100 km/h. Determine whether the driver was breaking the speed limit.   [2]

**5** A hot-air balloon rises vertically. At time $t=0$, a ball is released from the balloon. The graph shows the variation of the ball's velocity $v$ with $t$.

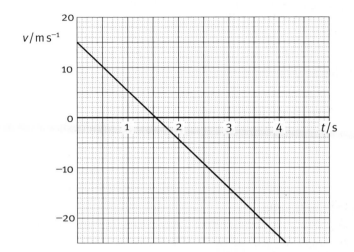

The ball hits the ground at $t=4.1$ s.
**a** Explain how the graph shows that the acceleration of the ball is constant. [1]
**b** Use the graph to:
  **i** determine the time at which the ball reaches its highest point [1]
  **ii** show that the ball rises for a further 12 m between release and its highest point [2]
  **iii** determine the distance between the highest point reached by the ball and the ground. [2]
**c** The equation relating $v$ and $t$ is $v=15-9.81t$. Explain the significance in the equation of:
  **i** the number 15 [1]
  **ii** the negative sign. [1]

**6** An aeroplane is travelling horizontally at a speed of $80 \text{ m s}^{-1}$ and drops a crate of emergency supplies. To avoid damage, the maximum vertical speed of the crate on landing is $20 \text{ m s}^{-1}$. You may assume air resistance is negligible.

80 m s⁻¹

**a** Calculate the maximum height of the aeroplane when the crate is dropped. [2]
**b** Calculate the time taken for the crate to reach the ground from this height. [2]
**c** The aeroplane is travelling at the maximum permitted height. Calculate the horizontal distance travelled by the crate after it is released from the aeroplane. [1]

# 3 Dynamics – explaining motion

## Objectives

After studying this chapter, you should be able to:

☐ state Newton's laws of motion

☐ identify the forces acting on a body in different situations

☐ describe how the motion of a body is affected by the forces acting on it

☐ solve problems using $F = ma$

## Force and acceleration

**Figure 3.1** An aircraft takes off – the force provided by the engines causes the aircraft to accelerate.

If you have ever flown in an aeroplane you will know how the back of the seat pushes you forwards when the aeroplane accelerates down the runway. The pilot must control many forces on the aeroplane to ensure a successful take-off.

In Chapters **1** and **2** we saw how motion can be **described** in terms of displacement, velocity, acceleration and so on. This is known as **kinematics**. Now we are going to look at how we can **explain** how an object moves in terms of the forces which change its motion. This is known as **dynamics**.

## Calculating the acceleration

Figure **3.2a** shows how we represent the force which the motors on a train provide to cause it to accelerate. The net force is represented by an arrow. The direction of the arrow shows the direction of the net force. The magnitude (size) of the net force of 20 000 N is also shown.

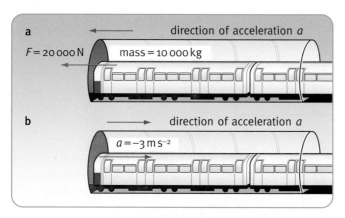

**Figure 3.2** A force is needed to make the train **a** accelerate, and **b** decelerate.

To calculate the acceleration $a$ of the train produced by the net force $F$, we must also know the train's mass $m$ (Table **3.1**). These quantities are related by:

$$a = \frac{F}{m} \quad \text{or} \quad F = ma$$

| Quantity | Symbol | Unit |
|----------|--------|------|
| net force | $F$ | N (newtons) |
| mass | $m$ | kg (kilograms) |
| acceleration | $a$ | $m\,s^{-2}$ (metres per second squared) |

**Table 3.1** The quantities related by $F = ma$.

In this example we have $F = 20\,000$ N and $m = 10\,000$ kg, and so:

$$a = \frac{F}{m} = \frac{20\,000}{10\,000} = 2\,m\,s^{-2}$$

In Figure **3.2b**, the train is decelerating as it comes into a station. Its acceleration is $-3.0 \, \text{m s}^{-2}$. What force must be provided by the braking system of the train?

$$F = ma = 10\,000 \times -3 = -30\,000 \, \text{N}$$

The minus sign shows that the force must act towards the right in the diagram, in the opposite direction to the motion of the train.

## Force, mass and acceleration

The equation we used above, $F = ma$, is a simplified version of **Newton's second law** of motion.

> For a body of constant mass, its acceleration is directly proportional to the net force applied to it.

An alternative form of Newton's second law is given in Chapter **6** when you have studied momentum. Since Newton's second law holds for objects that have a constant mass, this equation can be applied to a train whose mass remains constant during its journey. The equation $a = \dfrac{F}{m}$ relates acceleration, net force and mass. In particular, it shows that the bigger the force, the greater the acceleration it produces. You will probably feel that this is an unsurprising result. For a given object, the acceleration is directly proportional to the net force:

$$a \propto F$$

The equation also shows that the acceleration produced by a force depends on the mass of the object. The **mass** of an object is a measure of its **inertia**, or its ability to resist any change in its motion. The greater the mass, the smaller the acceleration which results. If you push your hardest against a Smart car (which has a small mass), you will have a greater effect than if you push against a more massive Rolls-Royce (Figure **3.3**). So for a constant force, the acceleration is inversely proportional to the mass:

$$a \propto \frac{1}{m}$$

The train driver knows that, when the train is full during the rush hour, it has a smaller acceleration. This

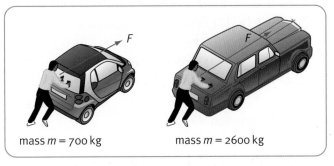

mass $m$ = 700 kg          mass $m$ = 2600 kg

**Figure 3.3** It is easier to make a small mass accelerate than a large mass.

is because its mass is greater when it is full of people. Similarly, it is more difficult to stop the train once it is moving. The brakes must be applied earlier to avoid the train overshooting the platform at the station.

## Worked examples

1   A cyclist of mass 60 kg rides a bicycle of mass 20 kg. When starting off, the cyclist provides a force of 200 N. Calculate the initial acceleration.

**Step 1** This is a straightforward example. First, we must calculate the combined mass $m$ of the bicycle and its rider:

$$m = 20 + 60 = 80 \, \text{kg}$$

We are given the force $F$:

force causing acceleration $F = 200 \, \text{N}$

**Step 2** Substituting these values gives:

$$a = \frac{F}{m} = \frac{200}{80} = 2.5 \, \text{m s}^{-2}$$

So the cyclist's acceleration is $2.5 \, \text{m s}^{-2}$.

2   A car of mass 500 kg is travelling at $20 \, \text{m s}^{-1}$. The driver sees a red traffic light ahead, and slows to a halt in 10 s. Calculate the braking force provided by the car.

*continued* ···▷

**Step 1** In this example, we must first calculate the acceleration required. The car's final velocity is $0\,\mathrm{m\,s^{-1}}$, so its change in velocity $\Delta v$ is $-20\,\mathrm{m\,s^{-1}}$. The time taken $\Delta t$ is $10\,\mathrm{s}$.

$$\text{acceleration } a = \frac{\text{change in velocity}}{\text{time taken}}$$

$$= \frac{\Delta v}{\Delta t} = \frac{-20}{10} = -2\,\mathrm{m\,s^{-2}}$$

**Step 2** To calculate the force, we use:

$$F = ma = 500 \times -2 = -1000\,\mathrm{N}$$

So the brakes must provide a force of $1000\,\mathrm{N}$. (The minus sign shows a force decreasing the velocity of the car.)

## Test yourself

1   Calculate the force needed to give a car of mass $800\,\mathrm{kg}$ an acceleration of $2.0\,\mathrm{m\,s^{-2}}$.

2   A rocket has a mass of $5000\,\mathrm{kg}$. At a particular instant, the net force acting on the rocket is $200\,000\,\mathrm{N}$. Calculate its acceleration.

3   (In this question, you will need to make use of the equations of motion which you studied in Chapter 2.) A motorcyclist of mass $60\,\mathrm{kg}$ rides a bike of mass $40\,\mathrm{kg}$. As she sets off from the lights, the forward force on the bike is $200\,\mathrm{N}$.

   Assuming the net force on the bike remains constant, calculate the bike's velocity after $5.0\,\mathrm{s}$.

# Understanding SI units

In physics, we mostly use units from the SI system. These units are all defined with extreme care, and for a good reason. In science and engineering, every measurement must be made on the same basis, so that measurements obtained in different laboratories can be compared. This is important for commercial reasons, too. Suppose an engineering firm in Taiwan is asked to produce a small part for the engine of a car which is to be assembled in India. The dimensions are given in millimetres and the part must be made with an accuracy of a tiny fraction of a millimetre. All concerned must know that the part will fit correctly – it wouldn't be acceptable to use a different millimetre scale in Taiwan and India.

Engineering measurements, as well as many other technical measurements, are made using SI units to ensure that customers get what they expected (and can complain if they don't). So governments around the world have set up standards laboratories to ensure that measuring instruments are as accurate as is required – scales weigh correctly, police speed cameras give reliable measurements, and so on. (Other, non-SI, units such as the foot, pound or hour, are defined in terms of SI units.)

## Base units, derived units

The metre, kilogram and second are three of the seven SI **base units**. These are defined with great precision so that every standards laboratory can reproduce them correctly.

Other units, such as units of speed ($\mathrm{m\,s^{-1}}$) and acceleration ($\mathrm{m\,s^{-2}}$) are known as **derived units** because they are combinations of base units. Some derived units, such as the newton and the joule, have special names which are more convenient to use than giving them in terms of base units. The definition of the newton will show you how this works.

## Defining the newton

Isaac Newton (1642–1727) played a significant part in developing the scientific idea of force. Building on Galileo's earlier thinking, he explained the relationship between force, mass and acceleration, which we now write as $F = ma$. For this reason, the SI unit of force is named after him.

We can use the equation $F = ma$ to define the **newton** (N).

One newton is the force that will give a $1\,\mathrm{kg}$ mass an acceleration of $1\,\mathrm{m\,s^{-2}}$ in the direction of the force.

$$1\,\mathrm{N} = 1\,\mathrm{kg} \times 1\,\mathrm{m\,s^{-2}} \quad \text{or} \quad 1\,\mathrm{N} = 1\,\mathrm{kg\,m\,s^{-2}}$$

## The seven base units

In mechanics (the study of forces and motion), the units we use are based on three base units: the metre, kilogram and second. As we move into studying electricity, we will need to add another base unit, the ampere. Heat requires another base unit, the kelvin (the unit of temperature).

Table **3.2** shows the seven base units of the SI system. Remember that all other units can be derived from these seven. The equations that relate them are the equations that you will learn as you go along (just as $F = ma$ relates the newton to the kilogram, metre and second). The unit of luminous intensity is not part of the A/AS course.

| Base unit | Symbol | Base unit |
|---|---|---|
| length | $x$, $l$, $s$ etc. | m (metre) |
| mass | $m$ | kg (kilogram) |
| time | $t$ | s (second) |
| electric current | $I$ | A (ampere) |
| thermodynamic temperature | $T$ | K (kelvin) |
| amount of substance | $n$ | mol (mole) |
| luminous intensity | $I$ | cd (candela) |

**Table 3.2** SI base quantities and units. In this course, you will learn about all of these except the candela.

## Test yourself

4 The pull of the Earth's gravity on an apple (its weight) is about 1 newton. We could devise a new international system of units by defining our unit of force as the weight of an apple. State as many reasons as you can why this would not be a very useful definition.

## Other SI units

Using only seven base units means that only this number of quantities have to be defined with great precision. There would be confusion and possible contradiction if more units were also defined. For example, if the density of water were **defined** as exactly $1\,\text{g}\,\text{cm}^{-3}$, then $1000\,\text{cm}^3$ of a sample of water would have a mass of exactly 1 kg. However, it is unlikely that the mass of this volume of water would equal exactly the mass of the standard kilogram. The standard kilogram, which is kept in France, is the one standard from which all masses can ultimately be measured.

All other units can be derived from the base units. This is done using the definition of the quantity. For example speed is defined as $\dfrac{\text{distance}}{\text{time}}$, and so the base units of speed in the SI system are $\mathbf{m\,s^{-1}}$.

Since the defining equation for force is $F = ma$, the base units for force are $\mathbf{kg\,m\,s^{-2}}$.

Equations that relate different quantities must have the same base units on each side of the equation. If this does not happen the equation must be wrong.

When each term in an equation has the same base units the equation is said to be **homogeneous**.

## Worked example

3 It is suggested that the time $T$ for one oscillation of a swinging pendulum is given by the equation $T^2 = 4\pi^2(l/g)$ where $l$ is the length of the pendulum and $g$ is the acceleration due to gravity. Show that this equation is homogeneous.

For the equation to be homogeneous, the term on the left-hand side must have the same base units as all the terms on the right-hand side.

**Step 1** The base unit of time $T$ is $\mathbf{s}$. The base unit of the left-hand side of the equation is therefore $\mathbf{s^2}$.

**Step 2** The base unit of $l$ is $\mathbf{m}$. The base units of $g$ are $\mathbf{m\,s^{-2}}$. Therefore the base unit of the right-hand side is $\dfrac{\mathbf{m}}{\mathbf{(m\,s^{-2})}} = \mathbf{s^2}$. (Notice that the constant $4\pi^2$ has no units.)

Since the base units on the left-hand side of the equation are the same as those on the right, the equation is homogeneous.

## Test yourself

5 Determine the base units of:

  **a** pressure $\left(= \dfrac{\text{force}}{\text{area}}\right)$

  **b** energy $(= \text{force} \times \text{distance})$

  **c** density $\left(= \dfrac{\text{mass}}{\text{volume}}\right)$

6 Use base units to prove that the following equations are homogeneous.

  **a** pressure = density × acceleration due to gravity × depth

  **b** distance travelled = initial speed × time + $\frac{1}{2}$ acceleration × time² $(s = ut + \frac{1}{2}at^2)$

## Prefixes

Each unit in the SI system can have **multiples** and **sub-multiples** to avoid using very high or low numbers. For example 1 millimetre (mm) is one thousandth of a metre and 1 micrometre (µm) is one millionth of a metre.

The **prefix** comes before the unit. In the unit mm, the first m is the prefix milli and the second m is the unit metre. You will need to recognise a number of prefixes for the A/AS course, as shown in Table **3.3**.

| Multiples | | | Sub-multiples | | |
|---|---|---|---|---|---|
| Multiple | Prefix | Symbol | Multiple | Prefix | Symbol |
| $10^3$ | kilo | k | $10^{-2}$ | centi | c |
| $10^6$ | mega | M | $10^{-3}$ | mill | m |
| $10^9$ | giga | G | $10^{-6}$ | micro | µ |
| $10^{12}$ | tera | T | $10^{-9}$ | nano | n |
| $10^{15}$ | peta | P | $10^{-12}$ | pico | p |

**Table 3.3** Multiples and sub-multiples

You must take care when using prefixes.

- Squaring or cubing prefixes – for example:
  $1\,cm = 10^{-2}\,m$
  so $1\,cm^2 = (10^{-2}\,m)^2 = 10^{-4}\,m^2$
  and $1\,cm^3 = (10^{-2}\,m)^3 = 10^{-6}\,m^3$.
- Writing units – for example, you must leave a small space between each unit when writing a speed such as $3\,m\,s^{-1}$, because if you write it as $3\,ms^{-1}$ it would mean $3$ millisecond$^{-1}$.

### Worked example

4  The density of water is $1.0\,g\,cm^{-3}$. Calculate this value in $kg\,m^{-3}$.

**Step 1** Find the conversions for the units:

$1\,g = 1 \times 10^{-3}\,kg$

$1\,cm^3 = 1 \times 10^{-6}\,m^3$

**Step 2** Use these in the value for the density of water:

$$1.0\,g\,cm^{-3} = \frac{1.0 \times 1 \times 10^{-3}}{1 \times 10^{-6}}$$

$$= 1.0 \times 10^3\,kg\,m^{-3}$$

# The pull of gravity

Now we need to consider some specific forces – such as weight and friction.

When Isaac Newton was confined to his rural home to avoid the plague which was rampant in other parts of England, he is said to have noticed an apple fall to the ground. From this, he developed his theory of gravity which relates the motion of falling objects here on Earth to the motion of the Moon around the Earth, and the planets around the Sun.

The force which caused the apple to accelerate was the pull of the Earth's gravity. Another name for this force is the **weight** of the apple. The force is shown as an arrow, pulling vertically downwards on the apple (Figure **3.4**). It is usual to show the arrow coming from the centre of the apple – its **centre of gravity**. The centre of gravity of an object is defined as the point where its entire weight appears to act.

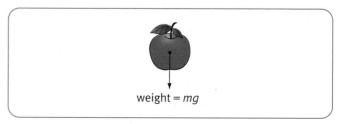

weight = *mg*

**Figure 3.4** The weight of an object is a force caused by the Earth's gravity. It acts vertically down on the object.

## Large and small

A large rock has a greater weight than a small rock, but if you push both rocks over a cliff at the same time, they will fall at the same rate. In other words, they have the **same** acceleration, regardless of their mass. This is a surprising result. Common sense may suggest that a heavier object will fall faster than a lighter one. It is said that Galileo dropped a large cannon ball and a small cannon ball from the top of the Leaning Tower of Pisa in Italy, and showed that they landed simultaneously. He may never actually have done this, but the story illustrates that the result is not intuitively obvious – if everyone thought that the two cannon balls would accelerate at the same rate, there would not have been any experiment or story.

In fact, we are used to lighter objects falling more slowly than heavy ones. A feather drifts down to the floor, while a stone falls quickly. However, we are being misled by the presence of **air resistance**. The force of air resistance has a large effect on the falling feather, and almost no effect on the falling stone. When astronauts visited the Moon (where there is virtually no atmosphere and so no air resistance), they were able to show that a feather and a stone fell side-by-side to the ground.

As we saw in Chapter 2, an object falling freely close to the Earth's surface has an acceleration of roughly $9.81 \, \text{m s}^{-2}$, the acceleration of free fall $g$.

We can find the force causing this acceleration using $F = ma$. This force is the object's **weight**. Hence the weight $W$ of an object is given by:

weight = mass × acceleration of free fall

or

$W = mg$

## Gravitational field strength

Here is another way to think about the significance of $g$. This quantity indicates how strong gravity is at a particular place. The Earth's gravitational field is stronger than the Moon's. On the Earth's surface, gravity gives an acceleration of free fall of about $9.81 \, \text{m s}^{-2}$. On the Moon, gravity is weaker; it only gives an acceleration of free fall of about $1.6 \, \text{m s}^{-2}$. So $g$ indicates the strength of the gravitational field at a particular place:

$g$ = gravitational field strength

and

weight = mass × gravitational field strength

(Gravitational field strength has unit $\text{N kg}^{-1}$. This unit is equivalent to $\text{m s}^{-2}$.)

## On the Moon

The Moon is smaller and has less mass than the Earth, and so its gravity is weaker. If you were to drop a stone on the Moon, it would have a smaller acceleration. Your hand is about 1 m above ground level; a stone takes about 0.45 s to fall through this distance on the Earth, but about 1.1 s on the surface of the Moon. The acceleration of free fall on the Moon is about one-sixth of that on the Earth:

$g_{\text{Moon}} = 1.6 \, \text{m s}^{-2}$

It follows that objects weigh less on the Moon than on the Earth. They are not completely weightless, because the Moon's gravity is not zero.

## Mass and weight

We have now considered two related quantities, mass and weight. It is important to distinguish carefully between these (Table 3.4).

| Quantity | Symbol | Unit | Comment |
|----------|--------|------|---------|
| mass | $m$ | kg | this does not vary from place to place |
| weight | $mg$ | N | this a force – it depends on the strength of gravity |

**Table 3.4** Distinguishing between mass and weight.

If your moon-buggy breaks down (Figure 3.5), it will be no easier to push it along on the Moon than on the Earth. This is because its mass does not change, because it is made from just the same atoms and molecules wherever it is. From $F = ma$, it follows that if

$m$ doesn't change, you will need the same force $F$ to start it moving.

However, your moon-buggy will be easier to lift on the Moon, because its weight will be less. From $W = mg$, since $g$ is less on the Moon, it has a smaller weight than when on the Earth.

**Figure 3.6** An elephant provides the force needed to drag this tree from the forest.

**Figure 3.5** The mass of a moon-buggy is the same on the Moon as on the Earth, but its weight is smaller.

# Mass and inertia

It took a long time for scientists to develop correct ideas about forces and motion. We will start by thinking about some wrong ideas, and then consider why Galileo, Newton and others decided new ideas were needed.

## Observations and ideas

Here are some observations to think about.

- The large tree trunk shown in Figure **3.6** is being dragged from a forest. The elephant provides the force needed to pull it along. If the elephant stops pulling, the tree trunk will stop moving.
- A horse is pulling a cart. If the horse stops pulling, the cart soon stops.
- You are riding a bicycle. If you stop pedalling, the bicycle will come to a halt.
- You are driving along the road. You must keep your foot on the accelerator pedal, otherwise the car will not keep moving.
- You kick a football. The ball rolls along the ground and gradually stops.

In each of these cases, there is a force which makes something move – the pull of the elephant or the horse, your push on the bicycle pedals, the force of the car engine, the push of your foot. Without the force, the moving object comes to a halt. So what conclusion might we draw?

**A moving object needs a force to keep it moving.**

This might seem a sensible conclusion to draw, but it is wrong. We have not thought about all the forces involved. The missing force is friction.

In each example above, friction (or air resistance) makes the object slow down and stop when there is no force pushing or pulling it forwards. For example, if you stop pedalling your cycle, air resistance will slow you down. There is also friction at the axles of the wheels and this too will slow you down. If you could lubricate your axles and cycle in a vacuum, you could travel along at a steady speed for ever, without pedalling!

In the 17th century, astronomers began to use telescopes to observe the heavens. They saw that objects such as the planets could move freely through space. They simply kept on moving, without anything providing a force to push them. Galileo came to the conclusion that this was the natural motion of objects.

- An object at rest will stay at rest, unless a force causes it to start moving.
- A moving object will continue to move at a steady speed in a straight line, unless a force acts on it.

So objects move with a constant velocity, unless a force acts on them. (Being stationary is simply a particular case of this, where the velocity is zero.) Nowadays it is much easier to appreciate this law of motion, because we have more experience of objects moving with little or no friction – roller-skates with low-friction bearings, ice skates, and spacecraft in empty space. In Galileo's day, people's everyday experience was of dragging things along the ground, or pulling things on carts with high-friction axles. Before Galileo, the orthodox scientific idea was that a force must act all the time to keep an object moving – this had been handed down from the time of the ancient Greek philosopher Aristotle. So it was a great achievement when scientists were able to develop a picture of a world without friction.

## The idea of inertia

The tendency of a moving object to carry on moving is sometimes known as **inertia**.

- An object with a large mass is difficult to stop moving – think about catching a cricket ball, compared with a tennis ball.
- Similarly, a stationary object with a large mass is difficult to start moving – think about pushing a car to get it started.
- It is difficult to make a massive object change direction – think about the way a fully laden supermarket trolley tries to keep moving in a straight line.

All of these examples suggest another way to think of an object's mass; it is a measure of its inertia – how difficult it is to change the object's motion. Uniform motion is the natural state of motion of an object. Here, **uniform motion** means 'moving with constant velocity' or 'moving at a steady speed in a straight line'. Now we can summarise these findings as **Newton's first law of motion**.

> An object will remain at rest or in a state of uniform motion unless it is acted on by a net external force.

In fact, this is already contained in the simple equation we have been using to calculate acceleration, $F = ma$. If no net force acts on an object ($F = 0$), it will not accelerate ($a = 0$). The object will either remain stationary or it will continue to travel at a constant velocity. If we rewrite the equation as $a = \dfrac{F}{m}$, we can see that the greater the mass $m$, the smaller the acceleration $a$ produced by a force $F$.

### Test yourself

10 Use the idea of inertia to explain why some large cars have power-assisted brakes.

11 A car crashes head-on into a brick wall. Use the idea of inertia to explain why the driver is more likely to come out through the windscreen if he or she is not wearing a seat belt.

## Top speed

The vehicle shown in Figure 3.7 is capable of speeds as high as 760 mph, greater than the speed of sound. Its streamlined shape is designed to cut down air

**Figure 3.7** The Thrust SSC rocket car broke the world land-speed record in 1997. It achieved a top speed of 763 mph (just over 340 m s⁻¹) over a distance of 1 mile (1.6 km).

resistance and its jet engines provide a strong forward force to accelerate it up to top speed. All vehicles have a top speed. But why can't they go any faster? Why can't a car driver keep pressing on the accelerator pedal, and simply go faster and faster?

To answer this, we have to think about the two forces mentioned above: air resistance and the forward thrust (force) of the engine. The vehicle will accelerate so long as the thrust is greater than the air resistance. When the two forces are equal, the net force on the vehicle is zero, and the vehicle moves at a steady velocity.

## Balanced and unbalanced forces

If an object has two or more forces acting on it, we have to consider whether or not they are 'balanced' (Figure 3.8). Forces on an object are balanced when the net force on the object is zero. The object will either remain at rest or have a constant velocity.

We can calculate the **resultant force** by adding up two (or more) forces which act in the same straight line. We must take account of the direction of each force. In the examples above, forces to the right are positive and forces to the left are negative.

When a car travels slowly, it encounters little air resistance. However, the faster it goes, the more air it has to push out of the way each second, and so the greater the air resistance. Eventually the backward force of air resistance equals the forward force provided between the tyres and the road, and the forces on the car are balanced. It can go no faster – it has reached top speed.

## Free fall

Skydivers (Figure 3.9) are rather like cars – at first, they accelerate freely. At the start of the fall, the only force acting on the diver is his or her weight. The acceleration of the diver at the start must therefore be $g$. Then increasing air resistance opposes their fall and their acceleration decreases. Eventually they reach a maximum velocity, known as the **terminal velocity**. At the terminal velocity the air resistance is equal to the weight. The terminal velocity is approximately 120 miles per hour (about $50\,\mathrm{m\,s^{-1}}$), but it depends on the diver's weight and orientation. Head-first is fastest.

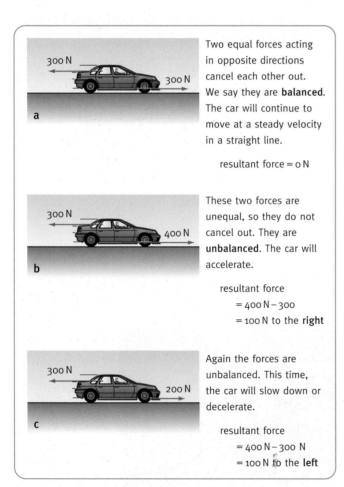

Two equal forces acting in opposite directions cancel each other out. We say they are **balanced**. The car will continue to move at a steady velocity in a straight line.

resultant force = 0 N

These two forces are unequal, so they do not cancel out. They are **unbalanced**. The car will accelerate.

resultant force
= 400 N – 300
= 100 N to the **right**

Again the forces are unbalanced. This time, the car will slow down or decelerate.

resultant force
= 400 N – 300 N
= 100 N to the **left**

**Figure 3.8** Balanced and unbalanced forces.

**Figure 3.9** A skydiver falling freely.

The idea of a parachute is to greatly increase the air resistance. Then terminal velocity is reduced, and the parachutist can land safely. Figure **3.10** shows how a parachutist's velocity might change during descent.

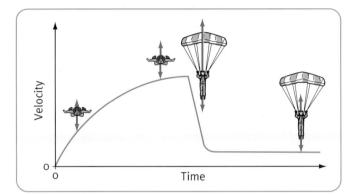

**Figure 3.10** The velocity of a parachutist varies during a descent.

Terminal velocity depends on the weight and surface area of the object. For insects, air resistance is much greater than for a human being and so their terminal velocity is quite low. Insects can be swept up several kilometres into the atmosphere by rising air streams. Later, they fall back to Earth uninjured. It is said that mice can survive a fall from a high building for the same reason.

# Moving through fluids

Air resistance is just one example of the resistive or **viscous forces** which objects experience when they move through a fluid – a liquid or a gas. If you have ever run down the beach and into the sea, or tried to wade quickly through the water of a swimming pool, you will have experienced the force of **drag**. The deeper the water gets, the more it resists your movement and the harder you have to work to make progress through it. In deep water, it is easier to swim than to wade.

You can observe the effect of drag on a falling object if you drop a key or a coin into the deep end of a swimming pool. For the first few centimetres, it speeds up, but for the remainder of its fall, it has a steady speed. (If it fell through the same distance in air, it would accelerate all the way.) The drag of water means that the falling object reaches its terminal velocity very soon after it is released. Compare this with a skydiver, who has to fall hundreds of metres before reaching terminal velocity.

# Moving through air

We rarely experience drag in air. This is because air is much less dense than water; its density is roughly $\frac{1}{800}$th that of water. At typical walking speed, we do not notice the effects of drag. However, if you want to move faster, they can be important. Racing cyclists, like the one shown in Figure **3.11**, wear tight-fitting clothing and streamlined helmets. Other athletes may take advantage of the drag of air. The runner in Figure **3.12** is undergoing resistance training. The parachute provides a backward force against which his muscles must work. This should help to develop his muscles.

**Figure 3.11** A racing cyclist adopts a posture which helps to reduce drag. Clothing, helmet and even the cycle itself are designed to allow them to go as fast as possible.

**Figure 3.12** A runner making use of air resistance to build up his muscles.

**5** A car of mass 500 kg is travelling along a flat road. The forward force provided between the car tyres and the road is 300 N and the air resistance is 200 N. Calculate the acceleration of the car.

**Step 1** Start by drawing a diagram of the car, showing the forces mentioned in the question (Figure 3.13). Calculate the resultant force on the car; the force to the right is taken as positive:

resultant force = 300 – 200 = 100 N

**Step 2** Now use $F = ma$ to calculate the car's acceleration:

$$a = \frac{F}{m} = \frac{100}{500} = 0.20 \, \text{m s}^{-2}$$

So the car's acceleration is $0.20 \, \text{m s}^{-2}$.

**Figure 3.13** For Worked example 5. The forces on an accelerating car.

**6** The maximum forward force a car can provide is 500 N. The air resistance $F$ which the car experiences depends on its speed according to $F = 0.2v^2$, where $v$ is the speed in m s⁻¹. Determine the top speed of the car.

**Step 1** From the equation $F = 0.2v^2$, you can see that the air resistance increases as the car goes faster. Top speed is reached when the forward force equals the air resistance. So, at top speed:

$$500 = 0.2v^2$$

continued ⋯⟩

**Step 2** Rearranging gives:

$$v^2 = \frac{500}{0.2} = 2500$$

$$v = 50 \, \text{m s}^{-1}$$

So the car's top speed is $50 \, \text{m s}^{-1}$ (this is about $180 \, \text{km h}^{-1}$).

**12** If you drop a large stone and a small stone from the top of a tall building, which one will reach the ground first Explain your answer.

**13** In a race, downhill skiers want to travel as quickly as possible. They are always looking for ways to increase their top speed. Explain how they might do this. Think about:
 **a** their skis
 **b** their clothing
 **c** their muscles
 **d** the slope.

**14** Skydivers jump from a plane at intervals of a few seconds. If two divers wish to join up as they fall, the second must catch up with the first.
 **a** If one diver is more massive than the other, which should jump first? Use the idea of forces and terminal velocity to explain your answer.
 **b** If both divers are equally massive, suggest what the second might do to catch up with the first.

# Identifying forces

It is important to be able to identify the forces which act on an object. When we know what forces are acting, we can predict how it will move. Figure 3.14 shows some important forces, how they arise, and how we represent them in diagrams.

| Diagram | Force | Important situations |
|---|---|---|
| 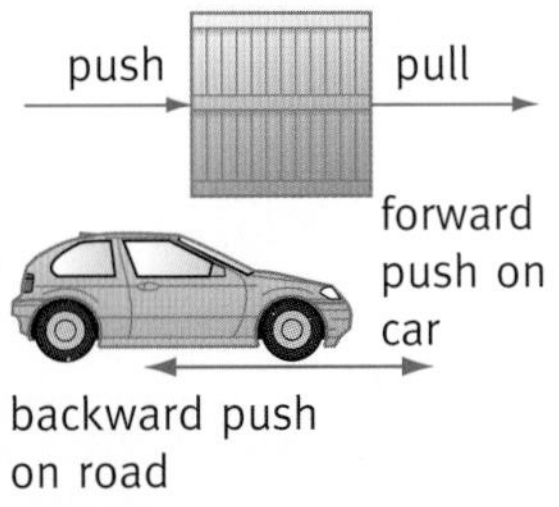 push  pull<br><br>forward push on car<br><br>backward push on road | **Pushes and pulls.** You can make an object accelerate by pushing and pulling it. Your force is shown by an arrow pushing (or pulling) the object.<br><br>The engine of a car provides a force to push backwards on the road. Frictional forces from the road on the tyre push the car forwards. | • pushing and pulling<br>• lifting<br>• force of car engine<br>• attraction and repulsion by magnets and by electric charges |
| 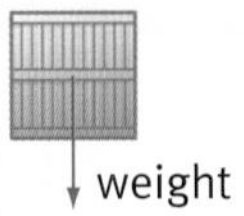 weight | **Weight.** This is the force of gravity acting on the object. It is usually shown by an arrow pointing vertically downwards from the object's centre of gravity. | • any object in a gravitational field<br>• less on the Moon |
| 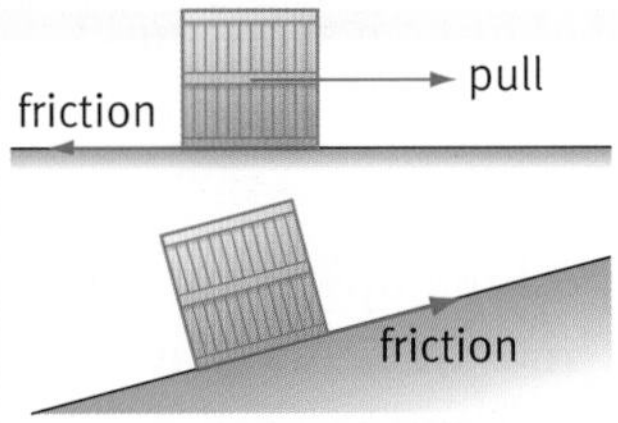 friction  pull<br><br>friction | **Friction.** This is the force which arises when two surfaces rub over one another. If an object is sliding along the ground, friction acts in the opposite direction to its motion. If an object is stationary, but tending to slide – perhaps because it is on a slope – the force of friction acts up the slope to stop it from sliding down. Friction always acts along a surface, never at an angle to it. | • pulling an object along the ground<br>• vehicles cornering or skidding<br>• sliding down a slope |
|  drag | **Drag.** This force is similar to friction. When an object moves through air, there is friction between it and the air. Also, the object has to push aside the air as it moves along. Together, these effects make up drag.<br><br>Similarly, when an object moves through a liquid, it experiences a drag force.<br><br>Drag acts to oppose the motion of an object; it acts in the opposite direction to the object's velocity. It can be reduced by giving the object a streamlined shape. | • vehicles moving<br>• aircraft flying<br>• parachuting<br>• objects falling thorugh air or water<br>• ships sailing |
| 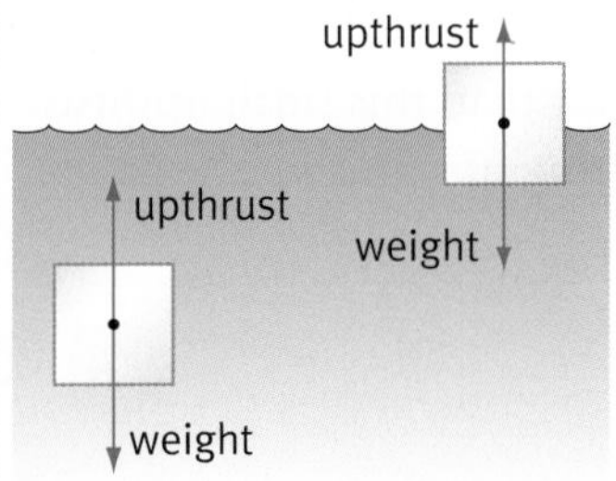 upthrust<br><br>upthrust  weight<br><br>weight | **Upthrust.** Any object placed in a fluid such as water or air experiences an upwards force. This is what makes it possible for something to float in water.<br><br>Upthrust arises from the pressure which a fluid exerts on an object. The deeper you go, the greater the pressure. So there is more pressure on the lower surface of an object than on the upper surface, and this tends to push it upwards. If upthrust is greater than the object's weight, it will float up to the surface. | • boats and icebergs floating<br>• people swimming<br>• divers surfacing<br>• a hot air balloon rising |
| 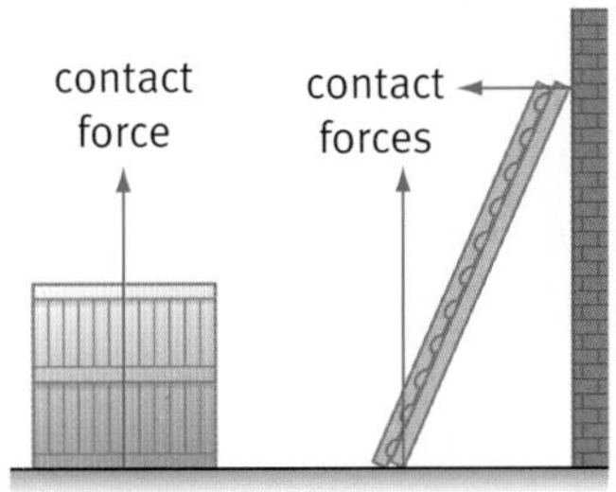 contact force  contact forces | **Contact force.** When you stand on the floor or sit on a chair, there is usually a force which pushes up against your weight, and which supports you so that you do not fall down. The contact force is sometimes known as the normal reaction of the floor or chair. (In this context, normal means 'perpendicular'.)<br><br>The contact force always acts at right angles to the surface which produces it. The floor pushes straight upwards; if you lean against a wall, it pushes back against you horizontally. | • standing on the ground<br>• one object sitting on top of another<br>• leaning against a wall<br>• one object bouncing off another |
| 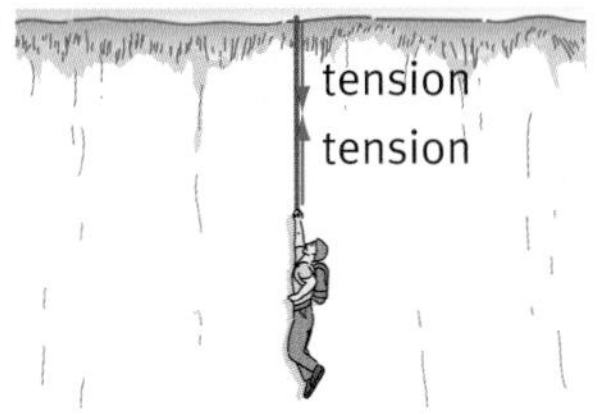 tension<br>tension | **Tension.** This is the force in a rope or string when it is stretched. If you pull on the ends of a string, it tends to stretch. The tension in the string pulls back against you. It tries to shorten the string.<br><br>Tension can also act in springs. If you stretch a spring, the tension pulls back to try to shorten the spring. If you squash (compress) the spring, the tension acts to expand the spring. | • pulling with a rope<br>• squashing or stretching a spring |

**Figure 3.14** Some important forces.

## Contact forces and upthrust

We will now think about the forces which act when two objects are in contact with each other. When two objects touch each other, each exerts a force on the other. These are called **contact forces**. For example, when you stand on the floor (Figure 3.15), your feet push downwards on the floor and the floor pushes back upwards on your feet. This is a vital force – the upward push of the floor prevents you from falling downwards under the pull of your weight.

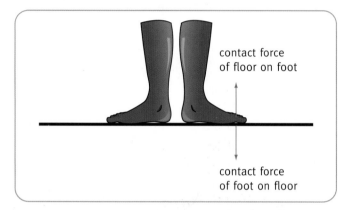

Figure 3.15 Equal and opposite contact forces act when you stand on the floor.

Where do these contact forces come from? When you stand on the floor, the floor becomes slightly compressed. Its atoms are pushed slightly closer together, and the interatomic forces push back against the compressing force. At the same time, the atoms in your feet are also pushed together so that they push back in the opposite direction. (It is hard to see the compression of the floor when you stand on it, but if you stand on a soft material such as foam rubber or a mattress you will be able to see the compression clearly.)

You can see from Figure 3.15 that the two contact forces act in opposite directions. They are also equal in magnitude. As we will see shortly, this is a consequence of Newton's third law of motion.

When an object is immersed in a fluid (a liquid or a gas), it experiences an upward force called **upthrust**. It is the upthrust of water which keeps a boat floating (Figure 3.16) and the upthrust of air which lifts a hot air balloon upwards.

The upthrust of water on a boat can be thought of as the contact force of the water on the boat. It is caused

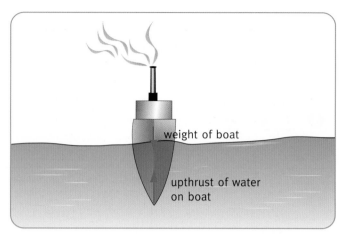

Figure 3.16 Without sufficient upthrust from the water, the boat would sink.

by the pressure of the water pushing upwards on the boat. Pressure arises from the motion of the water molecules colliding with the boat and the net effect of all these collisions is an upward force.

An object in air, such as a ball has a very small upthrust acting on it, because the density of the air around it is low. Molecules hit the top surface of the ball pushing down, but only a few more molecules push upwards on the bottom of the ball, so the resultant force upwards, or the upthrust is low. If the ball is falling, air resistance is greater than this small upthrust but both these forces are acting upwards on the ball.

### Test yourself

15 Name these forces:
   a the upward push of water on a submerged object
   b the force which wears away two surfaces as they move over one another
   c the force which pulled the apple off Isaac Newton's tree
   d the force which stops you falling through the floor
   e the force in a string which is holding up an apple
   f the force which makes it difficult to run through shallow water.

*continued* ⋯⊱

**16** Draw a diagram to show the forces which act on a car as it travels along a level road at its top speed.

**17** Imagine throwing a shuttlecock straight up in the air. Air resistance is more important for shuttlecocks than for a tennis ball. Air resistance always acts in the opposite direction to the velocity of an object.

Draw diagrams to show the two forces, weight and air resistance, acting on the shuttlecock:
**a** as it moves upwards
**b** as it falls back downwards.

# Newton's third law of motion

For completeness, we should now consider **Newton's third law of motion**. (There is more about this in Chapter **6**.)

When two objects interact, each exerts a force on the other. Newton's third law says that these forces are equal and opposite to each other:

> When two bodies interact, the forces they exert on each other are equal in magnitude and opposite in direction.

(These two forces are sometimes described as **action** and **reaction**, but this is misleading as it sounds as though one force arises as a consequence of the other. In fact, the two forces appear at the same time and we can't say that one caused the other.)

The two forces which make up a 'Newton's third law pair' have the following characteristics:

- They act on **different** objects.
- They are equal in magnitude.
- They are opposite in direction.
- They are forces **of the same type**.

What does it mean to say that the forces are 'of the same type'? We need to think about the type of interaction which causes the forces to appear.

- Two objects may attract each other because of the gravity of their masses – these are gravitational forces.
- Two objects may attract or repel because of their electrical charges – electrical forces.

- Two objects may touch – contact forces.
- Two objects may be attached by a string and pull on each other – tension forces.
- Two objects may attract or repel because of their magnetic fields – magnetic forces.

Figure **3.17** shows a person standing on the Earth's surface. The two gravitational forces are a Newton's third law pair, as are the two contact forces. Don't be misled into thinking that the person's weight and the contact force of the floor are a Newton's third law pair. Although they are 'equal and opposite', they do not act on different objects and they are not of the same type.

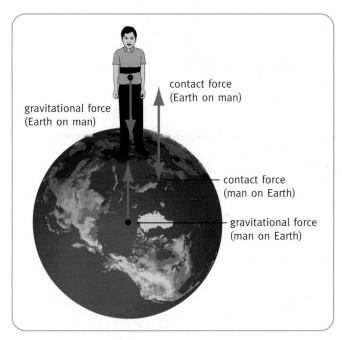

**Figure 3.17** For each of the forces that the Earth exerts on you, an equal and opposite force acts on the Earth.

## Test yourself

**18** Describe one 'Newton's third law pair' of forces involved in the following situations. In each case, state the object that each force acts on, the type of force and the direction of the force.
**a** You step on someone's toe.
**b** A car hits a brick wall and comes to rest.
**c** A car slows down by applying the brakes.
**d** You throw a ball upwards into the air.

# Summary

☐ An object will remain at rest or in a state of uniform motion unless it is acted on by an external force. This is Newton's first law of motion.

☐ For a body of constant mass, the acceleration is directly proportional to the net force applied to it. Net force $F$, mass $m$ and acceleration $a$ are related by the equation:

net force = mass × acceleration

$F = ma$.

This is a form of Newton's second law of motion.

☐ When two bodies interact, the forces they exert on each other are equal in magnitude and opposite in direction. This is Newton's third law of motion.

☐ The acceleration produced by a force is in the same direction as the force. Where there are two or more forces, we must determine the resultant force.

☐ A newton (N) is the force required to give a mass of 1 kg an acceleration of $1\,\text{m}\,\text{s}^{-2}$ in the direction of the force.

☐ The greater the mass of an object, the more it resists changes in its motion. Mass is a measure of the object's inertia.

☐ The weight of an object is a result of the pull of gravity on it:

weight = mass × acceleration of free fall ($W = mg$)
weight = mass × gravitational field strength

☐ An object falling freely under gravity has a constant acceleration provided the gravitational field strength is constant. However, fluid resistance (such as air resistance) reduces its acceleration. Terminal velocity is reached when the fluid resistance is equal to the weight of the object.

# End-of-chapter questions

1   When a golfer hits a ball his club is in contact with the ball for about 0.000 5 s and the ball leaves the club with a speed of $70\,\text{m}\,\text{s}^{-1}$. The mass of the ball is 46 g.
   a   Determine the mean accelerating force.
   b   What mass, resting on the ball, would exert the same force as in **a**?

2   The mass of a spacecraft is 70 kg. As the spacecraft takes off from the Moon, the upwards force on the spacecraft caused by the engines is 500 N. The gravitational field strength on the Moon is $1.6\,\text{N}\,\text{kg}^{-1}$.
   Determine
   a   the weight of the spacecraft on the Moon
   b   the resultant force on the spacecraft
   c   the acceleration of the spacecraft.

**3** A metal ball is dropped into a tall cylinder of oil. The ball initially accelerates but soon reaches a terminal velocity.
    **a** By considering the forces on the metal ball bearing, explain why it first accelerates but then reaches terminal velocity.
    **b** Describe how you would show that the metal ball reaches terminal velocity.

**4** Determine the speed in $m\,s^{-1}$ of an object that travels
    **a** $3\,\mu m$ in $5\,ms$
    **b** $6\,km$ in $3\,Ms$
    **c** $8\,pm$ in $4\,ns$

**5** Figure **3.18** shows a man who is just supporting the weight of a box. Two of the forces acting are shown in the diagram. According to Newton's third law, each of these forces is paired with **another** force.

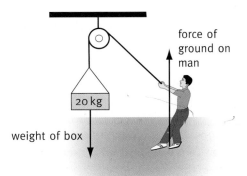

**Figure 3.18** For End-of-chapter Q **5**.

For **a** the weight of the box and **b** the force of the ground on the man, state:
    **i** the body that the other force acts upon
    **ii** the direction of the other force
    **iii** the type of force involved.

# Exam-style questions

**1** A car starts to move along a straight, level road. For the first $10\,s$, the driver maintains a constant acceleration of $1.5\,m\,s^{-2}$. The mass of the car is $1.1 \times 10^3\,kg$.
    **a** Calculate the driving force provided by the wheels, when:
        **i** the force opposing motion is negligible                                   **[1]**
        **ii** the total force opposing the motion of the car is $600\,N$.        **[1]**
    **b** Calculate the distance travelled by the car in the first $10\,s$.           **[2]**

**2** The diagram shows the speed–time graphs for two falling balls.
  **a** Determine the terminal velocity of the plastic ball.                                                     [1]
  **b** Both balls are of the same size and shape but the metal ball has a greater mass. Explain,
     in terms of Newton's laws of motion and the forces involved, why the plastic ball
     reaches a constant velocity but the metal ball does not.                                                    [3]
  **c** Explain why both balls have the same initial acceleration.                                               [2]

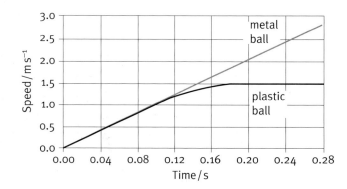

**3** A car of mass 1200 kg accelerates from rest to a speed of 8.0 m s$^{-1}$ in a time of 2.0 s
  **a** Calculate the forward driving force acting on the car while it is accelerating. Assume that,
     at low speeds, all frictional forces are negligible.                                                        [2]
  **b** At high speeds the resistive frictional force $F$ produced by air on a body moving with
     velocity $v$ is given by the equation $F = bv^2$ where $b$ is a constant.
     **i**   Derive the base units of force in the SI system.                                                     [1]
     **ii**  Determine the base units of $b$ in the SI system.                                                    [1]
     **iii** The car continues with same forward driving force and accelerates until it reaches a
         top speed of 50 m s$^{-1}$. At this speed the resistive force is given by the equation $F = bv^2$.
         Determine the value of $b$ for the car.                                                                  [2]
     **iv** Sketch a graph showing how the value of $F$ varies with $v$ over the range 0 to 50 m s$^{-1}$
         and use your graph to describe what happens to the acceleration of the car during
         this time.                                                                                              [2]

**4** **a** Explain what is meant by the **mass** of a body and the **weight** of a body.                         [3]
  **b** State and explain one situation in which the weight of a body changes while its
     mass remains constant.                                                                                      [2]
  **c** State the difference between the base units of mass and weight in the SI system.                          [2]

**5** **a** State Newton's second law of motion.                                                                 [2]
  **b** When jumping from a wall on to the ground, it is advisable to bend one's knees on
     landing.
     **i**  State how bending one's knees affects the time it takes to stop when hitting
        the ground.                                                                                              [1]
     **ii** Using Newton's second law of motion, explain why it is sensible to bend
        one's knees.                                                                                             [2]

## Objectives

After studying this chapter, you should be able to:

☐ add two or more coplanar forces

☐ resolve a force into perpendicular components

☐ define and apply the moment of a force and the torque of a couple

☐ apply the principle of moments

☐ state the conditions for a body to be in equilibrium

## Sailing ahead

Figure 4.1 Sailing into the wind.

Force is a vector quantity. Sailors know a lot about the vector nature of forces. For example, they can sail 'into the wind'. The sails of a yacht can be angled to provide a component of force in the forward direction and the boat can then sail at almost 45° to the wind. The boat tends to 'heel over' and the crew sit on the side of the boat to provide a turning effect in the opposite direction (Figure 4.1).

## Combining forces

You should recall that a vector quantity has both magnitude and direction. An object may have two or more forces acting on it and, since these are vectors, we must use vector addition (Chapter 1) to find their combined effect (their resultant).

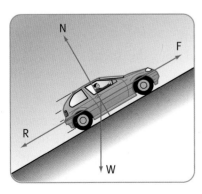

Figure 4.2 Four forces act on this car as it moves uphill.

There are several forces acting on the car (Figure 4.2) as it struggles up the steep hill. They are:

• its weight $W (= mg)$
• the contact force $N$ of the road (its normal reaction)
• air resistance $R$
• the forward force $F$ caused by friction between the car tyres and the road.

If we knew the magnitude and direction of each of these forces, we could work out their combined effect on the car. Will it accelerate up the hill? Or will it slide backwards down the hill? The combined effect of several forces is known as the **resultant force**. To see how to work out the resultant of two or more forces, we will start with a relatively simple example.

### Two forces in a straight line

We saw some examples earlier of two forces acting in a straight line. For example, a falling tennis ball may be acted on by two forces: its weight $mg$, downwards, and air resistance $R$, upwards (Figure 4.3). The resultant force is then:

$$\text{resultant force} = mg - R = 1.0 - 0.2 = 0.8\,\text{N}$$

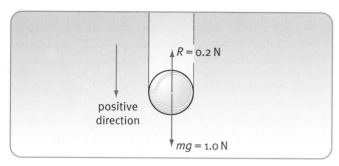

**Figure 4.3** Two forces on a falling tennis ball.

When adding two or more forces which act in a straight line, we have to take account of their directions. A force may be positive or negative; we adopt a **sign convention** to help us decide which is which.

If you apply a sign convention correctly, the sign of your final answer will tell you the direction of the resultant force (and hence acceleration).

## Two forces at right angles

Figure 4.4 shows a shuttlecock falling on a windy day. There are two forces acting on the shuttlecock: its weight vertically downwards, and the horizontal push of the wind. (It helps if you draw the force arrows of different lengths, to show which force is greater.) We must add these two forces together to find the resultant force acting on the shuttlecock.

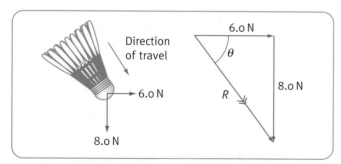

**Figure 4.4** Two forces act on this shuttlecock as it travels through the air; the vector triangle shows how to find the resultant force.

We add the forces by drawing two arrows, end-to-end, as shown on the right of Figure 4.4.

- First, a horizontal arrow is drawn to represent the 6.0 N push of the wind.

- Next, starting from the end of this arrow, we draw a second arrow, downwards, representing the weight of 8.0 N.
- Now we draw a line from the start of the first arrow to the end of the second arrow. This arrow represents the resultant force $R$, in both magnitude and direction.

The arrows are added by drawing them end-to-end; the end of the first arrow is the start of the second arrow. Now we can find the resultant force either by scale drawing, or by calculation. In this case, we have a 3–4–5 right-angled triangle, so calculation is simple:

$$R^2 = 6.0^2 + 8.0^2 = 36 + 64 = 100$$

$$R = 10\,\text{N}$$

$$\tan\theta = \frac{\text{opp}}{\text{adj}} = \frac{8.0}{6.0} = \frac{4}{3}$$

$$\theta = \tan^{-1}\frac{4}{3} = 53°$$

So the resultant force is 10 N, at an angle of 53° below the horizontal. This is a reasonable answer; the weight is pulling the shuttlecock downwards and the wind is pushing it to the right. The angle is greater than 45° because the downward force is greater than the horizontal force.

> If you draw a scale drawing be careful to:
> - state the scale used
> - draw a large diagram to reduce the uncertainty.

## Three or more forces

The spider shown in Figure 4.5 is hanging by a thread. It is blown sideways by the wind. The diagram shows the three forces acting on it:

- weight acting downwards
- the tension in the thread along the thread
- the push of the wind.

The diagram also shows how these can be added together. In this case, we arrive at an interesting result. Arrows are drawn to represent each of the three forces, end-to-end. The end of the third arrow coincides with the start of the first arrow, so the three arrows form a closed triangle. This tells us that the resultant force $R$ on the spider is zero, that is $R = 0$. The closed triangle in Figure 4.5 is known as a **triangle of forces.**

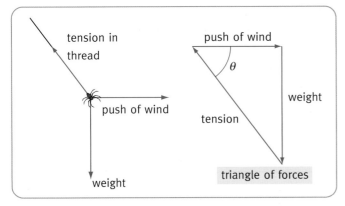

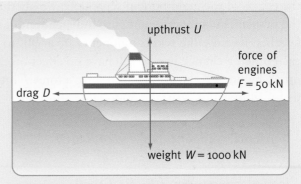

**Figure 4.6** For Test yourself Q **2**. The force $D$ is the frictional drag of the water on the boat. Like air resistance, drag is always in the opposite direction to the object's motion.

**Figure 4.5** Blowing in the wind – this spider is hanging in equilibrium.

So there is no resultant force. The forces on the spider balance each other out, and we say that the spider is in **equilibrium**. If the wind blew a little harder, there would be an unbalanced force on the spider, and it would move off to the right.

We can use this idea in two ways.

- If we work out the resultant force on an object, and find that it is zero, this tells us that the object is in equilibrium.
- If we know that an object is in equilibrium, we know that the forces on it must add up to zero. We can use this to work out the values of one or more unknown forces.

3 A stone is dropped into a fast-flowing stream. It does not fall vertically, because of the sideways push of the water (Figure 4.7).
  **a** Calculate the resultant force on the stone.
  **b** Is the stone in equilibrium?

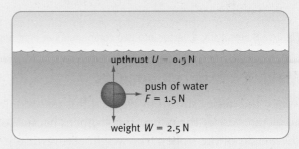

**Figure 4.7** For Test yourself Q **3**.

## Test yourself

1 A parachutist weighs 1000 N. When she opens her parachute, it pulls upwards on her with a force of 2000 N.
  **a** Draw a diagram to show the forces acting on the parachutist.
  **b** Calculate the resultant force acting on her.
  **c** What effect will this force have on her?

2 The ship shown in Figure 4.6 is travelling at a constant velocity.
  **a** Is the ship in equilibrium (in other words, is the resultant force on the ship equal to zero)? How do you know?
  **b** What is the upthrust $U$ of the water?
  **c** What is the drag $D$ of the water?

*continued* ···>}

## Components of vectors

Look back to Figure 4.5. The spider is in equilibrium, even though three forces are acting on it. We can think of the tension in the thread as having two effects:

- it is pulling upwards, to counteract the downward effect of gravity
- it is pulling to the left, to counteract the effect of the wind.

We can say that this force has two effects or **components**: an upwards (vertical) component and a sideways (horizontal) component. It is often useful to split up a vector quantity into components like this, just as we did with velocity in Chapter 2. The components are in two directions at right angles to each other, often horizontal and vertical. The process is called **resolving** the vector. Then we can think about the effects of each component separately; we say that the perpendicular components are **independent** of one another. Because the two components are at 90° to each other, a change in one will have no effect on the other. Figure 4.8 shows how to resolve a force $F$ into its horizontal and vertical components. These are:

horizontal component of $F = F_x = F\cos\theta$

vertical component of $F = F_y = F\sin\theta$

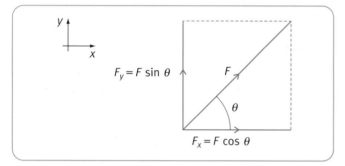

**Figure 4.8** Resolving a vector into two components at right angles.

## Making use of components

When the trolley shown in Figure 4.9 is released, it accelerates down the ramp. This happens because of the weight of the trolley. The weight acts vertically downwards. However, it does have a component which acts down the slope. By calculating the component of the trolley's weight down the slope, we can determine its acceleration.

**Figure 4.9** These students are investigating the acceleration of a trolley down a sloping ramp.

Figure 4.10 shows the forces acting on the trolley. To simplify the situation, we will assume there is no friction. The forces are:

• $W$, the weight of the trolley, which acts vertically downwards
• $R$, the contact force of the ramp, which acts at right angles to the ramp.

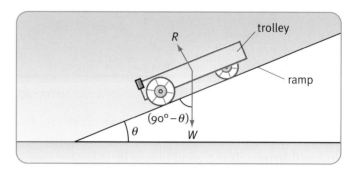

**Figure 4.10** A force diagram for a trolley on a ramp.

You can see at once from the diagram that the forces cannot be balanced, since they do not act in the same straight line.

To find the component of $W$ down the slope, we need to know the angle between $W$ and the slope. The slope makes an angle $\theta$ with the horizontal, and from the diagram we can see that the angle between the weight and the ramp is $(90° - \theta)$. Using the rule for calculating the component of a vector given above, we have:

component of $W$ down the slope
$$= W\cos(90° - \theta) = W\sin\theta$$

(A very helpful mathematical trick is $\cos(90° - \theta) = \sin\theta$; you can see this from Figure 4.10.)

Does the contact force $R$ help to accelerate the trolley down the ramp? To answer this, we must calculate its component down the slope. The angle between $R$ and the slope is 90°. So:

component of $R$ down the slope $= R\cos 90° = 0$

The cosine of 90° is zero, and so $R$ has no component down the slope. This shows why it is useful to think in terms of the components of forces; we don't know the value of $R$, but, since it has no effect down the slope, we can ignore it.

(There's no surprise about this result. The trolley runs down the slope because of the influence of its weight, not because it is pushed by the contact force $R$.)

## Changing the slope

If the students in Figure 4.9 increase the slope of their ramp, the trolley will move down the ramp with greater acceleration. They have increased $\theta$, and so the component of $W$ down the slope will have increased.

Now we can work out the trolley's acceleration. If the trolley's mass is $m$, its weight is $mg$. So the force $F$ making it accelerate down the slope is:

$$F = mg \sin \theta$$

Since from Newton's second law for constant mass we have $a = \dfrac{F}{m}$, the trolley's acceleration $a$ is given by:

$$a = \frac{mg \sin \theta}{m} = g \sin \theta$$

We could have arrived at this result simply by saying that the trolley's acceleration would be the component of $g$ down the slope (Figure 4.11). The steeper the slope, the greater the value of $\sin \theta$, and hence the greater the trolley's acceleration.

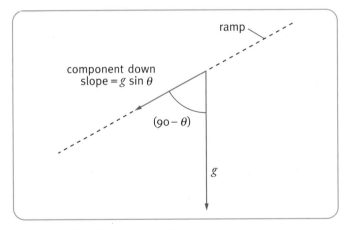

**Figure 4.11** Resolving $g$ down the ramp.

### Test yourself

4 The person in Figure 4.12 is pulling a large box using a rope. Use the idea of components of a force to explain why they are more likely to get the box to move if the rope is horizontal (as in **a**) than if it is sloping upwards (as in **b**).

*continued* ···▸

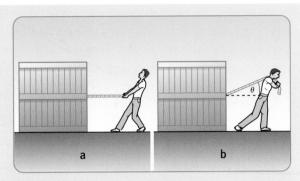

**Figure 4.12** Why is it easier to move the box with the rope horizontal? See Test yourself Q **4**.

5 A crate is sliding down a slope. The weight of the crate is 500 N. The slope makes an angle of 30° with the horizontal.
   **a** Draw a diagram to show the situation. Include arrows to represent the forces which act on the crate: the weight and the contact force of the slope.
   **b** Calculate the component of the weight down the slope.
   **c** Explain why the contact force of the slope has no component down the slope.
   **d** What third force might act to oppose the motion? In which direction would it act?

## Solving problems by resolving forces

A force can be resolved into two components at right angles to each other; these can then be treated independently of one another. This idea can be used to solve problems, as illustrated in Worked example 1.

### Worked example

1 A boy of mass 40 kg is on a waterslide which slopes at 30° to the horizontal. The frictional force up the slope is 120 N. Calculate the boy's acceleration down the slope. Take the acceleration of free fall $g$ to be 9.81 m s⁻².

*continued* ···▸

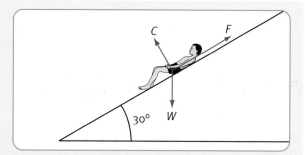

**Figure 4.13** For Worked example 1.

**Step 1** It is often helpful to draw a labelled diagram showing all the forces acting (Figure 4.13). This is known as a **free-body force diagram**. The forces are:

the boy's weight $W = 40 \times 9.81 = 392\,\text{N}$

the frictional force up the slope $F = 120\,\text{N}$

the contact force $C$ at 90° to the slope.

**Step 2** We are trying to find the resultant force on the boy which makes him accelerate down the slope. We resolve the forces down the slope, i.e. we find their components in that direction.

component of $W$ down the slope
$$= 392 \times \cos 60° = 196\,\text{N}$$

component of $F$ down the slope $= -120\,\text{N}$ (negative because $F$ is directed up the slope)

component of $C$ down the slope $= 0$ (because it is at 90° to the slope)

It is convenient that $C$ has no component down the slope, since we do not know the value of $C$.

**Step 3** Calculate the resultant force on the boy:
resultant force $= 196 - 120 = 76\,\text{N}$

**Step 4** Calculate his acceleration:

$$\text{acceleration} = \frac{\text{resultant force}}{\text{mass}} = \frac{76}{40} = 1.9\,\text{m s}^{-2}$$

continued ···⟫

So the boy's acceleration down the slope is $1.9\,\text{m s}^{-2}$. We could have arrived at the same result by resolving vertically and horizontally, but that would have led to two simultaneous equations from which we would have had to eliminate the unknown force $C$. It often helps to resolve forces at 90° to an unknown force.

## Test yourself

6  A child of mass 40 kg is on a water slide. The slide slopes down at 25° to the horizontal. The acceleration of free fall is $9.81\,\text{m s}^{-2}$. Calculate the child's acceleration down the slope:
   **a** when there is no friction and the only force acting on the child is his weight
   **b** if a frictional force of 80 N acts up the slope.

# Centre of gravity

We have weight because of the force of gravity of the Earth on us. Each part of our body – arms, legs, head, for example – experiences a force, caused by the force of gravity. However, it is much simpler to picture the overall effect of gravity as acting at a single point. This is our **centre of gravity**.

> The centre of gravity of an object is defined as the point where all the weight of the object may be considered to act.

For a person standing upright, the centre of gravity is roughly in the middle of the body, behind the navel. For a sphere, it is at the centre. It is much easier to solve problems if we simply indicate an object's weight by a single force acting at the centre of gravity, rather than a large number of forces acting on each part of the object. Figure 4.14 illustrates this point. The athlete performs a complicated manoeuvre. However, we can see that his centre of gravity follows a smooth, parabolic path through the air, just like the paths of projectiles we discussed in Chapter 2.

Figure 4.14 The dots indicate the athlete's centre of gravity, which follows a smooth trajectory through the air. With his body curved like this, the athlete's centre of gravity is actually outside his body, just below the small of his back. At no time is the whole of his body above the bar.

## Finding the centre of gravity

The centre of gravity of a thin sheet, or lamina, of cardboard or metal can be found by suspending it freely from two or three points (Figure 4.15).

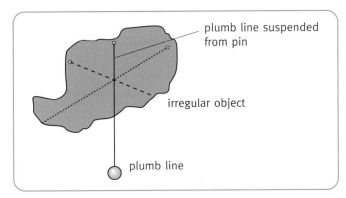

Figure 4.15 The centre of gravity is located at the intersection of the lines.

Small holes are made round the edge of the irregularly shaped object. A pin is put through one of the holes and held firmly in a clamp and stand so the object can swing freely. A length of string is attached to the pin. The other end of the string has a heavy mass attached to it. This arrangement is known as a **plumb line**. The object will stop swinging when its centre of gravity is vertically below the point of suspension. A line is drawn on the object along the vertical string of the plumb line. The centre of gravity must lie on this line. To find the position of the centre of gravity, the

process is repeated with the object suspended from different holes. The centre of gravity will be at the point of intersection of the lines drawn on the object.

# The turning effect of a force

Forces can make things accelerate. They can do something else as well: they can make an object turn round. We say that they can have a **turning effect**. Figure 4.16 shows how to use a spanner to turn a nut.

To maximise the turning effect of his force, the operator pulls close to the end of the spanner, as far as possible from the pivot (the centre of the nut) and at 90° to the spanner.

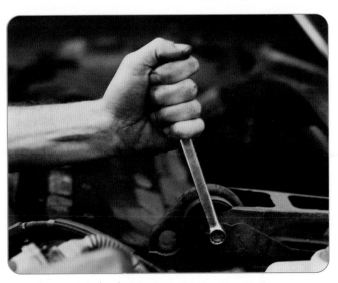

Figure 4.16 A mechanic turns a nut.

## Moment of a force

The quantity which tells us about the turning effect of a force is its **moment**. The moment of a force depends on two quantities:

- the magnitude of the force (the bigger the force, the greater its moment)
- the perpendicular distance of the force from the pivot (the further the force acts from the pivot, the greater its moment).

The moment of a force is defined as follows.

> The moment of a force = force × perpendicular distance of the pivot from the line of action of the force.

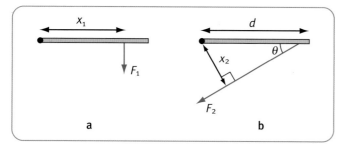

**Figure 4.17** The quantities involved in calculating the moment of a force.

Figure **4.17a** shows these quantities. The force $F_1$ is pushing down on the lever, at a perpendicular distance $x_1$ from the pivot. The moment of the force $F_1$ about the pivot is then given by:

moment = force × distance from pivot
$$= F_1 \times x_1$$

The unit of moment is the newton metre (N m). This is a unit which does not have a special name. You can also determine the moment of a force in N cm.

Figure **4.17b** shows a slightly more complicated situation. $F_2$ is pushing at an angle $\theta$ to the lever, rather than at 90°. This makes it have less turning effect. There are two ways to calculate the moment of the force.

**Method 1**

Draw a perpendicular line from the pivot to the line of the force. Find the distance $x_2$. Calculate the moment of the force, $F_2 \times x_2$. From the right-angled triangle, we can see that:

$$x_2 = d \sin \theta$$

Hence:

moment of force $= F_2 \times d \sin \theta = F_2 d \sin \theta$

**Method 2**

Calculate the component of $F_2$ which is at 90° to the lever. This is $F_2 \sin \theta$. Multiply this by $d$.

moment $= F_2 \sin \theta \times d$

We get the same result as Method 1:

moment of force $= F_2 d \sin \theta$

Note that any force (such as the component $F_2 \cos \theta$) which passes through the pivot has no turning effect, because the distance from the pivot to the line of the force is zero.

## Balanced or unbalanced?

We can use the idea of the moment of a force to solve two sorts of problem.

- We can check whether an object will remain balanced or start to rotate.
- We can calculate an unknown force or distance if we know that an object is balanced.

We can use the **principle of moments** to solve problems. The principle of moments states that:

> For any object that is in **equilibrium**, the sum of the clockwise moments about any point provided by the forces acting on the object equals the sum of the anticlockwise moments about that same point.

## *Worked examples*

2 Is the see-saw shown in Figure **4.18** in equilibrium (balanced), or will it start to rotate?

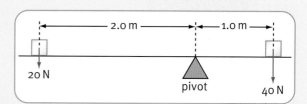

**Figure 4.18** Will these forces make the see-saw rotate, or are their moments balanced?

The see-saw will remain balanced, because the 20 N force is twice as far from the pivot as the 40 N force.

To prove this, we need to think about each force individually. Which direction is each force trying to turn the see-saw, clockwise or anticlockwise? The 20 N force is tending to turn the see-saw anticlockwise, while the 40 N force is tending to turn it clockwise.

*continued ⋯⟶*

**Step 1** Determine the anticlockwise moment:

moment of anticlockwise force
$$= 20 \times 2.0 = 40\,\text{N m}$$

**Step 2** Determine the clockwise moment:

moment of clockwise force
$$= 40 \times 1.0 = 40\,\text{N m}$$

**Step 3** We can see that:

clockwise moment = anticlockwise moment

So the see-saw is balanced and therefore does not rotate. The see-saw is in equilibrium.

**3** The beam shown in Figure **4.19** is in equilibrium. Determine the force $X$.

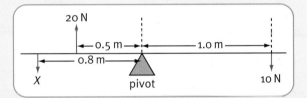

**Figure 4.19** For Worked example 3.

The unknown force $X$ is tending to turn the beam anticlockwise. The other two forces (10 N and 20 N) are tending to turn the beam clockwise. We will start by calculating their moments and adding them together.

**Step 1** Determine the clockwise moments:

sum of moments of clockwise forces
$$= (10 \times 1.0) + (20 \times 0.5)$$
$$= 10 + 10 = 20\,\text{N m}$$

**Step 2** Determine the anticlockwise moment:

moment of anticlockwise force $= X \times 0.8$

**Step 3** Since we know that the beam must be balanced, we can write:

sum of clockwise moments
$$= \text{sum of anticlockwise moments}$$

$$20 = X \times 0.8$$

$$X = \frac{20}{0.8} = 25\,\text{N}$$

So a force of 25 N at a distance of 0.8 m from the pivot will keep the beam still and prevent it from rotating (keep it balanced).

**4** Figure **4.20** shows the internal structure of a human arm holding an object. The biceps are muscles attached to one of the bones of the forearm. These muscles provide an upward force.

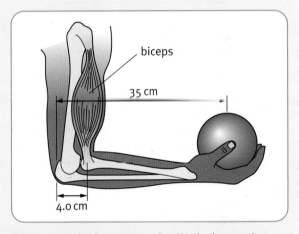

**Figure 4.20** The human arm. For Worked example 4.

An object of weight 50 N is held in the hand with the forearm at right angles to the upper arm. Use the principle of moments to determine the muscular force $F$ provided by the biceps, given the following data:

weight of forearm = 15 N

distance of biceps from the elbow = 4.0 cm

distance of centre of gravity
of forearm from elbow = 16 cm

distance of object in the hand
from elbow = 35 cm

**Step 1** There is a lot of information in this question. It is best to draw a simplified diagram of the forearm that shows all the forces and the relevant distances (Figure **4.21**). All distances must be from the pivot, which in this case is the elbow.

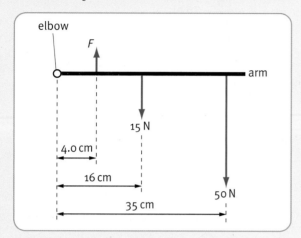

**Figure 4.21** Simplified diagram showing forces on the forearm. For Worked example 4.

**Step 2** Determine the clockwise moments:

sum of moments of clockwise forces
$$= (15 \times 0.16) + (50 \times 0.35)$$
$$= 19.9 \, \text{N m}$$

**Step 3** Determine the anticlockwise moment:

moment of anticlockwise force $= F \times 0.04$

**Step 4** Since the arm is in balance, according to the principle of moments we have:

sum of clockwise moments
$$= \text{sum of anticlockwise moments}$$

$$19.9 = 0.04 \, F$$

$$F = \frac{19.9}{0.04} = 497.5 \, \text{N} \approx 500 \, \text{N}$$

The biceps provide a force of 500 N – a force large enough to lift 500 apples!

7  A wheelbarrow is loaded as shown in Figure **4.22**.
   a Calculate the force that the gardener needs to exert to hold the wheelbarrow's legs off the ground.
   b Calculate the force exerted by the ground on the legs of the wheelbarrow (taken both together) when the gardener is not holding the handles.

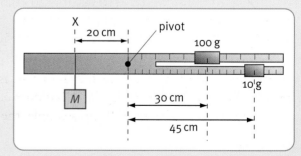

**Figure 4.22** For Test yourself Q **7**.

8  A traditional pair of scales uses sliding masses of 10 g and 100 g to achieve a balance. A diagram of the arrangement is shown in Figure **4.23**. The bar itself is supported with its centre of gravity at the pivot.
   a Calculate the value of the mass $M$, attached at X.
   b State **one** advantage of this method of measuring mass.

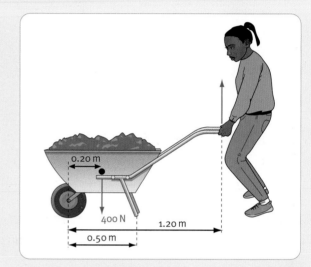

**Figure 4.23** For Test yourself Q **8**.

continued ⋯▸

**9** Figure **4.24** shows a beam with four forces acting on it
  **a** For each force, calculate the moment of the force about point P.
  **b** State whether each moment is clockwise or anticlockwise.
  **c** State whether or not the moments of the forces are balanced.

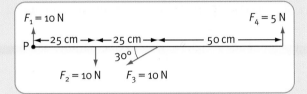

**Figure 4.24** For Test yourself Q **9**.

# The torque of a couple

Figure **4.25** shows the forces needed to turn a car's steering wheel. The two forces balance up and down (15 N up and 15 N down), so the wheel will not move up, down or sideways. However, the wheel is not in equilibrium. The pair of forces will cause it to rotate.

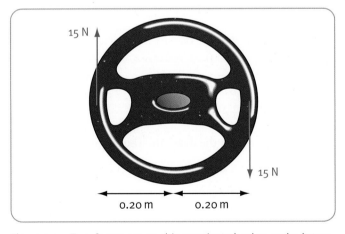

**Figure 4.25** Two forces act on this steering wheel to make it turn.

A pair of forces like that in Figure **4.25** is known as a **couple**. A couple has a turning effect, but does not cause an object to accelerate. To form a couple, the two forces must be:

• equal in magnitude
• parallel, but opposite in direction
• separated by a distance $d$.

The turning effect or moment of a couple is known as its torque. We can calculate the **torque** of the couple in Figure **4.25** by adding the moments of each force about the centre of the wheel:

$$\text{torque of couple} = (15 \times 0.20) + (15 \times 0.20)$$
$$= 6.0 \, \text{N m}$$

We could have found the same result by multiplying one of the forces by the perpendicular distance between them:

$$\text{torque of a couple} = 15 \times 0.4 = 6.0 \, \text{N m}$$

The torque of a couple is defined as follows:

> torque of a couple = one of the forces ×
> perpendicular distance between the forces

## Test yourself

**10** The driving wheel of a car travelling at a constant velocity has a torque of 137 N m applied to it by the axle that drives the car (Figure **4.26**). The radius of the tyre is 0.18 m. Calculate the driving force provided by this wheel.

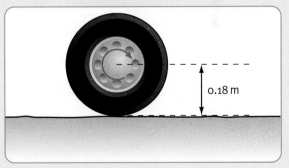

**Figure 4.26** For Test yourself Q **10**.

# Pure turning effect

When we calculate the moment of a single force, the result depends on the point or pivot about which the moment acts. The further the force is from the pivot, the greater the moment. A couple is different; the moment of a couple does not depend on the point about which it acts, only on the perpendicular distance between the two forces. A single force acting on an object will tend to make the object accelerate (unless there is another force to balance it). A couple, however, is a pair of equal and opposite forces, so it will not make the object accelerate. This means we can think of a couple as a pure 'turning effect', the size of which is given by its torque.

For an object to be in equilibrium, two conditions must be met at the same time.

• The resultant force acting on the object is zero.
• The resultant moment must be zero.

## Summary

☐ Forces are vector quantities that can be added by means of a vector triangle. Their resultant can be determined using trigonometry or by scale drawing.

☐ Vectors such as forces can be resolved into components. Components at right angles to one another can be treated independently of one another. For a force $F$ at an angle $\theta$ to the $x$-direction, the components are:

$x$-direction: $F \cos \theta$
$y$-direction: $F \sin \theta$

☐ The moment of a force = force × perpendicular distance of the pivot from the line of action of the force.

☐ The principle of moments states that, for any object that is in equilibrium, the sum of the clockwise moments about any point provided by the forces acting on the object equals the sum of the anticlockwise moments about that same point.

☐ A couple is a pair of equal, parallel but opposite forces whose effect is to produce a turning effect on a body without giving it linear acceleration.

torque of a couple = one of the forces × perpendicular distance between the forces

☐ For an object to be in equilibrium, the resultant force acting on the object must be zero and the resultant moment must be zero.

# End-of-chapter questions

1 A ship is pulled at a constant speed by two small boats A and B, as shown in the diagram. The engine of the ship does not produce any force.

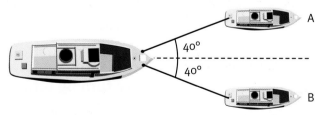

**Figure 4.27** For End-of-chapter Q 1.

The tension in each cable between A and B and the ship is 4000 N.
 **a** Draw a free-body diagram showing the three horizontal forces acting on the ship.
 **b** Draw a vector diagram to scale showing these three forces and use your diagram to find the value of the drag force on the ship.

**2** A book of mass 1.5 kg is at rest on a rough surface which is inclined at 20° to the horizontal.

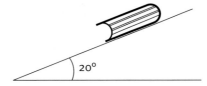

**Figure 4.28** For End-of-chapter Q **2**.

   **a** Draw a free-body diagram showing the three forces acting on the book.
   **b** Calculate the component of the weight that acts down the slope.
   **c** Use your answer to **b** to determine the force of friction that acts on the book.
   **d** Determine the normal contact force between the book and the surface.

**3** The free-body diagram shows three forces that act on a stone hanging at rest from two strings.

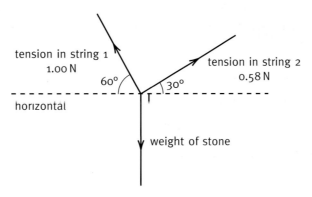

**Figure 4.29** For End-of-chapter Q **3**.

   **a** Calculate the horizontal component of the tension in each string. Why should these two components be equal in magnitude?
   **b** Calculate the vertical component of the tension in each string.
   **c** Use your answer to **b** to calculate the weight of the stone.
   **d** Draw a vector diagram of the forces on the stone. This should be a triangle of forces.
   **e** Use your diagram in **d** to calculate the weight of the stone.

**4** The force $F$ shown in the diagram has a moment of 40 N m about the pivot. Calculate the magnitude of the force $F$.

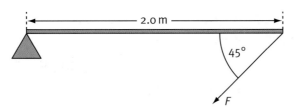

**Figure 4.30** For End-of-chapter Q **4**.

**5** The asymmetric bar shown in the diagram has a weight of 7.6 N and a centre of gravity that is 0.040 m from the wider end, on which there is a load of 3.3 N. It is pivoted a distance of 0.060 m from its centre of gravity. Calculate the force $P$ that is needed at the far end of the bar in order to maintain equilibrium.

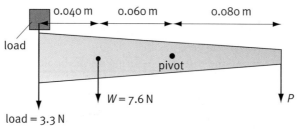

**Figure 4.31** For End-of-chapter Q 5.

# Exam-style questions

**1  a** Explain what is meant by:
   **i**  a couple                                                              [1]
   **ii** torque.                                                               [2]
  **b** The engine of a car produce a torque of 200 N m on the axle of the wheel in contact with the road. The car travels at a constant velocity towards the right.

   **i**  Copy the diagram above and show the direction of rotation of the wheel, and the horizontal component of the force that the road exerts on the wheel.        [2]
   **ii** State the resultant torque on the wheel. Explain your answer.         [2]
   **iii** The diameter of the car wheel is 0.58 m. Determine the value of the horizontal component of the road on the wheel.                                        [1]

**2  a** Explain what is meant by the **centre of gravity** of an object. [2]

**b** A flagpole of mass 25 kg is held in a horizontal position by a cable as shown in the diagram. The centre of gravity of the flagpole is at a distance of 1.5 m from the fixed end.

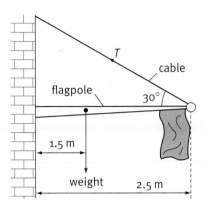

   **i** Write an equation to represent taking moments about the left-hand end of the flagpole. Use your equation to find the tension $T$ in the cable. [4]

   **ii** Determine the vertical component of the force at the left-hand end of the flagpole. [2]

**3  a** State the **two** conditions necessary for an object to be in equilibrium. [2]

**b** A metal rod of length 90 cm has a disc of radius 24 cm fixed rigidly at its centre, as shown in the diagram. The assembly is pivoted at its centre.

Two forces, each of magnitude 30 N, are applied normal to the rod at each end so as to produce a turning effect on the rod. A rope is attached to the edge of the disc to prevent rotation.

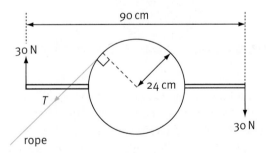

Calculate:
   **i** the torque of the couple produced by the 30 N forces [1]

   **ii** the tension $T$ in the rope. [3]

**4**  **a** Explain what is meant by the **torque of a couple**. [2]

**b** Three strings, A, B and C, are attached to a circular ring, as shown in the diagram.

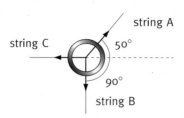

string A

string C        50°

90°

string B

The strings and the ring all lie on a smooth horizontal surface and are at rest. The tension in string A is 8.0 N.

Calculate the tension in strings B and C. [4]

**5**  The diagram shows a picture hanging symmetrically by two cords from a nail fixed to a wall. The picture is in equilibrium.

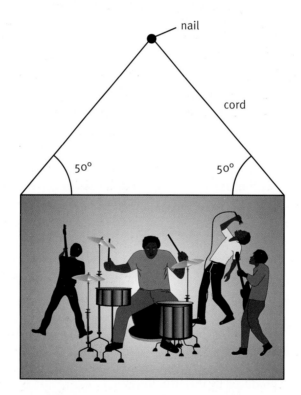

nail

cord

50°          50°

**a** Explain what is meant by **equilibrium**. [2]

**b** Draw a vector diagram to represent the three forces acting on the picture in the vertical plane. Label each force clearly with its name and show the direction of each force with an arrow. [2]

**c** The tension in the cord is 45 N and the angle that each end of the cord makes with the horizontal is 50°. Calculate:

  **i** the vertical component of the tension in the cord [1]

  **ii** the weight of the picture. [1]

# Objectives

After studying this chapter, you should be able to:

- understand and use the concept of work
- apply the principle of conservation of energy to simple examples
- derive and use the formulae for kinetic energy and potential energy
- understand the concept of internal energy and distinguish between other types of energy
- define and use the equation for power

# The idea of energy

**Figure 5.1** Anshan steel works, China.

The Industrial Revolution started in the late 18th century in the British Isles. Today, many other countries are undergoing the process of industrialisation (Figure **5.1**). Industrialisation began as engineers developed new machines which were capable of doing the work of hundreds of craftsmen and labourers. At first, they made use of the traditional techniques of water power and wind power. Water stored behind a dam was used to turn a wheel, which turned many machines. By developing new mechanisms, the designers tried to extract as much as possible of the energy stored in the water. Steam engines were developed, initially for pumping water out of mines. Steam engines use a fuel such as coal; there is much more energy stored in 1 kg of coal than in 1 kg of water held behind a dam. Steam engines soon powered the looms of the textile mills, and the British industry came to dominate world trade in textiles.

Nowadays, most factories and mills rely on electrical power, generated by burning coal or gas at a power station. The fuel is burnt to release its store of energy. High-pressure steam is generated, and this turns a turbine which turns a generator. Even in the most efficient coal-fired power station, only about 40% of the energy from the fuel is transferred to the electrical energy that the station supplies to the grid.

Engineers strove to develop machines which made the most efficient use of the energy supplied to them. At the same time, scientists were working out the basic ideas of energy transfer and energy transformations. The idea of energy itself had to be developed; it was not obvious at first that heat, light, electrical energy and so on could all be thought of as being, in some way, forms of the same thing. In fact, steam engines had been in use for 150 years before it was realised that their energy came from the heat supplied to them from their fuel.

The earliest steam engines had very low efficiencies – many converted less than 1% of the energy supplied to them into useful work. The understanding of the relationship between work and energy led to many ingenious ways of making the most of the energy supplied by fuel.

This improvement in energy efficiency has led to the design of modern engines such as the jet engines which have made long-distance air travel a commercial possibility (Figure **5.2**).

**Figure 5.2** The jet engines of this Airbus A380 aircraft are designed to make efficient use of their fuel. If they were less efficient, their thrust might only be sufficient to lift the empty aircraft, and the passengers would have to be left behind.

# Doing work, transferring energy

The weight-lifter shown in Figure 5.3 has powerful muscles. They can provide the force needed to lift a large weight above her head – about 2 m above the ground. The force exerted by the weight-lifter transfers energy from her to the weights. We know that the weights have gained energy because, when the athlete releases them, they come crashing down to the ground.

**Figure 5.3** It is hard work being a weight-lifter.

As the athlete lifts the weights and transfers energy to them, we say that her lifting force is doing work. 'Doing work' is a way of transferring energy from one object to another. In fact, if you want to know the scientific meaning of the word 'energy', we have to say it is 'that which is transferred when a force moves through a distance'. So work and energy are two closely linked concepts.

In physics, we often use an everyday word but with a special meaning. **Work** is an example of this. Table **5.1** describes some situations which illustrate the meaning of **doing work** in physics.

It is important to appreciate that our bodies sometimes mislead us. If you hold a heavy weight above your head for some time, your muscles will get tired. However, you are not doing any work **on the weights**, because you are not transferring energy to the weights once they are above your head. Your muscles get tired because they are constantly relaxing and contracting, and this uses energy, but none of the energy is being transferred to the weights.

## Calculating work done

Because **doing work** defines what we mean by **energy**, we start this chapter by considering how to calculate **work done**. There is no doubt that you do work if you push a car along the road. A force transfers energy from you to the car. But how much work do you do? Figure 5.4 shows the two factors involved:

- the size of the force $F$ – the bigger the force, the greater the amount of work you do
- the distance $s$ you push the car – the further you push it, the greater the amount of work done.

So, the bigger the force, and the further it moves, the greater the amount of work done.

| Doing work | Not doing work |
|---|---|
| Pushing a car to start it moving: your force transfers energy to the car. The car's kinetic energy (i.e. 'movement energy') increases. | Pushing a car but it does not budge: no energy is transferred, because your force does not move. The car's kinetic energy does not change. |
| Lifting weights: you are doing work as the weights move upwards. The gravitational potential energy of the weights increases. | Holding weights above your head: you are not doing work on the weights (even though you may find it tiring) because the force you apply on them is not moving. The gravitational potential energy of the weights is not changing. |
| A falling stone: the force of gravity is doing work. The stone's kinetic energy is increasing. | The Moon orbiting the Earth: the force of gravity is not doing work. The Moon's kinetic energy is not changing. |
| Writing an essay: you are doing work because you need a force to move your pen across the page, or to press the keys on the keyboard. | Reading an essay: this may seem like 'hard work', but no force is involved, so you are not doing any work. |

**Table 5.1** The meaning of 'doing work' in physics.

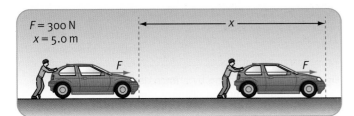
$F = 300\,\text{N}$
$x = 5.0\,\text{m}$

**Figure 5.4** You have to do work to start the car moving.

The **work done** by a force is defined as the product of the force and the distance moved in the direction of the force:

$$W = F \times s$$

where $s$ is the distance moved in the direction of the force.

In the example shown in Figure 5.4, $F = 300\,\text{N}$ and $s = 5.0\,\text{m}$, so:

work done $W = F \times s = 300 \times 5.0 = 1500\,\text{J}$

## Energy transferred

Doing work is a way of transferring energy. For both energy and work the correct SI unit is the joule (J). The amount of work done, calculated using $W = F \times s$, shows the amount of energy transferred:

work done = energy transferred

## Newtons, metres and joules

From the equation $W = F \times s$ we can see how the unit of force (the newton), the unit of distance (the metre) and the unit of work or energy (the joule) are related.

1 joule = 1 newton × 1 metre
$1\,\text{J} = 1\,\text{N}\,\text{m}$

The joule is defined as the amount of work done when a force of 1 newton moves a distance of 1 metre in the direction of the force. Since **work done = energy transferred**, it follows that a joule is also the amount of energy transferred when a force of 1 newton moves a distance of 1 metre in the direction of the force.

## Test yourself

1 In each of the following examples, explain whether or not any work is done by the force mentioned.
 a You pull a heavy sack along rough ground.
 b The force of gravity pulls you downwards when you fall off a wall.
 c The tension in a string pulls on a stone when you whirl it around in a circle at a steady speed.
 d The contact force of the bedroom floor stops you from falling into the room below.

2 A man of mass 70 kg climbs stairs of vertical height 2.5 m. Calculate the work done against the force of gravity. (Take $g = 9.81\,\text{m}\,\text{s}^{-2}$.)

*continued* ⋯➤

**3** A stone of weight 10 N falls from the top of a 250 m high cliff.

   **a** Calculate how much work is done by the force of gravity in pulling the stone to the foot of the cliff.

   **b** How much energy is transferred to the stone?

## Force, distance and direction

It is important to appreciate that, for a force to do work, there must be movement **in the direction of the force**. Both the force $F$ and the distance $s$ moved in the direction of the force are vector quantities, so you should know that their directions are likely to be important. To illustrate this, we will consider three examples involving gravity (Figure 5.5). In the equation for work done, $W = F \times s$, the distance moved $s$ is thus the displacement in the direction of the force.

Suppose that the force $F$ moves through a distance $s$ which is at an angle $\theta$ to $F$, as shown in Figure **5.6**. To determine the work done by the force, it is simplest to determine the component of $F$ in the direction of $s$. This component is $F \cos \theta$, and so we have:

work done $= (F \cos \theta) \times s$

Or simply:

work done $= Fs \cos \theta$

Worked example **1** shows how to use this.

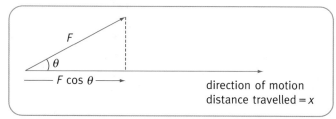

**Figure 5.6** The work done by a force depends on the angle between the force and the distance it moves.

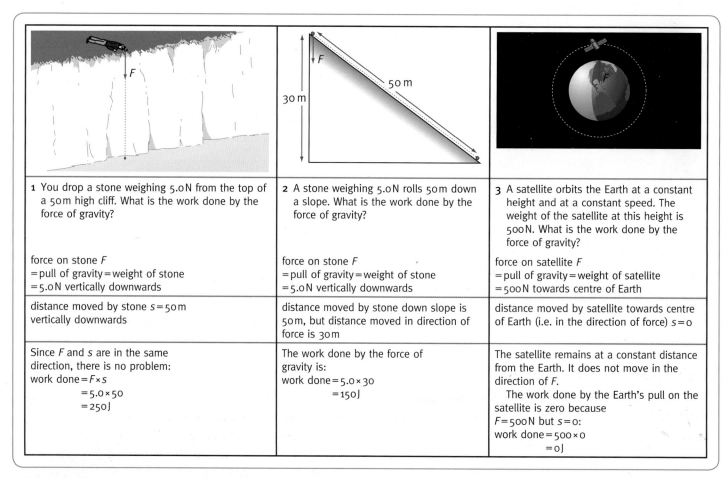

| 1 You drop a stone weighing 5.0 N from the top of a 50 m high cliff. What is the work done by the force of gravity? | 2 A stone weighing 5.0 N rolls 50 m down a slope. What is the work done by the force of gravity? | 3 A satellite orbits the Earth at a constant height and at a constant speed. The weight of the satellite at this height is 500 N. What is the work done by the force of gravity? |
|---|---|---|
| force on stone $F$<br>= pull of gravity = weight of stone<br>= 5.0 N vertically downwards | force on stone $F$<br>= pull of gravity = weight of stone<br>= 5.0 N vertically downwards | force on satellite $F$<br>= pull of gravity = weight of satellite<br>= 500 N towards centre of Earth |
| distance moved by stone $s = 50$ m vertically downwards | distance moved by stone down slope is 50 m, but distance moved in direction of force is 30 m | distance moved by satellite towards centre of Earth (i.e. in the direction of force) $s = 0$ |
| Since $F$ and $s$ are in the same direction, there is no problem:<br>work done $= F \times s$<br>$\quad\quad = 5.0 \times 50$<br>$\quad\quad = 250$ J | The work done by the force of gravity is:<br>work done $= 5.0 \times 30$<br>$\quad\quad = 150$ J | The satellite remains at a constant distance from the Earth. It does not move in the direction of $F$.<br>   The work done by the Earth's pull on the satellite is zero because<br>$F = 500$ N but $s = 0$:<br>work done $= 500 \times 0$<br>$\quad\quad = 0$ J |

**Figure 5.5** Three examples involving gravity.

## Worked example

1. A man pulls a box along horizontal ground using a rope (Figure 5.7). The force provided by the rope is 200 N, at an angle of 30° to the horizontal. Calculate the work done if the box moves 5.0 m along the ground.

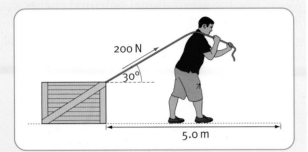

**Figure 5.7** For Worked example 1.

**Step 1** Calculate the component of the force in the direction in which the box moves. This is the horizontal component of the force:

horizontal component of force

$= 200 \cos 30° = 173\,\text{N}$

$F \cos \theta$ is the component at an angle $\theta$ to the force $F$.

**Step 2** Now calculate the work done:

work done = force × distance moved
$= 173 \times 5.0 = 865\,\text{J}$

Note that we could have used the equation work done = $Fs \cos \theta$ to combine the two steps into one.

## A gas doing work

Gases exert pressure on the walls of their container. If a gas expands, the walls are pushed outwards – the gas has done work on its surroundings. In a steam engine, expanding steam pushes a piston to turn the engine, and in a car engine, the exploding mixture of fuel

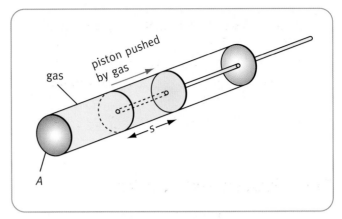

**Figure 5.8** When a gas expands, it does work on its surroundings.

and air does the same thing, so this is an important situation.

Figure 5.8 shows a gas at pressure $p$ inside a cylinder of cross-sectional area $A$. The cylinder is closed by a moveable piston. The gas pushes the piston a distance $s$. If we know the force $F$ exerted by the gas on the piston, we can deduce an expression for the amount of work done by the gas.

From the definition of pressure ( pressure = $\dfrac{\text{force}}{\text{area}}$ ), the force exerted by the gas on the piston is given by:

force = pressure × area

$F = p \times A$

and the work done is force × displacement:

$W = p \times A \times s$

But the quantity $A \times s$ is the **increase** in volume of the gas; that is, the shaded volume in Figure 5.8. We call this $\Delta V$, where the $\Delta$ indicates that it is a **change** in $V$. Hence the work done by the gas in expanding is:

$W = p\Delta V$

Notice that we are assuming that the pressure $p$ does not change as the gas expands. This will be true if the gas is expanding against the pressure of the atmosphere, which changes only very slowly.

## Test yourself

4   The crane shown in Figure **5.9** lifts its 500 N
    load to the top of the building from A to
    B. Distances are as shown on the diagram.
    Calculate how much work is done by the crane.

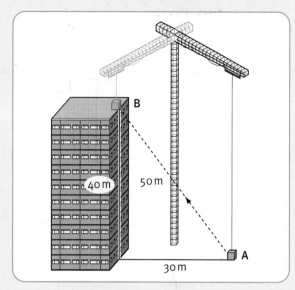

**Figure 5.9** For Test yourself Q **4**. The dotted line shows
the track of the load as it is lifted by the crane.

5   Figure **5.10** shows the forces acting on a box
    which is being pushed up a slope. Calculate
    the work done by each force if the box moves
    0.50 m up the slope.

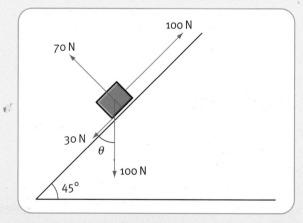

**Figure 5.10** For Test yourself Q **5**.

6   When you blow up a balloon, the expanding
    balloon pushes aside the atmosphere. How much
    work is done against the atmosphere in blowing
    up a balloon to a volume of 2 litres (0.002 m³)?
    (Atmospheric pressure = $1.0 \times 10^5$ N m⁻².)

# Gravitational potential energy

If you lift a heavy object, you do work. You are
providing an upward force to overcome the downward
force of gravity on the object. The force moves the
object upwards, so the force is doing work.

In this way, energy is transferred from you to the
object. You lose energy, and the object gains energy.
We say that the **gravitational potential energy** $E_p$
of the object has increased. Worked example **2** shows
how to calculate a change in gravitational potential
energy – or g.p.e. for short.

## Worked example

2   A weight-lifter raises weights with a mass of
    200 kg from the ground to a height of 1.5 m.
    Calculate how much work he does. By how
    much does the g.p.e. of the weights increase?

**Step 1** As shown in Figure **5.11**, the downward
force on the weights is their weight $W = mg$. An
equal, upward force $F$ is required to lift them.

**Figure 5.11** For Worked example **2**.

$$W = F = mg = 200 \times 9.81 = 1962 \, \text{N}$$

It helps to draw a diagram of the situation.

**Step 2** Now we can calculate the work done by
the force $F$:

continued ⋯⟶

work done = force × distance moved
= 1962 × 1.5 ≈ 2940 J

Note that the distance moved is in the same direction as the force. So the work done on the weights is about 2940 J. This is also the value of the increase in their g.p.e.

## An equation for gravitational potential energy

The change in the gravitational potential energy (g.p.e.) of an object, $E_p$, depends on the change in its height, $h$. We can calculate $E_p$ using this equation:

change in g.p.e. = weight × change in height

$$E_p = (mg) \times h$$

or simply

$$E_p = mgh$$

It should be clear where this equation comes from. The force needed to lift an object is equal to its weight $mg$, where $m$ is the mass of the object and $g$ is the acceleration of free fall or the gravitational field strength on the Earth's surface. The work done by this force is given by force × distance moved, or weight × change in height. You might feel that it takes a force greater than the weight of the object being raised to lift it upwards, but this is not so. Provided the force is equal to the weight, the object will move upwards at a steady speed.

Note that $h$ stands for the vertical height through which the object moves. Note also that we can only use the equation $E_p = mgh$ for relatively small changes in height. It would not work, for example, in the case of a satellite orbiting the Earth. Satellites orbit at a height of at least 200 km and $g$ has a smaller value at this height.

## Other forms of potential energy

Potential energy is the energy an object has because of its position or shape. So, for example, an object's gravitational potential energy changes when it moves through a gravitational field. (There is much more about gravitational fields in Chapter 19.)

We can identify other forms of potential energy. An electrically charged object has electric potential energy when it is placed in an electric field (see Chapter 9). An object may have elastic potential energy when it is stretched, squashed or twisted – if it is released it goes back to its original shape (see Chapter 8).

### Test yourself

7 Calculate how much gravitational potential energy is gained if you climb a flight of stairs. Assume that you have a mass of 52 kg and that the height you lift yourself is 2.5 m.

8 A climber of mass 100 kg (including the equipment she is carrying) ascends from sea level to the top of a mountain 5500 m high. Calculate the change in her gravitational potential energy.

9 a A toy car works by means of a stretched rubber band. What form of potential energy does the car store when the band is stretched?
  b A bar magnet is lying with its north pole next to the south pole of another bar magnet. A student pulls them apart. Why do we say that the magnets' potential energy has increased? Where has this energy come from?

## Kinetic energy

As well as lifting an object, a force can make it accelerate. Again, work is done by the force and energy is transferred to the object. In this case, we say that it has gained kinetic energy, $E_k$. The faster an object is moving, the greater its kinetic energy (k.e.).

For an object of mass $m$ travelling at a speed $v$, we have:

kinetic energy = $\frac{1}{2}$ × mass × speed$^2$

$$E_k = \frac{1}{2}mv^2$$

## Deriving the formula for kinetic energy

The equation for k.e., $E_k = \frac{1}{2}mv^2$, is related to one of the equations of motion. We imagine a car being accelerated from rest ($u = 0$) to velocity $v$. To give it acceleration $a$, it is pushed by a force $F$ for a distance s. Since $u = 0$, we can write the equation $v^2 = u^2 + 2as$ as:

$$v^2 = 2as$$

Multiplying both sides by $\frac{1}{2}m$ gives:

$$\tfrac{1}{2}mv^2 = mas$$

Now, $ma$ is the force $F$ accelerating the car, and $mas$ is the force × the distance it moves, that is, the work done by the force. So we have:

$$\tfrac{1}{2}mv^2 = \text{work done by force } F$$

This is the energy transferred to the car, and hence its kinetic energy.

## Worked example

3   Calculate the increase in kinetic energy of a car of mass 800 kg when it accelerates from $20\,\mathrm{m\,s^{-1}}$ to $30\,\mathrm{m\,s^{-1}}$.

**Step 1** Calculate the initial k.e. of the car:

$$E_k = \tfrac{1}{2}mv^2 = \tfrac{1}{2} \times 800 \times (20)^2 = 160\,000\,\mathrm{J}$$
$$= 160\,\mathrm{kJ}$$

**Step 2** Calculate the final k.e. of the car:

$$E_k = \tfrac{1}{2}mv^2 = \tfrac{1}{2} \times 800 \times (30)^2 = 360\,000\,\mathrm{J}$$
$$= 360\,\mathrm{kJ}$$

**Step 3** Calculate the change in the car's k.e.:

$$\text{change in k.e.} = 360 - 160 = 200\,\mathrm{kJ}$$

Take care! You can't calculate the **change** in k.e. by squaring the change in speed. In this example, the change in speed is $10\,\mathrm{m\,s^{-1}}$, and this would give an incorrect value for the change in k.e.

## Test yourself

10  Which has more k.e., a car of mass 500 kg travelling at $15\,\mathrm{m\,s^{-1}}$ or a motorcycle of mass 250 kg travelling at $30\,\mathrm{m\,s^{-1}}$?

11  Calculate the change in kinetic energy of a ball of mass 200 g when it bounces. Assume that it hits the ground with a speed of $15.8\,\mathrm{m\,s^{-1}}$ and leaves it at $12.2\,\mathrm{m\,s^{-1}}$.

# g.p.e.–k.e. transformations

A motor drags the roller-coaster car to the top of the first hill. The car runs down the other side, picking up speed as it goes (see Figure **5.12**). It is moving just fast enough to reach the top of the second hill, slightly lower than the first. It accelerates downhill again. Everybody screams!

The motor provides a force to pull the roller-coaster car to the top of the hill. It transfers energy to the car. But where is this energy when the car is waiting at the top of the hill? The car now has gravitational potential energy; as soon as it is given a small push to set it moving, it accelerates. It gains kinetic energy and at the same time it loses g.p.e.

As the car runs along the roller-coaster track (Figure **5.13**), its energy changes.

1   At the top of the first hill, it has the most g.p.e.
2   As it runs downhill, its g.p.e. decreases and its k.e. increases.

**Figure 5.12** The roller-coaster car accelerates as it comes downhill. It's even more exciting if it runs through water.

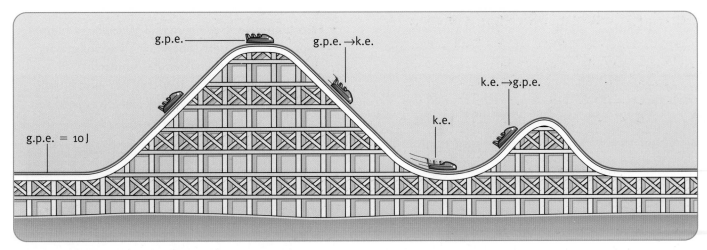

**Figure 5.13** Energy changes along a roller-coaster.

**3** At the bottom of the hill, all but 10 J of its g.p.e. has been changed to k.e. and heat and sound energy.

**4** As it runs back uphill, the force of gravity slows it down. K.e. is being changed to g.p.e.

Inevitably, some energy is lost by the car. There is friction with the track, and air resistance. So the car cannot return to its original height. That is why the second hill must be slightly lower than the first. It is fun if the car runs through a trough of water, but that takes even more energy, and the car cannot rise so high. There are many situations where an object's energy changes between gravitational potential energy and kinetic energy. For example:

- a high diver falling towards the water – g.p.e. changes to k.e.
- a ball is thrown upwards – k.e. changes to g.p.e.
- a child on a swing – energy changes back and forth between g.p.e. and k.e.

# Down, up, down – energy changes

When an object falls, it speeds up. Its g.p.e. decreases and its k.e. increases. Energy is being transformed from gravitational potential energy to kinetic energy. Some energy is likely to be lost, usually as heat because of air resistance. However, if no energy is lost in the process, we have:

decrease in g.p.e. = gain in k.e.

We can use this idea to solve a variety of problems, as illustrated by Worked example 4.

## Worked example

**4** A pendulum consists of a brass sphere of mass 5.0 kg hanging from a long string (see Figure 5.14). The sphere is pulled to the side so that it is 0.15 m above its lowest position. It is then released. How fast will it be moving when it passes through the lowest point along its path?

**Step 1** Calculate the loss in g.p.e. as the sphere falls from its highest position.

$$E_p = mgh = 5.0 \times 9.81 \times 0.15 = 7.36 \, \text{J}$$

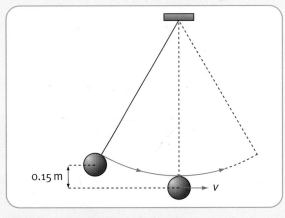

**Figure 5.14** For Worked example 4.

**Step 2** The gain in the sphere's k.e. is 7.36 J. We can use this to calculate the sphere's speed. First calculate $v^2$, then $v$:

$$\tfrac{1}{2}mv^2 = 7.36$$

*continued ⋯⟩*

$$\tfrac{1}{2} \times 5.0 \times v^2 = 7.36$$

$$v^2 = 2 \times \frac{7.36}{5.0} = 2.944$$

$$v = \sqrt{2.944} = 1.72\,\mathrm{m\,s^{-1}} \approx 1.7\,\mathrm{m\,s^{-1}}$$

Note that we would obtain the same result in Worked example 4 no matter what the mass of the sphere. This is because both k.e. and g.p.e. depend on mass $m$. If we write:

change in g.p.e. = change in k.e.

$$mgh = \tfrac{1}{2}mv^2$$

we can cancel $m$ from both sides. Hence:

$$gh = \frac{v^2}{2}$$

$$v^2 = 2gh$$

Therefore:

$$v = \sqrt{2gh}$$

The final speed $v$ only depends on $g$ and $h$. The mass $m$ of the object is irrelevant. This is not surprising; we could use the same equation to calculate the speed of an object falling from height $h$. An object of small mass gains the same speed as an object of large mass, provided air resistance has no effect.

## Test yourself

12 Re-work Worked example 4 for a brass sphere of mass 10 kg, and show that you get the same result. Repeat with any other value of mass.

13 Calculate how much gravitational potential energy is lost by an aircraft of mass 80 000 kg if it descends from an altitude of 10 000 m to an altitude of 1000 m. What happens to this energy if the pilot keeps the aircraft's speed constant?

*continued ⋯⟶*

14 A high diver (see Figure 5.15) reaches a highest point in her jump where her centre of gravity is 10 m above the water. Assuming that all her gravitational potential energy becomes kinetic energy during the dive, calculate her speed just before she enters the water.

**Figure 5.15** A high dive is an example of converting (transforming) gravitational potential energy to kinetic energy.

# Energy transfers
## Climbing bars

If you are going to climb a mountain, you will need a supply of energy. This is because your gravitational potential energy is greater at the top of the mountain than at the base. A good supply of energy would be some bars of chocolate. Each bar supplies 1200 kJ. Suppose your weight is 600 N and you climb a 2000 m high mountain. The work done by your muscles is:

work done = $Fs$ = 600 × 2000 = 1200 kJ

So one bar of chocolate will do the trick. Of course, in reality, it would not. Your body is inefficient. It

## Energy conservation and internal energy

When we use the idea that g.p.e. is changing to k.e., we are using the idea that energy is conserved; that is to say, there is as much energy at the end of the process as there was at the beginning. Where did this idea come from?

Figure 5.16 shows James Joule, the English scientist after whom the unit of energy is named. Joule is famous among physicists for having taken a thermometer on his honeymoon in the Alps. He knew that water at the top of a waterfall had gravitational potential energy.

Figure 5.16 James Prescott Joule; he helped to develop our idea of energy.

What happens to this energy when the water stops at the bottom of the waterfall? As the water falls, its molecules are accelerating downwards, but after they have landed in the pool at the bottom of the waterfall they move in random directions. The molecules are now moving faster than they did at the top of the waterfall but in random directions. We say that the internal energy of the water has increased.

Internal energy is the sum of the random potential and kinetic energies of all the molecules in a body.

If the temperature increases then the molecules have larger kinetic energy. This is what happens to the gravitational energy of the falling water – it becomes internal energy of the water. The temperature rises slightly because temperature is a measure of the average kinetic energy of the molecules.

You may have thought that the energy becomes thermal energy or heat, but internal energy is the correct scientific term in this case. Heat is what is provided, for example, by a Bunsen burner heating some water. The gases coming into the burner do not have any 'heat' as they are cold. They do have chemical energy which, when they are burnt, produces the 'heat' that passes into the water and becomes internal energy of the water.

The potential energy of the molecules can increase if, for example, liquid molecules evaporate. They are further apart in the gas than in the liquid and so they have more potential energy.

cannot convert 100% of the energy from food into gravitational potential energy. A lot of energy is wasted as your muscles warm up, you perspire, and your body rises and falls as you walk along the path. Your body is perhaps only 5% efficient as far as climbing is concerned, and you will need to eat 20 chocolate bars to get you to the top of the mountain. And you will need to eat more to get you back down again.

Many energy transfers are inefficient. That is, only part of the energy is transferred to where it is wanted. The rest is wasted, and appears in some form that is not wanted (such as waste heat), or in the wrong place. You can determine the efficiency of any device or system using the following equation:

$$\text{efficiency} = \frac{\text{useful output energy}}{\text{total input energy}} \times 100\%$$

A car engine is more efficient than a human body, but not much more. Figure 5.17 shows how this can be represented by a Sankey diagram. The width of the arrow represents the fraction of the energy which is transformed to each new form. In the case of a car engine, we want it to provide kinetic energy to turn the wheels. In practice, 80% of the energy is transformed into heat: the engine gets hot, and heat escapes into the surroundings. So the car engine is only 20% efficient.

We have previously considered situations where an object is falling, and all of its gravitational potential energy changes to kinetic energy. In Worked example 5, we will look at a similar situation, but in this case the energy change is not 100% efficient.

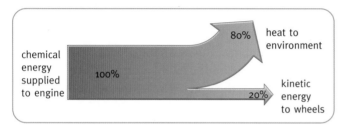

**Figure 5.17** We want a car engine to supply kinetic energy. This Sankey diagram shows that only 20% of the energy supplied to the engine ends up as kinetic energy – it is 20% efficient.

## Worked example

5 Figure 5.18 shows a dam which stores water. The outlet of the dam is 20 m below the surface of the water in the reservoir. Water leaving the dam is moving at 16 m s⁻¹. Calculate the percentage of the gravitational potential energy that is lost when converted into kinetic energy.

**Step 1** We will picture 1 kg of water, starting at the surface of the lake (where it has g.p.e., but no k.e.) and flowing downwards and out at the foot (where it has k.e., but less g.p.e.). Then:

$$\text{change in g.p.e. of water between surface and outflow} = mgh = 1 \times 9.81 \times 20 = 196\,\text{J}$$

*continued* ⋯⟩

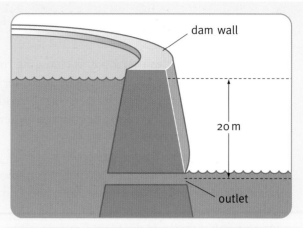

**Figure 5.18** Water stored behind the dam has gravitational potential energy; the fast-flowing water leaving the foot of the dam has kinetic energy.

**Step 2** Calculate the k.e. of 1 kg of water as it leaves the dam:

$$\begin{aligned} \text{k.e. of water leaving dam} &= \tfrac{1}{2}mv^2 \\ &= \tfrac{1}{2} \times 1 \times (16)^2 \\ &= 128\,\text{J} \end{aligned}$$

**Step 3** For each kilogram of water flowing out of the dam, the loss of energy is:

$$\text{loss} = 196 - 128 = 68\,\text{J}$$

$$\text{percentage loss} = \frac{68}{196} \times 100\% \approx 35\%$$

If you wanted to use this moving water to generate electricity, you would have already lost more than a third of the energy which it stores when it is behind the dam.

## Conserving energy

Where does the lost energy from the water in the reservoir go? Most of it ends up warming the water, or warming the pipes that the water flows through. In other words, the internal energy of the water and pipes has been increased. The outflow of water is probably noisy, so some sound is produced.

Here, we are assuming that all of the energy ends up somewhere. None of it disappears. We assume the same thing when we draw a Sankey diagram. The total thickness of the arrow remains constant. We could not have an arrow which got thinner (energy disappearing) or thicker (energy appearing out of nowhere).

We are assuming that **energy is conserved**. This is a principle, known as the **principle of conservation of energy**, which we expect to apply in all situations.

> Energy cannot be created or destroyed. It can only be converted from one form to another.

We should always be able to add up the total amount of energy at the beginning, and be able to account for it all at the end. We cannot be sure that this is always the case, but we expect it to hold true.

We have to think about energy changes **within a closed system**; that is, we have to draw an imaginary boundary around all of the interacting objects which are involved in an energy transfer.

Sometimes, applying the principle of conservation of energy can seem like a scientific fiddle. When physicists were investigating radioactive decay involving beta particles, they found that the particles after the decay had less energy in total than the particles before. They guessed that there was another, invisible particle which was carrying away the missing energy. This particle, named the neutrino, was proposed by the theoretical physicist Wolfgang Pauli in 1931. The neutrino was not detected by experimenters until 25 years later.

Although we cannot prove that energy is always conserved, this example shows that the principle of conservation of energy can be a powerful tool in helping us to understand what is going on in nature, and that it can help us to make fruitful predictions about future experiments.

## Power

The word **power** has several different meanings – political power, powers of ten, electrical power from power stations. In physics, it has a specific meaning which is related to these other meanings. Figure **5.19** illustrates what we mean by power in physics.

The lift shown in Figure **5.19** can lift a heavy load of people. The motor at the top of the building provides a force to raise the lift car, and this force does work against the force of gravity. The motor transfers energy to the lift car. The **power** $P$ of the motor is the rate at which it does work. Power is defined as the rate of work done. As a word equation, power is given by:

$$\text{power} = \frac{\text{work done}}{\text{time taken}}$$

$$\text{or } P = \frac{W}{t}$$

where $W$ is the work done in a time $t$.

**Figure 5.19** A lift needs a powerful motor to raise the car when it has a full load of people. The motor does many thousands of joules of work each second.

### Test yourself

**15** A stone falls from the top of a cliff, 80 m high. When it reaches the foot of the cliff, its speed is $38\,\text{m}\,\text{s}^{-1}$.
  **a** Calculate the proportion of the stone's initial g.p.e. that is converted to k.e.
  **b** What happens to the rest of the stone's initial energy?

## Units of power: the watt

Power is measured in watts, named after James Watt, the Scottish engineer famous for his development of the steam engine in the second half of the 18th century. The watt is defined as a rate of working of 1 joule per second. Hence:

1 watt = 1 joule per second

or $1\,W = 1\,J\,s^{-1}$

In practice we also use kilowatts (kW) and megawatts (MW).

1000 watts = 1 kilowatt (1 kW)

1 000 000 watts = 1 megawatt (1 MW)

You are probably familiar with the labels on light bulbs which indicate their power in watts, for example 60 W or 100 W. The values of power on the labels tell you about the energy transferred by an electrical current, rather than by a force doing work.

### Worked example

6  The motor of the lift shown in Figure 5.19 provides a force of 20 kN; this force is enough to raise the lift by 18 m in 10 s. Calculate the output power of the motor.

**Step 1** First, we must calculate the work done:

work done = force × distance moved
= 20 × 18 = 360 kJ

**Step 2** Now we can calculate the motor's output power:

$$\text{power} = \frac{\text{work done}}{\text{time taken}} = \frac{360 \times 10^3}{10} = 36\,kW$$

> Take care not to confuse the two uses of the letter 'W':
> W = watt (a unit)
> $W$ = work done (a quantity)

continued ···▸

So the lift motor's power is 36 kW. Note that this is its mechanical power output. The motor cannot be 100% efficient since some energy is bound to be wasted as heat due to friction, so the electrical power input must be more than 36 kW.

### Test yourself

16 Calculate how much work is done by a 50 kW car engine in a time of 1.0 minute.

17 A car engine does 4200 kJ of work in one minute. Calculate its output power, in kilowatts.

18 A particular car engine provides a force of 700 N when the car is moving at its top speed of $40\,m\,s^{-1}$.
   a Calculate how much work is done by the car's engine in one second.
   b State the output power of the engine.

## Moving power

An aircraft is kept moving forwards by the force of its engines pushing air backwards. The greater the force and the faster the aircraft is moving, the greater the power supplied by its engines.

Suppose that an aircraft is moving with velocity $v$. Its engines provide the force $F$ needed to overcome the drag of the air. In time $t$, the aircraft moves a distance $s$ equal to $v \times t$. So the work done by the engines is:

work done = force × distance

$$W = F \times v \times t$$

and the power $P \left(= \frac{\text{work done}}{\text{time taken}}\right)$ is given by:

$$P = \frac{W}{t} = \frac{F \times v \times t}{t}$$

and we have:

$$P = F \times v$$

power = force × velocity

It may help to think of this equation in terms of units. The right-hand side is in $N \times m\,s^{-1}$, and $N\,m$ is the same as J. So the right-hand side has units of $J\,s^{-1}$, or W, the unit of power. If you look back to Q **18** above, you will see that, to find the power of the car engine, rather than considering the work done in 1 s, we could simply have multiplied the engine's force by the car's speed.

## Human power

Our energy supply comes from our food. A typical diet supplies 2000–3000 kcal (kilocalories) per day. This is equivalent (in SI units) to about 10 MJ of energy. We need this energy for our daily requirements – keeping warm, moving about, brainwork, and so on. We can determine the average power of all the activities of our body:

average power = 10 MJ per day

$$= 10 \times \frac{10^6}{86\,400} = 116\,W$$

So we dissipate energy at the rate of about 100 W. We supply roughly as much energy to our surroundings as a 100 W light bulb. Twenty people will keep a room as warm as a 2 kW electric heater.

Note that this is our average power. If you are doing some demanding physical task, your power will be greater. This is illustrated in Worked example 7.

## Worked example

7 A person who weighs 500 N runs up a flight of stairs in 5.0 s (Figure **5.20**). Their gain in height is 3.0 m. Calculate the rate at which work is done against the force of gravity.

continued ⋯➔

**Figure 5.20** Running up stairs can require a high rate of doing work. You may have investigated your own power in this way.

**Step 1** Calculate the work done against gravity:

work done $W = F \times s = 500 \times 3.0 = 1500\,J$

**Step 2** Now calculate the power:

$$\text{power } P = \frac{W}{t} = \frac{1500}{5.0} = 300\,W$$

So, while the person is running up the stairs, they are doing work against gravity at a greater rate than their average power – perhaps three times as great. And, since our muscles are not very efficient, they need to be supplied with energy even faster, perhaps at a rate of 1 kW. This is why we cannot run up stairs all day long without greatly increasing the amount we eat. The inefficiency of our muscles also explains why we get hot when we exert ourselves.

## Test yourself

19 In an experiment to measure a student's power, she times herself running up a flight of steps. Use the data below to work out her useful power.

number of steps = 28

height of each step = 20 cm

acceleration of free fall = 9.81 m s⁻²

mass of student = 55 kg

time taken = 5.4 s

# Summary

- [ ] The work done $W$ when a force $F$ moves through a displacement $s$ in the direction of the force:

    $$W = Fs \quad \text{or} \quad W = Fs\cos\theta$$

    where $\theta$ is the angle between the force and the displacement.
- [ ] A joule is defined as the work done (or energy transferred) when a force of 1N moves a distance of 1m in the direction of the force.
- [ ] When an object of mass $m$ rises through a height $h$, its gravitational potential energy $E_p$ increases by an amount:

    $$E_p = mgh$$

- [ ] The kinetic energy $E_k$ of a body of mass $m$ moving at speed $v$ is:

    $$E_k = \tfrac{1}{2}mv^2$$

- [ ] The principle of conservation of energy states that, for a closed system, energy can be transformed to other forms but the total amount of energy remains constant.
- [ ] Internal energy is the sum of the potential and kinetic energies of the molecules.
- [ ] The efficiency of a device or system is determined using the equation:

    $$\text{efficiency} = \frac{\text{useful output energy}}{\text{total input energy}} \times 100\%$$

- [ ] Power is the rate at which work is done (or energy is transferred):

    $$P = \frac{W}{t} \quad \text{and} \quad P = Fv$$

- [ ] A watt is defined as a rate of transfer of energy of one joule per second.

# End-of-chapter questions

1   In each case below, discuss the energy changes taking place.
    a   An apple falling towards the ground.
    b   A car decelerates when the brakes are applied.
    c   A space probe fall towards the surface of a planet.

2   A 120 kg crate is dragged along the horizontal ground by a 200 N force acting at an angle of 30° to
    the horizontal, as shown in Figure **5.21**. The crate moves along the surface with a constant velocity
    of 0.5 m s$^{-1}$. The 200 N force is applied for a time of 16 s.

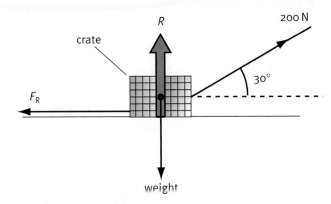

**Figure 5.21** For End-of-chapter question **2**.

    a   Calculate the work done on the crate by:
        i    the 200 N force
        ii   the weight of the crate
        iii  the normal contact force $R$.
    b   Calculate the rate of work done against the frictional force $F_R$.

3   Which of the following has greater kinetic energy?
    a   A 20-tonne truck travelling at a speed of 30 m s$^{-1}$.
    b   A 1.2 g dust particle travelling at 150 km s$^{-1}$ through space.

4   A 950 kg sack of cement is lifted to the top of a building 50 m high by an electric motor.
    a   Calculate the increase in the gravitational potential energy of the sack of cement.
    b   The output power of the motor is 4.0 kW. Calculate how long it took to raise the sack to the top
        of the building.
    c   The electrical power transferred by the motor is 6.9 kW. In raising the sack to the top of the
        building, how much energy is wasted in the motor as heat?

5   a   Define **power** and state its unit.
    b   Write a word equation for the kinetic energy of a moving object.
    c   A car of mass 1100 kg starting from rest reaches a speed of 18 m s$^{-1}$ in 25 s.
        Calculate the average power developed by the engine of the car.

# Exam-style questions

1  A cyclist pedals a long slope which is at 5.0° to the horizontal.

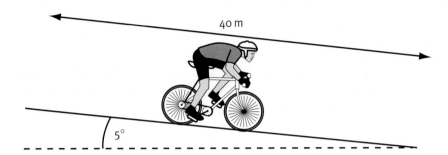

The cyclist starts from rest at the top of the slope and reaches a speed of $12\,\mathrm{m\,s^{-1}}$ after a time of $67\,\mathrm{s}$, having travelled $40\,\mathrm{m}$ down the slope. The total mass of the cyclist and bicycle is $90\,\mathrm{kg}$.

  **a** Calculate:

    **i** the loss in gravitational potential energy as he travels down the slope     [3]

    **ii** the increase in kinetic energy as he travels down the slope.     [2]

  **b i** Use your answers to **a** to determine the useful power output of the cyclist.     [3]

    **ii** Suggest **one** reason why the actual power output of the cyclist is larger than your value in **i**.     [2]

2  **a** Explain what is meant by **work**.     [2]

  **b i** Explain how the principle of conservation of energy applies to a man sliding from rest down a vertical pole, if there is a constant force of friction acting on him.     [2]

    **ii** The man slides down the pole and reaches the ground after falling a distance $h = 15\,\mathrm{m}$. His potential energy at the top of the pole is $1000\,\mathrm{J}$. Sketch a graph to show how his gravitational potential energy $E_p$ varies with $h$. Add to your graph a line to show the variation of his kinetic energy $E_k$ with $h$.     [3]

3  **a** Use the equations of motion to show that the kinetic energy of an object of mass $m$ moving with velocity $v$ is $\frac{1}{2}mv^2$.     [2]

  **b** A car of mass $800\,\mathrm{kg}$ accelerates from rest to a speed of $20\,\mathrm{m\,s^{-1}}$ in a time of $6.0\,\mathrm{s}$.

    **i** Calculate the average power used to accelerate the car in the first $6.0\,\mathrm{s}$.     [2]

    **ii** The power passed by the engine of the car to the wheels is constant. Explain why the acceleration of the car decreases as the car accelerates.     [2]

4  **a i** Define **potential energy**.     [1]

    **ii** Distinguish between gravitational potential energy and elastic potential energy.     [2]

**b** Sea water is trapped behind a dam at high tide and then released through turbines. The level of the water trapped by the dam falls 10.0 m until it is all at the same height as the sea.

   **i** Calculate the mass of sea water covering an area of $1.4 \times 10^6$ m$^2$ and depth 10.0 m. (Density of sea water = 1030 kg m$^{-3}$) [1]

   **ii** Calculate the maximum loss of potential energy of the sea water in **i** when passed through the turbines. [2]

   **iii** The potential energy of the sea water, calculated in **ii**, is lost over a period of 6.0 hours. Estimate the average power output of the power station over this time period, given that the efficiency of the power station is 50%. [3]

**5** **a** Explain what is meant by the **internal energy** of a substance. [2]

   **b** State and explain what happens to the internal energy of the water in the following cases. In your answer use ideas about molecules.

   **i** Water is heated from 20 °C to 60 °C, without evaporation. [2]

   **ii** Water evaporates at constant temperature. [2]

# 6 Momentum

## Objectives

After studying this chapter, you should be able to:

- [ ] define linear momentum
- [ ] relate force to rate of change of momentum
- [ ] state and apply the principle of conservation of momentum
- [ ] discuss energy changes in perfectly elastic and inelastic collisions

## Understanding collisions

**Figure 6.1** A high-speed photograph of a crash test. The cars collide head-on at 56 km h⁻¹ with dummies as drivers.

To improve the safety of cars the motion of a car during a crash must be understood and the forces on the driver minimised. In this way safer cars have been developed and many lives have been saved.

In this chapter, we will explore how the idea of **momentum** can allow us to predict how objects move after colliding (interacting) with each other. We will also see how Newton's laws of motion can be expressed in terms of momentum.

## The idea of momentum

Snooker players can perform some amazing moves on the table, without necessarily knowing Newton's laws of motion – see Figure 6.2. However, the laws of physics can help us to understand what happens when two snooker balls collide or when one bounces off the side cushion of the table.

Here are some examples of situations involving collisions:

- two cars collide head-on
- a fast-moving car runs into the back of a slower car in front
- a footballer runs into an opponent
- a hockey stick strikes a ball
- a comet or an asteroid collides with a planet as it orbits the Sun
- the atoms of the air collide constantly with each other, and with the walls of their surroundings
- electrons that form an electric current collide with the vibrating ions that make up a metal wire
- two distant galaxies collide over millions of years.

From these examples, we can see that collisions are happening all around us, all the time. They happen on the microscopic scale of atoms and electrons, they happen in our everyday world, and they also happen on the cosmic scale of our Universe.

**Figure 6.2** If you play pool often enough, you will be able to predict how the balls will move on the table. Alternatively, you can use the laws of physics to predict their motion.

# Modelling collisions

## Springy collisions

Figure **6.3a** shows what happens when one snooker ball collides head-on with a second, stationary ball. The result can seem surprising. The moving ball stops dead. The ball initially at rest moves off with the same velocity as that of the original ball. To achieve this, a snooker player must observe two conditions.

- The collision must be head-on. (If one ball strikes a glancing blow on the side of the other, they will both move off at different angles.)
- The moving ball must not be given any spin. (Spin is an added complication which we will ignore in our present study, although it plays a vital part in the games of pool and snooker.)

You can mimic the collision of two snooker balls in the laboratory using two identical trolleys, as shown in Figure **6.3b**. The moving trolley has its spring-load released, so that the collision is springy. As one trolley runs into the other, the spring is at first compressed, and then it pushes out again to set the second trolley moving. The first trolley comes to a complete halt. The 'motion' of one trolley has been transferred to the other.

You can see another interesting result if two moving identical trolleys collide head-on. If the collision is springy, both trolleys bounce backwards. If a fast-moving trolley collides with a slower one, the fast trolley bounces back at the speed of the slow one, and the slow one bounces back at the speed of the fast one. In this collision, it is as if the velocities of the trolleys have been swapped.

## Sticky collisions

Figure **6.4** shows another type of collision. In this case, the trolleys have adhesive pads so that they stick together when they collide. A sticky collision like this is the opposite of a springy collision like the ones described above.

If a single moving trolley collides with a single stationary one, they both move off together. After the collision, the speed of the combined trolleys is half that of the original trolley. It is as if the 'motion' of the original trolley has been shared between the two. If a

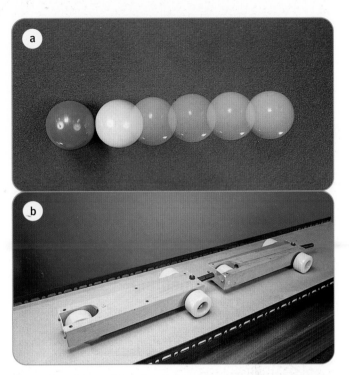

Figure 6.3 **a** The red snooker ball, coming from the left, has hit the yellow ball head-on. **b** You can do the same thing with two trolleys in the laboratory.

Figure 6.4 If a moving trolley sticks to a stationary trolley, they both move off together.

single moving trolley collides with a stationary double trolley (twice the mass), they move off with one-third of the original velocity.

From these examples of sticky collisions, you can see that, when the mass of the trolley increases as a result of a collision, its velocity decreases. Doubling the mass halves the velocity, and so on.

1 Here are two collisions to picture in your mind. Answer the question for each.
  a Ball A, moving towards the right, collides with stationary ball B. Ball A bounces back; B moves off slowly to the right. Which has the greater mass, A or B?
  b Trolley A, moving towards the right, collides with stationary trolley B. They stick together, and move off at less than half A's original speed. Which has the greater mass, A or B?

## Defining linear momentum

From the examples discussed above, we can see that two quantities are important in understanding collisions:

• mass $m$ of the object
• velocity $v$ of the object.

These are combined to give a single quantity, called the **linear momentum** (or simply momentum) $p$ of an object. The momentum of an object is defined as the product of the mass of the object and its velocity. Hence:

$$\text{momentum} = \text{mass} \times \text{velocity}$$

$$p = mv$$

The unit of momentum is $\text{kg m s}^{-1}$. There is no special name for this unit in the SI system.

Momentum is a vector quantity because it is a product of a vector quantity (velocity) and a scalar quantity (mass). Momentum has both magnitude and direction. Its direction is the same as the direction of the object's velocity.

In the earlier examples, we described how the 'motion' of one trolley appeared to be transferred to a second trolley, or shared with it. It is more correct to say that it is the trolley's momentum that is transferred or shared. (Strictly speaking, we should refer to linear momentum, because there is another quantity called **angular momentum** which is possessed by spinning objects.)

Like energy, we find that momentum is also conserved. We have to consider objects which form a **closed system** – that is, no external force acts on them. The principle of **conservation of momentum** states that:

> Within a closed system, the total momentum in any direction is constant.

The principle of conservation of momentum can also be expressed as follows:

> For a closed system, in any direction:
>   total momentum of objects before collision
>     = total momentum of objects after collision

A group of colliding objects always has as much momentum after the collision as it had before the collision. This principle is illustrated in Worked example 1.

## Worked example

1 In Figure 6.5, trolley A of mass 0.80 kg travelling at a velocity of $3.0 \text{ m s}^{-1}$ collides head-on with a stationary trolley B. Trolley B has twice the mass of trolley A. The trolleys stick together and have a common velocity of $1.0 \text{ m s}^{-1}$ after the collision. Show that momentum is conserved in this collision.

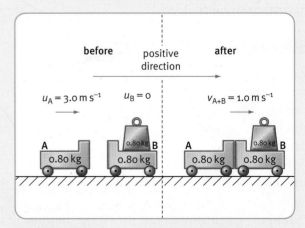

**Figure 6.5** The state of trolleys A and B, before and after the collision.

continued ⋯⟶

**Step 1** Make a sketch using the information given in the question. Notice that we need two diagrams to show the situations, one before and one after the collision. Similarly, we need two calculations – one for the momentum of the trolleys before the collision and one for their momentum after the collision.

**Step 2** Calculate the momentum before the collision:

momentum of trolleys before collision

$$= m_A \times u_A + m_B \times u_B$$
$$= (0.80 \times 3.0) + 0$$
$$= 2.4 \, \text{kg m s}^{-1}$$

Trolley B has no momentum before the collision, because it is not moving.

**Step 3** Calculate the momentum after the collision:

momentum of trolleys after collision

$$= (m_A + m_B) \times v_{A+B}$$
$$= (0.80 + 1.60) \times 1.0$$
$$= 2.4 \, \text{kg m s}^{-1}$$

So, both before and after the collision, the trolleys have a combined momentum of $2.4 \, \text{kg m s}^{-1}$. Momentum has been conserved.

## Test yourself

2 Calculate the momentum of each of the following objects.
   **a** A 0.50 kg stone travelling at a velocity of $20 \, \text{m s}^{-1}$.
   **b** A 25 000 kg bus travelling at $20 \, \text{m s}^{-1}$ on a road.
   **c** An electron travelling at $2.0 \times 10^7 \, \text{m s}^{-1}$. (The mass of the electron is $9.1 \times 10^{-31}$ kg.)

3 Two balls, each of mass 0.50 kg, collide as shown in Figure 6.6. Show that their total momentum before the collision is equal to their total momentum after the collision.

*continued* ⋯⋗

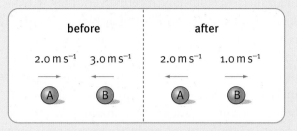

**Figure 6.6** For Test yourself Q **3**.

# Understanding collisions

The cars in Figure 6.7 have been badly damaged by a collision. The front of a car is designed to absorb the impact of the crash. It has a 'crumple zone', which collapses on impact. This absorbs most of the kinetic energy that the car had before the collision. It is better that the car's kinetic energy should be transferred to the crumple zone than to the driver and passengers.

Motor manufacturers make use of test labs to investigate how their cars respond to impacts. When a car is designed, the manufacturers combine soft, compressible materials that absorb energy with rigid structures that protect the car's occupants. Old-fashioned cars had much more rigid structures. In a collision, they were more likely to bounce back and the violent forces involved were much more likely to prove fatal.

**Figure 6.7** The front of each car has crumpled in, as a result of a head-on collision.

## Two types of collision

When two objects collide, they may crumple and deform. Their kinetic energy may also disappear completely as they come to a halt. This is an example of an inelastic collision. Alternatively, they may spring apart, retaining all of their kinetic energy. This is a perfectly elastic collision. In practice, in most collisions, some kinetic energy is transformed into other forms (e.g. heat or sound) and the collision is inelastic. Previously we described the collisions as being 'springy' or 'sticky'. We should now use the correct scientific terms **perfectly elastic** and **inelastic**.

We will look at examples of these two types of collision and consider what happens to linear momentum and kinetic energy in each.

### A perfectly elastic collision

Two identical objects A and B, moving at the same speed but in opposite directions, have a head-on collision, as shown in Figure 6.8. This is a perfectly elastic collision. Each object bounces back with its velocity reversed.

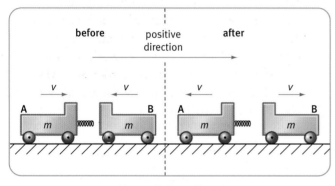

**Figure 6.8** Two objects may collide in different ways: this is an elastic collision. An inelastic collision of the same two objects is shown in Figure **6.9**.

You should be able to see that, in this collision, both momentum and kinetic energy are conserved. Before the collision, object A of mass $m$ is moving to the right at speed $v$ and object B of mass $m$ is moving to the left at speed $v$. Afterwards, we still have two masses $m$ moving with speed $v$, but now object A is moving to the left and object B is moving to the right. We can express this mathematically as follows.

### Before the collision

object A:  mass = $m$   velocity = $v$   momentum = $mv$
object B:  mass = $m$   velocity = $-v$   momentum = $-mv$

Object B has negative velocity and momentum because it is travelling in the opposite direction to object A. Therefore we have:

total momentum before collision
$$= \text{momentum of A} + \text{momentum of B}$$
$$= mv + (-mv) = 0$$

total kinetic energy before collision = k.e. of A + k.e. of B

$$= \tfrac{1}{2}mv^2 + \tfrac{1}{2}mv^2 = mv^2$$

The magnitude of the momentum of each object is the same. Momentum is a vector quantity and we have to consider the directions in which the objects travel. The combined momentum is zero. On the other hand, kinetic energy is a scalar quantity and direction of travel is irrelevant. Both objects have the same kinetic energy and therefore the combined kinetic energy is twice the kinetic energy of a single object.

**After the collision**, both objects have their velocities reversed, and we have:

total momentum after collision $= (-mv) + mv = 0$

total kinetic energy after collision $= \tfrac{1}{2}mv^2 + \tfrac{1}{2}mv^2 = mv^2$

So the total momentum and the total kinetic energy are unchanged. They are both conserved in a perfectly elastic collision such as this.

In this collision, the objects have a **relative speed** of $2v$ before the collision. After their collision, their velocities are reversed so their relative speed is $2v$ again. This is a feature of perfectly elastic collisions.

The relative speed of approach is the speed of one object measured relative to another. If two objects are travelling directly towards each other with speed $v$, as measured by someone stationary on the ground, then each object 'sees' the other one approaching with a speed of $2v$. Thus if objects are travelling in opposite directions we add their speeds to find the relative speed. If the objects are travelling in the same direction then we subtract their speeds to find the relative speed.

In a perfectly elastic collision, relative speed of approach = relative speed of separation.

### An inelastic collision

In Figure **6.9**, the same two objects collide, but this time they stick together after the collision and come to a halt. Clearly, the total momentum and the total kinetic energy are both zero after the collision, since neither mass is moving. We have:

|  | Before collision | After collision |
|---|---|---|
| momentum | 0 | 0 |
| kinetic energy | $mv^2$ | 0 |

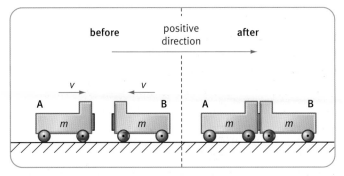

**Figure 6.9** An inelastic collision between two identical objects. The trolleys are stationary after the collision.

Again we see that momentum is conserved. However, kinetic energy is not conserved. It is lost because work is done in deforming the two objects.

In fact, **momentum is always conserved** in all collisions. There is nothing else into which momentum can be converted. Kinetic energy is usually not conserved in a collision, because it can be transformed into other forms of energy – sound energy if the collision is noisy, and the energy involved in deforming the objects (which usually ends up as internal energy – they get warmer). Of course, the total amount of energy remains constant, as prescribed by the principle of conservation of energy.

## Test yourself

4   Copy Table **6.1** below, choosing the correct words from each pair.

| Type of collision | Momentum | Kinetic energy | Total energy |
|---|---|---|---|
| perfectly elastic | conserved / not conserved | conserved / not conserved | conserved / not conserved |
| inelastic | conserved / not conserved | conserved / not conserved | conserved / not conserved |

**Table 6.1** For Test Yourself Q 4.

## Solving collision problems

We can use the idea of conservation of momentum to solve numerical problems, as illustrated by Worked example 2.

### Worked example

2   In the game of bowls, a player rolls a large ball towards a smaller, stationary ball. A large ball of mass 5.0 kg moving at 10.0 m s⁻¹ strikes a stationary ball of mass 1.0 kg. The smaller ball flies off at 10.0 m s⁻¹.

   a   Determine the final velocity of the large ball after the impact.

   b   Calculate the kinetic energy 'lost' in the impact.

**Step 1** Draw two diagrams, showing the situations before and after the collision. Figure 6.10 shows the values of masses and velocities; since we don't know the velocity of the large ball after the collision, this is shown as $v$. The direction from left to right has been assigned the 'positive direction'.

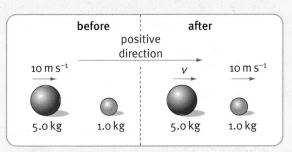

**Figure 6.10** When solving problems involving collisions, it is useful to draw diagrams showing the situations before and after the collision. Include the values of all the quantities that you know.

**Step 2** Using the principle of conservation of momentum, set up an equation and solve for the value of $v$:

total momentum before collision
= total momentum after collision

*continued* ⋯⟩

$$(5.0 \times 10) + (1.0 \times 0) = (5.0 \times v) + (1.0 \times 10)$$

$$50 + 0 = 5.0v + 10$$

$$v = \frac{40}{5.0} = 8.0\,\text{m s}^{-1}$$

So the speed of the large ball decreases to $8.0\,\text{m s}^{-1}$ after the collision. Its direction of motion is unchanged – the velocity remains positive.

**Step 3** Knowing the large ball's final velocity, calculate the change in kinetic energy during the collision:

total k.e. before collision
$$= \tfrac{1}{2} \times 5.0 \times 10^2 + 0 = 250\,\text{J}$$

total k.e. after collision
$$= \tfrac{1}{2} \times 5.0 \times 8.0^2 + \tfrac{1}{2} \times 1.0 \times 10^2 = 210\,\text{J}$$

k.e. 'lost' in the collision
$$= 250\,\text{J} - 210\,\text{J} = 40\,\text{J}$$

This lost kinetic energy will appear as internal energy (the two balls get warmer) and as sound energy (we hear the collision between the balls).

## Test yourself

5 Figure **6.11** shows two identical balls A and B about to make a head-on collision. After the collision, ball A rebounds at a speed of $1.5\,\text{m s}^{-1}$ and ball B rebounds at a speed of $2.5\,\text{m s}^{-1}$. The mass of each ball is $4.0\,\text{kg}$.
  a Calculate the momentum of each ball before the collision.
  b Calculate the momentum of each ball after the collision.
  c Is the momentum conserved in the collision?
  d Show that the total kinetic energy of the two balls is conserved in the collision.
  e Show that the relative speed of the balls is the same before and after the collision.

*continued ···▶*

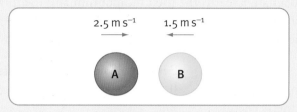

**Figure 6.11** For Test yourself Q **5**.

6 A trolley of mass $1.0\,\text{kg}$ is moving at $2.0\,\text{m s}^{-1}$. It collides with a stationary trolley of mass $2.0\,\text{kg}$. This second trolley moves off at $1.2\,\text{m s}^{-1}$.
  a Draw 'before' and 'after' diagrams to show the situation.
  b Use the principle of conservation of momentum to calculate the speed of the first trolley after the collision. In what direction does it move?

# Explosions and crash-landings

There are situations where it may appear that momentum is being created out of nothing, or that it is disappearing without trace. Do these contradict the principle of conservation of momentum?

The rockets shown in Figure **6.12** rise high into the sky. As they start to fall, they send out showers of chemical packages, each of which explodes to produce a brilliant sphere of burning chemicals. Material flies out in all directions to create a spectacular effect.

**Figure 6.12** These exploding rockets produce a spectacular display of bright sparks in the night sky.

Does an explosion create momentum out of nothing? The important point to note here is that the burning material spreads out equally in all directions. Each tiny spark has momentum, but for every spark, there is another moving in the opposite direction, i.e. with opposite momentum. Since momentum is a vector quantity, the total amount of momentum created is zero.

At the same time, kinetic energy is created in an explosion. Burning material flies outwards; its kinetic energy has come from the chemical potential energy stored in the chemical materials before they burn.

## More fireworks

A roman candle fires a jet of burning material up into the sky. This is another type of explosion, but it doesn't send material in all directions. The firework tube directs the material upwards. Has momentum been created out of nothing here?

Again, the answer is no. The chemicals have momentum upwards, but at the same time, the roman candle pushes downwards on the Earth. An equal amount of downwards momentum is given to the Earth. Of course, the Earth is massive, and we don't notice the tiny change in its velocity which results.

## Down to Earth

If you push a large rock over a cliff, its speed increases as it falls. Where does its momentum come from? And when it lands, where does its momentum disappear to?

The rock falls because of the pull of the Earth's gravity on it. This force is its weight and it makes the rock accelerate towards the Earth. Its weight does work and the rock gains kinetic energy. It gains momentum downwards. Something must be gaining an equal amount of momentum in the opposite (upward) direction. It is the Earth, which starts to move upwards as the rock falls downwards. The mass of the Earth is so great that its change in velocity is small – far too small to be noticeable.

When the rock hits the ground, its momentum becomes zero. At the same instant, the Earth also stops moving upwards. The rock's momentum cancels out the Earth's momentum. At all times during the rock's fall and crash-landing, momentum has been conserved.

If a rock of mass 60 kg is falling towards the Earth at a speed of 20 m s$^{-1}$, how fast is the Earth moving towards it? Figure 6.13 shows the situation. The mass of the Earth is $6.0 \times 10^{24}$ kg. We have:

total momentum of Earth and rock = 0

Hence:

$$(60 \times 20) + (6.0 \times 10^{24} \times v) = 0$$

$$v = -2.0 \times 10^{-22} \text{ m s}^{-1}$$

The minus sign shows that the Earth's velocity is in the opposite direction to that of the rock. The Earth moves very slowly indeed. In the time of the rock's fall, it will move much less than the diameter of the nucleus of an atom!

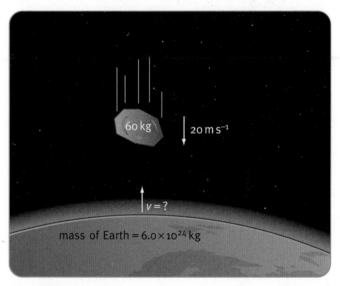

Figure 6.13 The rock and Earth gain momentum in opposite directions.

### Test yourself

7  Discuss whether momentum is conserved in each of the following situations.
   a A star explodes in all directions – a supernova.
   b You jump up from a trampoline. As you go up, your speed decreases; as you come down again, your speed increases.

continued ⋯⟶

**8** A ball of mass 0.40 kg is thrown at a wall. It strikes the wall with a speed of 1.5 m s$^{-1}$ perpendicular to the wall and bounces off the wall with a speed of 1.2 m s$^{-1}$. Explain the changes in momentum and energy which happen in the collision between the ball and the wall. Give numerical values where possible.

# Momentum and Newton's laws

The big ideas of physics are often very simple; that is to say, it takes only a few words to express them and they can be applied in many situations. However, 'simple' does not usually mean 'easy'. Concepts such as force, energy and voltage, for example, are not immediately obvious. They usually took someone to make a giant leap of imagination to first establish them. Then the community of physicists spent decades worrying away at them, refining them until they are the fundamental ideas which we use today.

Take Isaac Newton's work on motion. He published his ideas in a book commonly known as the *Principia* (see Figure **6.14**); its full title translated from Latin is *Mathematical Principles of Natural Philosophy*.

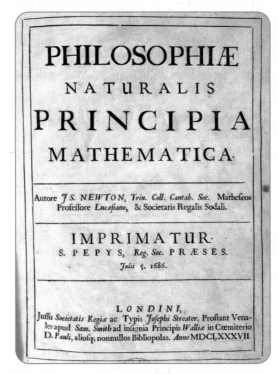

**Figure 6.14** The title page of Newton's *Principia* in which he outlined his theories of the laws that governed the motion of objects.

The *Principia* represents the results of 20 years of thinking. Newton was able to build on Galileo's ideas and he was in correspondence with many other scientists and mathematicians. Indeed, there was an ongoing feud with Robert Hooke as to who was the first to come up with certain ideas. Among scientists, this is known as 'priority', and publication is usually taken as proof of priority.

Newton wanted to develop an understanding of the idea of 'force'. You may have been told in your early studies of science that 'a force is a push or a pull'. That doesn't tell us very much. Newton's idea was that forces are interactions between bodies and that they change the motion of the body that they act on. Forces acting on an object can produce acceleration. For an object of constant mass, this acceleration is directly proportional to the net force acting on the object. That is much more like a scientific definition of force.

# Understanding motion

In Chapter **3**, we looked at Newton's laws of motion. We can get further insight into these laws by thinking about them in terms of momentum.

## Newton's first law of motion

In everyday speech, we sometimes say that something has momentum when we mean that it has a tendency to keep on moving of its own free will. An oil tanker is difficult to stop at sea, because of its momentum. We use the same word in a figurative sense: 'The election campaign is gaining momentum.' This idea of keeping on moving is just what we discussed in connection with **Newton's first law of motion**:

An object will remain at rest or keep travelling at constant velocity unless it is acted on by an external force.

An object travelling at constant velocity has constant momentum. Hence the first law is really saying that the momentum of an object remains the same unless the object experiences an external force.

## Newton's second law of motion

**Newton's second law of motion** links the idea of the net force acting on an object and its momentum. A statement of Newton's second law is:

> The net force acting on an object is directly proportional to the rate of change of the linear momentum of that object. The net force and the change in momentum are in the same direction.

Hence:

net force $\propto$ rate of change of momentum

This can be written as:

$$F \propto \frac{\Delta p}{\Delta t}$$

where $F$ is the net force and $\Delta p$ is the change in momentum taking place in a time interval of $\Delta t$. (Remember that the Greek letter delta, $\Delta$, is a shorthand for 'change in ...', so $\Delta p$ means 'change in momentum'.) The change in momentum and force are both vector quantities, hence these two quantities must be in the same direction.

The unit of force (the newton N) is defined to make the constant of proportionality equal to one, so we can write the second law of motion mathematically as:

$$F = \frac{\Delta p}{\Delta t}$$

If the forces acting on an object are balanced, there is no resultant or net force and the object's momentum will remain constant. If a net force acts on an object, its momentum (velocity and/or direction) will change. The equation above gives us another way of stating Newton's second law of motion:

> The net force acting on an object is equal to the rate of change of its momentum. The net force and the change in momentum are in the same direction.

This statement effectively defines what we mean by a force; it is an interaction that causes an object's momentum to change. So, if an object's momentum is changing, there must be a force acting on it. We can find the size and direction of the force by measuring the rate of change of the object's momentum.

> force = rate of change of momentum
>
> $$F = \frac{\Delta p}{\Delta t}$$

Worked example **3** shows how to use this equation.

## Worked example

3 Calculate the average force acting on a 900 kg car when its velocity changes from 5.0 m s$^{-1}$ to 30 m s$^{-1}$ in a time of 12 s.

**Step 1** Write down the quantities given:

$m = 900$ kg

initial velocity $u = 5.0$ m s$^{-1}$

$\Delta t = 12$ s

**Step 2** Calculate the initial momentum and the final momentum of the car.

momentum = mass × velocity

initial momentum
$$= mu = 900 \times 5.0 = 4500 \text{ kg m s}^{-1}$$

final momentum
$$= mv = 900 \times 30 = 27\,000 \text{ kg m s}^{-1}$$

**Step 3** Use Newton's second law of motion to calculate the average force on the car:

$$F = \frac{\Delta p}{\Delta t}$$

$$= \frac{27\,500 - 4500}{12}$$

$$= 1875 \text{ N} \approx 1900 \text{ N}$$

The average force acting on the car is about 1.9 kN.

## A special case of Newton's second law of motion

Imagine an object of constant mass $m$ acted upon by a net force $F$. The force will change the momentum of the object. According to Newton's second law of motion, we have:

$$F = \frac{\Delta p}{\Delta t} = \frac{mv - mu}{t}$$

where $u$ is the initial velocity of the object, $v$ is the final velocity of the object and $t$ is the time taken for the change in velocity. The mass $m$ of the object is a constant; hence the above equation can be rewritten as:

$$F = \frac{m(v - u)}{t}$$

The term in brackets is the acceleration $a$ of the object. Therefore a special case of Newton's second law is:

$$F = ma$$

We have already met this equation in Chapter **3**. In Worked example **3**, you could have determined the average force acting on the car using this simplified equation for Newton's second law of motion. Remember that the equation $F = ma$ is a special case of $F = \frac{\Delta p}{\Delta t}$ which only applies when the mass of the object is constant. There are situations where the mass of an object changes as it moves, for example a rocket, which burns a phenomenal amount of chemical fuel as it accelerates upwards.

### Test yourself

9 A car of mass 1000 kg is travelling at a velocity of $10\,\text{m s}^{-1}$. It accelerates for 15 s, reaching a velocity of $24\,\text{m s}^{-1}$. Calculate:
  a the change in the momentum of the car in the 15 s period.
  b the average force acting on the car as it accelerates.

*continued ⋯⟶*

10 A ball is kicked by a footballer. The average force on the ball is 240 N, and the impact lasts for a time interval of 0.25 s.
  a Calculate the change in the ball's momentum.
  b State the direction of the change in momentum.

11 Water pouring from a broken pipe lands on a flat roof. The water is moving at $5.0\,\text{m s}^{-1}$ when it strikes the roof. The water hits the roof at a rate of $10\,\text{kg s}^{-1}$. Calculate the force of the water hitting the roof. (Assume that the water does not bounce as it hits the roof. If it did bounce, would your answer be greater or smaller?)

12 A golf ball has a mass of 0.046 kg. The final velocity of the ball after being struck by a golf club is $50\,\text{m s}^{-1}$. The golf club is in contact with the ball for a time of 1.3 ms. Calculate the average force exerted by the golf club on the ball.

## Newton's third law of motion

Newton's third law of motion is to do with interacting objects. These could be two magnets attracting or repelling each other, two electrons repelling each other, etc. Newton's third law states:

> When two bodies interact, the forces they exert on each other are equal and opposite.

How can we relate this to the idea of momentum? Picture holding two magnets, one in each hand. You gradually bring them towards each other (Figure **6.15**) so that they start to attract each other. Each feels a force pulling it towards the other. The two forces are the same size, even if one magnet is stronger than the other. Indeed, one magnet could be replaced by an unmagnetised piece of steel and they would still attract each other equally.

If you release the magnets, they will gain momentum as they are pulled towards each other. One gains momentum to the left while the other gains equal momentum to the right.

Each is acted on by the same force, and for the same time. Hence momentum is conserved.

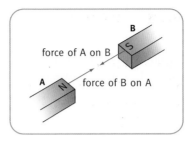

**Figure 6.15** Newton's third law states that the forces these two magnets exert one each other must be equal and opposite.

## Summary

☐ Linear momentum is the product of mass and velocity:

momentum = mass × velocity   or   $p = mv$

☐ The principle of conservation of momentum:
For a **closed system**, in any direction, the total momentum before an interaction (e.g. collision) is equal to the total momentum after the interaction.

☐ In all interactions or collisions, momentum and total energy are conserved.

☐ Kinetic energy is conserved in a perfectly elastic collision; relative speed is unchanged in a perfectly elastic collision.

☐ In an inelastic collision, kinetic energy is not conserved. It is transferred into other forms of energy (e.g. heat or sound). Most collisions are inelastic.

☐ The net force acting on a body is equal to the rate of change of its momentum:

net force = rate of change of momentum   or   $F = \dfrac{\Delta p}{\Delta t}$

☐ The equation $F = ma$ is a special case of Newton's second law of motion when mass $m$ remains constant.

## End-of-chapter questions

1  An object is dropped to the ground and its momentum increases. Explain how the law of conservation of momentum and Newton's third law of motion can be applied to this situation.

2  A ball of mass 2 kg, moving at 3.0 m s$^{-1}$, strikes a wall and rebounds with the same speed. State and explain whether there is a change in:
   a  the momentum of the ball
   b  the kinetic energy of the ball.

3  a  Define **linear momentum**.
   b  Determine the base units of linear momentum in the SI system.
   c  A car of mass 900 kg starting from rest has a constant acceleration of 3.5 m s$^{-2}$. Calculate its momentum after travelling a distance of 40 m.

**d** Figure **6.16** shows two identical objects about to make a head-on collision. The objects stick together during the collision. Determine the final speed of the objects. State the direction in which they move.

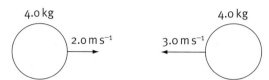

**Figure 6.16** For End-of-chapter Q **3**.

4 **a** Explain what is meant by an:
  **i** elastic collision
  **ii** inelastic collision.
  **b** A snooker ball of mass 0.35 kg hits the side of a snooker table at right angles and bounces off also at right angles. Its speed before collision is 2.8 m s$^{-1}$ and its speed after is 2.5 m s$^{-1}$. Calculate the change in the momentum of the ball.
  **c** Explain whether or not momentum is conserved in the situation described in **b**.

5 A car of mass 1100 kg is travelling at 24 m s$^{-1}$. The driver applies the brakes and the car decelerates uniformly and comes to rest in 20 s.
  **a** Calculate the change in momentum of the car.
  **b** Calculate the braking force on the car.
  **c** Determine the braking distance of the car.

# Exam-style questions

1 A cricket bat strikes a ball of mass 0.16 kg travelling towards it. The ball initially hits the bat at a speed of 25 m s$^{-1}$ and returns along the same path with the same speed. The time of impact is 0.0030 s.
  **a** Determine the change in momentum of the cricket ball. [2]
  **b** Determine the force exerted by the bat on the ball. [2]
  **c** Describe how the law of conservation of energy and momentum apply to this impact and state whether the impact is elastic or inelastic. [4]

2 **a** State the principle of conservation of momentum and state the conditions under which it is valid. [2]
  **b** An arrow of mass 0.25 kg is fired horizontally towards an apple of mass 0.10 kg which is hanging on a string.

The horizontal velocity of the arrow as it enters the apple is $30\,\mathrm{m\,s^{-1}}$. The apple was initially at rest and the arrow sticks in the apple.

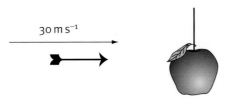

i Calculate the horizontal velocity of the apple and arrow immediately after the impact. [2]
ii Calculate the change in momentum of the arrow during the impact. [2]
iii Calculate the change in total kinetic energy of the arrow and apple during the impact. [2]
iv An identical arrow is fired at the centre of a stationary ball of mass 0.25 kg. The collision is perfectly elastic. Describe what happens and state the relative speed of separation of the arrow and the ball. [2]

3 a State what is meant by:
   i a perfectly elastic collision [1]
   ii a completely inelastic collision. [1]
   b A stationary uranium nucleus disintegrates, emitting an alpha-particle of mass $6.65 \times 10^{-27}$ kg and another nucleus X of mass $3.89 \times 10^{-25}$ kg.

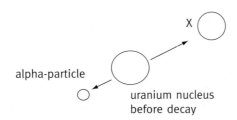

   i Explain why the alpha-particle and nucleus X must be emitted in exactly opposite directions. [2]
   ii Using the symbols $v_\alpha$ and $v_X$ for velocities, write an equation for the conservation of momentum in this disintegration. [1]
   iii Using your answer to ii, calculate the ratio $v_\alpha/v_X$ after the disintegration. [1]

4 a State **two** quantities that are conserved in an elastic collision. [1]
   b A machine gun fires bullets of mass 0.014 kg at a speed of $640\,\mathrm{m\,s^{-1}}$.
   i Calculate the momentum of each bullet as it leaves the gun. [1]
   ii Explain why a soldier holding the machine gun experiences a force when the gun is firing. [2]
   iii The maximum steady horizontal force that a soldier can exert on the gun is 140 N. Calculate the maximum number of bullets that the gun can fire in one second. [2]

5    Two railway trucks are travelling in the same direction and collide. The mass of truck X is $2.0 \times 10^4$ kg and the mass of truck Y is $3.0 \times 10^4$ kg. The diagram shows how the velocity of each truck varies with time.

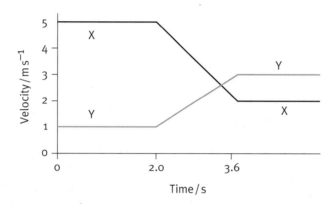

a  Copy and complete the table.                                                                    [6]

|            | Change in momentum/kg m s$^{-1}$ | Initial kinetic energy/J | Final kinetic energy/J |
|------------|----------------------------------|--------------------------|------------------------|
| truck X    |                                  |                          |                        |
| truck Y    |                                  |                          |                        |

b  State and explain whether the collision of the two trucks is an example of an elastic collision.                                                                                  [2]
c  Determine the force that acts on each truck during the collision.                                [2]

## Modelling the microscopic

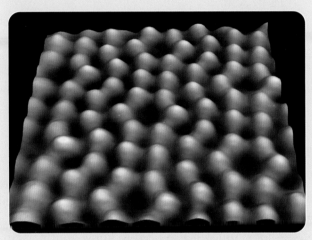

**Figure 7.1** The silicon atoms in a silicon chip imaged with a scanning tunnelling microscope.

Figure 7.1 is a remarkable image. It shows individual atoms on the surface of a piece of the element silicon, used for making the 'chips' which are the basis of modern electronic devices such as computers and mobile phones. Today, the idea that matter is made of particles called atoms is well established. In this chapter, we are going to look at the **particle model** of matter in order to see some of the different aspects of the behaviour of matter that it can explain.

We live in a macroscopic world. '**Macro**' means large, and our large-scale world includes rocks, trees, buildings, people and other animals, the atmosphere, planets and so on. We can simplify this complex world by focusing on particular materials – metals, stone, plastic, water, air. We can make measurements of many macroscopic properties of these materials – density, temperature, strength, viscosity, elasticity, pressure. However, in science, we are always looking for underlying explanations.

You will be familiar with a microscopic description of matter as being made up of particles. '**Micro**' means small, and these tiny particles may be atoms (Figure 7.1) or ions or molecules. By developing a simple picture of the way in which these particles behave, we can arrive at explanations of many of the macroscopic properties of matter listed above.

There is a great deal of satisfaction for a scientist in the way in which a simple microscopic model can explain a very diverse range of macroscopic phenomena. Nowadays we have techniques for showing up the particles from which matter is made, at least at the level of atoms and molecules. But bear in mind that many of these ideas were developed long before there was any possibility of 'seeing' atoms.

## Macroscopic properties of matter

In this chapter, we will look at the behaviour of matter on a macroscopic scale and use a microscopic model to explain our observations. You will already be familiar with two important properties of matter: density and pressure.

### Density

**Density** is a macroscopic property of matter. It is something we can measure and use without having to think about microscopic particles. It tells us about how concentrated the matter is. Density is a constant for a given material.

Density is defined as the mass per unit volume of a substance:

$$\text{density} = \frac{\text{mass}}{\text{volume}}$$

$$\rho = \frac{m}{V}$$

The symbol used here for density, $\rho$, is the Greek letter rho.

The standard unit for density in the SI system is $\text{kg m}^{-3}$, but you may also find values quoted in $\text{g cm}^{-3}$. It is useful to remember that these units are related by:

$$1000 \text{ kg m}^{-3} = 1 \text{ g cm}^{-3}$$

and that the density of water is approximately $1000 \text{ kg m}^{-3}$.

## Test yourself

1  A cube of copper has a mass of 240 g. Each side of the cube is 3.0 cm long. Calculate the density of copper in $\text{g cm}^{-3}$ and in $\text{kg m}^{-3}$.

2  The density of steel is $7850 \text{ kg m}^{-3}$. Calculate the mass of a steel sphere of radius 0.15 m. (First calculate the volume of the sphere using the formula $V = \frac{4}{3}\pi r^3$ and then use the density equation.)

## Pressure

When you stand on the floor, your feet exert **pressure** on the floor. The contact force of your feet on the floor is spread over the area of contact between feet and floor. Similarly, a gas exerts pressure on the walls of its container.

Pressure tells you about how the force is shared out over the area it acts on. For example, a flat shoe exerts a smaller pressure on the ground than a stiletto heel. The larger the area, the smaller the pressure, for a given force.

Pressure is defined as the normal force acting per unit cross-sectional area.

We can write this as a word equation:

$$\text{pressure} = \frac{\text{normal force}}{\text{cross-sectional area}}$$

$$p = \frac{F}{A}$$

The units of pressure are newtons per square metre $(\text{N m}^{-2})$, which are given the special name of pascals (Pa).

$$1 \text{ Pa} = 1 \text{ N m}^{-2}$$

## Test yourself

3  A chair stands on four feet, each of area $10 \text{ cm}^2$. The chair weighs 80 N. Calculate the pressure it exerts on the floor.

4  Estimate the pressure you exert on the floor when you stand on both feet. (You could draw a rough rectangle around both your feet placed together to find the area in contact with the floor. You will also need to know your mass in order to deduce your weight.)

## Pressure in a fluid

The pressure in a fluid (a liquid or gas) increases with depth. Divers know this: the further down they dive, the greater the water pressure acting on them. Pilots know this: the higher they fly, the less is the pressure of the atmosphere. The atmospheric pressure we experience down here on the surface of the Earth is due to the weight of the atmosphere above us, pressing downwards. It is pulled downwards by gravity.

The pressure in a fluid depends on three factors:

• the depth $h$ below the surface
• the density of the fluid $\rho$
• the acceleration due to gravity $g$.

In fact, pressure $p$ is proportional to each of these and we have:

$$p = \rho g h$$

$$\text{pressure} = \text{density} \times \text{acceleration due to gravity} \times \text{depth}$$

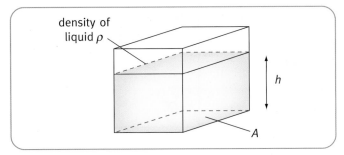

**Figure 7.2** The weight of water in a tank exerts pressure on its base.

We can derive this relationship using Figure 7.2. The force acting on the shaded area $A$ on the bottom of the tank is caused by the weight of water above it, pressing downwards. We can calculate this force and hence the pressure as follows:

$$\text{volume of water} = A \times h$$

$$\text{mass of water} = \text{density} \times \text{volume} = \rho \times A \times h$$

$$\text{weight of water} = \text{mass} \times g = \rho \times A \times h \times g$$

$$\text{pressure} = \frac{\text{force}}{\text{area}} = \rho \times A \times h \times \frac{g}{A}$$

$$= \rho \times g \times h$$

## Worked examples

**1** A cube of side 0.20 m floats in water with 0.15 m below the surface of the water. The density of water is 1000 kg m$^{-3}$. Calculate the pressure of the water acting on the bottom surface of the cube and the force upwards on the cube caused by this pressure. (This force is the upthrust on the cube.)

**Step 1** Use the equation for pressure:

$$P = \rho \times g \times h = 1000 \times 9.81 \times 0.15 = 1470\,\text{Pa}$$

**Step 2** Calculate the area of the base of the cube, and use this area in the equation for force.

$$\text{area of base of cube} = 0.2 \times 0.2 = 0.04\,\text{m}^2$$

$$\text{force} = \text{pressure} \times \text{area} = 1470 \times 0.04 = 58.8\,\text{N}$$

*continued* ⋯⟶

**2** Figure 7.3 shows a manometer used to measure the pressure of a gas supply. Calculate the pressure difference between the gas inside the pipe and atmospheric pressure.

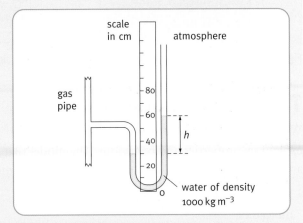

**Figure 7.3** For Worked example 2.

**Step 1** Determine the difference in height $h$ of the water on the two sides of the manometer.

$$h = 60 - 30 = 30\,\text{cm}$$

**Step 2** Because the level of water on the side of the tube next to the gas pipe is lower than on the side open to the atmosphere, the pressure in the gas pipe is above atmospheric pressure.

$$\text{pressure difference}$$
$$= \rho g h = 1000 \times 9.81 \times 0.30 = 2940\,\text{Pa}$$

## Test yourself

**5** Calculate the pressure of water on the bottom of a swimming pool if the depth of water in the pool varies between 0.8 m and 2.4 m. (Density of water = 1000 kg m$^{-3}$.) If atmospheric pressure is $1.01 \times 10^5$ Pa, calculate the maximum total pressure at the bottom of the swimming pool.

**6** Estimate the height of the atmosphere if atmospheric density at the Earth's surface is 1.29 kg m$^{-3}$. (Atmospheric pressure = 101 kPa.)

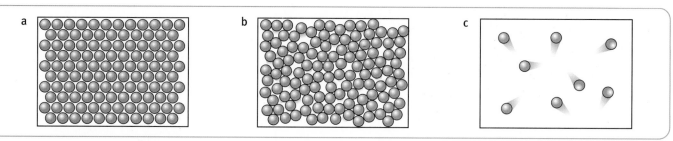

**Figure 7.4** Typical arrangements of atoms in **a** a solid, **b** a liquid and **c** a gas.

# The kinetic model

We can use a particle model to describe matter and explain its properties and behaviour. The model that we are going to use is based on the following assumptions.

- Matter is made up of tiny particles – atoms or molecules.
- These particles tend to move about. (The word 'kinetic' means moving.)

For simplicity, we will refer to these particles as 'atoms'. We picture the atoms as small, hard spheres. Figure 7.4 shows the model for the three states of matter: solid, liquid and gas. We describe the differences between these three states in terms of three criteria.

- The **spacing** of the atoms – how far apart are they, on average?
- The **ordering** of the atoms – are they arranged in an orderly or a random way?
- The **motion** of the atoms – are they moving quickly, slowly or not at all?

You should be familiar with the idea that, as a material changes from solid to liquid to gas, there is a change from close spacing to greater spacing, from order to disorder, and from restricted motion to free, fast motion. The increase in inter-atomic spacing explains why liquids are generally less dense than the solids from which they form, and why gases are much less dense than solids or liquids.

## Order and disorder

Solid materials may be classified according to how the atoms (or molecules) of which they are made are arranged. In a **crystalline material**, the atoms are arranged in a regular pattern. Pure metals are typically crystalline. They are made of many identical, spherical atoms packed closely together in a regular, repeating array. Figure 7.4a could represent the structure of a metal such as copper or iron.

In a non-crystalline material, the atoms are arranged in a random, haphazard way. Such a material is described as **amorphous**. A **polymer** is a solid made up of very long molecules containing many atoms in a chain, sometimes with cross-links between the chains, which means that one chain cannot move on its own. As a result, when a force is applied the rubber will deform, but upon release of the force, the rubber article will go back to its original shape.

If all the chains are parallel to each other, then the polymer may be a crystalline polymer. However, many polymers are amorphous because their long-chain molecules do not pack easily together to form a crystalline structure – see Figure 7.5. Glass is also amorphous; it consists of several types and sizes of atom randomly packed together. 'Crystalline' and 'amorphous' are at the extreme ends of the range of possible solid structures. In practice, many polymers have an in-between structure, with some regions of disorder and others where the molecular chains lie neatly side-by-side.

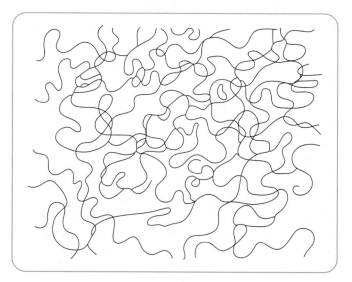

**Figure 7.5** The randomly coiled chains of an amorphous polymer.

## Atoms of a gas

We picture the atoms of a gas as being fast-moving. They bounce off the walls of their container (and off each other) as they travel around at high speed. How do we know that these atoms are moving like this?

It is much harder to visualise the atoms of a gas than those of a solid, because they move about in such a disordered way, and most of a gas is empty space. The movement of gas particles was investigated in the 1820s by a Scottish botanist, Robert Brown. He was using a microscope to look at pollen grains suspended in water, and saw very small particles moving around inside the water. He then saw the same motion in particles of dust in the air. It is easier in the laboratory to look at the movement of tiny particles of smoke in air.

## Observing Brownian motion

The oxygen and nitrogen molecules that make up most of the air are far too small to see; they are much smaller than the wavelength of light. To observe the effect of the air molecules we have to look at something bigger. In this experiment (Figure 7.6), the smoke cell contains air into which a small amount of smoke has been introduced. The cell is lit from the side, and the microscope is used to view the smoke particles.

The smoke particles show up as tiny specks of reflected light, but they are too small to see any detail of their shape. What is noticeable is the way they move. If you can concentrate on a single particle, you will see that it follows a somewhat jerky and erratic path. This is a consequence of the

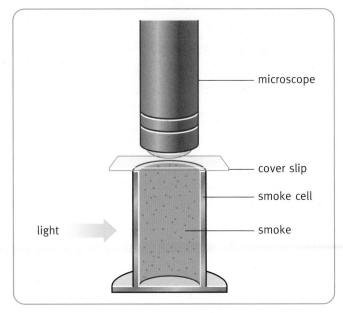

**Figure 7.6** Experimental arrangement for observing Brownian motion.

repeated collisions between the smoke particles and the air molecules. The erratic motion of the smoke particles provides direct evidence that the air molecules must:

• be moving
• also have haphazard motion.

Since the air molecules are much smaller than the smoke grain, we can deduce that they must be moving much faster than the smoke grain if they are to affect it in this way.

(Note that you may observe that all of the smoke particles in your field of view have a tendency to travel in one particular direction. This is a consequence of convection currents in the air. Also, you may have to adjust the focus of the microscope to keep track of an individual particle, as it moves up or down in the cell.)

Figure 7.7 shows the sort of path followed by a particle showing Brownian motion. In fact, this is from a scientific paper by the French physicist Jean Perrin, published in 1911. He was looking at the movement of a single pollen grain suspended in water. He recorded its position every 30 s; the grid spacing is approximately 3 μm. From this he could deduce the average speed of the grain and hence work out details of the movement of water molecules.

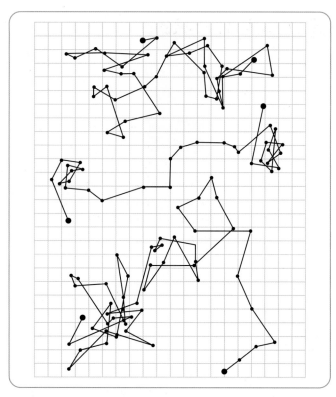

**Figure 7.7** Brownian motion of pollen grains, as drawn by the French scientist Jean Perrin.

## Fast molecules

For air at standard temperature and pressure (STP – 0 °C and 100 kPa), the average speed of the molecules is about 400 m s⁻¹. At any moment, some are moving faster than this and others more slowly. If we could follow the movement of a single air molecule, we would find that, some of the time, its speed was greater than this average; at other times it would be less. The velocity (magnitude and direction) of an individual molecule changes every time it collides with anything else.

This value for molecular speed is reasonable. It is comparable to (but greater than) the speed of sound in air (approximately 330 m s⁻¹ at STP). Very fast-moving particles can easily escape from the Earth's gravitational field. The required escape velocity is about 11 km s⁻¹. Since we still have an atmosphere, on average the air molecules must be moving much slower than this value.

## Explaining pressure

A gas exerts pressure on any surface with which it comes into contact. Pressure is a macroscopic property, defined as the force exerted per unit area of the surface.

The pressure of the atmosphere at sea level is approximately 100 000 Pa. The surface area of a typical person is 2.0 m². Hence the force exerted on a person by the atmosphere is about 200 000 N. This is equivalent to the weight of about 200 000 apples! Fortunately, air inside the body presses outwards with

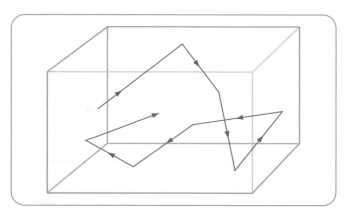

**Figure 7.8** The path of a single molecule in an otherwise empty box.

an equal and opposite force, so we do not collapse under the influence of this large force. We can explain the macroscopic phenomenon of pressure by thinking about the behaviour of the microscopic particles that make up the atmosphere.

Figure 7.8 shows the movement of a single molecule of air in a box. It bounces around inside, colliding with the various surfaces of the box. At each collision, it exerts a small force on the box. The pressure on the box is a result of the forces exerted by the vast number of molecules in the box. Two factors affect the force, and hence the pressure, that the gas exerts on the box:

- the number of molecules that hit each side of the box in one second
- the force with which one molecule collides with the wall.

If a molecule of mass $m$ hits the wall head-on with a speed $v$ it will rebound with a speed $v$ in the opposite direction. The change in momentum of the molecule is $2mv$. Since force is equal to rate of change of momentum, the higher the speed of the molecule the greater the force that each molecule exerts as it collides with the wall. Hence the pressure on the wall will increase if the molecules move faster.

If the piston in a bicycle pump is pushed inwards but the temperature of the gas inside is kept constant, then more molecules will hit the piston in each second but each collision will produce the same force, because the temperature and therefore the average speed of the molecules is the same. The increased rate of collision alone means that the force on the piston increases and thus the pressure rises. If the temperature of the gas in a container rises then the molecules move faster and hit the sides faster and more often; both of these factors cause the pressure to rise.

## Test yourself

12 State and explain in terms of the kinetic model what happens to the pressure inside a tyre when more molecules at the same temperature are pumped into the tyre.

13 Explain, using the kinetic model, why a can containing air may explode if the temperature rises.

# Changes of state

Many solid materials, when heated, undergo a change of state. They first become a liquid, and then a gas. Some materials change directly from the solid state into a gas.

Figure 7.9 represents these changes of state at the molecular level. Consider first what happens when a solid melts. The atoms of the solid gain enough energy to break some of the bonds with their neighbours. They adopt a more disordered arrangement, and usually their average spacing increases. The atoms are more free to move around within the bulk of the material. The solid has melted.

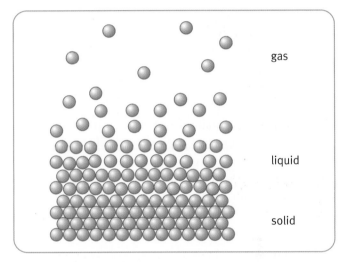

Figure 7.9 Changes of state.

As the liquid is heated further, the atoms become more disordered, further apart and faster moving. Eventually, at the boiling point, the atoms have sufficient energy to break free from their neighbours. They are now much further apart, moving rapidly about in a disordered state. The liquid has boiled to become a gas. Boiling occurs at a fixed temperature for any given atmospheric pressure.

When a liquid boils at atmospheric pressure, its volume increases by a factor of about 1000. In the liquid state, the molecules were closely packed; now they are occupying 1000 times as much space. If the diameter of a single molecule is $d$, it follows that the average separation of molecules in the gas is about

10*d*. It follows that about 99.9% of the volume of a gas is empty space.

When the volume increases by a factor of 1000 then the spacing between the molecules increases by the cube root of 1000 or by a factor of 10. Thus the molecules in a gas are about 10 times as far apart as in the liquid state.

## Evaporation

A liquid does not have to boil to change into a gas. A puddle of rain water dries up without having to be heated to 100 °C. When a liquid changes to a gas without boiling, we call this **evaporation**. The gas formed is called a **vapour** – this is the term used to describe a gas below its boiling point.

Any liquid has some vapour associated with it. If we think about the microscopic picture of this, we can see why (Figure 7.10). Within the liquid, molecules are moving about. Some move faster than others, and can break free from the bulk of the liquid. They form the vapour above the liquid. Some molecules from the vapour may come back into contact with the surface of the liquid, and return to the liquid. However, there is a net outflow of energetic molecules from the liquid, and eventually it will evaporate away completely.

You may have had your skin swabbed with alcohol or ether before an injection. You will have noticed how cold your skin becomes as the volatile liquid evaporates. Similarly, you can become very cold if you get wet and stand around in a windy place. This cooling of a liquid is a very important aspect of evaporation. When a liquid evaporates, it is the most energetic molecules that are most likely to escape. This leaves molecules with a below-average kinetic energy. Since temperature is a measure of the average kinetic energy of the molecules, it follows that the temperature of the evaporating liquid must fall.

## Test yourself

**14** Explain what happens to the atoms in a solid as the solid is heated and turns to liquid.

**15** Explain why only the more energetic molecules escape from a liquid.

**16** Explain why evaporation increases if the temperature of a liquid is higher.

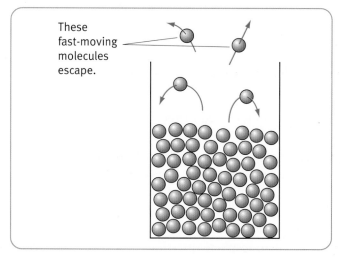

These fast-moving molecules escape.

**Figure 7.10** Fast-moving molecules leave the surface of a liquid – this is evaporation.

# Summary

☐ Density is defined as the mass per unit volume:

$$density = \frac{mass}{volume}$$

☐ Pressure is defined as the normal force acting per unit cross-sectional area:

$$pressure = \frac{force}{area}$$

☐ Pressure in a fluid increases with depth:

$$p = \rho g h$$

☐ Solid materials may be classified as crystalline or amorphous.
☐ Brownian motion provides evidence for the movement of molecules.
☐ The kinetic model allows us to explain the behaviour of matter (e.g. changes of state) and macroscopic properties of matter (e.g. density, pressure) in terms of the behaviour of molecules.

# End-of-chapter questions

1  What evidence is there that:
   a  the distance between the molecules in ice is roughly the same as the distance between the molecules in liquid water?
   b  the forces between the molecules of a solid are strong?

2  When air is pumped into a bicycle tyre, the pressure inside the tyre increases. Explain, in terms of the molecules of air:
   a  why there is a pressure inside the tyre
   b  why the pressure in the tyre increases as more air is pumped in.

3  A syringe is sealed at one end and contains air at atmospheric pressure. It is heated and the piston inside the syringe moves outwards so that the pressure of the trapped air inside is kept constant.

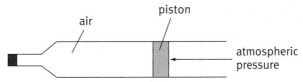

**Figure 7.11** For End-of-chapter Q 3.

   State what happens to:
   a  the average speed of the molecules
   b  the force that each molecule exerts on the piston as it hits the piston once

    c  the number of collisions of the molecules each second with the piston

    d  the force exerted on the piston by all the molecules that hit it.

4  Figure **7.12** shows smoke particles suspended in air. The smoke particles are observed to be in random motion.

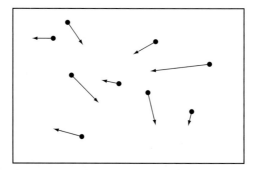

**Figure 7.12** For End-of-chapter Q 4.

    a  Explain why the smoke particles move.

    b  State **two** conclusions about air molecules and their motion that may be made from this observation.

5  a  Explain how a manometer may be adapted to measure large pressures.

    b  Explain why the pressure measured by a manometer does not depend on the cross-sectional area of the tube used in the manometer.

# Exam-style questions

1  The density of water vapour at atmospheric pressure is $0.60 \, \text{kg m}^{-3}$. The mass of one molecule of water is $3.0 \times 10^{-26} \, \text{kg}$.

    a  Calculate the volume available for each molecule of water in water vapour at atmospheric pressure.  [1]

    b  By considering the volume available for each molecule of water in the vapour to be a cube, calculate the side of the cube.  [1]

    c  The density of liquid water is $1000 \, \text{kg m}^{-3}$. Calculate the ratio

$$\frac{\text{mean distance between molecules in liquid water}}{\text{mean distance between molecules in water vapour}}$$

  [2]

2  a  Liquid of density $\rho$ fills a cylinder of base area $A$ and height $h$.

      i  Using the symbols provided, state the mass of liquid in the container.  [1]

      ii  Using your answer to **i** derive a formula for the pressure exerted on the base of the cylinder.  [2]

    b  A boy stands on a platform of area $0.050 \, \text{m}^2$ and a manometer measures the pressure created in a flexible plastic container by the weight $W$ of the boy.

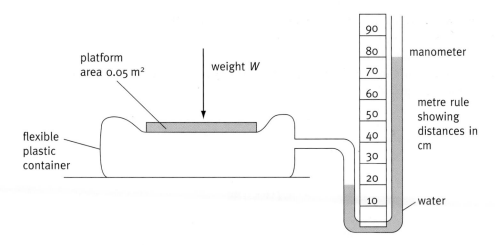

The density of water is $1000 \, \text{kg m}^{-3}$. Determine:

  **i**  the pressure difference between the inside of the plastic container and the atmosphere outside [2]

  **ii**  the weight $W$ of the boy. [2]

**3**  **a**  Draw a diagram of apparatus that may be used to observe the Brownian motion of small particles. [2]

  **b**  Explain what is meant by Brownian motion and suggest why Brownian motion provides evidence for the kinetic theory of gases. [4]

  **c**  Explain why Brownian motion is not observed in the motion of large particles such as a 10 g mass suspended on a string. [2]

**4**  **a**  **i**  Define **density**. [1]

     **ii**  State the base units in the SI system in which density is measured. [1]

  **b**  The diagram shows water in a container filled to a depth of 0.50 m. The density of water is $1000 \, \text{kg m}^{-3}$.

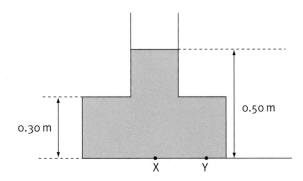

  **i**  Calculate the pressure at X on the base of the container. [2]

  **ii**  Explain why the pressure at X must be equal to the pressure at Y. [1]

  **iii**  Explain why the force downwards on the base of the container is larger than the weight of the liquid in the container. [2]

5  **a** Describe why the pressure of the atmosphere is less at the top of a mountain than at the bottom. **[1]**

   **b** The diagram shows a U-tube, open at both ends, which contains two different liquids X and Y that do not mix. The numbers on the metre rule are distances in centimetres. The density of liquid Y is $800 \, kg \, m^{-3}$.

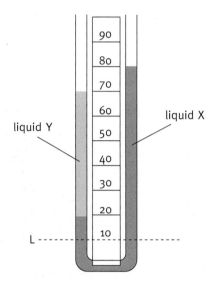

   **i** Explain how the diagram shows that liquid Y has a greater density than liquid X. **[2]**
   **ii** Calculate the density of liquid X. **[3]**
   **iii** Explain why the pressure in the U-tube is the same on both sides of the manometer at level L. **[1]**
   **iv** Calculate the pressure caused by liquid in the U-tube at level L. **[2]**

# Objectives

After studying this chapter, you should be able to:

☐ understand how tensile and compressive forces cause deformation

☐ be able to describe the behaviour of springs and understand Hooke's law

☐ define and use stress, strain and the Young modulus

☐ describe an experiment to measure the Young modulus

☐ be able to distinguish between elastic and plastic deformation

☐ demonstrate knowledge of force–extension graphs for typical ductile, brittle and polymeric materials and be able to deduce the strain energy

## Springy stuff

In everyday life, we make great use of elastic materials. The term elastic means **springy**; that is, the material deforms when a force is applied and returns to its original shape when the force is removed. Rubber is an elastic material. This is obviously important for a bungee jumper (Figure **8.1**). The bungee rope must have the correct degree of elasticity. The jumper must be brought gently to a halt. If the rope is too stiff, the jumper will be jerked violently so that the deceleration is greater than their body can withstand. On the other hand, if the rope is too stretchy, they may bounce up and down endlessly, or even strike the ground.

**Figure 8.1** The stiffness and elasticity of rubber are crucial factors in bungee jumping.

## Compressive and tensile forces

A pair of forces is needed to change the shape of a spring. If the spring is being squashed and shortened, we say that the forces are **compressive**. More usually, we are concerned with stretching a spring, in which case the forces are described as **tensile** (Figure **8.2**).

When a wire is bent some parts become longer and are in tension whilst other parts become shorter and are in compression. Figure **8.3** shows that the line AA becomes longer when the wire is bent and the line BB becomes shorter. The thicker the wire, the greater the compression and tension forces along its edges.

It is simple to investigate how the length of a helical spring is affected by the applied force or load.

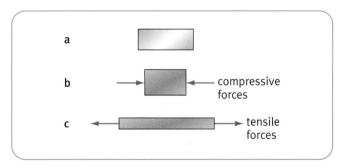

**Figure 8.2** The effects of compressive and tensile forces.

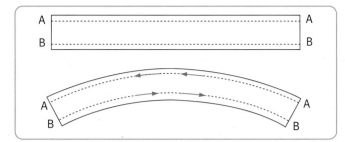

**Figure 8.3** Bending a straight wire or beam results in tensile forces along the upper surface (the outside of the bend) and compressive forces on the inside of the bend.

The spring hangs freely with the top end clamped firmly (Figure **8.4**). A load is added and gradually increased. For each value of the load, the extension of the spring is measured. Note that it is important to determine the increase in length of the spring, which we call the **extension**. We can plot a graph of force against extension to find the stiffness of the spring, as shown in Figure **8.5**.

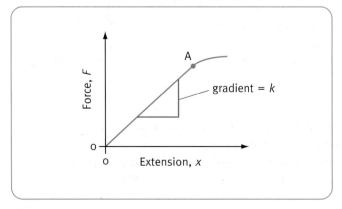

**Figure 8.4** Stretching a spring.

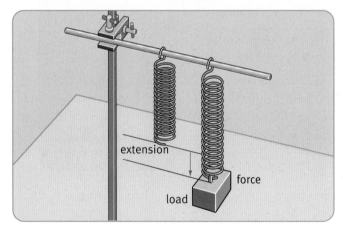

**Figure 8.5** Force–extension graph for a spring.

## Hooke's law

The conventional way of plotting the results would be to have the force along the horizontal axis and the extension along the vertical axis. This is because we are changing the force (the independent variable) and this results in a change in the extension (the dependent variable). The graph shown in Figure **8.5** has extension on the horizontal axis and force on the vertical axis. This is a departure from the convention because the **gradient** of the straight section of this graph turns out to be an important quantity known as the **force constant** of the spring. For a typical spring, the first section of this graph OA is a straight line passing through the origin. The extension $x$ is directly proportional to the applied force (load) $F$. The behaviour of the spring in the linear region OA of the graph can be expressed by the following equation:

$$x \propto F$$

or $F = kx$

where $k$ is the force constant of the spring (sometimes called either the stiffness or the spring constant of the spring). The force constant is the force per unit extension. The force constant $k$ of the spring is given by the equation:

$$k = \frac{F}{x}$$

The SI unit for the force constant is newton per metre or $N\,m^{-1}$. We can find the force constant $k$ from the gradient of section OA of the graph:

$$k = \text{gradient}$$

A stiffer spring will have a large value for the force constant $k$. Beyond point A, the graph is no longer a straight line. This is because the spring has become permanently deformed. It has been stretched beyond its **elastic limit**. The meaning of the term elastic limit is discussed further on page **124**.

If a spring or anything else responds to a pair of tensile forces in the way shown in section OA of Figure **8.5**, we say that it obeys **Hooke's law**:

A material obeys Hooke's law if the extension produced in it is proportional to the applied force (load). This is true as long as the elastic limit of the material is not exceeded.

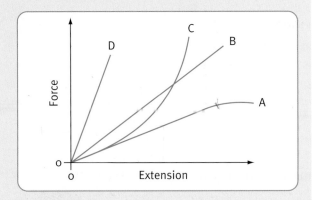
## Investigating springs

Springs can be combined in different ways (Figure 8.7): end-to-end (in series) and side-by-side (in parallel). Using identical springs, you can measure the force constant of a single spring, and of springs in series and in parallel. Before you do this, predict the outcome of such an experiment. If the force constant of a single spring is $k$, what will be the equivalent force constant of:

• two springs in series?
• two springs in parallel?

This approach can be applied to combinations of three or more springs.

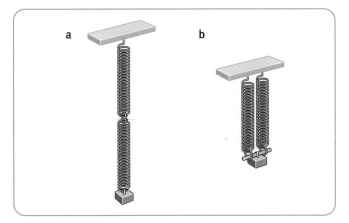

**Figure 8.7** Two ways to combine a pair of springs: **a** in series; **b** in parallel.

# Stretching materials

When we determine the force constant of a spring, we are only finding out about the stiffness of that particular spring. However, we can talk about the stiffnesses of different **materials**. For example, steel is stiffer than copper, but copper is stiffer than lead.

## Stress and strain

Figure **8.8** shows a simple way of assessing the stiffness of a wire in the laboratory. As the long wire is stretched, the position of the sticky tape pointer can be read from the scale on the bench.

Why do we use a long wire? Obviously, this is because a short wire would not stretch as much as a long one. We need to take account of this in our calculations, and we do this by calculating the strain

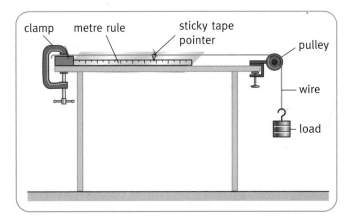

**Figure 8.8** Stretching a wire in the laboratory. WEAR EYE PROTECTION and be careful not to overload the wire.

produced by the load. The **strain** is defined as the fractional increase in the original length of the wire. That is:

$$\text{strain} = \frac{\text{extension}}{\text{original length}}$$

This may be written as:

$$\text{strain} = \frac{x}{L}$$

where $x$ is the extension of the wire and $L$ is its original length.

Note that both extension and original length must be in the same units and so strain is a ratio, without units. Sometimes strain is given as a percentage. For example, a strain of 0.012 is equivalent to 1.2%.

Why do we use a thin wire? This is because a thick wire would not stretch as much for the same force. Again, we need to take account of this in our calculations, and we do this by calculating the stress produced by the load. The **stress** is defined as the force applied per unit cross-sectional area of the wire. That is:

$$\text{stress} = \frac{\text{force}}{\text{cross-sectional area}}$$

This may be written as:

$$\text{stress} = \frac{F}{A}$$

where $F$ is the applied force on a wire of cross-sectional area $A$.

Force is measured in newtons and area is measured in square metres. Stress is similar to pressure, and has the same units: $N\,m^{-2}$ or pascals, Pa. If you imagine compressing a bar of metal rather than stretching a wire, you will see why stress or pressure is the important quantity.

## The Young modulus

We can now find the **stiffness** of the **material** we are stretching. Rather than calculating the ratio of force to extension as we would for a spring or a wire, we calculate the ratio of stress to strain. This ratio is a constant for a particular material and does not depend

on its shape or size. The ratio of stress to strain is called the **Young modulus** of the material. That is:

$$\text{Young modulus} = \frac{\text{stress}}{\text{strain}}$$

or

$$E = \frac{\sigma}{\varepsilon}$$

where $E$ is the Young modulus of the material, $\sigma$ (Greek letter sigma) is the stress and $\varepsilon$ (epsilon) is the strain.

The unit of the Young modulus is the same as that for stress, $N\,m^{-2}$ or Pa. In practice, values may be quoted in MPa or GPa. These units are related as:

$$1\,\text{MPa} = 10^6\,\text{Pa}$$

$$1\,\text{GPa} = 10^9\,\text{Pa}$$

Usually, we plot a graph with stress on the vertical axis and strain on the horizontal axis (Figure 8.9). It is drawn like this so that the gradient is the Young modulus of the material. It is important to consider only the first, linear section of the graph. In the linear section stress is proportional to strain and the wire under test obeys Hooke's law.

Table **8.1** gives some values of the Young modulus for different materials.

| Material | Young modulus / GPa |
|---|---|
| aluminium | 70 |
| brass | 90–110 |
| brick | 7–20 |
| concrete | 40 |
| copper | 130 |
| glass | 70–80 |
| iron (wrought) | 200 |
| lead | 18 |
| Perspex | 3 |
| polystyrene | 2.7–4.2 |
| rubber | 0.01 |
| steel | 210 |
| tin | 50 |
| wood | 10 approx. |

Table **8.1** The Young modulus of various materials. Many of these values depend on the precise composition of the material concerned. (Remember, $1\,\text{GPa} = 10^9\,\text{Pa}$.)

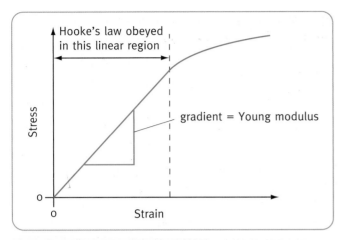

**Figure 8.9** Stress–strain graph, and how to deduce the Young modulus.

## Test yourself

2 List the metals in Table **8.1** from stiffest to least stiff.

3 Which of the non-metals in Table **8.1** is the stiffest?

4 Figure **8.10** shows stress–strain graphs for two materials, A and B. Use the graphs to determine the Young modulus of each material.

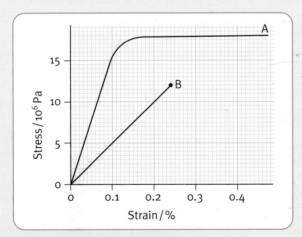

**Figure 8.10** Stress–strain graph for two different materials. For Test yourself Q **4**.

5 A piece of steel wire, 200.0 cm long and having cross-sectional area 0.50 mm², is stretched by a force of 50 N. Its new length is found to be

*continued* ⋯➔

200.1 cm. Calculate the stress and strain, and the Young modulus of steel.

6 Calculate the extension of a copper wire of length 1.00 m and diameter 1.00 mm when a tensile force of 10 N is applied to the end of the wire. (Young modulus $E$ of copper = 130 GPa.)

## Determining the Young modulus

Metals are not very elastic. In practice, they can only be stretched by about 0.1% of their original length. Beyond this, they become permanently deformed. As a result, some careful thought must be given to getting results that are good enough to give an accurate value of the Young modulus.

First, the wire used must be long. The increase in length is proportional to the original length, and so a longer wire gives larger and more measurable extensions. Typically, extensions up to 1 mm must be measured for a wire of length 1 m. To get suitable measurements of extension there are two possibilities: use a very long wire, or use a method that allows measurement of extensions that are a fraction of a millimetre.

The apparatus shown in Figure **8.8** can be used with a travelling microscope placed above the wire and focused on the sticky tape pointer. When the pointer moves, the microscope is adjusted to keep the pointer at the middle of the cross-wires on the microscope. The distance that the pointer has moved can then be measured accurately from the scale on the microscope.

In addition, the cross-sectional area of the wire must be known accurately. The diameter of the wire is measured using a micrometer screw gauge. This is reliable to within ±0.01 mm. Once the wire has been loaded in increasing steps, the load must be gradually decreased to ensure that there has been no permanent deformation of the wire.

Other materials such as glass and many plastics are also quite stiff, and so it is difficult to measure their Young modulus. Rubber is not as stiff, and strains of several hundred per cent can be achieved. However, the stress–strain graph for rubber is not a straight line. This means the value of the Young modulus found is not very precise, because it only has a very small linear region on a stress–strain graph.

## Test yourself

7  In an experiment to measure the Young modulus of glass, a student draws out a glass rod to form a fibre 0.800 m in length. Using a travelling microscope, she estimates its diameter to be 0.40 mm. Unfortunately it proves impossible to obtain a series of readings for load and extension. The fibre snaps when a load of 1.00 N is hung on the end. The student judges that the fibre extended by no more than 1 mm before it snapped. Use these values to obtain an estimate for the Young modulus of the glass used. Explain how the actual or accepted value for the Young modulus might differ from this estimate.

# Describing deformation

The Young modulus of a material describes its stiffness. This only relates to the initial, straight-line section of the stress–strain graph. In this region, the material is behaving in an elastic way and the straight line means that the material obeys Hooke's law. However, if we continue to increase the force beyond the elastic limit, the graph may cease to be a straight line. Figures **8.11**, **8.12** and **8.13** show stress–strain graphs for some typical materials. We will discuss what these illustrate in the paragraphs below.

## Glass, cast iron

Glass and cast iron (Figure **8.11**) behave in a similar way. If you increase the stress on them, they stretch slightly. However, there comes a point where the material breaks. Both glass and cast iron are **brittle**; if you apply a large stress, they shatter. They also show elastic behaviour up to the **breaking point**. If you apply a stress and then remove it, they return to their original length.

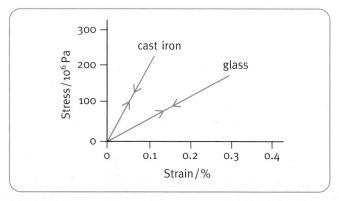

**Figure 8.11** Stress–strain graphs for two brittle materials.

## Copper, gold

Copper and gold (Figure **8.12**) show a different form of behaviour. If you have stretched a copper wire to determine its Young modulus, you will have noticed that, beyond a certain point (the elastic limit), the wire stretches more and more and will not return to its original length when the load is removed. It has become permanently deformed. We describe this as **plastic deformation**. Copper and gold are both metals that can be shaped by stretching, rolling, hammering and squashing. This makes them very useful for making wires, jewellery, and so on. They are described as **ductile** metals. Pure iron is also a ductile metal. Cast iron has carbon in it – it's really a form of steel – and this changes its properties so that it is brittle.

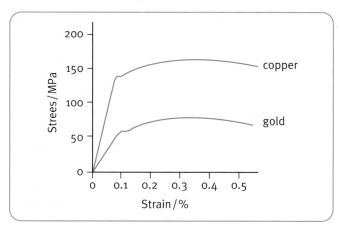

**Figure 8.12** Stress–strain graphs for two ductile materials.

## Polythene, Perspex

Different polymers behave differently, depending on their molecular structure and their temperature. This graph (Figure **8.13**) shows two typical forms of stress–strain graph for polymers. Polythene is easy to deform, as you will know if you have ever tried to stretch a polythene bag. The material stretches (plastic deformation), and then eventually becomes much stiffer and snaps. This is rather like the behaviour of a ductile metal. Perspex behaves in a brittle way. It stretches elastically up to a point, and then it breaks.

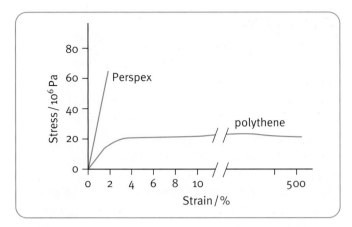

Figure 8.13 Stress–strain graphs for two polymeric materials.

## Rubber

Figure 8.14 shows a force–extension graph for rubber. After a small initial extension, a rubber cord becomes easy to stretch but when it is many times its initial length it becomes hard to stretch. This is because of the long chain of molecules in the polymer structure as described on page 110. The maximum strain can easily exceed 600% before the rubber breaks. Another difference between a metal wire and a sample of rubber is that when the stretching force is removed the rubber sample does not return to its original length by the same path. This is known as **elastic hysteresis**. You will see later that the area between the two paths on the graph is the work done on the rubber that is not returned when the stretching force is removed. This work becomes internal energy in the rubber and causes a rise in temperature.

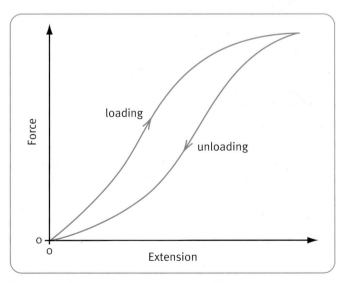

Figure 8.14 Force–extension graph for rubber.

We can summarise the way materials behave as follows.

- All materials show **elastic** behaviour up to the elastic limit; they return to their original length when the force is removed.
- **Brittle** materials break at the elastic limit.
- **Ductile** materials become permanently deformed if they are stretched beyond the elastic limit; they show **plastic** behaviour.

### Test yourself

8   Use the words **elastic**, **plastic**, **brittle** and **ductile** to deduce what the following observations tell you about the materials described.
   a If you tap a cast iron bath gently with a hammer, the hammer bounces off. If you hit it hard, the bath shatters.
   b Aluminium drinks cans are made by forcing a sheet of aluminium into a mould at high pressure.

## Strength of a material

The **strength** of a material tells us about how much stress is needed to break the material. On a stress–strain graph (Figure 8.15), we look for the value of the stress at which the material breaks. This value of breaking stress is called the **ultimate tensile stress (UTS)**. The term **ultimate** is used because this is the top of the graph, and **tensile** because the material is being stretched. For brittle materials the UTS is the stress at the breaking point.

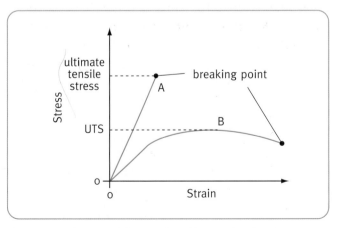

Figure 8.15 The material represented by graph A has a greater value for the ultimate tensile stress, hence it is stronger than the material represented by graph B.

## Test yourself

9 For each of the materials whose stress–strain graphs are shown in Figure **8.16**, deduce the values of the Young modulus and the ultimate tensile stress (breaking stress).

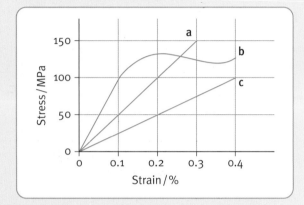

**Figure 8.16** Stress–strain graphs for three materials.

# Elastic potential energy

Whenever you stretch a material, you are doing work. This is because you have to apply a **force** and the material **extends** in the direction of the force. You will know this if you have ever used an exercise machine with springs intended to develop your muscles (Figure **8.17**). Similarly, when you push down on the end of a springboard before diving, you are doing work. You transfer energy to the springboard, and you recover the energy when it pushes you up into the air.

We call the energy in a deformed solid the **elastic potential energy** or **strain energy**. If the material has been strained elastically (the elastic limit has not been exceeded), the energy can be recovered. If the material has been plastically deformed, some of the work done has gone into moving atoms past one another, and the energy cannot be recovered. The material warms up slightly. We can determine how much elastic potential energy is involved from a force–extension graph, see Figure **8.18**. We need to use the equation that defines the amount of work done by a force. That is:

work done = force × distance moved in the direction of the force

**Figure 8.17** Using an exercise machine is hard work.

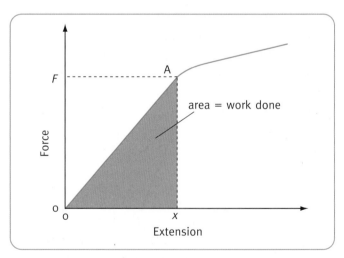

**Figure 8.18** Elastic potential energy is equal to the area under the force–extension graph.

First, consider the linear region of the graph where Hooke's law is obeyed, OA. The graph in this region is a straight line through the origin. The extension $x$ is directly proportional to the applied force $F$. There are two ways to find the work done.

## Method 1

We can think about the average force needed to produce an extension $x$. The average force is half the final force $F$, and so we can write:

elastic potential energy = work done

$$\text{elastic potential energy} = \frac{\text{final force}}{2} \times \text{extension}$$

$$\text{elastic potential energy} = \tfrac{1}{2}Fx$$

or

$$E = \tfrac{1}{2}Fx$$

## Method 2

The other way to find the elastic potential energy is to recognise that we can get the same answer by finding the area under the graph. The area shaded in Figure **8.17** is a triangle whose area is given by:

$$\text{area} = \tfrac{1}{2} \times \text{base} \times \text{height}$$

This again gives:

$$\text{elastic potential energy} = \tfrac{1}{2}Fx$$

or

$$E = \tfrac{1}{2}Fx$$

The **work done** in **stretching** or **compressing** a material is always equal to the area under the graph of force against extension. This is true whatever the shape of the graph, provided we draw the graph with extension on the horizontal axis. If the graph is not a straight line, we cannot use the $\tfrac{1}{2}Fx$ relationship, so we have to resort to counting squares or some other technique to find the answer. However, the elastic potential energy relates to the elastic part of the graph (i.e. up to the elastic limit), so we can only consider the linear section of the force–extension graph.

There is an alternative equation for elastic potential energy. We know that, according to Hooke's law (page **120**), applied force $F$ and extension $x$ are related by $F = kx$, where $k$ is the force constant. Substituting for $F$ gives:

$$\text{elastic potential energy} = \tfrac{1}{2}Fx = \tfrac{1}{2} \times kx \times x$$

$$\text{elastic potential energy} = \tfrac{1}{2}kx^2$$

## Worked example

1. Figure **8.19** shows a simplified version of a force–extension graph for a piece of metal. Find the elastic potential energy when the metal is stretched to its elastic limit and the total work that must be done to break the metal.

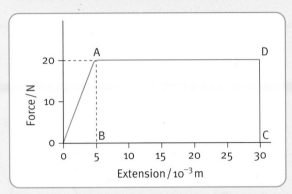

**Figure 8.19** For Worked example **1**.

**Step 1** The elastic potential energy when the metal is stretched to its elastic limit is given by the area under the graph up to the elastic limit. The graph is a straight line up to $x = 5.0\,\text{mm}$, $F = 20\,\text{N}$, so the elastic potential energy is the area of triangle OAB:

$$\begin{aligned}\text{elastic potential energy} &= \tfrac{1}{2}Fx \\ &= \tfrac{1}{2} \times 20 \times 5.0 \times 10^{-3} \\ &= 0.050\,\text{J}\end{aligned}$$

**Step 2** To find the work done to break the metal, we need to add on the area of the rectangle ABCD:

$$\begin{aligned}\text{work done} &= \text{total area under the graph} \\ &= 0.05 + (20 \times 25 \times 10^{-3}) \\ &= 0.05 + 0.50 = 0.55\,\text{J}\end{aligned}$$

## Test yourself

10 A force of 12 N extends a length of rubber band by 18 cm. Estimate the energy stored in this rubber band. Explain why your answer can only be an estimate.

*continued* ⋯➔

**11** A spring has a force constant of $4800\,\text{N}\,\text{m}^{-1}$. Calculate the elastic potential energy when it is compressed by 2.0 mm.

**12** Figure **8.20** shows force–extension graphs for two pieces of polymer. For each of the following questions, explain how you deduce your answer from the graphs.
  **a** State which polymer has the greater stiffness.
  **b** State which polymer requires the greater force to break it.
  **c** State which polymer requires the greater amount of work to be done in order to break it.

*continued* ⋯⟩

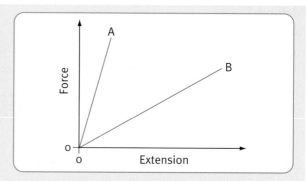

**Figure 8.20** For Test yourself Q 12.

# Summary

- ☐ Hooke's law states that the extension of a material is directly proportional to the applied force as long as its elastic limit is not exceeded.
- ☐ For a spring or a wire, $F = kx$, where $k$ is the force constant. The force constant has unit $\text{N}\,\text{m}^{-1}$.
- ☐ Stress is defined as:

$$\text{stress} = \frac{\text{force}}{\text{cross-sectional area}}$$

  or $\sigma = \dfrac{F}{A}$

- ☐ Strain is defined as:

$$\text{strain} = \frac{\text{extension}}{\text{original length}}$$

  or $\varepsilon = \dfrac{x}{L}$

- ☐ To describe the behaviour of a material under tensile and compressive forces, we have to draw a graph of stress against strain. The gradient of the initial linear section of the graph is equal to the Young modulus. The Young modulus is an indication of the stiffness of the material.
- ☐ The Young modulus $E$ is given by:

$$E = \frac{\text{stress}}{\text{strain}} = \frac{\sigma}{\varepsilon}$$

  The unit of the Young modulus is pascal (Pa) or $\text{N}\,\text{m}^{-2}$.

- ☐ Beyond the elastic limit, brittle materials break. Ductile materials show plastic behaviour and become permanently deformed.
- ☐ The area under a force–extension graph is equal to the work done by the force.
- ☐ For a spring or a wire obeying Hooke's law, the elastic potential energy $E$ is given by:

$$E = \tfrac{1}{2}\,Fx = \tfrac{1}{2}kx^2$$

# End-of-chapter questions

1 Sketch a force–extension graph for a spring which has a spring constant of $20\,\mathrm{N\,m^{-1}}$ and which obeys Hooke's law for forces up to 5 N. Your graph should cover forces between 0 and 6 N and show values on both axes.

2 Two springs, each with a spring constant $20\,\mathrm{N\,m^{-1}}$, are connected in series. Draw a diagram of the two springs connected in series and determine the total extension if a mass, with weight 2.0 N, is hung on the combined springs.

3 A sample of fishing line is 1.0 m long and is of circular cross-section of radius 0.25 mm. When a weight is hung on the line, the extension is 50 mm and the stress is $2.0 \times 10^8\,\mathrm{Pa}$. Calculate:
   a the cross-sectional area of the line
   b the weight added
   c the strain in the line
   d the Young modulus.

4 Give an example of a brittle material and of a ductile material not mentioned in the chapter and explain whether being brittle or ductile is an advantage or disadvantage for a particular use of this material.

5 Figure **8.21** shows the force–extension graph for a metal wire of length 2.0 m and cross-sectional area $1.5 \times 10^{-7}\,\mathrm{m^2}$

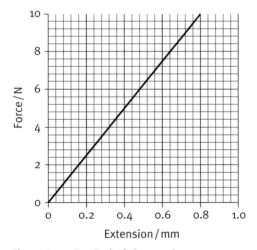

**Figure 8.21** For End-of-chapter Q 5.

   a Calculate the Young modulus.
   b Determine the energy stored in the wire when the extension is 0.8 mm.
   c Calculate the work done in stretching the wire between 0.4 mm and 0.8 mm.

# Exam-style questions

**1** **a** The diagram shows the stress–strain curves for a sample of three different materials P, Q and R.

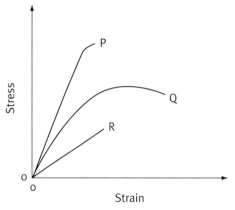

    **i** State and explain which material is likely to be made of glass and which of copper. [4]
    **ii** State and explain which material is strongest. [2]
    **iii** State and explain which material has the greatest Young modulus. [2]
   **b** Describe an experiment to determine the Young modulus for a material in the form of a wire. Include a labelled diagram and explain how you make the necessary measurements. Show how you would use your measurements to calculate the Young modulus. [7]

**2** **a** State the meaning of **tensile stress** and **tensile strain**. [2]
   **b** A vertical steel wire of length 1.6 m and cross-sectional area $1.3 \times 10^{-6}\,\text{m}^2$ carries a weight of 60 N. The Young modulus for steel is $2.1 \times 10^{11}\,\text{Pa}$. Calculate:
    **i** the stress in the wire [2]
    **ii** the strain in the wire [2]
    **iii** the extension produced in the wire by the weight. [2]

**3** To allow for expansion in the summer when temperatures rise, a steel railway line laid in cold weather is pre-stressed by applying a force of $2.6 \times 10^5\,\text{N}$ to the rail of cross-sectional area $5.0 \times 10^{-3}\,\text{m}^2$. If the railway line is not pre-stressed then a strain of $1.4 \times 10^{-5}$ is caused by each degree Celsius rise in temperature. The Young modulus of the steel is $2.1 \times 10^{11}\,\text{Pa}$.
   **a** State and explain whether the force applied to the rail when it is laid should be tensile or compressive. [2]
   **b** Calculate:
    **i** the strain produced when the rail is laid [3]
    **ii** the temperature rise when the rail becomes unstressed. [2]

**4** The diagram on the next page shows the stress–strain graph for a metal wire. The wire has a diameter of 0.84 mm and a natural length of 3.5 m. Use the graph to determine:
   **a** the Young modulus of the wire [3]
   **b** the extension of the wire when the stress is 0.6 GPa [2]

**c** the breaking force, assuming that the cross-sectional area of the wire
remains constant [3]

**d** the energy stored when the wire has a stress of 0.6 GPa. [3]

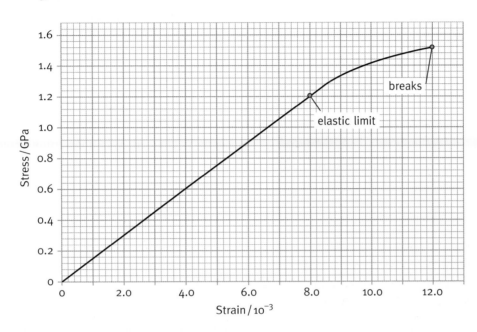

**5** The diagram shows the force–extension graph for a spring.

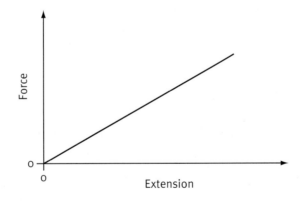

**a** State what is represented by:
   **i** the gradient of the graph [1]
   **ii** the area under the graph. [1]
**b** The spring has force constant $k = 80\,\text{N}\,\text{m}^{-1}$. The spring is compressed by 0.060 m
   and placed between two trolleys that run on a friction-free, horizontal track. Each trolley
   has a mass of 0.40 kg. When the spring is released the trolleys fly apart with equal speeds
   but in opposite directions.
   **i** How much energy is stored in the spring when it is compressed by 0.060 m? [2]
   **ii** Explain why the two trolleys must fly apart with equal speeds. [2]
   **iii** Calculate the speed of each trolley. [2]

## Objectives

After studying this chapter, you should be able to:

- [ ] show an understanding of the concept of an electric field
- [ ] define electric field strength
- [ ] draw field lines to represent an electric field

- [ ] calculate the strength of a uniform electric field
- [ ] calculate the force on a charge in a uniform field
- [ ] describe how charged particles move in a uniform electric field

## Electricity in nature

**Figure 9.1** Lightning flashes, dramatic evidence of natural electric fields.

The lower surface of a thundercloud is usually negatively charged. When lightning strikes, an intense electric current is sent down to the ground below. You may have noticed a 'strobe' effect – this is because each lightning strike usually consists of four or five flashes at intervals of 50 milliseconds or so. You will already know a bit about electric (or electrostatic) fields, from your experience of static electricity in everyday life, and from your studies in science. In this chapter, you will learn how we can make these ideas more formal. We will look at how electric forces are caused, and how we can represent their effects in terms of electric fields. Then we will find mathematical ways of calculating electric forces and field strengths.

## Attraction and repulsion

Static electricity can be useful – it is important in the process of photocopying, in dust precipitation to clean up industrial emissions, and in crop-spraying, among many other applications. It can also be a nuisance. Who hasn't experienced a shock, perhaps when getting out of a car or when touching a door handle? Static electric charge has built up and gives us a shock when it discharges.

We explain these effects in terms of **electric charge**. Simple observations in the laboratory give us the following picture:

- Objects are usually electrically neutral (uncharged), but they may become electrically charged, for example when one material is rubbed against another.
- There are two types of charge, which we call positive and negative.

- Opposite types of charge attract one another; like charges repel (Figure **9.2**).
- A charged object may also be able to attract an uncharged one; this is as a result of electrostatic induction.

**Figure 9.2** Attraction and repulsion between electric charges.

These observations are macroscopic. They are descriptions of phenomena that we can observe in the laboratory, without having to consider what is happening on the microscopic scale, at the level of particles such as atoms and electrons. However, we can give a more subtle explanation if we consider the microscopic picture of static electricity.

Using a simple model, we can consider matter to be made up of three types of particles: electrons (which have negative charge), protons (positive) and neutrons (neutral). An uncharged object has equal numbers of protons and electrons, whose charges therefore cancel out.

When one material is rubbed against another, there is friction between them, and electrons may be rubbed off one material onto the other (Figure **9.3**). The material that has gained electrons is now negatively charged, and the other material is positively charged.

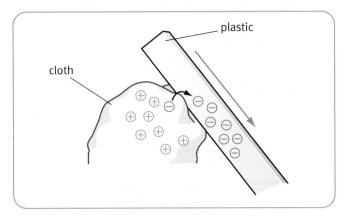

**Figure 9.3** Friction can transfer electrons from one material to another.

## The idea of positive and negative

If you lived in certain parts of Canada, the science curriculum would suggest that your teacher should allow you to play with plastic and glass rods so that you could discover for yourself the existence of positive and negative electric charges. This is a tall order, since it took some of the best scientific minds several decades to establish this idea!

By about 1730, physicists knew that, when rubbed, glass rods and pieces of amber appeared to have gained opposite types of electricity. These were known as **vitreous electricity** (vitreous means glassy) and **resinous electricity** (amber is a type of resin). Nowadays we would say that vitreous electricity is positive charge while resinous is negative. Two competing theories were developed to explain this:

- The **two fluids theory** proposed that there were two different electrical fluids at work, vitreous and resinous. An uncharged object had equal amounts of both, so their effects cancelled out. Adding vitreous fluid to an uncharged object made it positive, while adding resinous fluid made it negative.
- The **alternative single fluid theory** was proposed by Benjamin Franklin (Figure **9.4**) in about 1750. He thought that all objects contained an electrical fluid. Uncharged objects contained a standard amount; adding excess fluid made them positively charged.

**Figure 9.4** Benjamin Franklin. In this illustration, published long after his death, he is shown experimenting with static electricity. This work led him to invent the lightning conductor.

Franklin's idea wasn't accepted immediately. It was only in 1839 that Michael Faraday managed to show that static electricity and current electricity were aspects of the same phenomenon, together with 'bioelectricity' – electrical phenomena associated with living creatures.

Today, we accept Franklin's idea that there is only one type of electric 'fluid', and that it comes in positive and negative forms. No-one knows why Franklin chose to label 'vitreous electricity' as positive. This has proved something of an inconvenience, since it means that an electric current flowing from positive to negative in a metal wire actually consists of electrons flowing from negative to positive.

If a positively charged object is brought close to an uncharged one, the electrons in the second object may be attracted. We observe this as a force of attraction between the two objects. (This phenomenon is known as electrostatic induction.)

It is important to appreciate that it is usually electrons that are involved in moving within a material, or from one material to another. This is because electrons, which are on the outside of atoms, are less strongly held within a material than are protons. They may be free to move about within a material (like the conduction electrons in a metal), or they may be relatively weakly bound within atoms.

# Investigating electric fields

If you rub a strip of plastic so that it becomes charged, and then hold it close to your hair, you feel your hair being pulled upwards. The influence of the charged plastic spreads into the space around it; we say that there is an **electric field** around the charge. To produce an electric field, we need unbalanced charges (as with the charged plastic). To observe the field, we need to put something in it that will respond to the field (as your hair responded). There are two simple ways in which you can do this in the laboratory. The first uses a charged strip of gold foil, attached to an insulating handle (Figure 9.5). The second uses grains

of a material such as semolina; these line up in an electric field, rather like the way in which iron filings line up in a magnetic field (Figure 9.6).

**Figure 9.6** Apparatus showing a uniform electric field between two parallel charged plates.

## The concept of an electric field

A charged object experiences a force in an electric field. This is what an electric field is. We say that there is an electric field anywhere where an electric charge experiences a force. An electric field is a **field of force**.

This is a rather abstract idea. You will be more familiar with the idea of a 'field of force' from your experience of magnets. There is a magnetic field around a permanent magnet; another magnet placed nearby will experience a force. In your earlier studies, you will have plotted the field lines which we use to represent the field around a magnet. There is a third type of force field which we are all familiar with, because we live in it. This is a gravitational field. Our weight is the force exerted on us because of our mass by the gravitational field of the Earth.

So we have:

• electric fields – act on objects with electric charge
• magnetic fields – act on magnets (and on electric currents)
• gravitational fields – act on objects with mass.

Later in the course we will see that the electric force and the magnetic force are closely linked. They are generally considered to be a single entity, known as the electromagnetic force.

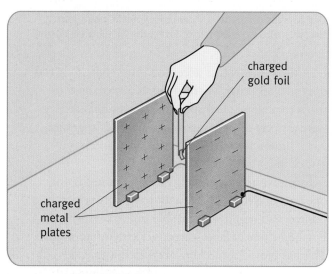

**Figure 9.5** Investigating the electric field between two charged metal plates.

## Representing electric fields

We can draw electric fields in much the same way that we can draw magnetic fields, by showing **field lines** (sometimes called lines of force). The three most important shapes are shown in Figure **9.7**.

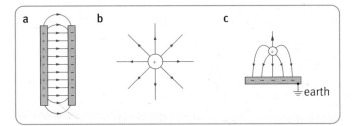

**Figure 9.7** Field lines representing electric fields. **a** A uniform electric field is produced between two oppositely charged plates. **b** A radial electric field surrounds a charged sphere. **c** The electric field between a charged sphere and an earthed plate.

As with magnetic fields, this representation tells us two things about the field: its direction (from the direction of the lines), and how strong it is (from the separation of the lines). The arrows go from positive to negative; they tell us the direction of the force on a positive charge in the field.

- A uniform field has the same strength at all points. Example: the electric field between oppositely charged parallel plates.
- A radial field spreads outwards in all directions. Example: the electric field around a point charge or a charged sphere.

We can draw electric fields for other arrangements. Note the symbol for an earth, which is assumed to be uncharged (i.e. at zero volts).

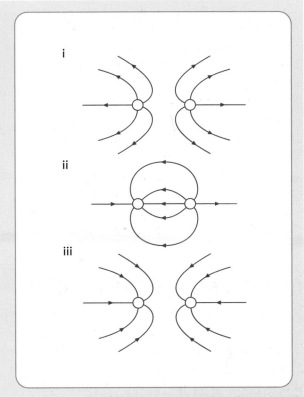

**Figure 9.8** Electric fields between charges – see Test yourself Q **1**.

## Test yourself

1 Which of the three field diagrams in Figure **9.8** represents:
   **a** two positive charges repelling each other?
   **b** two negative charges?
   **c** two opposite charges?

*continued ⋯⟶*

2 Many molecules are described as polar; that is, they have regions that are positively or negatively charged, though they are neutral overall. Draw a diagram to show how sausage-shaped polar molecules like those shown in Figure **9.9** might realign themselves in a solid.

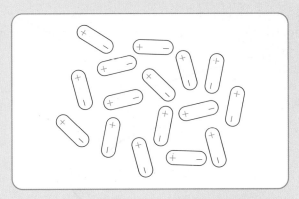

**Figure 9.9** Polar molecules – see Test yourself Q **2**.

3 Figure **9.10** shows the electric field pattern between a thundercloud and a building. State and explain where the electric field strength is greatest.

*continued ⋯⟶*

**Figure 9.10** Predict where the electric field will be strongest – that's where lightning may strike – see Test yourself Q 3.

# Electric field strength

For an electric field, we define electric field strength $E$ as follows:

> The **electric field strength** at a point is the force per unit charge exerted on a stationary positive charge at that point.

So, to define electric field strength, we imagine putting a positive test charge $+Q$ in the field and measuring the electric force $F$ that it feels (Figure **9.11**). (If you have used a charged gold leaf to investigate a field, this illustrates the principle of testing the field with a charge.)

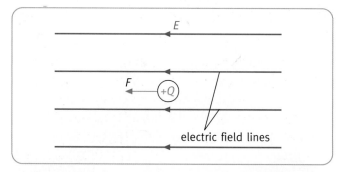

**Figure 9.11** A field of strength $E$ exerts force $F$ on charge $+Q$.

From this definition, we can write an equation for $E$:

$$E = \frac{F}{Q}$$

It follows that the unit of electric field strength is the newton per coulomb ($N\,C^{-1}$).

## The strength of a uniform field

You can set up a uniform field between two parallel metal plates by connecting them to the terminals of a high-voltage power supply (Figure **9.12**). The strength of the field between them depends on two factors:

- the voltage $V$ between the plates – the higher the voltage, the stronger the field: $E \propto V$;
- the separation $d$ between the plates – the greater their separation, the weaker the field: $E \propto \frac{1}{d}$.

These factors can be combined to give an equation for $E$:

$$E = -\frac{V}{d}$$

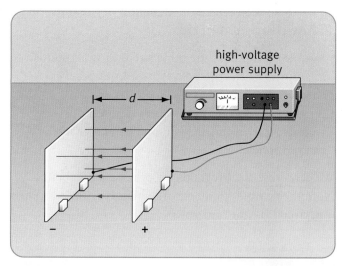

**Figure 9.12** There is a uniform field between two parallel, charged plates.

Worked example **1** shows a derivation of this. Note that the minus sign is necessary because, in Figure **9.12**, the voltage $V$ increases towards the right while the force $F$ acts in the opposite direction, towards the left. $E$ is a vector quantity. In calculations, we are often interested in the **magnitude** of the electric field strength, hence we can write:

$$E = \frac{V}{d}$$

From this equation, we can see that we could have given the units of electric field strength as volts per metre ($V\,m^{-1}$). Note:

$$1\,V\,m^{-1} = 1\,N\,C^{-1}$$

Worked example 2 shows how to solve problems involving uniform fields.

## Worked examples

1  Two metal plates are separated by a distance $d$. The potential difference between the plates is $V$. A positive charge $Q$ is pulled at a constant speed with a constant force $F$ from the negative plate all the way to the positive plate. Using the definition for electric field strength and the concept of work done, show that the magnitude of the electric field strength $E$ is given by the equation:

$$E = \frac{V}{d}$$

**Step 1** We have:

work done on charge = energy transformed

From their definitions, we can write:

work done = force × distance or $W = Fd$

energy transformed = $VQ$

**Step 2** Substituting gives:

$$Fd = VQ$$

and rearranging gives:

$$\frac{F}{Q} = \frac{V}{d}$$

**Step 3** The left-hand side of the equation is the electric field strength $E$. Hence:

$$E = \frac{V}{d}$$

*continued* ⋯⟩

2  Two parallel metal plates separated by 2.0 cm have a potential difference of 5.0 kV. Calculate the electric force acting on a dust particle between the plates that has a charge of $8.0 \times 10^{-19}$ C.

**Step 1** Write down the quantities given in the question.

$$d = 2.0 \times 10^{-2}\,m$$

$$V = 5.0 \times 10^{3}\,V$$

$$Q = 8.0 \times 10^{-19}\,C$$

When you write down the quantities it is important to include the units and to change them into base units. We have used powers of ten to do this.

**Step 2** To calculate the force $F$, you first need to determine the strength of the electric field.

$$E = \frac{V}{d}$$

$$E = \frac{50 \times 10^{3}}{2.0 \times 10^{-2}} = 2.5 \times 10^{5}\,V\,m^{-1}$$

**Step 3** Now calculate the force on the dust particle.

$$F = EQ$$

$$F = 2.5 \times 10^{5} \times 8.0 \times 10^{-19}$$
$$= 2.0 \times 10^{-13}\,N$$

## Test yourself

4  Figure **9.13** shows an arrangement of parallel plates, each at a different voltage. The electric field lines are shown in the space between the first pair. Copy and complete the diagram to show the electric field lines in the other two spaces.

*continued* ⋯⟩

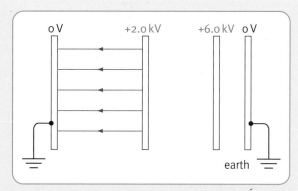

**Figure 9.13** An arrangement of parallel plates – see Test yourself Q 4.

5 Calculate the electric field strength at a point where a charge of 20 mC experiences a force vertically downwards of 150 N.

6 Calculate the electric field strength between two parallel charged plates, separated by 40 cm and with a potential difference between them of 1000 V.

7 An electron is situated in a uniform electric field. The electric force that acts on it is $8 \times 10^{-16}$ N. What is the strength of the electric field? (Electron charge $e = -1.6 \times 10^{-19}$ C.)

8 Air is usually a good insulator. However, a spark can jump through dry air when the electric field strength is greater than about 40 000 V cm$^{-1}$. This is called electrical breakdown. The spark shows that electrical charge is passing through the air – a current is flowing. (Do not confuse this with a chemical spark such as you might see when watching fireworks; in that case, small particles of a chemical substance are burning quickly.)
   a A Van de Graaff generator (Figure 9.14) is able to make sparks jump across a 4 cm gap. What is the voltage produced by the generator?
   b The highest voltage reached by the live wire of a conventional mains supply is 325 V. In theory (but DO NOT try this) how close would you have to get to a live wire to get a shock from it?

*continued* ⋯→

c Estimate the voltage of a thundercloud from which lightning strikes the ground 100 m below.

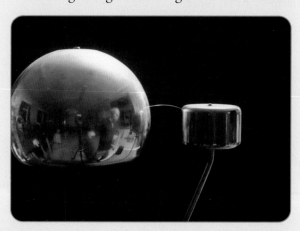

**Figure 9.14** A Van de Graaff generator produces voltages sufficient to cause sparks in air.

# Force on a charge

Now we can calculate the force $F$ on a charge $Q$ in the uniform field between two parallel plates. We have to combine the general equation for field strength $E = \dfrac{F}{Q}$ with the equation for the strength of a uniform field $E = -\dfrac{V}{d}$. This gives:

$$F = QE = -\frac{QV}{d}$$

For an electron with charge $-e$, this becomes:

$$F = \frac{eV}{d}$$

Figure 9.15 shows a situation where this force is important. A beam of electrons is entering the space between two charged parallel plates. How will the beam move?

We have to think about the force on a single electron. In the diagram, the upper plate is negative relative to the lower plate, and so the electron is pushed downwards. (You can think of this simply as the negatively charged electron being attracted by the positive plate, and repelled by the negative plate.)

If the electron were stationary, it would accelerate directly downwards. However, in this example, the electron is moving to the right. Its horizontal velocity will be unaffected by the force, but as it moves sideways

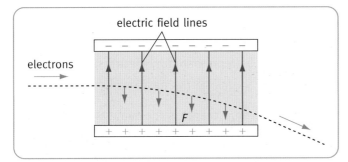

Figure 9.15 The parabolic path of a moving electron in a uniform electric field.

it will also accelerate downwards. It will follow a curved path, as shown. This curve is a parabola.

Note that the force on the electron is the same at all points between the plates, and it is always in the same direction (downwards, in this example).

This situation is equivalent to a ball being thrown horizontally in the Earth's uniform gravitational field (Figure 9.16). It continues to move at a steady speed horizontally, but at the same time it accelerates downwards. The result is the familiar curved trajectory shown. For the electron described above, the force of gravity is tiny – negligible compared to the electric force on it.

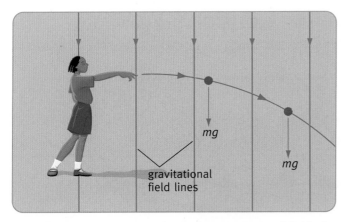

Figure 9.16 A ball, thrown in the uniform gravitational field of the Earth, follows a parabolic path.

## Test yourself

9  In Figure 9.17, two parallel plates are shown, separated by 25 cm.
   a  Copy the diagram and draw field lines to represent the field between the plates.
   b  What is the potential difference between points A and B?

*continued* ⋯⊹

c  What is the electric field strength at C, and at D?
d  Calculate the electric force on a charge of +5 µC placed at C. In which direction does the force act?

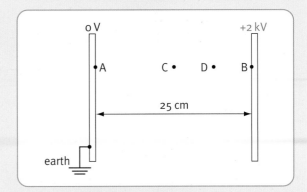

Figure 9.17 Two parallel, charged plates.

10  A particle of charge +2 µC is placed between two parallel plates, 10 cm apart, and with a potential difference of 5 kV between them. Calculate the field strength between the plates, and the force exerted on the charge.

11  We are used to experiencing accelerations that are usually less than $10\,m\,s^{-2}$. For example, when we fall, our acceleration is about $9.8\,m\,s^{-2}$. When a car turns a corner sharply at speed, its acceleration is unlikely to be more than $5\,m\,s^{-2}$. However, if you were an electron, you would be used to experiencing much greater accelerations than this. Calculate the acceleration of an electron in a television tube where the electric field strength is $50\,000\,V\,cm^{-1}$. (Electron charge $-e = -1.6 \times 10^{-19}\,C$; electron mass $m_e = 9.11 \times 10^{-31}\,kg$.)

12 a  Use a diagram to explain how the electric force on a charged particle could be used to separate a beam of electrons (e⁻) and positrons (e⁺) into two separate beams. (A positron is a positively charged particle that has the same mass as an electron but opposite charge. Positron–electron pairs are often produced in collisions in a particle accelerator.)
   b  Explain how this effect could be used to separate ions that have different masses and charges.

# Summary

☐ An electric field is a field of force, created by electric charges, and can be represented by electric field lines.

☐ The strength of the field is the force acting per unit positive charge at a point in the field, $E = \dfrac{F}{Q}$.

☐ In a uniform field (e.g. between two parallel charged plates), the force on a charge is the same at all points; the strength of the field is given by $E = -\dfrac{V}{d}$.

☐ An electric charge moving through a uniform electric field follows a parabolic path.

# End-of-chapter questions

1   Figure **9.5** on page **134** shows apparatus used to investigate the field between a pair of charged, parallel plates.
   **a**   Explain why the piece of gold foil deflects in the manner shown.
   **b**   State and explain what would be observed if the gold foil momentarily touched the negatively charged plate.

2   A charged dust particle in an electric field experiences a force of $4.4 \times 10^{-13}$ N. The charge on the particle is $8.8 \times 10^{-17}$ C. Calculate the electric field strength.

3   Calculate the potential difference that must be applied across a pair of parallel plates, placed 4 cm apart, to produce an electric field of $4000\,\text{V}\,\text{m}^{-1}$.

4   A potential difference of 2.4 kV is applied across a pair of parallel plates. The electric field strength between the plates is $3.0 \times 10^{4}\,\text{V}\,\text{m}^{-1}$.
   **a**   Calculate the separation of the plates.
   **b**   The plates are now moved so that they are 2.0 cm apart. Calculate the electric field strength produced in this new position.

5   A variable power supply is connected across a pair of parallel plates. The potential difference across the plates is doubled and the distance between the plates is decreased to one-third of the original. State by what factor the electric field changes. Explain your reasoning.

# Exam-style questions

1   The diagram shows a positively charged sphere close to an earthed metal plate.

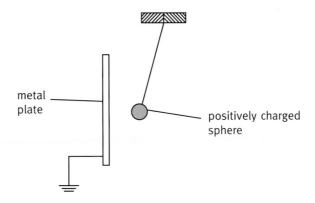

a   Copy the diagram and draw five lines to show the electric field near the plate and
    the sphere.                                                                             [3]
b   Explain why the sphere is attracted towards the metal plate.                            [2]
c   The sphere is now replaced with a similar negatively charged sphere.
    i   Explain what would be observed when the sphere is brought near to the earthed
        metal plate.                                                                        [2]
    ii  Describe any changes to the electric field that would occur.                        [1]

2   The diagram shows a proton as it moves between two charged parallel plates. The charge
    on the proton is $+1.6 \times 10^{-19}$ C.

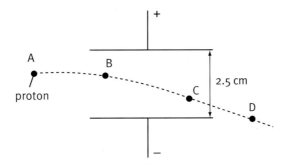

a   Copy the diagram and draw the electric field between the parallel plates.              [2]
    The force on the proton when it is at position B is $6.4 \times 10^{-14}$ N.
b   In which direction does the force on the proton act when it is at position B?          [1]
c   What will be the magnitude of the force on the proton when it is at position C?        [1]
d   Calculate the electric field strength between the plates.                              [2]
e   Calculate the potential difference between the plates.                                 [2]

3  **a** Define what is meant by the **electric field strength** at a point. [2]
In a particle accelerator a proton, initially at rest, is accelerated between two metal plates, as shown in the diagram.

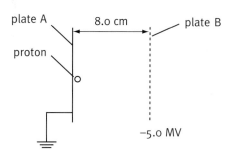

**b** Calculate the force on the proton due to the electric field. [3]
**c** Calculate the work done on the proton by the electric field when it moves from plate A to plate B. [2]
**d** State the energy gained by the proton. [1]
**e** Assuming that all this energy is converted to kinetic energy of the proton, calculate the speed of the proton when it reaches plate B. [3]
(Charge on a proton = $+1.6 \times 10^{-19}$ C; mass of a proton = $1.7 \times 10^{-27}$ kg.)

4  **a** Figure 1 shows the structure of a spark plug in an internal combustion engine.
Figure 2 is an enlarged version of the end of the spark plug, showing some of the lines of force representing the electric field.

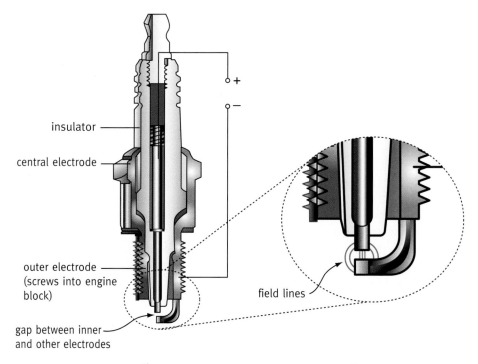

Figure 1                                   Figure 2

**a i** Copy the field lines from Figure **2**. On your copy, draw arrows on the lines of force to show the direction of the field. [1]

  **ii** What evidence does the diagram give that the field is strongest near the tip of the inner electrode? [1]

**b** The gap between the inner and outer electrodes is 1.25 mm and a field strength of $5.0 \times 10^6$ N C$^{-1}$ is required for electrical breakdown.

Estimate the minimum potential difference that must be applied across the inner and outer electrodes for a spark to be produced. (You may treat the two electrodes as a pair of parallel plates.) [2]

**c** When an electron is accelerated through a potential drop of approximately 20 V it will have sufficient energy to ionise a nitrogen atom.

Show that an electron must move 4.0 μm to gain this energy. [2]

# 10 Electric current, potential difference and resistance

## Objectives

After studying this chapter, you should be able to:

- [ ] show an understanding of the nature of electric current
- [ ] define charge and the coulomb
- [ ] solve problems using the equation $Q = It$
- [ ] define potential difference, e.m.f. and the volt
- [ ] use energy considerations to distinguish between p.d. and e.m.f.
- [ ] define resistance and the ohm
- [ ] solve problems using $V = IR$
- [ ] solve problems concerning energy and power in electric circuits

## Developing ideas

Electricity plays a vital part in our lives. We use electricity as a way of transferring energy from place to place – for heating, lighting and making things move. For people in a developing nation, the arrival of a reliable electricity supply marks a great leap forward. In Kenya, a microhydroelectric scheme has been built on Kabiri Falls, on the slopes of Mount Kenya.

Although this produces just 14 kW of power, it has given work to a number of people, as shown in Figures 10.1, 10.2 and 10.3.

**Figure 10.1** An operator controls the water inlet at the Kabiri Falls power plant. The generator is on the right.

**Figure 10.2** A metal workshop uses electrical welding equipment. This allows rapid repairs to farmers' machinery.

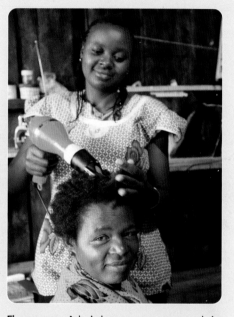

**Figure 10.3** A hairdresser can now work in the evenings, thanks to electrical lighting.

## Circuit symbols and diagrams

Before we go on to study electricity we need to introduce the concept of circuit diagrams. It is impossible to draw anything but the simplest circuits in a pictorial manner. To make it possible to draw complex circuits, a shorthand method using standard circuit symbols is used. You will have met many circuit components and their symbols in your previous studies. Some are shown in Table 10.1 and Figure 10.4.

The symbols in Table 10.1 are a small part of a set of internationally agreed conventional symbols for electrical components. It is essential that scientists, engineers, manufacturers and others around the world

| Symbol | Component name | Symbol | Component name |
|---|---|---|---|
| ——— | connecting lead | variable resistor | variable resistor |
| —|⊢— | cell | microphone | microphone |
| —|⊢--|⊢— | battery of cells | loudspeaker | loudspeaker |
| fixed resistor | fixed resistor | fuse | fuse |
| —o o— | power supply | earth | earth |
| junction of conductors | junction of conductors | ~ | alternating signal |
| crossing conductors (no connection) | crossing conductors (no connection) | —|⊢— | capacitor |
| ⊗ | filament lamp | thermistor | thermistor |
| Ⓥ | voltmeter | light-dependent resistor (LDR) | light-dependent resistor (LDR) |
| Ⓐ | ammeter | semiconductor diode | semiconductor diode |
| switch | switch | light-emitting diode (LED) | light-emitting diode (LED) |

**Table 10.1** Names of electrical components and their circuit symbols.

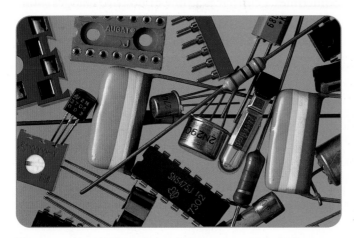

**Figure 10.4** A selection of electrical components, including resistors, fuses, capacitors and microchips.

use the same symbol for a particular component. In addition, many circuits are now designed by computers and these need a universal language in which to work and to present their results.

The International Electrotechnical Commission (IEC) is the body which establishes agreements on such things as electrical symbols, as well as for safety standards, working practices and so on. The circuit symbols used here form part of an international standard known as IEC 60617. Because this is

a shared 'language', there is less likelihood that misunderstandings will arise between people working in different organisations and different countries.

## What's in a word?

**Electricity** is a rather tricky word. In everyday life, its meaning may be rather vague – sometimes we use it to mean electric current; at other times, it may mean electrical energy or electrical power. In this chapter and the ones which follow, we will avoid using the word electricity and try to develop the correct usage of these more precise scientific terms.

## Electric current

You will have carried out many practical activities involving electric current. For example, if you connect a wire to a cell (Figure **10.5**), there will be current in the wire. And of course you make use of electric currents every day of your life – when you switch on a lamp or a computer, for example.

In the circuit of Figure **10.5**, the direction of the current is from the positive terminal of the cell, around the circuit to the negative terminal. This is a scientific convention: the direction of current is from

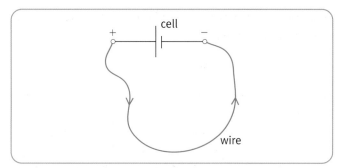

**Figure 10.5** There is current in the wire when it is connected to a cell.

positive to negative, and hence the current may be referred to as **conventional current**. But what is going on inside the wire?

A wire is made of metal. Inside a metal, there are negatively charged electrons which are free to move about. We call these **conduction** or **free** electrons, because they are the particles which allow a metal to conduct an electric current. The atoms of a metal bind tightly together; they usually form a regular array, as shown in Figure **10.6**. In a typical metal such as copper or silver, one electron from each atom breaks free to become a conduction electron. The atom remains as a positively charged ion. Since there are equal numbers of free electrons (negative) and ions (positive), the metal has no overall charge – it is neutral.

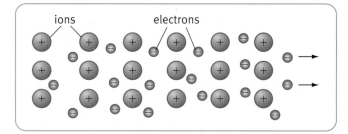

**Figure 10.6** In a metal, conduction electrons are free to move around the fixed positive ions. A cell connected across the ends of the metal causes the electrons to drift towards its positive terminal.

When the cell is connected to the wire, it exerts an electrical force on the conduction electrons that makes them travel along the length of the wire. Since electrons are negatively charged, they flow away from the negative terminal of the cell and towards the positive terminal. This is in the opposite direction to conventional current. This may seem a bit odd; it comes about because the direction of conventional

current was chosen long before anyone had any idea what was going on inside a piece of metal when carrying a current. If Benjamin Franklin (Chapter **9**) had allocated the names positive and negative the opposite way round, we would now label electrons as positively charged, and conventional current and electron flow would be in the same direction.

Note that there is a current at all points in the circuit as soon as the circuit is completed. We do not have to wait for charge to travel around from the cell. This is because the charged electrons are already present throughout the metal before the cell is connected.

We can use the idea of an electric field to explain why a current flows almost instantly. Connect the terminals of a cell to the two ends of a wire and we have a complete circuit. The cell produces an electric field in the wire; the field lines are along the wire, from the positive terminal to the negative. This means that there is a force on each electron in the wire, so each electron starts to move and the current exists almost instantly.

## Charge carriers

Sometimes a current is a flow of positive charges – for example, a beam of protons produced in a particle accelerator. The current is in the same direction as the particles. Sometimes a current is due to both positive and negative charges – for example, when charged particles flow through a solution. A solution which conducts is called an **electrolyte** and it contains both positive and negative ions. These move in opposite directions when the solution is connected to a cell (Figure **10.7**). Any charged particles which contribute to an electric current are known as **charge carriers**; these can be electrons, protons or ions.

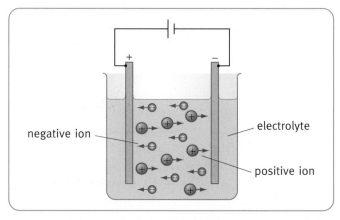

**Figure 10.7** Both positive and negative charges are free to move in a solution. Both contribute to the electric current.

## Test yourself

1 Look at Figure **10.7** and state the direction of the conventional current in the electrolyte (towards the left, towards the right, or in both directions at the same time).

2 Figure **10.8** shows a circuit with a conducting solution having both positive and negative ions.
   **a** Copy the diagram and draw in a cell between points A and B. Clearly indicate the positive and negative terminals of the cell.
   **b** Add an arrow to show the direction of the conventional current in the solution.
   **c** Add arrows to show the direction of the conventional current in the two connecting wires.

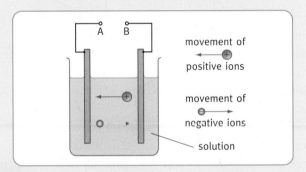

**Figure 10.8** For Test yourself Q **2**.

## Current and charge

When charged particles flow past a point in a circuit, we say that there is a current in the circuit. Electrical current is measured in **amperes** (A). So how much charge is moving when there is a current of 1 A? Charge is measured in **coulombs** (C). For a current of 1 A, the rate at which charge passes a point in a circuit is 1 C in a time of 1 s. Similarly, a current of 2 A gives a charge of 2 C in a time of 1 s. A current of 3 A gives a charge of 6 C in a time of 2 s, and so on. The relationship between charge, current and time may be written as the following word equation:

$$\text{current} = \frac{\text{charge}}{\text{time}}$$

This equation explains what we mean by current.

> Electric current is the rate of flow of electric charge past a point.

The equation for current can be rearranged to give an equation for charge:

$$\text{charge} = \text{current} \times \text{time}$$

This gives us the definition of the unit of charge, the coulomb.

One coulomb is the charge which flows past a point in a circuit in a time of 1 s when the current is 1 A.

In symbols, the charge flowing past a point is given by the relationship:

$$\Delta Q = I \Delta t$$

where $\Delta Q$ is the charge which flows during a time $\Delta t$ and $I$ is the current.

## Worked examples

1 There is a current of 10 A through a lamp for 1.0 hour. Calculate how much charge flows through the lamp in this time.

**Step 1** We need to find the time $t$ in seconds:

$$\Delta t = 60 \times 60 = 3600\,\text{s}$$

**Step 2** We know the current $I = 10\,\text{A}$, so the charge which flows is:

$$\Delta Q = I\Delta t = 10 \times 3600 = 36\,000\,\text{C} = 3.6 \times 10^4\,\text{C}$$

2 Calculate the current in a circuit when a charge of 180 C passes a point in a circuit in 2.0 minutes.

**Step 1** Rearranging $Q = It$ gives:

$$I = \frac{\Delta Q}{\Delta t} \quad \left( \text{or current} = \frac{\text{charge}}{\text{time}} \right)$$

**Step 2** With time in seconds, we then have:

$$\text{current } I = \frac{180}{120} = 1.5\,\text{A}$$

## Test yourself

3 The current in a circuit is 0.40 A. Calculate the charge that passes a point in the circuit in a period of 15 s.

continued ⋯⟩

**4** Calculate the current that gives rise to a charge flow of 150 C in a time of 30 s.

**5** In a circuit, a charge of 50 C passes a point in 20 s. Calculate the current in the circuit.

**6** A car battery is labelled '50 Ah'. This means that it can supply a current of 50 A for one hour.
 **a** For how long could the battery supply a continuous current of 200 A needed to start the car?
 **b** Calculate the charge which flows past a point in the circuit in this time.

## Charged particles

As we have seen, current is the flow of charged particles called charge carriers. But how much charge does each particle carry?

Electrons each carry a tiny negative charge of approximately $-1.6 \times 10^{-19}$ C. This charge is represented by $-e$. The magnitude of the charge is known as the **elementary charge**. This charge is so tiny that you would need about six million million million electrons – that's 6 000 000 000 000 000 000 of them – to have a charge equivalent to one coulomb.

> elementary charge $e = -1.6 \times 10^{-19}$ C

Protons are positively charged, with a charge $+e$. This is equal and opposite to that of an electron. Ions carry charges that are multiples of $+e$ and $-e$.

### Test yourself

**7** Calculate the number of protons which would have a charge of one coulomb. (Proton charge = $+1.6 \times 10^{-19}$ C.)

## The meaning of voltage

The term **voltage** is often used in a rather casual way. In everyday life, the word is used in a less scientific and often incorrect sense – for example, 'A big voltage can go through you and kill you.' In this section, we will consider a bit more carefully just what we mean by voltage and potential difference in relation to electric circuits.

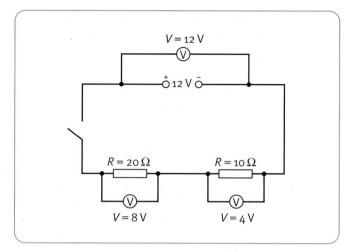

**Figure 10.9** Measuring voltages in a circuit. Note that each voltmeter is connected **across** the component.

Look at the simple circuit in Figure **10.9**. The power supply has negligible internal resistance. (We look at internal resistance later in Chapter **13**). The three voltmeters are measuring three voltages or potential differences. With the switch open, the voltmeter placed across the supply measures 12 V. With the switch closed, the voltmeter across the power supply still measures 12 V and the voltmeters placed across the resistors measure 8 V and 4 V. You will not be surprised to see that the voltage across the power supply is equal to the sum of the voltages across the resistors.

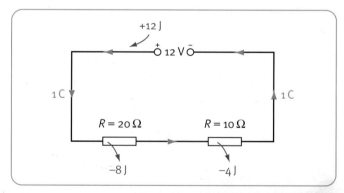

**Figure 10.10** Energy transfers as 1 C of charge flows round a circuit. This circuit is the same as that shown in Figure **10.9**.

Earlier in this chapter we saw that electric current is the rate of flow of electric charge. Figure **10.10** shows the same circuit as in Figure **10.9**, but here we are looking at the movement of one coulomb (1 C) of charge round the circuit. Electrical energy is transferred to the charge by the power supply. The charge flows round the circuit, transferring some of its electrical energy to heat in the first resistor, and the rest to the second resistor.

The voltmeter readings indicate the energy transferred to the component by each unit of charge. The voltmeter placed across the power supply measures the e.m.f. of the supply, whereas the voltmeters placed across the resistors measure the potential difference (p.d.) across these components. The terms e.m.f. and potential difference have different meanings – so you have to be very vigilant.

The term **potential difference** is used when charges **lose** energy by transferring electrical energy to other forms of energy in a component. Potential difference, $V$, is defined as the energy transferred per unit charge.

> The potential difference between two points, A and B, is the energy given up by unit charge as it moves from point A to point B.

The term the **e.m.f.** is used when charges **gain** electrical energy from a power supply or a battery. Electromotive force, $E$, is also defined as the energy transferred per unit charge.

> e.m.f. is formally defined as the total work done when unit charge goes round a complete circuit.

Note that e.m.f. stands for electromotive force. This is a misleading term. It has nothing at all to do with force. This term is a legacy from the past and we are stuck with it! It is best to forget where it comes from and simply use the term e.m.f.

# Electrical resistance

If you connect a lamp to a battery, a current in the lamp causes it to glow. But what determines the size of the current? This depends on two factors:

- the potential difference or voltage $V$ across the lamp – the greater the potential difference, the greater the current for a given lamp;
- the resistance $R$ of the lamp – the greater the resistance, the smaller the current for a given potential difference.

Now we need to think about the meaning of **electrical resistance**. The resistance of any component is defined as the ratio of the potential difference to the current. As a word equation, this is written as:

$$\text{resistance} = \frac{\text{potential difference}}{\text{current}}$$

or

$$R = \frac{V}{I}$$

where $R$ is the resistance of the component, $V$ is the potential difference across the component and $I$ is the current in the component. You can rearrange the equation above to give:

$$I = \frac{V}{R} \quad \text{and} \quad V = IR$$

Table **10.2** summarises these quantities and their units.

| Quantity | Symbol for quantity | Unit | Symbol for unit |
|---|---|---|---|
| current | $I$ | ampere (amp) | A |
| voltage (p.d., e.m.f.) | $V$ | volt | V |
| resistance | $R$ | ohm | Ω |

**Table 10.2** Basic electrical quantities, their symbols and SI units. Take care to understand the difference between V (in italics) meaning the quantity voltage and V meaning the unit volt.

## Defining the ohm

The unit of resistance, the ohm, can be determined from the equation that defines resistance:

$$\text{resistance} = \frac{\text{p.d.}}{\text{current}}$$

The ohm is equivalent to '1 volt per ampere'. That is:

$$1\,\Omega = 1\,V\,A^{-1}$$

> The ohm is the resistance of a component when a potential difference of 1 volt drives a current of 1 ampere through it.

**3** Calculate the current in a lamp given its resistance is $15\,\Omega$ and the potential difference across its ends is $3.0\,V$.

**Step 1** Here we have $V = 3.0\,V$ and $R = 15\,\Omega$.

**Step 2** Substituting in $I = \dfrac{V}{R}$ gives:

$$\text{current } I = \frac{3.0}{15} = 0.20\,A$$

So the current in the lamp is $0.20\,A$.

## Test yourself

**8** A car headlamp bulb has a resistance of $36\,\Omega$. Calculate the current in the lamp when connected to a '$12\,V$' battery.

**9** You can buy lamps of different brightness to fit in light fittings at home (Figure **10.11**). A '100 watt' lamp glows more brightly than a '60 watt' lamp. Explain which of the lamps has the higher resistance.

**Figure 10.11** Both of these lamps work from the 230 V mains supply, but one has a higher resistance than the other. For Test yourself Q 9.

continued ⋯⟩

**10 a** Calculate the potential difference across a motor carrying a current of $1.0\,A$ having a resistance of $50\,\Omega$.

**b** Calculate the potential difference across the same motor when the current is doubled. Assume its resistance remains constant.

**11** Calculate the resistance of a lamp carrying a current of $0.40\,A$ when connected to a $230\,V$ supply.

## Determining resistance

As we have seen, the equation for resistance is

$$R = \frac{V}{I}$$

To determine the resistance of a component, we therefore need to measure both the potential difference, $V$ across it and the current $I$ through it. To measure the current we need an ammeter. To measure the potential difference, we need a voltmeter. Figure **10.12** shows how these meters should be connected to determine the resistance of a metallic conductor, such as a length of wire.

- The ammeter is connected **in series** with the conductor, so that there is the same current in both.
- The voltmeter is connected across (**in parallel** with) the conductor, to measure the potential difference across it.

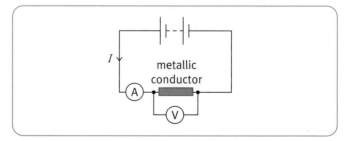

**Figure 10.12** Connecting an ammeter and a voltmeter to determine the resistance of a metallic conductor in a circuit.

12 In Figure **10.12** the reading on the ammeter
is 2.4 A and the reading on the voltmeter is
6.0 V. Calculate the resistance of the metallic
conductor.

# Electrical power

The rate at which energy is transferred is known as
power. Power $P$ is measured in watts (W). (If you are
not sure about this, refer back to Chapter **5**, where we
looked at the concept of power in relation to forces
and work done.)

$$\text{power} = \frac{\text{energy transferred}}{\text{time taken}}$$

$$P = \frac{\Delta W}{\Delta t}$$

where $P$ is the power and $\Delta W$ is the energy transferred
in a time $\Delta t$. Take care not to confuse $W$ for energy
transferred or work done with W for watts.

The rate at which energy is transferred in an
electrical component is related to two quantities:

• the current $I$ in the component
• the potential difference $V$ across the component.

We can derive an equation for electrical power from
the equations we have met so far. The amount of
energy $\Delta W$ transferred by a charge $\Delta Q$ when it moves
through a potential difference $V$ is given by:

$$\Delta W = V \Delta Q$$

Hence:

$$P = \frac{\Delta W}{\Delta t} = \frac{V \Delta Q}{\Delta t} = V \left( \frac{\Delta Q}{\Delta t} \right)$$

The ratio of charge to time, $\dfrac{\Delta Q}{\Delta t}$, is the current $I$ in
the component. Therefore:

$$P = VI$$

As a word equation, we have:

power = potential difference × current

and in units:

watts = amps × volts

4 Calculate the rate at which energy is transferred
by a 230 V mains supply which provides a
current of 8.0 A to an electric heater.

**Step 1** Use the equation for power:

$P = VI$ with $V = 230$ V and $I = 8.0$ A

**Step 2** Substitute values:

$P = 8 \times 230 = 1840$ W (1.84 kW)

13 Calculate the current in a 60 W light bulb
when it is connected to a 230 V supply.

14 A large power station supplies electrical energy
to the grid at a voltage of 25 kV. Calculate the
output power of the station when the current it
supplies is 40 kA.

## Fuses

A fuse is a device which is fitted in an electric circuit;
it is usually there to protect the wiring from excessive
currents. For example, the fuses in a domestic fuse box
will 'blow' if the current is too large. High currents
cause wires to get hot, and this can lead to damaged
wires, fumes from melting insulation, and even fires.

Fuses (Figure **10.13**) are usually marked with their
current rating; that is, the maximum current which they
will permit. Inside the fuse cartridge is a thin wire which
gets hot and melts if the current exceeds this value. This
breaks the circuit and stops any hazardous current. Worked
example **5** shows how an appropriate fuse is chosen.

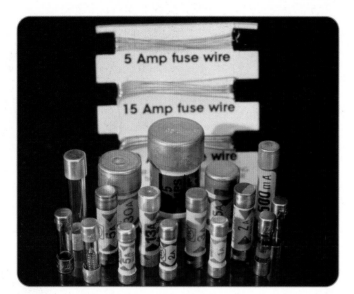

**Figure 10.13** Fuses of different current ratings.

## Worked example

5 An electric kettle is rated at 2.5 kW, 230 V. Determine a suitable current rating of the fuse to put in the three-pin plug. Choose from 1 A, 5 A, 13 A, 30 A.

**Step 1** Calculate the current through the kettle in normal operation. Rearranging $P = VI$ to make $I$ the subject gives:

$$I = \frac{P}{V}$$

So: $I = \dfrac{2500}{230} = 10.9\,\text{A}$

Don't forget to change the kilowatts into the base units, the watt.

**Step 2** Now we know that the normal current through the kettle is 10.9 A. We must choose a fuse with a **slightly higher** rating than this. Therefore the value of the fuse rating is 13 A.

A 5 A fuse would not be suitable because it would melt as soon as the kettle is switched on. A 30 A fuse would allow more than twice the normal current before blowing, which would not provide suitable protection.

15 An electric cooker is usually connected to the mains supply in a separate circuit from other appliances, because it draws a high current. A particular cooker is rated at 10 kW, 230 V.
  a Calculate the current through the cooker when it is fully switched on.
  b Suggest a suitable current rating for the fuse for this cooker.

## Power and resistance

A current $I$ in a resistor of resistance $R$ transfers energy to it. The resistor dissipates heat. The p.d. $V$ across the resistor is given by $V = IR$. Combining this with the equation for power, $P = VI$, gives us two further forms of the equation for power:

$$P = I^2 R$$

$$P = \frac{V^2}{R}$$

Which form of the equation we use in any particular situation depends on the information we have available to us. This is illustrated in Worked examples **6a** and **6b**, which relate to a power station and to the grid cables which lead from it (Figure **10.14**).

**Figure 10.14** A power station and electrical transmission lines. How much electrical power is lost as heat in these cables? (See Worked examples **6a** and **6b**.)

## Worked example

**6 a** A power station produces 20 MW of power at a voltage of 200 kV. Calculate the current supplied to the grid cables.

**Step 1** Here we have $P$ and $V$ and we have to find $I$, so we can use $P = VI$.

**Step 2** Rearranging the equation and substituting the values we know gives:

$$\text{current } I = \frac{P}{V} = \frac{20 \times 10^6}{200 \times 10^3} = 100 \text{ A}$$

> Remember to convert megawatts into watts and kilovolts into volts.

So the power station supplies a current of 100 A.

**b** The grid cables are 15 km long, with a resistance per unit length of $0.20\,\Omega\,\text{km}^{-1}$. How much power is wasted as heat in these cables?

**Step 1** First we must calculate the resistance of the cables:

$$\text{resistance } R = 15\,\text{km} \times 0.20\,\Omega\,\text{km}^{-1} = 3.0\,\Omega$$

**Step 2** Now we know $I$ and $R$ and we want to find $P$. We can use $P = I^2R$.

$$
\begin{aligned}
\text{power wasted as heat, } P &= I^2R \\
&= (100)^2 \times 3.0 \\
&= 3.0 \times 10^4\,\text{W} \\
&= 30\,\text{kW}
\end{aligned}
$$

Hence, of the 20 MW of power produced by the power station, 30 kW is wasted – just 0.15%.

## Test yourself

**16** A calculator is powered by a 3.0 V battery. The calculator's resistance is 20 kΩ. Calculate the power transferred to the calculator.

*continued* ⋯→

**17** An energy-efficient light bulb is labelled '230 V, 15 W'. This means that when connected to the 230 V mains supply it is fully lit and changes electrical energy to heat and light at the rate of 15 W. Calculate:
   **a** the current which flows through the bulb when fully lit
   **b** its resistance when fully lit.

**18** Calculate the resistance of a 100 W light bulb that draws a current of 0.43 A from a power supply.

## Calculating energy

We can use the relationship for power as energy transferred in unit time and the equation for electrical power to find the energy transferred in a circuit. Since

$$\text{power} = \text{current} \times \text{voltage}$$

and

$$\text{energy} = \text{power} \times \text{time}$$

we have:

$$\text{energy transferred} = \text{current} \times \text{voltage} \times \text{time}$$

$$\Delta W = IV\Delta t$$

Working in SI units, this gives energy transferred in joules.

## Test yourself

**19** A 12 V car battery can supply a current of 10 A for 5.0 hours. Calculate how many joules of energy the battery transfers in this time.

**20** A lamp is operated for 20 s. The current in the lamp is 10 A. In this time, it transfers 400 J of energy to the lamp. Calculate:
   **a** how much charge flows through the lamp
   **b** how much energy each coulomb of charge transfers to the lamp
   **c** the p.d. across the lamp.

# Summary

- Electric current is the rate of flow of charge. In a metal this is due to the flow of electrons. In an electrolyte, the flow of positive and negative ions produces the current.
- The direction of conventional current is from positive to negative; the direction of electron flow is from negative to positive.
- The SI unit of charge is the coulomb (C). One coulomb is the charge which passes a point when a current of 1A flows for 1s.

    charge = current × time; $\Delta Q = I \Delta t$

- The elementary charge, $e = -1.6 \times 10^{-19}$ C.
- The term potential difference (p.d.) is used when charges lose energy in a component. It is defined as the energy transferred per unit charge.

$$V = \frac{\Delta W}{\Delta Q} \quad \text{or} \quad \Delta W = V \Delta Q$$

- The term electromotive force (e.m.f.) is used when charges gain electrical energy from a battery or similar device. It is also defined as the energy transferred per unit charge.

$$E = \frac{\Delta W}{\Delta Q} \quad \text{or} \quad \Delta W = E \Delta Q$$

- A volt is a joule per coulomb. That is, $1V = 1JC^{-1}$.
- Power is the rate of energy transfer. In electrical terms, power is the product of voltage and current. That is, $P = VI$.
- Resistance is defined as the ratio of voltage to current. That is:

$$\text{resistance} = \frac{\text{voltage}}{\text{current}} \quad \left( R = \frac{V}{I} \right)$$

- The ohm is the resistance of a component when a potential difference of 1 volt is produced per ampere.
- For a resistance $R$, the power is given by:

$$P = I^2 R \quad \text{and} \quad P = \frac{V^2}{R}$$

- Energy transferred is given by the equation:

$$\Delta W = IV\Delta t$$

# End-of-chapter questions

1  Calculate the charge which passes through a lamp when there is a current of 150 mA for 40 minutes.

2  A generator produces a current of 40 A. How long will it take for a total of 2000 C to flow through the output?

3  In a lightning strike there is an average current of 30 kA, which lasts for 2000 μs. Calculate the charge which is transferred in this process.

**4** **a** A lamp of resistance $15\,\Omega$ is connected to a battery of e.m.f. $4.5\,V$. Calculate the current through the lamp.
   **b** Calculate the resistance of the filament of an electric fire which takes a current of $6.5\,A$ when it is connected across a mains supply of $230\,V$.
   **c** Calculate the voltage which is required to drive a current of $2.4\,A$ through a wire of resistance $3.5\,\Omega$.

**5** A battery of e.m.f. $6\,V$ produces a steady current of $2.4\,A$ for 10 minutes. Calculate:
   **a** the charge which it supplies
   **b** the energy that it transfers.

**6** Calculate the energy gained by an electron when it is accelerated through a potential difference of $50\,kV$. (Charge on the electron $= 1.6 \times 10^{-19}\,C$.)

**7** A woman has available $1\,A$, $3\,A$, $5\,A$, $10\,A$ and $13\,A$ fuses. Explain which fuse she should use for a $120\,V$, $450\,W$ hairdryer.

# Exam-style questions

**1** The diagram shows the principles of electrolysis of copper chloride.

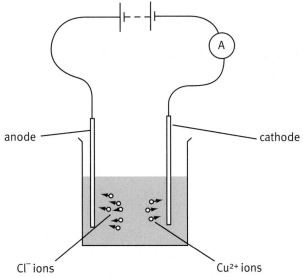

anode — — cathode

Cl⁻ ions        Cu²⁺ ions

   **a i** On a copy of the diagram, mark the direction of the conventional current in the electrolyte. Label it conventional current. [1]
   **ii** Mark the direction of the electron flow in the connecting wires. Label this electron flow. [1]
   **b** In a time period of 8 minutes $3.6 \times 10^{16}$ chloride ($Cl^-$) ions are neutralised and liberated at the anode and $1.8 \times 10^{16}$ copper ($Cu^{2+}$) ions are neutralised and deposited on the cathode.
   **i** Calculate the total charge passing through the electrolyte in this time. [2]
   **ii** Calculate the current in the circuit. [2]

2   The diagram shows an electron tube. Electrons move from the cathode to the anode carrying the current across the diode. The current in the milliammeter is 4.5 mA.

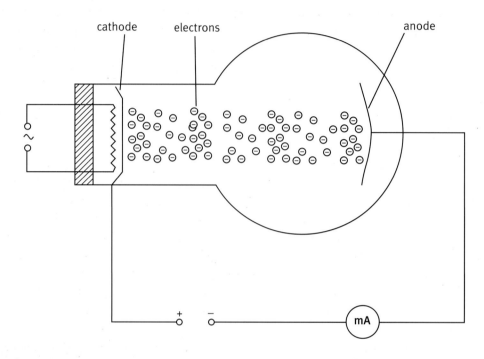

   cathode    electrons                              anode

   mA

a  Calculate the charge passing through the milliammeter in 3 minutes.                       [3]
b  Calculate the number of electrons which hit the anode in 3 minutes.                        [3]
c  The potential difference between the cathode and the anode is 75 V. Calculate
   the energy gained by an electron as it travels from the cathode to the anode.              [2]

3  a  Explain the difference between the terms **potential difference** of a cell and the **e.m.f.** of a cell.  [2]
   b  A battery has negligible internal resistance, an e.m.f. of 12.0 V and a capacity
      of 100 A h (ampere-hours). Calculate:
      i   the total charge that it can supply                                                 [2]
      ii  the total energy that it can transfer.                                              [2]
   c  The battery is connected to a 27 W lamp. Calculate the resistance of the lamp.          [3]

4   Some electricity generating companies use a unit called the kilowatt-hour (kWh) to calculate
    energy bills. 1 kWh is the energy a kilowatt appliance transfers in 1 hour.
    a  Show that 1 kWh is equal to 3.6 MJ.                                                     [2]
    b  An electric shower heater is rated at 230 V, 9.5 kW.
       i   Calculate the current it will take from the mains supply.                           [2]
       ii  Suggest why the shower requires a separate circuit from other appliances.           [1]
       iii Suggest a suitable current rating for the fuse in this circuit.                     [1]
    c  Calculate the energy transferred when a boy uses the shower for 5 minutes.              [2]

## Objectives

After studying this chapter you should be able to:

- [ ] recall and apply Kirchhoff's laws
- [ ] use Kirchhoff's laws to derive the formulae for the combined resistance of two or more resistors in series and in parallel
- [ ] recognise that ammeters are connected in series within a circuit and therefore should have low resistance
- [ ] recognise that voltmeters meters are connected in parallel across a component, or components, and therefore should have high resistance

## Circuit design

Over the years, electrical circuits have become increasingly complex, with more and more components combining to achieve very precise results (Figure 11.1). Such circuits typically include power supplies, sensing devices, potential dividers and output devices. At one time, circuit designers would start with a simple circuit and gradually modify it until the desired result was achieved. This is impossible today when circuits include many hundreds or thousands of components.

Instead, electronic engineers (Figure 11.2) rely on computer-based design software which can work out the effect of any combination of components. This is only possible because computers can be programmed with the equations which describe how current and voltage behave in a circuit. These equations, which include Ohm's law and Kirchhoff's two laws, were established in the 18th century, but they have come into their own in the 21st century through their use in computer-aided design (CAD) systems.

**Figure 11.2** A computer engineer in California uses a computer-aided design (CAD) software tool to design a circuit which will form part of a microprocessor, the device at the heart of every computer.

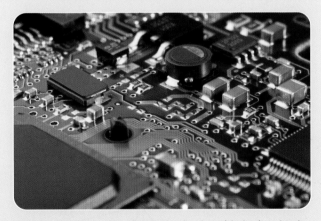

**Figure 11.1** A complex electronic circuit – this is the circuit board which controls a computer's hard drive.

## Kirchhoff's first law

You should be familiar with the idea that current may divide up where a circuit splits into two separate branches. For example, a current of 5.0 A may split at a junction or a point in a circuit into two separate currents of 2.0 A and 3.0 A. The total amount of current remains the same after it splits. We would not expect some of the current to disappear, or extra current to appear from nowhere. This is the basis of **Kirchhoff's first law**, which states that:

The sum of the currents entering any point in a circuit is equal to the sum of the currents leaving that same point.

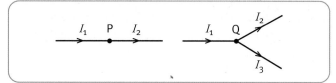

Figure 11.3 Kirchhoff's first law: current is conserved because charge is conserved.

This is illustrated in Figure 11.3. In the first part of the figure, the current into point P must equal the current out, so:

$$I_1 = I_2$$

In the second part of the figure, we have one current coming into point Q, and two currents leaving. The current divides at Q. Kirchhoff's first law gives:

$$I_1 = I_2 + I_3$$

Kirchhoff's first law is an expression of the **conservation of charge**. The idea is that the total amount of charge entering a point must exit the point. To put it another way, if a billion electrons enter a point in a circuit in a time interval of 1.0 s, then one billion electrons must exit this point in 1.0 s. The law can be tested by connecting ammeters at different points in a circuit where the current divides. You should recall that an ammeter must be connected in series so the current to be measured passes **through** it.

## Test yourself

1 Use Kirchhoff's first law to deduce the value of the current $I$ in Figure 11.4.

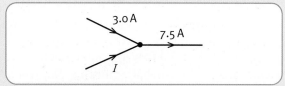

Figure 11.4 For Test yourself Q 1.

*continued* ···>

2 In Figure 11.5, calculate the current in the wire X. State the direction of this current (towards P or away from P).

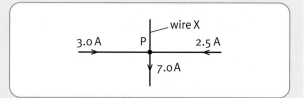

Figure 11.5 For Test yourself Q 2.

## Formal statement of Kirchhoff's first law

We can write Kirchhoff's first law as an equation:

$$\Sigma I_{in} = \Sigma I_{out}$$

Here, the symbol $\Sigma$ (Greek letter sigma) means 'the sum of all', so $\Sigma I_{in}$ means 'the sum of all currents entering into a point' and $\Sigma I_{out}$ means 'the sum of all currents leaving that point'. This is the sort of equation which a computer program can use to predict the behaviour of a complex circuit.

## Test yourself

3 Calculate $\Sigma I_{in}$ and $\Sigma I_{out}$ in Figure 11.6. Is Kirchhoff's first law satisfied?

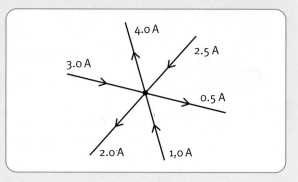

Figure 11.6 For Test yourself Q 3.

*continued* ···>

**4** Use Kirchhoff's first law to deduce the value and direction of the current $I_x$ in Figure **11.7**.

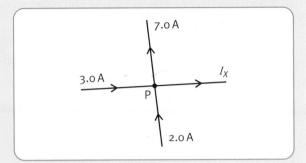

**Figure 11.7** For Test yourself Q 4.

# Kirchhoff's second law

This law deals with e.m.f.s and voltages in a circuit. We will start by considering a simple circuit which contains a cell and two resistors of resistances $R_1$ and $R_2$ (Figure 14.5). Since this is a simple series circuit, the current $I$ must be the same all the way around, and we need not concern ourselves further with Kirchhoff's first law. For this circuit, we can write the following equation:

$$E = IR_1 + IR_2$$

e.m.f. of battery = sum of p.d.s across the resistors

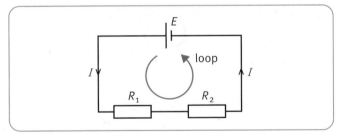

**Figure 11.8** A simple series circuit.

You should not find these equations surprising. However, you may not realise that they are a consequence of applying **Kirchhoff's second law** to the circuit. This law states that:

The sum of the e.m.f.s around any loop in a circuit is equal to the sum of the p.d.s around the loop.

You will see later (page **162**) that Kirchhoff's second law is an expression of the conservation of energy.

We shall look at another example of how this law can be applied, and then look at how it can be applied in general.

## Worked example

**1** Use Kirchhoff's laws to find the current in the circuit in Figure **11.9**.

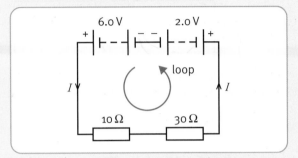

**Figure 11.9** A circuit with two opposing batteries.

This is a series circuit so the current is the same all the way round the circuit.

**Step 1** We calculate the sum of the e.m.f.s:

sum of e.m.f.s = 6.0 V – 2.0 V = 4.0 V

The batteries are connected in opposite directions so we must consider one of the e.m.f.s as negative.

**Step 2** We calculate the sum of the p.d.s:

sum of p.d.s = $(I \times 10) + (I \times 30) = 40I$

**Step 3** We equate these:

$$4.0 = 40I$$

and so    $I = 0.1$ A

No doubt, you could have solved this problem without formally applying Kirchhoff's second law, but you will find that in more complex problems the use of these laws will help you to avoid errors.

5 Use Kirchhoff's second law to deduce the p.d. across the resistor of resistance $R$ in the circuit shown in Figure **11.10**, and hence find the value of $R$. (Assume the battery of e.m.f. 10 V has negligible internal resistance.)

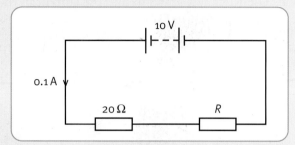

**Figure 11.10** Circuit for Test yourself Q **5**.

## An equation for Kirchhoff's second law

In a similar manner to the formal statement to the first law the second law can be written as an equation.

$$\Sigma E = \Sigma V$$

where $\Sigma E$ is the sum of the e.m.f.s and $\Sigma V$ is the sum of the potential drops.

# Applying Kirchhoff's laws

Figure **11.11** shows a more complex circuit, with more than one 'loop'. Again there are two batteries and two resistors. The problem is to find the current in each resistor. There are several steps in this; Worked example **2** shows how such a problem is solved.

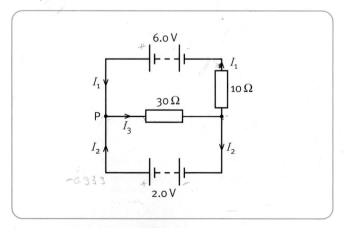

**Figure 11.11** Kirchhoff's laws are needed to determine the currents in this circuit.

2 Calculate the current in each of the resistors in the circuit shown in Figure **11.11**.

**Step 1** Mark the currents flowing. The diagram shows $I_1$, $I_2$ and $I_3$.

It does not matter if we mark these flowing in the wrong directions, as they will simply appear as negative quantities in the solutions.

**Step 2** Apply Kirchhoff's first law. At point P, this gives:

$$I_1 + I_2 = I_3 \tag{1}$$

**Step 3** Choose a loop and apply Kirchhoff's second law. Around the upper loop, this gives:

$$6.0 = (I_3 \times 30) + (I_1 \times 10) \tag{2}$$

**Step 4** Repeat step 3 around other loops until there are the same number of equations as unknown currents. Around the lower loop, this gives:

$$2.0 = I_3 \times 30 \tag{3}$$

We now have three equations with three unknowns (the three currents).

**Step 5** Solve these equations as simultaneous equations. In this case, the situation has been chosen to give simple solutions. Equation 3 gives $I_3 = 0.067$ A, and substituting this value in equation 2 gives $I_1 = 0.400$ A. We can now find $I_2$ by substituting in equation 1:

$$I_2 = I_3 - I_1 = 0.067 - 0.400 = -0.333 \text{ A}$$
$$\approx -0.33 \text{ A}$$

Thus $I_2$ is negative – it is in the opposite direction to the arrow shown in Figure **11.11**.

continued ⋯→

Note that there is a third 'loop' in this circuit; we could have applied Kirchhoff's second law to the outermost loop of the circuit. This gives a fourth equation:

$$6 - 2 = I_1 \times 10$$

However, this is not an independent equation; we could have arrived at it by subtracting equation 3 from equation 2.

## Signs and directions

Caution is necessary when applying Kirchhoff's second law. You need to take account of the ways in which the sources of e.m.f. are connected and the directions of the currents. Figure **11.12** shows a loop from a complicated circuit to illustrate this point. Only the components and currents within the loop are shown.

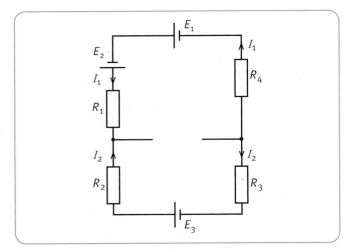

**Figure 11.12** A loop extracted from a complicated circuit.

### e.m.f.s

Starting with the cell of e.m.f. $E_1$ and working **anticlockwise** around the loop (because $E_1$ is 'pushing current' anticlockwise):

$$\text{sum of e.m.f.s} = E_1 + E_2 - E_3$$

Note that $E_3$ is opposing the other two e.m.f.s.

### p.d.s

Starting from the same point, and working **anticlockwise** again:

$$\text{sum of p.d.s} = I_1 R_1 - I_2 R_2 - I_2 R_3 + I_1 R_4$$

Note that the direction of current $I_2$ is clockwise, so the p.d.s that involve $I_2$ are negative.

6 You can use Kirchhoff's second law to find the current $I$ in the circuit shown in Figure **11.13**. Choosing the best loop can simplify the problem.
   **a** Which loop in the circuit should you choose?
   **b** Calculate the current $I$.

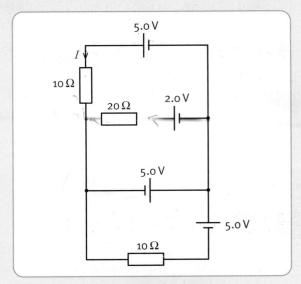

**Figure 11.13** Careful choice of a suitable loop can make it easier to solve problems like this. For Test yourself Q **6**.

7 Use Kirchhoff's second law to deduce the resistance $R$ of the resistor shown in the circuit loop of Figure **11.14**.

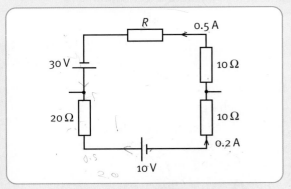

**Figure 11.14** For Test yourself Q **7**.

## Conservation of energy

Kirchhoff's second law is a consequence of the principle of conservation of energy. If a charge, say 1 C, moves around the circuit, it **gains** energy as it moves through each source of e.m.f. and loses energy as it passes through each p.d. If the charge moves all the way round the circuit, so that it ends up where it started, it must have the same energy at the end as at the beginning. (Otherwise we would be able to create energy from nothing simply by moving charges around circuits.) So:

> energy gained passing through sources of e.m.f. = energy lost passing through components with p.d.s

You should recall that an e.m.f. in volts is simply the energy gained per 1 C of charge as it passes through a source. Similarly, a p.d. is the energy lost per 1 C as it passes through a component.

> 1 volt = 1 joule per coulomb

Hence we can think of Kirchhoff's second law as:

> energy gained per coulomb = energy lost per coulomb
> around loop                        around loop

Here is another way to think of the meaning of e.m.f. A 1.5 V cell gives 1.5 J of energy to each coulomb of charge which passes through it. The charge then moves round the circuit, transferring the energy to components in the circuit. The consequence is that, by driving 1 C of charge around the circuit, the cell transfers 1.5 J of energy. Hence the e.m.f. of a source simply tells us the amount of energy (in joules) transferred by the source in driving unit charge (1 C) around a circuit.

### Test yourself

8 Use the idea of the energy gained and lost by a 1 C charge to explain why two 6 V batteries connected together in series can give an e.m.f. of 12 V or 0 V, but connected in parallel they give an e.m.f. of 6 V.

continued ⋯→

9 Apply Kirchhoff's laws to the circuit shown in Figure **11.15** to determine the current that will be shown by the ammeters $A_1$, $A_2$ and $A_3$.

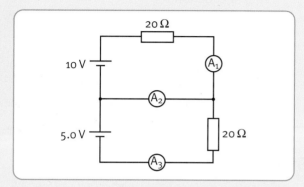

**Figure 11.15** Kirchhoff's laws make it possible to deduce the ammeter readings.

# Resistor combinations

You are already familiar with the formulae used to calculate the combined resistance $R$ of two or more resistors connected in series or in parallel. To derive these formulae we have to make use of Kirchhoff's laws.

## Resistors in series

Take two resistors of resistances $R_1$ and $R_2$ connected in series (Figure **11.16**). According to Kirchhoff's first law, the current in each resistor is the same. The p.d. $V$ across the combination is equal to the sum of the p.d.s across the two resistors:

$$V = V_1 + V_2$$

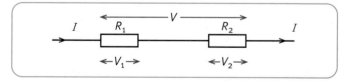

**Figure 11.16** Resistors in series.

Since $V = IR$, $V_1 = IR_1$ and $V_2 = IR_2$, we can write:

$$IR = IR_1 + IR_2$$

Cancelling the common factor of current $I$ gives:

$$R = R_1 + R_2$$

For three or more resistors, the equation for total resistance $R$ becomes:

$$R = R_1 + R_2 + R_3 + \cdots$$

## Test yourself

**10** Calculate the combined resistance of two $5\,\Omega$ resistors and a $10\,\Omega$ resistor connected in series.

**11** The cell shown in Figure **11.17** provides an e.m.f. of $2.0\,V$. The p.d. across one lamp is $1.2\,V$. Determine the p.d. across the other lamp.

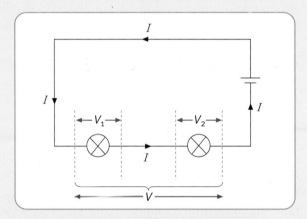

**Figure 11.17** A series circuit for Test yourself Q **11**.

**12** You have five $1.5\,V$ cells. How would you connect all five of them to give an e.m.f. of:
**a** $7.5\,V$  **b** $1.5\,V$  **c** $4.5\,V$?

## Resistors in parallel

For two resistors of resistances $R_1$ and $R_2$ connected in parallel (Figure **11.18**), we have a situation where the current divides between them. Hence, using Kirchhoff's first law, we can write:

$$I = I_1 + I_2$$

If we apply Kirchhoff's second law to the loop that contains the two resistors, we have:

$$I_1 R_1 - I_2 R_2 = 0\,V$$

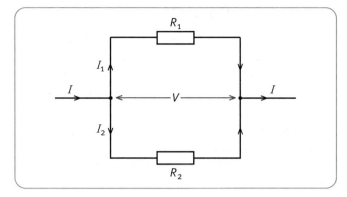

**Figure 11.18** Resistors connected in parallel.

(because there is no source of e.m.f. in the loop). This equation states that the two resistors have the same p.d. $V$ across them. Hence we can write:

$$I = \frac{V}{R}$$

$$I_1 = \frac{V}{R_1}$$

$$I_2 = \frac{V}{R_2}$$

Substituting in $I = I_1 + I_2$ and cancelling the common factor $V$ gives:

$$\frac{1}{R} = \frac{1}{R_1} + \frac{1}{R_2}$$

For three or more resistors, the equation for total resistance $R$ becomes:

$$\frac{1}{R} = \frac{1}{R_1} + \frac{1}{R_2} + \frac{1}{R_3} + \cdots$$

## Worked example

**3** Two $10\,\Omega$ resistors are connected in parallel. Calculate the total resistance.

**Step 1** We have $R_1 = R_2 = 10\,\Omega$, so:

$$\frac{1}{R} = \frac{1}{R_1} + \frac{1}{R_2}$$

$$\frac{1}{R} = \frac{1}{10} + \frac{1}{10} = \frac{2}{10} = \frac{1}{5}$$

*continued ⋯⟶*

**Step 2** Inverting both sides of the equation gives:

$$R = 5\,\Omega$$

> Take care not to forget this step – many students do! Nor should we write
>
> $$\frac{1}{R} = \frac{1}{5} = 5\,\Omega,\quad \text{as then you are saying } \frac{1}{5} = 5!$$

You can also determine the resistance as follows:

$$R = (R_1^{-1} + R_2^{-1})^{-1}$$
$$= (10^{-1} + 10^{-1})^{-1} = 5\,\Omega$$

To summarise, when components are connected in parallel:

- all have the same p.d. across their ends
- the current is shared between them
- we use the reciprocal formula to calculate their combined resistance.

## Test yourself

**13** Calculate the total resistance of four $10\,\Omega$ resistors connected in parallel.

**14** Calculate the resistances of the following combinations:
   **a** $100\,\Omega$ and $200\,\Omega$ in series
   **b** $100\,\Omega$ and $200\,\Omega$ in parallel
   **c** $100\,\Omega$ and $200\,\Omega$ in series and this in parallel with $200\,\Omega$.

**15** Calculate the current drawn from a 12 V battery of negligible internal resistance connected to the ends of the following:
   **a** $500\,\Omega$ resistor
   **b** $500\,\Omega$ and $1000\,\Omega$ resistors in series
   **c** $500\,\Omega$ and $1000\,\Omega$ resistors in parallel.

*continued ···⊁*

**16** You are given one $200\,\Omega$ resistor and two $100\,\Omega$ resistors. What total resistances can you obtain by connecting some, none, or all of these resistors in various combinations?

## Solving problems with parallel circuits

Here are some useful ideas which may prove helpful when you are solving problems with parallel circuits (or checking your answers to see whether they seem reasonable).

- When two or more resistors are connected in parallel, their combined resistance is smaller than any of their individual resistances. For example, three resistors of $2\,\Omega$, $3\,\Omega$ and $6\,\Omega$ connected together in parallel have a combined resistance of $1\,\Omega$. This is less than even the smallest of the individual resistances. This comes about because, by connecting the resistors in parallel, you are providing extra pathways for the current. Since the combined resistance is lower than the individual resistances, it follows that connecting two or more resistors in parallel will increase the current drawn from a supply. Figure **11.19** shows a hazard which can arise when electrical appliances are connected in parallel.
- When components are connected in parallel, they all have the same p.d. across them. This means that you can often ignore parts of the circuit which are not relevant to your calculation.
- Similarly, for resistors in parallel, you may be able to calculate the current in each one individually, then add them up to find the total current. This may be easier than working out their combined resistance using the reciprocal formula. (This is illustrated in Test yourself Q **19**.)

**Figure 11.19 a** Correct use of an electrical socket. **b** Here, too many appliances (resistances) are connected in parallel. This reduces the total resistance and increases the current drawn, to the point where it becomes dangerous.

## Test yourself

**17** Three resistors of resistances 20 Ω, 30 Ω and 60 Ω are connected together in parallel. Select which of the following gives their combined resistance:

110 Ω,    50 Ω,    20 Ω,    10 Ω

(No need to do the calculation!)

**18** In the circuit in Figure **11.20** the battery of e.m.f. 10 V has negligible internal resistance. Calculate the current in the 20 Ω resistor shown in the circuit.

*continued* ⋯⟶

**19** Determine the current drawn from the battery in Figure **11.20**.

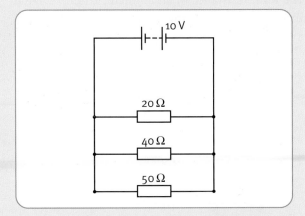

**Figure 11.20** Circuit diagram for Test yourself Q **18** and Q **19**.

**20** What value of resistor must be connected in parallel with a 20 Ω resistor so that their combined resistance is 10 Ω?

**21** You are supplied with a number of 100 Ω resistors. Describe how you could combine the minimum number of these to make a 250 Ω resistor.

**22** Calculate the current at each point (A–E) in the circuit shown in Figure **11.21**.

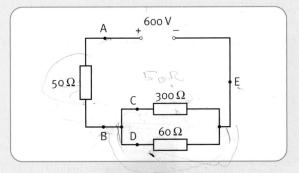

**Figure 11.21** For Test yourself Q **22**.

# Ammeters and voltmeters

Ammeters and voltmeters are connected differently in circuits (Figure **11.22**). Ammeters are always connected in series, since they measure the current through a circuit. For this reason, an ammeter should have as low a resistance as possible so that as little energy as possible is transferred in the ammeter itself. Inserting an ammeter with a higher resistance could significantly reduce the current flowing in the circuit. The ideal resistance of an ammeter is zero. Digital ammeters have very low resistances.

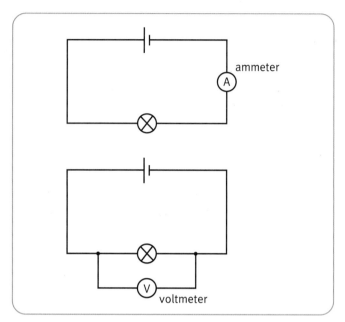

**Figure 11.22** How to connect up an ammeter and a voltmeter.

Voltmeters measure the potential difference between two points in the circuit. For this reason, they are connected in parallel (i.e. between the two points), and they should have a very high resistance to take as little current as possible. The ideal resistance of a voltmeter would be infinity. In practice, voltmeters have typical resistance of about $1\,M\Omega$. A voltmeter

with a resistance of $10\,M\Omega$ measuring a p.d. of $2.5\,V$ will take a current of $2.5 \times 10^{-7}\,A$ and dissipate just $0.625\,\mu J$ of heat energy from the circuit every second.

Some measuring instruments are shown in Figure **11.23**.

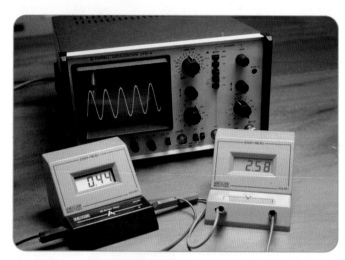

**Figure 11.23** Electrical measuring instruments: an ammeter, a voltmeter and an oscilloscope. The oscilloscope can display rapidly changing voltages.

### Test yourself

23 a A $10\,V$ power supply of negligible internal resistance is connected to a $100\,\Omega$ resistor. Calculate the current in the resistor.
  b An ammeter is now connected in the circuit, to measure the current. The resistance of the ammeter is $5.0\,\Omega$. Calculate the ammeter reading.

## Summary

- ☐ Kirchhoff's first law states that the sum of the currents entering any point in a circuit is equal to the sum of the currents leaving that point.
- ☐ Kirchhoff's second law states that the sum of the e.m.f.s around any loop in a circuit is equal to the sum of the p.d.s around the loop.
- ☐ The combined resistance of resistors in series is given by the formula:

$$R = R_1 + R_2 + \cdots$$

- ☐ The combined resistance of resistors in parallel is given by the formula:

$$\frac{1}{R} = \frac{1}{R_1} + \frac{1}{R_2} + \cdots$$

- ☐ Ammeters have a low resistance and are connected in series in a circuit.
- ☐ Voltmeters have a high resistance and are connected in parallel in a circuit.

# End-of-chapter questions

1  Use Kirchhoff's first law to calculate the unknown currents in the examples in Figure 11.24. In each example state the direction of the current.

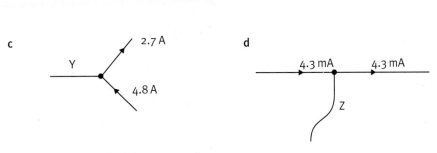
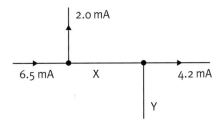

**Figure 11.24**  For End-of-chapter question 1.

2  Figure 11.25 shows a part of a circuit.

2.0 mA

6.5 mA     X          4.2 mA

Y

**Figure 11.25**  For End-of-chapter question 2.

Copy the circuit and write in the currents at X and at Y and show their directions.

**3** Figure **11.26** shows four circuits. Find the unknown potential difference (or differences) in each case.

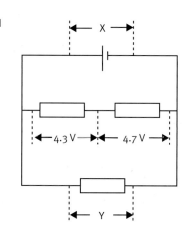

**Figure 11.26** For End-of-chapter question **3**.

**4** A filament lamp and a $220\,\Omega$ resistor are connected in series to a battery of e.m.f. 6.0 V. The battery has negligible internal resistance. A high-resistance voltmeter placed across the resistor measures 1.8 V.

Calculate:
**a** the current drawn from the battery
**b** the p.d. across the lamp
**c** the total resistance of the circuit
**d** the number of electrons passing through the battery in a time of 1.0 minute.
(The elementary charge is $1.6 \times 10^{-19}\,\text{C}$.)

5   The circuit diagram in Figure **11.27** shows a 12 V power supply connected to some resistors.

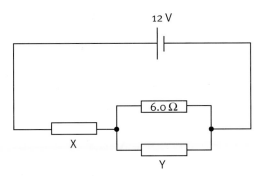

**Figure 11.27** For End-of-chapter question **5**.

The current in the resistor X is 2.0 A and the current in the 6.0 Ω resistor
is 0.5 A. Calculate:
a   the current in resistor Y
b   the resistance of resistor Y
c   the resistance of resistor X.

# Exam-style questions

1   a   Explain the difference between the terms **e.m.f.** and **potential difference**.                                        [2]
   b   The diagram shows a circuit containing batteries and resistors. You may assume
       that the batteries have negligible internal resistance.

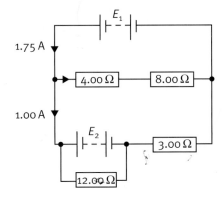

   i    Use Kirchhoff's first law to find the current through the 4.00 Ω and the 8.00 Ω resistors.   [1]
   ii   Calculate the e.m.f. of $E_1$.                                                                [2]
   iii  Calculate the value of $E_2$.                                                                [2]
   iv   Calculate the current through the 12.00 Ω resistor.                                          [2]

2  a  Explain why an ammeter is designed to have a low resistance. [2]
      A student builds the circuit in the diagram, using a battery of negligible
      internal resistance. The reading on the voltmeter is 9.0 V.

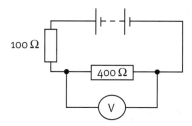

   b i   The voltmeter has a resistance of 1200 Ω. Calculate the e.m.f. of the battery. [4]
     ii  The student now repeats the experiment using a voltmeter of resistance
         12 kΩ. Show that the reading on this voltmeter would be 9.5 V. [3]
     iii Refer to your answers to **i** and **ii** and explain why a voltmeter should have
         as high a resistance as possible. [2]

3  a  Explain what is meant by the **resistance** of a resistor. [1]
   b  The figure shows a network of resistors connected to a cell of e.m.f. 6.0 V.

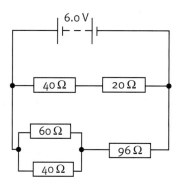

      Show that the resistance of the network of resistors is 40 Ω. [3]
   c  Calculate the current through the 60 Ω resistor. [3]

## Objectives

After studying this chapter, you should be able to:

- [ ] state Ohm's law
- [ ] sketch and explain the *I–V* characteristics for various components
- [ ] sketch the temperature characteristic for an NTC thermistor
- [ ] solve problems involving the resistivity of a material

## Superconductivity

**Figure 12.1** The Japanese JR-Maglev train, capable of speeds approaching $600\,\mathrm{km\,h^{-1}}$.

As metals are cooled, their resistance decreases. It was discovered as long ago as 1911 that when mercury was cooled using liquid helium to $4.1\,\mathrm{K}$ (4.1 degrees above absolute zero), its resistance suddenly fell to zero. This phenomenon was named **superconductivity**. Other metals, such as lead at $7.2\,\mathrm{K}$, also become superconductors.

When a current flows in a superconductor it can continue in that superconductor without the need for any potential difference and without dissipating any energy. This means that large currents can flow without the unwanted heating effect that would occur in a normal metallic or semiconducting conductor.

Initially superconductivity was only of scientific interest and had little practical use, as the liquid helium which was required to cool the superconductors is very expensive to produce. In 1986 it was discovered that particular ceramics became superconducting at much higher temperatures, above $77\,\mathrm{K}$, the boiling point of liquid nitrogen. This meant that liquid nitrogen, which is readily available, could be used to cool the superconductors and the expensive liquid helium was no longer needed. Consequently superconductor technology became a feasible proposition.

### Uses of superconductors

The JR-Maglev train in Japan's Yamanashi province floats above the track using superconducting magnets. This means that not only is the heating effect of the current in the magnet coils reduced to zero – it also means that the friction between the train and the track is eliminated and that the train can reach incredibly high speeds of up to $581\,\mathrm{km\,h^{-1}}$.

Particle accelerators, such as the Large Hadron Collider (LHC) at the CERN research facility in Switzerland, accelerate beams of charged particles to very high energies by making them orbit around a circular track many times. The particles are kept moving in the circular path by very strong magnetic fields produced by electromagnets whose coils are made from superconductors. Much of our understanding of the fundamental nature of matter is from doing experiments in which beams of these very high speed particles are made to collide with each other.

Magnetic resonance imaging (MRI) was developed in the 1940s. It is used by doctors to examine internal organs without invasive surgery. Superconducting magnets can be made much smaller than conventional magnets and this has enabled the magnetic fields produced to be much more precise, resulting in better imaging. You will find out more about MRI in Chapter 32.

# The *I–V* characteristic for a metallic conductor

In Chapter **10** we saw how we could measure the resistance of a resistor using a voltmeter and ammeter. In this section we are going to investigate the variation of the current, and hence resistance, as the potential difference across the conductor changes.

The potential difference across the metal conductor can be altered using a variable power supply or by having a variable resistor placed in series with the conductor. This allows us to measure the current at different potential differences across the conductor. The results of such a series of measurements is shown graphically in Figure **12.2b**.

Look at the graph of Figure **12.2b**. Such a graph is known as an *I–V* **characteristic**. The points are slightly scattered, but they clearly lie on a straight line. A line of best fit has been drawn. You will see that it passes through the origin of the graph. In other words, the current *I* is directly proportional to the voltage *V*.

The straight-line graph passing through the origin shows that the resistance of the conductor remains constant. If you double the current, the voltage will also double. However, its resistance, which is the ratio of the voltage to the current, remains the same. Instead of using:

$$R = \frac{V}{I}$$

to determine the resistance, for a graph of *I* against *V* which is a straight line passing through the origin, you can also use:

$$\text{resistance} = \frac{1}{\text{gradient of graph}}$$

(Take care! This is only true for an *I–V* graph which is a straight line through the origin.)

By reversing the connections to the resistor, the p.d. across it will be reversed, i.e. negative. The current will flow in the opposite direction – it is also negative. The graph is symmetrical, showing that if a p.d. of, say, 2.0 V produces a current of 0.5 A, then a p.d. of –2.0 V will produce a current of –0.5 A. This is true for most simple metallic conductors but is not true for some electronic components, such as diodes.

You get results similar to those shown in Figure **12.2b** for a commercial **resistor**. Resistors have different resistances, hence the gradient of the *I–V* graph will be different for different resistors.

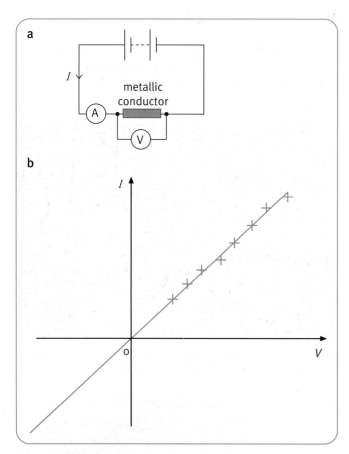

**Figure 12.2** To determine the resistance of a component, you need to measure both current and potential difference.

## Test yourself

1 Table **12.1** shows the results of an experiment to measure the resistance of a carbon resistor whose resistance is given by the manufacturer as $47\,\Omega \pm 10\%$.
   a Plot a graph to show the *I–V* characteristic of this resistor.
   b Do the points appear to fall on a straight line which passes through the origin of the graph?
   c Use the graph to determine the resistance of the resistor.
   d Does the value of the resistance fall within the range given by the manufacturer?

*continued* ⋯⋗

| Potential difference / V | Current / A |
|---|---|
| 2.1 | 0.040 |
| 4.0 | 0.079 |
| 6.3 | 0.128 |
| 7.9 | 0.192 |
| 10.0 | 0.202 |
| 12.1 | 0.250 |

**Table 12.1** Potential difference $V$ and current $I$ data for Test yourself Q 1.

# Ohm's law

For the metallic conductor whose $I$–$V$ characteristic is shown in Figure **12.2b**, the current through it is directly proportional to the p.d. across it. This is only true if the temperature of the conductor does not change. This means that its resistance is independent of both the current and the p.d. This is because the ratio $\dfrac{V}{I}$ is a constant. Any component which behaves like this is described as an **ohmic component**, and we say that it obeys **Ohm's law**. The statement of Ohm's law is very precise and you must not confuse this with the equation $\dfrac{V}{I} = R$.

> **Ohm's law**
> For a metallic conductor at constant temperature, the current in the conductor is directly proportional to the potential difference across its ends.

It is easier to see the significance of this if we consider a non-ohmic component. An example is a **semiconductor diode**. This is a component which allows electric current in only one direction. Nowadays, most diodes are made of semiconductor materials. One type, the **light-emitting diode** or LED, gives out light when it conducts.

Figure **12.3** shows the $I$–$V$ characteristic for a light-emitting diode. There are some points you should notice about this graph.

- We have included positive and negative values of current and voltage. This is because, when connected one way round (positively biased), the diode conducts and has a fairly low resistance. Connected the other way round (negatively biased), it allows only a tiny current through and has almost infinite resistance.

- For positive voltages less than about 2 V, the current is almost zero and hence the LED has almost infinite resistance. The LED starts to conduct suddenly at its **threshold voltage**. This depends on the colour of light it emits, but may be taken to be about 2 V. The resistance of the LED decreases dramatically for voltages greater than 2 V.

The resistance of a light-emitting diode depends on the potential difference across it. From this we can conclude that the LED does not obey Ohm's law; it is a **non-ohmic component**.

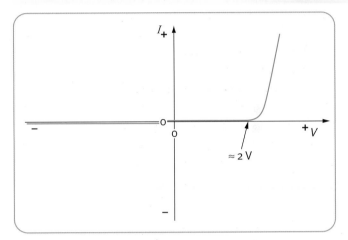

**Figure 12.3** The current against **potential difference** ($I$–$V$) characteristic for a light-emitting diode. The graph is not a straight line. An LED does not obey Ohm's law.

**Figure 12.4** This torch has seven white LEDs, giving a brighter, whiter light than a traditional filament lamp.

LEDs have traditionally been used as indicator lamps to show when an appliance is switched on. Newer versions, some of which produce white light, are replacing filament lamps, for example in traffic lights and torches (flashlights) – see Figure **12.4**.

This is because, although they are more expensive to manufacture, they are more energy-efficient and hence cheaper to run, so that the overall cost is less.

Diodes are also used as rectifiers. They allow current to pass in one direction only and so can be used to convert alternating current into direct current. Most modern diodes are made from silicon and will start conducting when there is a potential difference of about 0.6 V across them, rather less than the 2 V of the LED illustrated in the graph in Figure **12.3**.

### Test yourself

2 An electrical component allows a current of 10 mA through it when a voltage of 2.0 V is applied. When the voltage is increased to 8.0 V, the current becomes 60 mA. Does the component obey Ohm's law? Give numerical values for the resistance to justify your answer.

# Resistance and temperature

You should have noted earlier that, for a component to obey Ohm's law, the temperature must remain constant. You can see why this must be the case by considering the characteristics of a filament lamp. Figure **12.5** shows such a lamp; you can clearly see the wire filament glowing as the current passes through it. Figure **12.6** shows the $I$–$V$ characteristic for a similar lamp.

There are some points you should notice about the graph in Figure **12.6**.

- The line passes through the origin (as for an ohmic component).
- For very small currents and voltages, the graph is roughly a straight line.
- At higher voltages, the line starts to curve. The current is a bit less than we would have expected from a straight line. This suggests that the lamp's resistance has increased. You can also tell that the resistance has increased because the ratio $\dfrac{V}{I}$ is larger for higher voltages than for lower voltages.

The fact that the graph of Figure **12.6** is not a straight line shows that the resistance of the lamp depends on the temperature of its filament. Its resistance may increase by a factor as large as ten between when it is cold and when it is brightest (when its temperature may be as high as 1750 °C).

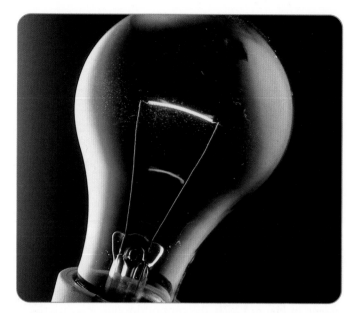

**Figure 12.5** The metal filament in a lamp glows as the current passes through it. It also feels warm. This shows that the lamp produces both heat and light.

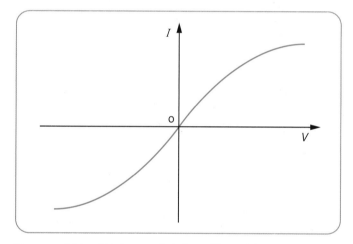

**Figure 12.6** The $I$–$V$ characteristic for a filament lamp.

### Test yourself

3 The two graphs in Figure **12.7** show the $I$–$V$ characteristics of a metal wire at two different temperatures, $\theta_1$ and $\theta_2$.
  a Calculate the resistance of the wire at each temperature.
  b State which is the higher temperature, $\theta_1$ or $\theta_2$.

4 The graph of Figure **12.8** shows the $I$–$V$ characteristics for two electrical components, a filament lamp and a length of steel wire.

*continued ⋯⟶*

**a** Identify which curve relates to each component.
**b** State at what voltage both have the same resistance.
**c** Determine the resistance at the voltage stated in **b**.

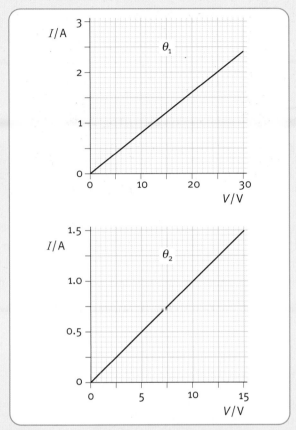

Figure 12.7 *I–V* graphs for a wire at two different temperatures. For Test yourself Q 3.

*continued* ⋯→

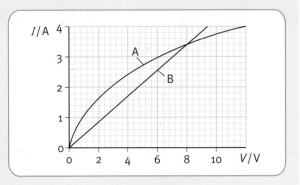

Figure 12.8 For Test yourself Q 4.

## Thermistors

Thermistors are components that are designed to have a resistance which changes rapidly with temperature. Thermistors ('**therm**al res**istors**') are made from metal oxides such as those of manganese and nickel. There are two distinct types of thermistor.

- Negative temperature coefficient (NTC) thermistors – the resistance of this type of thermistor decreases with increasing temperature. Those commonly used in schools and colleges may have a resistance of many thousands of ohms at room temperature, falling to a few tens of ohms at 100 °C. You are expected to recall the properties of NTC thermistors.
- Positive temperature coefficient (PTC) thermistors – the resistance of this type of thermistor rises abruptly at a definite temperature, usually around 100–150 °C.

## *Thermistors at work*

The change in their resistance with temperature gives thermistors many uses.

- Water temperature sensors in cars and ice sensors on aircraft wings – if ice builds up on the wings, the thermistor 'senses' this temperature drop and a small heater is activated to melt the ice.
- Baby alarms – the baby rests on an air-filled pad, and as he or she breathes, air from the pad passes over a thermistor, keeping it cool; if the baby stops breathing, the air movement stops, the thermistor warms up and an alarm sounds.
- Fire sensors – the rise in temperature activates an alarm.
- Overload protection in electric razor sockets – if the razor overheats, the thermistor's resistance rises rapidly and cuts off the circuit.

**5** The graph in Figure **12.9** was obtained by measuring the resistance $R$ of a particular thermistor as its temperature $\theta$ changed.

   **a** Determine its resistance at:

     **i** 20 °C

     **ii** 45 °C.

   **b** Determine the temperature when its resistance is:

     **i** 5000 Ω

     **ii** 2000 Ω.

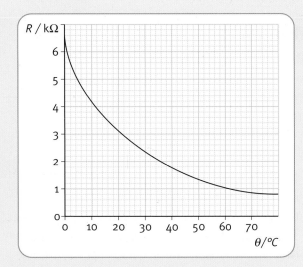

**Figure 12.9** The resistance of an NTC thermistor decreases as the temperature increases. For Test yourself Q **5**.

**6** A student connects a circuit with an NTC thermistor, a filament lamp and a battery in series. The lamp glows dimly. The student warms the thermistor with a hair dryer. What change will the student notice in the brightness of the lamp? Explain your answer.

## Understanding the origin of resistance

To understand a little more about the origins of resistance, it is helpful to look at how the resistance of a pure metal wire changes as its temperature is increased. This is shown in the graph of Figure **12.10**. You will see that the resistance of the pure metal increases linearly as the temperature increases from 0 °C to 100 °C. Compare this with the graph of Figure **12.8** for an NTC thermistor; the thermistor's resistance decreases very dramatically over a narrow temperature range.

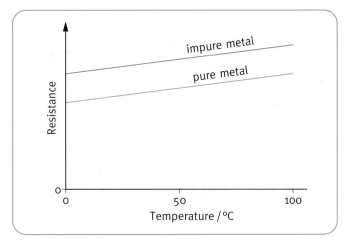

**Figure 12.10** The resistance of a metal increases gradually as its temperature is increased. The resistance of an impure metal wire is greater than that of a pure metal wire of the same dimensions.

Figure **12.10** also shows how the resistance of the metal changes if it is slightly impure. The resistance of an impure metal is greater than that of the pure metal and follows the same gradual upward slope. The resistance of a metal changes in this gradual way over a wide range of temperatures – from close to absolute zero up to its melting point, which may be over 2000 °C.

This suggests that there are two factors which affect the resistance of a metal:

- the temperature
- the presence of impurities.

Figure **12.11** shows a simple model which explains what happens in a metal when electrons flow through it.

In a metal, a current is due to the movement of free electrons. At low temperatures, they can move easily past the positive ions (Figure **12.11a**). However, as the temperature is raised, the ions vibrate with larger amplitudes. The electrons collide more frequently with the vibrating ions, and this decreases their mean drift velocity. They lose energy to the vibrating ions (Figure **12.11b**).

If the metal contains impurities, some of the atoms will be of different sizes (Figure **12.11c**). Again, this disrupts the free flow of electrons. In colliding with impurity atoms, the electrons lose energy to the vibrating atoms.

You can see that electrons tend to lose energy when they collide with vibrating ions or impurity atoms. They give up energy to the metal, so it gets hotter. The resistance of the metal increases with the temperature of the wire because of the decrease in the mean drift velocity of the electrons.

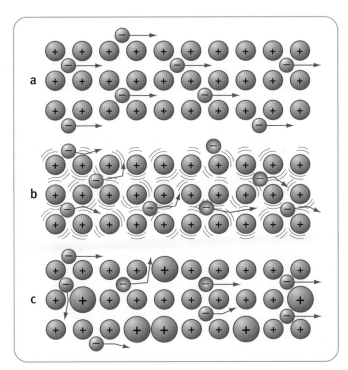

**Figure 12.11** A model of the origins of resistance in a metal. **a** At low temperatures, electrons flow relatively freely. **b** At higher temperatures, the electrons are obstructed by the vibrating ions and they make very frequent collisions with the ions. **c** Impurity atoms can also obstruct the free flow of electrons.

Conduction in semiconductors is different. At low temperatures, there are few delocalised, or free, electrons. For conduction to occur, electrons must have sufficient energy to free themselves from the atom they are bound to. As the temperature increases, a few electrons gain enough energy to break free of their atoms to become conduction electrons. The number of conduction electrons thus increases and so the material becomes a better conductor. At the same time, there are more electron–ion collisions, but this effect is small compared with the increase in the number of conduction electrons.

# Resistivity

The resistance of a particular wire depends on its size and shape. A long wire has a greater resistance than a short one, provided it is of the same thickness and material. A thick wire has less resistance than a thin one. For a metal in the shape of a wire, $R$ depends on the following factors:

- length $L$
- cross-sectional area $A$
- the material the wire is made from
- the temperature of the wire.

At a constant temperature, the resistance is directly proportional to the length of the wire and inversely proportional to its cross-sectional area. That is:

$$\text{resistance} \propto \text{length}$$

and

$$\text{resistance} \propto \frac{1}{\text{cross-sectional area}}$$

We can see how these relate to the formulae for adding resistors in series and in parallel.

- If we double the length of a wire it is like connecting two identical resistors in series; their resistances add to give double the resistance. The resistance is proportional to the length.
- Doubling the cross-sectional area of a wire is like connecting two identical resistors in parallel; their combined resistance is halved (since $\frac{1}{R_{total}} = \frac{1}{R} + \frac{1}{R}$).

  Hence the resistance is inversely proportional to the cross-sectional area.

Combining the two proportionalities for length and cross-sectional area, we get:

$$\text{resistance} \propto \frac{\text{length}}{\text{cross-sectional area}}$$

or

$$R \propto \frac{L}{A}$$

But the resistance of a wire also depends on the material it is made of. Copper is a better conductor than steel, steel is a better conductor than silicon, and so on. So if we are to determine the resistance $R$ of a particular wire, we need to take into account its length, its cross-sectional area and the material. The relevant property of the material is its **resistivity**, for which the symbol is $\rho$ (Greek letter **rho**). The word equation for resistance is:

$$\text{resistance} = \text{resistivity} \times \frac{\text{length}}{\text{cross-sectional area}}$$

$$R = \rho \frac{L}{A}$$

We can rearrange this equation to give an equation for resistivity. The resistivity of a material is defined by the following word equation:

$$\text{resistivity} = \text{resistance} \times \frac{\text{cross-sectional area}}{\text{length}}$$

$$\rho = \frac{RA}{L}$$

Values of the resistivities of some typical materials are shown in Table **12.2**. Notice that the units of resistivity are ohm metres ($\Omega\,m$); this is not the same as ohms per metre.

| Material | Resistivity /$\Omega\,m$ | Material | Resistivity /$\Omega\,m$ |
|---|---|---|---|
| silver | $1.60 \times 10^{-8}$ | mercury | $69.0 \times 10^{-8}$ |
| copper | $1.69 \times 10^{-8}$ | graphite | $800 \times 10^{-8}$ |
| nichrome[a] | $1.30 \times 10^{-8}$ | germanium | $0.65$ |
| aluminium | $3.21 \times 10^{-8}$ | silicon | $2.3 \times 10^{3}$ |
| lead | $20.8 \times 10^{-8}$ | Pyrex glass | $10^{12}$ |
| manganin[b] | $44.0 \times 10^{-8}$ | PTFE[d] | $10^{13} - 10^{16}$ |
| eureka[c] | $49.0 \times 10^{-8}$ | quartz | $5 \times 10^{16}$ |

[a] Nichrome – an alloy of nickel, copper and aluminium used in electric fires because it does not oxidise at 1000 °C.
[b] Manganin – an alloy of 84% copper, 12% manganese and 4% nickel.
[c] Eureka (constantan) – an alloy of 60% copper and 40% nickel.
[d] Poly(tetrafluoroethene) or Teflon.

**Table 12.2** Resistivities of various materials at 20 °C.

## Worked example

1  Find the resistance of a 2.6 m length of eureka wire with cross-sectional area $2.5 \times 10^{-7}\,m^2$.

**Step 1** Using the equation for resistance:

$$\text{resistance} = \text{resistivity} \times \frac{\text{length}}{\text{area}}$$

continued ···>

$$R = \frac{\rho L}{A}$$

**Step 2** Substituting values from the question and using the value for $\rho$ from Table **12.2**:

$$R = 49.0 \times 10^{-8} \times \frac{2.6}{2.5 \times 10^{-7}} = 5.1\,\Omega$$

So the wire has a resistance of $5.1\,\Omega$.

## Test yourself

8  Use the resistivity value quoted in Table **12.2** to calculate the lengths of 0.50 mm diameter manganin wire needed to make resistance coils with resistances of:
   a  $1.0\,\Omega$
   b  $5.0\,\Omega$
   c  $10\,\Omega$.

9  $1.0\,cm^3$ of copper is drawn out into the form of a long wire of cross-sectional area $4.0 \times 10^{-7}\,m^2$. Calculate its resistance. (Use the resistivity value for copper from Table **12.2**.)

10 A 1.0 m length of copper wire has a resistance of $0.50\,\Omega$.
   a  Calculate the resistance of a 5.0 m length of the same wire.
   b  What will be the resistance of a 1.0 m length of copper wire having half the diameter of the original wire?

11 A piece of steel wire has a resistance of $10\,\Omega$. It is stretched to twice its original length. Compare its new resistance with its original resistance.

## Resistivity and temperature

Resistivity, like resistance, depends on temperature. For a metal, resistivity increases with temperature. As we saw above, this is because there are more frequent collisions between the conduction electrons and the vibrating ions of the metal.

# Summary

- [ ] Ohm's law can be stated as: For a metallic conductor at constant temperature, the current in the conductor is directly proportional to the potential difference (voltage) across its ends.
- [ ] Ohmic components include a wire at constant temperature and a resistor.
- [ ] Non-ohmic components include a filament lamp and a light-emitting diode.
- [ ] A semiconductor diode allows current in one direction only.
- [ ] As the temperature of a metal increases, so does its resistance.
- [ ] A thermistor is a component which shows a rapid change in resistance over a narrow temperature range. The resistance of an NTC thermistor decreases as its temperature is increased.
- [ ] The resistivity $\rho$ of a material is defined as $\rho = \dfrac{RA}{L}$, where $R$ is the resistance of a wire of that material,

  $A$ is its cross-sectional area and $L$ is its length. The unit of resistivity is the ohm metre ($\Omega\,m$).

# End-of-chapter questions

1   The graph in Figure **12.12** shows the $I$–$V$ characteristic of an electrical component.

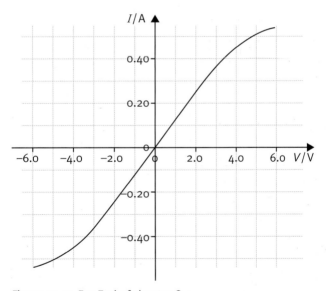

**Figure 12.12**  For End-of-chapter Q 1.

    **a** Calculate the resistance of the component when the potential difference across it is:
      **i**  2.0 V
      **ii** 5.0 V.
    **b** Suggest what the component is.

**2** A student connects a NTC thermistor to a battery and an ammeter. He places the thermistor in a beaker of water and gradually heats the water from 10 °C to its boiling point, recording the value of the current as he does so. He then plots a graph of the current through the thermistor against the temperature of the water.

    **a** Sketch the graph you would expect the student to obtain from the experiment.

    **b** Explain how the student could now use the thermistor as a thermometer.

**3**  **a** Describe the difference between the conduction process in copper and in the semiconductor, silicon.

    **b** Explain why the resistance of a metallic conductor increases with temperature while that of a semiconductor decreases.

**4** A nichrome wire has a length of 1.5 m and a cross-sectional area of 0.008 0 mm². Resistivity of nichrome = $1.30 \times 10^{-8}\,\Omega\,m$.

    **a** Calculate the resistance of the wire.

    **b** Calculate the length of this wire which would be needed to make an element of an electric fire of resistance 30 Ω.

# Exam-style questions

**1** The diagram shows a circuit.

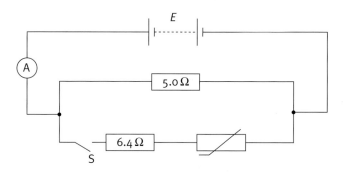

    **a** When switch S is open the current through ammeter A is 0.48 A. Calculate the e.m.f. of the battery. You may assume it has negligible internal resistance.   **[2]**

    **b** When switch S is closed the current in the ammeter increases to 0.72 A.

      **i** Deduce the current through the 6.4 Ω resistor.   **[1]**

      **ii** State the current through the thermistor.   **[1]**

    **c** State and explain how the reading on the ammeter changes when the temperature of the thermistor is increased.   **[3]**

**2**  **a** Explain why the resistance of a metal increases when its temperature increases.   **[2]**

    **b** State **two** other factors which determine the resistance of stated length of a wire.   **[2]**

    **c** When a potential difference of 1.5 V is applied across a 5.0 m length of insulated copper wire a current of 0.24 A passes through it.

> **i** Calculate the resistance of the length of wire. [2]
> **ii** The resistivity of copper is $1.69 \times 10^{-8}\,\Omega\,m$. Calculate the diameter
> of the wire. [3]
> **d** The wire is now made into a tight bundle. State and explain how you would expect
> the current through it to change. [3]

**3** The diagram shows a piece of silicon of width 32 mm and length 36 mm. The resistance
of the silicon between the points P and Q is $1.1\,M\Omega$. Silicon has a resistivity of $2.3 \times 10^{3}\,\Omega\,m$.

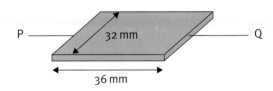

**a** Calculate the thickness of the piece of silicon. [3]
**b** Calculate the current which would pass through the silicon if a potential difference
of 12 V were applied across P and Q. [2]
**c** Discuss how the current would change if it were large enough to cause the silicon
to become significantly warmer. [3]

**4** A student is investigating the properties of a semiconducting diode. The diagram shows
the circuit she builds.

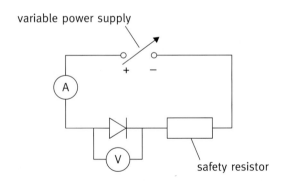

**a i** Sketch a graph to show how the current through the diode would vary as the
voltage across it is increased from 0 V to 1.0 V. [1]
**ii** The supply is now connected in the reverse direction and once more the potential
difference across the diode is increased from 0 V to 1.0 V. Complete the *I–V* graph. [1]
**b** Suggest why the safety resistor is required. [2]
**c** When the potential difference across the safety resistor is 1.4 V the current through it
is 20 mA. Calculate the resistance of the safety resistor. [2]

5   a   Explain what is meant by an **ohmic conductor**.                                    [2]
    b i   Sketch a graph of resistance $R$ against voltage $V$ for a wire of pure iron kept
          at constant temperature. Label this line X.                                       [1]
      ii  Sketch a graph of resistance $R$ against voltage $V$ for a second wire of impure iron,
          of the same diameter and the same length, which is kept at the same temperature.
          Label this line Y.                                                                [1]
      iii Explain how the graphs would change if the wires were kept at a higher, but still
          constant, temperature.                                                           [1]
    c   Deduce how the resistance of a wire made of pure iron would change if both the
        diameter and length were doubled.                                                  [3]

# 13 Practical circuits

## Objectives

After studying this chapter, you should be able to:

☐ explain the effects of internal resistance on terminal p.d. and power output of a source of e.m.f.

☐ explain the use of potential divider circuits

☐ solve problems involving the potentiometer as a means of comparing voltages

## The first electrical cell – an historical mystery

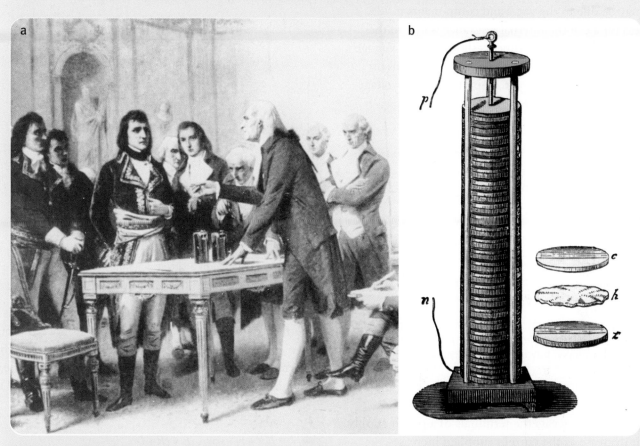

**Figure 13.1 a** Alessandro Volta demonstrating his newly invented pile (battery) to the French Emperor Napoleon. **b** Volta's pile, showing (top to bottom) discs of copper, wet felt and zinc.

The Italian Alessandro Volta (Figure **13.1a**) is generally credited with inventing the first battery. He devised it after his friend and rival Luigi Galvani had shown that a (dead) frog's leg could be made to twitch if an electrically charged plate was connected to it. Volta's battery consisted of alternate discs of copper and zinc, separated by felt soaked in brine – see Figure **13.1b**.

However, there is evidence that earlier technologists may have beaten him by over 1000 years. In 1936 a small pot was discovered during an archaeological dig near Baghdad. The pot was sealed with pitch, and inside the pot there was a copper cylinder surrounding an iron rod. When filled with an acid, perhaps vinegar, a potential difference of around 1.5 volts can be produced between the copper and the iron.

It has been suggested that this battery might have been used to electroplate metal objects with gold. So did Volta really invent the battery, or did he just rekindle an art that had been lost for more than a millennium?

# Internal resistance

You will be familiar with the idea that, when you use a power supply or other source of e.m.f., you cannot assume that it is providing you with the exact voltage across its terminals as suggested by the value of its e.m.f. There are several reasons for this. For example, the supply may not be made to a high degree of precision, batteries become flat, and so on. However, there is a more important factor, which is that all sources of e.m.f. have an **internal resistance**. For a power supply, this may be due to the wires and components inside, whereas for a cell the internal resistance is due to the chemicals within it. Experiments show that the voltage across the terminals of the power supply depends on the circuit of which it is part. In particular, the voltage across the power supply terminals decreases if it is required to supply more current.

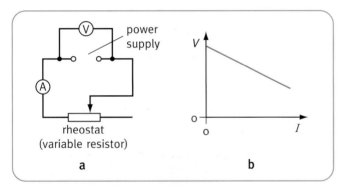

**Figure 13.2 a** A circuit for determining the e.m.f. and internal resistance of a supply; **b** typical form of results.

Figure **13.2** shows a circuit you can use to investigate this effect, and a sketch graph showing how the voltage across the terminals of a power supply might decrease as the current supplied increases.

The charges moving round a circuit have to pass through the external components **and** through the internal resistance of the power supply. These charges gain electrical energy from the power supply. This energy is lost as heat as the charges pass through the external components and through the internal resistance of the power supply. Power supplies and batteries get warm when they are being used. (Try using a cell to light a small torch bulb; feel the cell before connecting to the bulb, and then feel it again after the bulb has been lit for about 15 seconds.)

The reason for this heating effect is that some of the electrical potential energy of the charges is transformed to internal energy as they do work against the internal resistance of the cell.

It can often help to solve problems if we show the internal resistance $r$ of a source of e.m.f. explicitly in circuit diagrams (Figure **13.3**). Here, we are representing a cell as if it were a 'perfect' cell of e.m.f. $E$, together with a separate resistor of resistance $r$. The dashed line enclosing $E$ and $r$ represents the fact that these two are, in fact, a single component.

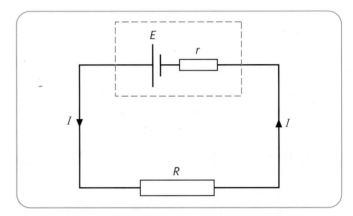

**Figure 13.3** It can be helpful to show the internal resistance $r$ of a cell (or a supply) in a circuit diagram.

Now we can determine the current when this cell is connected to an external resistor of resistance $R$. You can see that $R$ and $r$ are in series with each other. The current $I$ is the same for both of these resistors. The combined resistance of the circuit is thus $R + r$, and we can write:

$$E = I(R + r) \quad \text{or} \quad E = IR + Ir$$

We cannot measure the e.m.f. $E$ of the cell directly, because we can only connect a voltmeter across its terminals. This **terminal p.d.** $V$ across the cell is always the same as the p.d. across the external resistor. Therefore, we have:

$$V = IR$$

This will be less than the e.m.f. $E$ by an amount $Ir$. The quantity $Ir$ is the potential difference across the internal resistor and is referred to as the **lost volts**. If we combine these two equations, we get:

$V = E - Ir$

or

terminal p.d. = e.m.f. – 'lost volts'

The 'lost volts' indicates the energy transferred to the internal resistance of the supply. If you short-circuit a battery with a piece of wire, a large current will flow, and the battery will get warm as energy is transferred within it. This is also why you may damage a power supply by trying to make it supply a larger current than it is designed to give.

## Test yourself

**1** A battery of e.m.f. 5.0 V and internal resistance 2.0 Ω is connected to an 8.0 Ω resistor. Draw a circuit diagram and calculate the current in the circuit.

**2** **a** Calculate the current in each circuit in Figure 13.4.
**b** Calculate also the 'lost volts' for each cell and the terminal p.d.

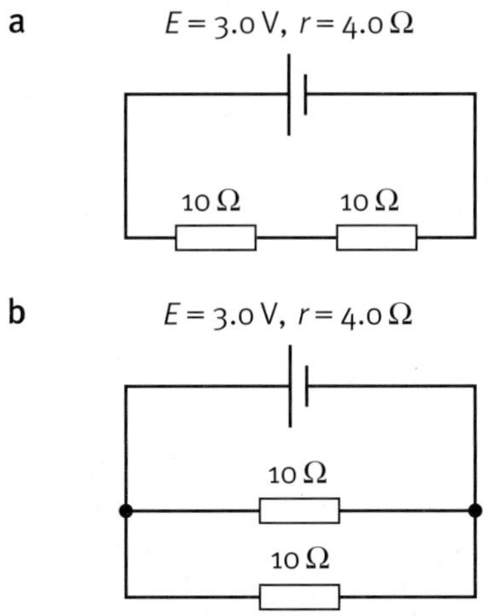


**Figure 13.4** For Test yourself Q 2.

**3** Four identical cells, each of e.m.f. 1.5 V and internal resistance 0.10 Ω, are connected in series. A lamp of resistance 2.0 Ω is connected across the four cells. Calculate the current in the lamp.

## Determining e.m.f. and internal resistance

You can get a good idea of the e.m.f. of an isolated power supply or a battery by connecting a digital voltmeter across it. A digital voltmeter has a very high resistance (~117 Ω), so only a tiny current will pass through it. The 'lost volts' will then only be a tiny fraction of the e.m.f. If you want to determine the internal resistance $r$ as well as the e.m.f. $E$, you need to use a circuit like that shown in Figure **13.2**. When the variable resistor is altered, the current in the circuit changes, and measurements can be recorded of the circuit current $I$ and terminal p.d. $V$. The internal resistance $r$ can be found from a graph of $V$ against $I$ (Figure **13.5**).

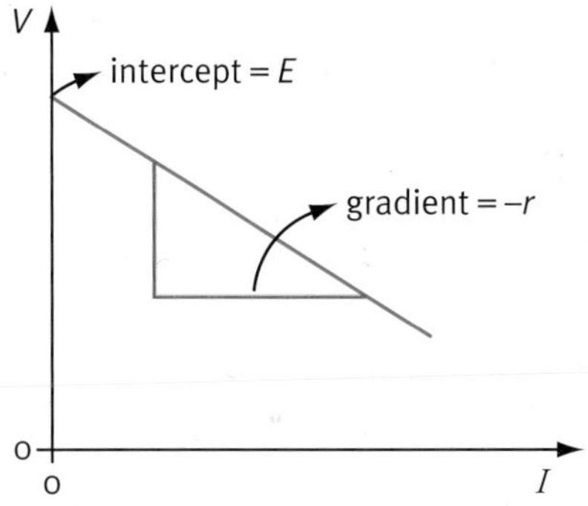


**Figure 13.5** $E$ and $r$ can be found from this graph.

Compare the equation $V = E - Ir$ with the equation of a straight line $y = mx + c$. By plotting $V$ on the $y$-axis and $I$ on the $x$-axis, a straight line should result. The intercept on the $y$-axis is $E$, and the gradient is $-r$.

## Worked example

**1** There is a current of 0.40 A when a battery of e.m.f. 6.0 V is connected to a resistor of 13.5 Ω. Calculate the internal resistance of the cell.

**Step 1** Substitute values from the question in the equation for e.m.f.:

$E = 6.0\,\text{V},\ I = 0.40\,\text{A},\ R = 13.5\,\Omega$

$E = IR + Ir$

*continued* ···›

$$6.0 = 0.40 \times 13.5 + 0.40 \times r$$
$$= 5.4 + 0.40r$$

**Step 2** Rearrange the equation to make $r$ the subject and solve:

$$6.0 - 5.4 = 0.40r$$

$$0.60 = 0.40r$$

$$r = \frac{0.60}{0.40} = 1.5\,\Omega$$

## Test yourself

4 When a high-resistance voltmeter is placed across an isolated battery, its reading is 3.0 V. When a 10 Ω resistor is connected across the terminals of the battery, the voltmeter reading drops to 2.8 V. Use this information to determine the internal resistance of the battery.

5 The results of an experiment to determine the e.m.f. $E$ and internal resistance $r$ for a power supply are shown in the Table 13.1. Plot a suitable graph and use it to find $E$ and $r$.

| $V/V$ | 1.43 | 1.33 | 1.18 | 1.10 | 0.98 |
|-------|------|------|------|------|------|
| $I/A$ | 0.10 | 0.30 | 0.60 | 0.75 | 1.00 |

**Table 13.1** Results for Test yourself Q 5.

## The effects of internal resistance

You cannot ignore the effects of internal resistance. Consider a battery of e.m.f. 3.0 V and of internal resistance 1.0 Ω. The **maximum current** that can be drawn from this battery is when its terminals are shorted-out. (The external resistance $R \approx 0$.) The maximum current is given by:

$$\text{maximum current} = \frac{E}{r} = \frac{3.0}{1.0} = 3.0\,\text{A}$$

The **terminal p.d.** of the battery depends on the resistance of the external resistor. For an external resistor of resistance 1.0 Ω, the terminal p.d. is 1.5 V – half of the e.m.f. The terminal p.d. approaches the value of the e.m.f. when the external resistance $R$ is very much greater than the internal resistance of the battery. For

example, a resistor of resistance 1000 Ω connected to the battery gives a terminal p.d. of 2.997 V. This is almost equal to the e.m.f. of the battery. The more current a battery supplies, the more its terminal p.d. will decrease. An example of this can be seen if a driver tries to start a car with the headlamps on. The starter motor requires a large current from the battery, the battery's terminal p.d. drops, and the headlamps dim.

## Test yourself

6 A car battery has an e.m.f. of 12 V and an internal resistance of 0.04 Ω. The starter motor draws a current of 100 A.
   a Calculate the terminal p.d. of the battery when the starter motor is in operation.
   b Each headlamp is rated as '12 V, 36 W'. Calculate the resistance of a headlamp.
   c To what value will the power output of each headlamp decrease when the starter motor is in operation? (Assume that the resistance of the headlamp remains constant.)

# Potential dividers

How can we get an output of 3.0 V from a battery of e.m.f. 6.0 V? Sometimes we want to use only part of the e.m.f. of a supply. To do this, we use an arrangement of resistors called a **potential divider** circuit.

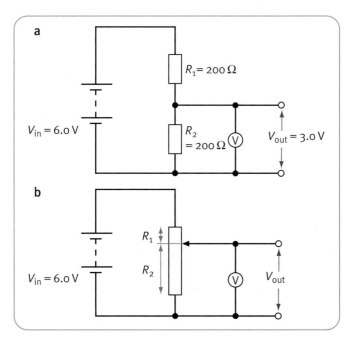

**Figure 13.6** Two potential divider circuits.

Figure **13.6** shows two potential divider circuits, each connected across a battery of e.m.f. 6.0 V and of negligible internal resistance. The high-resistance voltmeter measures the voltage across the resistor of resistance $R_2$. We refer to this voltage as the output voltage $V_{out}$ of the circuit. The first circuit, **a**, consists of two resistors of values $R_1$ and $R_2$. The voltage across the resistor of resistance $R_2$ is half of the 6.0 V of the battery. The second potential divider, **b**, is more useful. It consists of a single variable resistor. By moving the sliding contact, we can achieve any value of $V_{out}$ between 0.0 V (slider at the bottom) and 6.0 V (slider at the top).

The output voltage $V_{out}$ depends on the relative values of $R_1$ and $R_2$. You can calculate the value of $V_{out}$ using the following **potential divider equation**:

$$V_{out} = \left( \frac{R_2}{R_1 + R_2} \right) \times V_{in}$$

In this equation, $V_{in}$ is the total voltage across the two resistors.

## Test yourself

7 Determine the range for $V_{out}$ for the circuit in Figure **13.7** as the variable resistor $R_2$ is adjusted over its full range from 0 Ω to 40 Ω. (Assume the supply of e.m.f. 10 V has negligible internal resistance.)

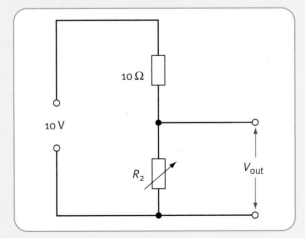

**Figure 13.7** For Test yourself Q 7.

## Potential dividers in use

Potential divider circuits are often used in electronic circuits. They are useful when a sensor is connected to a processing circuit. Suitable sensors include thermistors and **light-dependent resistors** (Figure **13.8**).

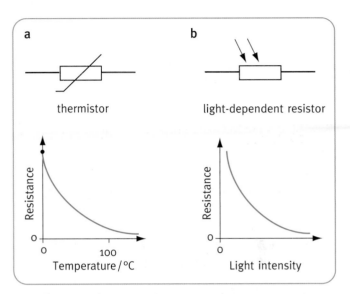

**Figure 13.8** Two components with variable resistances: **a** the thermistor's resistance changes with temperature; **b** the light-dependent resistor's resistance depends on the intensity of light.

These can be used as sensors because:

- the resistance of a negative temperature coefficient (NTC) thermistor **decreases** as its temperature **increases**
- the resistance of a light-dependent resistor (LDR) **decreases** as the incident intensity of light **increases**.

This means that a thermistor can be used in a potential divider circuit to provide an output voltage $V_{out}$ which depends on the temperature. A light-dependent resistor can be used in a potential divider circuit to provide an output voltage $V_{out}$ which depends on the intensity of light.

Figure **13.9** shows how a sensor can be used in a potential divider circuit. Here, a thermistor is being used to detect temperature, perhaps the temperature of a fish tank. If the temperature rises, the resistance of the thermistor decreases and the output voltage $V_{out}$ increases. If the output voltage $V_{out}$ is across the thermistor, as shown in Figure **13.9b**, it will decrease as the temperature rises. By changing the setting of the variable resistor $R_2$, you can control the range over which $V_{out}$ varies. This would allow you to set the temperature at which a heater operates, for example.

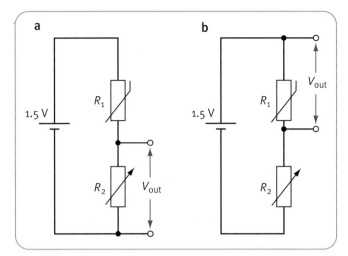

**Figure 13.9** Using a thermistor in a potential divider circuit. The output voltage $V_{out}$ may be **a** across the variable resistor, or **b** across the thermistor.

When designing a practical circuit like this, it is necessary to know how the voltage output depends on the temperature. You can investigate the voltage against temperature characteristics of such a circuit using a datalogger (Figure **13.10**). The temperature probe of the datalogger records the temperature of the water bath and the second input to the datalogger records the voltage output of the potential divider circuit. The temperature can be raised rapidly by pouring amounts of water into the water bath. The datalogger then records both temperature and voltage and the computer gives a display of the voltage against temperature. Dataloggers are very good at processing the collected data.

**Figure 13.10** Using a datalogger to investigate the characteristics of a thermistor in a potential divider circuit. During the experiment, the screen shows how temperature and output voltage change with time. After the experiment, the same data can be displayed as a graph of p.d. against temperature.

Potential divider circuits are especially useful in circuits with very small currents but where voltages are important. Electronic devices such as transistors and integrated circuits draw only very small currents, so potential dividers are very useful where these devices are used. Where large currents are involved, because there will be some current through both $R_1$ and $R_2$ (Figure **13.6**), there will be wasted power in the resistors of the potential divider circuit.

## Test yourself

8 An NTC thermistor is used in the circuit shown in Figure **13.11**. The supply has an e.m.f. of 10 V and negligible internal resistance. The resistance of the thermistor changes from $20\,k\Omega$ at 20 °C to $100\,\Omega$ at 60 °C. Calculate the output voltage $V_{out}$ at these two temperatures.

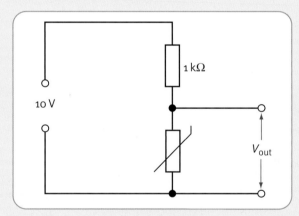

**Figure 13.11** Thermistor used in a potential divider circuit. For Test yourself Q **8** and Q **9**.

9 The thermistor in Figure **13.11** is replaced with a light-dependent resistor (LDR). Explain whether the output voltage $V_{out}$ will increase or decrease when a bright light is shone on to the LDR.

10 The light-dependent resistor (LDR) in Figure **13.12** has a resistance of $300\,\Omega$ in full sunlight and $1\,M\Omega$ in darkness. What values will the output voltage $V_{out}$ have in these two conditions?

*continued ⋯⋗*

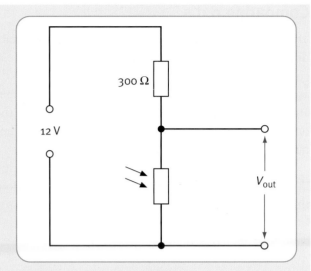

**Figure 13.12** For Test yourself Q **10.**

**11** A potential divider circuit is required which will give an output voltage that increases as the temperature increases. A thermistor is to be used whose resistance decreases as the temperature increases. Draw a suitable circuit for the potential divider, showing the connections for the output voltage.

# Potentiometer circuits

A **potentiometer** is a device used for comparing potential differences. For example, it can be used to measure the e.m.f. of a cell, provided you already have a source whose e.m.f. is known accurately. As we will see, a potentiometer can be thought of as a type of potential divider circuit.

A potentiometer consists of a metre length of resistance wire stretched horizontally between two points. In Figure **13.13**, the ends of the wire are labelled A and B. A **driver cell** is connected across the length of wire. Suppose this cell has an e.m.f. $E_o$ of 2.0 V. We can then say that point A is at a voltage of 2.0 V, B is at 0 V, and the midpoint of the wire is at 1.0 V. In other words, the voltage decreases steadily along the length of the wire.

Now, suppose we wish to measure the e.m.f. $E_X$ of cell X. This must have a value less than that of the driver cell. The positive terminal of cell X is connected to point A. (Note that both cells have their positive terminals connected to A.) A lead from the negative terminal is connected to a sensitive galvanometer (e.g.

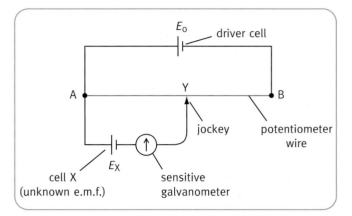

**Figure 13.13** A potentiometer connected to measure the e.m.f. of cell X.

a microammeter), and a lead from the other terminal of the galvanometer ends with a metal **jockey**. This is a simple connecting device with a very sharp edge that allows very precise positioning on the wire.

If the jockey is touched onto the metre wire close to point A, the galvanometer needle will deflect in one direction. If the jockey is touched close to B, the galvanometer needle will deflect in the opposite direction. Clearly there must be some point Y along the wire which, when touched by the jockey, gives zero deflection – the needle moves neither to the left nor the right.

In finding this position, the jockey must be touched gently and briefly onto the metre wire; the deflection of the galvanometer shows whether the jockey is too far to the left or right. It is important not to slide the jockey along the potentiometer wire as this may scrape its surface, making it non-uniform so that the voltage does not vary uniformly along its length.

When the jockey is positioned at Y, the galvanometer gives zero deflection showing that there is no current through it. This can only happen if the potential difference across the length of wire AY is equal to the e.m.f. of the cell. We can say that the potentiometer is balanced. If the balance point was exactly half-way along the wire, we would be able to say that the e.m.f. of X was half that of the driver cell.

To calculate the unknown e.m.f. $E_X$ we measure the length AY. Then we have:

$$E_X = \frac{AY}{AB} \times E_o$$

where $E_o$ is the e.m.f. of the driver cell.

The potentiometer can be thought of as a potential divider because the point of contact Y divides the resistance wire into two parts, equivalent to the two resistors of a potential divider.

## Comparing e.m.f.s with a potentiometer

When a potentiometer is balanced, no current flows from the cell being investigated. This means that its terminal p.d. is equal to its e.m.f.; we do not have to worry about any 'lost volts'. This is a great advantage that a potentiometer has over a voltmeter, which must draw a small current in order to work.

However, there is a problem: the driver cell is supplying current to the potentiometer, and so the p.d. between A and B will be less than the e.m.f. of the driver cell (some volts are lost because of its internal resistance). To overcome this problem, we use the potentiometer to compare p.d.s. Suppose we have two cells whose e.m.f.s $E_X$ and $E_Y$ we want to compare. Each is connected in turn to the potentiometer, giving balance points at C and D – see Figure **13.14**. (In the diagram, you can see immediately that $E_Y$ must be greater than $E_X$ because D is further to the right than C.)

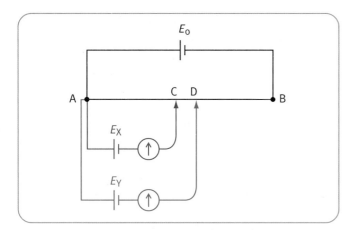

**Figure 13.14** Comparing two e.m.f.s using a potentiometer.

The ratio of the e.m.f.s of the two cells will be equal to the ratio of the two lengths AC and AD:

$$\frac{E_X}{E_Y} = \frac{AC}{AD}$$

If one of the cells used has an accurately known e.m.f., the other can be calculated with the same degree of accuracy.

## Comparing p.d.s

The same technique can be used to compare potential differences. For example, two resistors could be connected in series with a cell (Figure **13.15**). The p.d. across one resistor is first connected to the potentiometer and the balance length found. This is repeated with the other resistor and the new balance point is found. The ratio of the lengths is the ratio of the p.d.s.

Since both resistors have the same current flowing through them, the ratio of the p.d.s is also the ratio of their resistances.

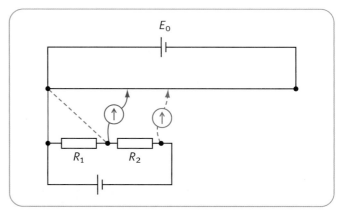

**Figure 13.15** Comparing two potential differences using a potentiometer.

# Summary

- [ ] A source of e.m.f., such as a battery, has an internal resistance. We can think of the source as having an internal resistance $r$ in series with an e.m.f. $E$.
- [ ] The terminal p.d. of a source of e.m.f. is less than the e.m.f. because of 'lost volts' across the internal resistor:

    terminal p.d. = e.m.f. – 'lost volts'

    $V = E - Ir$

- [ ] A potential divider circuit consists of two or more resistors connected in series to a supply. The output voltage $V_{out}$ across the resistor of resistance $R_2$ is given by:

$$V_{out} = \left( \frac{R_2}{R_1 + R_2} \right) V_{in}$$

- [ ] The resistance of a light-dependent resistor (LDR) decreases as the intensity of light falling on it increases. The resistance of a negative temperature coefficient (NTC) thermistor decreases as its temperature increases.
- [ ] Thermistors and light-dependent resistors can be used in potential divider circuits to provide output voltages that are dependent on temperature and light intensity, respectively.
- [ ] A potentiometer can be used to compare potential differences.

# End-of-chapter questions

1   A single cell of e.m.f. 1.5 V is connected across a $0.30\,\Omega$ resistor. The current in the circuit is 2.5 A.
   **a** Calculate the terminal p.d. and explain why it is not equal to the e.m.f. of the cell.
   **b** Show that the internal resistance $r$ of the cell is $0.30\,\Omega$.
   **c** It is suggested that the power dissipated in the external resistor is a maximum when its resistance $R$ is equal to the internal resistance $r$ of the cell.
     **i** Calculate the power dissipated when $R = r$.
     **ii** Show that the power dissipated when $R = 0.50\,\Omega$ and $R = 0.20\,\Omega$ is less than that dissipated when $R = r$, as the statement above suggests.

2   In order to switch on a heater when the temperature falls below a set value a potential divider is connected to a switching circuit. When the input voltage to the switching circuit falls below 0.5 V it switches the heater on.
   **a** Copy Figure **13.16** and add a suitable potential divider circuit to trigger the switching circuit.

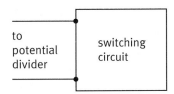

**Figure 13.16** For End-of-chapter Q 3.

   **b** Explain how the operator could lower the temperature at which the heater is switched on.

**3** Figure **13.17** shows a circuit used to monitor the variation of light intensity in a room.

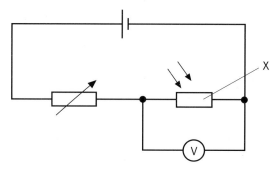

**Figure 13.17** For End-of-chapter Q 2.

    **a** Identify the component X and describe how the circuit works.
    **b** Suggest the reason for including the variable resistor in the circuit.

**4** A student is asked to compare the e.m.f.s of a standard cell and a test cell. He sets up the circuit shown in Figure **13.18** using the test cell.

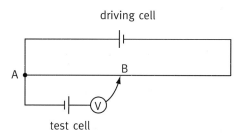

**Figure 13.18** For End-of-chapter Q 4.

    **a**  **i** Explain why he is unable to find a balance point and state the change he must make in order to achieve balance.
       **ii** State how he would recognise the 'balance point'.
    **b** He achieves balance when the distance AB is 22.5 cm. He repeats the experiment with the standard cell of e.m.f. of 1.434 V. The balance point using this cell is at 34.6 cm. Calculate the e.m.f. of the test cell.

# Exam-style questions

**1**  **a** Explain what is meant by the **internal resistance** of a cell.                                      [2]
    **b** When a dry cell is connected in series with a resistor of $2.00\,\Omega$ there is a current of $0.625\,A$. If a second resistor of $2.00\,\Omega$ is put in series with the first, the current falls to $0.341\,A$. Calculate:
       **i** the internal resistance of the cell                                            [3]
       **ii** the e.m.f. of the cell.                                                          [1]
    **c** A car battery needs to supply a current of $200\,A$ to turn over the starter motor. Explain why a battery made of a series of dry cells would not be suitable for a car battery.     [2]

**2**  **a**  State what is meant by the term **e.m.f. of a cell**. [2]

A student connects a high-resistance voltmeter across the terminals of a battery and observes a reading of 8.94 V. He then connects a 12 Ω resistor across the terminals and finds that the potential difference falls to 8.40 V.

**b**  Explain why the measured voltage falls. [2]

**c  i**  Calculate the current in the circuit. [2]

    **ii**  Calculate the internal resistance of the cell. [2]

    **iii**  State any assumptions you made in your calculations. [1]

**3**  The diagram shows two circuits which could be used to act as a dimmer switch for a lamp.

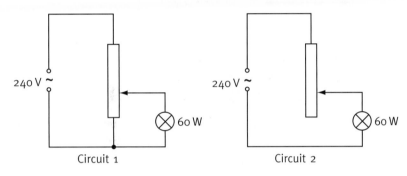

        Circuit 1                     Circuit 2

**a**  Explain **one** advantage circuit 1 has over circuit 2. [2]

**b**  One problem with circuit 1 is that there is always a current in the resistor. Explain how this problem could be rectified. [2]

**c  i**  The lamp is rated at 60 W at 240 V. Calculate the resistance of the lamp filament at its normal operating temperature. [2]

    **ii**  State and explain how the resistance of the filament at room temperature would compare with the value calculated in **c i**. [2]

**4**  The diagram shows a potential divider. The battery has negligible internal resistance and the voltmeter has infinite resistance.

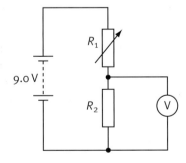

**a**  State and explain how the reading on the voltmeter will change when the resistance of the variable resistor is increased. [2]

**b**  Resistor $R_2$ has a resistance of 470 Ω. Calculate the value of the variable resistor when the reading on the voltmeter is 2.0 V. [2]

**c** The voltmeter is now replaced with one of resistance $2\,k\Omega$. Calculate the reading on this voltmeter. [2]

**d** $R_2$ is replaced with a light-dependent resistor. Explain how the reading on the voltmeter changes as light levels are reduced. [2]

5   The diagram shows a potentiometer circuit.

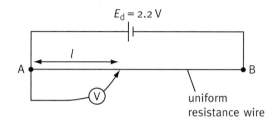

**a  i** Sketch a graph of the reading on the voltmeter against $l$ as the jockey is moved from point A to point B. [2]

   **ii** State the readings on the voltmeter when the jockey is connected to A and when it is connected to B. (You may assume that the driver cell has negligible internal resistance.) [1]

**b** Draw a circuit diagram to show how the potentiometer could be used to compare the e.m.f.s of two batteries. [3]

**c** When a pair of $4\,\Omega$ resistors are connected in series with a battery, there is a current of $0.60\,A$ current through the battery. When the same two resistors are connected in parallel and then connected across the battery, there is a current of $1.50\,A$ through it. Calculate the e.m.f. and the internal resistance of the battery. [4]

## Objectives

After studying this chapter, you should be able to:

- [ ] describe the motion of transverse and longitudinal waves, including polarised waves
- [ ] describe waves in terms of their wavelength, amplitude, frequency, speed and intensity
- [ ] determine the frequency of sound waves using a cathode-ray oscilloscope
- [ ] state the wavelengths of the principal radiations of the electromagnetic spectrum

## Vibrations making waves

The wind blowing across the surface of the sea produces waves. The surface of the water starts to move up and down, and these vibrations spread outwards – big waves may travel thousands of kilometres across the ocean before they break on a beach (Figure 14.1).

**Figure 14.1** This photograph shows a wave breaking on the shore and dissipating the energy it has drawn from the wind in its journey across the ocean. The two scientists are 'storm chasers' who are recording the waves produced by a hurricane in the Gulf of Mexico.

## Describing waves

When you pluck the string of a guitar, it vibrates. The vibrations create a wave in the air which we call sound. In fact, all vibrations produce **waves** of one type or another (Figure 14.2). Waves that move through a material (or a vacuum) are called **progressive waves**. A progressive wave transfers energy from one position to another.

At the seaside, a wave is what we see on the surface of the sea. The water moves around and a wave travels across the surface. In physics, we extend the idea of a wave to describe many other phenomena, including light, sound, etc. We do this by imagining an idealised wave, as shown in Figure 14.3 – you will never see such a perfect wave on the sea!

Figure 14.3 illustrates the following important definitions about waves and wave motion.

- The distance of a point on the wave from its undisturbed position or equilibrium position is called the **displacement** $x$.

**Figure 14.2** Radio telescopes detect radio waves from distant stars and galaxies; a rainbow is an effect caused by the reflection and refraction of light waves by water droplets in the atmosphere.

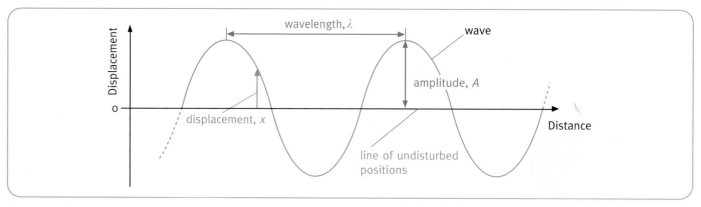

Figure 14.3 A displacement–distance graph illustrating the terms displacement, amplitude and wavelength.

- The maximum displacement of any point on the wave from its undisturbed position is called the **amplitude** $A$. Amplitude is measured in metres. The greater the amplitude of the wave, the louder the sound or the rougher the sea!
- The distance from any point on a wave to the next exactly similar point (e.g. crest to crest) is called the **wavelength** $\lambda$ (the Greek letter lambda). Wavelength is usually measured in metres.
- The time taken for one complete oscillation of a point in a wave is called the **period** $T$. It is the time taken for a point to move from one particular position and return to that same position, moving in the same direction. It is measured in seconds (s).
- The number of oscillations per unit time of a point in a wave is called its **frequency** $f$. For sound waves, the higher the frequency of a musical note, the higher is its pitch. Frequency is measured in hertz (Hz), where 1 Hz = one oscillation per second (1 kHz = $10^3$ Hz and 1 MHz = $10^6$ Hz). The frequency $f$ of a wave is the reciprocal of the period $T$:

$$f = \frac{1}{T}$$

Waves are called **mechanical waves** if they need a substance (medium) through which to travel. Sound is one example of such a wave. Other cases are waves on strings, seismic waves and water waves (Figure 14.4). Some properties of these waves are given on page **201** in Table **14.1**.

Figure 14.4 The impact of a droplet on the surface of a liquid creates a vibration, which in turn gives rise to waves on the surface.

## Test yourself

1 Determine the wavelength and amplitude of each of the two waves shown in Figure **14.5**.

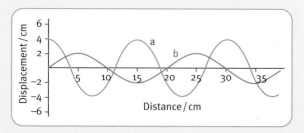

Figure 14.5 Two waves – for Test yourself Q **1**.

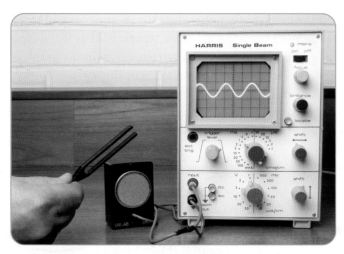

**Figure 14.6** Measuring the frequency of sound waves from a tuning fork.

## Measuring frequency

You can measure the frequency of sound waves using a cathode-ray oscilloscope (c.r.o.). Figure **14.6** shows how.

A microphone is connected to the input of the c.r.o. Sound waves are captured by the microphone and converted into a varying voltage which has the same frequency as the sound waves. This voltage is displayed on the c.r.o. screen.

It is best to think of a c.r.o. as a voltmeter which is capable of displaying a rapidly varying voltage. To do this, its spot moves across the screen at a steady speed, set by the time-base control. At the same time, the spot moves up and down according to the voltage of the input.

Hence the display on the screen is a graph of the varying voltage, with time on the (horizontal) *x*-axis. If we know the horizontal scale, we can determine the period and hence the frequency of the sound wave. Worked example **1** shows how to do this. (In Chapter **16** we will look at one method of measuring the wavelength of sound waves.)

### Worked example

1   Figure **14.7** shows the trace on an oscilloscope screen when sound waves are detected by a microphone. This time-base is set at $1\,\text{ms}\,\text{div}^{-1}$. Determine the frequency of the sound waves.

*continued* ┅┅⇢

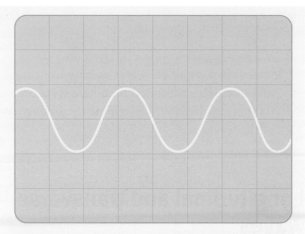

**Figure 14.7** A c.r.o. trace – what is the frequency of these waves?

**Step 1** Determine the period of the waves on the screen, in scale divisions. From Figure **14.7**, you can see that one complete wave occupies three scale divisions.

   period $T = 3.0\,\text{div}$

**Step 2** Determine the time interval represented by each scale division. The time-base control is set at $1\,\text{ms}\,\text{div}^{-1}$, and the variable control is set to the calibrated position. (If the variable control were set to an intermediate position, we would not know the calibration accurately.)

   scale factor $= 1.0\,\text{ms}\,\text{div}^{-1}$

**Step 3** Convert the period in divisions to ms:

   period $T = 3.0\,\text{div} \times 1\,\text{ms}\,\text{div}^{-1}$
   $= 3.0\,\text{ms} = 3.0 \times 10^{-3}\,\text{s}$

Notice how div and $\text{div}^{-1}$ cancel out.

**Step 4** Calculate the frequency from the period:

   frequency $f = \dfrac{1}{T} = \dfrac{1}{3.0 \times 10^{-3}} = 333\,\text{Hz}$

So the wave frequency is approximately $330\,\text{Hz}$.

# Longitudinal and transverse waves

There are two distinct types of wave, **longitudinal** and **transverse**. Both can be demonstrated using a slinky spring lying along a bench.

Push the end of the spring back and forth; the segments of the spring become compressed and then stretched out, along the length of the spring. Wave pulses run along the spring. These are longitudinal waves.

Waggle the end of the slinky spring from side to side. The segments of the spring move from side to side as the wave travels along the spring. These are transverse waves.

So the distinction between longitudinal and transverse waves is as follows.

- In longitudinal waves, the particles of the medium vibrate **parallel** to the direction of the wave velocity.
- In transverse waves, the particles of the medium vibrate at **right angles** to the direction of the wave velocity.

Sound waves are an example of a longitudinal wave. Light and all other electromagnetic waves are transverse waves. Waves in water are quite complex. Particles of the water may move both up and down and from side to side as a water wave travels through the water. You can investigate water waves in a ripple tank. There is more about this in Table 14.1 (page 201) and in Chapter 15.

## Representing waves

Figure 14.8 shows how we can represent longitudinal and transverse waves. The longitudinal wave shows how the material through which it is travelling is alternately compressed and expanded. This gives rise to high and low pressure regions respectively.

However, this is rather difficult to draw, so you will often see a longitudinal wave represented as if it were a sine wave. The displacement referred to in the graph is the displacement of the particles in the wave.

We can compare the **compressions** and **rarefactions** (or expansions) of the longitudinal wave with the peaks and troughs of the transverse wave.

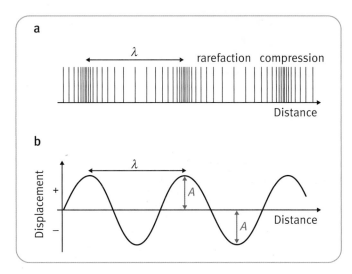

**Figure 14.8 a** Longitudinal waves and **b** transverse waves. $A$ = amplitude, $\lambda$ = wavelength.

## Phase and phase difference

All points along a wave have the same pattern of vibration. However, different points do not necessarily vibrate in step with one another. As one point on a stretched string vibrates up and down, the point next to it vibrates slightly out-of-step with it. We say that they vibrate out of phase with each other – there is a **phase difference** between them. This is the amount by which one oscillation leads or lags behind another.

Phase difference is measured in degrees.

As you can see from Figure 14.9, two points A and B, with a separation of one whole wavelength $\lambda$, vibrate in phase with each other. The phase difference between these two points is 360°. (You can also say it is 0°.) The phase difference between any other two points between A and B can have any value between 0° and 360°. A complete cycle of the wave is thought of as 360°. In Chapter 15 we will see what it means to say that two waves are 'in phase' or 'out of phase' with one another.

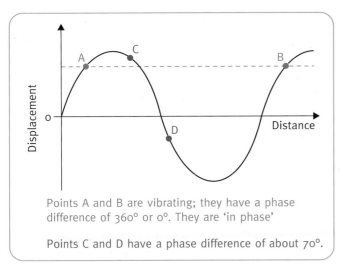

Points A and B are vibrating; they have a phase difference of 360° or 0°. They are 'in phase'

Points C and D have a phase difference of about 70°.

**Figure 14.9** Different points along a wave have different phases.

## Test yourself

3  Using axes of displacement and distance, sketch two waves A and B such that A has twice the wavelength and half the amplitude of B.

# Wave energy

It is important to realise that, for both types of mechanical wave, the particles that make up the material through which the wave is travelling do not move along – they only oscillate about a fixed point. It is **energy** that is transmitted by the wave. Each particle vibrates; as it does so, it pushes its neighbour, transferring energy to it. Then that particle pushes its neighbour, which pushes its neighbour. In this way, energy is transmitted from one particle to the next, to the next, and so on down the line.

# Intensity

The term **intensity** has a very precise meaning in physics. The intensity of a wave is defined as the rate of energy transmitted per unit area at right angles to the wave velocity.

$$\text{intensity} = \frac{\text{power}}{\text{cross-sectional area}}$$

Intensity is measured in watts per square metre ($\text{W m}^{-2}$). For example, when the Sun is directly overhead, the

intensity of its radiation is about $1.0\,\text{kW m}^{-2}$ (1 kilowatt per square metre). This means that energy arrives at the rate of about $1\,\text{kW}$ ($1000\,\text{J s}^{-1}$) on each square metre of the surface of the Earth. At the top of the atmosphere, the intensity of sunlight is greater, about $1.37\,\text{kW m}^{-2}$.

## Test yourself

4  A 100 W lamp emits electromagnetic radiation in all directions. Assuming the lamp to be a point source, calculate the intensity of the radiation:
   **a** at a distance of 1.0 m from the lamp
   **b** at a distance of 2.0 m from the lamp.

   Think of the area of a sphere at each of the two radii.

## Intensity and amplitude

The intensity of a wave generally decreases as it travels along. There are two reasons for this.

- The wave may 'spread out' (as in the example of light spreading out from a light bulb in Test yourself Q 4).
- The wave may be absorbed or scattered (as when light passes through the Earth's atmosphere).

As a wave spreads out, its amplitude decreases. This suggests that the intensity $I$ of a wave is related to its amplitude $A$. In fact, intensity is proportional to the square of the amplitude

$$\text{intensity} \propto \text{amplitude}^2$$

$$I \propto A^2$$

The relationship also implies that for a particular wave:

$$\frac{\text{intensity}}{\text{amplitude}^2} = \text{constant}$$

So, if one wave has **twice** the amplitude of another, it has **four** times the intensity. This means that it is carrying energy at four times the rate.

5 Waves from a source have an amplitude of
5.0 cm and an intensity of 400 W m$^{-2}$.
   a The amplitude of the waves is increased to
   10.0 cm. What is their intensity now?
   b The intensity of the waves is decreased to
   100 W m$^{-2}$. What is their amplitude?

# Wave speed

The speed with which energy is transmitted by a
wave is known as the wave speed $v$. This is measured
in m s$^{-1}$. The wave speed for sound in air at a pressure
of 10$^5$ Pa and a temperature of 0 °C is about
340 m s$^{-1}$, while for light in a vacuum it is almost
300 000 000 m s$^{-1}$.

## The wave equation

An important equation connecting the speed $v$ of a
wave with its frequency $f$ and wavelength $\lambda$ can be
determined as follows. We can find the speed of the
wave using:

$$\text{speed} = \frac{\text{distance}}{\text{time}}$$

But a wave will travel a distance of one whole
wavelength in a time equal to one period $T$. So:

$$\text{wave speed} = \frac{\text{wavelength}}{\text{period}}$$

## Shock waves

The energy carried by a wave can be considerable.
For example, the shock (seismic) waves from the
eruption of a volcano can cause serious structural
damage over a wide area. The energy carried in
such shock waves is of the order of 10$^{20}$ J!

Similarly, earthquakes, which are a mixture
of longitudinal and transverse waves, transmit
great amounts of energy from deep underground
up to the surface, often with devastating effects
(Figure 14.10).

Scientists produce small shock waves to help them
in their study of the Earth, for example in exploring
for underground resources (Figure 14.11). Most of
what we know about the internal structure of the
Earth, other planets, the Moon, and even the Sun,
has come from observations of shock waves moving
through these giant bodies.

Figure 14.10 The severe earthquake which struck Kashmir
in the North West province of Pakistan released vast
amounts of energy. Hundreds of buildings were destroyed
and roads washed away in the resulting landslips. Tens
of thousands of people were killed in Pakistan and many
more in neighbouring Indian Kashmir.

Figure 14.11 Machines like this send small shock waves
through the ground. The reflected waves are detected,
and the pattern of reflections shows up underground
features, such as layers of rock or trapped liquid. This
can help geologists to find new reserves of oil and other
natural resources.

or

$$v = \frac{\lambda}{T}$$

$$v = \left(\frac{1}{T}\right) \times \lambda$$

However, $f = \frac{1}{T}$ and so:

wave speed = frequency × wavelength

$$v = f \times \lambda$$

A numerical example may help to make this clear. Imagine a wave of frequency 5 Hz and wavelength 3 m going past you. In 1 s, five complete wave cycles, each of length 3 m, go past. So the total length of the waves going past in 1 s is 15 m. The distance covered by the wave in one second is its speed, therefore the speed of the wave is 15 m s⁻¹.

Clearly, for a given speed of wave, the greater the wavelength, the smaller the frequency and vice versa. The speed of sound in air is constant (for a given temperature and pressure). The wavelength of sound can be made smaller by increasing the frequency of the source of sound.

Table 14.1 gives typical values of speed ($v$), frequency ($f$) and wavelength ($\lambda$) for some mechanical waves. You can check for yourself that $v = f\lambda$ is satisfied.

## Worked example

2 Middle C on a piano tuned to concert pitch should have a frequency of 264 Hz (Figure 14.12). If the speed of sound is

*continued* ⋯⟩

330 m s⁻¹, calculate the wavelength of the sound produced when this key is played.

**Step 1** We use the above equation in slightly rewritten form:

$$\text{wavelength} = \frac{\text{speed}}{\text{frequency}}$$

**Step 2** Substituting the values for middle C we get:

$$\text{wavelength} = \frac{330}{264} = 1.25 \text{ m}$$

The human ear can detect sounds of frequencies between 20 Hz and 20 kHz, i.e. with wavelengths between 15 m and 15 mm.

Figure 14.12 Each string in a piano produces a different note.

## Test yourself

6 Sound is a mechanical wave that can be transmitted through a solid. Calculate the frequency of sound of wavelength 0.25 m that travels through steel at a speed of 5060 m s⁻¹.

*continued* ⋯⟩

| | Water waves in a ripple tank | Sound waves in air | Waves on a slinky spring |
|---|---|---|---|
| Speed / m s⁻¹ | about 0.12 | about 300 | about 1 |
| Frequency / Hz | about 6 | 20 to 20 000 (limits of human hearing) | about 2 |
| Wavelength / m | about 0.2 | 15 to 0.015 | about 0.5 |

Table 14.1 Speed ($v$), frequency ($f$) and wavelength ($\lambda$) data for some mechanical waves readily investigated in the laboratory.

7 A cello string vibrates with a frequency of 64 Hz. Calculate the speed of the transverse waves on the string given that their wavelength is 140 cm.

8 An oscillator is used to send waves along a stretched cord. Four complete wave cycles fit on a 20 cm length of the cord when the frequency of the oscillator is 30 Hz. For this wave, calculate:
a its wavelength
b its frequency
c its speed.

9 Copy and complete Table 14.2. (You may assume that the speed of radio waves is $3.0 \times 10^8 \, \mathrm{m\,s^{-1}}$.)

| Station | Wavelength / m | Frequency / MHz |
|---|---|---|
| Radio A (FM) | | 97.6 |
| Radio B (FM) | | 94.6 |
| Radio B (LW) | 1515 | |
| Radio C (MW) | 693 | |

Table 14.2 For Test yourself Q 9.

# Electromagnetic waves

You should be familiar with the idea that light is a region of the **electromagnetic spectrum**. It is not immediately obvious that light has any connection at all with electricity, magnetism and waves. These topics had been the subject of study by physicists for centuries before the connections between them became apparent.

An electric current always gives rise to a **magnetic field** (this is known as electromagnetism). A magnetic field is created by any **moving** charged particles such as electrons. Similarly, a changing magnetic field will induce a current in a nearby conductor. These observations led to the unification of the theories of electricity and magnetism by Michael Faraday in the mid-19th century. A vast technology based on the theories of electromagnetism developed rapidly, and continues to expand today (Figure **14.13**).

Faraday's studies were extended by James Clerk Maxwell. He produced mathematical equations that predicted that a changing electric or magnetic field would give rise to waves travelling through space. When he calculated the speed of these waves, it turned out to be the known speed of light. He concluded that light is a wave, known as an **electromagnetic wave**, that can travel through space (including a vacuum) as a disturbance of electric and magnetic fields.

Faraday had unified electricity and magnetism; now Maxwell had unified electromagnetism and light. In the 20th century, Abdus Salam (Figure **14.14**) managed to unify electromagnetic forces with the weak nuclear force, responsible for radioactive decay. Physicists continue to strive to

Figure 14.13 These telecommunications masts are situated 4500 metres above sea level in Ecuador. They transmit microwaves, a form of electromagnetic radiation, across the mountain range of the Andes.

Figure 14.14 Abdus Salam, the Pakistani physicist, won the 1979 Nobel Prize for Physics for his work on unification of the fundamental forces.

unify the big ideas of physics; you may occasionally hear talk of a **theory of everything**. This would not truly explain **everything**, but it would explain all known forces, as well as the existence of the various fundamental particles of matter.

# Electromagnetic radiation

By the end of the 19th century, several types of electromagnetic wave had been discovered:

• radio waves – these were discovered by Heinrich Hertz when he was investigating electrical sparks;
• infrared and ultraviolet waves – these lie beyond either end of the visible spectrum;
• X-rays – these were discovered by Wilhelm Röntgen and were produced when a beam of electrons collided with a metal target such as tungsten;
• γ-rays – these were discovered by Henri Becquerel when he was investigating radioactive substances.

We now regard all of these types of radiation as parts of the same electromagnetic spectrum, and we know that they can be produced in a variety of different ways.

## The speed of light

James Clerk Maxwell showed that the speed $c$ of electromagnetic radiation in a vacuum (free space) was independent of the frequency of the waves. In other words, all types of electromagnetic wave travel at the same speed in a vacuum. In the SI system of units, $c$ has the value:

$$c = 299\,792\,458\,\mathrm{m\,s^{-1}}$$

The approximate value for the speed of light in a vacuum (often used in calculations) is $3.0 \times 10^8\,\mathrm{m\,s^{-1}}$.

The wavelength $\lambda$ and frequency $f$ of the radiation are related by the equation:

$$c = f\lambda$$

When light travels from a vacuum into a material medium such as glass, its speed **decreases** but its frequency **remains the same**, and so we conclude that its wavelength must decrease. We often think of different forms of electromagnetic radiation as being characterised by their different wavelengths, but it is better to think of their different frequencies

as being their fundamental characteristic, since their wavelengths depend on the medium through which they are travelling.

**Test yourself**

**10** Red light of wavelength 700 nm in a vacuum travels into glass, where its speed decreases to $2.0 \times 10^8\,\mathrm{m\,s^{-1}}$. Determine:
  **a** the frequency of the light in a vacuum
  **b** its frequency and wavelength in the glass.

# Orders of magnitude

Table **14.3** shows the approximate ranges of wavelengths in a vacuum of the principal bands which make up the electromagnetic spectrum. This information is shown as a diagram in Figure **14.15** (see page **204**).

Here are some points to note:

• There are no clear divisions between the different ranges or bands in the spectrum. The divisions shown in Table **14.3** are somewhat arbitrary.
• The naming of subdivisions is also arbitrary. For example, microwaves are sometimes regarded as a subdivision of radio waves.
• The ranges of X-rays and γ-rays overlap. The distinction is that X-rays are produced when electrons decelerate rapidly or when they hit a target metal at high speeds. γ-rays are produced by nuclear reactions such as radioactive decay. There is no difference whatsoever in the radiation between an X-ray and a γ-ray of wavelength, say, $10^{-11}\,\mathrm{m}$.

| Radiation | Wavelength range / m |
|---|---|
| radio waves | $>10^6$ to $10^{-1}$ |
| microwaves | $10^{-1}$ to $10^{-3}$ |
| infrared | $10^{-3}$ to $7 \times 10^{-7}$ |
| visible | $7 \times 10^{-7}$ (red) to $4 \times 10^{-7}$ (violet) |
| ultraviolet | $4 \times 10^{-7}$ to $10^{-8}$ |
| X-rays | $10^{-8}$ to $10^{-13}$ |
| γ-rays | $10^{-10}$ to $10^{-16}$ |

Table **14.3** Wavelengths (in a vacuum) of the electromagnetic spectrum.

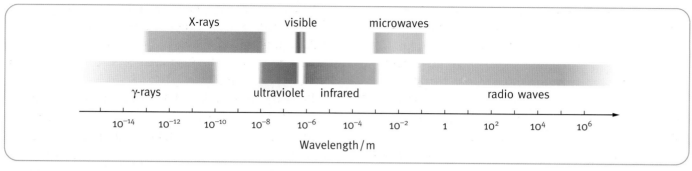

**Figure 14.15** Wavelengths of the electromagnetic spectrum. The boundaries between some regions are fuzzy.

# The nature of electromagnetic waves

An electromagnetic wave is a disturbance in the electric and magnetic fields in space. Figure 14.16 shows how we can represent such a wave. In this diagram, the wave is travelling from left to right.

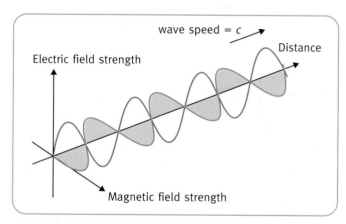

**Figure 14.16** An electromagnetic wave is a periodic variation in electric and magnetic fields.

The electric field is shown oscillating in the vertical plane. The magnetic field is shown oscillating in the horizontal plane. These are arbitrary choices; the point is that the two fields vary at right angles to each other, and also at right angles to the direction in which the wave is travelling. This shows that electromagnetic waves are transverse waves.

# Polarisation

**Polarisation** is a wave property which allows us to distinguish between transverse and longitudinal waves.
  Tie one end of a rubber rope to a post, get hold of the other end and pull the rope taut. If you move your

wrist up and down, a wave travels along the rope. The rope itself moves up and down vertically. Repeat the experiment, but this time move your wrist from side to side. Again a transverse wave is created, with bumps which move horizontally. Repeat again, this time moving your wrist diagonally. You have observed a characteristic of transverse waves: there are many different directions in which they can vibrate, all at right angles to the direction in which the wave travels. You cannot do this for a longitudinal wave because the oscillations are always parallel to the direction in which the wave travels.

The first wave you created on the rubber rope, by moving your wrist up and down, is said to be **vertically polarised**. The second was **horizontally polarised**. So the phenomenon of polarisation is something which distinguishes transverse waves from longitudinal ones. Only transverse waves can be polarised.

## Polarised light

Light can be shown to be a transverse wave by being polarised. Light consists of vibrations of electric and magnetic fields travelling through space. Light which is unpolarised (such as the light emitted by the Sun, or by a light bulb) has vibrations in all directions at right angles to the direction in which it is travelling.

When the light passes through a piece of Polaroid (a polarising filter), it becomes polarised. How does this work? Polaroid consists of long-chain molecules that absorb the energy from the oscillating electric field. If these molecules are arranged vertically, they absorb light waves which are polarised vertically, that is, light

waves whose electric field is oscillating up and down. Horizontally polarised light waves (whose electric field is oscillating from side to side) pass through unaffected (Figure **14.17a**). The light is now described as **plane polarised**.

Plane polarised light will be stopped by a second piece of Polaroid placed with its axis at 90° to the first, as shown in Figure **14.17b**. Polarisation can also be shown with other electromagnetic waves such as microwaves, radio and TV. The last of these can be demonstrated simply by rotating a set-top aerial and watching the effect on the picture.

You can show that a microwave transmitter used in the physics laboratory emits plane polarised microwaves. This can be done by rotating a metal grille between the transmitter and the receiver (Figure **14.18**). The metal rods of the grille behave very much like the long-chain molecules of a Polaroid.

The light we receive from the sky is sunlight which has been scattered by the atmosphere. This scattering polarises the light. We cannot see this, but many insects such as bees can, and perhaps some birds, too. This means that bees can tell the direction of the Sun even when it is overcast, and this helps them to navigate.

A good way to model the polarisation of scattered light in the atmosphere is to fill a transparent rectangular plastic tank with water and add a little milk to it (a few millilitres per litre should be sufficient). Shine a bright beam of light through the mixture (Figure **14.19**), and observe the polarisation at different points around the tank using a piece of Polaroid and a light meter.

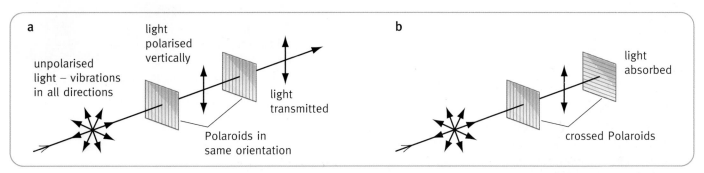

**Figure 14.17 a** Light, initially unpolarised, becomes vertically polarised after passing through the first Polaroid. **b** It is absorbed by a second Polaroid oriented at 90° to the first.

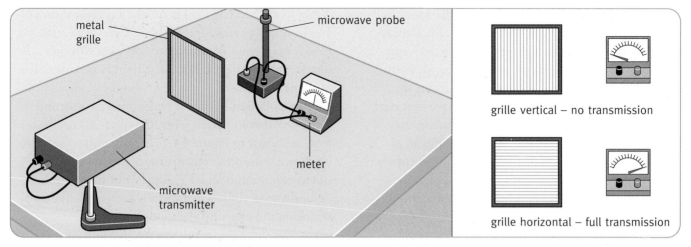

grille vertical – no transmission

grille horizontal – full transmission

**Figure 14.18** In one orientation, the metal grille blocks the microwaves; at 90°, it lets them through. This shows that the source produces polarised radiation. The microwave transmitter emits vertically plane polarised waves.

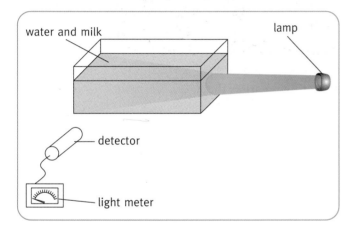

**Figure 14.19** A few drops of milk are mixed into water. The light is scattered by the tiny fat globules of the milk. Hold a light meter so that it detects scattered light coming from the side of the tank. Then place a Polaroid filter in front of the light meter and rotate it until you find the position at which it blocks the light.

## Effects that use polarisation of light

Some examples of effects which involve the polarisation of light are given below.

### Polaroid sunglasses

These reduce glare by one transmitting plane of polarisation of light waves only, so the amount of unpolarised light reaching the eyes is reduced. Light reflected from a shiny, level road or water surface is partially polarised in the horizontal plane, and the Polaroid in sunglasses is arranged to cut out this light (Figure **14.20**)

**Figure 14.20** A Polaroid filter can help in photography. By cutting out light reflected from the surface of the water, it allows us to see down to the seabed.

## Stresses in materials

When materials are stressed (for instance, when they form part of a structure such as a bridge), some parts may become more stressed than others. This can lead to unexpected failure of the structure. Engineers make models from transparent plastic; an example is shown in Figure **14.21**. If the model is viewed through a Polaroid, areas of stress concentration show up where the coloured bands are closest together.

## Liquid-crystal displays

The liquid-crystal displays of some calculators and laptop screens produce plane polarised light. You can investigate this effect by putting a piece of Polaroid over the display and rotating it.

**Figure 14.21** A plastic hook as seen through a polarising filter. The coloured pattern shows up places where stress is concentrated in the material.

# Summary

☐ Mechanical waves are produced by vibrating objects.

☐ A progressive wave carries energy from one place to another.

☐ Two points on a wave separated by a distance of one wavelength have a phase difference of 0° or 360°.

☐ There are two types of wave – longitudinal and transverse. Longitudinal waves have vibrations parallel to the direction in which the wave travels, whereas transverse waves have vibrations at right angles to the direction in which the wave travels. Surface water waves, waves on a string and light waves are all examples of transverse waves. Sound is a longitudinal wave.

☐ The frequency $f$ of a wave is related to its period $T$ by the equation:

$$f = \frac{1}{T}$$

☐ The frequency of a sound wave can be measured using a calibrated cathode-ray oscilloscope.

☐ The speed of all waves is given by the wave equation:

    wave speed = frequency × wavelength

$$v = f\lambda$$

- [ ] The intensity of a wave is defined as the wave power transmitted per unit area at right angles to the wave velocity. Hence intensity = power/cross-sectional area. Intensity has the unit $W\,m^{-2}$.
- [ ] The intensity $I$ of a wave is proportional to the square of the amplitude $A$ ($I \propto A^2$).
- [ ] All electromagnetic waves travel at the same speed of $3.0 \times 10^8\,m\,s^{-1}$ in a vacuum, but have different wavelengths and frequencies.
- [ ] The regions of the electromagnetic spectrum in order of increasing wavelength are: $\gamma$-rays, X-rays, ultraviolet, visible, infrared, microwaves and radio waves.
- [ ] Polarisation is a phenomenon which is only associated with transverse waves. A plane polarised wave has oscillations in only one plane.

# End-of-chapter questions

1  Figure 14.22 shows the screen of an oscilloscope. The time-base of the oscilloscope is set at $500\,\mu s\,div^{-1}$. Calculate the time period of the signal and hence its frequency.

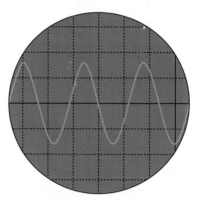

**Figure 14.22** For End-of-chapter Q 1.

2  **a**  State **two** main properties of electromagnetic waves.
   **b**  State **one** major difference between microwaves and radio waves.
   **c**  **i**  Estimate the wavelength in metres of X-rays.
       **ii**  Use your answer to **i** to determine the frequency of the X-rays.

3    a   Explain what is meant by **plane polarisation**.
     b   Name a type of wave that cannot be polarised. Explain your answer.
     c   A laser emits a plane polarised beam of light. A Polaroid (polarising filter) is placed at right angles to the laser beam and rotated. Describe how the transmitted intensity of laser light will change with the angle of rotation of the axis of the Polaroid.
     d   Other than using a Polaroid, state **two** examples of how light can be polarised.

4    Figure **14.23** shows a laboratory microwave transmitter T positioned directly opposite a microwave detector D, which is connected to a meter.

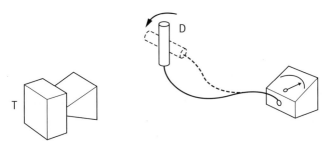

**Figure 14.23** For End-of-chapter Q 4.

Initially the meter shows a maximum reading. When the detector is rotated through 90° in a vertical plane as shown, the reading falls to zero.
   a   Explain why the meter reading falls.
   b   Predict what would happen to the meter reading if the detector is rotated a further 90°.
   c   State what the observations tell you about the nature of the microwaves.

# Exam-style questions

1    The diagram shows some air particles as a sound wave passes.

• • • • • •   • • • • • • • •   • • • •
P

   a   On a copy of the diagram, mark:
     i    a region of the wave which shows a compression – label it C.           [1]
     ii   a region of the wave which shows a rarefaction – label it R.         [1]
   b   Describe how the particle labelled P moves as the wave passes.          [2]
   c   The sound wave has a frequency of 240 Hz. Explain, in terms of the movement of an individual particle, what this means.          [2]
   d   The wave speed of the sound is $320\,\mathrm{m\,s^{-1}}$. Calculate the wavelength of the wave.          [2]

**2 a** Light is referred to as a type of electromagnetic wave. Explain what is meant by the term **electromagnetic wave.** [2]

**b i** Two stars emit radiation with the same power. Star A is twice as far from the Earth as star B. Explain how the intensities of the radiations compare to an observer on the Earth. [2]

**ii** State how the amplitudes of the two signals received by the observer compare. [2]

**c** The main signal from star A is in the ultraviolet region of the spectrum with a wavelength of $7.5 \times 10^{-8}$ m. Calculate the frequency of this radiation. [2]

**3** The diagram shows a loudspeaker producing a sound and a microphone connected to a cathode-ray oscilloscope.

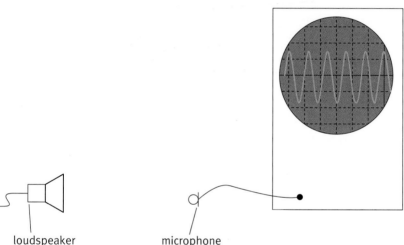

loudspeaker                    microphone

**a** Sound is described as a longitudinal wave. Explain how the trace on the oscilloscope relates to the movements of the air particles in the sound wave. [3]

**b** The time-base on the oscilloscope is set at $5\,\mathrm{ms\,div^{-1}}$. Calculate the frequency of the wave. [2]

**c** The wavelength of the wave is found to be 1.98 m. Calculate the speed of the wave. [2]

4   A motorist is driving along a wet road and is dazzled by the reflection of the sun from
    the road. She uses Polaroid sunglasses to reduce the glare.
    **a  i**  Explain what is meant by **polarised light.**                                    [2]
    **ii**  Explain why Polaroid sunglasses are more effective than plain dark glasses at reducing
            the glare.                                                                          [2]
    **b**  Explain why sound waves cannot be polarised.                                         [2]
    **c**  The diagram shows the traces of two sound waves displayed on an oscilloscope screen.

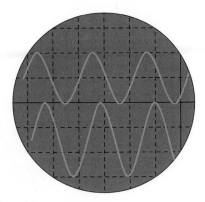

    **i**    Explain whether or not the waves are in phase.                                     [1]
    **ii**   State how their wavelengths compare.                                               [1]
    **iii**  Calculate the ratio of the intensities of the two waves.                           [2]

## Objectives

After studying this chapter, you should be able to:

☐ explain and use the principle of superposition of waves

☐ explain experiments that show diffraction and interference

☐ solve problems involving two-slit and multiple-slit interference

## Combining waves

Light travels as waves and can produce beautiful, natural effects such as the iridescent colours of a butterfly's wing (Figure 15.1). However, these colours do not come from pigments in the wing. Instead, they arise when light waves, scattered from different points on the wing, meet in your eye and combine to produce the colours that we see.

**Figure 15.1** The iridescent colours on a butterfly's wing demonstrate the beauty of nature. In this chapter we will study the effect known as interference, which leads to the production of these glorious colours.

## The principle of superposition of waves

In Chapter 14, we studied the production of waves and the difference between longitudinal and transverse waves and we saw how transverse waves can be polarised. In this chapter we are going to consider what happens when two or more waves meet at a point in space and combine together (Figure 15.2).

So what happens when two waves arrive together at the same place? We can answer this from our everyday experience. What happens when the beams of light waves from two torches cross over? They pass straight through one another. Similarly, sound waves pass through one another, apparently without affecting each other. This is very different from the behaviour of **particles**. Two bullets meeting in mid-air would ricochet off one another in a very un-wave-like way. If we look carefully at how two sets of waves interact when they meet, we find some surprising results.

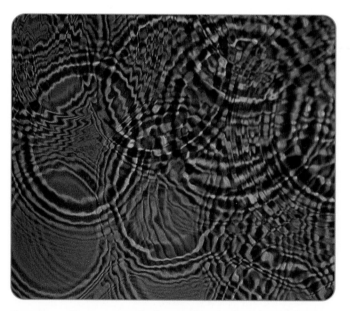

**Figure 15.2** Here we see ripples produced when drops of water fall into a swimming pool. The ripples overlap to produce a complex pattern of crests and troughs.

When two waves meet they combine, with the displacements of the two waves adding together. Figure 15.3 shows the displacement–distance graphs for two sinusoidal waves (blue and green) of different wavelengths. It also shows the resultant wave (red), which comes from combining these two. How do we find this resultant displacement shown in red?

Consider position A. Here the displacement of both waves is zero, and so the resultant must also be zero.

At position B, both waves have positive displacement. The resultant displacement is found by adding these together.

At position C, the displacement of one wave is positive while the other is negative. The resultant displacement lies between the two displacements. In fact, the resultant displacement is the algebraic sum of the displacements of waves A and B; that is, their sum, taking account of their signs (positive or negative).

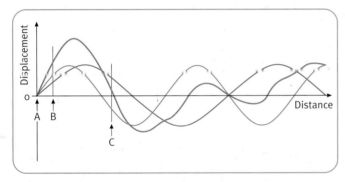

**Figure 15.3** Adding two waves by the principle of superposition – the red line is the resultant wave.

We can work our way along the distance axis in this way, calculating the resultant of the two waves by algebraically adding them up at intervals. Notice that, for these two waves, the resultant wave is a rather complex wave with dips and bumps along its length.

The idea that we can find the resultant of two waves which meet at a point simply by adding up the displacements at each point is called the **principle of superposition** of waves. This principle can be applied to more than two waves and also to all types of waves. A statement of the principle of superposition is shown below.

> When two or more waves meet at a point, the resultant displacement is the algebraic sum of the displacements of the individual waves.

**Test yourself**

1 On graph paper, draw two 'triangular' waves like those shown in Figure 15.4. (These are easier to work with than sinusoidal waves.) One should have wavelength 8 cm and amplitude 2 cm; the other wavelength 16 cm and amplitude 3 cm. Use the principle of superposition of waves to determine the resultant displacement at suitable points along the waves, and draw the complete resultant wave.

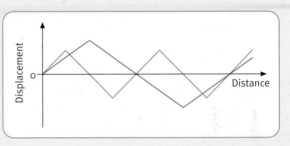

**Figure 15.4** Two triangular waves – for Test yourself Q 1.

# Diffraction of waves

You should be aware that all waves (such as sound and light) can be reflected and refracted. Transverse waves, such as light, can also be polarised (Chapter 14). Another wave phenomenon that applies to all waves is that they can be diffracted. **Diffraction** is the spreading of a wave as it passes through a gap or around an edge. It is easy to observe and investigate diffraction effects using water waves.

## Diffraction of ripples in water

A ripple tank can be used to show diffraction. Plane waves are generated using a vibrating bar, and **move towards** a gap in a barrier (Figure 15.5). Where the ripples strike the barrier, they are reflected back. Where they arrive at the gap, however, they pass through and spread out into the space beyond. It is this spreading out of waves as they travel through a gap (or past the edge of a barrier) that is called diffraction.

The extent to which ripples are diffracted depends on the width of the gap. This is illustrated in Figure 15.6. The lines in this diagram show the

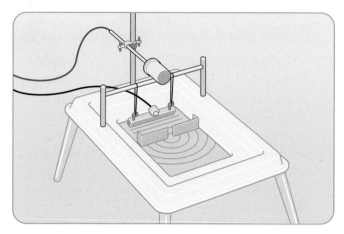

**Figure 15.5** Ripples, initially straight, spread out into the space beyond the gap in the barrier.

wavefronts. It is as if we are looking down on the ripples from above, and drawing lines to represent the tops of the ripples at some instant in time. The separation between adjacent wavefronts is equal to the wavelength $\lambda$ of the ripples.

Figure 15.6 shows the effect on the ripples when they encounter a gap in a barrier. The amount of diffraction depends on the width of the gap. There is hardly any noticeable diffraction when the gap is very much larger than the wavelength. As the gap becomes narrower, the diffraction effect becomes more pronounced. It is greatest when the width of the gap is equal to the wavelength of the ripples.

## Diffraction of sound and light

Diffraction effects are greatest when waves pass through a gap with a width equal to their wavelength. This is useful in explaining why we can observe diffraction readily for some waves, but not for others. For example, sound waves in the audible range have wavelengths from a few millimetres to a few metres. Thus we might expect to observe diffraction effects for sound in our environment. Sounds, for example, diffract as they pass through doorways. The width of a doorway is comparable to the wavelength of a sound and so a noise in one room spreads out into the next room.

Visible light has much shorter wavelengths (about $5 \times 10^{-7}$ m). It is not diffracted noticeably by doorways because the width of the gap is a million times larger than the wavelength of light. However, we can observe diffraction of light by passing it through a very narrow slit or a small hole. When laser light is directed onto a slit whose width is comparable to the wavelength of the incident light, it spreads out into the space beyond to form a smear on the screen (Figure 15.7). An adjustable slit allows you to see the effect of gradually narrowing the gap.

You can see the effects of diffraction for yourself by making a narrow slit with your two thumbs and looking through the slit at a distant light source (Figure 15.8). By gently pressing your thumbs together to narrow the gap between them you can see the effect of narrowing the slit.

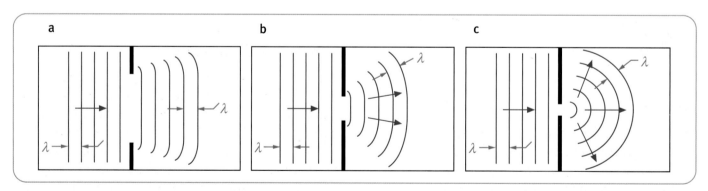

**Figure 15.6** The extent to which ripples spread out depends on the relationship between their wavelength and the width of the gap. In **a**, the width of the gap is very much greater than the wavelength and there is hardly any noticeable diffraction. In **b**, the width of the gap is greater than the wavelength and there is limited diffraction. In **c**, the gap width is equal to the wavelength and the diffraction effect is greatest.

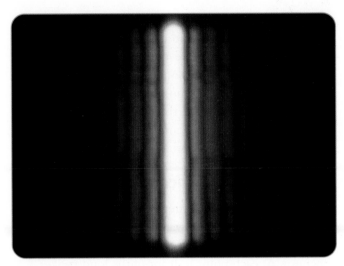

Figure 15.7 Light is diffracted as it passes through a slit.

Figure 15.8 You can see the effects of diffraction by looking through a narrow slit. What happens when you make the slit narrower? What happens to the amount of diffraction when you put different coloured filters in front of the lamp? What does this tell you about the wavelengths of the different colours?

## Diffraction of radio and microwaves

Radio waves can have wavelengths of the order of a kilometre. These waves are easily diffracted by the gaps in the hills and by the tall buildings around our towns and cities. Microwaves, used by the mobile phone network, have wavelengths of about 1 cm. These waves are not easily diffracted (because their wavelengths are much smaller than the dimensions of the gaps) and mostly travel through space in straight lines.

Cars need external radio aerials because radio waves have wavelengths longer than the size of the windows, so they cannot diffract into the car. If you try listening to a radio in a train without an external aerial, you will find that FM signals can be picked up weakly (their wavelength is about 3 m), but AM signals, with longer wavelengths, cannot get in at all.

### Test yourself

2  A microwave oven (Figure 15.9) uses microwaves whose wavelength is 12.5 cm. The front door of the oven is made of glass with a metal grid inside; the gaps in the grid are a few millimetres across. Explain how this design allows us to see the food inside the oven, while the microwaves are not allowed to escape into the kitchen (where they might cook us).

Figure 15.9 A microwave oven has a metal grid in the door to keep microwaves in and let light out.

## Explaining diffraction

Diffraction is a wave effect that can be explained by the principle of superposition. We have to think about what happens when a plane ripple reaches a gap in a barrier (Figure 15.10). Each point on the surface of the water in the gap is moving up and down. Each of these moving points acts as a source of new ripples spreading out into the space beyond the barrier. Now we have a lot of new ripples, and we can use the principle of superposition to find their resultant effect. Without trying to calculate the effect of an infinite number of ripples, we can say that in some directions the ripples add together while in other directions they cancel out.

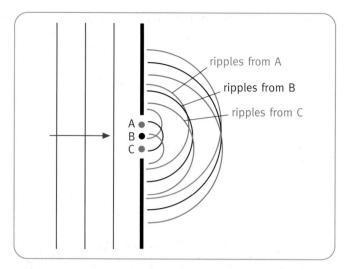

Figure 15.10 Ripples from all points across the gap contribute to the pattern in the space beyond.

# Interference

Adding waves of different wavelengths and amplitudes results in complex waves. We can find some interesting effects if we consider what happens when two waves of the same wavelength overlap at a point. Again, we will use the principle of superposition to explain what we observe.

A simple experiment shows the effect we are interested in here. Two loudspeakers are connected to a single signal generator (Figure 15.11). They each produce sound waves of the same wavelength. Walk around in the space in front of the loudspeakers; you

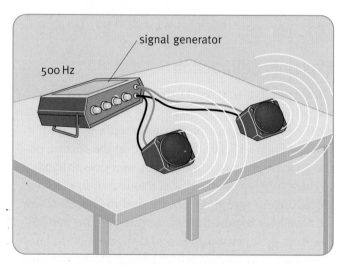

Figure 15.11 The sound waves from two loudspeakers combine to give an interference pattern. This experiment is best done outside so that reflections of sounds (or echoes) do not affect the results.

will hear the resultant effect. A naive view might be that we would hear a sound twice as loud as that from a single loudspeaker. However, this is not what we hear. At some points, the sound is **louder** than for a single speaker. At other points, the sound is much **quieter**. The space around the two loudspeakers consists of a series of loud and quiet regions. We are observing the phenomenon known as **interference**.

## Explaining interference

Figure 15.12 shows how interference arises. The loudspeakers are emitting waves that are in phase because both are connected to the same signal generator. At each point in front of the loudspeaker in Figure 15.11, waves are arriving from the two loudspeakers. At some points, the two waves arrive in phase (in step) with one another and with equal amplitude (Figure 15.12a). The principle of superposition predicts that the resultant wave has twice the amplitude of a single wave. We hear a louder sound.

At other points, something different happens. The two waves arrive completely out of phase or in antiphase (phase

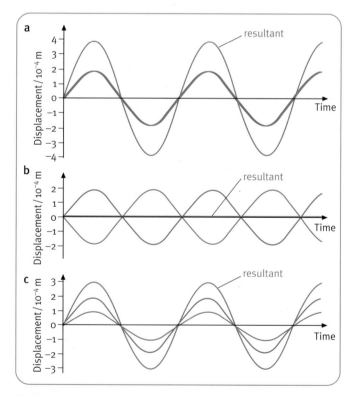

Figure 15.12 Adding waves by the principle of superposition. Blue and green waves of the same amplitude may give **a** constructive or **b** destructive interference, according to the phase difference between them. **c** Waves of different amplitudes can also interfere constructively.

difference is 180°) with one another (Figure **15.12b**). There is a cancelling out, and the resultant wave has zero amplitude. At this point, we would expect silence.

At other points again, the waves are neither perfectly out of step nor perfectly in step, and the resultant wave has amplitude less than that at the loudest point. Where two waves arrive at a point in phase with one another so that they add up, we call this effect **constructive interference**. Where they cancel out, the effect is known as **destructive interference**. Where two waves have different amplitudes (Figure **15.12c**), constructive interference results in a wave whose amplitude is the sum of the two individual amplitudes.

## Test yourself

3 Explain why the two loudspeakers must produce sounds of precisely the same frequency if we are to hear the effects of interference.

## Observing interference in a ripple tank

The two dippers in the ripple tank (Figure **15.13**) should be positioned so that they are just touching the surface of the water. When the bar vibrates, each dipper acts as a source of circular ripples spreading outwards. Where these sets of ripples overlap, we observe an interference pattern. Another way to observe interference in a ripple tank is to use plane waves passing through two gaps in a barrier. The water waves are diffracted at the two gaps and then interfere beyond the gaps.

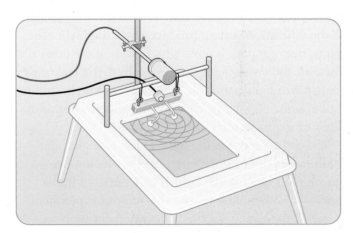

**Figure 15.13** A ripple tank can be used to show how two sets of circular ripples combine.

Figure **15.14** shows the interference pattern produced by two vibrating sources in a ripple tank. How can we explain such a pattern? Look at Figure **15.15** and compare it to Figure **15.14**. Figure **15.15** shows two sets of waves setting out from their sources. At a position such as A, ripples from the two sources arrive in phase with one another, and constructive interference occurs. At B, the two sets of ripples arrive out of phase, and there is destructive interference. Although waves are arriving at B, the surface of the water remains approximately flat.

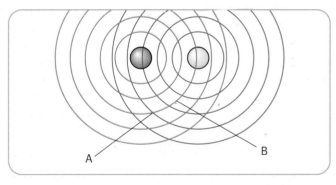

**Figure 15.14** Ripples from two point sources produce an interference pattern.

**Figure 15.15** The result of interference depends on the path difference between the two waves.

Whether the waves combine constructively or destructively at a point depends on the path difference of the waves from the two sources. The path difference is defined as the extra distance travelled by one of the waves compared with the other.

At point A in Figure **15.15**, the waves from the red source have travelled 3 whole wavelengths. The waves from the yellow source have travelled 4 whole wavelengths. The path difference between the two sets of waves is 1 wavelength. A path difference of 1 wavelength is equivalent to a phase difference of zero. This means that they are in phase so that they interfere constructively.

Now think about destructive interference. At point B, the waves from the red source have travelled 3 wavelengths; the waves from the yellow source have travelled 2.5 wavelengths. The path difference between the two sets of waves is 0.5 wavelengths, which is equivalent to a phase difference of 180°. The waves interfere destructively because they are in antiphase. In general, the conditions for constructive interference and destructive interference are outlined below. These conditions apply to **all** waves (water waves, light, microwaves, radio waves, sound, etc.) that show interference effects. In the equations below, $n$ stands for any integer (any whole number – including zero).

- For **constructive interference** the path difference is a whole number of wavelengths:

  path difference = $0$, $\lambda$, $2\lambda$, $3\lambda$, etc.

  or   path difference = $n\lambda$

- For **destructive interference** the path difference is an odd number of half wavelengths:

  path difference = $\frac{1}{2}\lambda$, $1\frac{1}{2}\lambda$, $2\frac{1}{2}\lambda$, etc.

  or   path difference = $(n + \frac{1}{2})\lambda$

## Interference of light

We can also show the interference effects produced by light. A simple arrangement involves directing the light from a laser through two slits (Figure **15.16**). The slits are two clear lines on a black slide, separated by a fraction of a millimetre. Where the light falls on the screen, a series of equally spaced dots of light are seen (see Figure **15.21**). These bright dots are referred to as interference 'fringes', and they are regions where light waves from the two slits are arriving in phase with each other, i.e. constructive interference. The dark regions in between are the result of destructive interference.

**Safety note**
If you carry out experiments using a laser, you should **follow correct safety procedures**. In particular, you should **wear eye protection** and **avoid allowing the beam to enter your eye directly**.

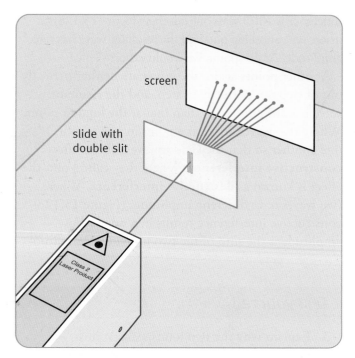

**Figure 15.16** Light beams from the two slits interfere in the space beyond.

These bright and dark fringes are the equivalent of the loud and quiet regions that you detected if you investigated the interference pattern of sounds from the two loudspeakers described above. Bright fringes correspond to loud sound, dark fringes to quiet sound or silence.

You can check that light is indeed reaching the screen from both slits as follows. Mark a point on the screen where there is a dark fringe. Now carefully cover up one of the slits so that light from the laser is only passing through one slit. You should find that the pattern of interference fringes disappears. Instead, a broad band of light appears across the screen. This broad band of light is the diffraction pattern produced by a single slit. The point that was dark is now light. Cover up the other slit instead, and you will see the same effect. You have now shown that light is arriving at the screen from both slits, but at some points (the dark fringes) the two beams of light cancel each other out.

You can achieve similar results with a bright light bulb rather than a laser, but a laser is much more convenient because the light is concentrated into a narrow, more intense beam. This famous experiment is called the Young double-slit experiment (see page **220**), but Thomas Young had no laser available to him when he first carried it out in 1801.

## Interference of microwaves

Using 2.8 cm wavelength microwave equipment (Figure 15.17), you can observe an interference pattern. The microwave transmitter is directed towards the double gap in a metal barrier. The microwaves are diffracted at the two gaps so that they spread out into the region beyond, where they can be detected using the probe receiver. By moving the probe around, it is possible to detect regions of high intensity (constructive interference) and low intensity (destructive interference). The probe may be connected to a meter, or to an audio amplifier and loudspeaker to give an audible output.

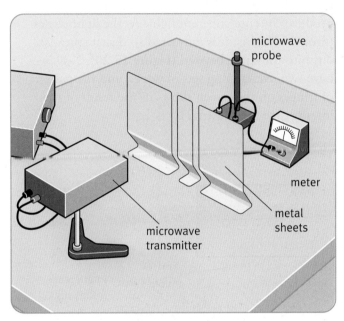

**Figure 15.17** Microwaves can also be used to show interference effects.

## Coherence

We are surrounded by many types of wave – light, infrared radiation, radio waves, sound, and so on. There are waves coming at us from all directions. So why do we not observe interference patterns all the time? Why do we need specialised equipment in a laboratory to observe these effects?

In fact, we can see interference of light occurring in everyday life. For example, you may have noticed haloes of light around street lamps or the Moon on a foggy night. You may have noticed light and dark bands of light if you look through fabric at a bright source of light. These are interference effects.

We usually need specially arranged conditions to produce interference effects that we can measure. Think about the demonstration with two loudspeakers. If they were connected to different signal generators with slightly different frequencies, the sound waves might start off in phase with one another, but they would soon go out of phase (Figure 15.18). We would hear loud, then soft, then loud again. The interference pattern would keep shifting around the room.

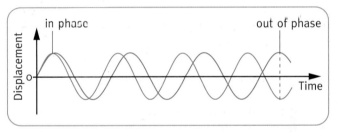

**Figure 15.18** Waves of slightly different wavelengths (and therefore frequencies) move in and out of phase with one another.

By connecting the two loudspeakers to the **same** signal generator, we can be sure that the sound waves that they produce are constantly in phase with one another. We say that they act as two **coherent** sources of sound waves (coherent means sticking together). Coherent sources emit waves that have a **constant phase difference**. Note that the two waves can only have a constant phase difference if their frequency is the same and remains constant.

Now think about the laser experiment. Could we have used two lasers producing exactly the same frequency and hence wavelength of light? Figure **15.19a** on page 220 represents the light from a laser. We can think of it as being made up of many separate bursts of light. We cannot guarantee that these bursts from two lasers will always be in phase with one another.

This problem is overcome by using a single laser and dividing its light using the two slits (Figure **15.19b**). The slits act as two coherent sources of light.

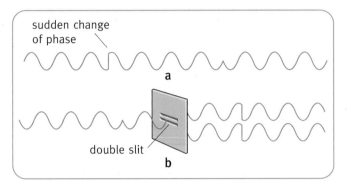

Figure **15.19** Waves must be coherent if they are to produce a clear interference pattern.

They are constantly in phase with one another (or there is a constant phase difference between them). If they were not coherent sources, the interference pattern would be constantly changing, far too fast for our eyes to detect. We would simply see a uniform band of light, without any definite bright and dark regions. From this you should be able to see that, in order to observe interference, we need two coherent sources of waves.

**Test yourself**

5 Draw sketches of displacement against time to illustrate the following:
  a two waves having the same amplitude and in phase with one another
  b two waves having the same amplitude and with a phase difference of 90°
  c two waves initially in phase but with slightly different wavelengths.
    Use your sketches to explain why two coherent sources of waves are needed to observe interference.

# The Young double-slit experiment

Now we will take a close look at a famous experiment which Thomas Young performed in 1801. He used this experiment to show the wave nature of light.

A beam of light is shone on a pair of parallel slits placed at right angles to the beam. Light diffracts and spreads outwards from each slit into the space beyond; the light from the two slits overlaps on a screen. An interference pattern of light and dark bands called 'fringes' is formed on the screen.

## Explaining the experiment

In order to observe interference, we need two sets of waves. The sources of the waves must be coherent – the phase difference between the waves emitted at the sources must remain constant. This also means that the waves must have the same wavelength. Today, this is readily achieved by passing a single beam of laser light through the two slits. A laser produces intense coherent light. As the light passes through the slits, it is diffracted so that it spreads out into the space beyond (Figure **15.20**). Now we have two overlapping sets of waves, and the pattern of fringes on the screen shows us the result of their interference (Figure **15.21**).

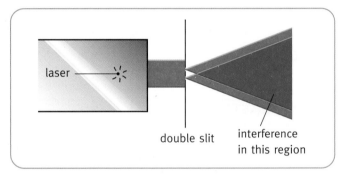

Figure **15.20** Interference occurs where diffracted beams from the two slits overlap.

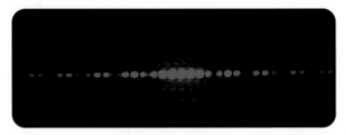

Figure **15.21** Interference fringes obtained using a laser and a double slit.

How does this pattern arise? We will consider three points on the screen (Figure **15.22**), and work out what we would expect to observe at each.

### Point A

This point is directly opposite the midpoint of the slits. Two rays of light arrive at A, one from slit 1 and the other from slit 2. Point A is equidistant from the two slits, and so the two rays of light have travelled the same distance. The path difference between the two rays of light is zero. If we assume that they were in phase (in step) with each other when they left the slits, then they will be in phase when they arrive at A. Hence they will interfere constructively, and we will observe a bright fringe at A.

### Point B

This point is slightly to the side of point A, and is the midpoint of the first dark fringe. Again, two rays of light arrive at B, one from each slit. The light from slit 1 has to travel slightly further than the light from slit 2, and so the two rays are no longer in step. Since point B is at the midpoint of the dark fringe, the two rays must be in antiphase (phase difference of 180°). The path difference between the two rays of light must be half a wavelength and so the two rays interfere destructively.

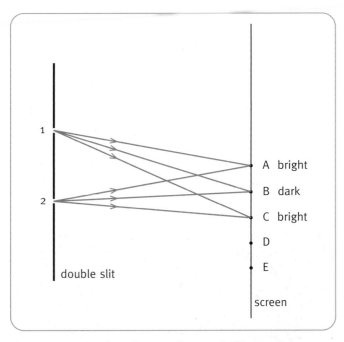

**Figure 15.22** Rays from the two slits travel different distances to reach the screen.

### Point C

This point is the midpoint of the next bright fringe with AB = BC. Again, ray 1 has travelled further than

ray 2; this time, it has travelled an extra distance equal to a whole wavelength $\lambda$. The path difference between the rays of light is now a whole wavelength. The two rays are in phase at the screen. They interfere constructively and we see a bright fringe.

The complete interference pattern (Figure **15.21**) can be explained in this way.

> ### Test yourself
>
> 6  Consider points D and E on the screen, where BC = CD = DE. State and explain what you would expect to observe at D and E.

## Determining wavelength $\lambda$

The double-slit experiment can be used to determine the wavelength $\lambda$ of light. The following three quantities have to be measured.

### Slit separation $a$

This is the distance between the centres of the slits, though it may be easier to measure between the edges of the slits. (It is difficult to judge the position of the centre of a slit. If the slits are the same width, the separation of their left-hand edges is the same as the separation of their centres.) A travelling microscope is suitable for measuring $a$.

### Fringe separation $x$

This is the distance between the centres of adjacent bright (or dark) fringes. It is best to measure across several fringes (say, ten) and then to calculate later the average separation. A metre rule or travelling microscope can be used.

### Slit-to-screen distance $D$

This is the distance from the midpoint of the slits to the central fringe on the screen. It can be measured using a metre rule or a tape measure.

Once these three quantities have been measured, the wavelength $\lambda$ of the light can be found using the relationship:

$$\lambda = \frac{ax}{D}$$

## Worked example

1  In a double-slit experiment using light from a helium–neon laser, a student obtained the following results:

> width of 10 fringes $10x = 1.5\,\text{cm}$

> separation of slits $a = 1.0\,\text{mm}$

> slit-to-screen distance $D = 2.40\,\text{m}$

Determine the wavelength of the light.

**Step 1** Work out the fringe separation:

$$\text{fringe separation } x = \frac{1.5 \times 10^{-2}}{10} = 1.5 \times 10^{-3}\,\text{m}$$

**Step 2** Substitute the values of $a$, $x$ and $D$ in the expression for wavelength $\lambda$:

$$\lambda = \frac{ax}{D}$$

Therefore:

$$\lambda = \frac{1.0 \times 10^{-3} \times 1.5 \times 10^{-3}}{2.40} = 6.3 \times 10^{-7}\,\text{m}$$

> Don't forget to convert all the distances into metres.

So the wavelength is $6.3 \times 10^{-7}$ m or 630 nm.

## Test yourself

7  If the student in Worked example **1** moved the screen to a distance of 4.8 m from the slits, what would the fringe separation become?

## Experimental details

An alternative arrangement for carrying out the double-slit experiment is shown in Figure **15.23**. Here, a white light source is used, rather than a laser. A monochromatic filter allows only one wavelength of light to pass through. A single slit diffracts the light. This diffracted light arrives in phase at the double slit, which ensures that the two parts of the double slit behave as coherent sources of light. The double slit is placed a centimetre or two beyond the single slit, and the fringes are observed on a screen a metre or so away. The experiment has to be carried out in a darkened room, as the intensity of the light is low and the fringes are hard to see.

There are three important factors involved in the way the equipment is set up.

- All slits are a fraction of a millimetre in width. Since the wavelength of light is less than a micrometre ($10^{-6}$ m), this gives a small amount of diffraction in the space beyond. If the slits were narrower, the intensity of the light would be too low for visible fringes to be achieved.
- The double slits are about a millimetre apart. If they were much further apart, the fringes would be too close together to be distinguishable.
- The screen is about a metre from the slits. This gives fringes which are clearly separated without being too dim.

With a laser, the light beam is more concentrated, and the initial single slit is not necessary. The greater intensity of the beam means that the screen can be further from the slits, so that the fringes are further apart; this reduces the percentage error in measurements of $x$ and $D$, and hence $\lambda$ can be determined more accurately.

A laser has a second advantage. The light from a laser is monochromatic; that is, it consists of a single wavelength. This makes the fringes very clear, and

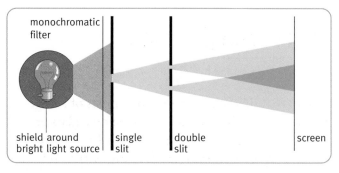

**Figure 15.23** To observe interference fringes with white light, it is necessary to use a monochromatic filter and a single slit before the double slit.

many of them are formed across the screen. With white light, a range of wavelengths are present. Different wavelengths form fringes at different points across the screen, smearing them out so that they are not as clear.

Using white light with no filter results in a central fringe which is white (because all wavelengths are in phase here), but the other fringes show coloured effects, as the different wavelengths interfere constructively at different points. In addition, only a few fringes are visible in the interference pattern.

## Test yourself

8 Use $\lambda = \dfrac{ax}{D}$ to explain the following observations.

   **a** With the slits closer together, the fringes are further apart.
   **b** Interference fringes for blue light are closer together than for red light.
   **c** In an experiment to measure the wavelength of light, it is desirable to have the screen as far from the slits as possible.

9 Yellow sodium light of wavelength 589 nm is used in the Young double-slit experiment. The slit separation is 0.20 mm, and the screen is placed 1.20 m from the slits. Calculate the separation of neighbouring fringes formed on the screen.

10 In a double-slit experiment, filters were placed in front of a white light source to investigate the effect of changing the wavelength of the light. At first, a red filter was used ($\lambda = 600$ nm) and the fringe separation was found to be 2.40 mm. A blue filter was then used ($\lambda = 450$ nm). Determine the fringe separation with the blue filter.

## Diffraction gratings

A transmission diffraction grating is similar to the slide used in the double-slit experiment, but with many more slits than just two. It consists of a large number of equally spaced lines ruled on a glass or plastic slide. Each line is capable of diffracting the incident light. There may be as many as 10 000 lines per centimetre. When light is shone through this grating, a pattern of interference fringes is seen.

In a reflection diffraction grating, the lines are made on a reflecting surface so that light is both reflected and diffracted by the grating. The shiny surface of a compact disc (CD) or DVD is an everyday example of a reflection diffraction grating. Hold a CD in your hand and twist it so that you are looking at the reflection of light from a lamp. You will observe coloured bands (Figure 15.24). A CD has thousands of equally spaced lines of microscopic pits on its surface; these carry the digital information. It is the diffraction from these lines that produces the coloured bands of light from the surface of the CD.

**Figure 15.24** A CD acts as a reflection diffraction grating. White light is reflected and diffracted at its surface, producing a display of spectral colours.

Monochromatic light from a laser is incident normally on a transmission diffraction grating. In the space beyond, interference fringes are formed. These can be observed on a screen, as with the double slit. However, it is usual to measure the angle $\theta$ at which they are formed, rather than measuring their separation (Figure 15.25). With double slits, the fringes are equally spaced and the angles are very small. With a diffraction grating, the angles are much greater and the fringes are not equally spaced.

The fringes are also referred to as **maxima**. The central fringe is called the zeroth-order maximum, the next fringe is the first-order maximum, and so on. The pattern is symmetrical, so there are two first-order maxima, two second-order maxima, and so on.

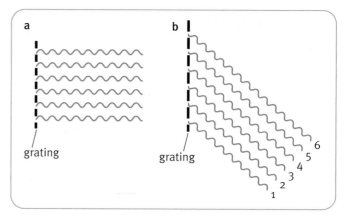

**Figure 15.26 a** Waves from each slit are in phase in the straight-through direction. **b** In the direction of the first-order maximum, the waves are in phase, but each one has travelled one wavelength further than the one below it.

an extra distance equal to one whole wavelength and is therefore in phase with ray 1. The path difference between ray 1 and ray 2 is equal to one wavelength $\lambda$. Ray 3 has travelled two extra wavelengths and is in phase with rays 1 and 2. In fact, the rays from all of the slits are in step in this direction, and a bright fringe results.

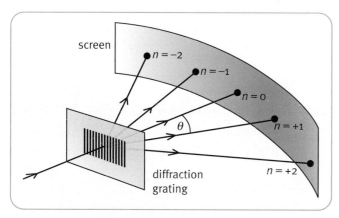

**Figure 15.25** The diffracted beams form a symmetrical pattern on either side of the undiffracted central beam.

## Explaining the experiment

The principle is the same as for the double-slit experiment, but here we have light passing through many slits. As it passes through each slit, it diffracts into the space beyond. So now we have many overlapping beams of light, and these interfere with one another. It is difficult to achieve constructive interference with many beams, because they all have to be in phase with one another.

There is a bright fringe, the zeroth-order maximum, in the straight-through direction ($\theta = 0$) because all of the rays here are travelling parallel to one another and in phase, so the interference is constructive (Figure 15.26a).

The first-order maximum forms as follows. Rays of light emerge from all of the slits; to form a bright fringe, all the rays must be in phase. In the direction of the first-order maximum, ray 1 has travelled the least distance (Figure 15.26b). Ray 2 has travelled

### Test yourself

11 Explain how the second-order maximum arises. Use the term **path difference** in your explanation.

## Determining wavelength $\lambda$ with a grating

By measuring the angles at which the maxima occur, we can determine the wavelength of the incident light. The wavelength $\lambda$ of the monochromatic light is related to the angle $\theta$ by:

$$d \sin \theta = n\lambda$$

where $d$ is the distance between adjacent lines of the grating and $n$ is known as the **order** of the maximum; $n$ can only have integer values 0, 1, 2, 3, etc. The distance $d$ is known as the grating element or grating spacing. This is illustrated in Worked example **2**.

**2** Monochromatic light is incident normally on a diffraction grating having 3000 lines per centimetre. The angular separation of the zeroth- and first-order maxima is found to be 10°. Calculate the wavelength of the incident light.

**Step 1** Calculate the slit separation (grating spacing) $d$. Since there are 3000 slits per centimetre, their separation must be:

$$d = \frac{1\,\text{cm}}{3000} = 3.33 \times 10^{-4}\,\text{cm} = 3.33 \times 10^{-6}\,\text{m}$$

**Step 2** Rearrange the equation $d\sin\theta = n\lambda$ and substitute values:

$$\theta = 10.0°, \; n = 1$$

$$\lambda = \frac{d\sin\theta}{n} = \frac{3.36 \times 10^{-6} \times \sin 10°}{1}$$

$$\lambda = 5.8 \times 10^{-7}\,\text{m} = 580\,\text{nm}$$

## Test yourself

**12 a** For the case described in Worked example **2**, at what angle would you expect to find the second-order maximum ($n = 2$)?

**b** Repeat the calculation of $\theta$ for $n = 3$, 4, etc. What is the limit to this calculation? How many maxima will there be altogether in this interference pattern?

**13** Consider the equation $d\sin\theta = n\lambda$. How will the diffraction pattern change if:

**a** the wavelength of the light is increased?

**b** the diffraction grating is changed for one with more lines per centimetre (slits that are more closely spaced)?

## Many slits are better than two

It is worth comparing the use of a diffraction grating to determine wavelength with the Young two-slit experiment.

• With a diffraction grating the maxima are very **sharp**.

• With a diffraction grating the maxima are also very **bright**. This is because rather than there being contributions from only two slits, there are contributions from a thousand or more slits.

• With two slits, there may be a large inaccuracy in the measurement of the slit separation $a$. The fringes are close together, so their separation may also be measured imprecisely.

• With a diffraction grating, there are many slits per centimetre, so $d$ can be measured accurately. Because the maxima are widely separated, the angle $\theta$ can be measured to a high degree of precision. So an experiment with a diffraction grating can be expected to give measurements of wavelength to a much higher degree of precision than a simple double-slit arrangement.

## Test yourself

**14** A student is trying to make an accurate measurement of the wavelength of green light from a mercury lamp ($\lambda - 546\,\text{nm}$). Using a double slit of separation 0.50 mm, he finds he can see ten clear fringes on a screen at a distance of 0.80 m from the slits. The student can measure their overall width to within ±1 mm. He then tries an alternative experiment using a diffraction grating that has 3000 lines per centimetre. The angle between the two second-order maxima can be measured to within ±0.1°.

**a** What will be the width of the ten fringes that he can measure in the first experiment?

**b** What will be the angle of the second-order maximum in the second experiment?

**c** Suggest which experiment you think will give the more accurate measurement of $\lambda$.

## Diffracting white light

A diffraction grating can be used to split white light up into its constituent colours (wavelengths). This splitting of light is known as **dispersion**, shown in Figure 15.27. A beam of white light is shone onto the grating. A zeroth-order, white maximum is observed at $\theta = 0°$, because all waves of each wavelength are in phase in this direction.

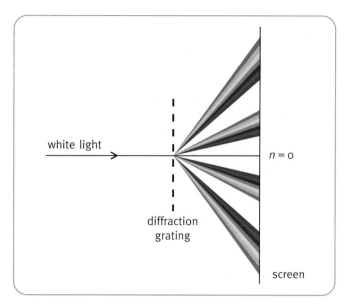

white light

n = 0

diffraction grating

screen

**Figure 15.27** A diffraction grating is a simple way of separating white light into its constituent wavelengths.

On either side, a series of spectra appear, with violet closest to the centre and red furthest away. We can see why different wavelengths have their maxima at

different angles if we rearrange the equation $d\sin\theta = n\lambda$ to give:

$$\sin\theta = \frac{n\lambda}{d}$$

From this it follows that the greater the wavelength $\lambda$, the greater the value of $\sin\theta$ and hence the greater the angle $\theta$. Red light is at the long wavelength end of the visible spectrum, and so it appears at the greatest angle.

## Test yourself

15 White light is incident normally on a diffraction grating with a slit separation $d$ of $2.00 \times 10^{-6}$ m.
   a Calculate the angle **between** the red and violet ends of the first-order spectrum. The visible spectrum has wavelengths between 400 nm and 700 nm.
   b Explain why the second- and third-order spectra overlap.

## Summary

☐ The principle of superposition states that when two or more waves meet at a point, the resultant displacement is the algebraic sum of the displacements of the individual waves.

☐ When waves pass through a slit, they may be diffracted so that they spread out into the space beyond. The diffraction effect is greatest when the wavelength of the waves is similar to the width of the gap.

☐ Interference is the superposition of waves from two coherent sources.

☐ Two sources are coherent when they emit waves that have a **constant phase difference**. (This can only happen if the waves have the same frequency or wavelength.)

☐ For **constructive interference** the path difference is a whole number of wavelengths:
   path difference = 0, $\lambda$, $2\lambda$, $3\lambda$, etc.   or   path difference = $n\lambda$

☐ For **destructive interference** the path difference is an odd number of half wavelengths:

   path difference = $\frac{1}{2}\lambda$, $1\frac{1}{2}\lambda$, $2\frac{1}{2}\lambda$, etc.   or   path difference = $(n+\frac{1}{2})\lambda$

☐ When light passes through a double slit, it is diffracted and an interference pattern of equally spaced light and dark fringes is observed. This can be used to determine the wavelength of light using the equation:

   $$\lambda = \frac{ax}{D}$$

   This equation can be used for all waves, including sound and microwaves.

☐ A diffraction grating diffracts light at its many slits or lines. The diffracted light interferes in the space beyond the grating. The equation for a diffraction grating is:

   $$d\sin\theta = n\lambda$$

# End-of-chapter questions

1  a  Copy the waves shown in Figure **15.28** onto a sheet of graph paper and use the principle
      of superposition to show the resultant wave.
   b  How does the wavelength of the resulting wave compare with that of the component waves?

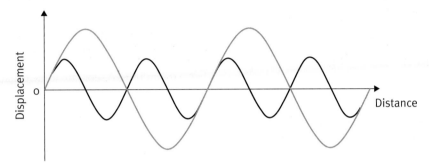

**Figure 15.28**  For End-of-chapter Q **1**.

2  Figure **15.29** shows a ripple tank being used to demonstrate diffraction of water waves.

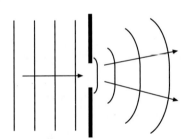

**Figure 15.29**  For End-of-chapter Q **2**.

Suggest how the diffracted wave shape will change if:
a  the wavelength of the incident wave is increased
b  the wavelength of the incident wave is decreased.

3  Explain why in the remote mountainous regions, such as the Hindu Kush, radio signals from
   terrestrial transmitters can be received, but television reception can only be received from
   satellite transmissions.

4  Damita and Jamal are organising a disco. Damita suggests that feeding the sound from the music centre to a second loudspeaker will increase the loudness of the music. Jamal says it won't work as there will be places where the sound will be very loud, due to constructive interference, and places where it will be much quieter, due to destructive interference. State who is correct and explain your reasoning.

5  The constant frequency signal from a signal generator is fed to two loudspeakers placed 1.5 m apart. A girl, who is 8.0 metres away from the speakers, walks across in a line parallel to the speakers. She finds that there is a distance of 1.2 m between successive spots where the sound is very quiet. Calculate the wavelength of the sound.

6  Two signal generators feed signals with slightly different frequencies to two separate loudspeakers. Suggest why a sound of continuously rising and falling loudness is heard.

7  A hydrogen discharge lamp produces a spectral line of wavelength 656 nm. Calculate the angles at which a diffraction grating, with 5000 lines cm$^{-1}$, would produce the first and second maxima for this light.

# Exam-style questions

1  **a** Explain what is meant by the term **superposition**.                                                                    [2]
   **b** In a Young double-slit experiment using the yellow light of wavelength 590 nm from a sodium discharge tube, a student sets up a screen 1.8 m from the double slit. He measures the distance between 12 fringes as 16.8 mm. Calculate the separation of the slits.                         [3]
   **c** State the effect of:
      **i**  using slits of narrower width (but the same separation)                                                             [2]
      **ii** using slits with a smaller separation but of the same width.                                                        [2]

2  **a** A laser light is described as producing light which is both highly coherent and highly monochromatic.
      Explain what is meant by the terms **coherent** and **monochromatic**.                                                     [2]
   **b** Figure 1 shows the set up used to analyse the spectrum of a sodium discharge lamp using a diffraction grating with 5000 lines cm$^{-1}$. Figure 2 shows the developed photographic film showing the spectral lines observed.

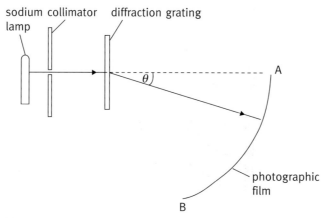

Figure 1

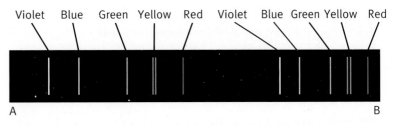

Violet  Blue  Green  Yellow  Red    Violet  Blue  Green Yellow  Red

A                                                          B

**Figure 2**

    **i**   Explain why two spectra are observed. [2]

    **ii**  Study the two spectra and describe **two** differences between them. [2]

   **iii** The green maximum near end A is at an angle $\theta$ of 15.5°. Calculate the wavelength
       of the green light. [3]

   **iv** Calculate the angle produced by the second green line. [2]

**3**  **a** Explain what is meant by the term **destructive interference**. [2]

   **b** A student sets up an experiment to investigate the interference pattern formed by
     microwaves of wavelength 1.5 cm. The apparatus is set up as in the Figure **15.17**
     on page **219**. The distance between the centres of the two slits is 12.5 cm. The detector
     is centrally placed 1.2 m from the metal plates where it detects a maximum. The student
     moves the detector 450 cm across the bench parallel to the plates. Calculate how many
     maxima the detector will be moved through. [3]

   **c** Calculate the frequency of these microwaves. [2]

   **d** The detector is moved back to the central position. When it is now rotated through
     90° the reading falls to zero. Explain what this tells us about the nature of the microwaves. [2]

**4**  **a** Explain what is meant by the **diffraction** of a wave. [2]

   **b** The diagram shows waves, in a ripple tank, spreading out from two slits.

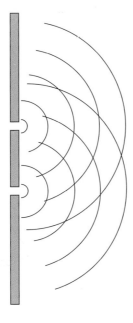

On a copy of the diagram, draw:
  i   a line showing points along the central maximum – label this line **0**                    [1]
  ii  a line showing the points along first maximum – label this line **1**                       [1]
  iii a line showing points along one of the first minima – label this line **min**.             [1]
c  The centres of the slits are 12 cm apart. At a distance of 60 cm from the barrier, the
   first maxima are 18 cm either side of the central maximum. Calculate the wavelength
   of the waves. You may assume that the formula developed for light waves is applicable
   in this example.                                                                                [2]

## Objectives

After studying this chapter, you should be able to:

☐ demonstrate and explain the formation of stationary waves

☐ determine the wavelength of sound waves using stationary waves

## The bridge that broke

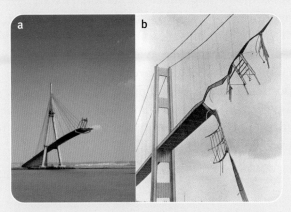

Figure **16.1 a** A suspension bridge under construction. **b** One that failed – the Tacoma Narrows bridge.

Figure **16.1a** shows the Normandy Bridge under construction in France. When designing bridges, engineers must take into account the possibility of the wind causing the build up of stationary waves, which cause the bridge to oscillate violently. Famously, this happened in October 1940 to the Tacoma Narrows bridge in Washington State, USA. High winds caused the bridge to vibrate with increasing amplitude until the bridge fell apart (Figure **16.1b**).

## From moving to stationary

The waves we have considered so far in Chapters **14** and **15** have been **progressive waves;** they start from a source and travel outwards, transferring energy from one place to another. A second important class of waves is **stationary waves** (standing waves). These can be observed as follows. Use a long spring or a slinky spring. A long rope or piece of rubber tubing will also do. Lay it on the floor and fix one end firmly. Move the other end from side to side so that transverse waves travel along the length of the spring and reflect off the fixed end (Figure **16.2**). If you adjust the frequency of the shaking, you should be able to achieve a stable pattern like one of those shown in Figure **16.3**. Alter the frequency in order to achieve one of the other patterns.

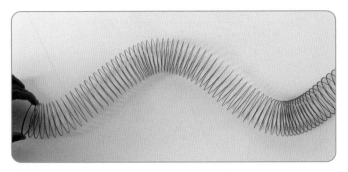

Figure **16.2** A slinky spring is used to generate a stationary wave pattern.

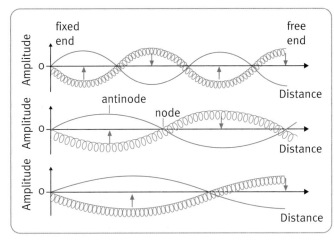

Figure **16.3** Different stationary wave patterns are possible, depending on the frequency of vibration.

You should notice that you have to move the end of the spring with just the right frequency to get one of these interesting patterns. The pattern disappears when the frequency of the shaking of the free end of the spring is slightly increased or decreased.

## Nodes and antinodes

What you have observed is a stationary wave on the long spring. There are points along the spring that remain (almost) motionless while points on either side are oscillating with the greatest amplitude. The points that do not move are called the **nodes** and the points where the spring oscillates with maximum amplitude are called the **antinodes**. At the same time, it is clear that the wave profile is not travelling along the length of the spring. Hence we call it a stationary wave or a standing wave.

We normally represent a stationary wave by drawing the shape of the spring in its two extreme positions (Figure **16.4a**). The spring appears as a series of loops, separated by nodes. In this diagram, point A is moving downwards. At the same time, point B in the next loop is moving upwards. The phase difference between points A and B is 180°. Hence the sections of spring in adjacent loops are always moving in antiphase; they are half a cycle out of phase with one another.

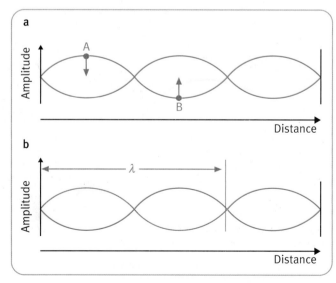

**Figure 16.4** The fixed ends of a long spring must be nodes in the stationary wave pattern.

## Formation of stationary waves

Imagine a string stretched between two fixed points, for example a guitar string. Pulling the middle of the string and then releasing it produces a stationary wave. There is a node at each of the fixed ends and an antinode in the middle. Releasing the string produces two progressive waves travelling in opposite directions. These are reflected at the fixed ends. The reflected waves combine to produce the stationary wave.

Figure **16.2** on page **231** shows how a stationary wave can be set up using a long spring. A stationary wave is formed whenever two progressive waves of the same amplitude and wavelength, travelling in **opposite** directions, superimpose. Figure **16.5** uses a displacement–distance graph (s–x) to illustrate the formation of a stationary wave along a long spring (or a stretched length of string).

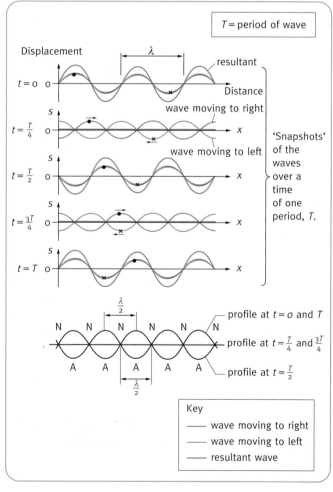

**Figure 16.5** The blue-coloured wave is moving to the left and the red-coloured wave to the right. The **principle of superposition** of waves is used to determine the resultant displacement. The profile of the long spring is shown in green.

- At time $t=0$, the progressive waves travelling to the left and right are in phase. The waves combine **constructively** giving amplitude twice that of each wave.
- After a time equal to one quarter of a period $\left(t = \dfrac{T}{4}\right)$, each wave travels a distance of one quarter of a wavelength to the left or right. Consequently, the two waves are in antiphase (phase difference = 180°). The waves combine **destructively** giving zero displacement.
- After a time equal to one half of a period $\left(t = \dfrac{T}{2}\right)$, the two waves are back in phase again. They once again combine **constructively**.
- After a time equal to three quarters of a period $t = \left(\dfrac{3T}{4}\right)$, the waves are in antiphase again. They combine **destructively** with the resultant wave showing zero displacement.
- After a time equal to one whole period ($t = T$), the waves combine **constructively**. The profile of the slinky spring is as it was at $t=0$.

This cycle repeats itself, with the long spring showing nodes and antinodes along its length. The separation between adjacent nodes or antinodes tells us about the progressive waves that produce the stationary wave.

A closer inspection of the graphs in Figure **16.5** shows that the separation between adjacent nodes or antinodes is related to the wavelength $\lambda$ of the progressive wave. The important conclusions are:

$$\text{separation between two adjacent nodes (or antinodes)} = \frac{\lambda}{2}$$

$$\text{separation between adjacent node and antinode} = \frac{\lambda}{4}$$

The wavelength $\lambda$ of **any** progressive wave can be determined from the separation between neighbouring nodes or antinodes of the resulting standing wave pattern. (This is $= \dfrac{\lambda}{2}$.) This can then be used to determine either the speed $v$ of the progressive wave or its frequency $f$ by using the wave equation:

$$v = f\lambda$$

It is worth noting that a stationary wave does not travel and therefore has no speed. It does not transfer energy between two points like a progressive wave. Table **16.1** shows some of the key features of a progressive wave and its stationary wave.

| | Progressive wave | Stationary wave |
|---|---|---|
| wavelength | $\lambda$ | $\lambda$ |
| frequency | $f$ | $f$ |
| speed | $v$ | zero |

**Table 16.1** A summary of progressive and stationary waves.

### Test yourself

1  A stationary (standing) wave is set up on a vibrating spring. Adjacent nodes are separated by 25 cm. Determine:
   **a** the wavelength of the stationary wave
   **b** the distance from a node to an adjacent antinode.

# Observing stationary waves
## Stretched strings

A string is attached at one end to a vibration generator, driven by a signal generator (Figure **16.6**). The other end hangs over a pulley and weights maintain the tension in the string. When the signal

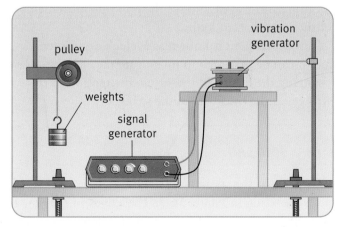

**Figure 16.6** Melde's experiment for investigating stationary waves on a string.

generator is switched on, the string vibrates with small amplitude. However, by adjusting the frequency, it is possible to produce stationary waves whose amplitude is much larger.

The pulley end of the string is unable to vibrate; this is a node. Similarly, the end attached to the vibrator is only able to move a small amount, and this is also a node. As the frequency is increased, it is possible to observe one loop (one antinode), two loops, three loops and more. Figure **16.7** shows a vibrating string where the frequency of the vibrator has been set to produce two loops.

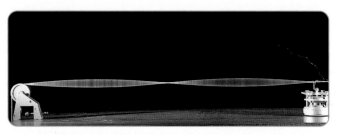

**Figure 16.7** When a stationary wave is established, one half of the string moves upwards as the other half moves downwards. In this photograph, the string is moving too fast to observe the effect.

A flashing stroboscope is useful to reveal the motion of the string at these frequencies, which look blurred to the eye. The frequency of vibration is set so that there are two loops along the string; the frequency of the stroboscope is set so that it almost matches that of the vibrations. Now we can see the string moving 'in slow motion', and it is easy to see the opposite movements of the two adjacent loops.

This experiment is known as **Melde's experiment**, and it can be extended to investigate the effect of changing the length of the string, the tension in the string and the thickness of the string.

## Test yourself

2 Look at the stationary (standing) wave on the string in Figure 16.7. The length of the vibrating section of the string is 60cm.
   **a** Determine the wavelength of the stationary wave and the separation of the two neighbouring antinodes.

continued ···➔

The frequency of vibration is increased until a stationary wave with three antinodes appears on the string.
   **b** Sketch a stationary wave pattern to illustrate the appearance of the string.
   **c** What is the wavelength of this stationary wave?

## Microwaves

Start by directing the microwave transmitter at a metal plate, which reflects the microwaves back towards the source (Figure **16.8**). Move the probe receiver around in the space between the transmitter and the reflector and you will observe positions of high and low intensity. This is because a stationary wave is set up between the transmitter and the sheet; the positions of high and low intensity are the antinodes and nodes respectively.

If the probe is moved along the direct line from the transmitter to the plate, the wavelength of the microwaves can be determined from the distance between the nodes. Knowing that microwaves travel at the speed of light $c$ $(3.0 \times 10^8 \, \text{ms}^{-1})$, we can then determine their frequency $f$ using the wave equation:

$$c = f\lambda$$

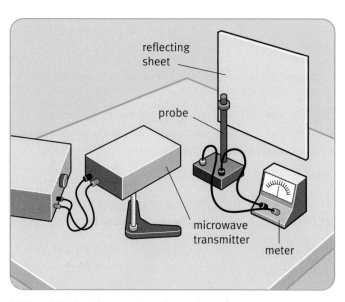

**Figure 16.8** A stationary wave is created when microwaves are reflected from the metal sheet.

## Test yourself

3 **a** Draw a stationary wave pattern for the microwave experiment above. Clearly show whether there is a node or an antinode at the reflecting sheet.
  **b** The separation of two adjacent points of high intensity is found to be 14 mm. Calculate the wavelength and frequency of the microwaves.

## An air column closed at one end

A glass tube (open at both ends) is clamped so that one end dips into a cylinder of water. By adjusting its height in the clamp, you can change the length of the column of air in the tube (Figure **16.9**). When you hold a vibrating tuning fork above the open end, the air column may be forced to vibrate, and the note of the tuning fork sounds much louder. This is an example of a phenomenon called **resonance**. The experiment described here is known as the **resonance tube.**

**Figure 16.9** A stationary wave is created in the air in the tube when the length of the air column is adjusted to the correct length.

For resonance to occur, the length of the air column must be just right. The air at the bottom of the tube is unable to vibrate, so this point must be a node. The air at the open end of the tube can vibrate most freely, so this is an antinode. Hence the length of

the air column must be one-quarter of a wavelength (Figure **16.10a**). (Alternatively, the length of the air column could be set to equal three-quarters of a wavelength – see Figure **16.10b**.)

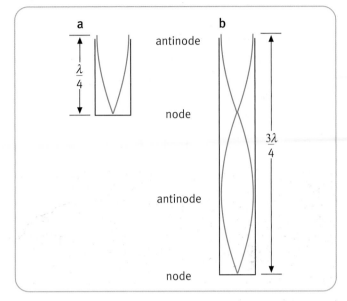

**Figure 16.10** Stationary wave patterns for air in a tube with one end closed.

Take care! The representation of standing sound waves can be misleading. Remember that a sound wave is a longitudinal wave, but the diagram we draw is more like a transverse wave. Figure **16.11a** on page 236 shows how we normally represent a standing sound wave, while Figure **16.11b** shows the direction of vibration of the particles along the wave.

## Test yourself

4 Explain how two sets of identical but oppositely travelling waves are established in the microwave and air column experiments described above.

## Open-ended air columns

The air in a tube which is open at both ends will vibrate in a similar way to that in a closed column. Take an open-ended tube and blow gently across the top. You should hear a note whose pitch depends on the length of the tube. Now cover the bottom of the tube with the palm of your hand and repeat the process. The pitch of the note now produced will be about an octave higher than the previous note, which means that the frequency is approximately twice the original frequency.

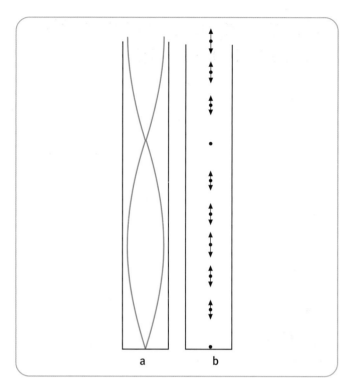

**Figure 16.11 a** The standard representation of a standing sound wave may suggest that it is a transverse wave. **b** A sound wave is really a longitudinal wave, so that the particles vibrate as shown.

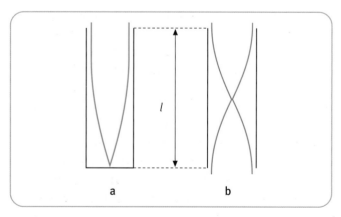

**Figure 16.12** Standing wave patterns for sound waves in **a** a closed tube, and **b** an open tube.

It is rather surprising that a standing wave can be set up in an open column of air in this way. What is going on? Figure 16.12 compares the situation for open and closed tubes. An open-ended tube has two open ends, so there must be an antinode at each end. There is a node at the midpoint.

For a tube of length $l$ you can see that in the closed tube the standing wave formed is one-quarter of a

wavelength, so the wavelength is $4l$, whereas in the open tube there is half a wavelength, giving a wavelength of $2l$. Closing one end of the tube thus halves the wavelength of the note and so the frequency doubles.

## Stationary waves and musical instruments

The production of different notes by musical instruments often depends on the creation of stationary waves (Figure 16.13). For a stringed instrument such as a guitar, the two ends of a string are fixed, so nodes must be established at these points. When the string is plucked half-way along its length, it vibrates with an antinode at its midpoint. This is known as the **fundamental mode of vibration** of the string. The **fundamental frequency** is the **minimum frequency** of a standing wave for a given system or arrangement.

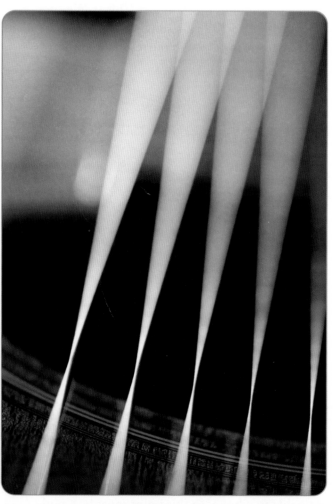

**Figure 16.13** When a guitar string is plucked, the vibrations of the strings continue for some time afterwards. Here you can clearly see a node close to the end of each string.

Similarly, the air column inside a wind instrument is caused to vibrate by blowing, and the note that is heard depends on a stationary wave being established. By changing the length of the air column, as in a trombone, the note can be changed. Alternatively, holes can be uncovered so that the air can vibrate more freely, giving a different pattern of nodes and antinodes.

In practice, the sounds that are produced are made up of several different stationary waves having different patterns of nodes and antinodes. For example, a guitar string may vibrate with two antinodes along its length. This gives a note having twice the frequency of the fundamental, and is described as a **harmonic** of the fundamental. The musician's skill is in stimulating the string or air column to produce a desired mixture of frequencies.

The frequency of a harmonic is always a multiple of the fundamental frequency. The diagrams show some of the modes of vibrations for a fixed length of string (Figure **16.14**) and an air column in a tube of a given length that is closed at one end (Figure **16.15**).

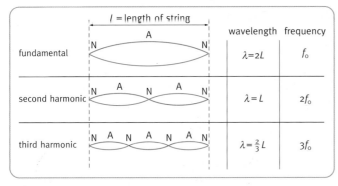

Figure **16.14** Some of the possible stationary waves for a fixed string of length $L$. The frequency of the harmonics is a multiple of the fundamental frequency $f_o$.

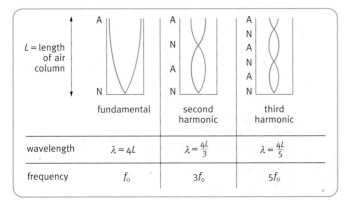

Figure **16.15** Some of the possible stationary waves for an air column, closed at one end. The frequency of each harmonic is an odd multiple of the fundamental frequency $f_o$.

# Determining the wavelength and speed of sound

Since we know that adjacent nodes (or antinodes) of a stationary wave are separated by half a wavelength, we can use this fact to determine the wavelength $\lambda$ of a progressive wave. If we also know the frequency $f$ of the waves, we can find their speed $v$ using the wave equation $v = f\lambda$.

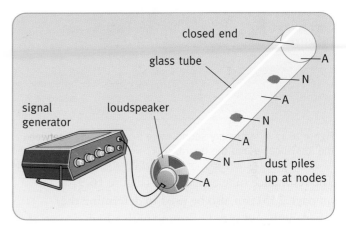

Figure **16.16** Kundt's dust tube can be used to determine the speed of sound.

One approach uses Kundt's dust tube (Figure **16.16**). A loudspeaker sends sound waves along the inside of a tube. The sound is reflected at the closed end. When a stationary wave is established, the dust (fine powder) at the antinodes vibrates violently. It tends to accumulate at the nodes, where the movement of the air is zero. Hence the positions of the nodes and antinodes can be clearly seen.

An alternative method is shown in Figure **16.17**; this is the same arrangement as used for microwaves. The loudspeaker produces sound waves, and these are reflected from the vertical board. The microphone detects the stationary sound wave in the space between the speaker and the board, and its output is displayed on the oscilloscope. It is simplest to turn off the time-base of the oscilloscope, so that the spot no longer moves across the screen. The spot moves up and down the screen, and the height of the vertical trace gives a measure of the intensity of the sound.

By moving the microphone along the line between the speaker and the board, it is easy to detect nodes and antinodes. For maximum accuracy, we do not measure the separation of adjacent nodes; it is better to measure the distance across several nodes.

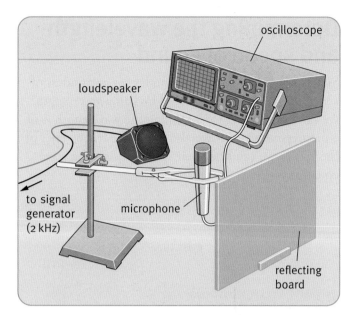

**Figure 16.17** A stationary sound wave is established between the loudspeaker and the board.

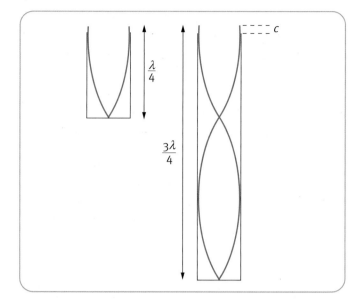

**Figure 16.18** The antinode at the open end of a resonance tube is formed at a distance $c$ beyond the open end of the tube.

The resonance tube experiment (Figure **16.9** on page **235**) can also be used to determine the wavelength and speed of sound with a high degree of accuracy. However, to do this, it is necessary to take account of a systematic error in the experiment, as discussed in the next section.

(Figure **16.9** on page **235**)

Figure **16.18**.

antinode at the top of the tube is shown extending slightly beyond the open end of the tube. This is because experiment shows that the air slightly beyond the end of the tube vibrates as part of the stationary wave. This is shown more clearly in Figure **16.18**.

The antinode is at a distance $c$ beyond the end of the tube, where $c$ is called the **end-correction**. Unfortunately, we do not know the value of $c$. It cannot be measured directly. However, we can write:

for the shorter tube, $= \dfrac{\lambda}{4} = l_1 + c$

for the longer tube, $\dfrac{3\lambda}{4} = l_2 + c$

Subtracting the first equation from the second equation gives:

$$\frac{3\lambda}{4} - \frac{\lambda}{4} = (l_2 + c) - (l_1 + c)$$

Simplifying gives:

$$\frac{\lambda}{2} = l_2 - l_1$$

Hence:

$$\lambda = 2(l_2 - l_1)$$

## Test yourself

**5** **a** For the arrangement shown in Figure **16.17**, suggest why it is easier to determine accurately the position of a node rather than an antinode.
   **b** Explain why it is better to measure the distance across several nodes.

**6** For sound waves of frequency 2500 Hz, it is found that two nodes are separated by 20 cm, with three antinodes between them.
   **a** Determine the wavelength of these sound waves.
   **b** Use the wave equation $v = f\lambda$ to determine the speed of sound in air.

# Eliminating errors

The resonance tube experiment illustrates an interesting way in which one type of experimental error can be reduced or even eliminated. Look at the representation of the stationary waves in the tubes shown in Figure **16.10** on page **235**. In each case, the

shown in Figure **16.10** on page **235**.

So, although we do not know the value of $c$, we can make two measurements ($l_1$ and $l_2$) and obtain an accurate value of $\lambda$. (You may be able to see from Figure **16.18** that the difference in lengths of the two tubes is indeed equal to half a wavelength.)

The end-correction $c$ is an example of a **systematic error**. When we measure the length $l$ of the tube, we are measuring a length which is consistently less than the quantity we really need to know ($l+c$). However, by understanding how the systematic error affects the results, we have been able to remove it from our measurements.

You will find more detailed discussion of systematic errors in Appendix **A1**: AS practical skills.

## Test yourself

7  In a resonance tube experiment, resonance is obtained for sound waves of frequency 630 Hz when the length of the air column is 12.6 cm and again when it is 38.8 cm. Determine:
   **a** the wavelength of the sound waves causing resonance
   **b** the end-correction for this tube
   **c** the speed of sound in air.

## Summary

- ☐ Stationary waves are formed when two identical waves travelling in opposite directions meet and superimpose. This usually happens when one wave is a reflection of the other.
- ☐ A stationary wave has a characteristic pattern of nodes and antinodes.
- ☐ A node is a point where the amplitude is always zero.
- ☐ An antinode is a point of maximum amplitude.
- ☐ Adjacent nodes (or antinodes) are separated by a distance equal to half a wavelength.
- ☐ We can use the wave equation $v = f\lambda$ to determine the speed $v$ or the frequency $f$ of a progressive wave. The wavelength $\lambda$ is found using the nodes or antinodes of the stationary wave pattern.

## End-of-chapter questions

1  Figure **16.19** shows a stationary wave on a string.

vibrator

**Figure 16.19** For End-of-chapter Q 1.

   **a** On a copy of the diagram, label one **node** (N) and one **antinode** (A).
   **b** Mark on your diagram the wavelength of the standing wave and label it $\lambda$.
   **c** The frequency of the vibrator is doubled. Describe the changes in the standing wave pattern.

2  A tuning fork which produces a note of 256 Hz is placed above tube which is nearly filled with water. The water level is lowered until resonance is first heard.
   **a** Explain what is meant by the term **resonance**.
   **b** The length of the column of air above the water, when resonance is first heard is 31.2 cm. Calculate the speed of the sound wave.

# Exam-style questions

1   a   State **two** similarities and **two** differences between progressive waves and stationary waves.   [4]
    b   The diagram shows an experiment to measure the speed of a sound in a string.
        The frequency of the vibrator is adjusted until the standing wave shown in the diagram
        is formed.

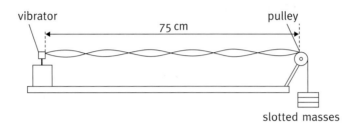

        i   On a copy of the diagram, mark a node (label it N) and an antinode (label it A).   [2]
        ii   The frequency of the vibrator is 120 Hz. Calculate the speed at which a progressive
             wave would travel along the string.   [3]
    c   The experiment is now repeated with the load on the string halved. In order to get a
        similar standing wave the frequency has to be decreased to 30 Hz.
        Explain, in terms of the speed of the wave in the string, why the frequency
        must be adjusted.   [3]

2   The diagram shows a standing wave, of frequency 400 Hz, produced by a loudspeaker
    in a closed tube.

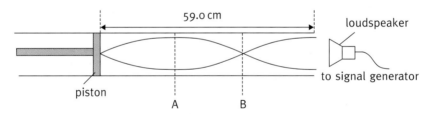

    a   Describe the movement of the air particles at:
        i   A   [2]
        ii   B.   [1]
    b   The piston is slowly moved outwards. The next resonant peak is heard when the length
        of the column of air is 99.4 cm.
        Calculate:
        i   the speed of the sound   [4]
        ii   the end correction which must be applied when using this tube.   [1]

3   a   Explain what is meant by:
        i   a **coherent** source of waves   [2]
        ii   **phase difference**.   [2]

**b** A student, experimenting with microwaves, sets up the arrangement shown in the diagram. With the metal plate at position A there is a very small signal. He slowly moves the plate back. As he does so he finds that the intensity initially rises until it becomes a maximum, then falls back to a minimum. This cycle repeats a total of five times until he reaches position B, where once again there is a minimum.

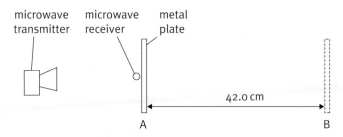

    **i**   Explain why a series of maxima and minima are heard.                                  [2]

    **ii**  Calculate the frequency of the microwaves.                                          [5]

**c** The student was surprised to find that there is a minimum when both plates are at position A. Suggest a reason for this.                           [2]

**4**    The diagram shows an experiment to measure the speed of sound in air.

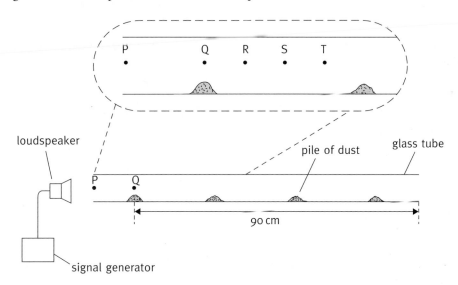

A small amount of dust is scattered along the tube. The loudspeaker is switched on. When the frequency is set at 512 Hz the dust collects in small piles as shown in the diagram.

**a** Determine the wavelength of the sound wave and calculate the speed of sound in the air in the tube.                                          [3]

**b** On a copy of the diagram, show the movement of the air particles at positions P, Q, R, S and T.                                          [3]

**c** Mark two points on your diagram where the movements of the air particles are 180° out of phase with each other – label them A and B.                     [1]

# 17 Radioactivity

## Objectives

After studying this chapter, you should be able to:

- [ ] describe the nuclear model of the atom and the evidence for it
- [ ] represent nuclides using their nucleon and proton numbers
- [ ] write simple nuclear decay equations and explain how they are balanced
- [ ] describe the spontaneous and random nature of radioactive decay
- [ ] show understanding of the nature and properties of α-, β and γ-radiations

## Radioactivity at work

Radioactive substances have many uses, for example in engineering and medicine. They must be handled with great care to ensure that no-one becomes contaminated and so exposed to the radiation which comes from these substances (Figure 17.1). In this chapter we will look at the nature of radioactive substances and the different types of radiation they produce.

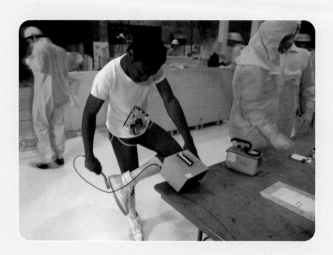

**Figure 17.1** A worker at a nuclear power station checks for any radioactive material on his body before he leaves for home at the end of his shift.

## Looking inside the atom

The idea that matter is composed of very small particles called atoms was first suggested by the Greeks some 2000 years ago. However, it was not until the middle of the 19th century that any ideas about the **inside** of the atom were proposed.

It was the English scientist J.J. Thomson who suggested that the atom is a neutral particle made of a positive charge with lumps of negative charge (electrons) in it. He could not determine the charge and the mass of the negative particles separately, but it was clear that a new particle, probably much smaller than the hydrogen atom, had been discovered. Since atoms are neutral and physicists had discovered a negatively charged part of an atom, it meant that there were both positive and negative charges in an atom. We now call this the **plum pudding model** of the atom (positive pudding with negative plums!).

Other experiments show that the electron has a mass of $9.11 \times 10^{-31}$ kg ($m_e$) and a charge of $-1.6 \times 10^{-19}$ C ($-e$). Today we use the idea of the electron to explain all sorts of phenomena, including electrostatics, current electricity and electronics.

## Alpha-particle scattering and the nucleus

Early in the 20th century, many physicists were investigating the recently discovered phenomenon of radioactivity, the process whereby unstable nuclei emit radiation. One kind of radiation they found consisted of what they called α-particles (alpha-particles).

These α-particles were known to be smaller than atoms, and had relatively high kinetic energies. Hence they were useful in experiments designed to discover the composition of atoms.

**Figure 17.2** Ernest Rutherford (on the right) in the Cavendish Laboratory, Cambridge, England. He had a loud voice that could disturb sensitive apparatus and so the notice was a joke aimed at him.

In 1906, while experimenting with the passage of α-particles through a thin mica sheet, Rutherford (Figure 17.2) noticed that most of the α-particles passed straight through. This suggested to him that there might be a large amount of empty space in the atom, and by 1909 he had developed what we now call the **nuclear model of the atom**.

In 1911 Rutherford carried out a further series of experiments, with Hans Geiger and Ernest Marsden at the University of Manchester, using gold foil in place of the mica. They directed parallel beams of α-particles at a piece of gold foil only $10^{-6}$ m thick. Most of the α-particles went straight through. Some were deflected slightly, but about 1 in 20 000 were deflected through an angle of more than 90°, so that they appeared to bounce back off the foil. This confirmed Rutherford in his thinking about the atom – that it was mostly empty space, with most of the mass and all of the positive charge concentrated in a tiny region at the centre. This central **nucleus** only affected the α-particles when they came close to it.

Later, when describing the results, Rutherford wrote: 'It was quite the most incredible event that has happened to me in my life. It was almost as incredible as if you fired a 15 inch shell at a piece of tissue paper and it came back and hit you.' In fact, he was not quite as surprised as this might suggest, because the results confirmed the ideas he had used in designing the experiment.

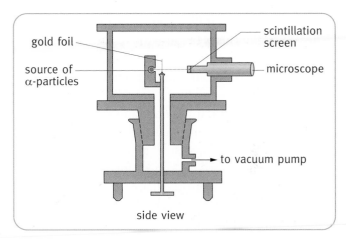

**Figure 17.3** The apparatus used for the α-scattering experiment. The microscope can be moved round to detect scattered radiation at different angles.

Figure **17.3** shows the apparatus used in the α-scattering experiment. Notice the following points:

- The α-particle source was encased in metal with a small aperture allowing a fine beam of α-particles to emerge.
- Air in the apparatus was pumped out to leave a vacuum; α-radiation is absorbed by a few centimetres of air.
- One reason for choosing gold was that it can be made into a very thin sheet or foil. Rutherford's foil was only a few hundreds of atoms thick.
- The α-particles were detected when they struck a solid 'scintillating' material. Each α-particle gave a tiny flash of light and these were counted by the experimenters (Geiger and Marsden).
- The detector could be moved round to detect the α-particles scattered through different angles.

Geiger and Marsden had the difficult task of observing and counting the tiny flashes of light produced by individual α-particles striking the scintillation screen. They had to spend several minutes in the darkened laboratory to allow the pupils of their eyes to become dilated so that they could see the faint flashes. Each experimenter could only stare into the detector for about a minute before the strain was too much and they had to change places.

## Explaining α-scattering

How can we explain the back-scattering of α-particles by the gold atoms?

If the atom was as Thomson pictured it, with negatively charged electrons scattered through a 'pudding' of positive charge, an individual α-particle would pass through it like a bullet, hardly being deflected at all. This is because the α-particles are more massive than electrons – they might push an electron out of the atom, but their own path would be scarcely affected.

On the other hand, if the mass and positive charge of the atom were concentrated at one point in the atom, as Rutherford suggested, an α-particle striking this part would be striking something more massive than itself and with a greater charge. A head-on collision would send the α-particle backwards.

A very simple analogy (or model) of the experiment is shown in Figure 17.4. When you roll a ball-bearing down a slope towards the 'cymbal' it may be deflected, but even if it is rolled directly at the cymbal's centre, it does not come back – it rolls over the centre and carries on to the other side. However, using the 'tin hat' shape, with a much narrower but higher central bulge, any ball-bearings rolled close to the centre will be markedly deflected, and those rolled directly towards it will come straight back.

The shape of the cymbal represents the shape of the electric field of an atom in the 'plum pudding' model: low central intensity and spread out. The 'tin hat' represents the shape of the electric field for the nuclear model: high central intensity and concentrated.

The paths of an α-particle near a nucleus are shown in Figure 17.5. Rutherford reasoned that the large deflection of the α-particle must be due to a very small charged nucleus. From his experiments he calculated that the diameter of the gold nucleus was about $10^{-14}$ m. It has since been shown that the very large deflection of the α-particle is due to the electrostatic repulsion between the positive charge of the α-particle and the positive charge of the nucleus of the atom. The closer the path of the α-particle gets to the nucleus, the greater will be this repulsion. An α-particle making a 'head-on' collision with a

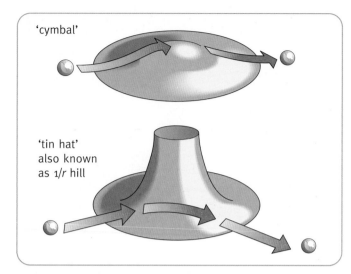

**Figure 17.4** An analogy for Rutherford's experiment.

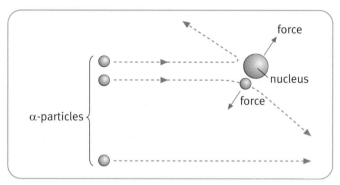

**Figure 17.5** Possible paths of an α-particle near a nucleus. The nucleus and the α-particle both experience electrostatic repulsion.

nucleus is back-scattered through 180°. The α-particle and nucleus both experience an equal but opposite repulsive electrostatic force $F$. This force has a much greater effect on the motion of the α-particle than on the massive nucleus of gold.

From the α-particle scattering experiment, Rutherford deduced the following.

- An α-particle is deviated due to the repulsive force between the α-particle and the positive charge in the atom.
- Most α-particles have little or no deviation – so most of an atom is empty space.
- A very few α-particles are deviated more than 90° – so most of the mass of an atom is concentrated in a small space (the nucleus) and most of an atom is empty space.

1 Rutherford's scattering experiments were done in an evacuated container. Explain why this is necessary.

2 In Rutherford's experiment, α-particles were directed at a thin gold foil. A small fraction of the α-particles were back-scattered through 180°.
   Describe and explain how the fraction back-scattered changes if each of the following changes are (separately) made.
   a A thicker foil is used.
   b Faster α-particles are used.
   c A silver foil is used – a silver nucleus has less positive charge than a gold nucleus.

# A simple model of the atom

After Rutherford had presented his findings, the nuclear model of the atom gained rapid acceptance. This was partly because it helped chemists to explain the phenomenon of chemical bonding (the way in which atoms bond together to form molecules). Subsequently, the proton was discovered. It had a positive charge, equal and opposite to that of the electron. However, its mass was too small to account for the entire mass of the atom and it was not until the early 1930s that this puzzle was solved by the discovery of the neutron, an uncharged particle with a similar mass to that of the proton. This suggests a model for the atom like the one shown in Figure 17.6.

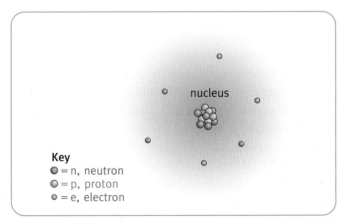

**Key**
- = n, neutron
- = p, proton
- = e, electron

**Figure 17.6** A simple model of the atom. If the nucleus were drawn to scale, it would be invisible (and the electrons are even smaller!).

- Protons and neutrons make up the nucleus of the atom.
- The electrons move around the nucleus in a cloud, some closer to and some further from the centre of the nucleus.

From this model it looks as though all matter, including ourselves, is mostly empty space. For example, if we scaled up the hydrogen atom so that the nucleus was the size of a 1 cm diameter marble, the orbiting electron would be a grain of sand some 800 m away!

## The scale of things

It is useful to have an idea of the approximate sizes of typical particles:

- radius of proton ~ radius of neutron ~ $10^{-15}$ m
- radius of nucleus ~ $10^{-15}$ m to $10^{-14}$ m
- radius of atom ~ $10^{-10}$ m
- size of molecule ~ $10^{-10}$ m to $10^{-6}$ m.

(Some molecules, such as large protein molecules, are very large indeed – compared to an atom!)
  The radii of nuclear particles are often quoted in femtometres (fm), where 1 fm = $10^{-15}$ m.

## Nuclear density

We can picture a proton as a small, positively charged sphere. Knowing its mass and radius, we can calculate its density:

mass of proton $m_p = 1.67 \times 10^{-27}$ kg

radius of proton $r = 0.80$ fm $= 0.80 \times 10^{-15}$ m

(In fact, the radius of the proton is not very accurately known; it is probably between $0.80 \times 10^{-15}$ m and $0.86 \times 10^{-15}$ m.)

$$\text{volume of proton} = \tfrac{4}{3}\pi r^3 = \tfrac{4}{3}\pi \times (0.80 \times 10^{-15})^3$$

$$= 2.14 \times 10^{-45}\,\text{m}^3 \approx 2.1 \times 10^{-45}\,\text{m}^3$$

$$\text{density} = \frac{\text{mass}}{\text{volume}}$$

$$\text{density} = \frac{1.67 \times 10^{-27}}{2.14 \times 10^{-45}} \approx 7.8 \times 10^{17}\,\text{kg m}^{-3}$$

So the proton has a density of roughly $10^{18}$ kg m$^{-3}$. This is also the density of an atomic nucleus, because nuclei are made of protons and neutrons held closely together.

Compare the density of nuclear material with that of water whose density is $1000\,\mathrm{kg\,m^{-3}}$ – the nucleus is $10^{15}$ times as dense. Nuclear matter the size of a tiny grain of sand would have a mass of about a million tonnes! This is a consequence of the fact that the nucleus occupies only a tiny fraction of the volume of an atom. The remainder is occupied by the cloud of orbiting electrons whose mass makes up less than one-thousandth of the atomic mass.

## Test yourself

3   Gold has a density of $19\,700\,\mathrm{kg\,m^{-3}}$. $193\,\mathrm{g}$ of gold contains $6.02\times10^{23}$ atoms. Use this information to estimate the volume of a gold atom, and hence its radius. State any assumptions you make.

# Nucleons and electrons

We will start this section with a summary of the particles mentioned so far (Table **17.1**). All nuclei, except the lightest form of hydrogen, contain protons and neutrons, and each nucleus is described by the number of protons and neutrons that it contains.

- Protons and neutrons in a nucleus are collectively called **nucleons**. For example, in a nucleus of gold, there are 79 protons and 118 neutrons, giving a total of 197 nucleons altogether.
- The total number of nucleons in a nucleus is called the **nucleon number** (or mass number) $A$.
- The nucleon number is equal to the sum of the number of neutrons in the nucleus, the **neutron number** $N$, and the number of protons, the **proton number** (or atomic number) $Z$, i.e.

$$A = N + Z$$

| Particle | Relative mass (proton = 1)[a] | Charge[b] |
|---|---|---|
| proton (p) | 1 | $+e$ |
| neutron (n) | 1 | 0 |
| electron (e) | 0.0005 | $-e$ |
| alpha-particle ($\alpha$) | 4 | $+2e$ |

[a] The numbers given for the masses are approximate.
[b] $e = 1.60\times10^{-19}\,\mathrm{C}$.

**Table 17.1** Summary of the particles that we have met so far in this chapter. The $\alpha$-particle is in fact a helium nucleus (with two protons and two neutrons).

Any nucleus of an atom can be represented by the symbol for the element along with the nucleon number and proton number as shown below:

$$\text{nucleon number} \atop \text{proton number} \quad \text{element symbol} \quad {}^{A}_{Z}X$$

oxygen ${}^{16}_{8}\mathrm{O}$         gold ${}^{197}_{79}\mathrm{Au}$         uranium ${}^{235}_{92}\mathrm{U}$

A specific combination of protons and neutrons in a nucleus is called a **nuclide**.

The proton and nucleon numbers of some common elements are shown in Table **17.2**.

## Test yourself

4   Table **17.2** shows the proton and nucleon numbers of several nuclei. Determine the number of neutrons in each of the following nuclei shown in the table:
   **a** nitrogen
   **b** bromine
   **c** silver
   **d** gold
   **e** mercury.

5   State the charge of each of the following in terms of the elementary charge $e$:
   **a** proton
   **b** neutron
   **c** nucleus
   **d** molecule
   **e** $\alpha$-particle.

# Isotopes

Although atoms of the same element may be identical chemically, their nuclei may be slightly different. The number of protons in the nucleus of an atom determines what element it is: helium always has 2 protons, carbon 6 protons, oxygen 8 protons, neon 10 protons, radium 88 protons, uranium 92 protons, and so on.

However, the number of neutrons in the nuclei for a given element can vary. Take neon as an

| Element | Nucleon number $A$ | Proton number $Z$ | Element | Nucleon number $A$ | Proton number $Z$ |
|---|---|---|---|---|---|
| hydrogen | 1 | 1 | bromine | 79 | 35 |
| helium | 4 | 2 | silver | 107 | 47 |
| lithium | 7 | 3 | tin | 120 | 50 |
| beryllium | 9 | 4 | iodine | 130 | 53 |
| boron | 11 | 5 | caesium | 133 | 55 |
| carbon | 12 | 6 | barium | 138 | 56 |
| nitrogen | 14 | 7 | tungsten | 184 | 74 |
| oxygen | 16 | 8 | platinum | 195 | 78 |
| neon | 20 | 10 | gold | 197 | 79 |
| sodium | 23 | 11 | mercury | 202 | 80 |
| magnesium | 24 | 12 | lead | 206 | 82 |
| aluminium | 27 | 13 | bismuth | 209 | 83 |
| chlorine | 35 | 17 | radium | 226 | 88 |
| calcium | 40 | 20 | uranium | 238 | 92 |
| iron | 56 | 26 | plutonium | 239 | 94 |
| nickel | 58 | 28 | americium | 241 | 95 |

**Table 17.2** Proton and nucleon numbers of some nuclides.

example. Three different naturally occurring forms of neon are:

$$^{20}_{10}\text{Ne} \qquad ^{21}_{10}\text{Ne} \qquad ^{22}_{10}\text{Ne}$$

The first has 10 neutrons in the nucleus, the second 11 neutrons and the third 12 neutrons. These three types of neon nuclei are called **isotopes** of neon. Each isotope has the same number of protons (for neon this is 10) but a different number of neutrons. The word 'isotope' comes from the Greek *isotopos* (same place), because all isotopes of the same element have the same place in the Periodic Table of elements.

> Isotopes are nuclei of the same element with a different number of neutrons but the same number of protons.

Any atom is electrically neutral (it has no net positive or negative charge), so the number of electrons surrounding the nucleus must equal the number of protons in the nucleus of the atom. If an atom gains or loses an electron, it is no longer electrically neutral and is called an **ion**.

For an atom, the number of protons (and hence the number of electrons) determines the chemical properties of the atom. The number of protons and the number of neutrons determine the nuclear

properties. It is important to realise that, since the number of protons, and therefore the number of electrons, in isotopes of the same element are identical, they will all have the same chemical properties but very different nuclear properties.

Hydrogen has three important isotopes, $^{1}_{1}\text{H}$, $^{2}_{1}\text{H}$ (deuterium) and $^{3}_{1}\text{H}$ (tritium) (Figure 17.7). $^{1}_{1}\text{H}$ and

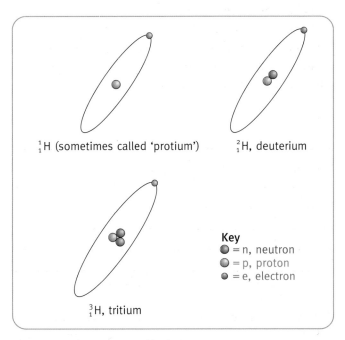

**Figure 17.7** The isotopes of hydrogen.

deuterium occur naturally, but tritium has to be made. Deuterium and tritium form the fuel of many fusion research reactors. Hydrogen is the most abundant element in the Universe (Figure 17.8), because it consists of just one proton and one electron, which is the simplest structure possible for an atom.

The different numbers of neutrons in the isotopes of en element means that the isotopes will have different relative atomic masses. There are differences too in some of their physical properties, such as density and boiling point. For example, heavy water, which is water containing deuterium, has a boiling point of 104 °C under normal atmospheric pressure.

Table 17.3 gives details of some other commonly occurring isotopes.

**Figure 17.8** The Horsehead Nebula in Orion. The large coloured regions are expanses of dust and gas, mostly hydrogen, that are ionised by nearby stars so that they emit light. The dark 'horse head' is where the areas of gas and dust remain in atomic form and block out the light from behind.

| Element | Nucleon number $A$ | Proton number $Z$ | Neutron number $N$ |
|---|---|---|---|
| hydrogen | 1 | 1 | 0 |
| | 2 | 1 | 1 |
| carbon | 12 | 6 | 6 |
| | 14 | 6 | 8 |
| oxygen | 16 | 8 | 8 |
| | 18 | 8 | 10 |
| neon | 20 | 10 | 10 |
| | 21 | 10 | 11 |
| potassium | 39 | 19 | 20 |
| | 40 | 19 | 21 |
| strontium | 88 | 38 | 50 |
| | 90 | 38 | 52 |
| caesium | 135 | 55 | 80 |
| | 137 | 55 | 82 |
| lead | 206 | 82 | 124 |
| | 208 | 82 | 126 |
| radium | 226 | 88 | 138 |
| | 228 | 88 | 140 |
| uranium | 235 | 92 | 143 |
| | 238 | 92 | 146 |

**Table 17.3** Some commonly occurring isotopes.

## Test yourself

6 Uranium has atomic number 92. Two of its common isotopes have nucleon numbers 235 and 238. Determine the number of neutrons for these isotopes.

7 There are seven naturally occurring isotopes of mercury with nucleon numbers (relative abundances) of 196 (0.2%), 198 (10%), 199 (16.8%), 200 (23.1%), 201 (13.2%), 202 (29.8%) and 204 (6.9%).
   a Determine the proton and neutron numbers for each isotope.
   b Determine the average relative atomic mass (equivalent to the 'average nucleon number') of naturally occurring mercury.

8 Group the following imaginary elements A–H into isotopes and name them using the Periodic Table in the back of the book (Appendix **D**).

| | A | B | C | D | E | F | G | H |
|---|---|---|---|---|---|---|---|---|
| Proton number | 20 | 23 | 21 | 22 | 20 | 22 | 22 | 23 |
| Nucleon number | 44 | 50 | 46 | 46 | 46 | 48 | 50 | 51 |

# Discovering radioactivity

The French physicist Henri Becquerel (Figure 17.9) is credited with the discovery of radioactivity in 1896. He had been looking at the properties of uranium compounds when he noticed that they affected photographic film – he realised that they were giving out radiation all the time and he performed several ingenious experiments to shed light on the phenomenon.

**Figure 17.9** Henri Becquerel, the discoverer of radioactivity, in his laboratory. His father and grandfather had been professors of physics in Paris before him.

# Radiation from radioactive substances

There are three types of radiation which are emitted by radioactive substances: alpha ($\alpha$), beta ($\beta$) and gamma ($\gamma$) radiations come from the unstable nuclei of atoms. Nuclei consist of protons and neutrons, and if the balance between these two types of particles is too far to one side, the nucleus may emit $\alpha$- or $\beta$-radiation as a way of achieving greater stability. Gamma radiation is usually emitted after $\alpha$- or $\beta$-decay, to release excess energy from the nuclei.

Table 17.4 shows the basic characteristics of the different types of radiation. The masses are given relative to the mass of a proton; charge is measured in units of $e$, the elementary charge.

| Radiation | Symbol | Mass (relative to proton) | Charge | Typical speed |
|---|---|---|---|---|
| $\alpha$-particle | $\alpha$, $^4_2\text{He}$ | 4 | $+2e$ | 'slow' ($10^6\,\text{m s}^{-1}$) |
| $\beta$-particle | $\beta$, $\beta^-$, e, $^0_{-1}\text{e}$ | $\dfrac{1}{1840}$ | $-e$ | 'fast' ($10^8\,\text{m s}^{-1}$) |
| $\gamma$-ray | $\gamma$ | 0 | 0 | speed of light ($3 \times 10^8\,\text{m s}^{-1}$) |

**Table 17.4** The basic characteristics of ionising radiations.

Note the following points:

- $\alpha$- and $\beta$-radiation are particles of matter. A $\gamma$-ray is a photon of electromagnetic radiation, similar to an X-ray. (X-rays are produced when electrons are decelerated; $\gamma$-rays are produced in nuclear reactions.)
- An $\alpha$-particle consists of two protons and two neutrons; it is a nucleus of helium-4. A $\beta$-particle is simply a fast-moving electron.
- The mass of an $\alpha$-particle is nearly 10 000 times that of an electron and it travels at roughly one-hundredth of the speed of a $\beta$-particle.

## Balanced equations

When an unstable nucleus undergoes radioactive decay, the nucleus before the decay is often referred to as the **parent** nucleus and the new nucleus after the decay of the alpha-particle is known as the **daughter** nucleus.

Radioactive decay processes can be represented by balanced equations. As for all equations representing nuclear processes, both nucleon number $A$ and proton number $Z$ are conserved.

- In $\alpha$-decay, the nucleon number decreases by 4 and the proton number decreases by 2.
- In $\beta$-decay, the nucleon number is unchanged and the proton number increases by 1.
- In $\gamma$-emission there is no change in nucleon or proton number.

The emission of $\alpha$- and $\beta$-particles can be shown on a graph of nucleon number plotted against proton number, as shown in Figure 17.10. The graph will appear different if neutron number is plotted against proton number.

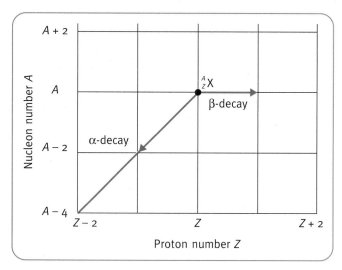

Figure 17.10 Emission of α- and β-particles.

## A note on β-decay

In β-decay an electron is emitted from a nucleus. How is this possible, since electrons are found outside the nucleus? What happens inside the nucleus is that a neutron decays to a proton and an electron. The neutron formed stays inside the nucleus but the electron is emitted as a β-particle. This makes the daughter nucleus more stable.

Free neutrons do indeed decay with the reaction:

$$^{1}_{0}n \rightarrow {}^{1}_{1}p + {}^{0}_{-1}e + \text{energy}$$

When a β-particle is emitted the nucleus loses one neutron and gains one proton. The overall nucleon number is unchanged.

## A third conserved quantity

We have seen that, in radioactive decay, both nucleon number $A$ and proton number $Z$ are conserved. However, if we add up the masses of the particles after decay and compare the total with the mass of the nucleus before decay, we find a surprising result. There is less mass after than before. How can mass 'disappear' like this? We can answer this by thinking about the energy which is carried away by the particles (α or β) and electromagnetic radiation (γ) produced in the decay. Albert Einstein realised that we can think of energy as having mass. So, if the mass of a nucleus decreases when it decays, we must look around and find the energy which is carrying away this mass.

The greater the apparent loss of mass, the greater the amount of energy which is escaping.

To sum this up, we talk about 'mass–energy'. In any closed system the total amount of mass–energy is conserved. If mass goes down, energy goes up, and vice versa, but the total is constant. (In Chapter **30** we will see how to use Einstein's mass–energy relationship $E = mc^2$ to calculate the amount of energy $E$ associated with mass $m$.)

## Worked examples

1  Radon is a radioactive gas that decays by α-emission to become polonium. Here is the equation for the decay of one of its isotopes, radon-222:

$$^{222}_{86}\text{Rn} \rightarrow {}^{218}_{84}\text{Po} + {}^{4}_{2}\text{He}$$

Show that $A$ and $Z$ are conserved.

Compare the nucleon and proton numbers on both sides of the equation for the decay:

nucleon number $A$    $222 = 218 + 4$

proton number $Z$    $86 = 84 + 2$

> Learn that in α-decay, $A$ decreases by 4 and $Z$ decreases by 2.
>  Don't confuse nucleon number $A$ with neutron number $N$.

In this case, radon-222 is the parent nucleus and polonium-218 is the daughter nucleus.

2  A carbon-14 nucleus (parent) decays by beta emission to become an isotope of nitrogen (daughter). Here is the equation that represents this decay:

$$^{14}_{6}\text{C} \rightarrow {}^{14}_{7}\text{N} + {}^{0}_{-1}\text{e}$$

continued ⋯⟩

Show that both nucleon number and proton number are conserved.

Compare the nucleon and proton numbers on both sides of the equation for the decay:

nucleon number $A$    $14 = 14 + 0$

proton number $Z$    $6 = 7 - 1$

> Learn that in β-decay, $A$ remains the same and $Z$ increases by 1.

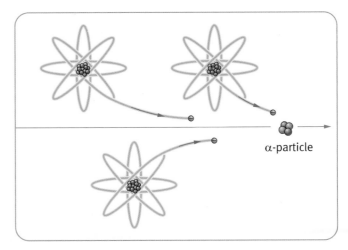

**Figure 17.11** As an α-particle passes through a material, it causes ionisation of atoms.

## Test yourself

9 Study the decay equations given in Worked examples **1** and **2**, and write balanced equations for the following:
   **a** A nucleus of radon-220 ($^{220}_{86}$Rn) decays by α-emission to form an isotope of polonium, Po.
   **b** A nucleus of a sodium isotope ($^{25}_{11}$Na) decays by β emission to form an isotope of magnesium, Mg.

10 Copy and complete this equation for the β-decay of a nucleus of argon:
   $^{41}_{18}$Ar → K + ?

# Properties of ionising radiation

Radiation affects the matter it passes through by causing ionisation. Both α- and β-particles are fast-moving charged particles, and if they collide with or pass close to atoms, they may knock or drag electrons away from the atoms (Figure 17.11). The resulting atoms are said to be **ionised**, and the process is called ionisation. In the process, the radiation loses some of its kinetic energy. After many ionisations, the radiation loses all of its energy and no longer has any ionising effect.

Alpha-radiation is the most strongly ionising, because the mass and charge of an α-particle are greater than those of a β-particle, and it usually travels more slowly. This means that an α-particle interacts more strongly with any atom that it passes, and so it is more likely to cause ionisation. Beta-particles are much lighter and faster, and so their effect is less. Gamma-radiation also causes ionisation, but not as strongly as α- and β particles, as γ-rays are not charged.

## Test yourself

11 a Explain why you would expect β-particles to travel further through air than α-particles.
   b Explain why you would expect β-particles to travel further through air than through metal.

## Behaviour of radiations in electric and magnetic fields

Because α-, β- and γ-radiations have different charges, or no charge, they behave differently in electric and magnetic fields. This can be used to distinguish one kind of radiation from another.

Figure **17.12** shows the effect of an electric field. A mixture of α-, β- and γ-radiations is passing through the gap between two parallel plates; the electric field in this space is uniform (Chapter **9**). Since α- and β-particles are charged, they are attracted to the plate that has the opposite charge to their own. Beta-particles are deflected more than α-particles, since their mass is so much less. Gamma-rays are undeflected since they are uncharged.

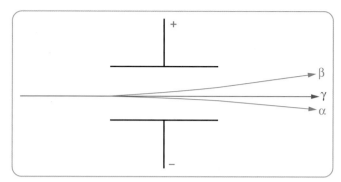

**Figure 17.12** An electric field can be used to separate α-, β- and γ-radiations.

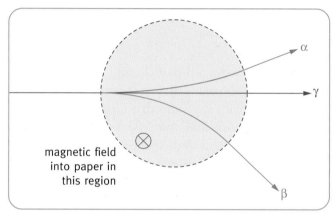

**Figure 17.13** A magnetic field may also be used to separate α-, β- and γ-radiations.

Figure **17.13** shows the effect of a magnetic field. In this case, the deflecting force on the particles is at right angles to their motion.

## Test yourself

**12 a** Some radioactive substances emit α-particles having two different speeds. Draw a diagram similar to Figure **17.12** to show how these particles would move in a uniform electric field. Label your diagram to show the tracks of the faster and slower α-particles.
**b** A β-emitting radioactive substance emits β-particles with a range of speeds. Add to the diagram you drew in **a** to show how these particles would behave in the uniform electric field.

## Radiation penetration

> **Safety note**
> When working with radioactive sources, it is essential to follow the relevant safety regulations, which your teacher will explain to you.

### Alpha-radiation

Because α-radiation is highly ionising, it cannot penetrate very far into matter. A cloud chamber can be used to show the tracks of α-particles in air (Figure **17.14**). The tracks are very dense, because of the dense concentration of ions produced, and they extend for only a few centimetres into the air. By the time the α-particles have travelled this far, they have lost virtually all of their kinetic energy. The α-particle, which is a nucleus of helium-4, grabs two drifting electrons in the air and becomes a neutral atom of helium gas.

Alpha-particles can also be detected by a solid-state detector, or by a Geiger–Müller (GM) tube with a thin end-window (Figure **17.15**) connected to an electronic counter. By moving the source back and forth in front of the detector, it is simple to show that

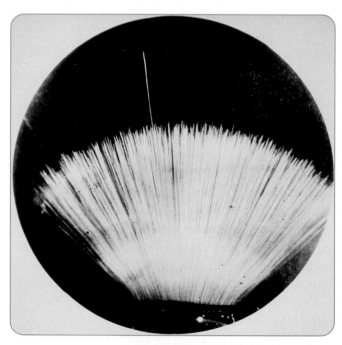

**Figure 17.14** Alpha-particle tracks show up in this photograph of a cloud chamber. Notice that all the particles travel roughly the same distance through the air, indicating that they all have roughly the same initial kinetic energy.

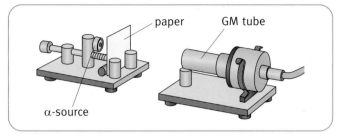

**Figure 17.15** Alpha-radiation can be absorbed by a single sheet of paper.

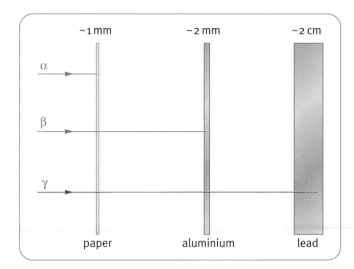

**Figure 17.16** A summary of the penetrating powers of α-, β- and γ-radiations. The approximate thickness of the absorbing material is also shown.

the particles only penetrate 5 or 6 cm of air. Similarly, with the source close to the detector, it can be shown that a single sheet of paper is adequate to absorb all of the α-radiation.

## Beta-radiation

A Geiger–Müller tube can detect β-radiation. The source is placed close to the tube, and different materials are positioned between source and tube. Paper has little effect; a denser material such as aluminium or lead is a more effective absorber. A few millimetres of aluminium will almost completely absorb β-radiation.

## Gamma-radiation

Since γ-radiation is the least strongly ionising, it is the most penetrating. Lead can be used to absorb γ-rays. The intensity of the radiation decreases gradually as it passes through the lead. In principle, an infinite thickness of lead would be needed to absorb the radiation completely; in practice, a couple of centimetres of lead will reduce the intensity by half and 10 cm will reduce the intensity to a safe level in most situations.

The different penetrating properties of α-, β- and γ-radiations can be summarised as follows:

- α-radiation is absorbed by a thin sheet of paper or a few centimetres of air
- β-radiation is absorbed by a few millimetres of metal
- γ-radiation is never completely absorbed but a few centimetres of lead, or several metres of concrete, greatly reduces the intensity.

This is illustrated in Figure 17.16.

## Test yourself

13 Explain why the most strongly ionising radiation (α-particles) is the least penetrating, while the least ionising (γ-rays) is the most penetrating.

14 A smoke detector (Figure 17.17) uses a source of α-radiation to detect the presence of smoke in the air. Find out how the smoke detector works and suggest why an α-source is more suitable for this than a β- or γ-source.

**Figure 17.17** A smoke detector that uses the absorption of α-radiation as the principle of its operation.

# Randomness and decay

Listen to a counter connected to a Geiger–Müller tube that is detecting the radiation from a weak source, so that the count rate is about one count per second. Each count represents the detection of a single α-particle or a β-particle or a γ-ray photon. You will notice that the individual counts do not come regularly. The counter beeps or clicks in a random, irregular manner. If you try to predict when the next clicks will come, you are unlikely to be right.

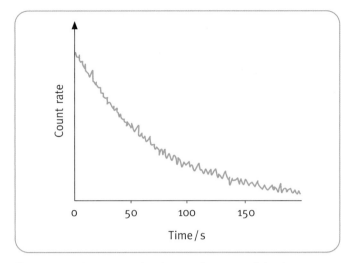

**Figure 17.19** Count rate showing randomness of decay.

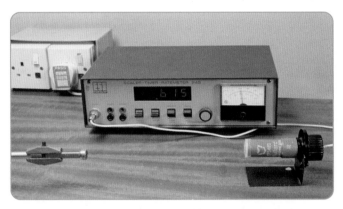

**Figure 17.18** The time constant of this ratemeter can be adjusted to smooth out rapid fluctuations in the count rate.

You can see the same effect if you have a ratemeter, which can measure faster rates (Figure **17.18**). The needle fluctuates up and down. Usually a ratemeter has a control for setting the 'time constant' – the time over which the meter averages out the fluctuations. Usually this can be set to 1 s or 5 s. The fluctuations are smoothed out more on the 5 s setting.

Figure **17.19** shows a graph of count rate against time, with a smoothing of a few seconds. The count rate decreases with time as the number of radioactive nuclei that are left decreases. The fluctuations either side are caused by the randomness of the decay.

So it is apparent that radioactive decay is a random, irregular phenomenon. But is it completely unpredictable? Well, not really. We can measure the average rate of decay. We might measure the number of counts detected in 1000 s, and then calculate the average number per second. We cannot be sure about this average rate either, because the number of counts in 1000 s will fluctuate, too. All of our measurements of radioactive decay are inherently uncertain and imprecise but, by taking averages over a sufficiently long time period, we can reduce or

smooth out the random fluctuations to reveal the underlying pattern.

## Spontaneous decay

Radioactive decay occurs within the unstable nucleus of an atom. A nucleus emits radiation and becomes the nucleus of an atom of a different element. This is a spontaneous process, which means that we cannot predict, for a particular nucleus, when it will happen. If we sit and stare at an individual nucleus, we cannot see any change that will tell us that it is getting ready to decay. And if it doesn't decay in the first hour when we are watching it, we cannot say that it is any more likely to decay in the next hour. What is more, we cannot affect the probability of an individual nucleus decaying, for example by changing its temperature.

This is slightly odd, because it goes against our everyday experience of the way things around us change. We observe things changing. They gradually age, die, rot away. But this is not how things are on the scale of atoms and nuclei. Many of the atoms of which we are made have existed for billions of years, and will still exist long after we are gone. The nucleus of an atom does not age.

If we look at a very large number of atoms of a radioactive substance, we will see the number of undecayed nuclei gradually decreases. However, we cannot predict when an **individual** nucleus will decay. Each nucleus 'makes up its own mind' when to decay, independently from its neighbours. This is because neighbouring nuclei do not interact with one another (unlike neighbouring atoms). The nucleus is a tiny fraction of the size of the atom, and the nuclear forces do not extend very far outside the nucleus. So one nucleus cannot affect a neighbouring nucleus by means of the nuclear force. Being inside a nucleus is a bit like living in a house in the middle of nowhere; you can just see out into the garden, but everything is darkness beyond, and the next house is 1000 km away.

The fact that individual nuclei decay spontaneously, and independently of their neighbours and of environmental factors, accounts for the random pattern of clicks that we hear from a Geiger counter and the fluctuations of the needle on the ratemeter.

To summarise, nuclear decay is **spontaneous** because:

- the decay of a particular nucleus is not affected by the presence of other nuclei;
- the decay of nuclei cannot be affected by chemical reactions or external factors such as temperature and pressure.

Nuclear decay is **random** because:

- it is impossible to predict when a particular nucleus in a sample is going to decay;
- each nucleus in a sample has the same chance of decaying per unit time.

## Summary

- [ ] The $\alpha$-particle scattering experiment provides evidence for the existence of a small, massive and positively charged nucleus at the centre of the atom.
- [ ] Most of the mass of an atom is concentrated in its nucleus.
- [ ] The nucleus consists of protons and neutrons, and is surrounded by a cloud of electrons.
- [ ] The number of protons and neutrons in the nucleus of an atom is called its nucleon number $A$.
- [ ] The number of protons in the nucleus of an atom is called its proton number (or atomic number) $Z$.
- [ ] Isotopes are nuclei of the same element with a different number of neutrons but the same number of protons.
- [ ] Different isotopes (or nuclides, if referring to the nucleus only) can be represented by the notation $^A_Z X$, where X is the chemical symbol for the element.
- [ ] There are three types of ionising radiation produced by radioactive substances: $\alpha$-particles, $\beta$-particles and $\gamma$-rays.
- [ ] In radioactive decay, the following quantities are conserved: proton number, nucleon number and mass–energy.
- [ ] The most strongly ionising, and hence the least penetrating, is $\alpha$-radiation. The least strongly ionising is $\gamma$-radiation.
- [ ] Because of their different charges, masses and speeds, the different types of radiation can be identified by the effect of an electric or magnetic field.
- [ ] Nuclear decay is a spontaneous and random process. This unpredictability means that count rates tend to fluctuate, and we have to measure average quantities.

# End-of-chapter questions

1 Before Rutherford's model, scientists believed that the atom was made up of negatively charged electrons embedded in a 'plum-pudding' of positive charge that was spread throughout the atom. Explain how the $\alpha$-particle scattering experiment proved that this old model of the atom was incorrect.

2 A nucleus of strontium has a nucleon number of 90 and a proton number of 38. Describe the structure of this strontium nucleus.

3 State the changes that take place in a nucleus when it emits an $\alpha$-particle and then two $\beta$-particles.

4 The nuclide of iodine with a nucleon number of 131 and a proton number 53 emits a $\beta$-particle. Write a nuclear equation for this decay.

5 The graph shown in Figure 17.19 shows how randomness affects count rate. State and explain what happens if the experiment is performed using the same amount of radioactive material but at a higher temperature.

# Exam-style questions

1 An isotope of carbon $^{14}_{6}C$ emits a $\beta$-particle and changes into an isotope of nitrogen (N).
   a What are $\beta$-particles? [1]
   b Write a nuclear decay equation for the decay. [2]
   c Draw a graph with the $y$-axis representing nucleon numbers between 10 and 16 and the $x$-axis representing proton numbers between 4 and 10. On your graph mark:
      i the isotope $^{14}_{6}C$ [2]
      ii the daughter nucleus produced in the decay. [1]

2 The radioactive decay of nuclei is random and spontaneous. Explain what is meant by:
   a **radioactive** decay [2]
   b **random** decay [2]
   c **spontaneous** decay. [2]

3 The isotopes of uranium U-236 and U-237 both emit radioactive particles. A nucleus of uranium-237 may be written as $^{237}_{92}U$ and emits a $\beta$-particle. A nucleus of uranium-236 emits an $\alpha$-particle. The number of protons in a nucleus of uranium is 92.
   a Describe the differences between an $\alpha$-particle and a $\beta$-particle. [4]
   b Explain how uranium can exist in a number of different isotopes. [2]
   c Write down the nuclear equation for the decay of U-236. [2]

4  Approximate values for the radius of a gold atom and the radius of a gold nucleus are $10^{-10}$ m and $10^{-15}$ m respectively.
   a  Estimate the ratio of the volume of a gold atom to the volume of a gold nucleus.  [2]
   b  The density of gold is $19\,000$ kg m$^{-3}$. Estimate the density of a gold nucleus, stating any assumptions that you make in your answer.  [3]

5  The nuclide of lead $^{210}_{82}$Pb decays in three separate stages by α- and β-emission to another lead nuclide $^{206}_{82}$Pb.
   a  Describe the structure of a nucleus of $^{210}_{82}$Pb.  [2]
   b  Alpha- and beta-particles are known as **ionising radiations**. State and explain why such radiations can be described as **ionising**.  [2]
   c  The two lead nuclides are shown on a graph of nucleon number, $A$, against proton number, $Z$.

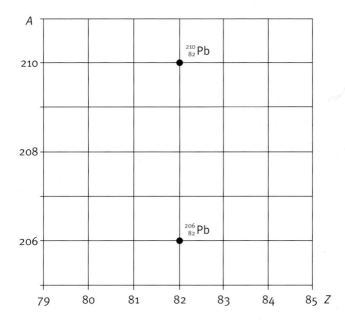

   Copy the graph and on your copy draw **three** arrows to represent one possible route for the three decays between the two isotopes of lead. Label each arrow to show whether an α-particle or a β-particle is emitted.  [3]

6  Geiger and Marsden carried out an experiment to investigate the structure of the atom. In this experiment α-particles were scattered by a thin film of gold.
   a  When Rutherford analysed their results, what conclusions did he draw about the distribution of mass and charge in the atom?  [2]
   b  Describe and explain the experimental observations that led to these conclusions.  [3]

# 18 Circular motion

## Objectives

After studying this chapter, you should be able to:

- [ ] express angular displacement in radians
- [ ] solve problems using the concept of angular velocity
- [ ] describe motion along a circular path as due to a perpendicular force which causes a centripetal acceleration

- [ ] recall and use equations for centripetal acceleration and for centripetal force

## Moving in circles

**Figure 18.1** Circular motion: the car's wheels go round in circles as the car itself follows a curved path.

The racing car in Figure **18.1** shows two examples of circular motion. The car's wheels spin around the axles, and the car follows a curved path as it speeds round the bend.

## Describing circular motion

Many things move in circles. Here are some examples:

- the wheels of a car or a bicycle
- the Earth in its (approximately circular) orbit round the Sun
- the hands of a clock
- a spinning DVD in a laptop
- the drum of a washing machine.

Sometimes, things move along a path that is part of a circle. For example, the car in Figure **18.1** is travelling around a bend in the road which is an arc of a circle.

Circular motion is different from the straight-line motion that we have discussed previously in our study of kinematics and dynamics in Chapters **1–6**. However, we can extend these ideas of dynamics to build up a picture of circular motion.

## Around the clock

The second hand of a clock moves steadily round the clock-face. It takes one minute for it to travel all the way round the circle. There are 360° in a complete circle and 60 seconds in a minute. So the hand moves 6° every second. If we know the angle $\theta$ through which the hand has moved from the vertical (12 o'clock) position, we can predict the position of the hand.

In the same way, we can describe the position of any object as it moves around a circle simply by stating the angle $\theta$ of the arc through which it has moved from its starting position. This is shown in Figure **18.2**.

The angle $\theta$ through which the object has moved is known as its **angular displacement**. For an object moving in a straight line, its position was defined by its displacement $s$, the **distance** it has travelled from its starting position. The corresponding quantity for circular motion is angular displacement $\theta$, the **angle** of the arc through which the object has moved from its starting position.

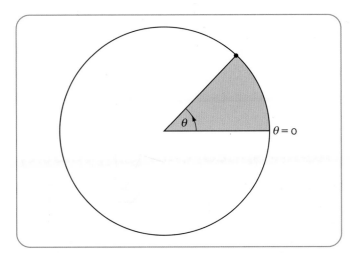

**Figure 18.2** To know how far an object has moved round the circle, we need to know the angle $\theta$.

## Test yourself

1  **a** By how many degrees does the angular displacement of the hour hand of a clock change each hour?
   **b** A clock is showing 3.30. Calculate the angular displacements in degrees from the 12.00 position of the clock to:
   **i** the minute hand
   **ii** the hour hand.

# Angles in radians

When dealing with circles and circular motion, it is more convenient to measure angles and angular displacements in units called radians rather than in degrees.

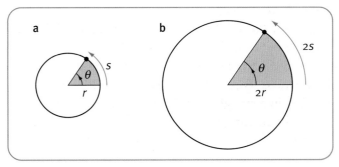

**Figure 18.3** The size of an angle depends on the radius and the length of the arc. Doubling both leaves the angle unchanged.

If an object moves a distance s around a circular path of radius $r$ (Figure **18.3a**), its angular displacement $\theta$ in **radians** is defined as follows:

$$\text{angle (in radians)} = \frac{\text{length of arc}}{\text{radius}}$$

or $\qquad \theta = \frac{s}{r}$

Since both $s$ and $r$ are distances measured in metres, it follows that the angle $\theta$ is simply a ratio. It is a dimensionless quantity. If the object moves twice as far around a circle of twice the radius (Figure **18.3b**), its angular displacement $\theta$ will still be the same.

$$\theta = \frac{\text{length of arc}}{\text{radius}} = \frac{2s}{2r} = \frac{s}{r}$$

When we define $\theta$ in this way, its units are radians rather than degrees. How are radians related to degrees? If an object moves all the way round the circumference of the circle, it moves a distance of $2\pi r$. We can calculate its angular displacement in radians:

$$\theta = \frac{\text{circumference}}{\text{radius}} = \frac{2\pi r}{r} = 2\pi$$

Hence a complete circle contains $2\pi$ radians. But we can also say that the object has moved through 360°. Hence:

$$360° = 2\pi \text{ rad}$$

Similarly, we have:

$$180° = \pi \text{ rad} \qquad 90° = \frac{\pi}{2} \text{ rad}$$

$$45° = \frac{\pi}{4} \text{ rad} \qquad \text{and so on}$$

## Defining the radian

An angle of one radian is defined as follows (see Figure **18.4**):

> One **radian** is the angle subtended at the centre of a circle by an arc of length equal to the radius of the circle.

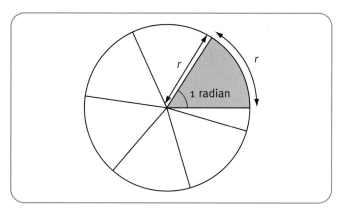

Figure 18.4 The length of the arc is equal to the radius when the angle is 1 radian.

An angle of 360° is equivalent to an angle of $2\pi$ radians. We can therefore determine what 1 radian is equivalent to in degrees.

$$1 \text{ radian} = \frac{360}{2\pi}$$

or    $1 \text{ radian} \approx 57.3°$

If you can remember that there are $2\pi$ rad in a full circle, you will be able to convert between radians and degrees:

• to convert from degrees to radians, multiply by $\frac{2\pi}{360°}$ or $\frac{\pi}{180°}$

• to convert from radians to degrees, multiply by $\frac{360°}{2\pi}$ or $\frac{180°}{\pi}$

Now look at Worked example 1.

## Worked example

1  If $\theta = 60°$, what is the value of $\theta$ in radians?

The angle $\theta$ is 60°. 360° is equivalent to $2\pi$ radians. Therefore:

$$\theta = 60 \times \frac{2\pi}{360}$$

$$= \frac{\pi}{3} = 1.05 \text{ rad}$$

(Note that it is often useful to express an angle as a multiple of $\pi$ radians.)

### Test yourself

2  a  Convert the following angles from degrees into radians: 30°, 90°, 105°.

   b  Convert these angles from radians to degrees: 0.5 rad, 0.75 rad, $\pi$ rad, $\frac{\pi}{2}$ rad.

   c  Express the following angles as multiples of $\pi$ radians: 30°, 120°, 270°, 720°.

# Steady speed, changing velocity

If we are to use Newton's laws of motion to explain circular motion, we must consider the **velocity** of an object going round in a circle, rather than its **speed**.

There is an important distinction between speed and velocity: **speed** is a scalar quantity which has magnitude only, whereas **velocity** is a vector quantity, with both magnitude and direction. We need to think about the direction of motion of an orbiting object.

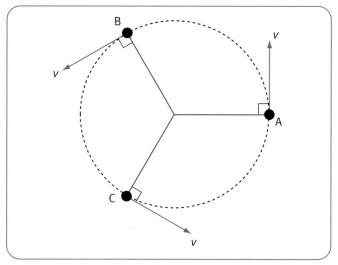

Figure 18.5 The velocity $v$ of an object changes direction as it moves along a circular path.

Figure 18.5 shows how we can represent the velocity of an object at various points around its circular path. The arrows are straight and show the direction of motion at a particular instant. They are drawn as tangents to the circular path. As the object travels through points A, B, C, etc., its speed remains constant but its direction changes. Since the direction of the velocity $v$ is changing, it follows that $v$ itself (a vector quantity) is changing as the object moves in a circle.

3 Explain why all the velocity arrows in Figure **18.5** are drawn the same length.

4 A toy train travels at a steady speed of $0.2\,\mathrm{m\,s^{-1}}$ around a circular track (Figure **18.6**). A and B are two points diametrically opposite to one another on the track.

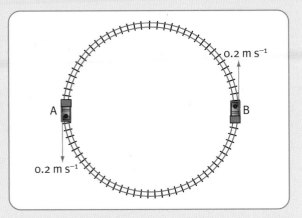

Figure **18.6** A toy train travelling around a circular track.

a Determine the change in the speed of the train as it travels from A to B.
b Determine the change in the velocity of the train as it travels from A to B.

# Angular velocity

As the hands of a clock travel steadily around the clock face, their velocity is constantly changing. The minute hand travels round 360° or $2\pi$ radians in 3600 seconds. Although its velocity is changing, we can say that its **angular velocity** is constant, because it moves round through the same angle each second.

$$\text{angular velocity} = \frac{\text{angular displacement}}{\text{time taken}}$$

$$\omega = \frac{\Delta\theta}{\Delta t}$$

We use the symbol $\omega$ (Greek letter omega) for angular velocity, measured in radians per second ($\mathrm{rad\,s^{-1}}$). For the minute hand of a clock, we have $\omega = \frac{2\pi}{3600} = 0.00175\,\mathrm{rad\,s^{-1}}$.

5 Show that the angular velocity of the second hand of a clock is $0.105\,\mathrm{rad\,s^{-1}}$.

6 The drum of a washing machine spins at a rate of 1200 rpm (revolutions per minute).
   a Determine the number of revolutions per second of the drum.
   b Determine the angular velocity of the drum.

## Relating velocity and angular velocity

Think again about the second hand of a clock. As it goes round, each point on the hand has the same angular velocity. However, different points on the hand have different velocities. The tip of the hand moves fastest; points closer to the centre of the clock face move more slowly.

This shows that the speed $v$ of an object travelling around a circle depends on two quantities: its angular velocity $\omega$ and its distance from the centre of the circle $r$. We can write the relationship as an equation:

$$\text{speed} = \text{angular velocity} \times \text{radius}$$

$$v = \omega r$$

Worked example **2** shows how to use this equation.

### Worked example

2 A toy train travels around a circular track of radius $2.5\,\mathrm{m}$ in a time of $40\,\mathrm{s}$. What is its speed?

**Step 1** Calculate the train's angular velocity $\omega$. One circuit of the track is equivalent to $2\pi$ radians. The rain travels around in $10\,\mathrm{s}$. Therefore:

$$\omega = \frac{2\pi}{40} = 0.157\,\mathrm{rad\,s^{-1}}$$

**Step 2** Calculate the train's speed:

$$v = \omega r = 0.157 \times 2.5 = 0.39\,\mathrm{m\,s^{-1}}$$

You could have arrived at the same answer by calculating the distance travelled (the circumference of the circle) and dividing by the time taken.

7 The angular velocity of the second hand of a clock is 0.105 rad s⁻¹. If the length of the hand is 1.8 cm, calculate the speed of the tip of the hand as it moves round.

8 A car travels around a 90° bend in 15 s. The radius of the bend is 50 m.
   **a** Determine the angular velocity of the car.
   **b** Determine the speed of the car.

9 A spacecraft orbits the Earth in a circular path of radius 7000 km at a speed of 7800 m s⁻¹. Determine its angular velocity.

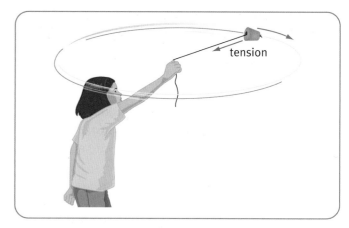

**Figure 18.7** Whirling a rubber bung.

# Centripetal forces

When an object's velocity is changing, it has acceleration. In the case of uniform circular motion, the acceleration is rather unusual because, as we have seen, the object's speed does not change but its velocity does. How can an object accelerate and at the same time have a steady speed?

One way to understand this is to think about what Newton's laws of motion can tell us about this situation. **Newton's first law** states that an object remains at rest or in a state of uniform motion (at constant speed in a straight line) unless it is acted on by an external force. In the case of an object moving at steady speed in a circle, we have a body whose velocity is not constant; therefore, there must be a resultant (unbalanced) force acting on it.

Now we can think about different situations where objects are going round in a circle and try to find the force that is acting on them.

• Consider a rubber bung on the end of a string. Imagine whirling it in a horizontal circle above your head (Figure 18.7). To make it go round in a circle, you have to pull on the string. The pull of the string on the bung is the unbalanced force, which is constantly acting to change the bung's velocity as it orbits your head. If you let go of the string, suddenly there is no tension in the string and the bung will fly off at a tangent to the circle.

• Similarly, as the Earth orbits the Sun, it has a constantly changing velocity. Newton's first law suggests that there must be an unbalanced force acting on it. That force is the gravitational pull of the Sun. If the force disappeared, the Earth would travel off in a straight line.

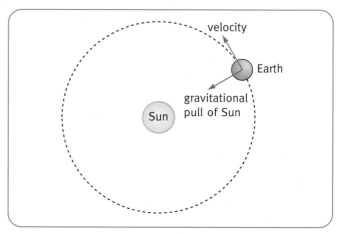

**Figure 18.8** The gravitational pull of the Sun provides the centripetal force that keeps the Earth in its orbit.

In both of these cases, you should be able to see why the direction of the force is as shown in Figure **18.8**. The force on the object is directed towards the centre of the circle. We describe each of these forces as a **centripetal force** – that is, directed towards the centre.

It is important to note that the word **centripetal** is an adjective. We use it to describe a force that is making something travel along a circular path. It does not tell us what causes this force, which might be gravitational, electrostatic, magnetic, frictional or whatever.

## Vector diagrams

Figure 18.9a shows an object travelling along a circular path, at two positions in its orbit. It reaches position B a short time after A. How has its velocity changed between these two positions?

The change in the velocity of the object can be determined using a vector triangle. This vector triangle in Figure 18.9b shows the difference between the final velocity $v_B$ and initial velocity $v_A$. The change in the velocity of the object between the points B and A is shown by the smaller arrow labelled $\Delta v$. Note that the change in the velocity of the object is (more or less):

• at right angles to the velocity at A
• directed towards the centre of the circle.

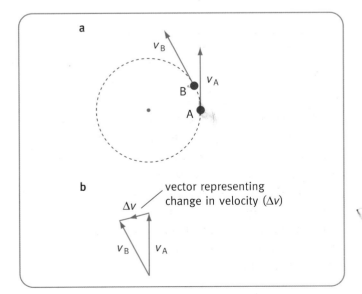

Figure 18.9 Changes in the velocity vector.

The object is accelerating because its velocity changes. Since acceleration is the rate of change of velocity

$$a = \frac{\Delta v}{\Delta t}$$

it follows that the acceleration of the object must be in the same direction as the change in the velocity – towards the centre of the circle. This is not surprising because, according to $F = ma$, the acceleration $a$ of the object is in the same direction as the centripetal force $F$.

## Acceleration at steady speed

Now that we know that the centripetal force $F$ and acceleration are always at right angles to the object's velocity, we can explain why its speed remains constant. If the force is to make the object change its speed, it must have a component in the direction of the object's velocity; it must provide a push in the direction in which the object is already travelling. However, here we have a force at 90° to the velocity, so it has no component in the required direction. (Its component in the direction of the velocity is $F\cos 90° = 0$.) It acts to pull the object around the circle, without ever making it speed up or slow down.

You can also use the idea of work done to show that the speed of the object moving in a circle remains the same. The work done by a force is equal to the product of the force and the distance moved by the object in the direction of the force. The distance moved by the object in the direction of the centripetal force is zero; hence the work done is zero. If no work is done on the object, its kinetic energy must remain the same and hence its speed is unchanged.

## Thinking like Newton

Isaac Newton devised an ingenious 'thought experiment' that allows us to think about circular motion, particularly in connection with objects orbiting the Earth. Consider a large cannon on some high point on the Earth's surface, capable of firing objects horizontally. Figure **18.10** shows what will happen if we fire them at different speeds.

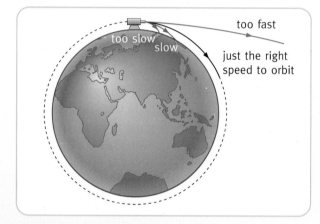

**Figure 18.10** Newton's 'thought experiment'.

If the object is fired too slowly, gravity will pull it down towards the ground and it will land at some distance from the cannon. A faster initial speed results in the object landing further from the cannon.

Now, if we try a bit faster than this, the object will travel all the way round the Earth. We have to get just the right speed to do this. As the object is pulled down towards the Earth, the curved surface of the Earth falls away beneath it. The object follows a circular path, constantly falling under gravity but never getting any closer to the surface.

If the object is fired too fast, it travels off into space, and fails to get into a circular orbit. So we can see that there is just one correct speed to achieve a circular orbit under gravity.

Note that we have ignored the effects of air resistance – that's easy to do in a thought experiment. The term 'thought experiment' (or *Gedankenexperiment* in German) was first used by Hans Christian Oersted in about 1812. Scientists have often made use of such an approach when developing their theories. The idea is to start with a hypothesis (an idea to be tested). Then ask the question, 'If the hypothesis is true, what would happen if we could do such-and-such…?' The experiment is not carried out, but the likely results show whether the hypothesis is possible or not.

Famous examples of thought experiments from physics include Galileo's Leaning Tower of Pisa experiment and Schrödinger's cat (an example from quantum physics). An internet search for 'thought experiments' will lead you to more examples.

# Calculating acceleration and force

If we spin a bung around in a circle (Figure **18.7**), we get a feeling for the factors which determine the centripetal force $F$ required to keep it in its circular orbit. The greater the mass $m$ of the bung and the greater its speed $v$, the greater is the force $F$ that is required. However if the radius $r$ of the circle is increased, $F$ is smaller.

Now we will deduce an expression for the centripetal acceleration of an object moving around a circle with a constant speed. Figure **18.11** shows a particle moving round a circle. In time $\Delta t$ it moves through

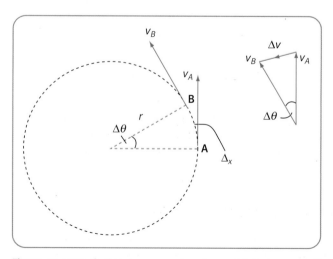

**Figure 18.11** Deducing an expression for centripetal acceleration.

an angle $\Delta\theta$ from A to B. Its speed remains constant but its velocity changes by $\Delta v$, as shown in the vector diagram. Since the narrow angle in this triangle is also $\Delta\theta$, we can say that:

$$\Delta\theta = \frac{\Delta v}{v}$$

Dividing both sides of this equation by $\Delta t$ and rearranging gives:

$$\frac{\Delta v}{\Delta t} = \frac{v\Delta\theta}{\Delta t}$$

The quantity on the left $\frac{\Delta v}{\Delta t} = a$, the particle's acceleration.

The quantity on the right $\frac{\Delta\theta}{\Delta t} = \omega$, the angular velocity.

Substituting for these gives:

$$a = v\omega$$

Using $v = \omega r$, we can eliminate $\omega$ from this equation:

$$a = \frac{v^2}{r}$$

## Test yourself

**13** Show that an alternative equation for the centripetal acceleration is $a = \omega^2 r$.

## Newton's second law of motion

Now that we have an equation for centripetal acceleration, we can use **Newton's second law** of motion to deduce an equation for centripetal force. If we write this law as $F = ma$, we find:

centripetal force $F = \dfrac{mv^2}{r} = mr\omega^2$

Remembering that an object accelerates in the direction of the resultant force on it, it follows that both $F$ and $a$ are in the same direction, towards the centre of the circle.

## Calculating orbital speed

We can use the force equation to calculate the speed that an object must have to orbit the Earth under gravity, as in Newton's thought experiment. The necessary

centripetal force $\dfrac{mv^2}{r}$ is provided by the Earth's gravitational pull $mg$.

Hence:

$$mg = \frac{mv^2}{r}$$

$$g = \frac{v^2}{r}$$

where $g = 9.81\,\mathrm{m\,s^{-2}}$ is the acceleration of free fall close to the Earth's surface. The radius of its orbit is equal to the Earth's radius, approximately 6400 km. Hence, we have:

$$9.81 = \frac{v^2}{(6.4 \times 10^6)}$$

$$v = \sqrt{9.81 \times 6.4 \times 10^6} = 7.92 \times 10^3\,\mathrm{m\,s^{-1}}$$

Thus if you were to throw or hit a ball horizontally at almost $8\,\mathrm{km\,s^{-1}}$, it would go into orbit around the Earth.

## Test yourself

**14** Calculate how long it would take a ball to orbit the Earth once, just above the surface, at a speed of $7920\,\mathrm{m\,s^{-1}}$. (The radius of the Earth is 6400 km.)

**15** A stone of mass 0.20 kg is whirled round on the end of a string of length 30 cm. The string will break when the tension in it exceeds 8.0 N. Calculate the maximum speed at which the stone can be whirled without the string breaking.

**16** The International Space Station (Figure **18.12**) has a mass of 350 tonnes, and orbits the Earth at an average height of 340 km, where the gravitational acceleration is $8.8\,\mathrm{m\,s^{-2}}$. The radius of the Earth is 6400 km. Calculate:
  **a** the centripetal force on the space station
  **b** the speed at which it orbits
  **c** the time taken for each orbit
  **d** the number of times it orbits the Earth each day.

*continued ⋯⟩*

Figure 18.12 The International Space Station orbiting Earth over Australia.

17 A stone of mass 0.40 kg is whirled round on the end of a string 0.50 m long. It makes three complete revolutions each second. Calculate:
   **a** its speed
   **b** its centripetal acceleration
   **c** the tension in the string.

18 Mars orbits the Sun once every 687 days at a distance of $2.3 \times 10^{11}$ m. The mass of Mars is $6.4 \times 10^{23}$ kg. Calculate:
   **a** its orbital speed
   **b** its centripetal acceleration
   **c** the gravitational force exerted on Mars by the Sun.

# The origins of centripetal forces

It is useful to look at one or two situations where the physical origin of the centripetal force may not be immediately obvious. In each case, you will notice that the forces acting on the moving object are not balanced – there is a net force. An object moving along a circular path is not in equilibrium and the resultant force acting on it is the centripetal force.

1 A car cornering on a level road (Figure **18.13**). Here, the road provides two forces. The force $N$ is the normal contact force which balances the weight $mg$ of the car – the car has no acceleration in the vertical direction. The second force is the force of friction $F$ between the tyres and the road surface. This is the unbalanced, centripetal force. If the road or tyres do not provide enough friction, the

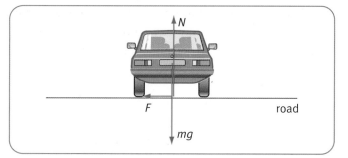

Figure 18.13 This car is moving away from us and turning to the left. Friction provides the centripetal force. $N$ and $F$ are the total normal contact and friction forces (respectively) provided by the contact of all four tyres with the road.

car will not go round the bend along the desired path. The friction between the tyres and the road provides the centripetal force necessary for the car's circular motion.

2 A car cornering on a banked road (Figure **18.14a**). Here, the normal contact force $N$ has a horizontal component which can provide the centripetal force. The vertical component of $N$ balances the car's weight. Therefore:

vertically $\qquad N\cos\theta = mg$

horizontally $\qquad N\sin\theta = \dfrac{mv^2}{r}$

where $r$ is the radius of the circular corner and $v$ is the car's speed.

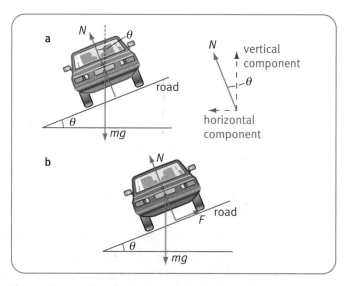

Figure 18.14 **a** On a banked road, the horizontal component of the normal contact force from the road can provide the centripetal force needed for cornering. **b** For a slow car, friction acts up the slope to stop it from sliding down.

If a car travels around the bend too slowly, it will tend to slide down the slope and friction will act up the slope to keep it on course (Figure **18.14b**). If it travels too fast, it will tend to slide up the slope. If friction is insufficient, it will move up the slope and come off the road.

3 An aircraft banking (Figure **18.15a**). To change direction, the pilot tips the aircraft's wings. The vertical component of the lift force $L$ on the wings balances the weight. The horizontal component of $L$ provides the centripetal force.

4 A stone being whirled in a horizontal circle on the end of a string – this arrangement is known as a conical pendulum (Figure **18.15b**). The vertical component of the tension $T$ is equal to the weight of the stone. The horizontal component of the tension provides the centripetal force for the circular motion.

5 At the fairground (Figure **18.15c**). As the cylinder spins, the floor drops away. Friction balances your weight. The normal contact force of the wall provides the centripetal force. You feel as though you are being pushed back against the wall; what you are feeling is the push of the wall on your back.

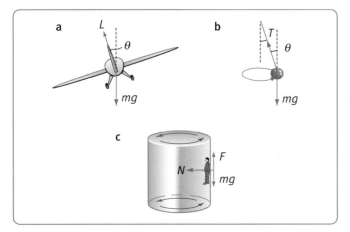

Figure **18.15** Three more ways of providing a centripetal force.

Note that the three situations shown in Figure **18.14a**, Figure **18.15a** and Figure **18.15b** are all equivalent. The moving object's weight acts downwards. The second force has a vertical component, which balances the weight, and a horizontal component, which provides the centripetal force.

## Test yourself

19 Explain why it is impossible to whirl a bung around on the end of a string in such a way that the string remains perfectly horizontal.

20 Explain why an aircraft will tend to lose height when banking, unless the pilot increases its speed to provide more lift.

21 If you have ever been down a water-slide (a flume) (Figure **18.16**) you will know that you tend to slide up the side as you go around a bend. Explain how this provides the centripetal force needed to push you around the bend. Explain why you slide higher if you are going faster.

Figure **18.16** A water-slide is a good place to experience centripetal forces.

## Summary

- ☐ Angles can be measured in radians. An angle of $2\pi\,\text{rad}$ is equal to 360°.
- ☐ An object moving at a steady speed along a circular path has uniform circular motion.
- ☐ The angular displacement $\theta$ is a measure of the angle through which an object moves in a circle.
- ☐ The angular velocity $\omega$ is the rate at which the angular displacement changes: $\omega = \frac{\theta}{t}$.
- ☐ For an object moving with uniform circular motion, speed and angular velocity are related by $v = \omega r$.

- An object moving in a circle is not in equilibrium; it has a net force acting on it.
- The net force acting on an object moving in a circle is called the centripetal force. This force is directed towards the centre of the circle and is at right angles to the velocity of the object.
- An object moving in a circle has a centripetal acceleration a given by:

$$a = \frac{v^2}{r} = r\omega^2$$

- The magnitude of the centripetal force $F$ acting on an object of mass $m$ moving at a speed $v$ in a circle of radius $r$ is given by:

$$F = \frac{mv^2}{r} = mr\omega^2$$

# End-of-chapter questions

1  **a**  Explain what is meant by a **radian**.
   **b**  A body moves round a circle at a constant speed and completes one revolution in 15 s. Calculate the angular velocity of the body.

2  Figure **18.17** shows part of the track of a roller-coaster ride in which a truck loops the loop. When the truck is at the position shown there is no reaction force between the wheels of the truck and the track. The diameter of the loop in the track is 8.0 m.

**Figure 18.17**  For End-of-chapter Q **2**.

   **a**  Explain what provides the centripetal force to keep the truck moving in a circle.
   **b**  Given that the acceleration due to gravity $g$ is $9.8\,\mathrm{m\,s^{-2}}$, calculate the speed of the truck.

3  **a**  Describe what is meant by **centripetal force**.

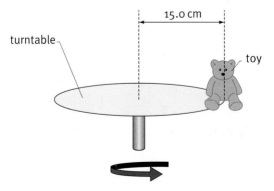

**Figure 18.18**  For End-of-chapter Q **3**.

**b** Figure **18.18** shows a toy of mass 60 g placed on the edge of a rotating turntable.

   **i** The diameter of the turntable is 15.0 cm. The turntable rotates, making 20 revolutions every minute. Calculate the centripetal force acting on the toy.

   **ii** Explain why the toy falls off when the speed of the turntable is increased.

**4** One end of a string is secured to the ceiling and a metal ball of mass 50 g is tied to its other end. The ball is initially at rest in the vertical position. The ball is raised through a vertical height of 70 cm (see Figure **18.19**). The ball is then released. It describes a circular arc as it passes through the vertical position.

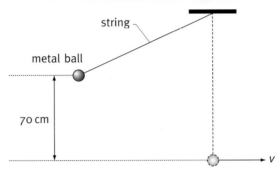

**Figure 18.19** For End-of-chapter Q 4.

The length of the string is 1.50 m.

**a** Ignoring the effects of air resistance, determine the speed $v$ of the ball as it passes through the vertical position.

**b** Calculate the tension $T$ in the string when the string is vertical.

**c** Explain why your answer to **b** is not equal to the weight of the ball.

**5** A car is travelling round a bend when it hits patch of oil. The car slides off the road onto the grass verge. Explain, using your understanding of circular motion why the car came off the road.

**6** Figure **18.20** shows an aeroplane banking to make a horizontal turn. The aeroplane is travelling at a speed of 75 m s$^{-1}$ and the radius of the turning circle is 80 m.

**a** Copy the diagram. On your copy, draw and label the forces acting on the aeroplane.

**b** Calculate the angle which the aeroplane makes with the horizontal.

**Figure 18.20** For End-of-chapter Q 6.

# Exam-style questions

**1**  **a** Explain what is meant by the term **angular velocity**. [2]

    **b** The diagram shows a rubber bung, of mass 200 g, on the end of a length of string being swung in a horizontal circle of radius 40 cm. The string makes an angle of 56° with the vertical.

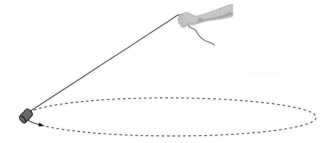

    Calculate:

    **i** the tension in the string [2]

    **ii** the angular velocity of the bung [3]

    **iii** the time it takes to make one complete revolution. [1]

**2**  **a** Explain what is meant by a **centripetal force**. [2]

    **b** A teacher swings a bucket of water, of total mass 5.4 kg, round in a vertical circle of diameter 1.8 m.

    **i** Calculate the minimum speed which the bucket must be swung at so that the water remains in the bucket at the top of the circle. [3]

    **ii** Assuming that the speed remains constant, what will be the force on the teacher's hand when the bucket is at the bottom of the circle? [2]

**3**  **a** Define a **radian**. [1]

    In training, military pilots are given various tests. One test puts them in a seat on the end of a large arm which is then spun round at a high speed, as shown in the diagram.

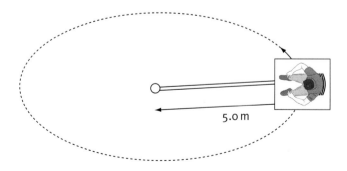

5.0 m

**b** Describe what the pilot will feel and relate this to the centripetal force. [3]

**c** At top speed the pilot will experience a centripetal force equivalent to six times his own weight (6 *mg*).

   **i** Calculate the of the speed pilot in this test. [3]

   **ii** Calculate the number of revolutions of the pilot per minute. [2]

**d** Suggest why it is necessary for pilots to be able to be able to withstand forces of this type. [2]

**4**  **a** Show that in one revolution there are $2\pi$ radians. [2]

   **b** The diagram shows a centrifuge used to separate solid particles suspended in a liquid of lower density.

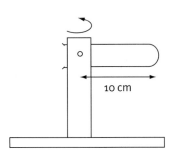

10 cm

   The container is spun at a rate of 540 revolutions per minute.

   **i** Calculate the angular velocity of the container. [2]

   **ii** Calculate the centripetal force on a particle of mass 20 mg at the end of the test tube. [2]

   **c** An alternative methods of separating the particles from the liquid is to allow them to settle to the bottom of a stationary container under gravity.

   By comparing the forces involved, explain why the centrifuge is a more effective method of separating the mixture. [2]

## Objectives

After studying this chapter, you should be able to:

- [ ] describe a gravitational field as a field of force and define gravitational field strength $g$
- [ ] recall and use Newton's law of gravitation
- [ ] solve problems involving the gravitational field strength of a uniform field and the field of a point mass

- [ ] define and solve problems involving gravitational potential $\varphi$
- [ ] analyse circular orbits in an inverse square law field, including geostationary orbits

## Gravitational forces and fields

**Figure 19.1** Skydivers balance the forces of gravity and air resistance.

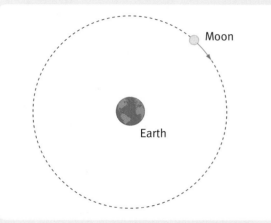

**Figure 19.2** The Moon orbits the Earth. There is an attractive gravitational force acting on the Moon due to its mass and the mass of the Earth.

We live our lives with the constant experience of gravity. We know that things fall when we drop them. The free-fall parachutists in Figure **19.1** are enjoying the experience of falling through the air under the influence of gravity.

The Earth's gravitational force extends well beyond its surface. The Moon stays in its orbit, at a distance of about 400 000 km away, because of the Earth's gravitational pull (Figure **19.2**). The Earth orbits the Sun at a distance of 150 000 000 km because of the gravitational force between them.

According to Newton, all masses create a **gravitational field** in the space around them. This field gives rise to a force on any

object having mass placed in this field. The Moon orbits the Earth because it experiences a gravitational force due to the Earth's gravitational field.

In physics, the idea of a field is a very general one. If an object is placed in a gravitational field, a force will act on the object because of its mass. In Chapter **9**, we saw that a charged object experiences a force when it is placed in an electric field. You are probably familiar with the idea that a magnet produces a magnetic field around itself, and that this will produce a force (attractive or repulsive) on another magnet placed nearby.

# Representing a gravitational field

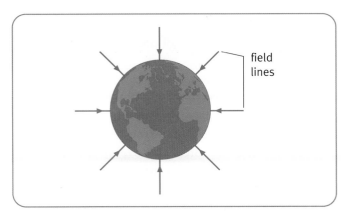

**Figure 19.3** The Earth's gravitational field is represented by field lines.

In Chapter **9** we saw how to represent an electric field using field lines. In a similar way, we can represent the Earth's gravitational field by drawing field lines, as shown in Figure **19.3**. The field lines show two things.

- The arrows on the field lines show us the direction of the gravitational force on a mass placed in the field.
- The spacing of the field lines indicates the strength of the gravitational field – the farther apart they are, the weaker the field.

The drawing of the Earth's gravitational field shows that all objects are attracted towards the centre of the Earth. This is true even if they are below the surface of the Earth. The gravitational force gets weaker as

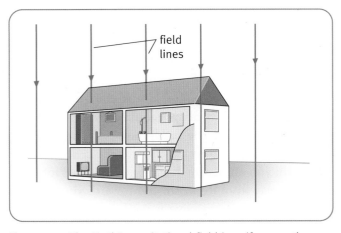

**Figure 19.4** The Earth's gravitational field is uniform on the scale of a building.

you get farther away from the Earth's surface – this is shown by the greater separation between the field lines. The Earth is almost a uniform spherical mass – it bulges a bit at the equator. The gravitational field of the Earth is as if its entire mass was concentrated at its centre. As far as any object beyond the Earth's surface is concerned, the Earth behaves as a **point mass**.

Figure **19.4** shows the Earth's gravitational field closer to its surface. The gravitational field in and around a building on the Earth's surface shows that the gravitational force is directed downwards everywhere and (because the field lines are parallel and evenly spaced) the strength of the gravitational field is the same at all points in and around the building. This means that your weight is the same everywhere in this gravitational field. Your weight does not get significantly less when you go upstairs. We describe the Earth's gravitational field as **radial**, since the field lines diverge (spread out) radially from the centre of the Earth. However, on the scale of a building, the gravitational field is **uniform**, since the field lines are equally spaced.

Jupiter is a more massive planet than the Earth and so we would represent its gravitational field by showing more closely spaced field lines.

## Newton's law of gravitation

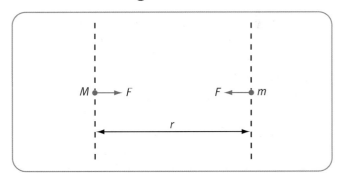

**Figure 19.5** Two point masses separated by distance $r$.

Newton used his ideas about mass and gravity to suggest a law of gravitation for two point masses (Figure **19.5**). He considered two point masses $M$ and $m$ separated by a distance $r$. Each point mass attracts the other with a force $F$. (According to Newton's third law of motion, the point masses interact with each other and therefore exert equal but opposite forces on each other.) A statement of **Newton's law of gravitation** is shown below.

Any two point masses attract each other with a force that is directly proportional to the product of their masses and inversely proportional to the square of their separation.

Note that the law refers to 'point masses' – you can alternatively use the term 'particles'. Things are more complicated if we think about solid bodies which occupy a volume of space. Each particle of one body attracts every particle of the other body and we would have to add all these forces together to work out the force each body has on the other. Newton was able to show that two uniform spheres attract one another with a force which is the same as if their masses were concentrated at their centres (provided their radii are much smaller than their separation).

According to Newton's law of gravitation, we have:

force ∝ product of the masses    or    $F \propto Mm$

force ∝ $\dfrac{1}{\text{distance}^2}$    or    $F \propto \dfrac{1}{r^2}$

Therefore:

$$F \propto \frac{Mm}{r^2}$$

To make this into an equation, we introduce the gravitational constant $G$. We also need a minus sign to show that the force is attractive.

$$F = -\frac{GMm}{r^2}$$

The gravitational constant $G$ is sometimes referred to as the **universal** gravitational constant because it is believed to have the same value, $6.67 \times 10^{-11}\,\text{N}\,\text{m}^2\,\text{kg}^{-2}$, throughout the Universe. This is important for our understanding of the history and likely long-term future of the Universe.

The equation above can also be applied to spherical objects (such as the Earth and the Moon) provided we remember to measure the separation $r$ between the centres of the objects. You may also come across the equation in the form:

$$F = -\frac{Gm_1 m_2}{r^2}$$

where $m_1$ and $m_2$ are the masses of the two bodies.

Let us examine this equation to see why it seems reasonable.

First, each of the two masses is important. Your weight (the gravitational force on you) depends on your mass and on the mass of the planet you happen to be standing on.

Second, the farther away you are from the planet, the weaker its pull. Twice as far away gives one-quarter of the force. This can be seen from the diagram of the field lines in Figure **19.6**. If the distance is doubled, the lines are spread out over four times the surface area, so their concentration is reduced to one-quarter. This is called an inverse square law – you may have come across a similar law for radiation such as light or γ-rays spreading out uniformly from a point source.

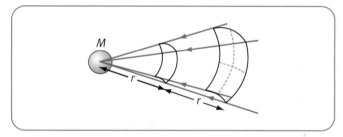

**Figure 19.6** Field lines are spread out over a greater surface area at greater distances, so the strength of the field is weaker.

As already mentioned, the minus sign represents the fact that the force is attractive. The radial distance $r$ is measured outwards from the attracting body; the force $F$ acts in the opposite direction, and so our sign convention requires that $F$ is negative.

We measure distances from the centre of mass of one body to the centre of mass of the other (Figure **19.7**). We treat each body as if its mass was concentrated at one point. The two bodies attract each other with equal and opposite forces, as required by Newton's third law of motion. The Earth pulls on you with a force (your weight) directed towards the centre of the Earth; you attract the Earth with an equal force, directed away from its centre and towards you. Your pull on an object as massive as the Earth has little effect on it. The Sun's pull on the Earth, however, has a very significant effect.

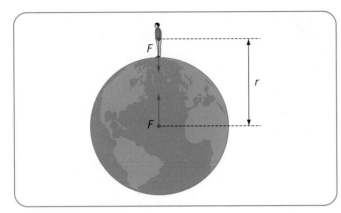

**Figure 19.7** A person and the Earth exert equal and opposite attractive forces on each other.

## Test yourself

1 Calculate the gravitational force of attraction between:
   a two objects separated by a distance of 1.0 cm and each having a mass of 100 g
   b two asteroids separated by a distance of $4.0 \times 10^9$ m and each having a mass of $5.0 \times 10^{10}$ kg
   c a satellite of mass $1.4 \times 10^4$ kg orbiting the Earth at a distance of 6800 km from the Earth's centre. (The mass of the Earth is $6.0 \times 10^{24}$ kg.)

2 Estimate the gravitational force of attraction between two people sitting side-by-side on a park bench. How does this force compare with the gravitational force exerted on each of them by the Earth, i.e. their weight?

# Gravitational field strength $g$

We can describe how strong or weak a gravitational field is by stating its **gravitational field strength**. We are used to this idea for objects on or near the Earth's surface. The gravitational field strength is the familiar quantity $g$. Its value is approximately $9.81 \, \text{m s}^{-2}$. The weight of a body of mass $m$ is $mg$.

To make the meaning of $g$ clearer, we should write it as $9.81 \, \text{N kg}^{-1}$. That is, each 1 kg of mass experiences a gravitational force of 9.81 N.

The gravitational field strength $g$ at any point in a gravitational field is defined as follows.

The gravitational field strength at a point is the gravitational force exerted per unit mass on a small object placed at that point.

This can be written as an equation:

$$g = \frac{F}{m}$$

where $F$ is the gravitational force on the object and $m$ is the mass of the object. Gravitational field strength has the unit $\text{N kg}^{-1}$. This is also equivalent to $\text{m s}^{-2}$.

We can use the definition above to determine the gravitational field strength for a point (or spherical) mass. The force between two point masses is given by:

$$F = -\frac{GMm}{r^2}$$

The gravitational field strength $g$ due to the mass $M$ at a distance of $r$ from its centre is thus:

$$g = \frac{F}{m} = -\frac{GM \cancel{m}}{r^2 \cancel{m}}$$

or

$$g = -\frac{GM}{r^2}$$

Since force is a vector quantity, it follows that gravitational field strength is also a vector. We need to give its direction as well as its magnitude in order to specify it completely. The field strength $g$ is not a constant; it decreases as the distance $r$ increases. The field strength obeys the inverse square law with distance. The field strength will decrease by a factor of four when the distance from the centre is doubled. Close to the Earth's surface, the magnitude of $g$ is about $9.81 \, \text{N kg}^{-1}$. Even if you climbed Mount Everest, which is 8.85 km high, the field strength will only decrease by 0.3%.

So the gravitational field strength $g$ at a point depends on the mass $M$ of the body causing the field, and the distance $r$ from its centre (see Worked example 1).

Gravitational field strength $g$ also has units $\text{m s}^{-2}$; it is an acceleration. Another name for $g$ is 'acceleration of free fall'. Any object that falls freely in a gravitational field has this acceleration, approximately $9.81 \, \text{m s}^{-2}$ near the Earth's surface.

In Chapter 2, you learned about different ways to determine an experimental value for $g$, the local gravitational field strength.

## Worked example

1 The Earth has radius 6400 km. The gravitational field strength on the Earth's surface is 9.81 N kg$^{-1}$. Use this information to determine the mass of the Earth and its mean density.

**Step 1** Write down the quantities given.

$$r = 6.4 \times 10^6 \, \text{m} \quad g = 9.81 \, \text{N kg}^{-1}$$

**Step 2** Use the equation $g = -\dfrac{GM}{r^2}$ to determine the mass of the Earth.

$$g = -\frac{GM}{r^2}$$

$$-9.8 = \frac{-6.67 \times 10^{-11} M}{(6.4 \times 10^6)^2}$$

The value of $g$ is negative because it is directed downwards, into the Earth, in the opposite direction to $r$.)

$$\text{mass of Earth} = M = 9.81 \times \frac{(6.4 \times 10^6)\,2}{6.67 \times 10^{-11}}$$

$$= 6.0 \times 10^{24} \, \text{kg}$$

**Step 3** Use the equation 'density = $\dfrac{\text{mass}}{\text{volume}}$' to determine the density of the Earth.

The Earth is a spherical mass. Its volume can be calculated using $\frac{4}{3}\pi r^2$.

$$\text{density} = \rho = \frac{M}{V} = \frac{6.0 \times 10^{24}}{\frac{4}{3} \times \pi \times (6.4 \times 10^6)^3}$$

$$\approx 5500 \, \text{kg m}^{-3}$$

## Test yourself

You will need the data in Table 19.1 to answer these questions.

| | Mass / kg | Radius / km | Distance from Earth / km |
|---|---|---|---|
| Earth | $6.0 \times 10^{24}$ | 6400 | – |
| Moon | $7.4 \times 10^{22}$ | 1740 | $3.8 \times 10^5$ |
| Sun | $2.0 \times 10^{30}$ | 700 000 | $1.5 \times 10^8$ |

**Table 19.1** Data for Test yourself Q 3–9.

3 Mount Everest is approximately 9.0 km high. Calculate how much less a mountaineer of mass 100 kg (including backpack) would weigh at its summit, compared to her weight at sea level. Would this difference be measurable with bathroom scales?

4 a Calculate the gravitational field strength:
   i close to the surface of the Moon
   ii close to the surface of the Sun.
   b Suggest how your answers above help to explain why the Moon has only a thin atmosphere, while the Sun has a dense atmosphere.

5 a Calculate the Earth's gravitational field strength at the position of the Moon.
   b Calculate the force the Earth exerts on the Moon. Hence determine the Moon's acceleration towards the Earth.

6 Jupiter's mass is 320 times that of the Earth and its radius is 11.2 times the Earth's. The Earth's surface gravitational field strength is 9.81 N kg$^{-1}$. Calculate the gravitational field strength close to the surface of Jupiter.

7 The Moon and the Sun both contribute to the tides on the Earth's oceans. Which has a bigger pull on each kilogram of seawater, the Sun or the Moon?

continued ⋯⟩

8 Astrologers believe that the planets exert an influence on us, particularly at the moment of birth. (They don't necessarily believe that this is an effect of gravity!)
  a Calculate the gravitational force on a 4.0 kg baby caused by Mars when the planet is at its closest to the Earth at a distance of 100 000 000 km. Mars has mass $6.4 \times 10^{23}$ kg.
  b Calculate the gravitational force on the same baby due to its 50 kg mother at a distance of 0.40 m.

9 There is a point on the line joining the centres of the Earth and the Moon where their combined gravitational field strength is zero. Is this point closer to the Earth or to the Moon? Calculate how far it is from the centre of the Earth.

# Energy in a gravitational field

As well as the force on a mass in a gravitational field, we can think about its energy. If you lift an object from the ground, you increase its gravitational potential energy (g.p.e.). The higher you lift it, the more work you do on it and so the greater its g.p.e. The object's change in g.p.e. can be calculated as $mg\Delta h$ where $\Delta h$ is the change in its height (as we saw in Chapter 5).

This approach is satisfactory when we are considering objects close to the Earth's surface. However, we need a more general approach to calculating gravitational energy, for two reasons:

1 If we use g.p.e. = $mg\Delta h$, we are assuming that an object's g.p.e. is zero on the Earth's surface. This is fine for many practical purposes but not, for example, if we are considering objects moving through space, far from Earth. For these, there is nothing special about the Earth's surface.
2 If we lift an object to a great height, $g$ decreases and we would need to take this into account when calculating g.p.e.

For these reasons, we need to set up a different way of thinking about gravitational potential energy. We start by picturing a mass at infinity, that is, at an infinite distance from all other masses. We say that here the mass has zero potential energy. This is a more convenient way of defining the zero of g.p.e. than using the surface of the Earth.

Now we picture moving the mass to the point where we want to know its g.p.e. As with lifting an object from the ground, we determine the work done to move the mass to the point. The work done on it is equal to the energy transferred to it, i.e. its g.p.e., and that is how we can determine the g.p.e. of a particular mass.

# Gravitational potential

In practice, it is more useful to talk about the **gravitational potential** at a point. This tells us the g.p.e. **per unit mass** at the point (just as field strength $g$ tells us the force **per unit mass** at a point in a field). The symbol used for potential is $\varphi$ (Greek letter phi), and **unit mass** means one kilogram. Gravitational potential is defined as follows.

> The gravitational potential at a point is the work done in bringing unit mass from infinity to the point.

For a point mass $M$, we can write an equation for $\varphi$ at a distance $r$ from $M$:

$$\varphi = -\frac{GM}{r}$$

where $G$ is the gravitational constant as before. Notice the minus sign; gravitational potential is always negative. This is because, as a mass is brought towards another mass, its g.p.e. decreases. Since g.p.e. is zero at infinity, it follows that, anywhere else, g.p.e. and potential are less than zero, i.e. they are negative.

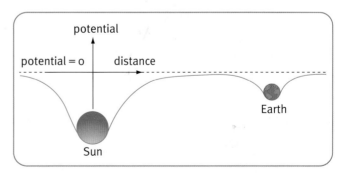

Figure 19.8 The gravitational potential is zero at infinity (far from any mass), and decreases as a mass is approached.

Picture a spacecraft coming from a distant star to visit the solar system. The variation of the gravitational potential along its path is shown in Figure 19.8. We will concentrate on three parts of its journey.

1 As the craft approaches the Earth, it is attracted towards it. The closer it gets to Earth, the lower its g.p.e. becomes and so the lower its potential.

2 As it moves away from the Earth, it has to work against the pull of the Earth's gravity. Its g.p.e. increases and so we can say that the potential increases. The Earth's gravitational field creates a giant 'potential well' in space. We live at the bottom of that well.

3 As it approaches the Sun, it is attracted into a much deeper well. The Sun's mass is much greater than the Earth's and so its pull is much stronger and the potential at its surface is more negative than on the Earth's surface.

## Test yourself

You will need the data for the mass and radius of the Earth and the Moon from Table **19.1** to answer this question.

Gravitational constant $G = 6.67 \times 10^{-11}\,\mathrm{N\,m^2\,kg^{-2}}$.

**10 a** Determine the gravitational potential at the surface of the Earth.

**b** Determine the gravitational potential at the surface of the Moon.

**c** Which has the shallower 'potential well', the Earth or the Moon? Draw a diagram similar to Figure **19.8** to compare the 'potential wells' of the Earth and the Moon.

**d** Use your diagram to explain why a large rocket is needed to lift a spacecraft from the surface of the Earth but a much smaller rocket can be used to launch from the Moon's surface.

## Fields – terminology

The words used to describe gravitational (and other) fields can be confusing. Remember:

• **field strength** tells us about the **force** on unit mass at a point;

• **potential** tells us about **potential energy** of unit mass at a point.

You have already learned about field strength in connection with electric fields, where it is the force on unit charge. Similarly, when we talk about the potential difference between two points in electricity,

we are talking about the difference in electrical potential energy of unit charge. You will learn more about this in Chapter **23**.

# Orbiting under gravity

For an object orbiting a planet, such as an artificial satellite orbiting the Earth, gravity provides the centripetal force which keeps it in orbit (Figure **19.9**).

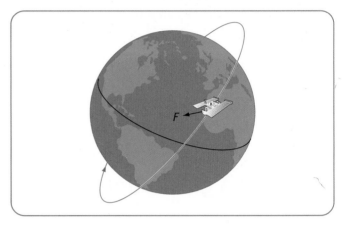

**Figure 19.9** The gravitational attraction of the Earth provides the centripetal force on an orbiting satellite.

This is a simple situation as there is only one force acting on the satellite – the gravitational attraction of the Earth. The satellite follows a circular path because the gravitational force is at right angles to its velocity.

From Chapter **18**, you know that the centripetal force $F$ on a body is given by:

$$F = \frac{mv^2}{r}$$

Consider a satellite of mass $m$ orbiting the Earth at a distance $r$ from the Earth's centre at a constant speed $v$. Since it is the gravitational force between the Earth and the satellite which provides this centripetal force, we can write:

$$\frac{GMm}{r^2} = \frac{mv^2}{r}$$

where $M$ is the mass of the Earth. (There is no need for a minus sign here as the gravitational force and the centripetal force are both directed towards the centre of the circle.)

Rearranging gives:

$$v^2 = \frac{GM}{r}$$

**Figure 19.10** During this space walk, both the astronaut and the spacecraft travel through space at over $8\,\text{km}\,\text{s}^{-1}$.

This equation allows us to calculate, for example, the speed at which a satellite must travel to stay in a circular orbit. Notice that the mass of the satellite $m$ has cancelled out. The implication of this is that all satellites, whatever their masses, will travel at the same speed in a particular orbit. You would find this very reassuring if you were an astronaut on a space walk outside your spacecraft (Figure **19.10**). You would travel at the same speed as your craft, despite the fact that your mass is a lot less than its mass. The equation above can be applied to the planets of our Solar System – $M$ becomes the mass of the Sun.

Now look at Worked example 2.

### Worked example

2 The Moon orbits the Earth at an average distance of $384\,000\,\text{km}$ from the centre of the Earth. Calculate its orbital speed. (The mass of the Earth is $6.0 \times 10^{24}\,\text{kg}$.)

**Step 1** Write down the known quantities.

$$r = 3.84 \times 10^8\,\text{m} \quad M = 6.0 \times 10^{24}\,\text{kg} \quad v = ?$$

**Step 2** Use the equation $v^2 = \dfrac{GM}{r}$ to determine the orbital speed $v$.

*continued* ⋯→

$$v^2 = \frac{GM}{r}$$

$$v^2 = \frac{6.67 \times 10^{-11} \times 6.0 \times 10^{24}}{3.84 \times 10^8}$$

$$v^2 = 1.04 \times 10^6$$

Don't forget to take the square root of $v^2$ to get $v$.

$$v = 1020\,\text{m}\,\text{s}^{-1} \approx 1.0 \times 10^3\,\text{m}\,\text{s}^{-1}$$

So the Moon travels around its orbit at a speed of roughly $1\,\text{km}\,\text{s}^{-1}$.

### Test yourself

11 Calculate the orbital speed of an artificial satellite travelling $200\,\text{km}$ above the Earth's surface. (The radius of Earth is $6.4 \times 10^6\,\text{m}$ and its mass is $6.0 \times 10^{24}\,\text{kg}$.)

# The orbital period

It is often more useful to consider the time taken for a complete orbit, the orbital **period** $T$. Since the distance around an orbit is equal to the circumference $2\pi r$, it follows that:

$$v = \frac{2\pi r}{T}$$

We can substitute this in the equation for $v^2$ on page **278**. This gives:

$$\frac{4\pi^2 r^2}{T^2} = \frac{GM}{r}$$

and rearranging this equation gives:

$$T^2 = \left(\frac{4\pi^2}{GM}\right) r^3$$

This equation shows that the orbital period $T$ is related to the radius $r$ of the orbit. The square of the period is directly proportional to the cube of the radius ($T^2 \propto r^3$). This is an important result. It was first discovered by Johannes Kepler, who analysed the available data for the planets of the solar system. It was an empirical law (one based solely on experiment) since he had no theory to explain why there should be this relationship between $T$ and $r$. It was not until Isaac Newton formulated his law of gravitation that it was possible to explain this fact.

# Orbiting the Earth

The Earth has one natural satellite – the Moon – and many thousands of artificial satellites – some spacecraft and a lot of debris. Each of these satellites uses the Earth's gravitational field to provide the centripetal force that keeps it in orbit. In order for a satellite to maintain a particular orbit, it must travel at the correct speed. This is given by the equation on page **278**:

$$v^2 = \frac{GM}{r}$$

It follows from this equation that the closer the satellite is to the Earth, the faster it must travel. If it travels too slowly, it will fall down towards the Earth's surface. If it travels too quickly, it will move out into a higher orbit.

## Test yourself

**12** A satellite orbiting a few hundred kilometres above the Earth's surface will experience a slight frictional drag from the Earth's (very thin) atmosphere. Draw a diagram to show how you would expect the satellite's orbit to change as a result. How can this problem be overcome if it is desired to keep a satellite at a particular height above the Earth?

## Observing the Earth

Artificial satellites have a variety of uses. Many are used for making observations of the Earth's surface for commercial, environmental, meteorological and military purposes. Others are used for astronomical observations, benefiting greatly from being above the Earth's atmosphere. Still others are used for navigation, telecommunications and broadcasting.

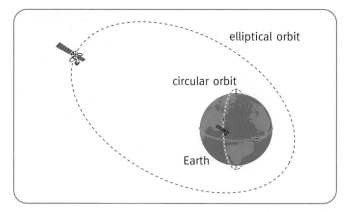

**Figure 19.11** Satellites orbiting the Earth.

Figure **19.11** shows two typical orbits. A satellite in a circular orbit close to the Earth's surface and passing over the poles, completes about 16 orbits in 24 hours. As the Earth turns below it, the satellite 'sees' a different strip of the Earth's surface during each orbit. A satellite in an elliptical orbit has a more distant view of the Earth.

## Geostationary orbits

A special type of orbit is one in which a satellite is positioned so that, as it orbits, the Earth rotates below it at the same rate. The satellite remains above a fixed point on the Earth's surface. This kind of orbit is called a **geostationary orbit**. This idea was first suggested in 1945 by the engineer and science fiction writer Arthur C. Clarke. He proposed setting up a series of communications satellites in a 'Clarke belt' above the equator. These would allow telecommunications signals to leap-frog around the world.

We can determine the distance of a satellite in a geostationary orbit using the equation:

$$T^2 = \left( \frac{4\pi^2}{GM} \right) r^3$$

For a satellite to stay above a fixed point on the equator, it must take exactly 24 hours to complete one orbit (Figure **19.12**). We know:

$G = 6.67 \times 10^{-11}\,\mathrm{N\,m^2\,kg^{-2}}$

$T = 24\ \text{hours} = 86\,400\,\mathrm{s}$

$M = 6.0 \times 10^{24}\,\mathrm{kg}$

## Parking in space

A geostationary orbit is sometimes known as a 'parking orbit'. There are over 300 satellites in such orbits. They are used for telecommunications (transmitting telephone messages around the world) and for satellite television transmission. A base station on Earth sends the TV signal up to the satellite, where it is amplified and broadcast back to the ground. Satellite receiver dishes are a familiar sight; you will have observed how, in a neighbourhood, they all point towards the same point in the sky. Because the satellite is in a geostationary orbit, the dish can be fixed. Satellites in any other orbits move across the sky so that a tracking system is necessary to communicate with them. Such a system is complex and expensive, and too demanding for the domestic market.

Geostationary satellites have a lifetime of perhaps ten years. They need a fuel supply to maintain them in the correct orbit, and to keep them pointing correctly towards the Earth. Eventually they run out of fuel and need to be replaced.

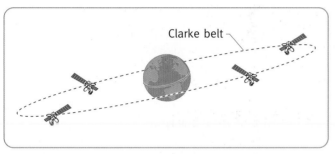

**Figure 19.12** Geostationary satellites are parked in the 'Clarke belt', high above the equator. This is a perspective view; the Clarke belt is circular.

Hence:

$$r^3 = \frac{GMT^2}{4\pi^2} = \frac{6.67 \times 10^{-11} \times 6.0 \times 10^{24} \times (86\,400)^2}{4\pi^2}$$

$$= 7.66 \times 10^{22}\,\text{m}^3$$

$$r = \sqrt[3]{7.66 \times 10^{22}} = 4.23 \times 10^7\,\text{m}$$

So, for a satellite to occupy a geostationary orbit, it must be at a distance of 42 300 km from the centre of the Earth and at a point directly above the equator. Note that the radius of the Earth is 6400 km, so the orbital radius is 6.6 Earth radii from the centre of the Earth (or 5.6 Earth radii from its surface). Figure **19.12** has been drawn to give an impression of the size of the orbit.

# Summary

☐ The force of gravity is an attractive force between any two objects due to their masses.
☐ The gravitational field strength $g$ at a point is the gravitational force exerted per unit mass on a small object placed at that point – that is:

$$g = \frac{F}{m}$$

☐ The external field of a uniform spherical mass is the same as that of an equal point mass at the centre of the sphere.
☐ Newton's law of gravitation states that:
Any two point masses attract each other with a force that is directly proportional to the product of their masses and inversely proportional to the square of their separation.
☐ The equation for Newton's law of gravitation is:

$$F = -\frac{GMm}{r^2}$$

☐ The gravitational field strength at distance $r$ from a point or spherical mass $M$ is given by:

$$g = -\frac{GM}{r^2}$$

☐ On or near the surface of the Earth, the gravitational field is uniform, so the value of $g$ is approximately constant. Its value is equal to the acceleration of free fall.
☐ The gravitational potential at a point is the work done in bringing unit mass from infinity to that point.
☐ The gravitational potential of a point mass is given by:

$$\varphi = -\frac{GM}{r}$$

☐ The orbital period of a satellite is the time taken for one orbit.
☐ The orbital period can be found by equating the gravitational force $\frac{GMm}{r^2}$ to the centripetal force $\frac{mv^2}{r}$.

☐ The orbital speed of a planet or satellite can be determined using the equation:

$$v^2 = \frac{GM}{r}$$

☐ Geostationary satellites have an orbital period of 24 hours and are used for telecommunications transmissions and for television broadcasting.

# End-of-chapter questions

1 Two small spheres each of mass 20 g hang side by side with their centres 5.00 mm apart. Calculate the gravitational attraction between the two spheres.

2 It is suggested that the mass of a mountain could be measured by the deflection from the vertical of a suspended mass. Figure **19.13** shows the principle.

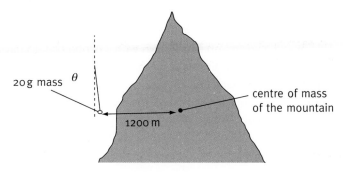

**Figure 19.13** For End-of-chapter Q **2**.

   **a** Copy Figure **19.13** and draw arrows to represent the forces acting on the mass. Label the arrows.
   **b** The whole mass of the mountain, $3.8 \times 10^{12}$ kg, may be considered to act at its centre of mass. Calculate the horizontal force on the mass due to the mountain.
   **c** Compare the force calculated in **b** with the Earth's gravitational force on the mass.

3 Figure **19.14** shows the Earth's gravitational field.

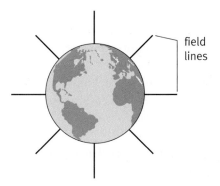

**Figure 19.14** For End-of-chapter Q **3**.

   **a** Copy the diagram and add arrows to show the direction of the field.
   **b** Explain why the formula potential energy gained = $mg\Delta h$ can be used to find the increase in potential energy when an aircraft climbs to a height of 10 000 m but cannot be used to calculate the increase in potential energy when a spacecraft travels from the Earth's surface to a height of 10 000 km.

4   Mercury, the smallest of the eight recognised planets, has a diameter of $4.88 \times 10^6$ m and a mean density of $5.4 \times 10^3$ kg m$^{-3}$.
   a   Calculate the gravitational field at its surface.
   b   A man has a weight of 900 N on the Earth's surface. What would his weight be on the surface of Mercury?

5   Calculate the potential energy of a spacecraft of mass 250 kg when it is 20 000 km from the planet Mars. (Mass of Mars = $6.4 \times 10^{23}$ kg, radius of Mars = $3.4 \times 10^6$ m.)

6   Ganymede is the largest of Jupiter's moons with a mass of $1.48 \times 10^{23}$ kg. It orbits Jupiter with an orbital radius of $1.07 \times 10^6$ km and it rotates on its own axis with a period of 7.15 days. It has been suggested that to monitor an unmanned landing craft on the surface of Ganymede a geostationary satellite should be placed in orbit around Ganymede.
   a   Calculate the orbital radius of the proposed geostationary satellite.
   b   Suggest a difficulty that might be encountered in achieving a geostationary orbit for this moon.

7   The Earth orbits the Sun with a period of 1 year at an orbital radius of $1.50 \times 10^{11}$ m. Calculate:
   a   the orbital speed of the Earth
   b   the centripetal acceleration of the Earth
   c   the Sun's gravitational field strength at the Earth.

# Exam-style questions

1   The planet Mars has a mass of $6.4 \times 10^{23}$ kg and a diameter of 6790 km.
   a   i   Calculate the acceleration due to gravity at the planet's surface.   [2]
       ii   Calculate the gravitational potential at the surface of the planet.   [2]
   b   A rocket is to return some samples of Martian material to Earth. Write down how much energy each kilogram of matter must be given to escape completely from Mars's gravitational field.   [1]
   c   Use you answer to b to show that the minimum speed that the rocket must reach to escape from the gravitational field is 5000 m s$^{-1}$.   [2]
   d   Suggest why it has been proposed that for a successful mission to Mars that the craft that takes the astronauts to Mars will be assembled at the space station and launched from there, rather than from the Earth's surface.   [2]

2   a   Explain what is meant by the **gravitational potential at a point**.   [2]
    b   The diagram shows the potential near a planet of mass $M$ and radius $R$.

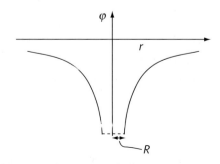

On a copy of the diagram, draw similar curves:
  i   for a planet of the same radius but of mass $2M$ – label this **i**.                    [2]
  ii  for a planet of the same mass but of radius $2R$ – label this **ii**.                    [2]
 c  Use the graphs to explain from which of the three planets it would require the least
    energy to escape.                                                                          [2]
 d  Venus has a diameter of $12\,100\,$km and a mass of $4.87 \times 10^{24}\,$kg.
    Calculate the energy needed to lift one kilogram from the surface of Venus to a space
    station in orbit $900\,$km from the surface.                                               [4]

3  a  Explain what is meant by the **gravitational field strength at a point**.                [2]

The diagram shows the dwarf planet, Pluto, and its moon, Charon. These can be
considered to be a double planetary system orbiting each other about their joint
centre of mass.

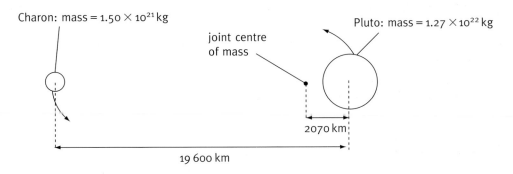

Charon: mass = $1.50 \times 10^{21}\,$kg

joint centre of mass

Pluto: mass = $1.27 \times 10^{22}\,$kg

2070 km

19 600 km

 b  Calculate the gravitational pull on Charon due to Pluto.                                   [3]
 c  Use your result to **b** to calculate Charon's orbital period.                             [3]
 d  Explain why Pluto's orbital period must be the same as Charon's.                           [1]

4  The graph shows the variation of the Earth's gravitational field strength with
   distance from its centre.

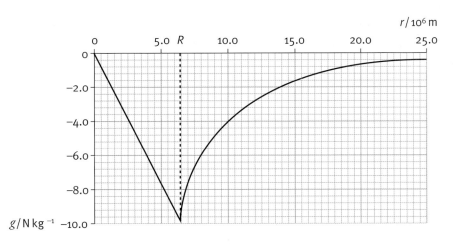

**a** Determine the gravitational field strength at a height equal to $2R$ above the Earth's surface, where $R$ is the radius of the Earth. [1]

**b** A satellite is put into an orbit at this height. State the centripetal acceleration of the satellite. [1]

**c** Calculate the speed at which the satellite must travel to remain in this orbit. [2]

**d i** The diagram shows the orbital path of the satellite. Frictional forces mean that the satellite gradually slows down.

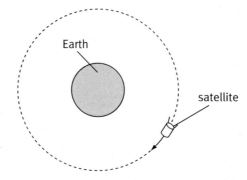

Copy the diagram and show on your copy the resulting path of the satellite. [1]

**ii** Suggest and explain why there is not a continuous bombardment of old satellites colliding with the Earth. [2]

## Objectives

After studying this chapter, you should be able to:

- [ ] describe examples of free and forced oscillations
- [ ] use appropriate terminology to describe oscillations
- [ ] define simple harmonic motion (s.h.m.)
- [ ] recall and use equations for displacement and velocity in s.h.m.
- [ ] draw and use graphical representations of s.h.m.

- [ ] describe energy changes during s.h.m.
- [ ] describe the effects of damping on oscillations, with practical examples
- [ ] describe examples of forced oscillations and resonance, together with the effects of damping on resonance

## Oscillations in an engine

Figure **20.1** shows a cut-away view of a modern car engine; there are four pistons which oscillate up to 5000 times per minute when the engine is operating at full power. Engineers need to understand the physics of oscillations to be able to calculate the stresses produced on the pistons when the engine is operating.

**Figure 20.1** The pistons inside this car engine oscillate up and down as the engine powers the car.

## Free and forced oscillations

Oscillations and vibrations are everywhere. A bird in flight flaps its wings up and down. An aircraft's wings also vibrate up and down, but this is not how it flies. The wings are long and thin, and they vibrate slightly because they are not perfectly rigid. Many other structures vibrate – bridges when traffic flows across, buildings in high winds.

A more specific term than vibration is **oscillation**. An object **oscillates** when it moves back and forth repeatedly, on either side of some equilibrium position. If we stop the object from oscillating, it returns to the equilibrium position.

We make use of oscillations in many different ways – for pleasure (a child on a swing), for music (the vibrations of a guitar string), for timing (the movement of a pendulum or the vibrations of

a quartz crystal). Whenever we make a sound, the molecules of the air oscillate, passing the sound energy along. The atoms of a solid vibrate more and more as the temperature rises.

These examples of oscillations and vibrations may seem very different from one another. In this chapter, we will look at the characteristics that are shared by all oscillations.

### Free or forced?

The easiest oscillations to understand are free oscillations. If you pluck a guitar string, it continues to vibrate for some time after you have released it. It vibrates at a particular frequency (the number of vibrations per unit time). This is called its **natural frequency** of vibration, and it gives rise to the particular note that you hear. Change the length of the string, and you change the natural frequency. In a similar way, the prongs of a tuning fork have a natural frequency of vibration, which you can observe when you strike it on a cork. Every oscillator has a natural frequency of vibration, the frequency with which it vibrates freely after an initial disturbance.

On the other hand, many objects can be forced to vibrate. If you sit on a bus, you may notice that the vibrations from the engine are transmitted to your body, causing you to vibrate with the same frequency. These are not free vibrations of your body; they are forced vibrations. Their frequency is not the natural frequency of vibration of your body, but the forcing frequency of the bus.

In the same way, you can force a metre ruler to oscillate by waving it up and down; however, its natural frequency of vibration will be much greater than this, as you will discover if you hold one end down on the bench and twang the other end (Figure **20.2**).

**Figure 20.2** A ruler vibrating freely at its natural frequency.

### Test yourself

1 State which of the following are free oscillations, and which are forced:
   **a** the wing beat of a mosquito
   **b** the movement of the pendulum in a grandfather clock

*continued ···▸*

**c** the vibrations of a cymbal after it has been struck
**d** the shaking of a building during an earthquake.

# Observing oscillations

Many oscillations are too rapid or too small for us to observe. Our eyes cannot respond rapidly enough if the frequency of oscillation is more than about 5 Hz (five oscillations per second); anything faster than this appears as a blur. In order to see the general characteristics of oscillating systems, we need to find suitable systems that oscillate slowly. Here are three suitable situations to look at.

## A mass–spring system

A trolley, loaded with extra masses, is tethered by identical springs in between two clamps (Figure **20.3**). Displace the trolley to one side and it will oscillate back and forth along the bench. Listen to the sound of the trolley moving. Where is it moving fastest? What happens to its speed as it reaches the ends of its oscillation? What is happening to the springs as the trolley oscillates?

**Figure 20.3** A trolley tethered between springs will oscillate freely from side to side.

## A long pendulum

A string, at least 2 m long, hangs from the ceiling with a large mass fixed at the end (Figure **20.4**). Pull the mass some distance to one side, and let go. The pendulum will swing back and forth at its natural frequency of oscillation. Try to note the characteristics of its motion. In what ways is it similar to the motion of the oscillating trolley? In what ways is it different?

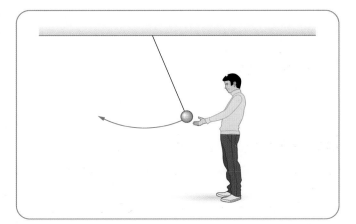

Figure 20.4 A long pendulum oscillates back and forth.

## A loudspeaker cone

A signal generator, set to a low frequency (say, 1 Hz), drives a loudspeaker so that it vibrates (Figure 20.5). You need to be able to see the cone of the loudspeaker. How does this motion compare with that of the pendulum and the mass–spring system? Try using a higher frequency (say, 100 Hz). Use an electronic stroboscope flashing at a similar frequency to show up the movement of the cone. (It may help to paint a white spot on the centre of the cone.) Do you observe the same pattern of movement?

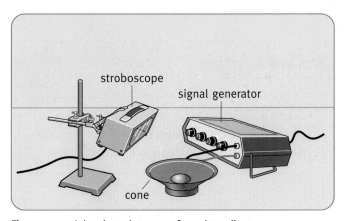

Figure 20.5 A loudspeaker cone forced to vibrate up and down.

## Test yourself

2   If you could draw a velocity–time graph for any of these oscillators, what would it look like? Would it be a curve like the one shown in

*continued* ⋯⋗

Figure **20.6a**, or triangular (saw-toothed) like the one shown in Figure **20.6b**?

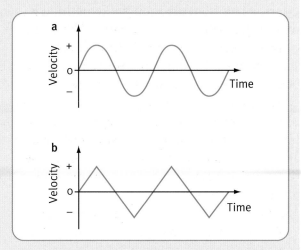

Figure 20.6 Two possible velocity–time graphs for vibrating objects.

# Describing oscillations

All of these examples show the same pattern of movement. The trolley accelerates as it moves towards the centre of the oscillation. It is moving fastest at the centre. It decelerates as it moves towards the end of the oscillation. At the extreme position, it stops momentarily, reverses its direction and accelerates back towards the centre again.

## Amplitude, period and frequency

Many oscillating systems can be represented by a displacement–time graph like that shown in Figure **20.7**. The displacement $x$ varies in a smooth way on either side of the midpoint. The shape of this graph is a sine curve, and the motion is described as **sinusoidal**.

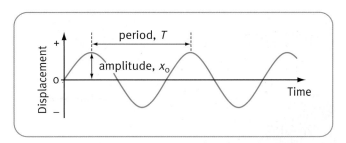

Figure 20.7 A displacement–time graph to show the meanings of amplitude and period.

Notice that the displacement changes between positive and negative values, as the object moves through the equilibrium position. The maximum displacement from the equilibrium position is called the **amplitude** $x_0$ of the oscillation.

The displacement–time graph can also be used to show the period and frequency of the oscillation. The period $T$ is the time for one complete oscillation. Note that the oscillating object must go from one side to the other and back again (or the equivalent). The frequency $f$ is the number of oscillations per unit time, and so $f$ is the reciprocal of $T$:

$$\text{frequency} = \frac{1}{\text{period}} \qquad \text{or} \qquad f = \frac{1}{T}$$

The equation above can also be written as:

$$\text{period} = \frac{1}{\text{frequency}} \qquad \text{or} \qquad T = \frac{1}{f}$$

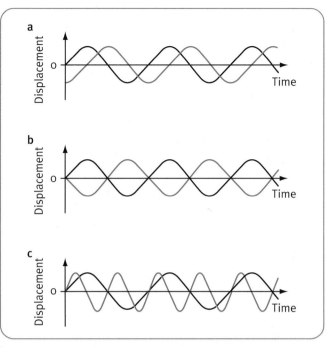

**Figure 20.9** Illustrating the idea of phase difference.

## Test yourself

3 From the displacement–time graph shown in Figure 20.8, determine the amplitude, period and frequency of the oscillations represented.

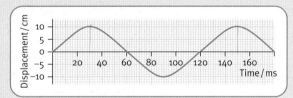

**Figure 20.8** A displacement–time graph for an oscillator.

## Phase

The term **phase** describes the point that an oscillating mass has reached within the complete cycle of an oscillation. It is often important to describe the **phase difference** between two oscillations. The graph of Figure 20.9a shows two oscillations which are identical except for their phase difference. They are out of step with one another. In this example, they have a phase difference of one-quarter of an oscillation. Phase difference can be measured as a fraction of an oscillation, in degrees or in radians (see Worked example 1).

## Test yourself

4 **a** Figure **20.9b** shows two oscillations which are out of phase. By what fraction of an oscillation are they out of phase?
 **b** Why would it not make sense to ask the same question about Figure **20.9c**?

## Worked example

1 Figure **20.10** shows displacement–time graphs for two identical oscillators. Calculate the phase difference between the two oscillations. Give your answer in degrees and in radians.

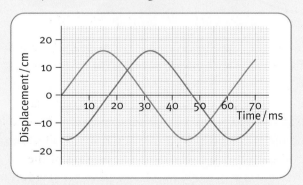

**Figure 20.10** The displacement–time graphs of two oscillators with the same period.

*continued ···*

**Step 1** Measure the time interval $t$ between two corresponding points on the graphs.

$t = 17$ ms

**Step 2** Determine the period $T$ for one complete oscillation.

$T = 60$ ms

Remember that a complete oscillation is when the object goes from one side to the other and back again.

**Step 3** Now you can calculate the phase difference as a fraction of an oscillation.

phase difference = fraction of an oscillation

Therefore:

phase difference $= \dfrac{t}{T} = \dfrac{17}{60} = 0.283$ oscillation

**Step 4** Convert to degrees and radians. There are 360° and $2\pi$ rad in one oscillation.

phase difference $= 0.283 \times 360° = 102° \approx 100°$

phase difference $= 0.283 \times 2\pi$ rad $= 1.78$ rad
$$\approx 1.8 \text{ rad}$$

# Simple harmonic motion

There are many situations where we can observe the special kind of oscillations called **simple harmonic motion** (s.h.m.). Some are more obvious than others. For example, the vibrating strings of a musical instrument show s.h.m. When plucked or bowed, the strings move back and forth about the equilibrium position of their oscillation. The motion of the tethered trolley in Figure **20.3** and of the pendulum in Figure **20.4** is also s.h.m. (Simple harmonic motion is defined in terms of the acceleration and displacement of an oscillator – see page **292**.)

Here are some other, less obvious, situations where simple harmonic motion can be found.

- When a pure (single tone) sound wave travels through air, the molecules of the air vibrate with s.h.m.
- When an alternating current flows in a wire, the electrons in the wire vibrate with s.h.m.
- There is a small alternating electric current in a radio or television aerial when it is tuned to a signal, in the form of electrons moving with s.h.m.
- The atoms that make up a molecule vibrate with s.h.m. (see for example the hydrogen molecule in Figure **20.11a**).

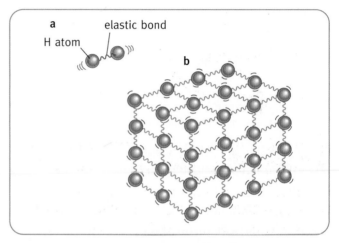

**Figure 20.11** We can think of the bonds between atoms as being springy; this leads to vibrations, **a** in a molecule of hydrogen and **b** in a solid crystal.

Oscillations can be very complex, with many different frequencies of oscillation occurring at the same time. Examples include the vibrations of machinery, the motion of waves on the sea, and the vibration of a solid crystal formed when atoms, ions or molecules bond together (Figure **20.11b**). It is possible to break down a complex oscillation into a sum of simple oscillations, and so we will focus our attention in this chapter on s.h.m. with only one frequency. We will also concentrate on large-scale mechanical oscillations, but you should bear in mind that this analysis can be extended to the situations mentioned above, and many more besides.

## The requirements for s.h.m.

If a simple pendulum is undisturbed, it is in equilibrium. The string and the mass will hang vertically. To start it swinging (Figure **20.12**), it must be pulled to one side of its equilibrium position. The forces on the mass are unbalanced and so it moves back towards its equilibrium position. The mass swings past this point and continues until it comes to rest momentarily at the other side; the process is then repeated in the opposite direction. Note that a complete oscillation is from right to left and back again.

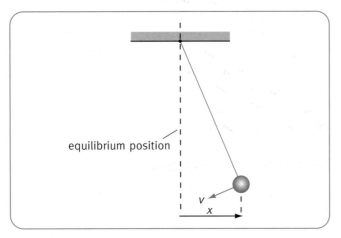

**Figure 20.12** This swinging pendulum has positive displacement *x* and negative velocity *v*.

The three requirements for s.h.m. of a mechanical system are:

1 a mass that oscillates;
2 a position where the mass is in equilibrium (conventionally, displacement *x* to the right of this position is taken as positive; to the left it is negative);
3 a restoring force that acts to return the mass to its equilibrium position; the restoring force *F* is directly proportional to the displacement *x* of the mass from its equilibrium position and is directed towards that point.

### The changes of velocity in s.h.m.

As the pendulum swings back and forth, its velocity is constantly changing. As it swings from right to left (as shown in Figure 20.12) its velocity is negative.

It accelerates towards the equilibrium position and then decelerates as it approaches the other end of the oscillation. It has positive velocity as it swings back from left to right. Again, it is has maximum speed as it travels through the equilibrium position and decelerates as it swings up to its starting position.

This pattern of acceleration – deceleration – changing direction – acceleration again is characteristic of simple harmonic motion. There are no sudden changes of velocity. In the next section we will see how we can observe these changes and how we can represent them graphically.

# Graphical representations of s.h.m.

If you set up a trolley tethered between springs (Figure 20.13) you can hear the characteristic rhythm of s.h.m. as the trolley oscillates back and forth. By adjusting the mass carried by the trolley, you can achieve oscillations with a period of about two seconds.

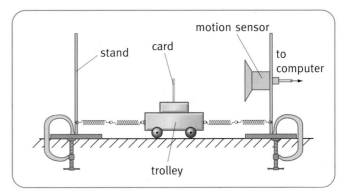

**Figure 20.13** A motion sensor can be used to investigate s.h.m. of a spring–trolley system.

The motion sensor allows you to record how the displacement of the trolley varies with time. Ultrasonic pulses from the sensor are reflected by the card on the trolley and the reflected pulses are detected. This 'sonar' technique allows the sensor to determine the displacement of the trolley. A typical screen display is shown in Figure 20.14.

The computer can then determine the velocity of the trolley by calculating the rate of change of displacement. Similarly, it can calculate the rate of change of velocity to determine the acceleration.

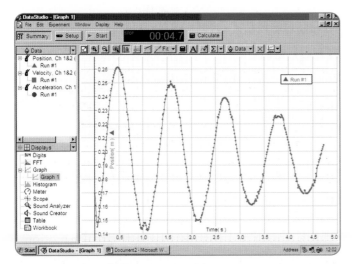

Figure 20.14 A typical displacement–time graph generated by a motion sensor.

Idealised graphs of displacement, velocity and acceleration against time are shown in Figure 20.15. We will examine these graphs in sequence to see what they tell us about s.h.m. and how the three graphs are related to one another.

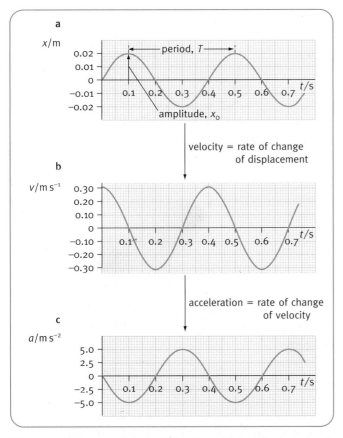

Figure 20.15 Graphs of displacement $x$, velocity $v$ and acceleration $a$ against time $t$ for s.h.m.

## Displacement–time ($x$–$t$) graph

The displacement of the oscillating mass varies according to the smooth curve shown in Figure 20.15a. Mathematically, this is a sine curve; its variation is described as **sinusoidal**. Note that this graph allows us to determine the amplitude $x_0$ and the period $T$ of the oscillations. In this graph, the displacement $x$ of the oscillation is shown as zero at the start, when $t$ is zero. We have chosen to consider the motion to start when the mass is at the midpoint of its oscillation (equilibrium position) and is moving to the right. We could have chosen any other point in the cycle as the starting point, but it is conventional to start as shown here.

## Velocity–time ($v$–$t$) graph

The velocity $v$ of the oscillator at any time can be determined from the gradient of the displacement–time graph:

$$v = \frac{\Delta x}{\Delta t}$$

Again, we have a smooth curve (Figure 20.15b), which shows how the velocity $v$ depends on time $t$. The shape of the curve is the same as for the displacement–time graph, but it starts at a different point in the cycle. When time $t=0$, the mass is at the equilibrium position and this is where it is moving fastest. Hence the velocity has its maximum value at this point. Its value is positive because at time $t=0$ it is moving towards the right.

## Acceleration–time ($a$–$t$) graph

Finally, the acceleration $a$ of the oscillator at any time can be determined from the gradient of the velocity–time graph:

$$a = \frac{\Delta v}{\Delta t}$$

This gives a third curve of the same general form (Figure 20.15c), which shows how the acceleration $a$ depends on time $t$. At the start of the oscillation, the mass is at its equilibrium position. There is no resultant force acting on it so its acceleration is zero. As it moves to the right, the restoring force acts towards the left, giving it a negative acceleration. The acceleration has its greatest value when the mass is displaced farthest from the equilibrium position. Notice that the acceleration graph is 'upside-down' compared with the displacement graph. This shows that:

acceleration ∝ –displacement

or

$a \propto -x$

In other words, whenever the mass has a positive displacement (to the right), its acceleration is to the left, and vice versa.

## Test yourself

7 Use the graphs shown in Figure 20.15 to determine the values of the following quantities:
   a amplitude
   b period
   c maximum velocity
   d maximum acceleration.

8 State at what point in an oscillation the oscillator has zero velocity but positive acceleration.

9 Look at the x–t graph of Figure 20.15a. When $t = 0.1$ s, what is the gradient of the graph? State the velocity at this instant.

10 Figure 20.16 shows the displacement–time (x–t) graph for an oscillating mass. Use the graph to determine the following quantities:
   a the velocity in $\mathrm{cm\,s^{-1}}$ when $t = 0$ s
   b the maximum velocity in $\mathrm{cm\,s^{-1}}$
   c the acceleration in $\mathrm{cm\,s^{-2}}$ when $t = 1.0$ s.

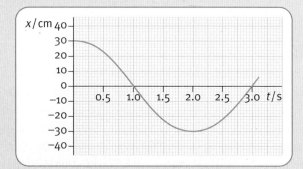

**Figure 20.16** A displacement–time graph for an oscillating mass – see Test yourself Q **10**.

# Frequency and angular frequency

The frequency $f$ of s.h.m. is equal to the number of oscillations per unit time. As we saw earlier, $f$ is related to the period $T$ by:

$$f = \frac{1}{T}$$

We can think of a complete oscillation of an oscillator or a cycle of s.h.m. as being represented by $2\pi$ radians. (This is similar to a complete cycle of circular motion, where an object moves round through $2\pi$ radians.) The phase of the oscillation changes by $2\pi$ rad during one oscillation. Hence, if there are $f$ oscillations in unit time, there must be $2\pi f$ radians in unit time. This quantity is the **angular frequency** of the s.h.m. and it is represented by the symbol $\omega$.

The angular frequency $\omega$ is thus related to frequency $f$ by the following equation:

$$\omega = 2\pi f$$

Since $f = \frac{1}{T}$, the angular frequency $\omega$ is related to the period $T$ of the oscillator by the equation:

$$\omega = \frac{2\pi}{T} \quad \text{or} \quad T = \frac{2\pi}{\omega}$$

In Figure 20.17, a single cycle of s.h.m. is shown, but with the x-axis marked with the phase of the motion in radians.

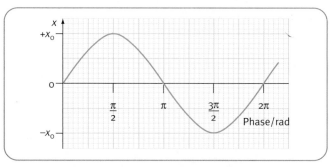

**Figure 20.17** The phase of an oscillation varies from 0 to $2\pi$ during one cycle.

11 An object moving with s.h.m. goes through two complete cycles in 1.0 s. Calculate:
  a the period $T$
  b the frequency $f$
  c the angular frequency $\omega$.

12 Figure **20.18** shows the displacement–time graph for an oscillating mass. Use the graph to determine the following:
  a amplitude
  b period
  c frequency

  d angular frequency
  e displacement at A
  f velocity at B
  g velocity at C.

13 An atom in a crystal vibrates with s.h.m. with a frequency of $10^{14}$ Hz. The amplitude of its motion is $2.0 \times 10^{-12}$ m.
  a Sketch a graph to show how the displacement of the atom varies during one cycle.
  b Use your graph to estimate the maximum velocity of the atom.

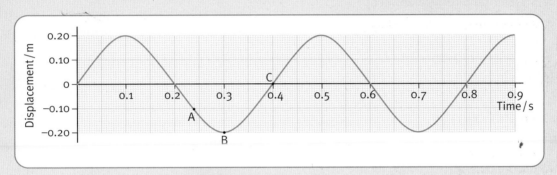

Figure **20.18** A displacement–time graph. For Test yourself Q **12**.

# Equations of s.h.m.

The graph of Figure **20.15a** shown earlier represents how the displacement of an oscillator varies during s.h.m. We have already mentioned that this is a sine curve. We can present the same information in the form of an equation. The relationship between the displacement $x$ and the time $t$ is as follows:

$$x = x_0 \sin \omega t$$

where $x_0$ is the amplitude of the motion and $\omega$ is its frequency. Sometimes the same motion is represented using a cosine function, rather than a sine function:

$$x = x_0 \cos \omega t$$

The difference between these two equations is illustrated in Figure **20.19**. The sine version starts at $x = 0$, i.e. the oscillating mass is at its equilibrium position when $t = 0$. The cosine version starts at $x = x_0$, so that the mass is at its maximum displacement when $t = 0$.

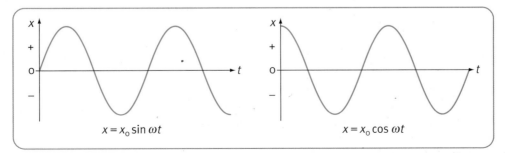

Figure **20.19** These two graphs represent the same simple harmonic motion. The difference in starting positions is related to the sine and cosine forms of the equation for $x$ as a function of $t$.

Note that, in calculations using these equations, the quantity $\omega t$ is in radians. Make sure that your calculator is in radian mode for any calculation (see Worked example). The presence of the $\pi$ in the equation should remind you of this.

## Worked example

2  A pendulum oscillates with frequency 1.5 Hz and amplitude 0.10 m. If it is passing through its equilibrium position when $t = 0$, write an equation to represent its displacement $x$ in terms of amplitude $x_0$, angular frequency $\omega$ and time $t$. Determine its displacement when $t = 0.50$ s.

**Step 1** Select the correct equation. In this case, the displacement is zero when $t = 0$, so we use the sine form:

$$x = x_0 \sin \omega t$$

**Step 2** From the frequency $f$, calculate the angular frequency $\omega$:

$$\omega = 2\pi f = 2 \times 1.5 \times \pi = 3.0\pi$$

**Step 3** Substitute values in the equation: $x_0 = 0.10$ m. So:

$$x = 0.10 \sin (3.0\pi t)$$

Don't forget to put your calculator into radian mode.

**Step 4** To find $x$ when $t = 0.50$ s, substitute for $t$ and calculate the answer:

$$x = 0.10 \sin (2\pi \times 1.5 \times 0.50)$$
$$= 0.10 \sin (4.713)$$
$$= -0.10 \text{ m}$$

This means that the pendulum is at the extreme end of its oscillation; the minus sign means that it is at the negative or left-hand

continued ···➔

end, assuming you have chosen to consider displacements to the right as positive.

(If your calculation went like this:

$$x = 0.1 \sin (2\pi \times 1.5 \times 0.5) = 0.1 \sin (4.713)$$
$$= -8.2 \times 10^{-3} \text{ m}$$

then your calculator was set to work in degrees, not radians.)

## Test yourself

14  The vibration of a component in a machine is represented by the equation:

$$x = 3.0 \times 10^{-4} \sin (240\pi t)$$

where the displacement $x$ is in metres. Determine the **a** amplitude, **b** frequency and **c** period of the vibration.

15  A trolley is at rest, tethered between two springs. It is pulled 0.15 m to one side and, when time $t = 0$, it is released so that it oscillates back and forth with s.h.m. The period of its motion is 2.0 s.
   **a** Write an equation for its displacement $x$ at any time $t$ (assume that the motion is not damped by frictional forces).
   **b** Sketch a displacement–time graph to show two cycles of the motion, giving values where appropriate.

## Acceleration and displacement

In s.h.m., an object's acceleration depends on how far it is displaced from its equilibrium position and on the magnitude of the restoring force. The greater the displacement $x$, the greater the acceleration $a$. In fact, $a$ is proportional to $x$. We can write the following equation to represent this:

$$a = -\omega^2 x$$

This equation shows that $a$ is proportional to $x$; the constant of proportionality is $\omega^2$. The minus sign shows that, when the object is displaced to the **right**, the direction of its acceleration is to the **left**. The acceleration is always directed towards the equilibrium position.

It should not be surprising that angular frequency $\omega$ appears in this equation. Imagine a mass hanging on a spring, so that it can vibrate up and down. If the spring is stiff, the force on the mass will be greater and it will be accelerated more for a given displacement and its frequency of oscillation will be higher. The equation:

$$a = -\omega^2 x$$

helps us to define simple harmonic motion. The acceleration $a$ is directly proportional to displacement $x$; and the minus sign shows that it is in the opposite direction.

Simple harmonic motion is defined as follows:

> A body executes simple harmonic motion if its acceleration is directly proportional to its displacement from its equilibrium position, and is always directed towards the equilibrium position.

If $a$ and $x$ were in the same direction (no minus sign), the body's acceleration would increase as it moved away from the fixed point and it would move away faster and faster, never to return.

Figure **20.20** shows the acceleration–displacement ($a$–$x$) graph for an oscillator executing s.h.m. Note the following:

• The graph is a straight line through the origin ($a \propto x$).
• It has a negative slope (the minus sign in the equation $a = -\omega^2 x$). This means that the acceleration is always directed towards the equilibrium position.
• The magnitude of the gradient of the graph is $\omega^2$.
• The gradient is independent of the amplitude of the motion. This means that the frequency $f$ or the period $T$ of the oscillator is independent of the amplitude and so a simple harmonic oscillator keeps steady time.

A mathematical note: we say that the equation $a = -\omega^2 x$ defines simple harmonic motion – it tells us what is required if a body is to perform s.h.m. The

equation $x = x_0 \sin \omega t$ is then described as a **solution** to the equation, since it tells us how the displacement of the body varies with time. If you have studied calculus you may be able to differentiate the equation for $x$ twice with respect to time to obtain an equation for acceleration and thereby show that the defining equation $a = -\omega^2 x$ is satisfied.

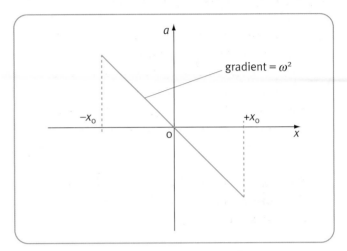

**Figure 20.20** Graph of acceleration $a$ against displacement $x$ for an oscillator executing s.h.m.

## Equations for velocity

The velocity $v$ of an oscillator varies as it moves back and forth. It has its greatest speed when it passes through the equilibrium position in the middle of the oscillation. If we take time $t = 0$ when the oscillator passes through the middle of the oscillation with its greatest speed $v_0$, then we can represent the changing velocity as an equation:

$$v = v_0 \cos \omega t$$

We use the cosine function to represent the velocity since it has its maximum value when $t = 0$.

The equation $v = v_0 \cos \omega t$ tells us how $v$ depends on $t$. We can write another equation to show how the velocity depends on the oscillator's displacement $x$:

$$v = \pm \omega \sqrt{(x_0^2 - x^2)}$$

This equation can be used to deduce the speed of an oscillator at any point in an oscillation, including its maximum speed.

## Maximum speed of an oscillator

If an oscillator is executing simple harmonic motion, it has maximum speed when it passes through its equilibrium position. This is when its displacement $x$ is zero. The maximum speed $v_0$ of the oscillator depends on the frequency $f$ of the motion and on the amplitude $x_0$. Substituting $x = 0$ in the equation

$v = \pm \omega \sqrt{(x_0^2 - x^2)}$ gives the maximum speed:

$$v_0 = \omega x_0$$

According to this equation, for a given oscillation:

$$v_0 \propto x_0$$

A simple harmonic oscillator has a period that is independent of the amplitude. A greater amplitude means that the oscillator has to travel a greater distance in the same time – hence it has a greater speed.

The equation also shows that:

$$v_0 \propto \omega$$

so that the maximum speed is proportional to the frequency. Increasing the frequency means a shorter period. A given distance is covered in a shorter time – hence it has a greater speed.

Have another look at Figure **20.15**. The period of the motion is 0.40 s and the amplitude of the motion is 0.02 m. The frequency $f$ can be calculated as follows:

$$f = \frac{1}{t} = \frac{1}{0.40} = 2.5\,\text{Hz}$$

We can now use the equation $v_0 = (2\pi f)x_0$ to determine the maximum speed $v_0$:

$$v_0 = (2\pi f)x_0 = (2\pi \times 2.5) \times 2.0 \times 10^{-2}$$

$$v_0 \approx 0.31\,\text{m s}^{-1}$$

This is how the values on Figure **20.15b** were calculated.

## Test yourself

**16** A mass secured at the end of a spring moves with s.h.m. The frequency of its motion is 1.4 Hz.

  **a** Write an equation of the form $a = -\omega^2 x$ to show how the acceleration of the mass depends on its displacement.

  **b** Calculate the acceleration of the mass when it is displaced 0.050 m from its equilibrium position.

**17** A short pendulum oscillates with s.h.m. such that its acceleration $a$ (in m s$^{-2}$) is related to its displacement $x$ (in m) by the equation $a = -300x$. Determine the frequency of the oscillations.

**18** The pendulum of a grandfather clock swings from one side to the other in 1.00 s. The amplitude of the oscillation is 12 cm. Calculate:

  **a** the period of its motion

  **b** the frequency

  **c** the angular frequency.

  **d** Write an equation of the form $a = -\omega^2 x$ to show how the acceleration of the pendulum weight depends on its displacement.

  **e** Calculate the maximum speed of the pendulum bob.

  **f** Calculate the speed of the bob when its displacement is 6 cm.

**19** A trolley of mass $m$ is fixed to the end of a spring. The spring can be compressed and extended. The spring has a force constant $k$. The other end of the spring is attached to a vertical wall. The trolley lies on a smooth horizontal table. The trolley oscillates when it is displaced from its equilibrium position.

  **a** Show that the motion of the oscillating trolley is s.h.m.

  **b** Show that the period $T$ of the trolley is given by the equation:

$$T = 2\pi \sqrt{\frac{m}{k}}$$

This study of simple harmonic motion illustrates some important aspects of physics.

- Physicists often take a complex problem (such as, how do the atoms in a solid vibrate?) and reduce it to a simpler, more manageable problem (such as, how does a mass–spring system vibrate?). This is simpler because we know that the spring obeys Hooke's law, so that force is proportional to displacement.
- Physicists generally feel happier if they can write mathematical equations which will give numerical answers to problems. The equation $a = -\omega^2 x$ which describes s.h.m. can be solved to give the sine and cosine equations we have considered above.
- Once physicists have solved one problem like this, they look around for other situations where they can use the same ideas all over again. So the mass–spring theory also works well for vibrating atoms and molecules, for objects bobbing up and down in water, and in many other situations.
- They also seek to modify the theory to fit a greater range of situations. For example, what happens if the spring doesn't obey Hooke's law? What happens if the vibrating mass experiences a frictional force as it oscillates? (The answer to this latter question appears later in this chapter.)

Your A level physics course will help you to build up your appreciation of some of these big ideas – fields (magnetic, electric, gravitational), energy and so on.

# Energy changes in s.h.m.

During simple harmonic motion, there is a constant interchange of energy between two forms: potential and kinetic. We can see this by considering the mass–spring system shown in Figure 20.21. When the mass is pulled to one side (to start the oscillations), one spring is compressed and the other is stretched. The springs store elastic potential energy. When the mass is released, it moves back towards the equilibrium position, accelerating as it goes. It has increasing kinetic energy. The potential energy stored in the springs decreases while the kinetic energy of the mass increases by the same amount (as long as there are no heat losses due to frictional forces). Once the mass has passed the equilibrium position, its kinetic energy decreases and the energy is transferred back to the springs. Provided the oscillations are undamped, the total energy in the system remains constant.

## Energy graphs

We can represent these energy changes in two ways. Figure 20.22 shows how the kinetic energy and elastic potential energy change with time. Potential energy is maximum when displacement is maximum (positive or negative). Kinetic energy is maximum when displacement is zero. The total energy remains constant throughout. Note that both kinetic energy and potential energy go through two complete cycles during one period of the oscillation. This is because kinetic energy is maximum when the mass is passing through the equilibrium position to the left and to the right. The potential energy is maximum at both ends of the oscillation.

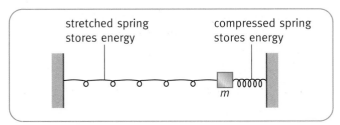

**Figure 20.21** The elastic potential energy stored in the springs is converted to kinetic energy when the mass is released.

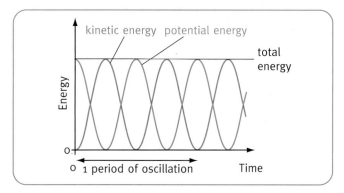

Figure 20.22 The kinetic energy and potential energy of an oscillator vary periodically, but the total energy remains constant if the system is undamped.

A second way to show this is to draw a graph of how potential energy and kinetic energy vary with displacement (Figure 20.23).

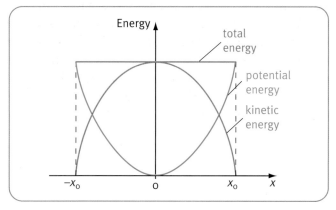

Figure 20.23 The kinetic energy is maximum at zero displacement; the potential energy is maximum at maximum displacement ($x_0$ and $-x_0$).

The graph shows that:

• kinetic energy is maximum when displacement $x = 0$
• potential energy is maximum when $x = \pm x_0$
• at any point on this graph, the total energy (k.e. + p.e.) has the same value.

## Test yourself

**20** To start a pendulum swinging, you pull it slightly to one side.
  **a** What kind of energy does this transfer to the mass?

*continued ⋯⟫*

**b** Describe the energy changes that occur when the mass is released.

**21** Figure **20.23** shows how the different forms of energy change with displacement during s.h.m. Copy the graph, and show how the graph would differ if the oscillating mass were given only half the initial input of energy.

**22** Figure **20.24** shows how the velocity $v$ of a 2.0 kg mass was found to vary with time $t$ during an investigation of the s.h.m. of a pendulum. Use the graph to estimate the following for the mass:
  **a** its maximum velocity
  **b** its maximum kinetic energy
  **c** its maximum potential energy
  **d** its maximum acceleration
  **e** the maximum restoring force that acted on it.

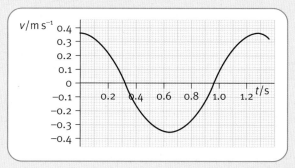

Figure **20.24** A velocity–time graph for a pendulum – see Test yourself Q **22**.

# Damped oscillations

In principle, oscillations can go on for ever. In practice, however, the oscillations we observe around us do not. They die out, either rapidly or gradually. A child on a swing knows that the amplitude of her swinging will decline until eventually she will come to rest, unless she can put some more energy into the swinging to keep it going.

This happens because of friction. On a swing, there is friction where the swing is attached to the frame and there is friction with the air. The amplitude of the child's oscillations decreases as the friction transfers energy away from her to the surroundings.

We describe these oscillations as **damped**. Their amplitude decreases according to a particular pattern. This is shown in Figure **20.25**.

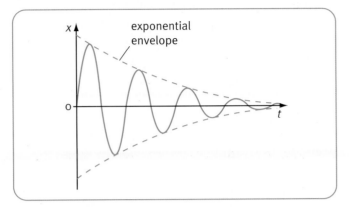

**Figure 20.25** Damped oscillations.

The amplitude of damped oscillations does not decrease linearly. It decays exponentially with time. An exponential decay is a particular mathematical pattern that arises as follows. At first, the swing moves rapidly. There is a lot of air resistance to overcome, so the swing loses energy quickly and its amplitude decreases at a high rate. Later, it is moving more slowly. There is less air resistance and so energy is lost more slowly – the amplitude decreases at a lower rate. Hence we get the characteristic curved shape, which is the 'envelope' of the graph in Figure **20.25**.

Notice that the frequency of the oscillations does not change as the amplitude decreases. This is a characteristic of simple harmonic motion. The child may swing back and forth once every two seconds, and this stays the same whether the amplitude is large or small.

## Investigating damping

You can investigate the exponential decrease in the amplitude of oscillations using a simple laboratory arrangement (Figure **20.26**). A hacksaw blade or other springy metal strip is clamped (vertically or horizontally) to the bench. A mass is attached to the free end. This will oscillate freely if you displace it to one side.

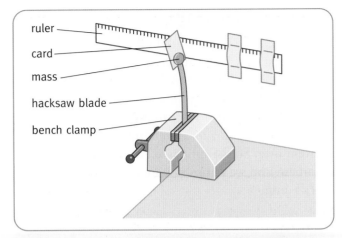

**Figure 20.26** Damped oscillations with a hacksaw blade.

A card is attached to the mass so that there is significant air resistance as the mass oscillates. The amplitude of the oscillations decreases and can be measured every five oscillations by judging the position of the blade against a ruler fixed alongside.

A graph of amplitude against time will show the characteristic exponential decrease. You can find the 'half-life' of this exponential decay graph by determining the time it takes to decrease to half its initial amplitude (Figure **20.27**).

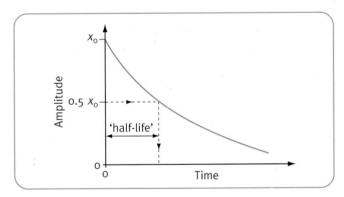

**Figure 20.27** A typical graph of amplitude against time for damped oscillations.

By changing the size of the card, it is possible to change the degree of damping, and hence alter the half-life of the motion.

## Energy and damping

Damping can be very useful if we want to get rid of vibrations. For example, a car has springs (Figure **20.28**) which make the ride much more comfortable for us when the car goes over a bump. However, we wouldn't want to spend every car journey vibrating up and down as a reminder of the last bump we went over. So the springs are damped by the shock absorbers, and we return rapidly to a smooth ride after every bump.

**Figure 20.28** The springs and shock absorbers in a car suspension system form a damped system.

Damping is achieved by introducing the force of friction into a mechanical system. In an undamped oscillation, the total energy of the oscillation remains constant. There is a regular interchange between potential and kinetic energy. By introducing friction, damping has the effect of removing energy from the oscillating system, and the amplitude and maximum speed of the oscillation decrease.

---

### Test yourself

**23 a** Sketch graphs to show how each of the following quantities changes during the course of a single complete oscillation of an undamped pendulum: kinetic energy, potential energy, total energy.
  **b** State how your graphs would be different for a lightly damped pendulum.

---

## Resonance

**Resonance** is an important physical phenomenon that can appear in a great many different situations. A dramatic example is the Millennium Footbridge in London, opened in June 2000 (Figure **20.29**). With up to 2000 pedestrians walking on the bridge, it started to sway dangerously. The people also swayed in time with the bridge, and this caused the amplitude of the bridge's oscillations to increase – this is resonance. After three days the bridge was closed. It took engineers two years to analyse the problem and then add 'dampers' to the bridge to absorb the energy of its oscillations. The bridge was then reopened and there have been no problems since.

**Figure 20.29** The 'wobbly' Millennium Footbridge in London was closed for nearly two years to correct problems caused by resonance.

You will have observed a much more familiar example of resonance when pushing a small child on a swing. The swing plus child has a natural frequency of oscillation. A small push on each swing results in the amplitude increasing until the child is swinging high in the air.

### Observing resonance

Resonance can be observed with almost any oscillating system. The system is forced to oscillate at a particular frequency. If the forcing frequency happens to match the natural frequency of oscillation of the system, the amplitude of the resulting oscillations can build up to become very large.

Barton's pendulums is a demonstration of this (Figure **20.30**). Several pendulums of different lengths hang from a horizontal string. Each has its own natural frequency of oscillation. The 'driver' pendulum at the end is different; it has a large mass at the end, and its length is equal to that of one of the others. When the driver is set swinging, the others gradually start to move. However, only the pendulum whose length matches that of the driver pendulum builds up a large amplitude so that it is resonating.

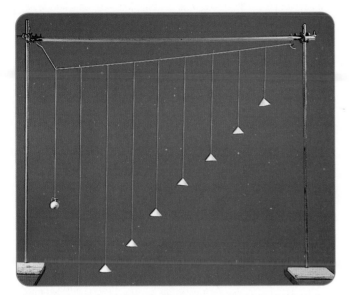

**Figure 20.30** Barton's pendulums.

What is going on here? All the pendulums are coupled together by the suspension. As the driver swings, it moves the suspension, which in turn moves the other pendulums. The frequency of the matching pendulum is the same as that of the driver, and so it gains energy and its amplitude gradually builds up. The other pendulums have different natural frequencies, so the driver has little effect.

In a similar way, if you were to push the child on the swing once every three-quarters of an oscillation, you would soon find that the swing was moving backwards as you tried to push it forwards, so that your push would slow it down.

You can observe resonance for yourself with a simple mass–spring system. You need a mass on the end of a spring (Figure **20.31**), chosen so that the mass oscillates up and down with a natural frequency of about 1 Hz. Now hold the top end of the spring and move your hand up and down rapidly, with an amplitude of a centimetre or two. Very little happens. Now move your hand up and down more slowly, close to 1 Hz. You should see the mass oscillating with gradually

increasing amplitude. Adjust your movements to the exact frequency of the natural vibrations of the mass and you will see the greatest effect.

**Figure 20.31** Resonance with a mass on a spring.

## Defining resonance

For resonance to occur, we must have a system that is capable of oscillating freely. We must also have some way in which the system is forced to oscillate. When the forcing frequency matches the natural frequency of the system, the amplitude of the oscillations grows dramatically.

If the driving frequency does not quite match the natural frequency, the amplitude of the oscillations will increase, but not to the same extent as when resonance is achieved. Figure **20.32** shows how the amplitude of oscillations depends on the driving frequency in the region close to resonance.

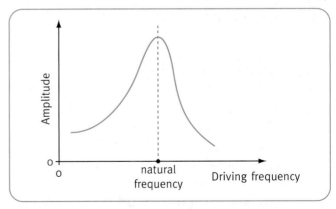

**Figure 20.32** Maximum amplitude is achieved when the driving frequency matches the natural frequency of oscillation.

In resonance, energy is transferred from the driver to the resonating system more efficiently than when resonance does not occur. For example, in the case of the Millennium Footbridge, energy was transferred from the pedestrians to the bridge, causing large-amplitude oscillations.

The following statements apply to any system in resonance:

- its natural frequency is equal to the frequency of the driver
- its amplitude is maximum
- it absorbs the greatest possible energy from the driver.

## Resonance and damping

During earthquakes, buildings are forced to oscillate by the vibrations of the Earth. Resonance can occur, resulting in serious damage (Figure **20.33**). In regions of the world where earthquakes happen regularly, buildings may be built on foundations that absorb the energy of the shock waves. In this way, the vibrations are 'damped' so that the amplitude of the oscillations cannot reach dangerous levels. This is an expensive business, and so far is restricted to the wealthier parts of the world.

**Figure 20.33** Resonance during the Mexico City earthquake of 19 September 1985 caused the collapse of many buildings. The earthquake, whose epicentre was in the Pacific Ocean, measured 8.1 on the Richter scale. Many lives were lost.

Damping is thus useful if we want to reduce the damaging effects of resonance. Figure **20.34** shows how damping alters the resonance response curve of Figure **20.32**. Notice that, as the degree of damping is increased, the amplitude of the resonant vibrations decreases. The resonance peak becomes broader. There is also an effect on the frequency at which resonance occurs, which becomes slightly lower for a lightly damped system.

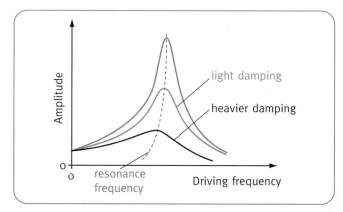

**Figure 20.34** Damping reduces the amplitude of resonant vibrations.

## Using resonance

As we have seen, resonance can be a problem in mechanical systems. However, it can also be useful. For example, many musical instruments rely on resonance.

Resonance is not confined to mechanical systems. It is made use of in, for example, microwave cooking. The microwaves used have a frequency that matches a natural frequency of vibration of water molecules (the microwave is the 'driver' and the molecule is the 'resonating system'). The water molecules in the food are forced to vibrate and they absorb the energy of the microwave radiation. The water gets hotter and the absorbed energy spreads through the food and cooks or heats it.

Magnetic resonance imaging (MRI) is increasingly used in medicine to produce images such as Figure **20.35**, showing aspects of a patient's internal organs. Radio waves having a range of frequencies are used, and particular frequencies are absorbed by particular atomic nuclei. The frequency absorbed depends on the type of nucleus and on its surroundings. By analysing the absorption of the radio waves, a computer-generated image can be produced. (There is much more about how MRI works in Chapter **32**.)

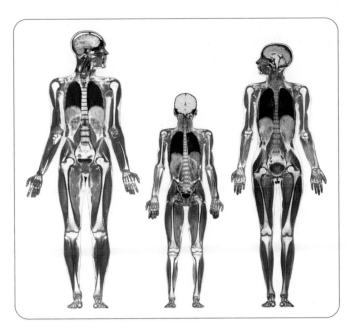

**Figure 20.35** This magnetic resonance imaging (MRI) picture shows a man, a woman and a nine-year-old child. The image has been coloured to show up the bones (white), lungs (dark) and other organs.

A radio or television also depends on resonance for its tuning circuitry. The aerial picks up signals of many different frequencies from many transmitters. The tuner can be adjusted to resonate at the frequency of the transmitting station you are interested in, and the circuit produces a large-amplitude signal for this frequency only.

### Test yourself

24 List **three** examples of situations where resonance is a problem, and three others where resonance is useful. In each case, state what the oscillating system is and what forces it to resonate.

# Summary

- ☐ Many systems, mechanical and otherwise, will oscillate freely when disturbed from their equilibrium position.
- ☐ Some oscillators have motion described as **simple harmonic motion** (s.h.m.). For these systems, graphs of displacement, velocity and acceleration against time are sinusoidal curves – see Figure **20.36**.

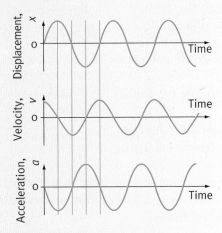

**Figure 20.36** Graphs for s.h.m.

- ☐ During a single cycle of s.h.m., the phase changes by $2\pi$ radians. The angular frequency $\omega$ of the motion is related to its period $T$ and frequency $f$ by the equations

$$\omega = \frac{2\pi}{T} \quad \text{and} \quad \omega = 2\pi f$$

- In s.h.m., displacement $x$ and velocity $v$ can be represented as a function of time $t$ by equations of the form:

$$x = x_0 \sin \omega t \quad \text{and} \quad v = v_0 \cos \omega t$$

- A body executes simple harmonic motion if its acceleration is directly proportional to its displacement from its equilibrium position. The acceleration is always directed towards the equilibrium position.
- Acceleration $a$ is related to displacement $x$ by the equation $a = -\omega^2 x$.
- The maximum speed $v_0$ is given by the equation $v_0 = \omega x_0$.
- The frequency or period of a simple harmonic oscillator is independent of its amplitude.
- In s.h.m., there is a regular interchange between kinetic energy and potential energy.
- Resistive forces remove energy from an oscillating system. This is known as damping. Damping causes the amplitude to decay with time.
- When an oscillating system is forced to vibrate close to its natural frequency, the amplitude of vibration increases rapidly. The amplitude is maximum when the forcing frequency matches the natural frequency of the system; this is resonance.
- Resonance can be a problem, but it can also be very useful.

# End-of-chapter questions

1 State and justify whether the following oscillators show simple harmonic motion:
   a a basketball being bounced repeatedly on the ground
   b a guitar string vibrating
   c a conducting sphere vibrating between two parallel, oppositely charged metal plates
   d the pendulum of a grandfather clock.

2 The pendulum of a clock is displaced by a distance of 4.0 cm and it oscillates in s.h.m. with a frequency of 1.0 s.
   a Write down an equation to describe the displacement $x$ of the pendulum bob with time $t$.
   b Calculate:
      i the maximum velocity of the pendulum bob
      ii its velocity when its displacement is 2.0 cm.

3 A 50 g mass is attached to is securely clamped spring. The mass is pulled downwards by 16 mm and released which causes it to oscillate with s.h.m. of time period of 0.84 s.
   a Calculate the frequency of the oscillation.
   b Calculate the maximum velocity of the mass.
   c Calculate the maximum kinetic energy of the mass and state at which point in the oscillation it will have this velocity.
   d Write down the maximum gravitational potential energy of the mass (relative to its equilibrium position). You may assume that the damping is negligible.

4 In each of the examples in Figure **20.37** give the phase difference as **i** a fraction of an oscillation, **ii** degrees and **iii** radians.

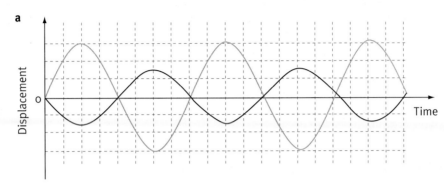

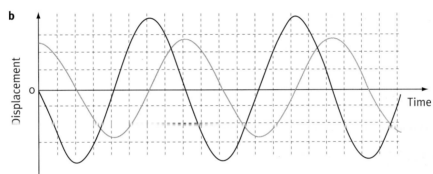

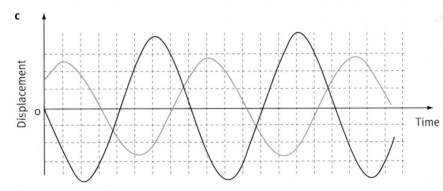

**Figure 20.37** For End-of-chapter Q 4.

5   a   Determine the frequency and the period of the oscillation described by the graph in Figure **20.38**.

    b   Use a copy of the graph and on the same axes sketch:
      i   the velocity of the particle
      ii   the acceleration of the particle.

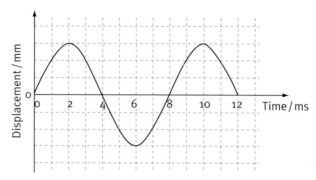

**Figure 20.38** For End-of-chapter Q **5**.

6   Figure **20.39** shows the displacement of a body as it vibrates between two points.
    a   State and explain if the body is moving with simple harmonic motion.
    b   Use a copy of the diagram.
      i   On the second set of axes show the velocity of the body as it vibrates.
      ii   On the third set of axes show the acceleration of the body.

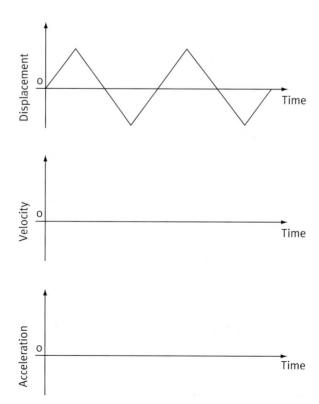

**Figure 20.39** For End-of-chapter Q **6**.

# Exam-style questions

1   The diagram shows the piston of a small car engine which oscillates in the cylinder with a motion which approximates to simple harmonic motion at 4200 revs per minute (1 rev = 1 cycle). The mass of the piston is 0.24 kg.

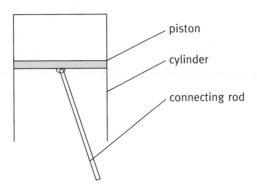

a   Explain what is meant by **simple harmonic motion**.                                    [2]
b   Calculate the frequency of the oscillation.                                             [1]
c   The amplitude of the oscillation is 12.5 cm. Calculate:
   i   the maximum speed at which the piston moves                                          [2]
   ii  the maximum acceleration of the piston                                              [2]
   iii the force required on the piston to produce the maximum acceleration.               [1]

2   The diagram on the next page shows a turntable with a rod attached to it a distance 15 cm from the centre. The turntable is illuminated from the side so that a shadow is cast on a screen. A simple pendulum is placed behind the turntable and it is set oscillating so that it has an amplitude equal to the distance of the rod from the centre of the turntable.

The speed of rotation of the turntable is adjusted. When it is rotating at 1.5 revolutions per second the shadow of the pendulum and the rod move back and forth across the screen exactly in phase.
a   Explain what is meant by the term **in phase**.                                          [1]
b   Write down an equation to describe the displacement $x$ of the pendulum from its equilibrium position and the angular frequency of the oscillation of the pendulum.                                              [1]

The turntable rotates through 60° from the position of maximum displacement shown in the diagram.
c   Calculate the displacement (from its equilibrium position) of the pendulum.            [3]
d   Calculate its speed at this point.                                                     [2]
e   Through what further angle must the turntable rotate before it has this speed again?    [2]

**View from front**

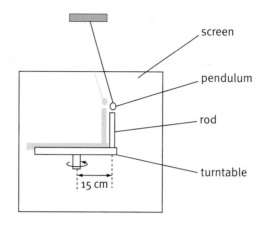

screen

pendulum

rod

turntable

15 cm

---

**View from above**

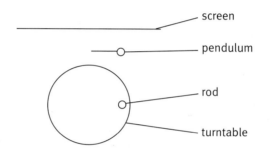

screen

pendulum

rod

turntable

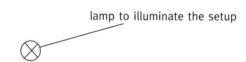

lamp to illuminate the setup

**3** When a cricket ball hits a cricket bat at high speed it can cause a standing wave to form on the bat. In one such example the handle of the bat moved with a frequency of 60 Hz with an amplitude of 2.8 mm.
The vibrational movement of the bat handle can be modelled on simple harmonic motion.

  **a** State the conditions for simple harmonic motion      [2]

  **b** Calculate the maximum acceleration of the bat handle.      [2]

  **c** Given that the part of the bat handle held by the cricketer has a mass of 0.48 kg, calculate the maximum force produced on his hands.      [1]

  **d** The oscillations are damped and die away after about five complete cycles. Sketch a displacement–time graph to show the oscillations.      [2]

**4** Seismometers are used to detect and measure the shock waves which travel through the Earth due to earthquakes.

Figure **1** shows the structure of a simple seismometer. The shock wave will cause the mass to vibrate, causing a trace to be drawn on the paper scroll.

**a** The typical frequency of a shock wave is between 30 and 40 Hz. Explain why the natural frequency of the spring–mass system in the seismometer should be very much less than this range of frequencies. [3]

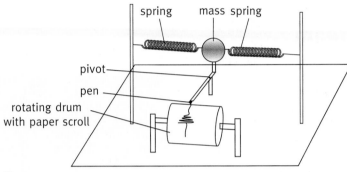

**Figure 1**

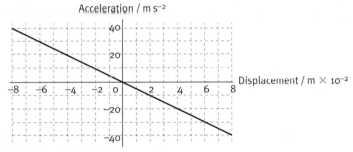

**Figure 2**

**b** The graph in Figure **2** shows the acceleration of the mass against its displacement when the seismometer is recording an earthquake. What evidence does the graph give that the motion is simple harmonic? [2]

**c** Use information from the graph to calculate the frequency of the oscillation. [4]

# Objectives

After studying this chapter, you should be able to:

- ☐ use a simple kinetic model of matter to explain phenomena associated with changes of state
- ☐ explain what is meant by temperature and outline how it can be measured
- ☐ outline the advantage of the thermodynamic scale of temperature

- ☐ relate the internal energy of an object to the energy of its particles
- ☐ use the first law of thermodynamics
- ☐ define and use specific heat capacity and specific latent heat, and outline how these quantities can be measured

# From water to steam

When water boils, it changes state – it turns to steam. A liquid has become a gas. This is a familiar process, but Figure 21.1 shows a dramatic example of such a change of state. This is a geyser in New Zealand, formed when water is trapped underground where it is in contact with hot rocks. The temperature and pressure of the water build up until it suddenly erupts above the surface to form a tall plume of scalding water and steam.

Figure 21.1 At regular intervals of time, the White Lady Geyser, near Rotorua in New Zealand, throws up a plume of water and steam.

# Changes of state

In Chapter 7, we saw how the kinetic model of matter can be used to describe the structures of solids, liquids and gases. You should recall that the kinetic model describes the behaviour of matter in terms of moving particles (atoms, molecules, etc.). Figure 7.4 on page **110** shows how we picture the three states of matter at the atomic scale.

- In a solid, the particles are close together, tightly bonded to their neighbours, and vibrating about fixed positions.
- In a gas, the particles have broken free from their neighbours; they are widely separated and are free to move around within their container.

In this chapter, we will extend these ideas to look at the energy changes involved when materials are heated and cooled.

**1** Describe a liquid in terms of the arrangement of its particles, the bonding between them and their motion.

# Energy changes

Energy must be supplied to raise the temperature of a solid, to melt it, to heat the liquid and to boil it. Where does this energy go to? It is worth taking a close look at a single change of state and thinking about what is happening on the atomic scale.

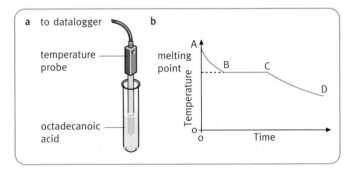

**Figure 21.2 a** Apparatus for obtaining a cooling curve, and **b** typical results.

Figure **21.2a** shows a suitable arrangement. A test tube containing octadecanoic acid (a white, waxy substance at room temperature) is warmed in a water bath. At 80 °C, the substance is a clear liquid. The tube is then placed in a rack and allowed to cool. Its temperature is monitored, either with a thermometer or with a temperature probe and datalogger. Figure **21.2b** shows typical results.

The temperature drops rapidly at first, then more slowly as it approaches room temperature. The important section of the graph is the region BC. The temperature remains steady for some time. The clear liquid is gradually returning to its white, waxy solid state. It is essential to note that energy is still being lost even though the temperature is not decreasing. When no liquid remains, the temperature starts to drop again.

From the graph, we can deduce the melting point of octadecanoic acid. This is a technique used to help identify substances by finding their melting points.

## Heating ice

In some ways, it is easier to think of the experiment above in reverse. What happens when we heat a substance?

Imagine taking some ice from the deep freeze. Put the ice in a well-insulated container and heat it at a steady rate. Its temperature will rise; eventually we will have a container of water vapour. (Note that water vapour is an invisible gas; the 'steam' that you see when a kettle boils is not a gas but a cloud of tiny droplets of liquid water.)

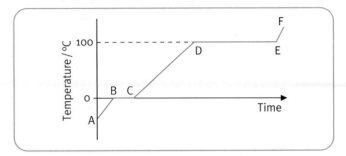

**Figure 21.3** A graph of temperature against time for water, heated at a steady rate.

Figure **21.3** shows the results we might expect if we could carry out this idealised experiment. Energy is supplied to the ice at a constant rate. We will consider the different sections of this graph in some detail, in order to describe where the energy is going at each stage.

We need to think about the kinetic and potential energies of the molecules. If they move around more freely and faster, their kinetic energy has increased. If they break free of their neighbours and become more disordered, their electrical potential energy has increased.

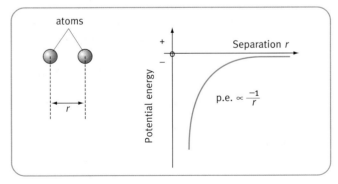

**Figure 21.4** The electrical potential energy of atoms is negative and increases as they get further apart.

You know that the kinetic energy of a particle is the energy it has due to its motion. Figure **21.4** shows how the electrical potential energy of two isolated atoms depends on their separation. Work must be done (energy must be put in) to separate neighbouring atoms – think about the work you must do to snap a piece of plastic or to tear a sheet of paper. The graph shows that:

- the electrical potential energy of two atoms very close together is large and negative
- as the separation of the atoms increases, their potential energy also increases
- when the atoms are completely separated, their potential energy is maximum and has a value of zero.

Now look at the graph shown in Figure 21.3.

### Section AB

The ice starts below 0 °C; its temperature rises. The molecules gain energy and vibrate more and more. Their vibrational kinetic energy is increasing. There is very little change in the mean separation between the molecules and hence there is very little change in their electrical potential energy.

### Section BC

The ice melts at 0 °C. The molecules become more disordered. There is a modest increase in the separation between the molecules and hence their electrical potential energy has increased.

### Section CD

The ice has become water. Its temperature rises towards 100 °C. The molecules move increasingly rapidly. Their kinetic energy is increasing. There is very little change in the mean separation between the molecules and therefore very little change in the electrical potential energy of the molecules.

### Section DE

The water is boiling. The molecules are becoming completely separate from one another. There is a large increase in the separation between the molecules and hence their electrical potential energy has increased greatly. Their movement becomes very disorderly.

### Section EF

The steam is being heated above 100 °C. The molecules move even faster. Their kinetic energy is increasing. The molecules have maximum electrical potential energy of zero.

From this analysis, you should see that, when water is heated, each change of state (melting, boiling) involves the following:

- there must be an input of energy
- the temperature does not change

- the molecules are breaking free of one another
- their potential energy is increasing.

In between the changes of state:

- the input of energy raises the temperature of the substance
- the molecules move faster
- their kinetic energy is increasing.

The hardest point to appreciate is that you can put energy into the system without its temperature rising. This happens during any change of state; the energy goes to breaking the bonds between neighbouring molecules. The energy which must be supplied to cause a change of state is sometimes called 'latent heat'. The word 'latent' means 'hidden' and refers to the fact that, when you melt something, its temperature does not rise and the energy that you have put in seems to have disappeared.

It may help to think of temperature as a measure of the average kinetic energy of the molecules. When you put a thermometer in some water to measure its temperature, the water molecules collide with the thermometer and share their kinetic energy with it. At a change of state, there is no change in kinetic energy, so there is no change in temperature.

Notice that melting the ice (section BC) takes much less energy than boiling the same amount of water (section DE). This is because, when a solid melts, the molecules are still bonded to most of their immediate neighbours. When a liquid boils, each molecule breaks free of all of its neighbours. Melting may involve the breaking of one or two bonds per molecule, whereas boiling involves breaking eight or nine.

## Evaporation

A liquid does not have to boil to change into a gas. A puddle of rain-water dries up without having to be heated to 100 °C. When a liquid changes to a gas without boiling, we call this **evaporation**.

Any liquid has some vapour associated with it. If we think about the microscopic picture of this, we can see why (Figure 21.5). Within the liquid, molecules are moving about. Some move faster than others, and can break free from the bulk of the liquid. They form the vapour above the liquid. Some molecules from the vapour may come back into contact with the surface of the liquid, and return to the liquid. However, there is a net outflow of energetic molecules from the liquid, and eventually it will evaporate away completely.

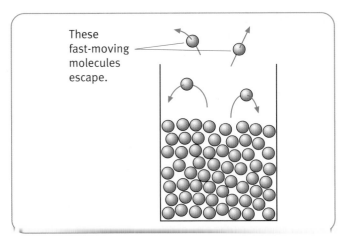

These fast-moving molecules escape.

Figure 21.5 Fast-moving molecules leave the surface of a liquid – this is evaporation.

You may have had your skin swabbed with alcohol or ether before an injection. You will have noticed how cold your skin becomes as the volatile liquid evaporates. Similarly, you can become very cold if you get wet and stand around in a windy place. This cooling of a liquid is a very important aspect of evaporation.

When a liquid evaporates, it is the most energetic molecules that are most likely to escape. This leaves molecules with a below-average kinetic energy. Since temperature is a measure of the average kinetic energy of the molecules, it follows that the temperature of the evaporating liquid must fall.

## Test yourself

2 Use the kinetic model of matter to explain the following:
  a If you leave a pan of water on the hob for a long time, it does not all boil away as soon as the temperature reaches 100 °C.
  b It takes less energy to melt a 1.0 kg block of ice at 0 °C than to boil away 1.0 kg of water at 100 °C.
  c When a dog is overheated, it pants.

# Internal energy

All matter is made up of particles, which we will refer to here as 'molecules'. Matter can have energy. For example, if we lift up a stone, it has gravitational potential energy. If we throw it, it has kinetic energy.

Kinetic and potential energies are the two general forms of energy. We consider the stone's potential and kinetic energies to be properties or attributes of the stone itself; we calculate their values ($mgh$ and $\frac{1}{2}mv^2$) using the mass and speed of the stone.

Now think about another way in which we could increase the energy of the stone: we could heat it (Figure 21.6). Now where does the energy from the heater go? The stone's gravitational potential and kinetic energies do not increase; it is not higher or faster than before. The energy seems to have disappeared into the stone.

Figure 21.6 Increasing the internal energy of a stone.

Of course, you already know the answer to this. The stone gets hotter, and that means that the molecules which make up the stone have more energy, both kinetic and electrical potential. They vibrate more and faster, and they move a little further apart. This energy of the molecules is known as the **internal energy** of the stone. The internal energy of a system (e.g. the heated stone) is defined as follows:

> The internal energy of a system is the sum of the random distribution of kinetic and potential energies of its atoms or molecules.

## Molecular energy

Earlier in this chapter, where we studied the phases of matter, we saw how solids, liquids and gases could be characterised by differences in the arrangement, order and motion of their molecules. We could equally have said that, in the three phases, the molecules have different amounts of kinetic and potential energies.

Now, it is a simple problem to find the internal energy of an amount of matter. We add up the kinetic and potential energies associated with all the molecules in that matter. For example, consider the gas shown in Figure 21.7. There are ten molecules in the box, each having kinetic and potential energy. We can work out what all of these are and add them together, to get the total internal energy of the gas in the box.

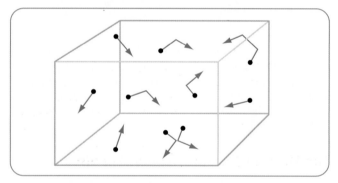

Figure 21.7 The molecules of a gas have both kinetic and potential energies.

## Changing internal energy

There are two obvious ways in which we can increase the internal energy of some gas: we can heat it, or we can do work on it by compressing it.

### Heating a gas (Figure 21.8a)
The walls of the container become hot and so its molecules vibrate more vigorously. The molecules of the cool gas strike the walls and bounce off faster. They have gained kinetic energy, and we say the temperature has risen.

### Doing work on a gas (Figure 21.8b)
In this case, a wall of the container is being pushed inwards. The molecules of the cool gas strike a moving

wall and bounce off faster. They have gained kinetic energy and again the temperature has risen. This explains why a gas gets hotter when it is compressed.

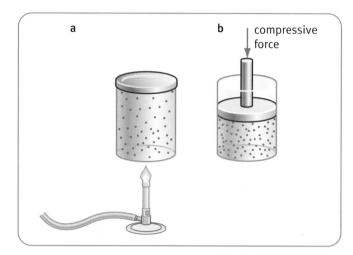

Figure 21.8 Two ways to increase the internal energy of a gas: a by heating it, and b by compressing it.

There are other ways in which the internal energy of a system can be increased; by passing an electric current through it, for example. However, doing work and heating are all we need to consider here.

The internal energy of a gas can also decrease; for example, if it loses heat to its surroundings, or if it expands so that it does work on its surroundings.

## First law of thermodynamics

You will be familiar with the idea that energy is **conserved**; that is, energy cannot simply disappear, or appear from nowhere. This means that, for example, all the energy we put into a gas by heating it and by doing work on it must end up in the gas; it increases the internal energy of the gas. We can write this as an equation:

increase in internal energy
= energy supplied by heating
+ energy supplied by doing work

In symbols:

$$\Delta U = \Delta Q + \Delta W$$

This statement is known as the **first law of thermodynamics** and is a formal statement of the principle of conservation of energy. (It applies to all situations, not simply to a mass of gas.) Since you have learned previously that energy is conserved, it may seem to be a simple idea, but it took scientists a good many decades to understand the nature of energy and to appreciate that it is conserved.

# The meaning of temperature

Picture a beaker of boiling water. You want to measure its temperature, so you pick up a thermometer which is lying on the bench. The thermometer reads 20 °C. You place the thermometer in the water and the reading goes up … 30 °C, 40 °C, 50 °C. This tells you that the thermometer is getting hotter; energy is being transferred from the water to the thermometer.

Eventually, the thermometer reading reaches 100 °C and it stops rising. Because the reading is steady, you can deduce that energy is no longer being transferred to the thermometer and so its scale tells you the temperature of the water.

This simple, everyday activity illustrates several points:

• We are used to the idea that a thermometer shows the temperature of something with which it is in contact. In fact, it tells you **its own temperature**. As the reading on the scale was rising, it wasn't showing the temperature of the water. It was showing that the temperature of the thermometer was rising.
• Energy is transferred from a hotter object to a cooler one. The temperature of the water was greater than the temperature of the thermometer, so energy transferred from one to the other.
• When two objects are at the same temperature, there is no transfer of energy between them. That is what happened when the thermometer reached the same temperature as the water, so it was safe to say that the reading on the thermometer was the same as the temperature of the water.

From this, you can see that temperature tells us about the direction in which energy flows. If two objects are placed in contact (so that energy can flow between them), it will flow from the hotter to the cooler. Energy flowing from a region of higher temperature to a region of lower temperature is called **thermal energy**. (Here, we are not concerned with the mechanism by which the energy is transferred. It may be by conduction, convection or radiation.)

When two objects, in contact with each other, are at the same temperature, there will be no transfer of thermal energy between them. We say that they are in **thermal equilibrium** with each other – see Figure **21.9**.

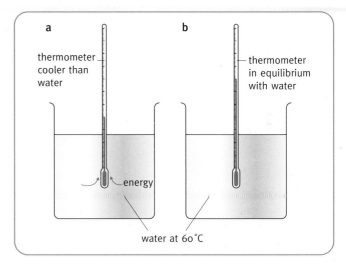

**Figure 21.9  a** Thermal energy is transferred from the hot water to the cooler thermometer because of the temperature difference between them. **b** When they are at the same temperature, there is no transfer of thermal energy and they are in thermal equilibrium.

## The thermodynamic (Kelvin) scale

The Celsius scale of temperature is a familiar, everyday scale of temperature. It is based on the properties of water. It takes two fixed points, the melting point of pure ice and the boiling point of pure water, and divides the range between them into 100 equal intervals.

There is nothing special about these two fixed points. In fact, both change if the pressure changes or if the water is impure. The **thermodynamic scale**, also known as the Kelvin scale, is a better scale in that one of its fixed points, **absolute zero**, has a greater significance than either of the Celsius fixed points.

It is not possible to have a temperature lower than 0 K. Sometimes it is suggested that, at this temperature, matter has no energy left in it. This is not strictly true; it is more correct to say that, for any matter at absolute zero, it is impossible to **remove** any more energy from it. Hence absolute zero is the temperature at which all substances have the minimum internal energy. (The kinetic energy of the atoms or molecules is zero and their electrical potential energy is minimum.)

We use different symbols to represent temperatures on these two scales: $\theta$ for the Celsius scale, and $T$ for the thermodynamic (Kelvin) scale. To convert between the two scales, we use these relationships:

$$\theta \, (°C) = T \, (K) - 273.15$$

$$T \, (K) = \theta \, (°C) + 273.15$$

For most practical purposes, we round off the conversion factor to 273 as shown in the conversion chart (Figure **21.10**).

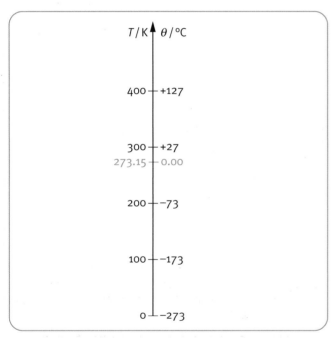

**Figure 21.10** A conversion chart relating temperatures on the thermodynamic (Kelvin) and Celsius scales.

The thermodynamic scale is different from other scales of temperature, such as the Celsius and Fahrenheit scales, because it does not depend on somewhat variable properties of substances such as the melting and boiling points of water. It has two fixed points:

• absolute zero, which is defined as 0 K
• the triple point of water, the temperature at which ice, water and water vapour can co-exist, which is defined as 273.16 K (equal to 0.01 °C).

So the gap between absolute zero and the triple point of water is divided into 273.16 equal divisions. Each

division is 1 K. The scale is defined in this slightly odd way so that the scale divisions on the thermodynamic scale are equal in size to the divisions on the Celsius scale, making conversions between the two scales relatively easy.

A **change** in temperature of 1 K is thus equal to a **change** in temperature of 1 °C.

## Test yourself

4  a  Convert each of the following temperatures from the Celsius scale to the thermodynamic scale: 0 °C, 20 °C, 120 °C, 500 °C, –23 °C, –200 °C.
   b  Convert each of the following temperatures from the thermodynamic scale to the Celsius scale: 0 K, 20 K, 100 K, 300 K, 373 K, 500 K.

5  The electrical resistance of a pure copper wire is mostly due to the vibrations of the copper atoms. Table **21.1** shows how the resistance of a length of copper wire is found to change as it is heated. Copy the table and add a column showing the temperatures in K. Draw a graph to show these data. (Start the temperature scale of your graph at 0 K.) Explain why you might expect the resistance of copper to be zero at this temperature.

| Temperature / °C | Resistance / Ω |
|---|---|
| 10 | 3120 |
| 50 | 3600 |
| 75 | 3900 |
| 100 | 4200 |
| 150 | 4800 |
| 220 | 5640 |
| 260 | 6120 |

**Table 21.1** The variation of resistance with temperature for a length of copper wire.

# Thermometers

A thermometer is any device which can be used to measure temperature. Each type of thermometer makes use of some physical property of a material which changes with temperature. The most familiar is the length of a column of liquid in a tube, which gets longer as the temperature increases because the liquid expands – this is how a liquid-in-glass thermometer works. Other properties which can be used as the basis of thermometers include:

• the resistance of an electrical resistor or thermistor
• the voltage produced by a thermocouple
• the colour of an electrically heated wire
• the volume of a fixed mass of gas at constant pressure.

In each case, the thermometer must be calibrated at two or more known temperatures (such as the melting and boiling points of water, which correspond to 0 °C and 100 °C), and the scale between divided into equal divisions. There is no guarantee that two thermometers will agree with each other except at these fixed points. Now we will look in detail at two types of electrical thermometer.

In Chapter 12, we saw that electrical resistance changes with temperature. For metals, resistance increases with temperature at a fairly steady rate. However, for a thermistor, the resistance changes rapidly over a relatively narrow range of temperatures. A small change in temperature results in a large change in resistance, so a thermometer based on a thermistor will be sensitive over that range of temperatures.

A **thermocouple** is another electrical device which can be used as the sensor of a thermometer. Figure **21.11** shows the principle. Wires of two different metals, X and Y, are required. A length of metal X has a length of metal Y soldered to it at each end. This produces two **junctions**, which are the important parts of the thermocouple. If the two junctions are at different temperatures, an e.m.f. will be produced between the two free ends of the thermocouple, and can be measured using a voltmeter. The greater the difference in

temperatures, the greater the voltage produced; however, this e.m.f. may not vary linearly with temperature, i.e. a graph of e.m.f. against temperature is not usually a straight line.

Electrical thermometers can measure across a great **range** of temperatures, from 0 K to hundreds or even thousands of kelvin.

Table **21.2** compares resistance and thermocouple thermometers.

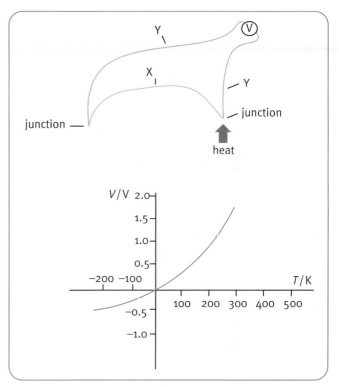

**Figure 21.11** The construction of a thermocouple thermometer; the voltage produced depends on the temperature (as shown in the calibration graph) and on the metals chosen.

| Feature | Resistance thermometer | Thermocouple thermometer |
|---|---|---|
| robustness | very robust | robust |
| range | resistance wire: wide range thermistor: narrow range | can be very wide |
| size | larger than thermocouple, has greater thermal capacity therefore slower acting | smaller than resistance thermometers, has smaller thermal capacity, therefore quicker acting and can measure temperature at a point |
| sensitivity | themistor: high sensitivity over narrow range resistance wire: less sensitive | can be sensitive if appropriate metals chosen |
| linearity | themistor: fairly linear over narrow range resistance wire: good linearity | non-linear so requires calibration |
| remote operation | long conducting wires allow the operator to be at a distance from the thermometer | long conducting wires allow the operator to be at a distance from the thermometer |

**Table 21.2** Comparing resistance and thermocouple thermometers.

6 Give **one** word for each of the following:
   a adding a scale to a thermometer
   b all the termperatures, from lowest to highest, which a thermometer can measure
   c the extent to which equal rises in temperature give equal changes in the thermometer's output
   d how big a change in ouput is produced by a given change in temperature.

# Calculating energy changes

So far, we have considered the effects of heating a substance in qualitative terms, and we have given an explanation in terms of a kinetic model of matter. Now we will look at the amount of energy needed to change the temperature of something, and to produce a change of state.

## Specific heat capacity

If we heat some material so that its temperature rises, the amount of energy we must supply depends on three things:

• the mass $m$ of the material we are heating
• the temperature change $\Delta\theta$ we wish to achieve
• the material itself.

Some materials are easier to heat than others. It takes more energy to raise the temperature of 1 kg of water by 1 °C than to raise the temperature of 1 kg of alcohol by the same amount.

   We can represent this in an equation. The amount of energy $E$ that must be supplied is given by:

$$E = mc\Delta\theta$$

where $c$ is the **specific heat capacity** of the material. Rearranging this equation gives:

$$c = \frac{E}{m\Delta\theta}$$

The specific heat capacity of a material can be defined as a word equation as follows:

$$\text{specific heat capacity} = \frac{\text{energy supplied}}{\text{mass} \times \text{temperature change}}$$

Alternatively, specific heat capacity can be defined in words as follows:

> The specific heat capacity of a substance is the energy required per unit mass of the substance to raise the temperature by 1 K (or 1 °C).

The word 'specific' here means 'per unit mass', i.e. per kg. From this form of the equation, you should be able to see that the units of $c$ are $J\,kg^{-1}\,K^{-1}$ (or $J\,kg^{-1}\,°C^{-1}$). Table **21.3** shows some values of specific heat capacity measured at 0 °C.

| Substance | $c$ / $J\,kg^{-1}\,K^{-1}$ |
|---|---|
| aluminium | 880 |
| copper | 380 |
| lead | 126 |
| glass | 500–680 |
| ice | 2100 |
| water | 4180 |
| sea water | 3950 |
| ethanol | 2500 |
| mercury | 140 |

Table **21.3** Values of specific heat capacity.

Specific heat capacity is related to the gradient of the sloping sections of the graph shown earlier in Figure **21.3**. The steeper the gradient, the faster the substance heats up, and hence the lower its specific heat capacity must be. Worked example **1** shows how to calculate the specific heat capacity of a substance.

## Worked example

1 When 26 400 J of energy is supplied to a 2.0 kg block of aluminium, its temperature rises from 20 °C to 35 °C. The block is well insulated so that there is no energy loss to the surroundings. Determine the specific heat capacity of aluminium.

**Step 1** We are going to use the equation:

$$c = \frac{E}{m\Delta\theta}$$

continued ···>

We need to write down the quantities that we know:

$$E = 26\,400\,\text{J} \qquad m = 2.0\,\text{kg}$$

$$\Delta\theta = (35 - 20)\,°\text{C} = 15\,°\text{C} \quad \text{(or 15 K)}$$

**Step 2** Now substitute these values and solve the equation:

$$c = \frac{E}{m\Delta\theta}$$

$$c = \frac{26\,400}{(2.0 \times 15)} = 880\,\text{J kg}^{-1}\,\text{K}^{-1}$$

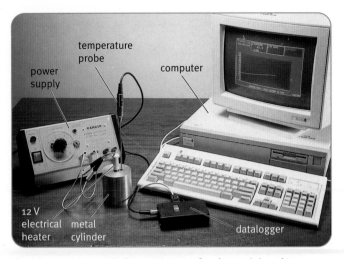

**Figure 21.12** A practical arrangement for determining the specific heat capacity of a metal.

## Test yourself

You will need to use data from Table **21.3** to answer these questions.

7  Calculate the energy which must be supplied to raise the temperature of 5.0 kg of water from 20 °C to 100 °C.

8  Which requires more energy, heating a 2.0 kg block of lead by 30 K, or heating a 4.0 kg block of copper by 5.0 K?

9  A well-insulated 1.2 kg block of iron is heated using a 50 W heater for 4.0 min. The temperature of the block rises from 22 °C to 45 °C. Find the experimental value for the specific heat capacity of iron.

## Determining specific heat capacity c

How can we determine the specific heat capacity of a material? The principle is simple: supply a known amount of energy to a known mass of the material and measure the rise in its temperature. Figure **21.12** shows one practical way of doing this for a metal.

The metal is in the form of a cylindrical block of mass 1.00 kg. An electrical heater is used to supply the energy. This type of heater is used because we can easily determine the amount of energy supplied –

more easily than if we heated the metal with a Bunsen flame, for example. An ammeter and voltmeter are used to make the necessary measurements.

A thermometer or temperature sensor is used to monitor the block's temperature as it is heated. The block must not be heated too quickly; we want to be sure that the energy has time to spread throughout the metal.

The block should be insulated by wrapping it in a suitable material – this is not shown in the illustration. It would be possible in principle to determine c by making just one measurement of temperature change, but it is better to record values of the temperature as it rises and plot a graph of temperature $\theta$ against time $t$. The method of calculating c is illustrated in Worked example **2**.

## Worked example

2  An experiment to determine the specific heat capacity c of a 1.00 kg aluminium block is carried out; the block is heated using an electrical heater. The current in the heater is 4.17 A and the p.d. across it is 12 V. Measurements of the rising temperature of the block are represented by the graph shown in Figure **21.13**. Determine a value for the specific heat capacity c of aluminium.

*continued* ⋯⟶

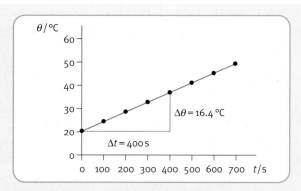

**Figure 21.13** Graph of temperature against time for an aluminium block as it is heated.

**Step 1** Write down the equation that relates energy change to specific heat capacity:

$$E = mc\Delta\theta$$

**Step 2** Divide both sides by a time interval $\Delta t$:

$$\frac{E}{\Delta t} = mc\left(\frac{\Delta\theta}{\Delta t}\right)$$

The quantity $\dfrac{E}{\Delta t}$ is the rate at which energy is supplied, i.e. the power $P$ of the heater. The quantity $\dfrac{\Delta\theta}{\Delta t}$ is the rate of rise of temperature of the block, i.e. the gradient of the graph of $\theta$ against $t$. Hence:

$$P = m \times c \times \text{gradient}$$

**Step 3** Calculate the power of the heater and the gradient of the graph.

$$\text{power} = \text{p.d.} \times \text{current}$$

$$P = VI = 12 \times 4.17 \approx 50\,\text{W}$$

$$\text{gradient} = \frac{\Delta\theta}{\Delta t} = \frac{16.4}{400} = 0.041\,°\text{C s}^{-1}$$

**Step 4** Substitute values, rearrange and solve.

$$50 = 1.00 \times c \times 0.041$$

$$c = \frac{50}{1.00 \times 0.041} = 1220\,\text{J kg}^{-1}\,\text{K}^{-1}$$

## Sources of error

This experiment can give reasonably good measurements of specific heat capacities. As noted earlier, it is desirable to have a relatively low rate of heating, so that energy spreads throughout the block. If the block is heated rapidly, different parts may be at different temperatures.

Thermal insulation of the material is also vital. Inevitably, some energy will escape to the surroundings. This means that **more** energy must be supplied to the block for each degree rise in temperature and so the experimental value for the specific heat capacity will be too high. One way around this is to cool the block below room temperature before beginning to heat it. Then, as its temperature rises past room temperature, heat losses will be zero in principle, because there is no temperature difference between the block and its surroundings.

### Test yourself

10 At higher temperature, the graph shown in Figure **21.13** deviates increasingly from a straight line. Suggest an explanation for this.

11 In measurements of the specific heat capacity of a metal, energy losses to the surroundings are a source of error. Is this a systematic error or random error? Justify your answer.

12 In an experiment to measure the specific heat capacity of water, a student used an electrical heater to heat some water. His results are shown below. Calculate a value for the heat capacity of water. Comment on any likely sources of error.

> mass of beaker = 150 g
> mass of beaker + water = 672 g
> current in the heater = 3.9 A
> p.d. across heater = 11.4 V
> initial temperature = 18.5 °C
> final temperature = 30.2 °C
> time taken = 13.0 min

*continued* ⋯➔

21 Thermal physics

**13** A block of paraffin wax was heated gently, at a steady rate. Heating was continued after the wax had completely melted. The graph of Figure **21.14** shows how the material's temperature varied during the experiment.

  **a** For each section of the graph (AB, BC and CD), describe the state of the material.

  **b** For each section, explain whether the material's internal energy was increasing, decreasing or remaining constant.

  **c** Consider the two sloping sections of the graph. State whether the material's specific heat capacity is greater when it is a solid or when it is a liquid. Justify your answer.

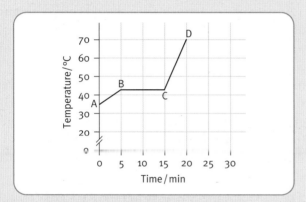

**Figure 21.14** Temperature variation of a sample of wax, heated at a constant rate.

## Specific latent heat

Energy must be supplied to melt or boil a substance. (In this case, there is no temperature rise to consider since the temperature stays constant during a change of state.) This energy is called latent heat.

> The specific latent heat of a substance is the energy required per kilogram of the substance to change its state without any change in temperature.

When a substance melts, this quantity is called the **specific latent heat of fusion**; for boiling, it is the **specific latent heat of vaporisation**.

To calculate the amount of energy $E$ required to melt or vaporise a mass $m$ of a substance, we simply need to know its specific latent heat $L$:

$$E = mL$$

$L$ is measured in $J\,kg^{-1}$. (Note that there is no 'per °C' since there is no change in temperature.) For water the values are:

- specific latent heat of fusion of water is $330\,kJ\,kg^{-1}$
- specific latent heat of vaporisation of water is $2.26\,MJ\,kg^{-1}$

You can see that $L$ for boiling water to form steam is roughly seven times the value for melting ice to form water. As we discussed earlier (page **314**), this is because, when ice melts, only one or two bonds are broken for each molecule; when water boils, several bonds are broken per molecule. Worked example **3** shows how to calculate these amounts of energy.

(page **314**)

---

### Worked example

**3** The specific latent heat of vaporisation of water is $2.26\,MJ\,kg^{-1}$. Calculate the energy needed to change $2.0\,g$ of water into steam at $100\,°C$.

**Step 1** We have been given the following quantities:

$$m = 2.0\,g = 0.002\,kg \quad \text{and} \quad L = 2.26\,MJ\,kg^{-1}$$

**Step 2** Substituting these values in the equation $E = mL$, we have:

$$\text{energy} = 0.002 \times 2.26 \times 10^{6} = 4520\,J$$

---

### Test yourself

**14** The specific latent heat of fusion of water is $330\,kJ\,kg^{-1}$. Calculate the energy needed to change $2.0\,g$ of ice into water at $0\,°C$. Suggest why the answer is much smaller than the amount of energy calculated in Worked example **3**.

## Determining specific latent heat L

How can we determine the specific latent heat of a material? The principle is similar to determining the specific heat capacity (but remember that there is no change in temperature).

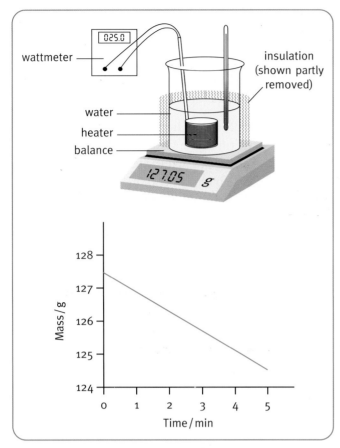

Figure 21.15 Determining the specific latent heat of vaporisation of water.

Figure 21.15 shows how to measure the specific latent heat of vaporisation of water. A beaker containing water is heated using an electrical heater. A wattmeter (or an ammeter and a voltmeter) determines the rate at which energy is supplied to the heater. The beaker is insulated to minimise energy loss, and it stands on a balance. A thermometer is included to ensure that the temperature of the water remains at 100 °C.

The water is heated at a steady rate and its mass recorded at equal intervals of time. Its mass decreases as it boils.

A graph of mass against time should be a straight line whose gradient is the rate of mass loss. The wattmeter shows the rate at which energy is supplied to the water via the heater. We thus have:

$$\text{specific latent heat} = \frac{\text{rate of supply of energy}}{\text{rate of loss of mass}}$$

A similar approach can be used to determine the specific latent heat of fusion of ice. In this case, the ice is heated electrically in a funnel; water runs out of the funnel and is collected in a beaker on a balance.

As with any experiment, we should consider sources of error in measuring $L$ and their effects on the final result. When water is heated to produce steam, some energy may escape to the surroundings so that the measured energy is greater than that supplied to the water. This systematic error gives a value of $L$ which is greater than the true value. When ice is melted, energy from the surroundings will conduct into the ice, so that the measured value of $L$ will be an underestimate.

## Test yourself

15 A sample of alcohol is heated with a 40 W heater until it boils. As it boils, its mass decreases at a rate of 2.25 g per minute. Assuming that 80% of the energy supplied by the heater is transferred to the alcohol, extimate the specific latent heat of vaporization of the alcohol. Give your answer in $J\,kg^{-1}$.

## Summary

- [ ] The kinetic model of matter allows us to explain behaviour (e.g. changes of state) and macroscopic properties (e.g. specific heat capacity and specific latent heat) in terms of the behaviour of molecules.
- [ ] The internal energy of a system is the sum of the random distribution of kinetic and potential energies associated with the atoms or molecules that make up the system.
- [ ] If the temperature of an object increases, there is an increase in its internal energy.
- [ ] Internal energy also increases during a change of state, but there is no change in temperature.

- [ ] The first law of thermodynamics expresses the the conservation of energy:

    increase in internal energy = energy supplied by heating + work done on the system

- [ ] Temperatures on the thermodynamic (Kelvin) and Celsius scales of temperature are related by:

    $T (\text{K}) = \theta \ (^\circ\text{C}) + 273.15$

    $\theta (^\circ\text{C}) = T \ (\text{K}) - 273.15$

- [ ] At absolute zero, all substances have a minimum internal energy.
- [ ] A thermometer makes use of a physical property of a material that varies with temperature.
- [ ] The word equation for the specific heat capacity of a substance is:

$$\text{specific heat capacity} = \frac{\text{energy supplied}}{\text{mass} \times \text{temperature change}}$$

The specific heat capacity of a substance is the energy required per unit mass of the substance to raise the temperature by 1 K (or 1 °C).
- [ ] The energy transferred in raising the temperature of a substance is given by $E = mc\Delta\theta$.
- [ ] The specific latent heat of a substance is the energy required per kilogram of the substance to change its state without any change in temperature: $E = mL$.

# End-of-chapter questions

1   Describe the changes to the kinetic energy, the potential energy and the total internal energy of the molecules of a block of ice as:
    a   it melts at 0 °C
    b   the temperature of the water rises from 0 °C to room temperature.

2   Explain, in terms of kinetic energy, why the temperature of a stone increases when it falls from a cliff and lands on the beach below.

3   Explain why the barrel of a bicycle pump gets very hot as the pump is used to pump up a bicycle tyre. (Hint: the work done against friction is not large enough to explain the rise in temperature.)

4   The zeroth law of thermodynamics states that if the temperature of body A is equal to the temperature of body B and the temperature of body B is the same as body C, then the temperature of body C equals the temperature of body A.
    Explain, in terms of energy flow, why the concept of temperature would be meaningless if this law was not obeyed.

5    Copy and complete the table which shows the melting and boiling points (at standard atmospheric pressure) of different materials in both degrees Celsius and kelvin.

| Substance | Melting point | | Boiling point | |
|---|---|---|---|---|
| | °C | K | °C | K |
| oxygen | −223 | | | 90 |
| hydrogen | | 14 | −253 | |
| lead | 327 | | | 2023 |
| mercury | | 234 | 357 | |

6    When a thermocouple has one junction in melting ice and the other junction in boiling water it produces an e.m.f. of $63\,\mu V$.
   a  What e.m.f. would be produced if the second junction was also placed in melting ice?
   b  When the second junction is placed in a cup of coffee, the e.m.f. produced is $49\,\mu V$. Calculate the temperature of the coffee.
   c  The second junction is now placed in a beaker of melting lead at $327\,°C$.
      i   Calculate the e.m.f which would be produced.
      ii  State the assumption you make.

7    The list gives four different types of thermometer.
         thermistor
         thermocouple
         constant pressure gas thermometer
         liquid-in-glass thermometer

   For each of the jobs below, state which type of thermometer you would use and justify your choice.
   a  A gardener measuring the temperature in a greenhouse.
   b  An engineer mapping the temperature at different points on the cylinder head of a car engine.
   c  A technician monitoring the temperatures in the core of a nuclear reactor.

8    a  A $500\,W$ kettle contains $300\,g$ of water at $20\,°C$. Calculate the time it would take to raise the temperature of the water to boiling point.
     b  The kettle is allowed to boil for 2 minutes. Calculate the mass of water that would remain in the kettle.
        State any assumptions that you make.
        (Specific heat capacity of water $= 4.18 \times 10^3\,J\,kg^{-1}\,°C^{-1}$, specific latent heat of vaporisation of water $= 2.26 \times 10^6\,J\,kg^{-1}$.)

# Exam-style questions

**1  a** Explain what is meant by the **specific heat capacity** of a substance. [2]

**b** The diagram shows the apparatus used to measure the specific heat capacity of a copper block of mass 850 g.

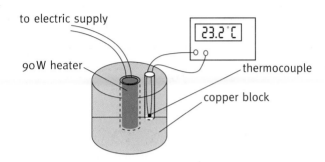

The block is initially at 12 °C. The heater is switched on and the time taken for the temperature to rise to 30 °C is recorded. The block is cooled to the original temperature, the potential difference across the heater is increased and the experiment is repeated.

The results are shown in the table.

| Power output of heater / W | Time taken / s |
|---|---|
| 40 | 190 |
| 60 | 114 |

**i**   Explain why a thermocouple thermometer is suitable for this experiment. [2]

**ii**  Explain why the experiment is repeated using a different power input. [2]

**iii** Calculate the specific heat capacity of copper. [5]

**2  a** A cylinder of carbon dioxide is at room temperature and at a pressure of 20 atmospheres. A cloth is placed over the outlet and the tap opened. Solid carbon dioxide is formed on the cloth.
Explain, using the first law of thermodynamics, why the carbon dioxide cools sufficiently for the solid to form. [3]

**b** Solid carbon dioxide sublimes to form carbon dioxide gas; that is, it changes directly from a solid to a gas. This change is called **sublimation**. The diagram on the next page shows the apparatus used to measure the specific latent heat of sublimation of carbon dioxide.

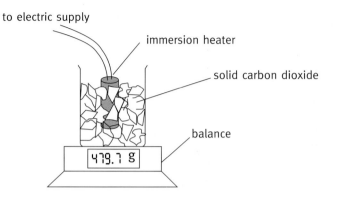

to electric supply

immersion heater

solid carbon dioxide

balance

479.7 g

Explain what is meant by the **latent heat of sublimation**. [2]

**c** The change in mass of the solid carbon dioxide in a time interval of 5 minutes is measured with the heater switched off. The change of mass, in the same time interval, is found with the heater switched on. The energy to supplied to the heater is also measured.
The results are shown in the table below.

| | Initial reading on balance / g | Final reading on balance / g | Energy supplied to the heater / J |
|---|---|---|---|
| heater off | 484.3 | 479.7 | 0 |
| heater on | 479.7 | 454.2 | 12 000 |

  **i** Explain why readings are taken with the heater switched off. [1]
  **ii** Calculate the specific latent heat of sublimation of carbon dioxide. [3]
**d** The specific latent heat of sublimation is greater than either the specific latent heat of fusion or the specific latent heat of vaporisation.
Suggest a reason for this. [2]

**3** **a** Explain why energy is needed for boiling even though the temperature of the liquid remains constant. [2]
The diagram shows apparatus that can be used to measure the specific latent heat of vaporisation of nitrogen.

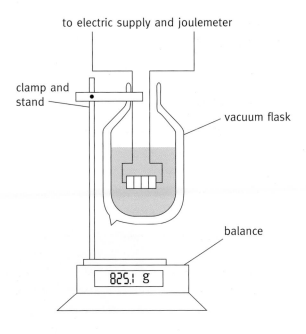

to electric supply and joulemeter

clamp and stand

vacuum flask

balance

825.1 g

**b** Suggest why the nitrogen is contained in a vacuum flask. [1]

**c** The change in mass of the nitrogen is measured with the heater switched off. The heater is switched on transferring energy at 40 W, and the change of mass is found once more. The results are shown in the table.

| | Initial reading on balance/g | Final reading on balance/g | Time/minute |
|---|---|---|---|
| heater off | 834.7 | 825.5 | 4 |
| heater on | 825.5 | 797.1 | 2 |

Calculate the specific latent heat of vaporisation of liquid nitrogen. [4]

**4 a i** Explain what is meant by **internal energy**. [2]

**ii** Explain what is meant by the **absolute zero of temperature**. [2]

**b** A electric hot water heater has a power rating of 9.0 kW. The water is heated as it passes through the heater. Water flows through the heater at a speed of $1.2\,\mathrm{m\,s^{-1}}$ through pipes which have a total cross-sectional area of $4.8 \times 10^{-5}\,\mathrm{m^2}$. The temperature of the water entering the heater is 15 °C.

**i** Calculate the mass of water flowing through the heater each second. [2]

**ii** Calculate the temperature at which the water leaves the heater. [3]

**iii** State any assumptions you have made when doing your calculation. [1]

**iv** It is possible to adjust the temperature of the water from the heater. Suggest how the temperature of the water could be increased. [1]

(Density of water = $1000\,\mathrm{kg\,m^{-3}}$, the specific heat capacity of water = $4200\,\mathrm{J\,kg^{-1}\,°C^{-1}}$.)

## Objectives

After studying this chapter, you should be able to:

- ☐ solve problems using the equation of state for an ideal gas
- ☐ interpret Brownian motion in terms of the movement of molecules
- ☐ state the assumptions of the kinetic theory of gases

- ☐ deduce a relationship between pressure, volume and the microscopic properties of the molecules of a gas
- ☐ relate the kinetic energy of the molecules of a gas to its temperature

## The idea of a gas

Figure 22.1 shows a weather balloon being launched. Balloons like this carry instruments high into the atmosphere from where measurements of pressure, temperature, wind speed and other variables are transmitted back to the ground.

The balloon is filled with helium so that its overall density is less than that of the surrounding air. The result is an upthrust on the balloon, greater than its weight, so that it rises upwards. As it moves upwards, the pressure of the surrounding atmosphere decreases so that the balloon expands. The temperature drops, which tends to make the gas in the balloon shrink. In this chapter we will look at the behaviour of gases as their pressure, temperature and volume change.

Figure 22.1 A weather balloon being launched.

## Molecules in a gas

In Chapter 7, we looked at observations of Brownian motion and saw that the jittery motion of smoke particles in air could be explained by saying that air consists of fast-moving molecules whose collisions with a smoke particle cause it to move around. Because the mass of the smoke particle is much greater than that of the air molecules, its speed is much less than theirs. Figure 22.2 shows an impression of the distribution of molecules of a gas in a container. You can see that the molecules of the gas are moving around at random – the word **gas** has the same origin as the word **chaos**.

Figure 22.2 Molecules of a gas – collisions with the walls of the container cause the gas's pressure on the container.

For air at standard temperature and pressure (s.t.p. – 0 °C and 100 kPa), the average speed of the molecules is about 400 m s$^{-1}$. At any moment, some are moving faster than this and others more slowly. If we could follow the movement of a single air molecule, we would find that, some of the time, its speed was greater than this average; at other times it would be less. The velocity (magnitude and direction) of an individual molecule changes every time it collides with anything else.

This value for molecular speed is reasonable. It is comparable to (but greater than) the speed of sound in air (approximately 330 m s$^{-1}$ at s.t.p.). Very fast-moving particles can easily escape from the Earth's gravitational field. The required escape velocity is about 11 km s$^{-1}$. Since we still have an atmosphere, on average the air molecules must be moving much slower than this value.

## Test yourself

1 An oxygen molecule is moving around inside a spherical container of diameter 0.10 m. The molecule's speed is 400 m s$^{-1}$. Estimate the number of times each second the molecule collides with the walls of the container. (You can assume that the molecule's speed is constant.)

# Measuring gases

We are going to picture a container of gas, such as the box shown in Figure 22.3. There are four properties of this gas that we might measure: pressure, temperature, volume and mass. In this chapter, you will learn how these quantities are related to one another.

## Pressure

This is the force exerted normally per unit area by the gas on the walls of the container. We saw in Chapter **6** that this pressure is the result of molecular collisions with the walls of the container. Pressure is measured in pascals, Pa (1 Pa = 1 N m$^{-2}$).

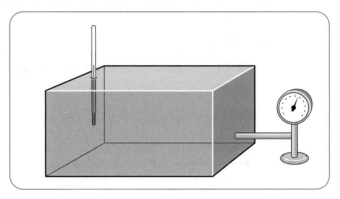

**Figure 22.3** A gas has four measurable properties, which are all related to one another: pressure, temperature, volume and mass.

## Temperature

This might be measured in °C, but in practice it is more useful to use the thermodynamic (Kelvin) scale of temperature. You should recall how these two scales are related:

$$T\,(\text{K}) = \theta\,(°\text{C}) + 273.15$$

## Volume

This is a measure of the space occupied by the gas. Volume is measured in m$^3$.

## Mass

This is measured in g or kg. In practice, it is more useful to consider the **amount** of gas measured in moles.

The mole is defined as follows:

One mole of any substance is the amount of that substance which contains the same number of particles as there are in 0.012 kg of carbon-12.

(In this definition, 'particles' may be atoms, molecules, ions, etc.)

One mole of any substance is equal to the relative atomic or molecular mass of the substance measured in grams. For example, one mole of oxygen ($O_2$) has a mass of about 32 g.

A mole of any substance (solid, liquid or gas) contains a standard number of particles (molecules or atoms). This number is known as the **Avogadro constant**, $N_A$. The experimental value for $N_A$ is $6.02 \times 10^{23}$ mol$^{-1}$. We can easily determine the number of atoms in a sample if we know how many moles it contains. For example:

2.0 mol of helium contains

$$2.0 \times 6.02 \times 10^{23} = 1.20 \times 10^{24} \text{ atoms}$$

10 mol of carbon contains

$$10 \times 6.02 \times 10^{23} = 6.02 \times 10^{24} \text{ atoms}$$

We will see later that, if we consider equal numbers of moles of two different gases under the same conditions, their properties are the same.

## Test yourself

2  The mass of one mole of carbon is 12 g. Determine:
   **a** the number of atoms in one mole of carbon
   **b** the number of moles and the number of atoms in 54 g of carbon
   **c** the number of atoms in 1.0 kg of carbon.

3  The molar mass of uranium is about 235 g mol⁻¹.
   **a** Calculate the mass of a single atom of uranium.
   **b** A small pellet of uranium has a mass of 20 mg. For this pellet, calculate:
      **i** the number of moles
      **ii** the number of uranium atoms.

4  'It can be useful to recall that 1.0 kg of matter contains of the order of $10^{26}$ atoms.' Making suitable estimates, test this statement.

# Boyle's law

This law relates the pressure $p$ and volume $V$ of a gas. It was discovered in 1662 by Robert Boyle. If a gas is compressed, its pressure increases and its volume decreases. Pressure and volume are inversely related.
   We can write **Boyle's law** as:

The pressure exerted by a fixed mass of gas is inversely proportional to its volume, provided the temperature of the gas remains constant.

Note that this law relates two variables, pressure and volume, and it requires that the other two, mass and temperature, remain constant.

Boyle's law can be written as:

$$p \propto \frac{1}{V}$$

or simply:

$$pV = \text{constant}$$

We can also represent Boyle's law as a graph, as shown in Figure **22.4**. A graph of $p$ against $\frac{1}{V}$ is a straight line passing through the origin, showing direct proportionality.

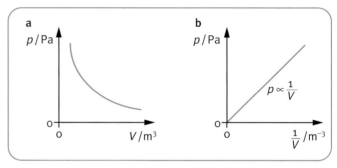

**Figure 22.4** Graphical representations of the relationship between pressure and volume of a gas (Boyle's law).

For solving problems, you may find it more useful to use the equation in this form:

$$p_1 V_1 = p_2 V_2$$

Here, $p_1$ and $V_1$ represent the pressure and volume of the gas before a change, and $p_2$ and $V_2$ represent the pressure and volume of the gas after the change. Worked example **1** shows how to use this equation.

## Worked example

1  A cylinder contains 0.80 dm³ of nitrogen gas at a pressure of 1.2 atmosphere (1 atm = $1.01 \times 10^5$ Pa). A piston slowly compresses the gas to a pressure of 6.0 atm. The temperature of the gas remains constant. Calculate the final volume of the gas.

Note from the question that the temperature of the gas is constant, and that its mass is fixed

*continued* ⋯⊁

(because it is contained in a cylinder). This means that we can apply Boyle's law.

**Step 1** We are going to use Boyle's law in the form $p_1V_1 = p_2V_2$. Write down the quantities that you know, and that you want to find out.

$p_1 = 1.2\,\text{atm}$      $V_1 = 0.80\,\text{dm}^3$
$p_2 = 6.0\,\text{atm}$      $V_2 = ?$

Note that we don't need to worry about the particular units of pressure and volume being used here, so long as they are the same on both sides of the equation. The final value of $V_2$ will be in $\text{dm}^3$ because $V_1$ is in $\text{dm}^3$.

**Step 2** Substitute the values in the equation, rearrange and find $V_2$.

$$p_1V_1 = p_2V_2$$

$$1.2 \times 0.8 = 6.0 \times V_2$$

$$V_2 = \frac{1.2 \times 0.8}{6.0} = 0.16\,\text{dm}^3$$

So the volume of the gas is reduced to $0.16\,\text{dm}^3$.

The pressure increases by a factor of 5, so the volume decreases by a factor of 5.

## Test yourself

5  A balloon contains $0.04\,\text{m}^3$ of air at a pressure of $120\,\text{kPa}$. Calculate the pressure required to reduce its volume to $0.025\,\text{m}^3$ at constant temperature.

# Changing temperature

Boyle's law requires that the temperature of a gas is fixed. What happens if the temperature of the gas is allowed to change? Figure 22.5 shows the results of an experiment in which a fixed mass of gas is cooled at constant pressure. The gas contracts; its volume decreases.

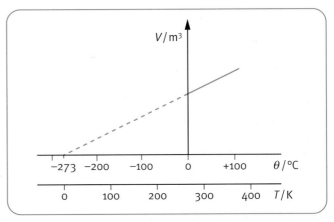

**Figure 22.5** The volume of a gas decreases as its temperature decreases.

This graph does not show that the volume of a gas is proportional to its temperature on the Celsius scale. If a gas contracted to zero volume at $0\,°\text{C}$, the atmosphere would condense on a cold day and we would have a great deal of difficulty in breathing! However, the graph **does** show that there is a temperature at which the volume of a gas does, in principle, shrink to zero. Looking at the lower temperature scale on the graph, where temperatures are shown in kelvin (K), we can see that this temperature is $0\,\text{K}$, or absolute zero. (Historically, this is how the idea of absolute zero first arose.)

We can represent the relationship between volume $V$ and thermodynamic temperature $T$ as:

$$V \propto T$$

or simply:

$$\frac{V}{T} = \text{constant}$$

Note that this relationship only applies to a fixed mass of gas and where the pressure remains constant.

The relationship above is an expression of **Charles's law**, named after the French physicist Jacques Charles who in 1787 experimented with different gases kept at constant pressure.

If we combine Boyle's law and Charles's law, we can arrive at a single equation for a fixed mass of gas:

$$\frac{pV}{T} = \text{constant}$$

Shortly, we will look at the constant quantity which appears in this equation, but first we will consider the extent to which this equation applies to real gases.

## Real and ideal gases

The relationships between $p$, $V$ and $T$ that we have considered above are based on experimental observations of gases such as air, helium, nitrogen, etc., at temperatures and pressures around room temperature and pressure. In practice, if we change to more extreme conditions, such as low temperatures or high pressures, gases start to deviate from these laws as the gas atoms exert significant electrical forces on each other. For example, Figure 22.6 shows what happens when nitrogen is cooled down towards absolute zero. At first, the graph of volume against temperature follows a good straight line. However, as it approaches the temperature at which it condenses, it deviates from ideal behaviour, and at 77 K it condenses to become liquid nitrogen.

Thus we have to attach a condition to the relationships discussed above. We say that they apply to an **ideal gas**. When we are dealing with real gases, we have to be aware that their behaviour may be significantly different from the ideal equation:

$$\frac{pV}{T} = \text{constant}$$

An ideal gas is thus defined as one for which we can apply the equation:

$$\frac{pV}{T} = \text{constant}$$

for a fixed mass of gas.

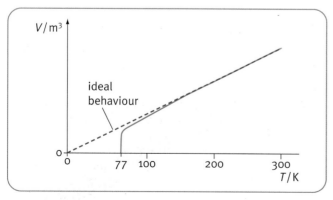

**Figure 22.6** A real gas (in this case, nitrogen) deviates from the behaviour predicted by Charles's law at low temperatures.

## Ideal gas equation

So far, we have seen how $p$, $V$ and $T$ are related. It is possible to write a single equation relating these quantities which takes into account the amount of gas being considered.

If we consider $n$ moles of an ideal gas, we can write the equation in the following form:

$$pV = nRT$$

This equation is called the **ideal gas equation** or the **equation of state** for an ideal gas. It relates all four of the variable quantities discussed at the beginning of this chapter. The constant of proportionality $R$ is called the universal molar gas constant. Its experimental value is:

$$R = 8.31\,\text{J}\,\text{mol}^{-1}\,\text{K}^{-1}$$

Note that it doesn't matter what gas we are considering – it could be a very 'light' gas like hydrogen, or a much 'heavier' one like carbon dioxide. So long as it is behaving as an ideal gas, we can use the same equation of state with the same constant $R$.

## Calculating the number $n$ of moles

Sometimes we know the mass of gas we are concerned with, and then we have to be able to find how many moles this represents. To do this, we use this relationship:

$$\text{number of moles} = \frac{\text{mass (g)}}{\text{molar mass (g mol}^{-1})}$$

For example: How many moles are there in 1.6 kg of oxygen?

$$\text{molar mass of oxygen} = 32\,\text{g mol}^{-1}$$

$$\text{number of moles} = \frac{1600\,\text{g}}{32\,\text{g mol}^{-1}} = 50\,\text{mol}$$

(Note that this tells us that there are 50 moles of oxygen **molecules** in 1.6 kg of oxygen. An oxygen molecule consists of two oxygen atoms – its formula is $O_2$ – so 1.6 kg of oxygen contains 100 moles of oxygen **atoms**.)

Now look at Worked examples **2** and **3**.

## Worked examples

**2** Calculate the volume occupied by one mole of an ideal gas at room temperature (20 °C) and pressure ($1.013 \times 10^5$ Pa).

**Step 1** Write down the quantities given.

$$p = 1.013 \times 10^5 \, \text{Pa} \qquad n = 1.0$$

$$T = 293 \, \text{K}$$

> Note that the temperature is converted to kelvin.

**Step 2** Substituting these values in the equation of state gives:

$$V = \frac{nRT}{p} = \frac{1 \times 8.31 \times 293}{1.103 \times 10^5}$$

$$V = 0.0240 \, \text{m}^3 = 2.40 \times 10^{-2} \, \text{m}^3$$
$$= 24.0 \, \text{dm}^3$$

> ($1 \, \text{dm} = 0.1 \, \text{m}$; hence $1 \, \text{dm}^3 = 10^{-3} \, \text{m}^3$)

This value, the volume of one mole of gas at room temperature and pressure, is well worth remembering. It is certainly known by most chemists.

---

**3** A car tyre contains 0.020 m³ of air at 27 °C and at a pressure of $3.0 \times 10^5$ Pa. Calculate the mass of the air in the tyre. (Molar mass of air = 28.8 g mol⁻¹.)

**Step 1** Here, we need first to calculate the number of moles of air using the equation of state. We have:

$$p = 3.0 \times 10^5 \, \text{Pa} \qquad V = 0.02 \, \text{m}^3$$

$$T = 27 \, °\text{C} = 300 \, \text{K}$$

> Don't forget to convert temperatures to kelvin.

*continued* ⋯➔

So, from the equation of state:

$$n = \frac{pV}{RT} = \frac{30 \times 10^5 \times 0.02}{8.31 \times 300}$$

$$n = 2.41 \, \text{mol}$$

**Step 2** Now we can calculate the mass of air:

mass = number of moles × molar mass

mass = $2.41 \times 28.8 = 69.4 \, \text{g} \approx 69 \, \text{g}$

## Test yourself

For the questions which follow, you will need the following value:

$$R = 8.31 \, \text{J mol}^{-1} \, \text{K}^{-1}$$

**6** At what temperature (in K) will 1.0 mol of a gas occupy 1.0 m³ at a pressure of $1.0 \times 10^4$ Pa?

**7** Nitrogen consists of molecules $N_2$. The molar mass of nitrogen is 28 g mol⁻¹. For 100 g of nitrogen, calculate:
   **a** the number of moles
   **b** the volume occupied at room temperature and pressure? (r.t.p. = 20 °C , $1.01 \times 10^5$ Pa.)

**8** Calculate the volume of 5.0 mol of an ideal gas at a pressure of $1.0 \times 10^5$ Pa and a temperature of 200 °C.

**9** A sample of gas contains $3.0 \times 10^{24}$ atoms. Calculate the volume of the gas at a temperature of 300 K and a pressure of 120 kPa.

**10** At what temperature would 1.0 kg of oxygen occupy 1.0 m³ at a pressure of $1.0 \times 10^5$ Pa? (Molar mass of $O_2 = 32$ g mol⁻¹.)

*continued* ⋯➔

11 A cylinder of hydrogen has a volume of 0.10 m³. Its pressure is found to be 20 atmospheres at 20 °C.
  a Calculate the mass of hydrogen in the cylinder.
  b If it was filled with oxygen instead to the same pressure, how much oxygen would it contain?
  (Molar mass of $H_2$ = 2.0 g mol⁻¹, molar mass of $O_2$ = 32 g mol⁻¹; 1 atmosphere = $1.01 \times 10^5$ Pa.)

# Modelling gases – the kinetic model

In this chapter, we are concentrating on the macroscopic properties of gases (pressure, volume, temperature). These can all be readily measured in the laboratory. The equation:

$$\frac{pV}{T} = \text{constant}$$

is an empirical relationship. In other words, it has been deduced from the results of experiments. It gives a good description of gases in many different situations. However, an empirical equation does not **explain** why gases behave in this way. An explanation requires us to think about the underlying nature of a gas and how this gives rise to our observations.

A gas is made of particles (atoms or molecules). Its pressure arises from collisions of the particles with the walls of the container; more frequent, harder collisions give rise to greater pressure. Its temperature indicates the average kinetic energy of its particles; the faster they move, the greater their average kinetic energy and the higher the temperature.

The **kinetic theory of gases** is a theory which links these microscopic properties of particles (atoms or molecules) to the macroscopic properties of a gas. Table 22.1 shows the assumptions on which the theory is based.

On the basis of these assumptions, it is possible to use Newtonian mechanics to show that pressure is inversely proportional to volume (Boyle's law), volume

| Assumption | Explanation/comment |
|---|---|
| A gas contains a very large number of spherical particles (atoms or molecules). | A small 'cube' of air can have as many as $10^{20}$ molecules. |
| The forces between particles are negligible, except during collisions. | If the particles attracted each other strongly over long distances, they would all tend to clump together in the middle of the container. The particles travel in straight lines between collisions. |
| The volume of the particles is negligible compared to the volume occupied by the gas. | When a liquid boils to become a gas, its particles become much farther apart. |
| Most of the time, a particle moves in a straight line at a constant velocity. The time of collision with another particle or with the container walls is negligible compared with the time between collisions. | The particles collide with the walls of the container and with each other, but for most of the time they are moving with constant velocity. |
| The collisions of particles with each other and with the container are perfectly elastic, so that no kinetic energy is lost. | Kinetic energy cannot be lost. The internal energy of the gas is the total kinetic energy of the particles. |

Table 22.1 The basic assumptions of the kinetic theory of gases.

is directly proportional to thermodynamic (kelvin) temperature (Charles's law), and so on. The theory also shows that the particles of a gas have a range of speeds – some move faster than others.

Things are different when a gas is close to condensing. At temperatures a little above the boiling point, the molecules of a gas are moving more slowly and they tend to stick together – a liquid is forming. So we cannot consider them to be moving about freely, and the kinetic theory of gases must be modified. This is often how physics progresses. A theory is developed which explains a simple situation. Then the theory is modified to explain more complex situations.

The kinetic theory has proved to be a very powerful model. It convinced many physicists of the existence of particles long before it was ever possible to visualise them.

## Molecules in a box

We can use the kinetic model to deduce an equation which relates the macroscopic properties of a gas (pressure, volume) to the microscopic properties of its molecules (mass and speed). We start by picturing a single molecule in a cube-shaped box of side $l$ (Figure 22.7). This molecule has mass $m$, and is moving with speed $c$ parallel to one side of the box ($c$ is not the speed of light in this case). It rattles back and forth, colliding at regular intervals with the ends of the box and thereby contributing to the pressure of the gas. We are going to work out the pressure this one molecule exerts on one end of the box and then deduce the total pressure produced by all the molecules.

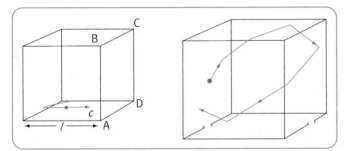

**Figure 22.7** A single molecule of a gas, moving in a box.

Consider a collision in which the molecule strikes side ABCD of the cube. It rebounds elastically in the opposite direction, so that its velocity is $-c$. its momentum changes from $mc$ to $-mc$. The change in momentum arising from this single collision is thus:

change in momentum $= -mc - (+mc)$
$$= -mc - mc = -2mc$$

Between consecutive collisions with side ABCD, the molecule travels a distance of $2l$ at speed $c$. Hence:

time between collisions with side ABCD $= \dfrac{2l}{c}$

Now we can find the force that this one molecule exerts on side ABCD, using Newton's second law of motion. This says that the force produced is equal to the rate of change of momentum:

force $= \dfrac{\text{change in momentum}}{\text{time taken}} = \dfrac{2mc}{2l/c} = \dfrac{mc^2}{l}$

(We use $+2mc$ because now we are considering the force of the molecule on side ABCD, which is in the opposite direction to the change in momentum of the molecule.)

The area of side ABCD is $l^2$. From the definition of pressure, we have:

pressure $= \dfrac{\text{force}}{\text{area}} = \dfrac{mc^2/l}{l^2} = \dfrac{mc^2}{l^3}$

This is for one molecule, but there is a large number $N$ of molecules in the box. Each has a different velocity, and each contributes to the pressure. We write the average value of $c^2$ as $<c^2>$, and multiply by $N$ to find the total pressure:

pressure $p = \dfrac{Nm <c^2>}{l^3}$

But this assumes that all the molecules are travelling in the same direction and colliding with the same pair of opposite faces of the cube. In fact they will be moving in all three dimensions equally, so we need to divide by 3 to find the pressure exerted.

pressure $p = \dfrac{1}{3} \dfrac{Nm <c^2>}{l^3}$

Here, $l^3$ is equal to the volume $V$ of the cube, so we can write:

$p = \dfrac{1}{3} \dfrac{Nm}{V} <c^2>$   or   $pV = \dfrac{1}{3} Nm <c^2>$

(Notice that, in the second form of the equation, we have the macroscopic properties of the gas – pressure and volume – on one side of the equation and the microscopic properties of the molecules on the other side.)

Finally, the quantity $Nm$ is the mass of all the molecules of the gas, and this is simply equal to the mass $M$ of the gas. So $\dfrac{Nm}{V}$ is equal to the density $\rho$ of the gas, and we can write

$p = \dfrac{1}{3} \rho <c^2>$

So the pressure of a gas depends only on its density and the mean square speed of its molecules.

## A plausible equation?

It is worth thinking a little about whether the equation $p = \frac{1}{3}\frac{Nm}{V}<c^2>$ seems to make sense. It should be clear to you that the pressure is proportional to the number of molecules, $N$. More molecules mean greater pressure. Also, the greater the mass of each molecule, the greater the force it will exert during a collision.

The equation also suggests that pressure $p$ is proportional to the average value of the speed squared. This is because, if a molecule is moving faster, not only does it strike the container harder, but it also strikes the container more often.

The equation suggests that the pressure $p$ is inversely proportional to volume occupied by the gas. Here, we have deduced Boyle's law. If we think in terms of the kinetic model, we can see that if a mass of gas occupies a larger volume, the molecules will spend more time in the bulk of the gas, and less time colliding with the walls. So, the pressure will be lower.

These arguments should serve to convince you that the equation is plausible; this sort of argument cannot prove the equation.

---

### Test yourself

**12** Check that the units on the left-hand side of the equation $p = \frac{1}{3}\frac{Nm<c^2>}{V}$ are the same as those on the right-hand side.

**13** The quantity $Nm$ is the total mass of the molecules of the gas, i.e. the mass of the gas. At room temperature, the density of air is about $1.29\,\mathrm{kg\,m^{-3}}$ at a pressure of $10^5\,\mathrm{Pa}$.
   **a** Use these figures to deduce the value of $<c^2>$ for air molecules at room temperature.
   **b** Find a typical value for the speed of a molecule in the air by calculating $\sqrt{<c^2>}$. How does this compare with the speed of sound in air, approximately $330\,\mathrm{m\,s^{-1}}$?

---

## Temperature and molecular kinetic energy

Now we can compare the equation $pV = \frac{1}{3}Nm<c^2>$ with the ideal gas equation $pV = nRT$. The left-hand sides are the same, so the two right-hand sides must also be equal:

$$\tfrac{1}{3}Nm<c^2> = nRT$$

We can use this equation to tell us how the absolute temperature of a gas (a macroscopic property) is related to the mass and speed of its molecules. If we focus on the quantities of interest, we can see the following relationship:

$$m<c^2> = \frac{3nRT}{N}$$

The quantity $\frac{N}{n} = N_A$ is the Avogadro constant, the number of particles in 1 mole. So:

$$m<c^2> = \frac{3RT}{N_A}$$

It is easier to make sense of this if we divide both sides by 2, to get the familiar expression for kinetic energy:

$$\tfrac{1}{2}m<c^2> = \frac{3RT}{2N_A}$$

The quantity $\frac{1}{2}m<c^2>$ is the average kinetic energy of a molecule in the gas, and $R$ **and** $N_A$ are constants. Hence the thermodynamic temperature $T$ is proportional to the average kinetic energy of a molecule.

> The mean translational kinetic energy of an atom (or molecule) of an ideal gas is proportional to the thermodynamic temperature.

It is easier to recall this as:

mean translational kinetic energy of atom $\propto T$

We need to consider two of the terms in this statement. Firstly, we talk about **translational** kinetic energy. This is the energy that the molecule has because it is moving along; a molecule made of two or more atoms may also spin or tumble around, and is then said to have rotational kinetic energy – see Figure 22.8.

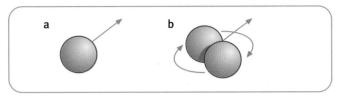

Figure 22.8 **a** A monatomic molecule has only translational kinetic energy. **b** A diatomic molecule can have both translational and rotational kinetic energy.

Secondly, we talk about **mean** (or average) translational kinetic energy. There are two ways to find the average translational kinetic energy (k.e.) of a molecule of a gas: add up all the kinetic energies of the individual molecules of the gas and then calculate the average k.e. per molecule. Alternatively, watch an individual molecule over a period of time as it moves about, colliding with other molecules and the walls of the container and calculate its average k.e. over this time. Both should give the same answer.

## Test yourself

14 a The quantity $\frac{R}{N_A}$ is called the Boltzmann constant, $k$. Show that it has the value $1.38 \times 10^{-23}\,\text{J K}^{-1}$.
   b Write down an equation linking the Boltzmann constant, the thermodynamic temperature and the average kinetic energy of a molecule.

## Mass, kinetic energy and temperature

Since mean k.e. $\propto T$, it follows that if we double the thermodynamic temperature of an ideal gas (e.g. from 300 K to 600 K), we double the mean k.e. of its molecules. It doesn't follow that we have doubled their speed; because k.e. $\propto v^2$, their mean speed has increased by a factor of $\sqrt{2}$.

Air is a mixture of several gases: nitrogen, oxygen, carbon dioxide, etc. In a sample of air, the mean k.e. of the nitrogen molecules is the same as that of the oxygen molecules and that of the carbon dioxide molecules. This comes about because they are all repeatedly colliding with one another, sharing their energy. Carbon dioxide molecules have greater mass than oxygen molecules; since their mean translational k.e. is the same, it follows that the carbon dioxide molecules move more slowly than the oxygen molecules.

## Test yourself

15 Calculate the mean translational k.e. of atoms in an ideal gas at 27 °C.

16 The atoms in a gas have a mean translational k.e. equal to $5.0 \times 10^{-21}$ J. Calculate the temperature of the gas in K and in °C.

17 Show that, if the mean speed of the molecules in an ideal gas is doubled, the thermodynamic temperature of the gas increases by a factor of 4.

18 A fixed mass of gas expands to twice its original volume at a constant temperature. How do the following change:
   a the pressure of the gas
   b the mean translational kinetic energy of its molecules?

19 Air consists of molecules of oxygen (molar mass = 32 g mol⁻¹) and nitrogen (molar mass = 28 g mol⁻¹). Calculate the mean translational k.e. of these molecules in air at 20 °C. Use your answer to estimate a typical speed for each type of molecule.

20 Show that the change in the internal energy of one mole of an ideal gas per unit change in temperature is always a constant. What is this constant?

## Summary

- ☐ Brownian motion provides evidence for the fast, random movement of molecules in a gas.
- ☐ For an ideal gas:

$$\frac{pV}{T} = \text{constant}$$

- ☐ One mole of any substance contains $N_A$ particles (atoms or molecules).
  $N_A = $ Avogadro constant $= 6.02 \times 10^{23}\,\text{mol}^{-1}$.
- ☐ The equation of state for an ideal gas is:

$$pV = nRT \quad \text{for } n \text{ moles}$$

- ☐ From the kinetic model of a gas, we can deduce the relationship:

$$p = \frac{1}{3}\frac{Nm\langle c^2 \rangle}{V} = \frac{1}{3}\rho\langle c^2 \rangle$$

where $\langle c^2 \rangle$ is the mean square molecular speed and $\rho$ is the density of the gas.

- ☐ The mean translational kinetic energy $E$ of a particle (atom or molecule) of an ideal gas is proportional to the thermodynamic temperature $T$.

# End-of-chapter questions

1   a   State how many atoms there are in:
    **i**   a mole of helium gas
    **ii**   a mole of chlorine gas
    **iii**   a kilomole of neon gas.
  **b**   A container holds four moles of carbon dioxide. Calculate:
    **i**   the number of carbon dioxide molecules there are in the container
    **ii**   the number of carbon atoms there are in the container
    **iii**   the number of oxygen atoms there are in the container.

2   A bar of gold has a mass of 1.0 kg. Calculate:
  **a**   the number of moles of gold in the bar
  **b**   the number of gold atoms in the bar
  **c**   the mass of one gold atom.
  (Relative atomic mass of gold = 197.)

3   A cylinder holds 140 dm³ of nitrogen at room temperature and pressure. Moving slowly so that there is no change in temperature, a piston is pushed to reduce the volume of the nitrogen to 42 dm³.
  **a**   Calculate the pressure of the nitrogen after compression.
  **b**   Explain the effect on the temperature and pressure of the nitrogen if the piston were pushed in very quickly.

4  The atmospheric pressure is 100 kPa, equivalent to the pressure exerted by a column of water 10 m high. A bubble of oxygen of volume 0.42 cm³ is released by a water plant at a depth of 25 m. Calculate the volume of the bubble when it reaches the surface. State any assumptions you make.

5  A cylinder contains 40 dm³ of carbon dioxide at a pressure of $4.8 \times 10^5$ Pa at room temperature. Calculate:
   a  the number of moles of carbon dioxide
   b  the mass of carbon dioxide.
   (Relative molecular mass of carbon dioxide = 44.)

6  Calculate the volume of 1 mole of ideal gas at a pressure of $1.01 \times 10^5$ Pa and at a temperature of 0 °C.

7  A vessel of volume 200 dm³ contains $3.0 \times 10^{26}$ molecules of gas at a temperature of 127 °C. Calculate the pressure exerted by the gas on the vessel walls.

8  a  Calculate the average speed of helium molecules at room temperature and pressure.
   b  Comment on how this speed compares with the average speed of air molecules at the same temperature and pressure.

9  A sample of neon is contained in a cylinder at 27 °C. Its temperature is raised to 243 °C.
   a  Calculate the kinetic energy of the neon atoms at:
      i   27 °C
      ii  243 °C.
   b  Compare the speeds of the molecules at the two temperatures.

## Exam-style questions

1  A lorry is to cross the Sahara desert. The journey begins just before dawn when the temperature is 3 °C. The volume of air held in each tyre is 1.50 m³ and the pressure in the tyres is $3.42 \times 10^5$ Pa.
   a  Explain how the air molecules in the tyre exert a pressure on the tyre walls.  [3]
   b  Calculate the number of moles of air in the tyre.  [3]
   c  By midday the temperature has risen to 42 °C.
      i   Calculate the pressure in the tyre at this new temperature. You may assume that no air escapes and the volume of the tyre is unchanged.  [2]
      ii  Calculate the increase in the average translational kinetic energy of an air molecule due to this temperature rise.  [2]

2  a  Explain what is meant by **Brownian motion** and how it provides evidence for the existence of molecules.  [3]
   b  The density of air at room temperature and pressure, r.t.p. (20 °C and $1.03 \times 10^5$ Pa), is 1.21 kg m⁻³. Calculate the average speed of air molecules at r.t.p.  [4]
   c  State and explain the effect on the average speed of the air molecules of:
      i   raising the temperature of the air  [2]
      ii  going to a higher altitude (but keeping the temperature constant).  [1]

3   **a** Explain what is meant by an **ideal gas.**                                    [2]

   **b** A cylinder contains 500 g of helium at a pressure of $5.0 \times 10^5$ Pa and a temperature
     of 27 °C. You may assume helium acts as an ideal gas.
     Calculate:

     **i**  the number of moles of helium the cylinder holds                          [1]

     **ii**  the number of atoms of helium the cylinder holds.                        [1]

   **c** Calculate the volume of the cylinder.                                         [3]

   **d** When the tap of the cylinder is opened for a short time a small amount of the helium
     escapes into atmosphere. As it does so, the temperature of the helium drops significantly.

     **i**  Explain why the temperature drops.                                       [2]

     **ii**  Describe what happens to the average speed of the atoms of the escaped helium.   [1]
     (Relative atomic mass of helium = 4.)

4   A hot air balloon, its basket and passengers has a total mass of 450 kg. The inflated balloon
   holds 3000 m³ of air.

   **a** Calculate the minimum force needed to lift the balloon off the ground.          [1]

   **b** The atmospheric pressure is $1.03 \times 10^5$ Pa and the density of the air is 1.23 kg m⁻³.

     **i**  Calculate the mass of 3000 m³ of air.                                   [1]

     **ii**  Calculate the number of moles of air in the balloon. You may consider air to act as
     an ideal gas with a relative molecular mass of 29.                          [1]

   **c** As the air is heated it expands and some of it is expelled through a vent at the top of the
     balloon.
     Calculate the maximum mass of air that can remain in the balloon to give sufficient
     upthrust for the balloon to just leave the ground.                              [2]

   **d** Calculate the minimum temperature the air inside the balloon must be heated to for
     the balloon to just lift off the ground.                                        [4]

# 23 Coulomb's law

## Objectives

After studying this chapter, you should be able to:

☐ recall and use Coulomb's law
☐ calculate the field strength and potential due to a point charge

☐ define electric potential and relate field strength to the potential gradient
☐ compare and contrast electric and gravitational fields

## Living in a field

The scientist in the photograph (Figure 23.1) is using a detector to measure the electric field produced by a mobile phone mast. People often worry that the electric field produced by a mobile phone transmitter may be harmful, but detailed studies have yet to show any evidence for this. If you hold a mobile phone close to your ear, the field strength will be far greater than that produced by a nearby mast.

**Figure 23.1** Mobile phone masts produce weak electric fields – this scientist is using a small antenna to detect and measure the field of a nearby mast to ensure that it is within safe limits.

## Electric fields

In Chapter **9**, we presented some fundamental ideas about electric fields:

- An electric field is a field of force and can be represented by field lines.
- The electric field strength at a point is the force per unit positive charge that acts on a stationary charge:

$$\text{field strength} = \frac{\text{force}}{\text{charge}} \qquad E = \frac{F}{Q}$$

- There is a uniform field between charged parallel plates:

$$\text{field strength} = \frac{\text{potential difference}}{\text{separation}} \qquad E = \frac{V}{d}$$

In this chapter, we will extend these ideas to consider how electric fields arise from electric charges. We will also compare electric fields with gravitational fields (Chapter **19**).

## Coulomb's law

Any electrically charged object produces an electric field in the space around it. It could be something as small as an electron or a proton, or as large as a planet or star. To say that it produces an electric field means that it will exert a force on any other charged object which is in the field. How can we determine the size of such a force?

The answer to this was first discovered by Charles Coulomb, a French physicist. He realised that it was important to think in terms of **point charges**; that is, electrical charges which are infinitesimally small so that we need not worry about their shapes. In 1785 Coulomb proposed a law that describes the force that one charged particle exerts on another. This law is remarkably similar in form to Newton's law of gravitation (page **274**).

A statement of **Coulomb's law** is as follows:

> Any two point charges exert an electrical force on each other that is proportional to the product of their charges and inversely proportional to the square of the distance between them.

We consider two point charges $Q_1$ and $Q_2$ separated by a distance $r$ (Figure **23.2**). The force each charge exerts on the other is $F$. According to Newton's third law of motion, the point charges interact with each other and therefore exert equal but opposite forces on each other.

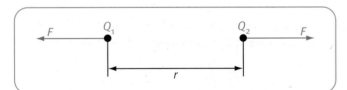

**Figure 23.2** The variables involved in Coulomb's law.

According to Coulomb's law, we have:

force ∝ product of the charges     $F \propto Q_1 Q_2$

force ∝ $\dfrac{1}{\text{distance}^2}$     $F \propto \dfrac{1}{r^2}$

Therefore:

$$F \propto \frac{Q_1 Q_2}{r^2}$$

We can write this in a mathematical form:

$$F = \frac{k Q_1 Q_2}{r^2}$$

The constant of proportionality is:

$$k = \frac{1}{4\pi \varepsilon_0}$$

where $\varepsilon_0$ is known as the **permittivity of free space** ($\varepsilon$ is the Greek letter epsilon). The value of $\varepsilon_0$ is approximately $8.85 \times 10^{-12}\,\text{F m}^{-1}$. An equation for Coulomb's law is thus:

$$F = \frac{Q_1 Q_2}{4\pi \varepsilon_0 r^2}$$

By substituting for $\pi$ and $\varepsilon_0$, we can show that the force $F$ can also be given by the equation:

$$F \approx 9.0 \times 10^9 \, \frac{Q_1 Q_2}{r^2}$$

i.e. the constant $k$ has the approximate numerical value of $9.0 \times 10^9\,\text{N m}^2\,\text{C}^{-2}$.

This approximation can be useful for making rough calculations, but more precise calculations require that the value of $\varepsilon_0$ given above is used.

Following your earlier study of Newton's law of gravitation, you should not be surprised by this relationship. The force depends on each of the properties producing it (in this case, the charges), and it is an inverse square law with distance – if the particles are twice as far apart, the electrical force is a quarter of its previous value (Figure **23.3**).

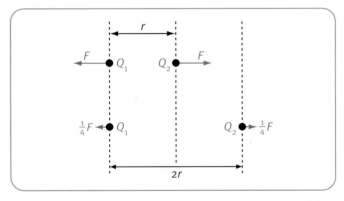

**Figure 23.3** Double the separation results in one-quarter of the force, a direct consequence of Coulomb's law.

Note also that, if we have a positive and a negative charge, then the force $F$ is negative. We interpret this as an attraction. Positive forces, as between two like charges, are repulsive. In gravity, we only have attraction.

So far we have considered point charges. If we are considering uniformly charged spheres we measure the distance from the centre of one to the centre of the other – they behave as if their charge was all concentrated at the centre. Hence we can apply the equation for Coulomb's law for both point charges (e.g. protons, electrons, etc.) and uniform charged spheres as long as we use the **centre-to-centre** distance between the objects.

## Investigating Coulomb's law

It is quite tricky to investigate the force between charged objects, because charge tends to leak away into the air or to the Earth during the course of any experiment. The amount of charge we can investigate is difficult to measure, and usually small, giving rise to tiny forces.

Figure **23.4** shows one method for investigating the inverse square law for two charged metal balls (polystyrene balls coated with conducting silver paint). As one charged ball is lowered down towards the other, their separation decreases and so the force increases, giving an increased reading on the balance.

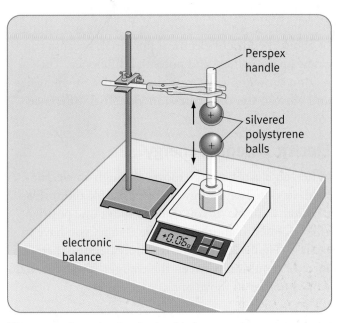

**Figure 23.4** Investigating Coulomb's law.

# Electric field strength for a radial field

In Chapter **9**, we saw that the electric field strength at a point is defined as the force per unit charge exerted on a positive charge placed at that point, $E = \dfrac{F}{Q}$

So, to find the field strength near a point charge $Q_1$ (or outside a uniformly charged sphere), we have to imagine a small positive test charge $Q_2$ placed in the field, and determine the force per unit charge on it. We can then use the definition above to determine the electric field strength for a point (or spherical) charge.

The force between the two point charges is given by:

$$F = \frac{Q_1 Q_2}{4\pi\varepsilon_0 r^2}$$

The electric field strength $E$ due to the charge $Q_1$ at a distance of $r$ from its centre is thus:

$$E = \frac{\text{force}}{\text{test charge}} = \frac{Q_1 Q_2}{4\pi\varepsilon_0 r^2 Q_2}$$

or

$$E = \frac{Q}{4\pi\varepsilon_0 r^2}$$

The field strength $E$ is not a constant; it decreases as the distance $r$ increases. The field strength obeys the inverse square law with distance – just like the gravitational field strength for a point mass. The field strength will decrease by a factor of four when the distance from the centre is doubled.

Note also that, since force is a vector quantity, it follows that electric field strength is also a vector. We need to give its direction as well as its magnitude in order to specify it completely. Worked example **1** shows how to use the equation for field strength near a charged sphere.

### Worked example

1 A spherical metal dome of diameter 12 cm is positively charged. The electric field strength at the surface of the dome is $4.0 \times 10^5\,\text{V m}^{-1}$. Draw the electric field pattern for the dome and determine the total surface charge.

**Step 1** Draw the electric field pattern (Figure 23.5). The electric field lines must be normal to the surface and radial.

*continued ⋯⋗*

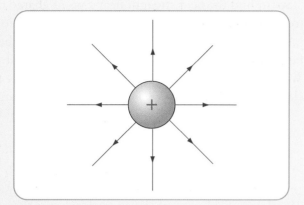

**Figure 23.5** The electric field around a charged sphere.

**Step 2** Write down the quantities given:

electric field strength $E = 4.0 \times 10^5 \, \text{V m}^{-1}$

$$\text{radius } r = \frac{0.12}{2} = 0.06 \, \text{m}$$

**Step 3** Use the equation for the electric field strength to determine the surface charge:

$$E = \frac{Q}{4\pi\varepsilon_0 r^2}$$

$$Q = 4\pi\varepsilon_0 r^2 \times E$$

$$Q = 4\pi \times 8.85 \times 10^{-12} \times (0.06)^2 \times 4.0 \times 10^5$$

$$Q = 1.6 \times 10^{-7} \, \text{C} \; (0.16 \, \mu\text{C})$$

---

### Test yourself

You will need the data below to answer the following questions.

$$\varepsilon_0 = 8.85 \times 10^{-12} \, \text{F m}^{-1}$$

1  A metal sphere of radius 20 cm carries a positive charge of 2.0 μC.
   **a** What is the electric field strength at a distance of 25 cm from the centre of the sphere?
   **b** An identical metal sphere carrying a negative charge of 1.0 μC is placed next to the first sphere. There is a gap of 10 cm between

*continued* ⋯➔

them. Calculate the electric force that each sphere exerts on the other.

> Remember to calculate the centre-to-centre distance between the two spheres.

   **c** Determine the electric field strength midway along a line joining the centres of the spheres.

2  A Van de Graaff generator produces sparks when the field strength at its surface is $4.0 \times 10^4 \, \text{V cm}^{-1}$. If the diameter of the sphere is 40 cm, what is the charge on it?

# Electric potential

When we discussed gravitational potential (page 277), we started from the idea of potential energy. The potential at a point is then the potential energy of unit mass at the point. We will approach the idea of electrical potential in the same way. However, you may be relieved to find that you already know something of about the idea of electrical potential, because you know about voltage and potential difference. This section shows how we formalise the idea of voltage, and why we use the expression 'potential difference' for some kinds of voltage.

## Electric potential energy

When an electric charge moves through an electric field, its potential energy changes. Think about this concrete example: if you want to move one positive charge closer to another positive charge, you have to push it (Figure 23.6). This is simply because there is a force of repulsion between the charges. You have to do work in order to move one charge closer to the other.

**Figure 23.6** Work must be done to push one positive charge towards another.

In the process of doing work, energy is transferred from you to the charge that you are pushing. Its potential energy increases. If you let go of the charge, it will move away from the repelling charge. This is analogous to lifting up a mass; it gains gravitational potential energy as you lift it, and it falls if you let go.

## Energy changes in a uniform field

We can also think about moving a positive charge in a uniform electric field between two charged parallel plates. If we move the charge towards the positive plate, we have to do work. The potential energy of the charge is therefore increasing. If we move it towards the negative plate, its potential energy is decreasing (Figure **23.7**).

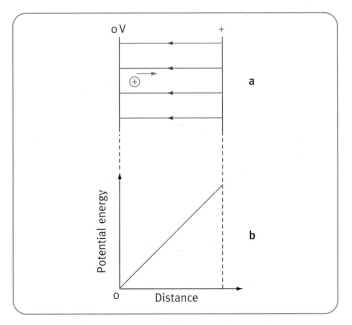

**Figure 23.7** Electrostatic potential energy changes in a uniform field.

Since the force is the same at all points in a uniform electric field, it follows that the energy of the charge increases steadily as we push it from the negative plate to the positive plate. The graph of potential energy against distance is a straight line, as shown in Figure **23.7**.

We can calculate the change in potential energy of a charge $Q$ as it is moved from the negative plate to the positive plate very simply. Potential difference is defined as the energy change per coulomb between two points (recall from Chapter **10** that one volt is one joule per coulomb). Hence, for charge $Q$, the

work done in moving it from the negative plate to the positive plate is:

$$W = QV$$

We can rearrange this equation as

$$V = \frac{W}{Q}$$

This is really how voltage $V$ is defined. It is the energy per unit charge at a point in an electric field. By analogy with gravitational potential, we call this the electric potential at a point. Now you should be able to see that what we regard as the familiar idea of voltage should more correctly be referred to as electric potential. The difference in potential between two points is the potential difference (p.d.) between them.

Just as with gravitational fields, we must define the zero of potential (this is the point where we consider a charge to have zero potential energy). Usually, in a laboratory situation, we define the Earth as being at a potential of zero volts. If we draw two parallel charged plates arranged horizontally, with the lower one earthed (Figure **23.8**), you can see immediately how similar this is to our idea of gravitational fields. The diagram also shows how we can include equipotential lines in a representation of an electric field.

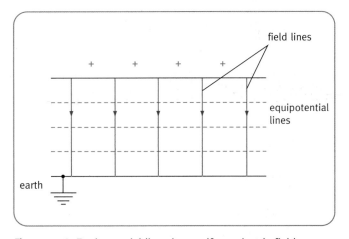

**Figure 23.8** Equipotential lines in a uniform electric field.

We can extend the idea of electric potential to measurements in electric fields. In Figure **23.9**, the power supply provides a potential difference of 10 V. The value of the potential at various points is shown. You can see that the middle resistor has a potential difference across it of $(8 - 2)\,V = 6\,V$.

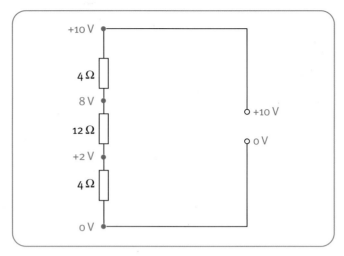

**Figure 23.9** Changes in potential (shown in red) around an electric circuit.

## Energy in a radial field

Imagine again pushing a small positive test charge towards a large positive charge. At first, the repulsive force is weak, and you have only to do a small amount of work. As you get closer, however, the force increases (Coulomb's law), and you have to work harder and harder.

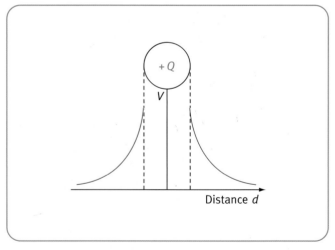

**Figure 23.10** The potential decreases according to an inverse law near a charged sphere.

The potential energy of the test charge increases as you push it. It increases more and more rapidly the closer you get to the repelling charge. This is shown by the graph in Figure **23.10**. We can write an equation for the potential $V$ at a distance $r$ from a charge $Q$:

$$V = \frac{Q}{4\pi\varepsilon_0 r^2}$$

(This comes from the calculus process of integration, applied to the Coulomb's law equation.) You should be able to see how this relationship parallels the equivalent formula for gravitational potential in a radial field:

$$\varphi = -\frac{GM}{r}$$

Note that we do not need the minus sign in the electric equation as it is included in the charge. A negative charge gives an attractive (negative field) whereas a positive charge gives a repulsive (positive field).

We can show these same ideas by drawing field lines and equipotential lines. The equipotentials get closer together as we get closer to the charge (Figure **23.11**).

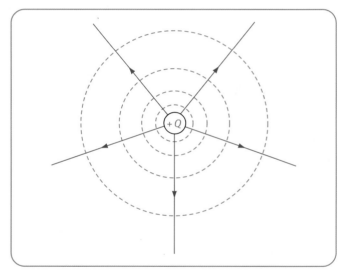

**Figure 23.11** The electric field around a positive charge. The dashed equipotential lines are like the contour lines on a map; they are spaced at equal intervals of potential.

To arrive at the result above, we must again define our zero of potential. Again, we say that a charge has zero potential energy when it is at infinity (some place where it is beyond the influence of any other charges). If we move towards a positive charge, the potential is positive. If we move towards a negative charge, the potential is negative.

This allows us to give a strict definition of electric potential:

> The **electric potential** at a point is equal to the work done in bringing unit positive charge from infinity to that point.

## Field strength and potential gradient

We can picture electric potential in the same way that we thought about gravitational potential. A negative charge attracts a positive test charge, so we can regard it as a potential 'well'. A positive charge is the opposite – a 'hill' (Figure **23.12**). The strength of the field is shown by the slope of the hill or well:

field strength = –potential gradient

The minus sign is needed because, if we are going up a potential hill, the force on us is pushing us back down the slope, in the opposite direction.

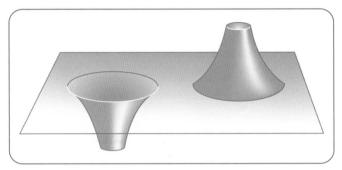

**Figure 23.12** A 'potential well' near a negative charge, and a 'potential hill' near a positive charge.

This relationship applies to all electric fields. You can see that, for a uniform field, the potential gradient is $\frac{V}{d}$, and hence:

$$E = \frac{V}{d}$$

This is the relationship quoted without proof in Chapter **9** (page **136**).

Worked example **2** shows how to determine the field strength from a potential–distance graph.

### Worked example

2  The graph (Figure **23.13**) shows how the electric potential varies near a charged object. Calculate the electric field strength at a point 5 cm from the centre of the object.

*continued* ⋯⟩

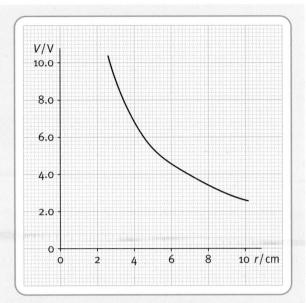

**Figure 23.13** Variation of the potential $V$ near a positively charged object.

**Step 1** Draw the tangent to the graph at the point 5.0 cm. This is shown in Figure **23.14**.

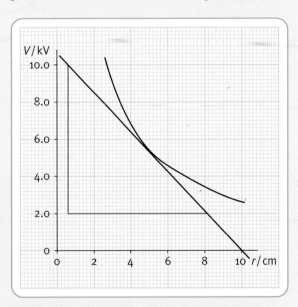

**Figure 23.14** Drawing the tangent to the $V$–$r$ graph to find the electric field strength $E$.

**Step 2** Calculate the gradient of the tangent:

$$\text{gradient} = \frac{\Delta V}{\Delta r}$$

$$= \frac{(10.0 - 2.0)}{(0.6 - 8.2)}$$

*continued* ⋯⟩

$$= -1.05\,\text{kV cm}^{-1} = -1.05 \times 10^5\,\text{V m}^{-1}$$
$$\approx -1.1 \times 10^5\,\text{V m}^{-1}$$

The electric field strength is therefore $+1.1 \times 10^5\,\text{V m}^{-1}$ or $+1.1 \times 10^5\,\text{N C}^{-1}$.

Remember $E = -$potential gradient.

## Test yourself

3  **a** What would be the electrical potential energy of a charge of $+1\,\text{C}$ placed at each of the points A, B, C, D between the charged, parallel plates shown in Figure **23.15**?

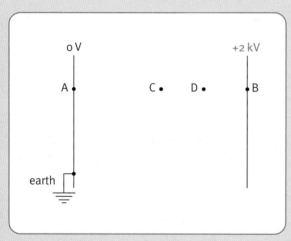

**Figure 23.15** A uniform electric field – see Test yourself Q **3**.

**b** What would be the potential energy of a $+2\,\text{C}$ charge at each of these points? (C is half-way between A and B; D is half-way between C and B.)

4  A Van de Graaff generator has a dome of radius $10\,\text{cm}$. It is charged up to a potential of $100\,000\,\text{V}$ ($100\,\text{kV}$). How much charge does it store? What is the potential at a distance of $10\,\text{cm}$ from the dome?

*continued* ⋯▸

5  **a** How much work would be done in moving a $+1\,\text{C}$ charge along the following paths shown in Figure **23.16**: from E to H; from E to F; from F to G; from H to E?
   **b** How would your answers differ for:
   **i** a $-1\,\text{C}$ charge
   **ii** a $+2\,\text{C}$ charge?

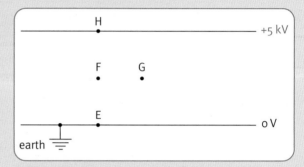

**Figure 23.16** A uniform electric field – see Test yourself Q **5**.

# Comparing gravitational and electric fields

There are obvious similarities between the ideas we have used in this chapter to describe electric fields and those we used in Chapter **19** for gravitational fields. This can be helpful, or it can be confusing! The summary given in Table **23.1** is intended to help you to sort them out.

An important difference is this: electric charges can be positive or negative, so they can attract and repel. There are no negative masses so there is only attraction in a gravitational field.

| Gravitational fields | Electric fields |
| --- | --- |
| **Origin** arise from masses | **Origin** arise from electric charges |
| **Vector forces** only gravitational attraction, no repulsion | **Vector forces** both electrical attraction and repulsion are possible (because of positive and negative charges) |
| **All gravitational fields** field strength $g = \dfrac{F}{m}$ i.e. field strength is force per unit mass | **All electric fields** field strength $F = \dfrac{F}{Q}$ i.e. field strength is force per unit positive charge |
| **Units** $F$ in N, $g$ in $N\,kg^{-1}$ or $m\,s^{-2}$ | **Units** $F$ in N, $E$ in $N\,C^{-1}$ or $V\,m^{-1}$ |
| **Uniform gravitational fields** parallel gravitational field lines $g = $ constant | **Uniform electric fields** parallel electric field lines $E = \dfrac{V}{d} = $ constant |
| **Spherical gravitational fields** radial field lines force given by Newton's law: $F = -\dfrac{GMm}{r^2}$ field strength is therefore: $g = -\dfrac{GM}{r^2}$ (The minus sign indicates an attractive field.) force and field strength obey an inverse square law with distance | **Spherical electric fields** radial field lines force given by Coulomb's law: $F = \dfrac{Q_1 Q_2}{4\pi\varepsilon_0 r^2}$ field strength is therefore: $E = \dfrac{Q}{4\pi\varepsilon_0 r^2}$ (A negative charge gives an attractive field, a positive charge gives a repulsive field.) force and field strength obey an inverse square law with distance |

| Gravitational fields | Electric fields |
| --- | --- |
| gravitational potential is given by: $\varphi = -\dfrac{GM}{r}$ | electric potential is given by: $V = \dfrac{Q}{4\pi\varepsilon_0 r}$ |
| potential obeys an inverse relationship with distance and is zero at infinity | potential obeys an inverse relationship with distance and is zero at infinity |

Table 23.1 Gravitational and electric fields compared.

## Test yourself

You will need the data below to answer the question.

proton mass $= 1.67 \times 10^{-27}$ kg
proton charge $= +1.6 \times 10^{-19}$ C
$\varepsilon_0 = 8.85 \times 10^{-12}$ F m$^{-1}$
$G = 6.67 \times 10^{-11}$ N m$^2$ kg$^{-2}$

6 Two protons in the nucleus of an atom are separated by a distance of $10^{-15}$ m. Calculate the electrostatic force of repulsion between them, and the force of gravitational attraction between them. (Assume the protons behave as point charges and point masses.) Is the attractive gravitational force enough to balance the repulsive electrical force? What does this suggest to you about the forces between protons within a nucleus?

# Summary

☐ Coulomb's law states that two point charges exert an electrical force on each other that is proportional to the product of their charges and inversely proportional to the square of the distance between them.

☐ The equation for Coulomb's law is:

$$F = \frac{Q_1 Q_2}{4\pi\varepsilon_0 r^2}$$

☐ A point charge $Q$ gives rise to a radial field. The electric field strength is given by the equation:

$$E = \frac{Q}{4\pi\varepsilon_0 r^2}$$

☐ The electric potential at a point is defined as the work done in bringing unit positive charge from infinity to the point.

☐ For a point charge, the electric potential is given by:

$$V = \frac{Q}{4\pi\varepsilon_0 r}$$

# End-of-chapter questions

1  On a copy of Figure **23.17**, draw the electric fields between the charged objects.

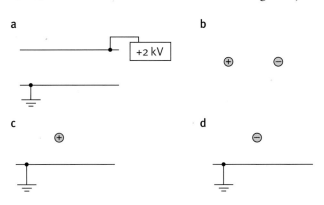
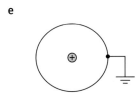

**Figure 23.17**  For End-of-chapter Q 1.

2   Two parallel plates are 4 cm apart and have a potential difference of 2.5 kV between them.
    a   Calculate the electric field strength between the plates.
    b   A small piece of dust carrying a charge of +2.4 nC moves into the space between the plates.
        i   Calculate the force on the dust particle.
        ii  The mass of the dust particle is 4.2 μg. Calculate the acceleration of the particle
            towards the negative plate.

3   A small sphere carries a charge of $2.4 \times 10^{-9}$ C. Calculate the electric field strength at
    a distance of:
    a   2 cm from the centre of the sphere
    b   4 cm from the centre of the sphere.

4   A conducting sphere of diameter 6.0 cm is mounted on an insulating base. The sphere is
    connected to a power supply which has an output voltage of 20 kV.
    a   Calculate the charge on the sphere.
    b   Calculate the electric field strength at the surface of the sphere.

5   The nucleus of a hydrogen atom carries a charge of $+1.6 \times 10^{-19}$ C. Its electron is at
    a distance of $1.05 \times 10^{-10}$ m from the nucleus.
    Calculate the ionisation potential of hydrogen.
    (Hint: This is equal to the work per unit charge when removing the electron to infinity.)

# Exam-style questions

1   a   Define **electric field strength**.                                                    [2]
    b   Two charged conducting spheres each of radius 1.0 cm are placed with their centres
        10 cm apart, as shown in the diagram.

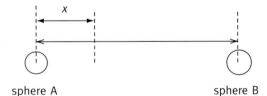

    Sphere A carries a charge of $+2 \times 10^{-9}$ C.

The graph below shows how the electric field strength between the two spheres varies with distance $x$.

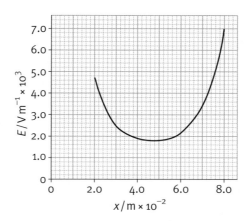

i  Calculate the field produced by sphere A at the 5.0 cm mark. [2]

ii  Use your result to **b i** to calculate the charge on sphere B. [3]

**c**  i  Sphere B is now removed. Calculate the potential at the surface of sphere A. [2]

ii  Suggest and explain how the potential at the surface of sphere A would compare before and after sphere B was removed. [2]

**2**  An $\alpha$-particle emitted in the radioactive decay of radium has an energy of $8.0 \times 10^{-13}$ J.

  **a**  i  Calculate the potential difference that an $\alpha$-particle, initially at rest, would have to be accelerated through to gain this energy. [2]

  ii  Calculate the speed of the $\alpha$-particle at this energy. [3]

  **b**  The diagram shows the path of the $\alpha$-particle of this energy as it approaches a gold nucleus.

  i  State the speed of the $\alpha$-particle at its point of closest approach to the gold nucleus. [1]

  ii  Write down the kinetic energy of the $\alpha$-particle at this point. [1]

  iii  Write down the potential energy of the $\alpha$-particle at this point. [1]

  **c**  Use your answer to **b iii** to show that the $\alpha$-particle will reach a distance of $4.5 \times 10^{-14}$ m from the centre of the gold nucleus. [2]

  **d**  Suggest and explain what this information tells us about the gold nucleus. [2]

  (Mass of an $\alpha$-particle $= 6.65 \times 10^{-27}$ kg, charge on an $\alpha$-particle $= +2e$, charge on an gold nucleus $= +79e$)

**3** **a** Define **electric potential at a point.** [2]

**b** The graph shows the potential well near a hydrogen nucleus.

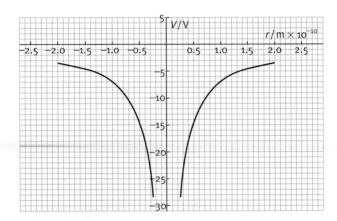

The first electron orbital can be considered to be a circle of diameter $1.04 \times 10^{-10}$ m.

**i** Determine the potential at a point on this orbital. [2]

**ii** Calculate the energy required to ionise the atom. [2]

**c** Use the graph to estimate the electric field strength at a distance of $1.0 \times 10^{-10}$ m from the centre of the nucleus. [2]

**4** The diagram shows a conducting sphere of radius 0.80 cm carrying a charge of $+6.0 \times 10^{-8}$ C resting on a balance.

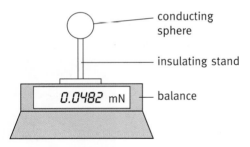

conducting sphere

insulating stand

0.0482 mN — balance

**a** Calculate the electric field at the surface of the sphere. [2]

**b** A identical sphere carrying a charge of $-4.5 \times 10^{-8}$ C held so that its centre is 5.0 cm vertically above the centre of the first sphere.

**i** Calculate the electric force between the two spheres. [2]

**ii** Calculate the new reading on the balance. [1]

**c** The second sphere is moved vertically downwards through 1.5 cm.
Calculate the work done against the electric field, in moving the sphere. [3]

# 24 Capacitance

## Capacitors

Most electronic devices, such as radios, computers
and MP3 players, make use of components called
capacitors. These are usually quite small, but
Figure 24.1 shows a giant capacitor, specially
constructed to store electrical energy at the
Fermilab particle accelerator in the United States.

Figure 24.1 One of the world's largest capacitors, built to store
energy at the Fermilab particle accelerator.

## Capacitors in use

Capacitors are used to store electrical charge (and energy)
in electrical and electronic circuits. This means that they
have many valuable applications. For example, capacitors
are used in computers; they are charged up in normal
use, and then they gradually discharge if there is a power
failure, so that the computer will operate long enough to
save valuable data. The photograph (Figure 24.2) shows a
variety of shapes and sizes of capacitors.

Every capacitor has two leads, connected to two metal
plates where the charge is stored. Between the plates is an
insulating material called the **dielectric**. Figure 24.3 shows
a simplified version of the construction of a capacitor; in
practice, many have a spiral 'Swiss-roll' form.

To charge a capacitor, it must be connected to a
voltage supply. The negative terminal of the supply
pushes electrons onto one plate, making it negatively
charged. Electrons are repelled from the other plate,
making it positively charged. Figure 24.4 shows that

Figure 24.2 A variety of capacitors.

there is a flow of electrons all the way round the
circuit. The ammeters show the current in the circuit.
The current eventually stops when the capacitor
is fully charged. When this happens, the potential
difference (p.d.) across the capacitor is equal to the
electromotive force (e.m.f.) of the supply.

Note: The convention is that current is the flow of
positive charge. Here, it is free electrons that flow.
Electrons are negatively charged; the current flows in
the opposite direction to the electrons (Figure 24.5).

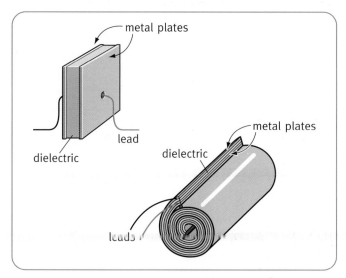

Figure 24.3 The construction of two types of capacitor.

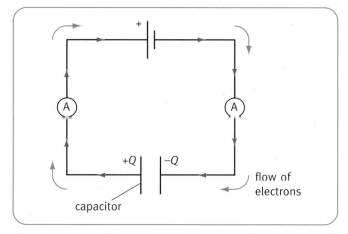

Figure 24.4 The flow of charge when a capacitor is charged up.

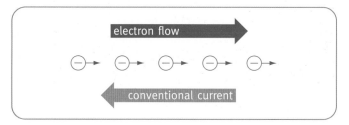

Figure 24.5 A flow of electrons to the right constitutes a conventional current to the left.

## Stored charge

If one plate of the capacitor stores charge $+Q$, then the other stores an equal and opposite charge $-Q$. We say that the charge stored by the capacitor is $Q$. (In fact, the total charge on the capacitor is zero. We focus our attention on one of the capacitor plates where there is an excess or deficiency of electrons. Connecting the capacitor to a supply **separates** the charges into $+Q$ and $-Q$.)

To make the capacitor store more charge, we would have to use a supply of higher e.m.f. If we connect the leads of the charged capacitor together, electrons flow back around the circuit and the capacitor is discharged.

You can observe a capacitor discharging as follows: Connect the two leads of a capacitor to the terminals of a battery. Disconnect, and then reconnect the leads to a light-emitting diode (LED). It is best to have a protective resistor in series with the LED. The LED will glow briefly as the capacitor discharges.

In any circuit, the charge that flows past a point in a given time is equal to the area under a current–time graph (just as distance is equal to the area under a speed–time graph). So the charge stored by a capacitor is given by the area under the current–time graph recorded while the capacitor is being charged up.

## The meaning of capacitance

If you look at some capacitors, you will see that they are marked with the value of their **capacitance**. The greater the capacitance, the greater is the charge stored by the capacitor for a given potential difference across it. The capacitance $C$ of a capacitor is defined by:

$$\text{capacitance} = \frac{\text{charge}}{\text{potential difference}}$$

or $\qquad C = \dfrac{Q}{V}$

where $Q$ is the charge stored by the capacitor and $V$ is the potential difference across it.

> The capacitance of a capacitor is the charge stored per unit of potential difference across it.

The charge on the capacitor may be calculated using the equation:

$$Q = VC$$

This equation shows that the charge stored depends on two things: the capacitance $C$ and the voltage $V$ (double the voltage stores double the charge).

## Units of capacitance

The unit of capacitance is the **farad**, F. From the equation that defines capacitance, you can see that this must be the same as the units of charge (coulombs, C) divided by volts (V):

$$1\,\text{F} = 1\,\text{C V}^{-1}$$

(It is unfortunate that the letter 'C' is used for both capacitance and coulomb. There is room for confusion here!)

In practice, a farad is a large unit. Few capacitors are big enough to store 1 C when charged up to 1 V. Capacitors usually have their values marked in picofarads (pF) or microfarads (µF):

$$\text{pF} = 10^{-12}\,\text{F} \qquad 1\,\text{µF} = 10^{-6}\,\text{F}$$

## Other markings on capacitors

Many capacitors are marked with their highest safe working voltage. If you exceed this value, charge may leak across between the plates, and the dielectric will cease to be an insulator. Some capacitors (electrolytic ones) must be connected correctly in a circuit. They have an indication to show which end must be connected to the positive of the supply. Failure to connect correctly will damage the capacitor, and can be extremely dangerous.

### Test yourself

1  Calculate the charge stored by a 220 µF capacitor charged up to 15 V. Give your answer in microcoulombs (µC) and in coulombs (C).

2  A capacitor stores $1.0 \times 10^{-3}$ C of charge when charged to 500 V. Calculate its capacitance in farads (F), microfarads (µF) and picofarads (pF).

3  Calculate the average current required to charge a 50 µF capacitor to a p.d. of 10 V in a time interval of 0.01 s.

4  A student connects an uncharged capacitor of capacitance $C$ in series with a resistor, a cell and a switch. The student closes the switch and records the current $I$ at intervals of 10 s. The results are shown in Table 24.1. The potential difference across the capacitor after 60 s was

continued ⋯⇥

8.5 V. Plot a current–time graph, and use it to estimate the value of $C$.

| $t\,/\,\text{s}$ | 0 | 10 | 20 | 30 | 40 | 50 | 60 |
|---|---|---|---|---|---|---|---|
| $I\,/\,\text{µA}$ | 200 | 142 | 102 | 75 | 51 | 37 | 27 |

**Table 24.1** Data for Test yourself Q 4.

## Energy stored in a capacitor

When you charge a capacitor, you use a power supply to push electrons onto one plate and off the other. The power supply does work on the electrons, so their potential energy increases. You recover this energy when you discharge the capacitor.

If you charge a large capacitor (1000 µF or more) to a potential difference of 6.0 V, disconnect it from the supply, and then connect it across a 6.0 V lamp, you can see the lamp glow as energy is released from the capacitor. The lamp will flash briefly. Clearly, such a capacitor does not store much energy when it is charged.

In order to charge a capacitor, work must be done to push electrons onto one plate and off the other (Figure 24.6). At first, there is only a small amount of negative charge on the left-hand plate. Adding more electrons is relatively easy, because there is not much repulsion. As the charge stored increases, the repulsion between the electrons on the plate and the new electrons increases, and a greater amount of work must be done to increase the charge stored.

This can be seen qualitatively in Figure 24.7a. This graph shows how the p.d. $V$ increases as the amount of charge stored $Q$ increases. It is a straight line because $Q$ and $V$ are related by:

$$V = \frac{Q}{C}$$

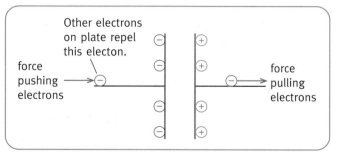

**Figure 24.6** When a capacitor is charged, work must be done to push additional electrons against the repulsion of the electrons that are already present.

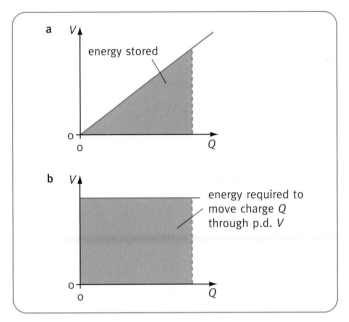

Figure 24.7 The area under a graph of voltage against charge gives a quantity of energy. The area in **a** shows the energy stored in a capacitor; the area in **b** shows the energy required to drive a charge through a resistor.

We can use Figure 24.7a to calculate the work done in charging up the capacitor.

First, consider the work done $W$ in moving charge $Q$ through a constant p.d. $V$. This is given by:

$$W = QV$$

(You studied this equation in Chapter **10**.) From the graph of $Q$ against $V$ (Figure **24.7b**), we can see that the quantity $Q \times V$ is given by the area under the graph.

> The area under a graph of p.d. against charge is equal to work done.

If we apply the same idea to the capacitor graph (Figure **24.7a**), then the area under the graph is the shaded triangle, with an area of $\frac{1}{2}$ base × height. Hence the work done in charging a capacitor to a particular p.d. is given by:

$$W = \frac{1}{2} QV$$

Substituting $Q = CV$ into this equation gives two further equations:

$$W = \frac{1}{2} QV^2$$

and

$$W = \frac{1}{2} \frac{Q^2}{C}$$

These three equations show the work done in charging up the capacitor. This is equal to the energy stored by the capacitor, since this is the amount of energy released when the capacitor is discharged.

We can also see from the second formula ($W = \frac{1}{2}CV^2$) that the energy $W$ that a capacitor stores depends on its capacitance $C$ and the potential difference $V$ to which it is charged.

The energy $W$ stored is proportional to the square of the potential difference $V$ ($W \propto V^2$) It follows that doubling the charging voltage means that four times as much energy is stored. This comes about because, when you double the voltage, not only is twice as much charge stored, but it is stored at twice the voltage.

## Test yourself

5 State the quantity represented by the gradient of the straight line shown in Figure **24.7a**.

6 The graph of Figure **24.8** shows how $V$ depends on $Q$ for a particular capacitor.

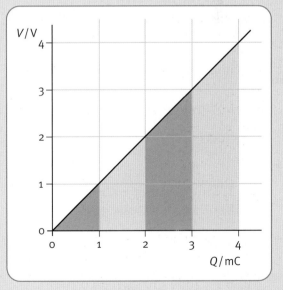

Figure 24.8 The energy stored by a capacitor is equal to the area under the graph of voltage against charge.

*continued* ⋯⇾

The area under the graph has been divided into strips to make it easy to calculate the energy stored. The first strip (which is simply a triangle) shows the energy stored when the capacitor is charged up to 1.0 V. The energy stored is:

$$\tfrac{1}{2}QV = \tfrac{1}{2} \times 1.0 \, \text{mC} \times 1.0 \, \text{V} = 0.5 \, \text{mJ}$$

a Calculate the capacitance $C$ of the capacitor.
b Copy Table 24.2 and complete it by calculating the areas of successive strips, to show how $W$ depends on $V$.
c Plot a graph of $W$ against $V$. Describe the shape of this graph.

| $Q/\text{mC}$ | $V/\text{V}$ | Area of strip $\Delta W/\text{mJ}$ | Sum of areas $W/\text{mJ}$ |
|---|---|---|---|
| 1.0 | 1.0 | 0.5 | 0.5 |
| 2.0 | 2.0 | 1.5 | 2.0 |
| 3.0 | | | |
| 4.0 | | | |

Table 24.2 Data for Test yourself Q 6.

## Worked example

1 A 2000 µF capacitor is charged to a p.d. of 10 V. Calculate the energy stored by the capacitor.

Step 1 Write down the quantities we know:

$C = 2000 \, \mu\text{F}$
$V = 10 \, \text{V}$

Step 2 Write down the equation for energy stored and substitute values:

$$W = \tfrac{1}{2}CV^2$$

$$W = \tfrac{1}{2} \times 2000 \times 10^{-6} \times 10^2 = 0.10 \, \text{J}$$

Don't forget to change the µF into F.

continued ···▸

This is a small amount of energy – compare it with the energy stored by a rechargeable battery, typically of the order of 10 000 J. A charged capacitor will not keep an MP3 player running for any length of time.

## Investigating energy stored

If you have a sensitive joulemeter (capable of measuring millijoules, mJ), you can investigate the equation for energy stored. A suitable circuit is shown in Figure 24.9.

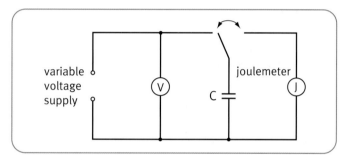

Figure 24.9 With the switch to the left, the capacitor C charges up; to the right, it discharges through the joulemeter.

The capacitor is charged up when the switch connects it to the power supply. When the switch is altered, the capacitor discharges through the joulemeter. (It is important to wait for the capacitor to discharge completely.) The joulemeter will measure the amount of energy released by the capacitor.

By using capacitors with different values of $C$, and by changing the charging voltage $V$, you can investigate how the energy $W$ stored depends on $C$ and $V$.

## Test yourself

7 Calculate the energy stored for the following capacitors:
a a 5000 µF capacitor charged to 5.0 V
b a 5000 pF capacitor charged to 5.0 V
c a 200 µF capacitor charged to 230 V.

continued ···▸

8 Which stores more charge, a 100 µF capacitor charged to 200 V or a 200 µF capacitor charged to 100 V? Which stores more energy?

9 A 10 000 µF capacitor is charged to 12 V, and then connected across a lamp rated at '12 V, 36 W'.
  a Calculate the energy stored by the capacitor.
  b Estimate the time the lamp stays fully lit. Assume that energy is dissipated in the lamp at a steady rate.

10 In a simple photographic flashgun, a 0.20 F capacitor is charged by a 9.0 V battery. It is then discharged in a flash of duration 0.01 s. Calculate:
  a the charge and energy stored by the capacitor
  b the average power dissipated during the flash
  c the average current in the flash bulb
  d the approximate resistance of the bulb.

# Capacitors in parallel

Capacitors are used in electric circuits to store charge and energy. Situations often arise where two or more capacitors are connected together in a circuit. In this section, we will look at capacitors connected in parallel. The next section deals with capacitors in series.

When two capacitors are connected in parallel (Figure 24.10), their combined or total capacitance $C_{total}$ is simply the sum of their individual capacitances $C_1$ and $C_2$:

$$C_{total} = C_1 + C_2$$

This is because, when two capacitors are connected together, they are equivalent to a single capacitor with larger plates. The bigger the plates, the more charge that can be stored for a given voltage, and hence the greater the capacitance.

The total charge $Q$ stored by two capacitors connected in parallel and charged to a potential difference $V$ is simply given by:

$$Q = C_{total} \times V$$

For three or more capacitors connected in parallel, the equation for their total capacitance becomes:

$$C_{total} = C_1 + C_2 + C_3 + \cdots$$

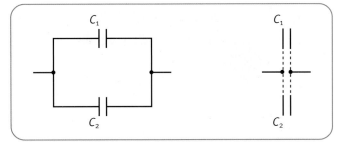

Figure 24.10 Two capacitors connected in parallel are equivalent to a single, larger capacitor.

## Capacitors in parallel: deriving the formula

We can derive the equation for capacitors in parallel by thinking about the charge stored by the two capacitors. As shown in Figure 24.11, $C_1$ stores charge $Q_1$ and $C_2$ stores charge $Q_2$. Since the p.d. across each capacitor is $V$, we can write:

$$Q_1 = C_1 V \quad \text{and} \quad Q_2 = C_2 V$$

The total charge stored is given by the sum of these:

$$Q = Q_1 + Q_2 = C_1 V + C_2 V$$

Since $V$ is a common factor:

$$Q = (C_1 + C_2) V$$

Comparing this with $Q = C_{total} V$ gives the required $C_{total} = C_1 + C_2$. It follows that for three or more capacitors connected in parallel, we have:

$$C_{total} = C_1 + C_2 + C_3 + \cdots$$

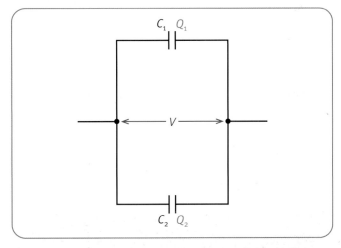

Figure 24.11 Two capacitors connected in parallel have the same p.d. across them, but store different amounts of charge.

## Capacitors in parallel: Summary

For capacitors in parallel, the following rules apply:

- The p.d. across each capacitor is the same.
- The total charge stored by the capacitors is equal to the sum of the charges:

$$Q_{total} = Q_1 + Q_2 + Q_3 + \cdots$$

- The total capacitance $C_{total}$ is given by:

$$C_{total} = C_1 + C_2 + C_3 + \cdots$$

### Test yourself

**11 a** Calculate the total capacitance of two $100\,\mu\text{F}$ capacitors connected in parallel.
   **b** Calculate the total charge they store when charged to a p.d. of $20\,\text{V}$.

**12** A capacitor of capacitance $50\,\mu\text{F}$ is required, but the only values available to you are $10\,\mu\text{F}$, $20\,\mu\text{F}$ and $100\,\mu\text{F}$ (you may use more than one of each value). How would you achieve the required value by connecting capacitors in parallel? Give at least two answers.

# Capacitors in series

In a similar way to the case of capacitors connected in parallel, we can consider two or more capacitors connected in series (Figure **24.12**). The total capacitance $C_{total}$ of two capacitors of capacitances $C_1$ and $C_2$ is given by:

$$\frac{1}{C_{total}} = \frac{1}{C_1} + \frac{1}{C_2}$$

Here, it is the reciprocals of the capacitances that must be added to give the reciprocal of the total capacitance. For three or more capacitors connected in series, the equation for their total capacitance is:

$$\frac{1}{C_{total}} = \frac{1}{C_1} + \frac{1}{C_2} + \frac{1}{C_3} + \cdots$$

**Figure 24.12** Two capacitors connected in series.

## Capacitors in series: deriving the formula

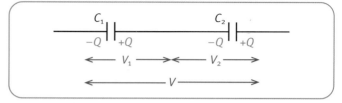

**Figure 24.13** Capacitors connected in series store the same charge, but they have different p.d.s across them.

This follows the same principles apply here as for the case of capacitors in parallel. Figure **24.13** shows the situation. $C_1$ and $C_2$ are connected in series, and there is a p.d. $V$ across them. This p.d. is divided (it is shared between the two capacitors), so that the p.d. across $C_1$ is $V_1$ and the p.d. across $C_2$ is $V_2$. It follows that:

$$V = V_1 + V_2$$

Now we must think about the charge stored by the combination of capacitors. In Figure **24.13**, you will see that both capacitors are shown as storing the same charge $Q$. How does this come about? When the voltage is first applied, charge $-Q$ arrives on the left-hand plate of $C_1$. This repels charge $-Q$ off the right-hand plate, leaving it with charge $+Q$. Charge $-Q$ now arrives on the left-hand plate of $C_2$, and this in turn results in charge $+Q$ on the right-hand plate.

Note that charge is not arbitrarily created or destroyed in this process – the total amount of charge in the system is constant. This is an example of the conservation of charge.

Notice also that there is a central isolated section of the circuit between the two capacitors. Since this is initially uncharged, it must remain so at the end. This requirement is satisfied, because there is charge $-Q$ at one end and $+Q$ at the other. Hence we conclude that capacitors connected in series store the same charge. This allows us to write equations for $V_1$ and $V_2$:

$$V_2 = \frac{Q}{C_1} \quad \text{and} \quad V_2 = \frac{Q}{C_2}$$

The combination of capacitors stores charge $Q$ when charged to p.d. $V$, and so we can write:

$$V = \frac{Q}{C_{total}}$$

Substituting these in $V = V_1 + V_2$ gives:

$$\frac{Q}{C_{total}} = \frac{Q}{C_1} + \frac{Q}{C_2}$$

Cancelling the common factor of $Q$ gives the required equation:

$$\frac{1}{C_{total}} = \frac{1}{C_1} + \frac{1}{C_2}$$

Worked example 2 shows how to use this relationship.

## Worked example

2   Calculate the total capacitance of a 300 µF capacitor and a 600 µF capacitor connected in series.

**Step 1** The calculation should be done in two steps; this is relatively simple using a calculator with a '$\frac{1}{x}$' or $x^{-1}$ key.

Substitute the values into the equation:

$$\frac{1}{C_{total}} = \frac{1}{C_1} + \frac{1}{C_2}$$

This gives:

$$\frac{1}{C_{total}} = \frac{1}{300} + \frac{1}{600}$$

$$\frac{1}{C_{total}} = 0.005 \ \mu F^{-1}$$

**Step 2** Now take the reciprocal of this value to determine the capacitance in µF:

$$\frac{1}{C_{total}} = \frac{1}{0.005} = 200 \ \mu F$$

Notice that the total capacitance of two capacitors in series is less than either of the individual capacitances.

Using the $x^{-1}$ key on your calculator, you can also do this calculation in one step:

$$C_{total} = (300^{-1} + 600^{-1})^{-1} = 200 \ \mu F$$

# Comparing capacitors and resistors

It is helpful to compare the formulae for capacitors in series and parallel with the corresponding formulae for resistors (Table 24.3).

| | Capacitors | Resistors |
|---|---|---|
| **In series** | store same charge | have same current |
| | $\frac{1}{C_{total}} = \frac{1}{C_1} + \frac{1}{C_2} + \frac{1}{C_3} + \cdots$ | $R_{total} = R_1 + R_2 + R_3 + \cdots$ |
| **In parallel** | have same p.d. | have same p.d. |
| | $C_{total} = C_1 + C_2 + C_3 + \cdots$ | $\frac{1}{R_{total}} = \frac{1}{R_1} + \frac{1}{R_2} + \frac{1}{R_3} + \cdots$ |

**Table 24.3** Capacitors and resistors compared.

Notice that the reciprocal formula applies to capacitors in series but to resistors in parallel. This comes from the definitions of capacitance and resistance. Capacitance indicates how good a capacitor is at storing charge for a given voltage, and resistance indicates how **bad** a resistor is at letting current through for a given voltage.

## Test yourself

15 The conductance $G$ of a resistor indicates how **good** a resistor is at letting current through for a given voltage. It is the reciprocal of the resistance: $G = \dfrac{1}{R}$.

Write down equations for the combined conductance $G_{total}$ of two resistors whose conductances are $G_1$ and $G_2$, connected:
a in series
b in parallel.

# Capacitor networks

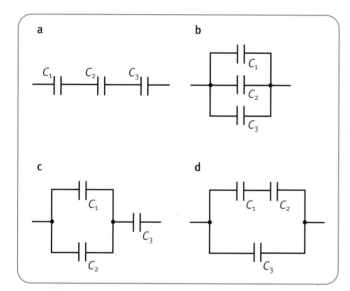

**Figure 24.14** Four ways to connect three capacitors.

There are four ways in which three capacitors may be connected together. These are shown in Figure **24.14**. The combined capacitance of the first two arrangements (three capacitors in series, three in parallel) can be calculated using the formulae above. The other combinations must be dealt with in a different way:

- Figure **24.14a** – All in series. Calculate $C_{total}$ as in Table **24.3**.
- Figure **24.14b** – All in parallel. Calculate $C_{total}$ as in Table **24.3**.
- Figure **24.14c** – Calculate $C_{total}$ for the two capacitors of capacitances $C_1$ and $C_2$, which are connected in

parallel, and then take account of the third capacitor of capacitance $C_3$, which is connected in series.
- Figure **24.14d** – Calculate $C_{total}$ for the two capacitors of capacitances $C_1$ and $C_2$, which are connected in series, and then take account of the third capacitor of capacitance $C_3$, which is connected in parallel.

These are the same approaches as would be used for networks of resistors.

## Test yourself

16 For each of the four circuits shown in Figure 24.14, calculate the total capacitance in μF if each capacitor has capacitance 100 μF.

17 Given a number of 100 μF capacitors, how might you connect networks to give the following values of capacitance:
a 400 μF
b 25 μF
c 250 μF?

(Note that, in each case, there is more than one correct answer; try to find the answer that requires the minimum number of capacitors.)

18 You have three capacitors of capacitances 100 pF, 200 pF and 600 pF. Determine the maximum and minimum values of capacitance that you can make by connecting them together to form a network. State how they should be connected in each case.

19 Calculate the capacitance in μF of the network of capacitors shown in Figure 24.15.

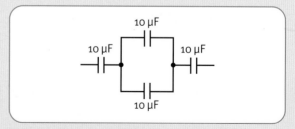

**Figure 24.15** A capacitor network – see Test yourself Q **19**.

## Sharing charge, sharing energy

If a capacitor is charged and then connected to a second capacitor (Figure **24.16**), what happens to the charge and the energy that it stores? Note that, when the capacitors are connected together, they are in parallel, because they have the same p.d. across them. Their combined capacitance $C_{total}$ is equal to the sum of their individual capacitances. Now we can think about the charge stored, $Q$. This is shared between the two capacitors; the total amount of charge stored must remain the same, since charge is conserved. The charge is shared between the two capacitors in proportion to their capacitances. Now the p.d. can be calculated from $V = \dfrac{Q}{C}$ and the energy from $W = \frac{1}{2}CV^2$

If we look at a numerical example, we find an interesting result (Worked example 3).

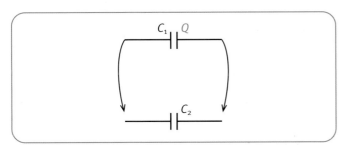

**Figure 24.16** Capacitor of capacitance $C_1$ is charged and then connected across $C_2$.

### Worked example

3 Consider two 100 mF capacitors. One is charged to 10 V, disconnected from the power supply, and then connected across the other. Calculate the energy stored by the combination.

**Step 1** Calculate the charge and energy stored for the single capacitor.

initial charge $Q = VC = 10 \times 100 \times 10^{-3} = 1.0\,C$

initial stored energy $\frac{1}{2}CV^2 = \frac{1}{2} \times 100 \times 10^2$

$$= 5.0\,J$$

*continued* ⋯⟶

**Step 2** Calculate the final p.d. across the capacitors. The capacitors are in parallel and have a total charge stored of 1.0 C.

$$C_{total} = C_1 + C_2 = 100 + 100 = 200\,mF$$

The p.d. $V$ can be determined using $Q = VC$.

$$V = \frac{Q}{C} = \frac{1.0}{200} \times 10^{-3} = 5.0\,V$$

This is not surprising because the charge is shared equally, with the original capacitor losing half of its charge.

**Step 3** Now calculate the total energy stored by the capacitors.

total energy $\frac{1}{2}CV^2 = \frac{1}{2} \times 200 \times 10^{-3} \times 5.0^2$

$$= 2.5\,J$$

The charge stored remains the same, but half of the stored energy is lost. This energy is lost in the connecting wires as heat as electrons migrate between the capacitors.

Figure **24.17** shows an analogy to the situation described in Worked example **3**. Capacitors are represented by containers of water. A wide (high capacitance) container is filled to a certain level (p.d.). It is then connected to a container with a smaller capacitance, and the levels equalise. (The p.d. is the same for each.) Notice that the potential energy of the water has decreased, because the height of its centre of gravity above the base level has decreased. Energy is dissipated as heat, as there is friction both within the moving water and between the water and the container.

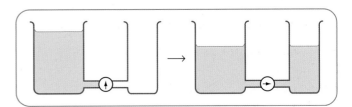

**Figure 24.17** An analogy for the sharing of charge between capacitors.

20 Three capacitors, each of capacitance $120\,\mu F$, are connected together in series. This network is then connected to a $10\,kV$ supply. Calculate:
   a their combined capacitance in $\mu F$
   b the charge stored
   c the total energy stored.

21 A $20\,\mu F$ capacitor is charged up to $200\,V$ and then disconnected from the supply. It is then connected across a $5.0\,\mu F$ capacitor. Calculate:
   a the combined capacitance of the two capacitors in $\mu F$
   b the charge they store
   c the p.d. across the combination
   d the energy dissipated when they are connected together.

## Capacitance of isolated bodies

It is not just capacitors that have capacitance – all bodies have capacitance. Yes, even you have capacitance! You may have noticed that, particularly in dry conditions, you may become charged up, perhaps by rubbing against a synthetic fabric. You are at a high voltage and store a significant amount of charge. Discharging yourself by touching an earthed metal object would produce a spark.

If we consider a conducting sphere of radius $r$ insulated from its surroundings and carrying a charge $Q$ it will have a potential at its surface of $V$, where

$$V = \frac{1}{4\pi\varepsilon_0}\,\frac{Q}{r}$$

Since $C = \dfrac{Q}{V}$, it follows that the capacitance of a sphere $C = 4\pi\varepsilon_0 r$.

22 Estimate the capacitance of the Earth given that it has a radius of $6.4 \times 10^6\,m$.

## Summary

☐ Capacitors are constructed from two metal sheets ('plates'), separated by an insulating material. They store charge.
☐ For a capacitor, the charge stored is directly proportional to the p.d. between the plates: $Q = VC$.
☐ Capacitance is the charge stored per unit of p.d.
☐ A farad is a coulomb per volt: $1\,F = 1\,C\,V^{-1}$.
☐ Capacitors store energy. The energy $W$ stored at p.d. $V$ is:

$$W = \tfrac{1}{2}QV = \tfrac{1}{2}CV^2 = \tfrac{1}{2}\frac{Q^2}{C}$$

The formula $W = \tfrac{1}{2}QV$ is deduced from the area under a graph of potential difference against charge.
☐ For capacitors connected in parallel and in series, the combined capacitances are as follows:

parallel:   $C_{total} = C_1 + C_2 + C_3 + \cdots$

series:   $\dfrac{1}{C_{total}} = \dfrac{1}{C_1} + \dfrac{1}{C_2} + \dfrac{1}{C_3} + \cdots$

These formulae are derived from conservation of charge and addition of p.d.s.

# End-of-chapter questions

1   A 470 µF capacitor is connected across the terminals of a battery of e.m.f. 9 V.
    Calculate the charge on the plates of the capacitor.

2   Calculate the p.d. across the terminals of a 2200 µF capacitor when it has a charge of 0.033 C
    on its plates.

3   Calculate the capacitance of a capacitor if it stores a charge of 2.0 C when there is a
    potential difference of 5000 V across its plates.

4   Calculate the energy stored when a 470 µF capacitor has a potential difference of 12 V
    across its plates.

5   Calculate the energy stored on a capacitor if it stores 1.5 mC of charge when there is
    a potential difference of 50 V across it.

6   A 5000 µF capacitor has a p.d. of 24 V across its plates.
    a   Calculate the energy stored on the capacitor.
    b   The capacitor is briefly connected across a bulb and half the charge flows off the capacitor. Calculate
        the energy dissipated in the lamp.

7   A 4700 µF capacitor has a p.d. of 12 V across its terminals. It is connected to a resistor
    and the charge leaks away through the resistor in 2.5 s.
    a   Calculate the energy stored on the capacitor.
    b   Calculate the charge stored on the capacitor.
    c   Estimate the average current through the resistor.
    d   Estimate the resistance of the resistor.
    e   Suggest why the last two quantities can only be estimates.

8   An electronic engineer is designing a circuit in which a capacitor of capacitance of 4700 µF is to
    be connected across a potential difference of 9.0 V. He has four 4700 µF, 6 V capacitors available.

    Draw a diagram to show how the four capacitors could be used for this purpose.

9   Calculate the different capacitances that can be made from three 100 µF capacitors. For each value,
    draw the network that is used.

**10** Figure 24.18 shows three capacitors connected in series with a cell of e.m.f. 1.5 V.

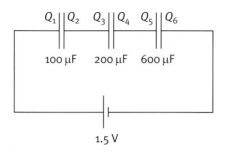

Figure 24.18 For End-of-chapter Q 10.

    **a** Calculate the charges $Q_1$ to $Q_6$ on each of the plates.
    **b** Calculate the p.d. across each capacitor.

# Exam-style questions

**1**   **a** State **one** use of a capacitor in a simple electric circuit.                                              [1]
      **b** The diagram shows a circuit used to investigate the discharge of a capacitor and the graph shows the change in current with time when the capacitor is discharged.

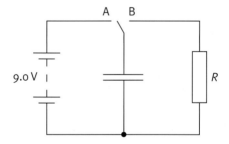

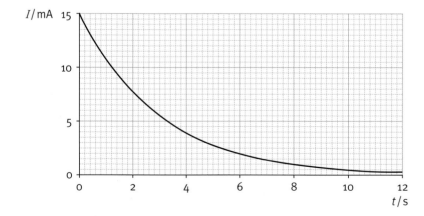

      **i** Deduce the resistance $R$ of the resistor.                                            [2]
      **ii** Explain why the current decreases as the capacitor discharges.              [2]

   **iii** The charge on the capacitor is equal to the area under the graph. Estimate the charge on the capacitor when the potential difference across it is 9.0 V. [2]

   **iv** Calculate the capacitance of the capacitor. [2]

**2** The spherical dome on a Van de Graaff generator is placed near an earthed metal plate. The dome has a diameter of 40 cm and the potential at its surface is 54 kV.

   **a i** Calculate the charge on the dome. [2]

    **ii** Calculate the capacitance of the dome. [2]

The metal plate is moved slowly towards the dome and it discharges through the plate. The graph in the diagram shows how the potential at the surface of the sphere changes during the discharge.

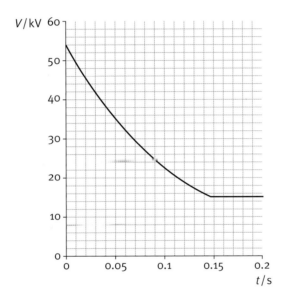

   **b** Calculate the energy that is dissipated during the discharge. [4]

   **c** Suggest why the discharge ceases while there is still some charge on the dome. [2]

**3** **a** Show that the capacitance $C$ of an isolated conducting sphere is given by the formula:

$$C = 4\pi\varepsilon_0 r$$ [2]

The diagram shows two identical conducting brass spheres of radius 10 cm mounted on insulating stands. Sphere A has a charge of $+5.0 \times 10^{-8}$ C and sphere B is uncharged.

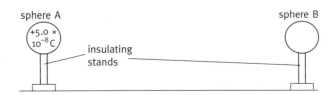

**b i** Calculate the potential at the surface of sphere A. [2]
   **ii** Calculate the energy stored on sphere A. [2]

Sphere B is brought up to sphere A and is touched on it so that the charge is shared between the two spheres, before being removed to its original position.

**c i** Calculate the energy stored on each sphere. [3]
   **ii** Suggest why there is a change in the total energy of the system. [1]

**4 a** Define the term **capacitance** of a capacitor. [2]
   **b** The diagram shows a circuit which can be used to measure the capacitance of a capacitor.

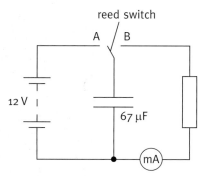

The reed switch vibrates back and forth at a frequency of 50 Hz. Each time it makes contact with A the capacitor is charged by the battery so that there is a p.d. of 12 V across it. Each time it makes contact with B it is fully discharged through the resistor.

   **i** Calculate the charge that is stored on the capacitor when there is a p.d. of 12 V across it. [2]
   **ii** Calculate the current in the resistor. [2]
   **iii** Calculate the power in the milliammeter. [3]
   **c** A second capacitor of the same value is connected in series with the first capacitor. Discuss the effect on both the current recorded and the power dissipated in the resistor. [4]

## Objectives

After studying this chapter, you should be able to:

- [ ] describe a magnetic field as a field of force and use field lines to represent a field
- [ ] determine the magnitude and direction of the force on a current-carrying conductor in a magnetic field
- [ ] define magnetic flux density and describe how it can be measured using a current balance
- [ ] explain the forces between current-carrying conductors

## Magnets and currents

The train shown in Figure 25.1 is supported at a precise distance above the track by computer-controlled electromagnets. In this chapter, we will look at magnetic forces and fields, how they arise, and how they interact.

Figure 25.1 This high-speed train is magnetically levitated so that it avoids friction with the track.

## Producing and representing magnetic fields

A magnetic field exists wherever there is force on a magnetic pole. As we saw with electric and gravitational fields, a magnetic field is a field of force.

You can make a magnetic field in two ways: using a permanent magnet, or using an electric current. You should be familiar with the magnetic field patterns of bar magnets (Figure 25.2). These can be shown using iron filings or plotting compasses.

We represent magnetic field patterns by drawing magnetic field lines.

- The magnetic field lines come out of north poles and go into south poles.
- The direction of a field line at any point in the field shows the direction of the force that a 'free' magnetic north pole would experience at that point.
- The field is strongest where the field lines are closest together.

An electromagnet makes use of the magnetic field created by an electric current (Figure 25.3a). A coil is used because this concentrates the magnetic field. One end becomes a north pole (field lines emerging), while the other end is the south pole. Another name for a coil like this is a **solenoid**. The field pattern for the solenoid looks very similar to that of a bar magnet (see Figure 25.2a), with field lines emerging from a north pole at one end and returning to a south pole at the other. The strength of the magnetic field of a solenoid can be greatly increased by adding a core made of a ferrous (iron-rich) material. For example, an iron rod placed inside the solenoid can act as a core; when the current flows through the solenoid, the iron core itself becomes magnetised and this produces a much stronger field. A flat coil (Figure 25.3b) has a similar field to that of a solenoid.

If we unravel an electromagnet, we get a weaker field. This, too, can be investigated using iron filings or compasses. The magnetic field pattern for a long current-carrying wire is very different from that

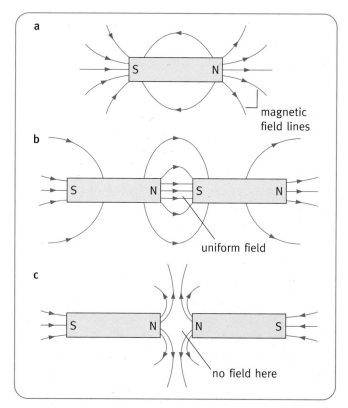

Figure 25.2 Magnetic field patterns: **a** for a bar magnet; **b** for two attracting bar magnets; **c** for two repelling bar magnets.

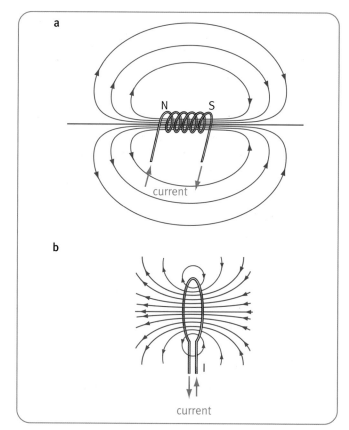

Figure 25.3 Magnetic field patterns for **a** a soleniod, and **b** a flat circular coil.

of a solenoid. The magnetic field lines shown in Figure 25.4 are circular, centred on the long current-carrying wire. Farther away from the wire, the field lines are drawn farther apart, representing the weaker field at this distance. Reversing the current reverses the direction of the field.

All magnetic fields are created by **moving** charges. (In the case of a wire, the moving charges are free electrons.) This is even true for a permanent bar magnet. In a permanent magnet, the magnetic field

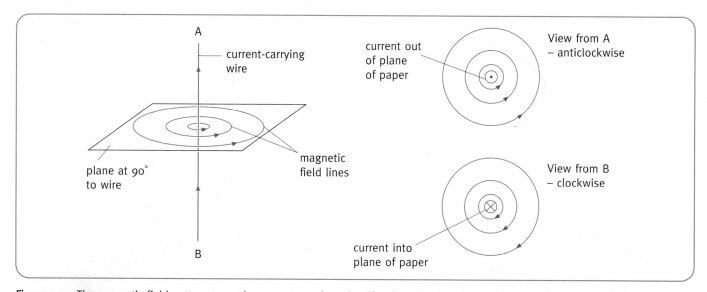

Figure 25.4 The magnetic field pattern around a current-carrying wire. The diagram also shows the convention used to indicate the direction of current.

is produced by the movement of electrons within the atoms of the magnet. Each electron represents a tiny current as it circulates around within its atom, and this current sets up a magnetic field. In a ferrous material such as iron, the weak fields due to all the electrons combine together to make a strong field which spreads out into the space beyond the magnet. In non-magnetic materials, the fields produced by the electrons cancel each other out.

## Field direction

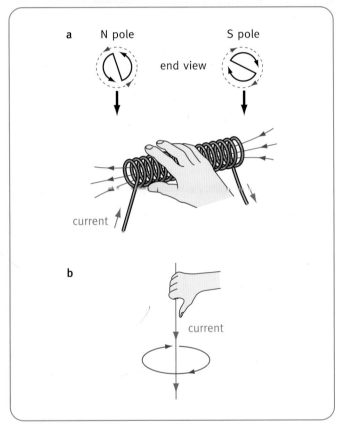

**Figure 25.5** Two rules for determining the direction of a magnetic field, **a** inside a solenoid and **b** around a current-carrying wire.

The idea that magnetic field lines emerge from north poles and go into south poles is simply a convention. Figure 25.5 shows some useful rules for remembering the direction of the magnetic field produced by a current.

The **right-hand grip rule** gives the direction of magnetic field lines in an electromagnet. Grip the coil, so that your fingers go around it following the direction of the current. Your thumb now points in

the direction of the field lines inside the coil, i.e. it points towards the electromagnet's north pole.

Another way to identify the poles of an electromagnet is to look at it end on, and decide which way round the current is flowing. The top diagrams in Figure 25.5 show how you can remember that clockwise is a south pole, anticlockwise is a north pole.

The circular field around a wire carrying a current does not have magnetic poles. To find the direction of the magnetic field you need to use another rule, the **right-hand rule**. Grip the wire with your right hand, pointing your thumb in the direction of the current. Your fingers curl around in the direction of the magnetic field.

For the straight wire in Figure 25.5, the thumb points downwards in the direction of the current. The fingers curl round clockwise as viewed from above. The curling around from the palm of the hand to the fingers shows you the direction of the magnetic field. This rule can also be applied to the solenoid in Figure 25.5. If you grip the solenoid at one end with the thumb of your right hand pointing in the direction of the current, your fingers curl round and point down the middle of the solenoid in the direction of the field.

Notice that the right-hand grip rule and the right-hand rule are slightly different rules, but each can give the direction of the magnetic field around a current-carrying wire.

### Test yourself

1 Sketch the magnetic field pattern around a long straight wire carrying an electric current. Now, alongside this first sketch, draw a second sketch to show the field pattern if the current flowing is doubled and its direction reversed.

2 Sketch the diagram in Figure 25.6, and label the north and south poles of the electromagnet. Show on your sketch the direction of the magnetic field (as shown by the needle of a plotting compass) at each of the positions A, B, C and D.

*continued* ⋯⟶

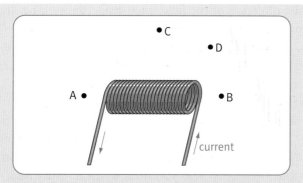

**Figure 25.6** A current-carrying solenoid. For Test yourself Q 2.

**3** State which of the pairs of electromagnets shown in Figure 25.7 attract one another, and which repel.

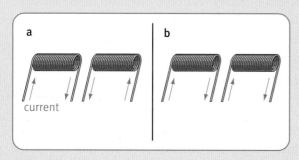

**Figure 25.7** Two pairs of solenoids. For Test yourself Q 3.

# Magnetic force

A current-carrying wire is surrounded by a magnetic field. This magnetic field interacts with an external magnetic field, giving rise to a force on the conductor, just like the fields of two interacting magnets. The simplest situation is shown in Figure 25.8.

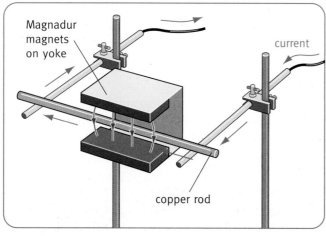

**Figure 25.8** The copper rod is free to roll along the two horizontal aluminium 'rails'.

The magnets create a fairly uniform magnetic field. As soon as the current in the copper rod is switched on, the rod starts to roll, showing that a force is acting on it.

We use **Fleming's left-hand (motor) rule** to predict the direction of the force on the current-carrying conductor. There are three things here, all of which are mutually at right angles to each other – the magnetic field, the current in the rod, and the force on the rod. These can be represented by holding the thumb and the first two fingers of your left hand so that they are mutually at right angles (Figure 25.9). Your thumb and fingers then represent:

- thuMb – direction of Motion
- First finger – direction of external magnetic Field
- seCond finger – direction of conventional Current

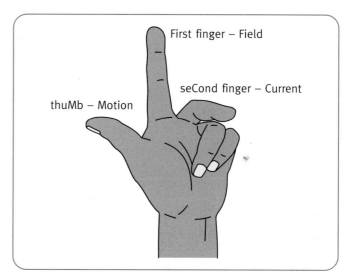

**Figure 25.9** Fleming's left-hand (motor) rule.

If the thumb and first two fingers of the left hand are held at right angles to one another, with the First finger pointing in the direction of the Field and seCond finger in the direction of the Current, then the thuMb points in the direction of the Motion or force.

You should practise using your left hand to check that the rule correctly predicts these directions.

We can explain this force by thinking about the magnetic fields of the magnets and the current-carrying conductor. These fields combine or interact to produce the force on the rod.

Figure 25.10 shows:

- the external magnetic field of the magnets
- the magnetic field of the current-carrying conductor
- the combined fields of the current-carrying conductor and the magnets.

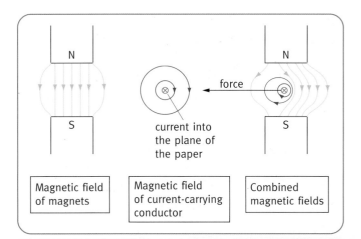

**Figure 25.10** In the field of a permanent magnet, a current-carrying conductor experiences a force in accordance with Fleming's left-hand rule. The fields due to the permanent magnet and the current (left and centre) combine as shown on the right.

If you think of the magnetic field lines as elastic bands then you can see why the wire is pushed out in the direction shown.

The production of this force is known as the **motor effect**, because this force is used in electric motors. In a simple motor, a current in a coil produces a magnetic field; this field interacts with a second field produced by a permanent magnet.

## Test yourself

4 Figure 25.11 shows three examples of current-carrying conductors in magnetic fields. For each example, decide whether there will be a magnetic force on the conductor. If there is a force, in what direction will it act?

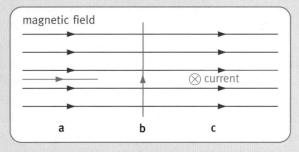

**Figure 25.11** Three conductors in a magnetic field.

# Magnetic flux density

In electric or gravitational field diagrams, the strength of the field is indicated by the separation between the field lines. The field is strongest where the field lines are closest together. The same is also true for magnetic fields. The **strength** of a magnetic field is known as its **magnetic flux density**. (You can imagine this quantity to represent the number of magnetic field lines passing through a region per unit area.) The magnetic flux density is greater close to the pole of a bar magnet, and gets smaller as you move away from it.

The symbol used for magnetic flux density is $B$ and its unit is the **tesla** (T).

We define gravitational field strength $g$ at a point as the force per unit mass:

$$g = \frac{F}{m}$$

Electric field strength $E$ is defined as the force per unit positive charge:

$$E = \frac{F}{Q}$$

In a similar way, magnetic flux density is defined in terms of the magnetic force experienced by a current-carrying conductor placed at **right angles** to a magnetic field. For a uniform magnetic field, the flux density $B$ is defined by the equation:

$$B = \frac{F}{Il}$$

where $F$ is the force experienced by a current-carrying conductor, $I$ is the current in the conductor and $l$ is the length of the conductor in the uniform magnetic field of flux density $B$. The direction of the force $F$ is given by Fleming's left-hand rule.

Magnetic flux density is defined as follows:

The magnetic flux density at a point in space is the force experienced per unit length by a long straight conductor carrying unit current and placed at right angles to the field at that point.

The unit for magnetic flux density is $\mathrm{N\,A^{-1}\,m^{-1}}$ or simply tesla (T). Note that $1\,\mathrm{T} = 1\,\mathrm{N\,A^{-1}\,m^{-1}}$.

The tesla is defined as follows:

The magnetic flux density is $1\,\mathrm{T}$ when a wire carrying a current of $1\,\mathrm{A}$ placed at right angles to the magnetic field experiences a force of $1\,\mathrm{N}$ per metre of its length.

The force on the conductor is given by the equation:

$$F = BIl$$

Note that you can only use this equation when the field is at right angles to the current.

# Measuring magnetic flux density

The simplest device for measuring magnetic flux density $B$ is a Hall probe (Figure 25.12). When the probe is held so that the field lines are passing at right angles through the flat face of the probe, the meter gives a reading of the value of $B$. Some instruments are calibrated so that they give readings in microteslas (μT) or milliteslas (mT). Others are not calibrated, so you must either calibrate them, or use them to obtain relative measurements of $B$.

A Hall probe must be held so that the field lines are passing directly through it, at right angles to the flat surface of the probe (Figure 25.13). If the probe is not held in the correct orientation, the reading on the meter will be reduced.

A Hall probe works as follows: The probe itself is a slice of semiconductor (Figure 25.14). This material

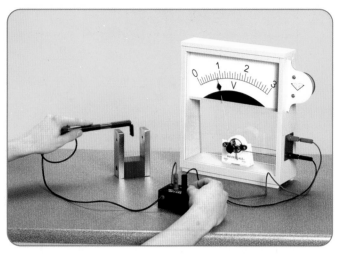

Figure 25.12 Using a Hall probe to measure the flux density between two magnets.

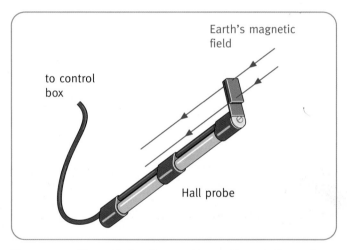

Figure 25.13 Magnetic flux lines must pass through the probe at 90° to the surface.

is used because the electrons move much faster in a semiconductor than in a metal for a given current, and so the effect is much greater. A small current flows through the probe from one end to the other. When a magnetic field is applied, the electrons are pushed sideways by the $BIl$ force, so that they accumulate along one side of the probe. This is detected as a small voltage across the probe – the greater the flux density of the field, the greater the voltage. The control box amplifies the voltage and it is displayed by the meter.

## The current balance

Figure 25.15 shows a simple arrangement that can be used to determine the flux density between two magnets. The magnetic field between these magnets is (roughly) uniform. The length $l$ of the current-carrying wire in the uniform magnetic field can be measured using a ruler.

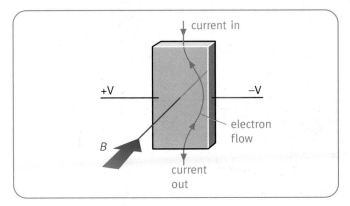

**Figure 25.14** Electrons are deflected as they move through the Hall probe.

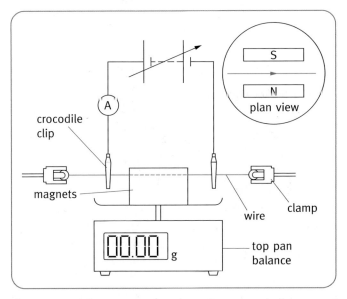

**Figure 25.15** An arrangement to determine magnetic flux density in the laboratory.

When there is no current in the wire, the magnet arrangement is placed on the top pan and the balance is zeroed. Now, when a current $I$ flows in the wire, its value is shown by the ammeter. The wire experiences an upward force and, according to Newton's third law of motion, there is an equal and opposite force on the magnets. The magnets are pushed downwards and a reading appears on the scale of the balance. The force $F$ is given by $mg$, where $m$ is the mass indicated on the balance in kilograms and $g$ is the acceleration of free fall ($9.81\,\mathrm{m\,s^{-2}}$).

Knowing $F$, $I$ and $l$, the magnetic flux density $B$ between the magnets can be determined using the equation:

$$B = \frac{F}{Il}$$

You can also use the arrangement in Figure **25.15** to show that force is directly proportional to the current.

A system like this in effect 'weighs' the force on the current-carrying conductor and is an example of a current balance. Another version of a current balance is shown in Figure **25.16**. This consists of a wire frame which is balanced on two pivots. When a current flows through the frame, the magnetic field pushes the frame downwards. By adding small weights to the other side of the frame, you can restore it to a balanced position.

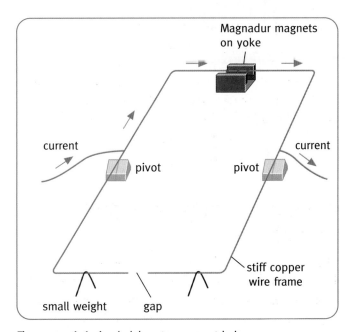

**Figure 25.16** A simple laboratory current balance

## Test yourself

8  In the examples shown in the diagrams in Figure **25.17**, which current balances will tilt? Will the side carrying the current tilt upwards or downwards?

*continued ⋯⟶*

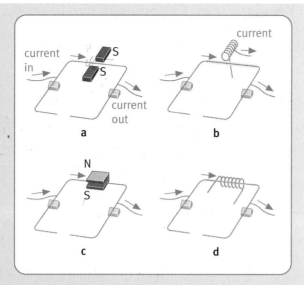

Figure 25.17 Four current balances – will they tip? For Test yourself Q **8**.

9 In the current balance shown in Figure 25.18, a current of 0.50 A is flowing. A student finds that a counterweight of mass 0.02 g is needed to restore balance. The section of the conductor in the field is 5.0 cm long. What is the flux density of the field?

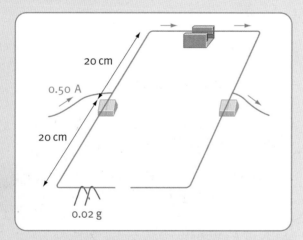

Figure 25.18 A current balance – see Test yourself Q **9**.

# Currents crossing fields

## At right angles

We explained the force on a current-carrying conductor in a field in terms of the interaction of the two magnetic fields: the field due to the current and the external field. Here is another, more abstract, way of thinking of this.

Whenever an electric current cuts across magnetic field lines (Figure **25.19**), a force is exerted on the current-carrying conductor. This helps us to remember that a conductor experiences no force when the current is parallel to the field.

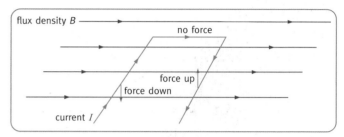

Figure 25.19 The force on a current-carrying conductor crossing a magnetic field.

This is a useful idea, because it saves us thinking about the field due to the current. In Figure **25.19**, we can see that there is only a force when the current cuts across the magnetic field lines.

This force is very important – it is the basis of electric motors. Worked example **1** shows why a current-carrying coil placed in a magnetic field rotates.

## Worked example

1 An electric motor has a rectangular loop of wire with the dimensions shown in Figure **25.20**. The loop is in a magnetic field of flux density 0.10 T. The current in the loop is 2.0 A. Calculate the torque that acts on the loop in the position shown.

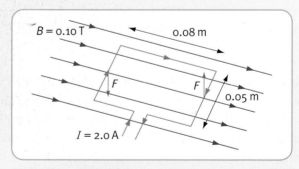

Figure 25.20 A simple electric motor – a current-carrying loop in a magnetic field.

**Step 1** The quantities we know are:

$$B = 0.10 \text{ T}, I = 2.0 \text{ A and } l = 0.05 \text{ m}$$

*continued ···▷*

**Step 2** Now we can calculate the force on one side of the loop using the equation $F = BIl$:

$$F = 0.10 \times 2.0 \times 0.05$$
$$= 0.01\,\text{N}$$

**Step 3** The two forces on opposite sides of the loop are equal and anti-parallel. In other words, they form a couple. From Chapter 4, you should recall that the torque (moment) of a couple is equal to the magnitude of one of the forces times the perpendicular distance between them. The two forces are separated by 0.08 m, so:

$$\text{torque} = \text{force} \times \text{separation}$$
$$= 0.01 \times 0.08 = 8.0 \times 10^{-4}\,\text{N m}$$

## Test yourself

10 A wire of length 50 cm carrying a current of 2.4 A lies at right angles to a magnetic field of flux density 5.0 mT. Calculate the force on the wire.

11 The coil of an electric motor is made up of 200 turns of wire carrying a current of 1.0 A. The coil is square, with sides of length 20 cm, and it is placed in a magnetic field of flux density 0.05 T.
   **a** Determine the maximum force exerted on the side of the coil.
   **b** In what position must the coil be for this force to have its greatest turning effect?
   **c** List four ways in which the motor could be made more 'powerful' – that is, have greater torque.

## At an angle other than 90°

Now we must consider the situation where the current-carrying conductor cuts across a magnetic field at an angle other than a right angle. In Figure 25.21, the force gets weaker as the conductor is moved round from OA to OB, to OC and finally

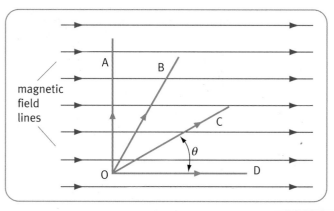

**Figure 25.21** The force on a current-carrying conductor depends on the angle it makes with the magnetic field lines.

to OD. In the position OD, there is no force on the conductor. To calculate the force, we need to find the component of the magnetic flux density $B$ at right angles to the current. This component is $B\sin\theta$, where $\theta$ is the angle between the magnetic field and the current or the conductor. Substituting this into the equation $F = BIl$ gives:

$$F = (B\sin\theta)Il$$

or simply:

$$F = BIl\sin\theta$$

Now look at Worked example 2.

## Worked example

2 A conductor OC (see Figure 25.21) of length 0.20 m lies at an angle $\theta$ of 25° to a magnetic field of flux density 0.050 T. Calculate the force on the conductor when it carries a current of 400 mA.

   **Step 1** Write down what you know, and what you want to know:

   $B = 0.050\,\text{T}$        $l = 0.20\,\text{m}$

   $I = 400\,\text{mA} = 0.40\,\text{A}$     $\theta = 25°$

   $F = ?$

*continued* ⋯→

**25 Magnetic fields and electromagnetism**    379

**Step 2** Write down the equation, substitute values and solve:

$$F = BIl\sin\theta$$

$$F = 0.050 \times 0.40 \times 0.20 \times \sin 25° \approx 1.7 \times 10^{-3} \, \text{N}$$

**Step 3** Give the direction of the force. The force acts at 90° to the field and the current, i.e. perpendicular to the page. The left-hand rule shows that it acts downwards into the plane of the paper.

Note that the component of $B$ parallel to the field is $B\cos\theta$, but this does not contribute to the force; there is no force when the field and current are parallel. The force $F$ is at right angles to both the current and the field.

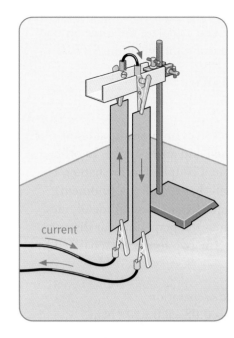
**Figure 25.23** Current flowing through two aluminium strips – their magnetic fields interact.

## Test yourself

12 What force will be exerted on each of the currents shown in Figure 25.22, and in what direction will each force act?

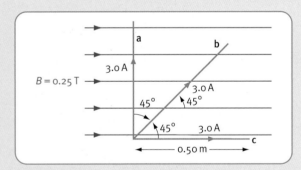

**Figure 25.22** Three currents in a magnetic field.

# Forces between currents

Any electric current has a magnetic field around it. If we have two currents, each will have its own magnetic field, and we might expect these to interact. You can observe the attraction and repulsion between two parallel currents using the equipment shown in Figure 25.23.

Two long thin strips of aluminium foil are mounted so that they are parallel and a small distance apart. By connecting them in series with a power supply, you can make a current flow through first one and then the other. By changing the connections, you can make the current flow first in the same direction through both strips (parallel currents) and then in opposite directions (anti-parallel currents).

If you try this out, you will observe the strips of foil either bending towards each other or away from each other. (Foil is used because it is much more flexible than wire.)

You should find that parallel currents attract one another, while anti-parallel currents repel. This may seem surprising, since we are used to opposite charges attracting, and opposite magnetic poles attracting. Now we have found that opposite currents repel one another.

## Explaining the forces

There are two ways to understand the origin of these forces. In the first, we draw the magnetic fields around two current-carrying conductors (Figure 25.24). The first part of the diagram shows two unlike (anti-parallel) currents, one flowing into the page, the other flowing out of the page. Their magnetic fields circle round, and in the space between the wires there is an extra-strong field. We imagine the field lines squashed together, and the result is that they push the wires apart. The diagram shows the resultant field, and the repulsive forces on the two wires.

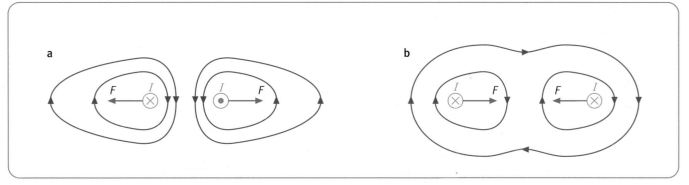

**Figure 25.24** The forces on parallel currents.

The second part of Figure 25.24 shows the same idea, but for two like (parallel) currents. In the space between the two wires, the magnetic fields cancel out. The wires are pushed together.

The other way to explain the forces between the currents is to use the idea of the motor effect. Figure 25.25 again shows two like currents, $I_1$ and $I_2$, but this time we only consider the magnetic field of one of them, $I_1$. The second current $I_2$ is flowing across the magnetic field of $I_1$; from the diagram, you can see that $B$ is at right angles to $I_2$. Hence there will be a force on $I_2$ (the $BIl$ force), and we can find its direction using Fleming's left-hand rule. The arrow shows the direction of the force, which is towards $I_1$. Similarly, there will be a $BIl$ force on $I_1$, directed towards $I_2$.

These two forces are equal and opposite to one another. They are an example of an action and reaction pair, as described by Newton's third law of motion.

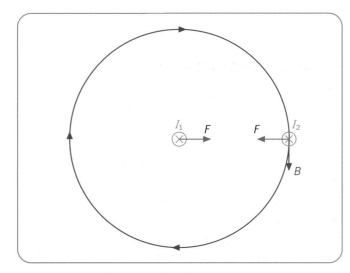

**Figure 25.25** Explaining the force between two currents.

## Test yourself

13 Two flat circular coils of wire are set up side by side, as shown in Figure 25.26. They are connected in series so that the same current flows around each, and in the same direction. Will the coils attract or repel one another? Explain your answer, first by describing the coils as electromagnets, and secondly by considering the forces between parallel currents. What will happen if the current is reversed in both coils?

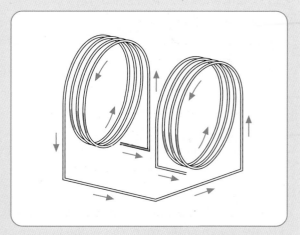

**Figure 25.26** Two coils carrying the same current – see Test yourself Q 13.

# Relating SI units

In this chapter, we have seen how one SI unit, the tesla, is defined in terms of three others, the amp, the metre and the newton. It is an essential feature of the SI system that all units are carefully defined; in particular, derived units such as the newton and tesla must be defined in terms of a set of more fundamental units called **base units**.

We met the idea of base units in Chapter 3. The SI system of units has seven base units of which you have met six. These are:

m    kg    s    A    K    mol

(The seventh is the candela, cd, the unit of luminous intensity.) Each base unit is carefully defined; for example, the ampere can be defined in terms of the magnetic force between two parallel wires carrying a current. The exact definition is not required, but you should know that the ampere is itself a base unit. Other units are known as **derived units**, and can be deduced from the base units. For example, as shown in Chapter 3, the newton is given by:

$$1\,N = 1\,kg\,m\,s^{-2}$$

Similarly, in this chapter, you have learned about the tesla, the unit of magnetic flux density, given by:

$$1\,T = 1\,N\,A^{-1}\,m^{-1} \text{ or } 1\,T = 1\,kg\,A^{-1}\,s^{-2}$$

If you learn formulae relating physical quantities, you can replace the quantities by their units to see how the units are defined. For example:

$$\text{force} = \text{mass} \times \text{acceleration} \quad F = ma \quad N = kg\,m\,s^{-2}$$

You should be able to picture how the different derived units form a logical sequence, as shown in Table 25.1.

| Base units | Derived units | because |
|---|---|---|
| m, kg, s | newton $N = kg\,m\,s^{-2}$ | $F = ma$ |
| | joule $J = kg\,m^2\,s^{-2}$ | $W = Fd$ |
| | watt $W = kg\,m^2\,s^{-3}$ | $P = \dfrac{W}{t}$ |
| m, kg, s, A | coulomb $C = A\,s$ | $Q = It$ |
| | volt $V = kg\,m^2\,A^{-1}\,s^{-3}$ | $V = \dfrac{W}{Q}$ |
| | tesla $T = kg\,A^{-1}\,s^{-2}$ | $B = \dfrac{F}{Il}$ |

**Table 25.1** How derived units relate to base units in the SI system.

## Summary

- ☐ Moving charges produce a magnetic field; this is electromagnetism.
- ☐ A current-carrying conductor has concentric magnetic field lines. The magnetic field pattern for a solenoid or flat coil resembles that of a bar magnet.
- ☐ The separation between magnetic field lines is an indication of the field's strength.
- ☐ Magnetic flux density $B$ is defined by the following equation:

$$B = \frac{F}{Il}$$

  where $F$ is the force experienced by a current-carrying conductor, $I$ is the current in the conductor and $l$ is the length of the conductor in the uniform magnetic field.
- ☐ The unit of magnetic flux density is the tesla (T). $1\,T = 1\,N\,A^{-1}\,m^{-1}$.
- ☐ The magnetic flux density is $1\,T$ when a wire carrying a current of $1\,A$ placed at right angles to the magnetic field experiences a force of $1\,N$ per metre of its length.
- ☐ The magnetic force on a current-carrying conductor is given by $F = BIl$ or $F = BIl\sin\theta$.
- ☐ The force on a current-carrying conductor can be used to measure the flux density of a magnetic field using a current balance.
- ☐ A force acts between current-carrying conductors due to the interaction of their magnetic fields.

# End-of-chapter questions

1  A current-carrying wire is placed in a uniform magnetic field.
   a  When does the wire experience the maximum force due to the magnetic field?
   b  When does the current-carrying wire experience no force due to the magnetic field?

2  A current-carrying conductor placed at right angles to a uniform magnetic field, experiences a force of $4.70 \times 10^{-3}$ N. Determine the force on the wire when, separately:
   a  the current in the wire is increased by a factor of 3.0
   b  the magnetic flux density is halved
   c  the length of the wire in the magnetic field is reduced to 40% of its original length.

3  A copper wire carrying a current of 1.2 A has 3.0 cm of its length placed in a uniform magnetic field, as shown in Figure 25.27. The force experienced by the wire is $3.8 \times 10^{-3}$ N when the angle between the wire and the magnetic field is 50°.

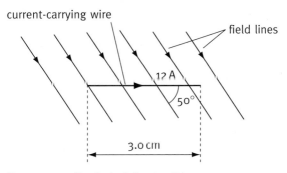

current-carrying wire

field lines

1.2 A

50°

3.0 cm

**Figure 25.27** For End-of-chapter Q 3.

   a  Calculate the magnetic field strength.
   b  What is the direction of the force experienced by the wire?

4  Figure 25.28 shows a view from above of two long, parallel strips of aluminium foil A and B, carrying a current downwards into the paper.

A                    B

**Figure 25.28** For End-of-chapter Q 4.

   a  On a copy of the diagram, draw the magnetic field around and between the two strips.
   b  State and explain the direction of the forces caused by the current in the strips.

5   Figure 25.29 shows a wire XY which carries a direct current. Plotting compass R, placed alongside the wire, points due north. Compass P is placed below the wire and compass Q is placed above the wire.

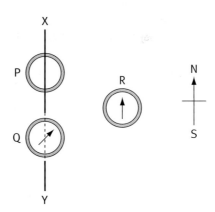

**Figure 25.29** For End-of-chapter Q 5.

   **a**  State the direction of the current in the wire.
   **b**  State in which direction compass P points.
   **c**  State in which direction compass Q points if the current in the wire is reversed.

# Exam-style questions

1   The diagram shows a rectangular metal frame PQRS placed in a uniform magnetic field.

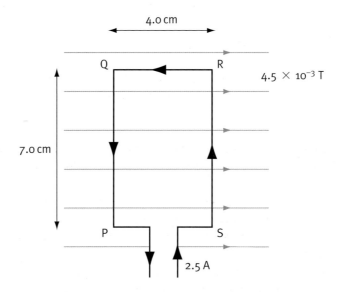

The magnetic flux density is $4.5 \times 10^{-3}$ T.

The current in the metal frame is 2.5 A.

a  Calculate the force experienced by side PQ of the frame. [3]

b  Suggest why side QR does not experience a force. [1]

c  Describe the motion of the frame immediately after the current in the frame is switched on. [2]

d  Calculate the maximum torque (moment) exerted about an axis parallel to side PQ. [2]

2   The diagram shows a current-carrying wire frame placed between a pair of Magnadur magnets on a yoke.

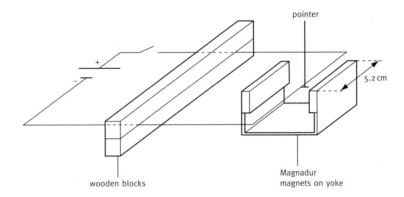

A current of 8.5 A in the wire causes the pointer to move vertically upwards. A small paper tape is attached on to the pointer. The paper tape is found to have a mass of 60 mg when the pointer returns to its initial position. The section of the wire between the poles of the magnetic has a length of 5.2 cm.

a  State the direction of the magnetic field. [1]

b  Calculate the force on the wire due to the magnetic field when it carries a current of 8.5 A. [2]

c  Calculate the magnetic flux density of the magnetic field between the poles of the magnet. [3]

d  Describe what happens to the frame if low-frequency alternating current passes through the wire. [1]

3   a  The size of the force acting on a wire carrying a current in a magnetic field is proportional to the size of the current in the wire. With the aid of a diagram describe how this can be demonstrated in a school laboratory. [5]

b  At a point on the Earth's surface the horizontal component of the Earth's magnetic field is $1.6 \times 10^{-5}$ T. A piece of wire 3.0 m long and of weight 0.020 N lies in an east–west direction on a laboratory bench. When a large current flows in the wire, the wire just lifts off the surface of the bench.

  i  State the direction of the current in the wire. [1]

  ii  Calculate the minimum current needed to lift the wire from the bench. [3]

**4** The diagram shows a fixed horizontal wire passing centrally between the poles of a permanent magnet that is placed on a top-pan balance. With no current flowing, the balance records a mass of 102.45 g. When a current of 4.0 A flows in the wire, the balance records a mass of 101.06 g.

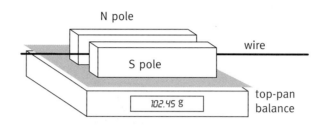

**a** Explain why the reading on the top-pan balance decreases when the current is switched on. [2]

**b** State and explain the direction of the current flow in the wire. [2]

**c** The length of the wire in the magnetic field is 5.0 cm. Calculate the average magnetic flux density between the poles of the magnet. [2]

**d** Sketch a graph, with balance reading on the vertical axis and current on the horizontal axis, to show how the balance reading changes when the current is altered. [2]

**5 a** Define **magnetic flux density** and explain the similarity with the definition of electric field strength. [3]

**b** Two thin horizontal wires are placed in a north–south direction. One wire is placed on a bench and the other wire is held 3.0 cm directly above the first wire.

   **i** Explain why the force exerted by the wire on the bench decreases when a current flows in the two wires. [3]

   **ii** The magnetic flux density $B$ at a distance $x$ from a long straight wire carrying a current $I$ is given by the expression $B = 2.0 \times 10^{-7}\dfrac{I}{x}$, where $x$ is in metres and $I$ in amps. When the current in each wire is 4.0 A, calculate the force per unit length on one wire due to the current in the other. [3]

# Charged particles

## Objectives

After studying this chapter, you should be able to:

☐ determine the magnitude and direction of the force on a charge moving in a magnetic field

☐ analyse the deflection of beams of charged particles in electric and magnetic fields

☐ explain the principles of methods of measuring speed, charge and charge-to-mass ratio for electrons

## Moving particles

The world of atomic physics is populated by a great variety of particles – electrons, protons, neutrons, positrons and many more. Many of these particles are electrically charged, and so their motion is influenced by electric and magnetic fields. Indeed, we use this fact to help us to distinguish one particle from another. Figure **26.1** shows the tracks of particles in a detector called a bubble chamber. A photon (no track) has entered from the top and collided with a proton; the resulting spray of nine particles shows up as the gently curving tracks moving downwards. The tracks curve because the particles are charged and are moving in a magnetic field. The tightly wound spiral tracks are produced by electrons which, because their mass is small, are more dramatically affected by the field.

In this chapter, we will look at how charged particles behave in electric and magnetic fields and how this knowledge can be used to control beams of

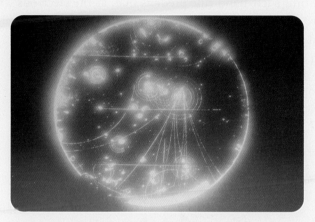

**Figure 26.1** A bubble chamber image of the tracks of sub-atomic particles. The tracks curve because the charged particles are affected by the presence of a magnetic field.

charged particles. At the end of the chapter, we will look at how this knowledge was used to discover the electron and to measure its charge and mass.

## Observing the force

You can use your knowledge of how charged particles and electric currents are affected by fields to interpret diagrams of moving particles. You must bear in mind that, by convention, the direction of conventional electric current is the direction of flow of positive charge. When electrons are moving, the conventional current is regarded as flowing in the opposite direction.

An electron beam tube (Figure **26.2**) can be used to demonstrate the magnetic force on a moving charge. A beam of electrons is produced by an 'electron gun', and magnets or electromagnets are used to apply a magnetic field.

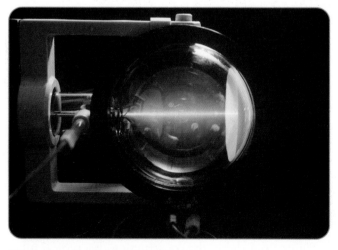

**Figure 26.2** An electron beam tube.

You can use such an arrangement to observe the effect of changing the strength and direction of the magnetic field, and the effect of reversing the field.

If you are able to observe a beam of electrons like this, you should find that the force on the electrons moving through the magnetic field can be predicted using Fleming's left-hand rule. In Figure **26.3**, a beam of electrons is moving from right to left, into a region where a magnetic field is directed into the plane of the paper. Since electrons are negatively charged, they represent a conventional current from left to right. Fleming's left-hand rule predicts that, as the electrons enter the field, the force on them will be upwards and so the beam will be deflected up the page. As the direction of the beam changes, so does the direction of the force. The force due to the magnetic field is always at 90° to the velocity of the electrons.

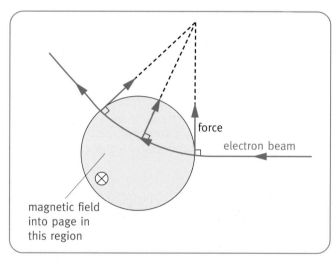

**Figure 26.3** A beam of electrons is deflected as it crosses a magnetic field. The magnetic field into the plane of the paper is represented by the cross in the circle.

It is this force that gives rise to the motor effect. The electrons in a wire experience a force when they flow across a magnetic field, and they transfer the force to the wire itself.

## Using electron beams

Oscilloscopes, as well as some computer monitors and television sets, make use of beams of electrons. Electrons are moved about using magnetic and electric fields, and the result can be a rapidly changing image on the screen.

Figure **26.4** shows the construction of a typical tube. The electron gun has a heated cathode. The positively

charged anode attracts electrons from the negative cathode, and they pass through the anode to form a narrow beam in the space beyond. The direction of the beam can be changed using an electric field between two plates (as shown in Figure **26.4**), or a magnetic field created by electromagnetic coils.

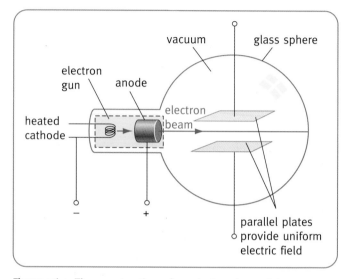

**Figure 26.4** The construction of an electron beam tube.

### Test yourself

1  In the diagram in Figure **26.5**, radiation from a radioactive material passes through a region of uniform magnetic field. Identify which tracks are those of α-particles (alpha-particles, positive charge), β-particles (beta-particles, negative charge) and γ-rays (gamma-rays, no charge).

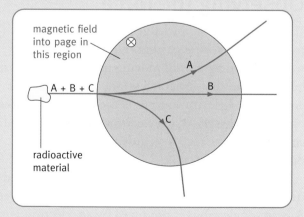

**Figure 26.5** Three types of radiation passing through a magnetic field.

## The magnetic force on a moving charge

We can make an intelligent guess about the factors that determine the size of the force on a moving charge in a uniform magnetic field (Figure 26.6). It will depend on:

- the magnetic flux density $B$ (strength of the magnetic field)
- the charge $Q$ on the particle
- the speed $v$ of the particle.

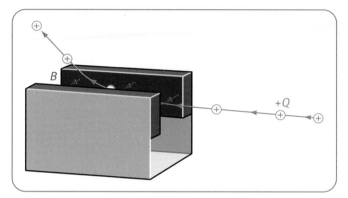

**Figure 26.6** The path of a charged particle is curved in a magnetic field.

The magnetic force $F$ on a moving particle at right angles to a magnetic field is given by the equation:

$$F = BQv$$

The direction of the force can be determined from Fleming's left-hand rule. The force $F$ is always at 90° to the velocity of the particle. Consequently, the path described by the particle will be an arc of a circle.

If the charged particle is moving at an angle $\theta$ to the magnetic field, this equation becomes:

$$F = BQv\sin\theta$$

We can show that the two equations $F = BIl$ and $F = BQv$ are consistent with one another, as follows.

Since current $I$ is the rate of flow of charge, we can write:

$$I = \frac{Q}{t}$$

Substituting in $F = BIl$ gives:

$$F = \frac{BQl}{t}$$

Now, $\frac{l}{t}$ is the speed $v$ of the moving particle, so we can write:

$$F = BQv$$

For an electron, whose charge is $-e$, the magnitude of the force on it is:

$$F = Bev \quad (e = 1.6 \times 10^{-19}\,\text{C})$$

The force on a moving charge is sometimes called 'the $Bev$ force', and it is really no different from 'the $BIl$ force'.

Here is an important reminder: The force $F$ is always at right-angles to the particle's velocity $v$, and its direction can be found using the left-hand rule (Figure 26.7).

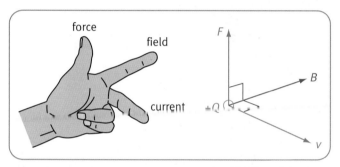

**Figure 26.7** Fleming's left hand rule, applied to a moving positive charge.

## Orbiting charges

Consider a charged particle moving at right angles to a uniform magnetic field. It will describe a circular path because the magnetic force $F$ is always perpendicular to its velocity. We can describe $F$ as a **centripetal force**, because it is always directed towards the centre of the circle.

Figure **26.8** shows a fine-beam tube. In this tube, a beam of fast-moving electrons is produced by an electron gun. This is similar to the cathode and anode shown in Figure **26.4,** but in this case the beam is directed vertically downwards as it emerges from the gun. It enters the spherical tube, which has a uniform horizontal magnetic field. The beam is at right angles to the field and the *Bev* force pushes it round in a circle.

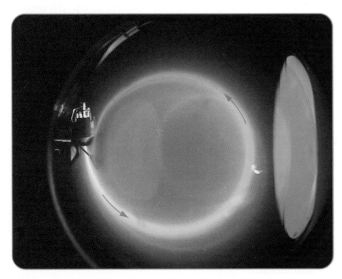

**Figure 26.8** In this fine-beam tube, a beam of electrons is bent around into a circular orbit by an external magnetic field. The beam is shown up by the presence of a small amount of gas in the tube. (The electrons travel in an anticlockwise direction.)

The fact that the *Bev* force acts as a centripetal force gives us a clue as to how we can calculate the radius of the orbit of a charged particle in a uniform magnetic field. The centripetal force on the charged particle is given by:

$$\text{centripetal force} = \frac{mv^2}{r}$$

The centripetal force is provided by the magnetic force *Bev*. Therefore:

$$Bev = \frac{mv^2}{r}$$

Cancelling and rearranging to find $r$ gives:

$$r = \frac{mv}{Be}$$

You can also write this equation in terms of the momentum $p$ of the particle, that is:

$$p = Ber$$

The equation $r = \dfrac{mv}{Be}$ shows that:

- faster-moving particles move in bigger circles ($r \propto v$);
- particles with greater masses also move in bigger circles (they have more inertia: $r \propto m$);
- a stronger field makes the particles move in tighter circles ($r \propto \dfrac{1}{B}$).

This is made use of in a variety of scientific applications, such as particle accelerators and mass spectrometers. It can also be used to find the charge-to-mass ratio $\dfrac{e}{m}$ of an electron.

## The charge-to-mass ratio of an electron

Experiments to find the mass of an electron first involve finding the charge-to-mass ratio $\dfrac{e}{m}$. This is known as the specific charge on the electron – the word 'specific' here means 'per unit mass'.

Using the equation for an electron travelling in a circle in a magnetic field, $\dfrac{e}{m_e} = \dfrac{v}{Br}$. Clearly, measurements of $v$, $B$ and $r$ are needed to measure $\dfrac{e}{m}$. There are difficulties in measuring $B$ and $r$. For example, it is difficult to measure $r$ with a rule outside the tube in Figure **26.8** because of parallax error. Also, $v$ must be measured, and you need to know how this is done. One way is to use the cathode–anode voltage $V_{ca}$. This p.d. causes each electron to accelerate as it moves from the cathode to the anode. If an individual electron has charge $-e$ then an amount of work $e \times V_{ca}$ is done on each electron. This is its kinetic energy as it leaves the anode:

$$eV_{ca} = \tfrac{1}{2} m_e v^2$$

where $m_e$ is electron mass and $v$ is the speed of the electron

Eliminating $v$ from the two equations, $eV_{ca} = \tfrac{1}{2} m_e v^2$ and $r = \dfrac{m_e v}{Be}$, gives:

$$\frac{e}{m_e} = \frac{2V_{ca}}{r^2 B^2}$$

Hence, if we measure $V_{ca}$, $r$ and $B$, we can calculate $\frac{e}{m_e}$. As we shall see shortly, the electron charge $e$ can be measured more directly, and this allows us to calculate the electron mass $m_e$ from the value of $\frac{e}{m_e}$.

## Worked example

1  An electron is travelling at right angles to a uniform magnetic field of flux density 1.2 mT. The speed of the electron is $8.0 \times 10^6\,\mathrm{m\,s^{-1}}$. Calculate the radius of circle described by this electron. (For an electron, charge $e = 1.6 \times 10^{-19}\,\mathrm{C}$ and mass $m_e = 9.11 \times 10^{-31}\,\mathrm{kg}$.)

**Step 1** Calculate the magnetic force on the electron.

$$F = Bev = 1.2 \times 10^{-3} \times 1.6 \times 10^{-19} \times 8.0 \times 10^6$$

$$F = 1.536 \times 10^{-15}\,\mathrm{N} \approx 1.5 \times 10^{-15}\,\mathrm{N}$$

**Step 2** Use your knowledge of motion in a circle to determine the radius $r$.

$$F = \frac{mv^2}{r}$$

Therefore:

$$r = \frac{mv^2}{F} = \frac{9.11 \times 10^{-31} \times (8.0 \times 10^6)^2}{1.536 \times 10^{15}}$$

$$r \approx 3.8 \times 10^{-2}\,\mathrm{m} \quad (3.8\,\mathrm{cm})$$

Note: The same result could have been obtained simply by using the equation:

$$r = \frac{mv}{Be}$$

## Test yourself

4  Look at the photograph of the electron beam in the fine-beam tube (Figure **26.8**). In which direction is the magnetic field (into or out of the plane of the photograph)?

*continued* ⋯➔

5  The particles in the circular beam shown in Figure **26.8** all travel round in the same orbit. What can you deduce about their mass, charge and speed?

6  An electron beam in a vacuum tube is directed at right angles to a magnetic field, so that it travels along a circular path. Predict the effect on the size and shape of the path that would be produced (separately) by each of the following changes:
   **a** increasing the magnetic flux density
   **b** reversing the direction of the magnetic field
   **c** slowing down the electrons
   **d** tilting the beam, so that the electrons have a component of velocity along the magnetic field.

# Electric and magnetic fields

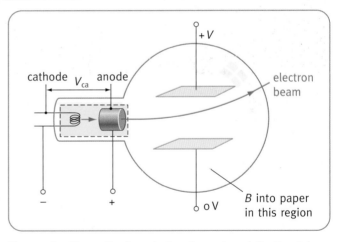

Figure **26.9** The path of an electron beam in a deflection tube.

A deflection tube (Figure **26.9**) is designed to show a beam of electrons passing through a combination of electric and magnetic fields. By adjusting the strengths of the electric and magnetic fields, you can balance the two forces on the electrons, and the beam will remain horizontal. The magnetic field is provided by two coils, called Helmholtz coils (Figure **26.10**), which give a very uniform field in the space between them.

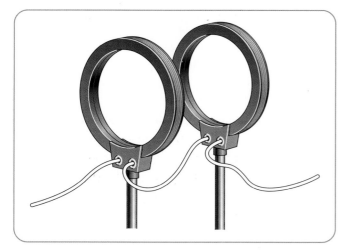

**Figure 26.10** A pair of Helmholtz coils is used to give a uniform magnetic field.

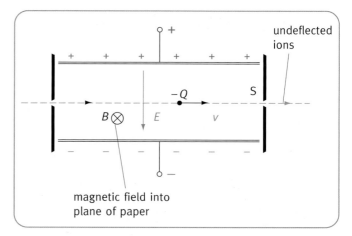

**Figure 26.11** A velocity selector – only particles with the correct combination of charge, mass and velocity will emerge through the slit S.

If the electron beam remains straight, it follows that the electric and magnetic forces on each electron must have the same magnitude and act in opposite directions. Therefore:

electric force = magnetic force
(upward)          (downward)

$$eE = Bev$$

where $E$ is the electric field strength between the parallel plates with a p.d of $V$. The speed $v$ of the electrons is simply related to the strengths of the two fields. That is:

$$v = \frac{E}{B}$$

The electric field strength is given by:

$$E = \frac{V}{d}$$

therefore:

$$v = \frac{V}{Bd}$$

## Velocity selection

Balancing the effects of electric and magnetic fields is also used in a device called a velocity selector. This is used in devices such as mass spectrometers where it is desired to produce a beam of charged particles all moving with the same velocity. The construction of a velocity selector is shown in Figure **26.11**.

The apparatus is very similar to the deflection tube in Figure **26.9**. Two parallel plates are situated in an evacuated chamber. They provide a uniform electric field of strength $E$. The region between the plates is also occupied by a uniform magnetic field of flux density $B$ which is at right angles to the electric field. Charged particles (electrons or ions) enter from the left. Only those travelling at the desired speed $v$ emerge undeflected from the slit S. If a negative ion has a speed greater than $\frac{V}{Bd}$ it will be deflected up less by the electric field than it is deflected down by the magnetic field and it will hit the bottom part of slit S.

---

### Test yourself

7  This question is about the velocity selector shown in Figure **26.11**.
   a  State the directions of the magnetic and electric forces on a positively charged ion travelling towards the slit S.
   b  The speed of the ion is given by the equation:

   $$v = \frac{E}{B}$$

   Calculate the speed of an ion emerging from the slit S when the magnetic flux density is 0.30 T and the electric field strength is $1.5 \times 10^3\,\mathrm{V\,m^{-1}}$.
   c  Explain why ions travelling at a speed greater than your answer to **b** will not emerge from the slit.

---

# Discovering the electron

Today, a great deal is known about electrons and we use the idea of electrons to explain all sorts of phenomena, including electric current and chemical bonding. However, at the end of the 19th century, physicists were only just beginning to identify the tiny particles which make up matter.

**Figure 26.12** Joseph Thomson – in 1897 he discovered the electron using the vacuum tube shown here.

One of the leaders in this field was the English physicist J.J. Thomson (Figure 26.12). In the photograph he is shown with the deflection tube which he used in his discovery of the electron. His tube was similar in construction to the deflection tube shown in Figure 26.9. At one end was an electron gun that produced a beam of electrons (which he called 'cathode rays'). Two metal plates allowed him to apply an electric field to deflect the beam, and he could place magnets outside the tube to apply a magnetic force to the beam. Here is a summary of his observations and what he concluded from them:

- The beam in his tube was deflected towards a positive plate and away from a negative plate, so the particles involved must have negative charge. This was confirmed by the deflection of the beam by a magnetic field.
- When the beam was deflected, it remained as a tight, single beam rather than spreading out into a broad beam. This showed that, if the beam consisted of particles, they must all have the same mass, charge and speed. (Lighter particles would have been deflected more than heavier ones; particles with greater charge would be deflected more; and faster particles would be deflected less.)

- By applying both electric and magnetic fields, Thomson was able to balance the electric and magnetic forces so that the beam in the tube remained straight. He could then calculate the charge-to-mass ratio $\frac{e}{m_e}$ for the particles he had discovered. Although he did not know the value of either $e$ or $m_e$ individually, he was able to show that the particles concerned must be much lighter than atoms. They were the particles which we now know as electrons. In fact, for a while, Thomson thought that atoms were made up of thousands of electrons, although his ideas could not explain how so many negatively charged particles could combine to produce a neutral atom.

## Measuring *e*

The charge $e$ of an electron is very small ($-1.6 \times 10^{-19}$ C) and difficult to measure. The American physicist Robert Millikan devised an ingenious way to do it, publishing his results in 1913. He used tiny, charged droplets of oil suspended in a uniform electric field (Figure 26.13). If a particular droplet was stationary, he knew that the electric force acting on it upwards was equal to the force of gravity acting downwards on it. For a droplet of charge $Q$ and mass $m$:

gravitational force downwards = electric force upwards

$$mg = QE = \frac{QV}{d}$$

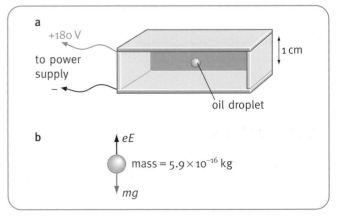

**Figure 26.13** Millikan's oil-drop experiment to determine the charge of an electron.

Millikan's procedure was as follows:

- He used an atomiser spray to produce a small number of tiny oil drops in the chamber. These drops were charged by friction with the nozzle of the spray.
- With the electric field switched off, he observed a single drop falling. If its velocity was constant, he knew that it was falling at terminal velocity. By timing its fall against a scale, he could determine its velocity and from this he could work out its mass (heavier drops fall with a greater terminal velocity).
- He then switched on the electric field and adjusted it until the drop remained stationary. Then he knew that the drop's weight was balanced by the electric force on it.
- To alter the charge on an oil drop, Millikan included a source of β-radiation in his apparatus. Beta-radiation is simply fast-moving electrons. An oil drop which absorbed an electron would gain negative charge and so the electric force on it would change.

Millikan determined the charges on many oil drops (a tricky procedure) and found that they were all small multiples of a particular value, which he took to be the charge on a single electron, $e$. Having established a value for $e$, he could easily combine this with Thomson's value for $\frac{e}{m_e}$ to calculate the electron mass $m_e$.

## Quantisation of charge

Millikan's value of $e$ was within 1% of today's known value. The fact that his oil drops all had charges equal to a multiple of this value suggested that it was something very fundamental. It suggested that electric charge is **quantised**, that is to say, that charge cannot take any value; rather, it must have a value which is a multiple of this fundamental value $e$. We now know that particles such as protons and many others from the 'particle zoo' of sub-atomic particles have charges which are multiples of $e$. The exception is quarks, which have charges which are multiples of $\frac{1}{3}e$.

### Test yourself

8 If the electron charge is $1.60 \times 10^{-19}$ C and the charge-to-mass ratio $\frac{e}{m}$ is $1.76 \times 10^{11}$ C kg$^{-1}$, calculate the electron mass.

9 This question is about Millikan's apparatus as shown in Figure **26.13**. Study the diagram, and use the information it contains to help you answer the questions that follow.
   a The upper plate in the diagram is connected to the positive terminal of the supply. What does this tell you about the sign of the charge on the droplet?
   b What is the electric field strength between the two plates?
   c What is the weight of the droplet?
   d What is the electric force acting on it when it is stationary?
   e What is the charge on the droplet? What is the significance of this value?
   f In Millikan's experiment, he included a source of β-radiation. When an oil droplet was irradiated, it was suddenly observed to start moving upwards. What explanation can you give for this?
   g Assuming that the charge on the oil droplet had increased because it had captured a single electron, what new value of voltage between the plates would you now expect to hold it stationary?

# Summary

☐ The magnetic force on a moving charged particle is given by the equation $F = BQv$. For an electron the equation is $F = Bev$.

☐ A charged particle entering at right angles to a uniform magnetic field describes a circular path because the magnetic force is perpendicular to the velocity.

☐ The equation for an electron travelling in a uniform magnetic field is:

$$\frac{m_e v^2}{r} = Bev$$

☐ The velocity of an undeflected charged particle in a region where electric and magnetic fields are at right angles is given by the equation:

$$v = \frac{E}{B}$$

# End-of-chapter questions

1  The magnetic force $BQv$ causes an electron to travel in a circle in a uniform magnetic field. Explain why this force does not cause an increase in the speed of the electron.

2  An electron beam is produced from an electron gun in which each electron is accelerated through a p.d. of 1.6 kV. When these electrons pass at right angles through a magnetic field of flux density 8.0 mT, the radius of curvature of the electron beam is 0.017 m. Determine the specific charge of the electron, $\frac{e}{m_e}$.

3  An $\alpha$-particle and a $\beta$-particle with the same velocity travel at right angles through the same magnetic field. Determine the ratio of:
   a  the masses of the two particles
   b  the charges on the two particles
   c  the forces created by the magnetic field on the two particles
   d  the radii of the circular orbits of the two particles in the magnetic field.

4  A moving charged particle experiences a force in an electric field and in a magnetic field. State **two** differences between the forces experienced in the two types of field.

5  In a measurement of the electron charge using Millikan's experiment, the weight of the oil drop was $1.0 \times 10^{-13}$ N. A p.d. of 1.25 kV applied between the plates, which are 12 mm apart, keeps the oil drop stationary. Calculate the number of excess electrons on the oil drop.

# Exam-style questions

**1** The diagram shows the path of an electron as it travels in air. The electron rotates clockwise around a uniform magnetic field into the plane of the paper, but the radius of the orbit decreases in size.

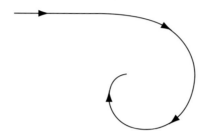

  **a i** Explain the origin of the force that causes the electron to spiral in this manner. [2]

    **ii** Explain why the radius of the circle gradually decreases. [2]

  **b** At one point in the path, the speed of the electron is $1.0 \times 10^7 \, \text{m s}^{-1}$ and the magnetic flux density is 0.25 T. Calculate:

    **i** the force on an electron at this point due to the magnetic field [2]

    **ii** the radius of the path at this point. [2]

**2** The diagram shows an arrangement to deflect protons from a source to a detector using a magnetic field. A uniform magnetic field exists only within the area shown. Protons move from the source to the detector in the plane of the paper.

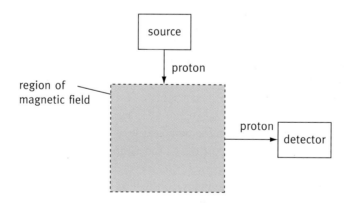

  **a i** Copy the diagram and sketch the path of a proton from the source to the detector. Draw an arrow at **two** points on the path to show the direction of the force on the proton produced by the magnetic field. [3]

    **ii** State the direction of the magnetic field within the area shown. [1]

  **b** The speed of a proton as it enters the magnetic field is $4.0 \times 10^6 \, \text{m s}^{-1}$. The magnetic flux density is 0.25 T. Calculate:

    **i** the magnitude of the force on the proton caused by the magnetic field [1]

    **ii** the radius of curvature of the path of the proton in the magnetic field. [2]

**c** Two changes to the magnetic field in the area shown are made. These changes allow an electron with the same speed as the proton to be deflected along the same path as the proton. State the **two** changes made. [2]

**3** The diagram shows an electron tube. Electrons emitted from the cathode accelerate towards the anode and then pass into a uniform electric field created by two oppositely charged parallel metal plates.

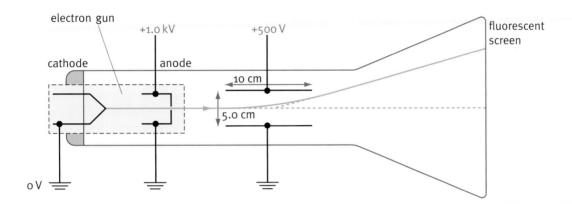

**a i** Explain why the beam curves upwards. [2]
  **ii** Explain how the pattern formed on the fluorescent screen shows that all the electrons have the same speed as they leave the anode. [2]
**b** Write down an equation relating the speed of the electrons $v$ to the potential difference $V_{ac}$ between the anode and the cathode. [1]
**c** The deflection of the beam upwards can be cancelled by applying a suitable uniform magnetic field in the space between the parallel plates.
  **i** State the direction of the magnetic field for this to happen. [1]
  **ii** Write down an equation relating the speed of the electrons, $v$, the electric field $E$ that exists between the plates and the magnetic flux density $B$ needed to make the electrons pass undeflected between the plates. [2]
  **iii** Calculate the value of $B$ required, using the apparatus shown in the diagram, given that the specific charge on an electron $\dfrac{e}{m_e}$ is $1.76 \times 10^{11}\,\mathrm{C\,kg^{-1}}$. [2]

**4** Protons and helium nuclei from the Sun pass into the Earth's atmosphere above the poles, where the magnetic flux density is $6.0 \times 10^{-5}\,\mathrm{T}$. The particles are moving at a speed of $1.0 \times 10^{6}\,\mathrm{m\,s^{-1}}$ at right angles to the magnetic field in this region. The magnetic field can be assumed to be uniform.
**a** Calculate the radius of the path of a proton as it passes above the Earth's pole. [3]
**b** Draw a diagram to show the deflection caused by the magnetic field on a proton and on a helium nucleus which both have the same initial velocity as they enter the magnetic field. State on the diagram the radius of the path of each particle. [2]
  Mass of a helium nucleus = $6.8 \times 10^{-27}\,\mathrm{kg}$
  Charge on a helium nucleus = $3.2 \times 10^{-19}\,\mathrm{C}$

5    In Millikan's oil drop experiment, an oil drop of weight $1.5 \times 10^{-14}$ N is held stationary between plates 10 mm apart by a p.d. between the plates of 470 V.

    **a**  Draw a diagram of the apparatus and explain why the oil drop remains stationary.    [3]

    **b**  **i**  Calculate the charge on the oil drop.    [3]

        **ii**  Explain what is meant by **quantisation of charge**.    [2]

    **c**  When the charge on the oil drop is changed, the p.d. needed to keep the drop stationary also changes. Values of 940 V and 313 V are also obtained.

        **i**  Describe how the charge on the oil drop can be changed while the drop remains between the plates.    [1]

        **ii**  Explain why only certain values of p.d. are found in this experiment and predict another value of the p.d. that may be required when the charge on the oil drop is changed.    [3]

# 27 Electromagnetic induction

## Objectives

After studying this chapter, you should be able to:

- define magnetic flux and its unit
- describe experiments which illustrate aspects of electromagnetic induction
- solve problems using Faraday's and Lenz's laws of electromagnetic induction

- explain simple applications of electromagnetic induction

## Generating electricity

Most of the electricity we use is generated by electromagnetic induction. This process goes on in the generators at work in power stations and in wind turbines (Figure 27.1) and, on a much smaller scale, in bicycle dynamos. It is the process whereby a conductor and a magnetic field are moved relative to each other to induce, or generate, a current or electromotive force (e.m.f.).

Figure 27.1 This giant wind turbine uses electromagnetic induction to produce electricity. Look for the two engineers at work. (You can identify them by their white helmets.) This gives you an idea of the size of the generator.

## Observing induction

Here are some simple experiments in which you can observe some of the features of electromagnetic induction. In each case, try to predict what you will observe before you try the experiment.

### Experiment 1

Connect a small electric motor to a moving-coil voltmeter (Figure 27.2). Spin the shaft of the motor and observe the deflection of the voltmeter. What happens when you spin the motor more slowly? What happens when you stop? Usually, we connect a motor to a power supply and it turns. In this experiment, you have turned the motor and it generates a voltage across its terminals. A generator is like a motor working in reverse.

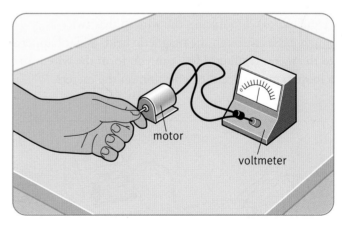

Figure 27.2 A motor works in reverse as a generator.

## Experiment 2

Connect a coil to a sensitive microammeter (Figure 27.3). Move a bar magnet in towards the coil. Hold it still, and then remove it. How does the deflection on the meter change? Try different speeds, and the opposite pole of the magnet. Try weak and strong magnets.

With the same equipment, move the coil towards the magnet and observe the deflection of the meter.

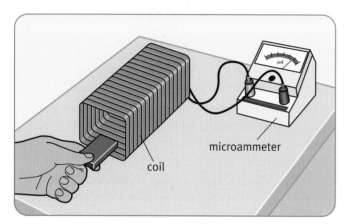

**Figure 27.3** A magnet moving near a coil generates a small current.

## Experiment 3

Connect a long wire to a sensitive microammeter. Move the middle section of the wire up and down through the magnetic field between the magnets (Figure 27.4). Double up the wire so that twice as much passes through the magnetic field. What happens to the meter reading? How can you form the wire into a loop to give twice the deflection on the meter?

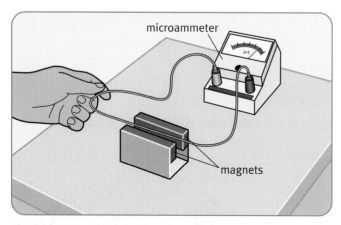

**Figure 27.4** Investigating the current induced when a wire moves through a magnetic field.

In all these experiments, you have seen an electric current or an e.m.f. induced. In each case, there is a magnetic field and a conductor. When you move the magnet or the conductor, there is an induced current. When you stop, the current stops.

From the three experiments, you should see that the size of the induced current or e.m.f. depends on several factors.

For a straight wire, the induced current or e.m.f. depends on:

• the magnitude of the magnetic flux density
• the length of the wire in the field
• the speed of movement of the wire.

For a coil of wire, the induced current or e.m.f. depends on:

• the magnitude of the magnetic flux density
• the cross-sectional area of the coil
• the number of turns of wire
• the rate at which the coil turns in the field.

# Explaining electromagnetic induction

You have seen that relative movement of a conductor and a magnetic field induces a current in the conductor when it is part of a complete circuit. (In the experiments above, the meter was used to complete the circuit.) Now we need to think about how to explain these observations, using what we know about magnetic fields.

## Cutting magnetic field lines

Start by thinking about a simple bar magnet. It has a magnetic field in the space around it. We represent this field by magnetic field lines. Now think about what happens when a wire is moved into the magnetic field (Figure 27.5). As it moves, it **cuts across** the magnetic field. Remove the wire from the field, and again it must cut across the field lines, but in the opposite direction.

We think of this cutting of magnetic field by a conductor as the effect that gives rise to an induced current in the conductor. It doesn't matter whether the conductor is moved through the field, or the magnet is moved past the conductor, the result is the same – there will be an induced current.

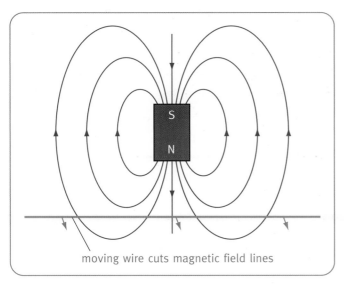

Figure 27.5 Inducing a current by moving a wire through a magnetic field.

The effect is magnified if we use a coil of wire. For a coil of $N$ turns, the effect is $N$ times greater than for a single turn of wire. With a coil, it is helpful to imagine the number of field lines **linking** the coil. If there is a change in the number of field lines which pass through the coil, an e.m.f. will be induced across the ends of the coil (or there will be an induced current if the coil forms part of a complete circuit).

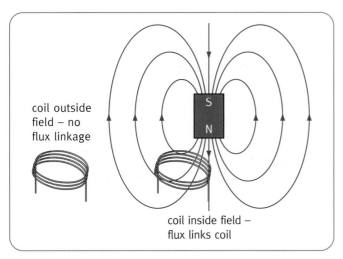

Figure 27.6 The flux passing through a coil changes as it is moved into and out of a magnetic field.

Figure 27.6 shows a coil near a magnet. When the coil is outside the field, there are no magnetic field lines linking the coil. When it is inside the field, field lines link the coil. Moving the coil into or out of the field changes this linkage, and this induces an e.m.f. across the ends of the coil.

## Test yourself

1 Use the idea of a conductor cutting magnetic field lines to explain how a current is induced in a bicycle generator (Figure 27.7).

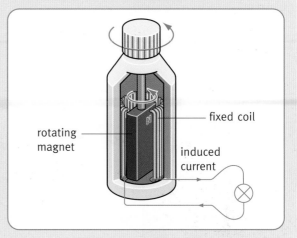

Figure 27.7 In a bicycle generator, a permanent magnet rotates inside a fixed coil of wire. For Test yourself Q 1.

## Current direction

How can we predict the direction of the induced current? For the motor effect in Chapter 25, we used Fleming's left-hand (motor) rule. Electromagnetic induction is like the mirror image of the motor effect. Instead of a current producing a force on a current-carrying conductor in a magnetic field, we provide an external force on a conductor by moving it through a magnetic field and this induces a current in the conductor. So you should not be too surprised to find that we use the mirror image of the left-hand rule: **Fleming's right-hand (generator) rule.**

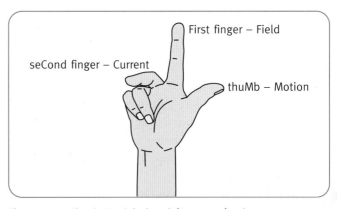

Figure 27.8 Fleming's right-hand (generator) rule.

The three fingers represent the same things again (Figure 27.8):

- thuMb – direction of Motion
- First finger – direction of external magnetic Field
- seCond finger – direction of (conventional) induced Current

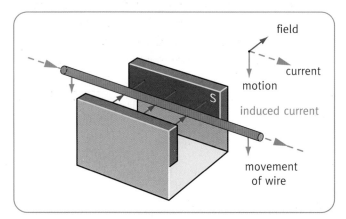

Figure 27.9 Deducing the direction of the induced current using Fleming's right-hand rule.

In the example shown in Figure 27.9, the conductor is being moved downwards across the magnetic field. There is an induced current in the conductor as shown. Check this with your own right hand. You should also check that reversing the movement or the field will result in the current flowing in the opposite direction.

## Induced e.m.f.

When a conductor is not part of a complete circuit, there cannot be an induced current. Instead, negative charge will accumulate at one end of the conductor, leaving the other end positively charged. We have induced an e.m.f. across the ends of the conductor.

Is e.m.f. the right term? Should it be voltage? In Chapter 10 you saw the distinction between voltage and e.m.f. The latter is the correct term here because, by pushing the wire through the magnetic field, work is done and this is transformed into electrical energy. Think of this in another way. Since we could connect the ends of the conductor so that there is a current in some other component, such as a lamp, which would light up, it must be an e.m.f. – a source of electrical energy.

Figure 27.10 shows how the induced current gives rise to an induced e.m.f. Notice that, within the

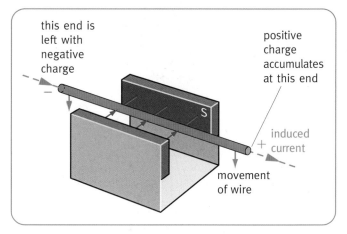

Figure 27.10 An e.m.f. is induced across the ends of the conductor.

conductor, conventional current is from negative to positive, in the same way as inside a battery or any other source of e.m.f. In reality, the free electrons within the conductor travel from right to left, making the left-hand side of the conductor negative. What causes these electrons to move? Moving the conductor is equivalent to giving an electron within the conductor a velocity in the direction of this motion. This electron is in an external magnetic field and hence experiences a magnetic force *Bev* from right to left. Check this out for yourself.

## Test yourself

2 The coil in Figure 27.11 is rotating in a uniform magnetic field. Deduce the direction of the induced current in sections AB and CD. State which terminal, X or Y, will become positive.

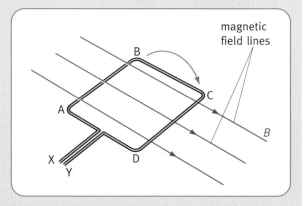

Figure 27.11 A coil rotated in a magnetic field.

*continued* ⋯⟶

**3** When an aircraft flies from east to west, its wings are an electrical conductor cutting across the Earth's magnetic flux. In the northern hemisphere, which wingtip will become positively charged? Why will this wingtip be negative in the southern hemisphere?

## Magnetic flux and magnetic flux linkage

So far in this chapter we have looked at the ideas of electromagnetic induction in a descriptive way. Now we will see how to calculate the value of the induced e.m.f. and look at a general way of determining its direction.

In Chapter 25, we saw how magnetic flux density $B$ is defined by the equation

$$B = \frac{F}{Il}$$

Now we can go on to define **magnetic flux** as a quantity. We picture **magnetic flux density** $B$ as the number of magnetic field lines passing through a region **per unit area**. Similarly, we can picture magnetic flux as the total number of magnetic field lines passing through an area $A$. For a magnetic field normal to $A$, the magnetic flux $\Phi$ (Greek letter phi) must therefore be equal to the product of magnetic flux density and the area $A$ (Figure 27.12a).

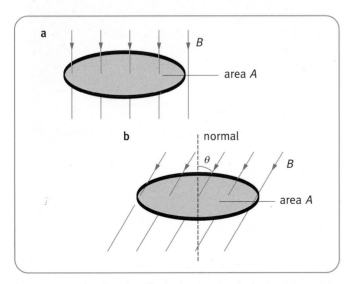

**Figure 27.12 a** The magnetic flux is equal to $BA$ when the field is normal to the area. **b** The magnetic flux becomes $BA\cos\theta$ when the field is at an angle $\theta$ to the normal of the area.

The magnetic flux $\Phi$ through area $A$ is defined as:

$$\Phi = BA$$

where $B$ is the component of the magnetic flux density perpendicular to the area.

How can we calculate the magnetic flux when $B$ is not perpendicular to $A$? You can easily see that when the field is parallel to the plane of the area, the magnetic flux through $A$ is zero. To find the magnetic flux in general, we need to find the component of the magnetic flux density perpendicular to the area. Figure 27.12b shows a magnetic field at an angle $\theta$ to the normal. In this case:

magnetic flux $= (B\cos\theta) \times A$

or simply:

magnetic flux $= BA\cos\theta$

(Note that, when $\theta = 90°$, flux $= 0$ and when $\theta = 0°$, flux $= BA$.)

For a coil with $N$ turns, the **magnetic flux linkage** is defined as the product of the magnetic flux and the number of turns; that is:

magnetic flux linkage $= N\Phi$

or

magnetic flux linkage $= BAN\cos\theta$

(Note that, if the angle $\theta$ is measured between the magnetic field and the surface, the equation becomes magnetic flux linkage $= BAN\sin\theta$.)

The unit for magnetic flux or flux linkage is the weber (Wb).

One weber is equal to one tesla metre-squared; $1\,\text{Wb} = 1\,\text{T}\,\text{m}^2$.

An e.m.f. is induced in a circuit whenever there is a **change** in the magnetic flux linking the circuit. Since magnetic flux is equal to $BA\cos\theta$, there are three ways an e.m.f. can be induced:

• changing the magnetic flux density $B$
• changing the area $A$ of the circuit
• changing the angle $\theta$.

Now look at Worked example 1.

## Worked example

1 Figure **27.13** shows a solenoid with a cross-sectional area $0.10\,m^2$. It is linked by a magnetic field of flux density $2.0 \times 10^{-3}\,T$ and has 250 turns. Calculate the magnetic flux and flux linkage for this solenoid.

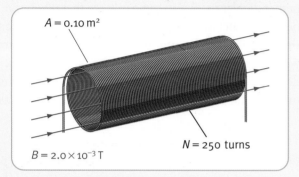

$A = 0.10\,m^2$

$N = 250$ turns

$B = 2.0 \times 10^{-3}\,T$

**Figure 27.13** A solenoid in a magnetic field.

**Step 1** We have $B = 2.0 \times 10^{-3}\,T$, $A = 0.10\,m^2$, $\theta = 0°$ and $N = 250$ turns. Hence we can calculate the flux $\Phi$.

$$\Phi = BA$$

$$\Phi = 2.0 \times 10^{-3} \times 0.10 = 2.0 \times 10^{-4}\,Wb$$

**Step 2** Now calculate the flux linkage.

magnetic flux linkage $= N\Phi$

magnetic flux linkage $= 2.0 \times 10^{-4} \times 250$
$$= 5.0 \times 10^{-2}\,Wb$$

## Test yourself

4 Use the idea of magnetic flux linkage to explain why, when a magnet is moved into a coil, the e.m.f. induced depends on the strength of the magnet and the speed at which it is moved.

5 In an experiment to investigate the factors that affect the magnitude of an induced e.m.f.,

*continued* ⋯▸

a student moves a wire back and forth between two magnets, as shown in Figure **27.14**. Explain why the e.m.f. generated in this way is much smaller than if the wire is moved up and down in the field.

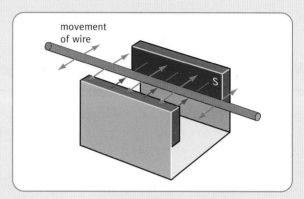

movement of wire

S

**Figure 27.14** A wire is moved horizontally in a horizontal magnetic field. For Test yourself Q **5**.

6 In the type of generator found in a power station (Figure **27.15**), a large electromagnet is made to rotate inside a fixed coil. An e.m.f. of 25 kV is generated; this is an alternating voltage of frequency 50 Hz. What factor determines the frequency? What factors do you think would affect the magnitude of the e.m.f.?

**Figure 27.15** The generators of this power station produce electricity at an induced e.m.f. of 25 kV. For Test yourself Q **6**.

7 A bar magnet produces a uniform flux density of 0.15 T at the surface of its north pole. The pole measures 1.0 cm × 1.5 cm. Calculate the magnetic flux at this pole.

*continued* ⋯▸

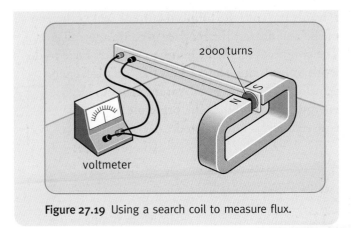

**Figure 27.19** Using a search coil to measure flux.

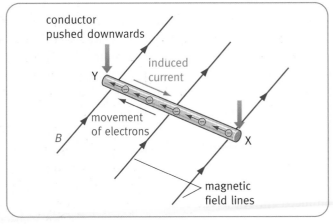

**Figure 27.20** Showing the direction of the induced current.

## Lenz's law

We use Faraday's law to calculate the magnitude of an induced e.m.f. Now we can go on to think about the direction of the e.m.f. – in other words, which end of a wire or coil moving in a magnetic field becomes positive, and which becomes negative.

Fleming's right-hand rule gives the direction of an induced current. This is a particular case of a more general law, Lenz's law, which will be explained in this section. First, we will see how the motor effect and the generator effect are related to each other.

### The origin of electromagnetic induction

So far, we have not given an explanation of electromagnetic induction. You have seen, from the experiments at the beginning of this chapter, that it does occur, and you know the factors that affect it. But what is the origin of the induced current?

Figure 27.20 gives an explanation. A straight wire XY is being pushed downwards through a horizontal magnetic field of flux density $B$. Now, think about the free electrons in the wire. They are moving downwards, so they are in effect an electric current. Of course, because electrons are negatively charged, the conventional current is flowing upwards.

We now have a current flowing across a magnetic field, and the motor effect will therefore come into play. Each electron experiences a force of magnitude $Bev$. Using Fleming's left-hand rule, we can find the direction of the force on the electrons. The diagram

shows that the electrons will be pushed in the direction from X to Y. So a current has been induced to flow in the wire; the direction of the conventional current is from Y to X.

Now we can check that Fleming's right-hand rule gives the correct directions for motion, field and current, which indeed it does.

So, to summarise, there is an induced current because the electrons are pushed by the motor effect. Electromagnetic induction is simply a consequence of the motor effect.

In Figure 27.20, electrons are found to accumulate at Y. This end of the wire is thus the negative end of the e.m.f. and X is positive. If the wire was connected to an external circuit, electrons would flow out of Y, round the circuit, and back into X. Figure 27.21 shows how the moving wire is equivalent to a cell (or any other source of e.m.f.).

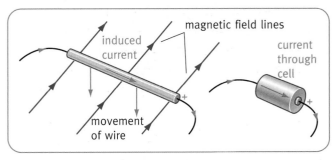

**Figure 27.21** A moving conductor in a magnetic field is a source of e.m.f., equivalent to a cell.

## Forces and movement

Electromagnetic induction is how we generate most of our electricity. We turn a coil in a magnetic field, and the mechanical energy we put in is transferred to electrical energy. By thinking about these energy transfers, we can deduce the direction of the induced current.

Figure 27.22 shows one of the experiments from earlier in this chapter. The north pole of a magnet is being pushed towards a coil of wire. There is an induced current in the coil, but what is its direction? The diagram shows the two possibilities.

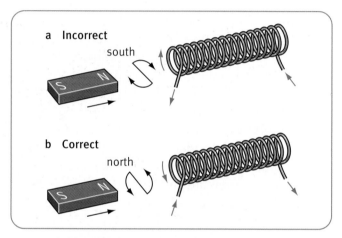

**Figure 27.22** Moving a magnet towards a coil: the direction of the induced current is as shown in **b**, not **a**.

The current in the coil turns it into an electromagnet. One end becomes the north pole, the other the south pole. In Figure 27.22a, if the induced current is in this direction, the coil end nearest the approaching north pole of the magnet would be a south pole. These poles will attract one another, and you could let go of the magnet and it would be dragged into the coil. The magnet would accelerate into the coil, the induced current would increase further, and the force of attraction between the two would also escalate.

In this situation, we would be putting no energy into the system, but the magnet would be gaining kinetic energy, and the current would be gaining electrical energy. A nice trick if you could do it, but against the principle of conservation of energy!

It follows that Figure 27.22b must show the correct situation. As the north pole of the magnet is pushed

towards the coil, the induced current makes the end of the coil nearest the magnet become a north pole. The two poles repel one another, and you have to do work to push the magnet into the coil. The energy transferred by your work is transferred to electrical energy of the current. The principle of energy conservation is not violated.

Figure 27.23 shows how we can apply the same reasoning to a straight wire being moved in a downward direction through a magnetic field. There will be an induced current in the wire, but in which direction? Since this is a case of a current across a magnetic field, a force will act on it (the motor effect), and we can use Fleming's left-hand rule to deduce its direction.

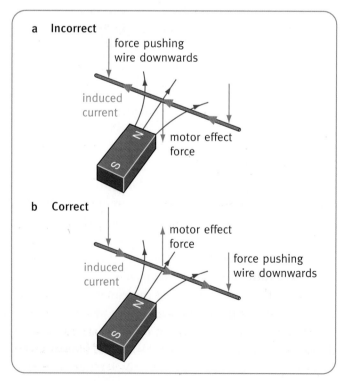

**Figure 27.23** Moving a conductor through a magnetic field: the direction of the induced current is as shown in **b**, not **a**.

First we will consider what happens if the induced current is in the wrong direction. This is shown in Figure **27.23a**. The left-hand rule shows that the force that results would be downward – in the direction in which we are trying to move the wire. The wire would thus be accelerated, the current would increase, and again we would be getting both kinetic and electrical energy for no energy input.

The induced current must be as shown in Figure **27.23b**. The force that acts on it due to the motor effect pushes against you as you try to move the wire through the field. You have to do work to move the wire, and hence to generate electrical energy. Once again, the principle of energy conservation is not violated.

## Test yourself

**14** Draw a diagram to show the directions of the induced current and of the opposing force if you now try to move the wire shown in Figure **27.23** upwards through the magnetic field.

## A general law for induced e.m.f.

Lenz's law summarises this general principle of energy conservation. The direction of an induced current is such that it always produces a force that opposes the motion that is being used to produce it. If the direction of the current were opposite to this, we would be getting energy for nothing. Here is a statement of **Lenz's law**:

> Any induced current or induced e.m.f. will be established in a direction so as to produce effects which oppose the change that is producing it.

The idea of this opposition to change is encapsulated in the **minus** sign in the equation for Faraday's law:

$$E = -\frac{\Delta(N\Phi)}{\Delta t}$$

This law can be shown to be correct in any experimental situation. For example, in Figure **27.22**, a sensitive ammeter connected in the circuit shows the direction of the current as the magnet is moved in and out. If a battery is later connected to the coil to make a larger and constant current in the same direction, a compass will show what the poles are at the end of the solenoid. If a north pole is moved into the solenoid then the solenoid itself will have a north pole at that end. If a north pole is moved out of the solenoid, then the solenoid will have a south pole at that end.

## Test yourself

**15** A bar magnet is dropped vertically downwards through a long solenoid, which is connected to an oscilloscope (Figure **27.24**). The oscilloscope trace shows how the e.m.f. induced in the coil varies as the magnet accelerates downwards.

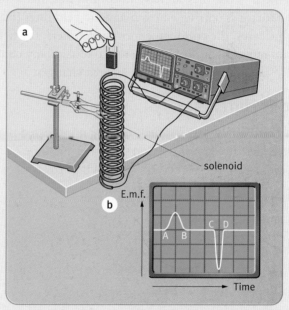

**Figure 27.24 a** A bar magnet falls through a long coil. **b** The oscilloscope trace shows how the induced e.m.f. varies with time.

**a** Explain why an e.m.f. is induced in the coil as the magnet enters it (section AB of the trace).
**b** Explain why no e.m.f. is induced while the magnet is entirely inside the coil (section BC).
**c** Explain why section CD shows a negative trace, why the peak e.m.f. is greater over this section, and why CD represents a shorter time interval than AB.

*continued* ⋯➔

# Using induction: eddy currents, generators and transformers

An induced e.m.f. can be generated in a variety of ways. What they all have in common is that a conductor is cutting across magnetic field lines (in some cases, the conductor moves; in others, the field lines move). The alternative way to look at any change is to say that the flux linking an area changes.

## Eddy currents

Induced e.m.f.s are formed in some unexpected places. Consider the demonstration shown in Figure 27.25. A metal disc on the end of a rod swings freely between two opposite magnetic poles.

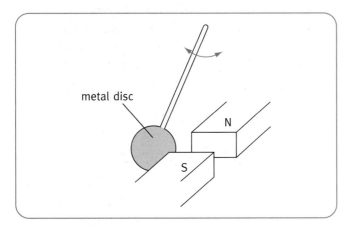

Figure 27.25 Demonstrating eddy current damping.

Without the magnets, the disc oscillates from side to side for a long time. This is because air resistance is small and it takes a long time for the energy of the disc to be lost. When the magnets are present, the oscillation of the disc dies away quickly. As the disc enters the magnetic field, one side of the disc is cutting the

magnetic field lines and so an induced e.m.f. is created in that side but not in the side that has not yet entered. Since the disc is a conductor, the induced e.m.f. creates currents in the disc itself. These currents are known as eddy currents. They flow in a circular fashion inside the disc. Lenz's law predicts that the induced currents that flow in the disc will produce a force that opposes the motion, just as in Figure 27.23. Eddy currents, like other electrical currents, cause heating and the energy of the oscillation dies away quickly. The oscillation is damped by the eddy currents.

This principle can be used in some types of electromagnetic or eddy-current braking systems. For example, a large electromagnet suspended under a train can cause eddy currents in the rails and slow the train down. Better still, if the train has an electric motor, then the kinetic energy of the train can be used to turn the electric motor to generate an induced e.m.f.. With the appropriate electronics the energy from the induced current can be passed back to the power supply that runs the train. This is an example of regenerative braking.

## Generators

We can generate electricity by spinning a coil in a magnetic field. This is equivalent to using an electric motor backwards. Figure 27.26 shows such a coil in three different orientations as it spins. Notice that the rate of change of flux linkage is maximum when the coil is moving through the horizontal position – one side is cutting rapidly downwards through the field lines, the other is cutting rapidly upwards. In this position, we get a large induced e.m.f. As the coil moves through the vertical position, the rate of

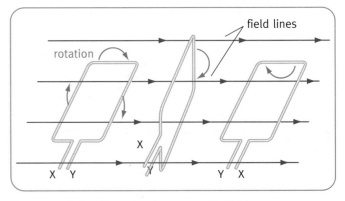

Figure 27.26 A coil rotating in a magnetic field.

change of flux is zero – the sides of the coil are moving parallel to the field lines, not cutting them, so that there is hardly any change in the flux linkage.

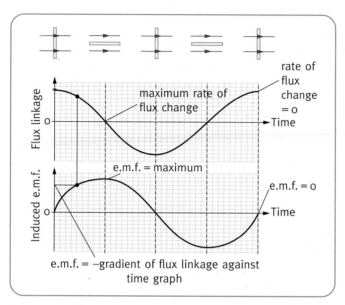

Figure 27.27 The magnetic flux linking a rotating coil as it changes. This gives rise to an alternating e.m.f. The orientation of the coil is shown above the graphs.

Figure 27.27 shows how the flux linkage varies with time for a rotating coil. According to Faraday's law, the induced e.m.f. is equal to minus the gradient of the flux linkage against time graph.

- When the flux linking the coil is maximum, the rate of change of flux is zero and hence the induced e.m.f. is zero.
- When the flux linking the coil is zero, the rate of change of flux is maximum (the graph is steepest) and hence the induced e.m.f. is also maximum.

Hence, for a coil like this we get a varying e.m.f. – this is how alternating current is generated. In practice, it is simpler to keep the large coil fixed and spin an electromagnet inside it (Figure 27.28). A bicycle generator (see Figure 27.7) is similar, but in this case a permanent magnet is made to spin inside a fixed coil. This makes for a very robust device.

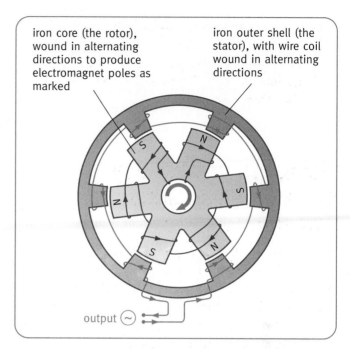

Figure 27.28 In a generator, an electromagnet rotates inside a coil.

## Test yourself

17 Figure 27.29 represents a coil of wire ABCD being rotated in a uniform horizontal magnetic field. Copy and complete the diagram to show the direction of the induced current in the coil, and the directions of the forces on sides AB and CD that oppose the rotation of the coil.

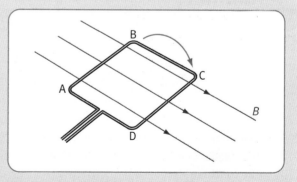

Figure 27.29 A coil rotating in a magnetic field.

18 Does a bicycle generator (Figure 27.7) generate alternating or direct current? Justify your answer.

*continued ⋯⟶*

**19** The peak e.m.f. induced in a rotating coil in a magnetic field depends on four factors: magnetic flux density $B$, area of the coil $A$, number of turns $N$, and frequency $f$ of rotation. Use Faraday's law to explain why the e.m.f. must be proportional to each of these quantities.

## Transformers

Another use of electromagnetic induction is in transformers. An alternating current is supplied to the primary coil and produces a varying magnetic field in the soft iron core (Figure 27.30). The secondary coil is also wound round this core, so the magnetic flux linking the secondary coil is constantly changing. Hence, according to Faraday's law, a varying e.m.f. is induced across the secondary coil. The core is laminated – it is made up of thin sheets of soft iron. Using soft iron in the core increases the amount of the magnetic flux and, hopefully, all of the magnetic flux from the primary coil passes to the secondary coil. The thin sheets of iron in the core are separated by a non-conductor so eddy currents cannot flow from one sheet to the next. This reduces the eddy currents and the thermal energy that they create in the core.

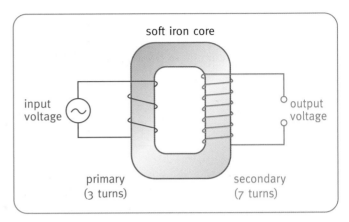

**Figure 27.30** The construction of a transformer.

There is much more about transformers in Chapter **28**, where we will look at how they are used to change voltages in circuits which make use of alternating currents.

### Test yourself

**20** Explain why, if a transformer is connected to a steady (d.c.) supply, no e.m.f. is induced across the secondary coil.

# Summary

- ☐ In a magnetic field of magnetic flux density $B$, the magnetic flux passing through an area $A$ is given by $\Phi = BA$.
- ☐ The magnetic flux linking a coil of $N$ turns is the magnetic flux linkage, $N\Phi$.
- ☐ Flux and flux linkage are measured in webers (Wb).
- ☐ One weber is equal to one tesla metre-squared. $1\,\text{Wb} = 1\,\text{T}\,\text{m}^2$.
- ☐ When a conductor moves so that it cuts across a magnetic field, an e.m.f. is induced across its ends. When the magnetic flux linking a coil changes, an e.m.f. is induced in the coil.
- ☐ Faraday's law states that the magnitude of the induced e.m.f. is equal to the rate of change of magnetic flux linkage:

$$E = -\frac{\Delta(N\Phi)}{\Delta t}$$

- ☐ Lenz's law states that the induced current or e.m.f. is in a direction so as to produce effects which oppose the change that is producing it.
- ☐ In an a.c. generator, an e.m.f. is induced because the rotating coil changes the magnetic flux linking the coil.

# End-of-chapter questions

1  A student thinks that electrical current passes through the core in a transformer to the secondary coil. Describe how you might demonstrate that this is not true and explain how an electrical current is actually induced in the secondary coil. Use Faraday's law in your explanation.

2  A square coil of 100 turns of wire has sides of length 5.0 cm. It is placed in a magnetic field of flux density 20 mT, so that the flux is perpendicular to the plane of the coil.
   a  Calculate the flux through the coil.
   b  The coil is now pulled from the magnetic field in a time of 0.10 s. Calculate the average e.m.f. induced in it.

3  An aircraft of wingspan 40 m flies horizontally at a speed of 300 m s$^{-1}$ in an area where the vertical component of the Earth's magnetic field is $5.0 \times 10^{-5}$ T. Calculate the e.m.f. generated between the aircraft's wingtips.

4  What is an eddy current? State **one** example where eddy currents are useful and one where they are a disadvantage.

5  Figure 27.27 shows the magnetic flux linkage and induced e.m.f. as a coil rotates. Explain why the induced e.m.f. is a maximum when there is no flux linkage and the induced e.m.f. is zero when the flux linkage is a maximum.

# Exam-style questions

1  a  Explain what is meant by a magnetic flux linkage of 1 Wb.                               [2]
   b  The diagram shows how the magnetic flux density through a 240 turn coil with a cross-sectional area $1.2 \times 10^{-4}$ m$^2$ varies with time.

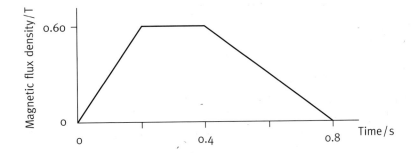

   i    Determine the maximum rate of change of flux in the coil.                              [2]
   ii   Determine the induced e.m.f. in the coil.                                              [2]
   iii  Sketch a diagram to show the induced e.m.f. varies with time. Mark values on both the e.m.f. and time axes.    [2]

2  The diagram shows a square coil about to enter a region of uniform magnetic field of magnetic flux density 0.30 T. The magnetic field is at right-angles to the plane of the coil. The coil has 150 turns and each side is 2.0 cm in length. The coil moves at a constant speed of $0.50\,\mathrm{m\,s^{-1}}$.

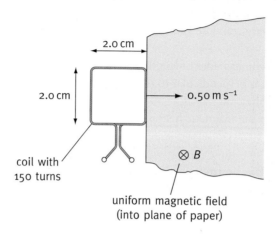

a  i  Calculate the time taken for the coil to enter completely the region of magnetic field.  [1]
   ii  Determine the magnetic flux linkage through the coil when it is all within the region of magnetic field.  [2]
b  Explain why the induced e.m.f. is constant while the coil is entering the magnetic field.  [1]
c  Use your answer to a to determine the induced e.m.f. across the ends of the coil.  [4]
d  What is the induced e.m.f. across the ends of the coil when it is completely within the magnetic field? Explain your answer.  [2]
e  Sketch a graph to show the variation of the induced e.m.f. with time from the instant that the coil enters the magnetic field. Your time axis should go from 0 to 0.08 s.  [2]

3  a  State Faraday's law of electromagnetic induction.  [2]
   b  A circular coil of diameter 200 mm has 600 turns. It is placed with its plane perpendicular to a horizontal magnetic field of uniform flux density 50 mT. The coil is then rotated through 90° about a vertical axis in a time of 120 ms.

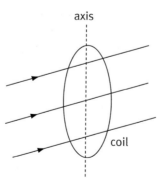

Calculate:
i  the magnetic flux passing through the coil before the rotation  [2]
ii  the change of magnetic flux linkage produced by the rotation  [2]
iii  the average e.m.f. induced in the coil during the rotation.  [2]

**4  a** State Lenz's law and explain how you would use a coil and a magnet to demonstrate
        the law. Make clear any other apparatus that you use.                                    [4]

   **b** A vehicle brake consists of an aluminium disc attached to a car axle. Electromagnets
        cause an e.m.f. to be induced in the disc.

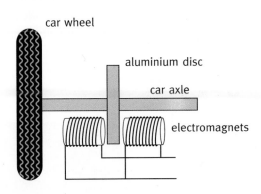

   **i** Explain how the induction of an e.m.f. causes the vehicle to slow down.                 [3]
   **ii** Explain why the braking effect increases when the speed of the car increases.          [2]

**5** A bicycle wheel is mounted vertically on a metal axle in a horizontal magnetic field.
     Sliding connections are made to the metal edge of the wheel and to the metal axle.

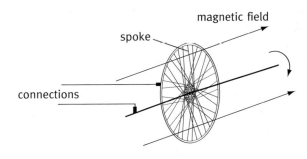

   **a i** Explain why an e.m.f. is induced when the wheel rotates.                              [2]
   **ii** State and explain two ways in which this e.m.f. can be increased.                      [2]
   **b** The wheel rotates five times per second and has a radius of 15 cm. The magnetic
        flux density may be assumed to be uniform and of value $5.0 \times 10^{-3}$ T.
        Calculate:
   **i** the area swept out each second by one spoke                                             [2]
   **ii** the induced e.m.f. between the contacts.                                               [2]

## Objectives

After studying this chapter, you should be able to:

- ☐ know how to measure frequency and voltage using a cathode-ray oscilloscope
- ☐ describe an alternating current or voltage in terms of period, frequency, peak value and r.m.s. values
- ☐ relate r.m.s. and peak values for sinusoidal currents

- ☐ solve problems involving transformers
- ☐ explain the benefits of transmission of electrical energy at high voltages
- ☐ explain how diodes and capacitors can be used to produce rectified, smoothed currents and voltages

## Describing alternating current

In developed countries, mains electricity is a supply of alternating current (a.c.). The first mains electricity supplies were developed towards the end of the 19th century; at that time, a great number of different voltages and frequencies were used in different places. In some places, the supply was direct current (d.c.). Nowadays this has been standardised across much of the world, with standard voltages of 110 V or 230 V (or similar), and frequencies of 50 Hz or 60 Hz.

In this chapter we will look at some of the reasons why a.c. has been chosen as standard. First, however, we must take a close look at the nature of alternating currents.

Figure 28.1 Public electricity supplies made possible new forms of street lighting and advertising.

## Sinusoidal current

An alternating current can be represented by a graph such as that shown in Figure 28.2. This shows that the current varies cyclically. During half of the cycle, the current is positive, and in the other half it is negative. This means that the current flows alternately one way and then the other in the wires in which it is travelling. Whenever you use a mains appliance, current flows backwards and forwards in the wires between you and the power station where it is being generated. At any instant in time, the current has a particular magnitude and direction given by the graph.

The graph has the same shape as the graphs used to represent simple harmonic motion (see Chapter 20), and it can be interpreted in the same way. The electrons in a wire carrying a.c. thus move back and forth with s.h.m. The current varies like a sine wave

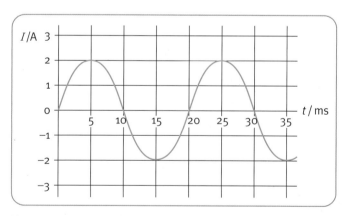

Figure 28.2 A graph to represent a sinusoidal alternating current.

and so it is described as **sinusoidal**. (In principle, any current whose direction changes between positive and negative can be described as **alternating**, but we will only be concerned with those which have a regular, sinusoidal pattern.)

Since the *x*-axis measures time, the c.r.o. trace can be used to measure frequency. In the above example, since

$$\text{period} = \frac{1}{\text{frequency}}$$

$$\text{frequency} = \frac{1}{0.02} = 50\,\text{Hz}$$

## Test yourself

5  If the Y-sensitivity and time-base for the trace shown in Figure **28.6** are 5 V/cm and 10 ms/cm, what are the amplitude, period and frequency of the signal to the Y-input?

6  Draw the c.r.o. trace for a sinusoidal voltage of frequency 100 Hz and amplitude 10 V, when the time-base is 10 ms/cm and the Y-sensitivity is 10 V/cm.

# Power and a.c.

We use mains electricity to supply us with energy. If the current and voltage are varying all the time, does this mean that the power is varying all the time too? The answer to this is yes, it is. You may have noticed that some fluorescent lamps flicker continuously, especially if you observe them out of the corner of your eye. A tungsten filament lamp would flicker too, but the frequency of the mains has been chosen so that the filament does not have time to cool down noticeably between peaks in the supply.

## Comparing a.c. and d.c.

Because power supplied by an alternating current is varying all the time, we need to have some way of describing the **average power** which is being supplied. To do this, we compare an alternating current with a direct current, and try to find the direct current that supplies the same average power as the alternating current.

Figure **28.7** shows how this can be done in practice. Two lamps are placed side-by-side; one is connected to an a.c. supply (on the right) and the other to a d.c. supply (the batteries on the left). The a.c. supply is adjusted so that the two lamps are equally bright, indicating that the two supplies are providing energy at the same average rate. The output voltages are then compared on the double-beam oscilloscope.

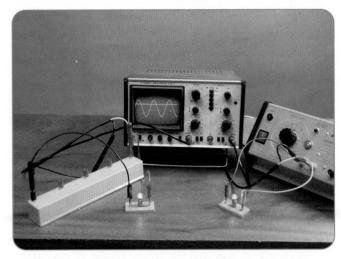

**Figure 28.7** Comparing direct and alternating currents that supply the same power. The lamps are equally bright.

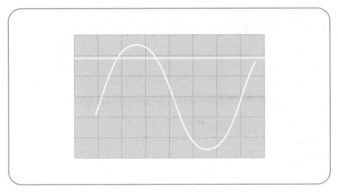

**Figure 28.8** The oscilloscope trace from the experiment shown in Figure **28.7**.

A typical trace is shown in Figure **28.8**. This shows that the a.c. trace sometimes rises above the steady d.c. trace, and sometimes falls below it. This makes sense: sometimes the a.c. is delivering more power than the d.c., and sometimes less, but the average power is the same for both.

There is a mathematical relationship between the d.c. voltage and the peak value $V_0$ of the alternating voltage. The d.c. voltage is about 70% of $V_0$. (You might have expected it to be about half, but it is more than this, because of the shape of the sine graph.) This steady d.c. voltage is known as the root-mean-square (r.m.s.) value of the alternating voltage. In the same way, we can think of the root-mean-square value of an alternating current, $I_{rms}$:

The root-mean-square value of an alternating current is that steady current which delivers the same average power as the a.c. to a resistive load.

(The lamps in the experiment above are the 'resistive loads'.) A full analysis, which we will come to shortly, shows that $I_{rms}$ is related to $I_0$ by:

$$I_{rms} = \frac{I_0}{\sqrt{2}} \qquad \text{or} \qquad I_{rms} = 0.707 \times I_0$$

This is where the factor of 70% comes from. Note that this factor only applies to sinusoidal alternating currents.

## Test yourself

7 What is the r.m.s. value of an alternating current represented (in amps) by the equation $I = 2.5 \sin(100\pi t)$?

8 The mains supply to domestic consumers in many European countries has an r.m.s. voltage $V_{rms}$ of 230 V. (Note that it is the r.m.s. value which is generally quoted, not the peak value.) What is the peak value of the supply?

## Calculating power

The importance of r.m.s. values is that they allow us to apply equations from our study of direct current to situations where the current is alternating. So, to calculate the average power dissipated in a resistor, we can use the usual formulae for power:

$$P = I^2 R = IV = \frac{V^2}{R}$$

Remember that it is essential to use the r.m.s. values of $I$ and $V$, as in Worked example 1. If you use peak values, your answer will be too great by a factor of 2.

## Worked example

1  A sinusoidal p.d. of peak value 25 V is connected across a 20 Ω resistor. What is the average power dissipated in the resistor?

   **Step 1** Calculate the r.m.s. value of the p.d.:

$$V_{rms} = \frac{V_0}{\sqrt{2}} = \frac{25}{\sqrt{2}} = 17.7\,\text{V}$$

continued ···➔

**Step 2** Now calculate the average power dissipated:

$$P = \frac{V^2}{R} = \frac{17.7^2}{20} = 15.6\,\text{W}$$

(Note that, if we had used $V_0$ rather than $V_{rms}$, we would have found $P = \frac{25^2}{20} = 31.3\,\text{W}$, which is double the correct answer.)

## Test yourself

9 What is the average power dissipated when a sinusoidal alternating current with a peak value of 3.0 A flows through a 100 Ω resistor?

10 A sinusoidal voltage of peak value 325 V is connected across a 1 kΩ resistor.
   a What is the r.m.s. value of this voltage?
   b Use $V = IR$ to calculate the r.m.s. current which flows through the resistor.
   c What is the average power dissipated in the resistor?

## Root-mean-square

We will now briefly consider the origin of the term root-mean-square and show how the factor of $\sqrt{2}$ comes about. The equation $P = I^2 R$ tells us that the power $P$ is proportional to the square of the current $I$. Figure 28.9 shows how we can calculate $I^2$ for an alternating current. The current $I$ varies sinusoidally, and during half of each cycle it is negative. However, $I^2$ is always positive (because the square of a negative number is positive). Notice that $I^2$ varies up and down, and that it has twice the frequency of the current.

Now, if we consider $\langle I^2 \rangle$, the average (mean) value of $I^2$, we find that its value is half the peak value (because the graph is symmetrical):

$$\langle I^2 \rangle = \tfrac{1}{2} I^2$$

To find the r.m.s. value of $I$, we now take the square root of $\langle I^2 \rangle$. This introduces a factor of the square root of $\tfrac{1}{2}$, or $\frac{1}{\sqrt{2}}$.

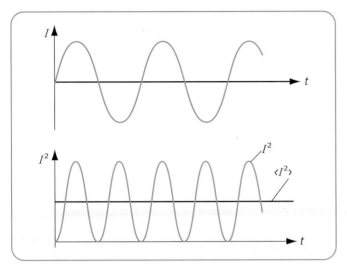

Figure 28.9 An alternating current $I$ is alternately positive and negative, while $I^2$ is always positive.

Summarising this process: to find the r.m.s. value of the current, we find the root of mean of the square of the current – hence r.m.s.

# Why use a.c. for electricity supply?

There are several reasons for preferring alternating voltages for a national electricity supply system. The most important reason is that a.c. can be transformed

Figure 28.10 Power lines carry electricity from power station to consumer.

to high voltages, so that the current flowing is reduced, and this leads to lower power losses in the transmission lines. Typically, the generators at a power station produce electrical power at a voltage of 25 kV. This is transformed up to a voltage of perhaps 400 kV (and as much as 1 MV in some countries). The power is then transmitted along many kilometres of high-voltage power lines (Figure 28.10) before being transformed down to a lower voltage for supply to the millions of consumers. The transformers used for increasing and decreasing the voltage are discussed in detail in the next section.

This high voltage brings problems: the lines must be suspended high above the ground between pylons, and high-quality insulators are needed to prevent current passing from the cables to the pylons. As current flows through transmission lines (wires), it loses power because of the resistance of the lines. The wires become warm; this is resistive or ohmic heating, as discussed in Chapter 10. The smaller the current, the smaller the losses. This is illustrated in Worked example 2.

## Worked example

2 A power station generates electrical power at a rate of 10 MW. This power is to be transmitted along cables whose total resistance is 10 Ω. Calculate the power losses in the cable if the power is transmitted at 50 kV and at 250 kV.

**Step 1** Using $I = \dfrac{P}{V}$, calculate the current flowing in each case:

for 50 kV: $I = \dfrac{10 \times 10^6}{5 \times 10^4} = 200\,\text{A}$

for 250 kV: $I = \dfrac{10 \times 10^6}{25 \times 10^4} = 40\,\text{A}$

*continued* ⋯⟩

**Step 2** Using $P = I^2R$, calculate the power losses in each case:

for 50 kV: $P = 200^2 \times 10 = 4 \times 10^5 = 400\,\text{kW}$

for 250 kV: $P = 40^2 \times 10 = 1.6 \times 10^4 = 16\,\text{kW}$

Take care! Note that we have two quantities for which we are using the symbol $P$: the total power being transmitted, and the power lost in the wires. Notice that using a higher voltage does not change the resistance of the cables.

We have shown that, by increasing the voltage by a factor of 5, we have reduced the power losses by a factor of 25.

## Economic savings

The resistive heating of power lines is a waste of money, in two ways. Firstly, it costs money to generate power because of the fuel needed. Secondly, more power stations are required, and power stations are expensive. The use of transformers to transform power to high voltages saves a few per cent of a national bill for electrical power, and means that fewer expensive power stations are needed.

It is claimed that having a few, very large power stations gives economies of scale, but this is debated by many environmentalists who would prefer to see many small, local power stations. It is also the case that new developments in technology are making it easier to transform direct current to high voltages. This is more compatible with sustainable electricity generating systems such as photovoltaics (solar cells), so we may see the development of d.c. grid systems in the near future.

## Transformers

Figure **28.11** shows the construction of a simple transformer. The primary coil of $N_p$ turns of wire is wound around the iron core. The secondary coil of $N_s$ turns is wound on the opposite side of the core. (Many different configurations are possible, with different shapes of core and with the coils wound separately or one on top of the other.)

The p.d. $V_p$ across the primary coil causes an alternating current $I_p$ to flow. This produces an alternating magnetic field in the soft iron core. The secondary coil is thus in a changing magnetic field, and an alternating current $I_s$ is induced in it. There is thus an alternating e.m.f. $V_s$ across the secondary coil.

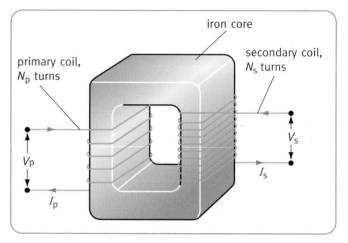

**Figure 28.11** Defining quantities for a simple iron-cored transformer.

Note that there is no **electrical** connection between the primary coil and the secondary coil. Energy is transferred from one to the other via the magnetic field in the core.

## Step-up, step-down

The transformer represented in Figure **28.11** has 5 turns on its primary coil and 10 on its secondary coil. It is described as a **step-up transformer** because the output voltage is greater than the input voltage (the voltage has been 'stepped up').

How does this happen? We have 5 turns producing magnetic flux. This flux links the 10 turns of the secondary coil. Because flux linkage $N\varphi$ is proportional to the number of turns, it follows that there is more magnetic flux – twice as much – linking the secondary coil than the primary. As the magnetic flux changes (because we are using alternating voltages), the e.m.f. induced in the secondary coil is greater than the voltage across the primary coil.

We can write an equation relating the voltages across the coils to the number of turns in each coil:

$$\frac{V_s}{V_p} = \frac{N_s}{N_p}$$

The equation above is known as the **turns-ratio equation** for a transformer.

In words, the ratio of the voltages is equal to the ratio of the turns of the transformer. For the transformer in Figure **28.11**, a voltage of 1.0 V applied to the primary coil will result in an output of 2.0 V across the secondary coil; 50 V will give 100 V, and so on.

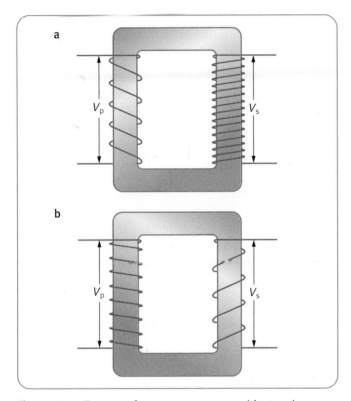

a

$V_p$

$V_s$

b

$V_p$

$V_s$

**Figure 28.12** Two transformers: **a** step-up, and **b** step-down.

A transformer with fewer turns on the secondary coil than on the primary coil is described as a **step-down transformer**. It lowers the voltage at the primary coil. Figure **28.12** shows both types of transformer. Worked example **3** shows how to use the turns-ratio equation.

## Worked example

**3** A radio requires a 6.0 V supply but has to be operated from a 230 V mains supply. It is fitted with a transformer to reduce the mains voltage. Calculate the turns ratio for this transformer. If the primary coil has 5000 turns, how many turns must the secondary have?

**Step 1** The turns ratio $\dfrac{N_s}{N_p}$ is given by:

$$\frac{V_s}{V_p} = \frac{N_s}{N_p}$$

Hence:

$$\frac{N_s}{N_p} = \frac{V_s}{V_p} = \frac{6.0}{230} = 0.026$$

This ratio is less than one because we are reducing the voltage.

**Step 2** We know that $N_p = 5000$, so we can calculate $N_s$.

$$N_s = N_p \times 0.026 = 5000 \times 0.026 = 130$$

So the secondary coil must have 130 turns. Check that this seems reasonable: the voltage has to be reduced by a factor of about 40, so the number of turns must be reduced by the same factor.

## Test yourself

11 a What is the turns ratio of the transformer shown in Figure **28.12a**?
   b What is the turns ratio of the transformer shown in Figure **28.12b**?
   c If an alternating p.d. of value 10.0 V is connected across the primary coil of each, what will be the induced e.m.f. across each secondary?

12 A power station generates electricity at a voltage of 25 kV. This must be transformed for onward transmission at 400 kV. If the primary coil of the transformer used has 2000 turns, how many turns must the secondary coil have?

## Voltage, current, power

If there is no power lost in a transformer, it follows that the quantity $I \times V$ is the same for both primary and secondary coils:

$$I_p V_p = I_s V_s \quad \text{or} \quad \frac{V_s}{V_p} = \frac{I_p}{I_s}$$

In other words, the ratio of the voltages is the **inverse** ratio of the currents. If the voltage is stepped up, the current is stepped down, and vice versa. This explains the function of transformers in power transmission, as discussed earlier.

Note that this relationship assumes that no power is lost in the transformer. In practice, some power is lost because of the resistance of the transformer coil windings; some power is also lost as the magnetic flux in the core flows back and forth. The windings and the core tend to become warm. Large transformers

**Figure 28.13** Installing a new transformer in a gold mine in Ghana.

such as the one shown in Figure **28.13** handle a large amount of power. A small percentage is wasted, and the resulting heat is carried away by cooling fluid pumped around the transformer and through the fins which are visible in the photograph.

The transformers used in the electricity supply industry must be designed with great care to minimise energy losses. The electricity supply may pass through as many as ten transformers between the generator and the consumer. If each transformer wasted just 1% of the power, that would give an overall loss of 10%. Since there are roughly 100 big power stations in the UK, that would require ten power stations just to cope with the losses in transformers. Today's well-designed transformers have losses of under 0.1%. This contributes greatly to energy savings in the power transmission industry.

# Rectification

Many electrical appliances work with alternating current. Some, like electrical heaters, will work equally well with d.c. or a.c. However, there are many appliances such as electronic equipment which require d.c. For these, the alternating mains must be converted to d.c. by the process of **rectification**.

A simple way to do this is to use a diode, which is a component that will only allow current to flow in one direction. Figure 28.14 shows a circuit for doing this, together with a graph to show the effect. You will see that the output voltage is always positive, but it goes up and down. This is still technically direct current, because the current only flows in one direction.

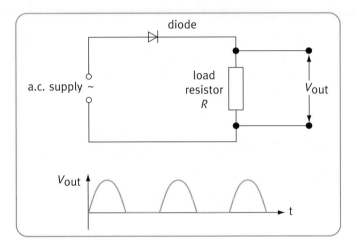

Figure 28.14 Half-wave rectification of a.c. requires a single diode.

This type of rectification is known as half-wave rectification. For one half of the time the voltage is zero, and this means that the power available from a half-wave rectified supply is reduced.

## The bridge rectifier

To overcome this problem of reduced power, a bridge rectifier circuit is used. This consists of four diodes connected across the alternating voltage, as shown in Figure 28.15. The resulting output voltage across the load resistor $R$ is full-wave rectified.
The way in which this works is shown in Figure 28.16.

- During the first half of the a.c. cycle, terminal A is positive. Current flows through diode 2, downwards through $R$ and through diode 3 to terminal B. In this half of the cycle, current cannot flow through diodes 1 or 4 because they are pointing the wrong way.
- In the second half of the cycle, terminal B is positive. Current flows through diode 4, downwards through $R$, and through diode 1 to terminal A. Diodes 2 and 3 do not conduct because they are pointing the wrong way.

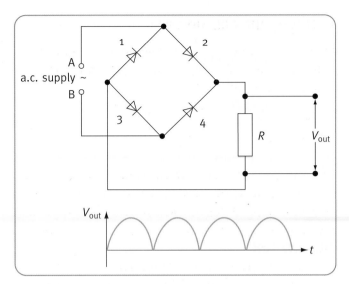

Figure 28.15 Full-wave rectification of a.c. using a diode bridge.

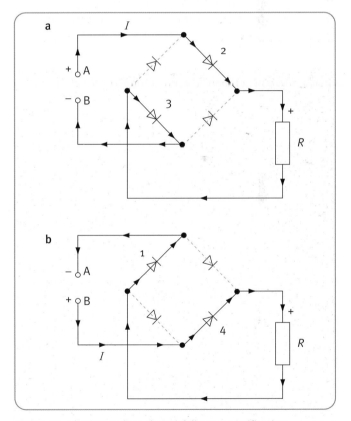

Figure 28.16 Current flow during full-wave rectification.

Note that in both halves of the cycle, current flows the same way (downwards) through $R$, so the top end of $R$ must be positive.

You can construct a bridge rectifier using light-emitting diodes (LEDs) which light up when current flows through them. By connecting this bridge to a slow a.c. supply (for instance 1 Hz from a signal generator), you can see the sequence in which the diodes conduct during rectification.

## Test yourself

15 Explain why, when terminal B in Figure **28.16** is positive (during the second half of the cycle), the current flows through diodes 1 and 4, but not through diodes 2 and 3.

## Smoothing

In order to produce steady d.c. from the 'bumpy' d.c. that results from rectification, a smoothing capacitor must be incorporated in the circuit, in parallel with the load resistor $R$. This is shown in Figure **28.17**. The idea is that the capacitor charges up and maintains the voltage at a high level. It discharges gradually when the rectified voltage drops, but the voltage soon rises again and the capacitor charges up again. The result is an output voltage with 'ripple'.

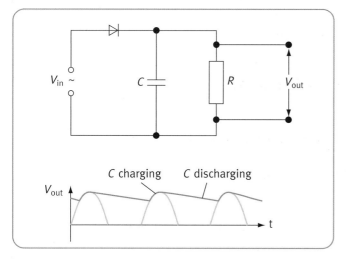

**Figure 28.17** A smoothing capacitor is connected across (in parallel with) the load resistor.

The amount of ripple can be controlled by careful choice of the values of $C$ and $R$. A large capacitor discharges more slowly than a small capacitor, so will give less ripple. Similarly, if $R$ has a large value, $C$ will discharge more slowly. In practice, the greater the value of the quantity $R \times C$, the smoother the rectified a.c. However, if $R$ and $C$ have large values, it will be difficult to change the value of the voltage quickly.

## Test yourself

16 Sketch the following voltage patterns:
   **a** a sinusoidal alternating voltage
   **b** the same voltage as **a**, but half-wave rectified
   **c** the same voltage as **b**, but smoothed
   **d** the same voltage as **a**, but full-wave rectified
   **e** the same voltage as **d**, but smoothed.

17 A student wires a bridge rectifier incorrectly as shown in Figure **28.18**. Explain what you would expect to observe when an oscilloscope is connected across the load resistor $R$.

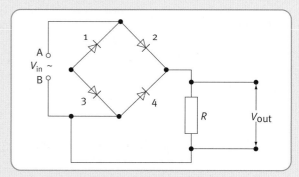

**Figure 28.18** A bridge rectifier circuit that is wired incorrectly – see Test yourself Q **17**.

18 A bridge rectifier circuit is used to rectify an alternating current through a resistor $R$. A smoothing capacitor $C$ is connected across $R$. Figure **28.19** shows how the current varies. Use sketches to show the changes you would expect:
   **a** if $R$ was increased
   **b** if $C$ was decreased.

**Figure 28.19** A smoothed, rectified current – see Test yourself Q **18**.

# Summary

- A sinusoidal alternating current can be represented by $I = I_o \sin \omega t$, where $I_o$ is the peak value of the current.
- The root-mean-square value of an alternating current is that steady current which delivers the same average power as the a.c. to a resistive load; for a sinusoidal a.c., $I_{rms} = \dfrac{I_o}{\sqrt{2}}$.
- Electrical power is usually transmitted at high voltages; this allows the current to be reduced, and so resistive losses are less.
- Transformers are used to change an alternating voltage. The voltage is stepped up or down in proportion to the turns ratio of the transformer.
- For a transformer, $\dfrac{V_s}{V_p} = \dfrac{N_s}{N_p}$. If it is 100% efficient, then $V_p I_p = V_s I_s$.
- Diodes are used to convert a.c. to d.c. A single diode gives half-wave rectification. A bridge of four diodes gives full-wave rectification. A capacitor smoothes the rectified voltage.

# End-of-chapter questions

1   Write down a general expression for the sinusoidal variation with time $t$ of:
   a   an alternating voltage $V$
   b   an alternating current $I$ (you may assume that $I$ and $V$ are in phase)
   c   the power $P$ dissipated due to this current and voltage.

2   The value of an alternating current in A is represented by the equation $I = 2 \sin (50\pi t)$
   a   What is the peak value of the current?
   b   What is the frequency of the supply?
   c   Sketch a graph to show two cycles of the variation of current with time. Mark the axes with suitable values.
   d   Calculate $I_{rms}$, the r.m.s. value of current, and mark this on your graph.
   e   Find **two** values of $t$ at which $I = I_{rms}$.

3   The a.c. mains of 240 V r.m.s. is connected to the primary coil of a transformer, which contains 1200 turns. The r.m.s. output of the transformer is 6.0 V.
   a   Calculate the number of turns on the secondary coil.
   b   A resistance of $6.0\,\Omega$ is connected across the secondary coil. Calculate:
      i   the average power dissipated in the resistor
      ii  the peak current in the primary coil.

**4** The graph in Figure **28.20** shows the sinusoidal variation of current in the primary current of a transformer. The current in the secondary coil is zero.

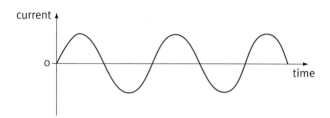

**Figure 28.20** For End-of-chapter Q **4.**

    **a** Copy the graph and on your copy draw, on the same axes, the variation with time of:
       **i** the magnetic flux in the core of the transformer – label this A.
      **ii** the induced e.m.f. in the primary coil of the transformer – label this B.
    **b** State how the two graphs in **a i** and **ii** are related to each other.

**5** An oscilloscope is used to measure the voltage waveform across a $200\,\Omega$ resistor. The waveform is shown in Figure **28.21**. The time-base of the oscilloscope is set at $5\,\text{ms division}^{-1}$ and the Y-gain at $0.5\,\text{V division}^{-1}$.

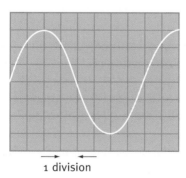

1 division

**Figure 28.21** For End-of-chapter Q **5.**

Determine:
**a** the period and hence the frequency of the waveform
**b** the peak voltage and hence the r.m.s. voltage
**c** the r.m.s. current in the resistor
**d** the mean power dissipated in the resistor.

# Exam-style questions

1  **a** State the relationship between the peak current $I_0$ and the r.m.s. current $I_{rms}$ for a
sinusoidally varying current. [1]
   **b** When connected to a steady d.c. supply, the current in a resistor is 2.0 A. When
connected to an a.c. supply, the current in the same resistor has a peak value
of 2.0 A. The heating effects of the two currents in the resistor are different.
   **i** Explain why the heating effects are different and state which heating effect is the greater. [2]
   **ii** Calculate the ratio of the power dissipated in the resistor by the d.c. current to the power
dissipated in the resistor by the a.c. current. [2]
   **c** State **one** advantage of using alternating current in the home. [1]

2  A sinusoidal voltage of 6.0 V r.m.s. and frequency 50 Hz is connected to a diode and a resistor R of
resistance 400 Ω as shown in the diagram.

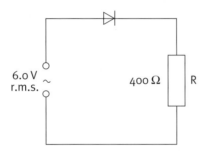

   **a** Draw a sketch graph showing the variation with time of both the supply waveform
(use a dotted line) and the voltage across R (use a solid line). Put numerical scales on
both the voltage and time axes. [4]
   **b** An uncharged capacitor C is connected across R. When the 6.0 V r.m.s. supply is
switched on, the capacitor charges fully during the first quarter of a cycle. You may
assume that p.d. across the diode is zero when it conducts. For the next three-quarters
of the first cycle, the diode stops conducting and the p.d. across R falls to one half of the
peak value. During this time the mean p.d. across R is 5.7 V.
   For the last three-quarters of the first cycle, calculate:
   **i** the time taken [1]
   **ii** the mean current in R [2]
   **iii** the charge flowing through R [2]
   **iv** the capacitance of C. [2]
   **c** Explain why the diode stops conducting during part of each cycle in **b**. [2]

3  The rectified output from a transformer is connected to a resistor R of resistance 1000 Ω.
Graph **A** on the next page shows the variation with time $t$ of the p.d. $V$ across the resistor.
Graph **B** shows the variation of $V$ when a capacitor is placed across R to smooth the output.

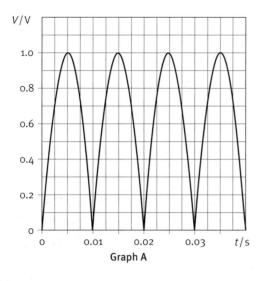

Graph A

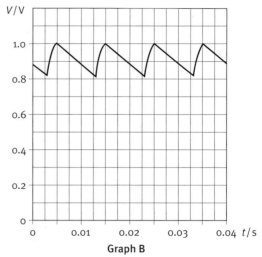

Graph B

**a** Explain how the rectification is achieved. Draw a circuit diagram to show the components involved. [6]

**b** Explain the action of the capacitor in smoothing the output. [3]

**c** Using graph B, between $t = 0.005$ and $t = 0.015\,\text{s}$, determine:

   **i** the time during which the capacitor is charging [1]

   **ii** the mean value of the p.d. across R [1]

   **iii** the average power dissipated in R. [2]

**4** An ideal transformer is used to produce an output of **peak** value 12 V from the 230 V r.m.s. mains supply.

  **a** The primary coil of the transformer contains 2000 turns. Calculate the number of turns in the secondary coil. [3]

  **b** The output from the secondary coil is half-wave rectified, and connected to a resistor R and capacitor C in parallel.

    Sketch a graph on the same axes to show the variation with time of:

   **i** the output p.d. of the secondary coil [1]

   **ii** the p.d. across R. [2]

  **c** State and explain what happens to the p.d. across R when another capacitor of equal value is placed in parallel with C. [3]

**5** Electrical energy is supplied by a high voltage power line which has a total resistance of $4.0\,\Omega$. At the input to the line, the root-mean-square (r.m.s.) voltage has a value of 400 kV and the input power is 500 MW.

  **a i** Explain what is meant by **root-mean-square voltage**. [2]

   **ii** Calculate the minimum voltage that the insulators which support the line must withstand without breakdown. [2]

  **b i** Calculate the value of the r.m.s. current in the power line. [2]

   **ii** Calculate the power loss on the line. [2]

   **iii** Explain why it is an advantage to transmit the power at a high voltage. [2]

  **c** Power at 400 kV is converted to power at 124 kV by a step-down transformer. Describe the basic principle of a step-down transformer. [2]

# 29 Quantum physics

## Objectives

After studying this chapter you should be able to:

- [ ] appreciate the particulate nature of electromagnetic radiation
- [ ] interpret the photoelectric effect in terms of photons
- [ ] describe electron diffraction and the evidence it provides for the wave nature of matter
- [ ] explain line spectra in terms of discrete electron energy levels in atoms

## What is light?

When the first laser was made in 1960, it seemed like a clever idea, but it was a long time before it found any useful application. Today, lasers are everywhere – in CD and DVD machines, computer disc drives, supermarket barcode scanners – there are probably more lasers than people. Figure **29.1** shows a patient undergoing laser eye surgery.

The invention of the laser was only possible when scientists had cracked the mystery of the nature of light. Does light behave as particles or as waves? As we shall see in this chapter, the answer is – a bit of both.

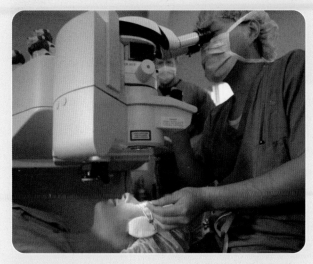

**Figure 29.1** This patient is undergoing laser eye surgery which improves the focusing of the eye by modifying the shape of the surface of the eyeball.

## Modelling with particles and waves

In this chapter, we will study two very powerful scientific models – particles and waves – to see how they can help us to understand more about both light and matter. First we will take a closer look at each of these models in turn.

### Particle models

In order to explain the properties of matter, we often think about the particles of which it is made and the ways in which they behave. We imagine particles as being objects that are hard, have mass, and move about according to the laws of Newtonian mechanics (Figure **29.2**). When two particles collide, we can predict how they will move after the collision, based on knowledge of their masses and velocities before the collision. If you have played snooker or pool, you will have a pretty good idea of how particles behave.

Particles are a macroscopic model. Our ideas of particles come from what we observe on a macroscopic scale – when we are walking down the street, or observing the motion of stars and planets, or working with trolleys and balls in the laboratory. But what else can we explain using a particle model?

The importance of particle models is that we can apply them to the microscopic world, and explain more phenomena.

**Figure 29.2** Pool balls provide a good model for the behaviour of particles on a much smaller scale.

We can picture gas molecules as small, hard particles, rushing around and bouncing haphazardly off one another and the walls of their container. This is the kinetic model of a gas which we studied in depth in Chapter 22. We can explain the macroscopic (larger scale) phenomena of pressure and temperature in terms of the masses and speeds of the microscopic particles. This is a very powerful model, which has been refined to explain many other aspects of the behaviour of gases.

Table **29.1** shows how, in particular areas of science, we can use a particle model to interpret and make predictions about macroscopic phenomena.

| Area | Model | Macroscopic phenomena |
|---|---|---|
| electricity | flow of electrons | current |
| gases | kinetic theory | pressure, temperature and volume of a gas |
| solids | crystalline materials | mechanical properties |
| radioactivity | nuclear model of atom | radioactive decay, fission and fusion reactions |
| chemistry | atomic structure | chemical reactions |

**Table 29.1** Particle models in science.

## Wave models

Waves are something that we see on the sea. There are tidal waves, and little ripples. Some waves have foamy tops, others are breaking on the beach.

Physicists have an idealised picture of a wave – it is shaped like a sine graph. You will not see any waves quite this shape on the sea. However, it is a useful picture, because it can be used to represent some simple phenomena. More complicated waves can be made up of several simple waves, and physicists can cope with the mathematics of sine waves. (This is the principle of superposition, which we looked at in detail in Chapter 15.)

Waves are a way in which energy is transferred from one place to another. In any wave, something is changing in a regular way, while energy is travelling along. In water waves, the surface of the water moves up and down periodically, and energy is transferred horizontally.

Table **29.2** shows some other phenomena that we explain in terms of waves.

| Phenomenon | Varying quantity |
|---|---|
| sound | pressure (or density) |
| light (and other electromagnetic waves) | electric and magnetic field strengths |
| waves on strings | displacement |

**Table 29.2** Wave models in science.

The characteristic properties of waves are that they all show reflection, refraction, diffraction and interference. Waves also do not have mass or charge. Since particle models can also explain reflection and refraction, it is diffraction and interference that we regard as the defining characteristics of waves. If we can show diffraction and interference, we know that we are dealing with waves (Figure **29.3**).

**Figure 29.3** A diffraction grating splits up light into its component colours and can produce dramatic effects in photographs.

## Waves or particles?

Wave models and particle models are both very useful. They can explain a great many different observations. But which should we use in a particular situation? And what if both models seem to work when we are trying to explain something?

This is just the problem that physicists struggled with for over a century, in connection with light. Does light travel as a wave or as particles?

For a long time, Newton's view prevailed – light travels as particles. This was set out in 1704 in his famous book *Opticks*. He could use this model to explain both reflection and refraction. His model suggested that light travels faster in glass than in air. In 1801 Thomas Young, an English physicist, demonstrated that light showed diffraction and

interference effects. Physicists were still very reluctant to abandon Newton's particle model of light. The ultimate blow to Newton's model came from the work carried out by the French physicist Léon Foucault in 1853. His experiments on the speed of light showed that light travelled more slowly in water than in air. Newton's model was in direct contradiction with experimental results. Most scientists were convinced that light travelled through space as a wave.

## Particulate nature of light

We expect light to behave as waves, but can light also behave as particles? The answer is yes, and you are probably already familiar with some of the evidence.

If you place a Geiger counter next to a source of gamma radiation you will hear an irregular series of clicks. The counter is detecting γ-rays (gamma-rays). But γ-rays are part of the electromagnetic spectrum. They belong to the same family of waves as visible light, radio waves, X-rays, etc.

So, here are waves giving individual or discrete clicks, which are indistinguishable from the clicks given by α-particles (alpha-particles) and β-particles (beta-particles). We can conclude that γ-rays behave like particles when they interact with a Geiger counter.

This effect is most obvious with γ-rays, because they are at the most energetic end of the electromagnetic spectrum. It is harder to show the same effect for visible light.

### Photons

The **photoelectric effect**, and Einstein's explanation of it, convinced physicists that light could behave as a stream of particles. Before we go on to look at this in detail, we need to see how to calculate the energy of photons.

Newton used the word **corpuscle** for the particles which he thought made up light. Nowadays, we call them **photons** and we believe that all electromagnetic radiation consists of photons. A photon is a 'packet of energy' or a quantum of electromagnetic energy. Gamma-photons (γ-photons) are the most energetic. According to Albert Einstein, who based his ideas on the work of another German physicist Max Planck, the energy $E$ of a photon in joules (J) is related to the frequency $f$ in hertz (Hz) of the electromagnetic radiation of which it is part, by the equation:

$$E = hf$$

The constant $h$ has an experimental value equal to $6.63 \times 10^{-34}$ J s.

This constant $h$ is called the **Planck constant**. It has the unit joule seconds (J s), but you may prefer to think of this as 'joules per hertz'. The energy of a photon is directly proportional to the frequency of the electromagnetic waves, that is:

$$E \propto f$$

Hence, high-frequency radiation means high-energy photons.

Notice that the equation $E = hf$ tells us the relationship between a particle property (the photon energy $E$) and a wave property (the frequency $f$). It is called the **Einstein relation** and applies to all electromagnetic waves.

The frequency $f$ and wavelength $\lambda$ of an electromagnetic wave are related to the wave speed $c$ by the wave equation $c = f\lambda$, so we can also write this equation as:

$$E = \frac{hc}{\lambda}$$

It is worth noting that the energy of the photon is inversely proportional to the wavelength. Hence the short-wavelength X-ray photon is far more energetic than the long-wavelength photon of light.

Now we can work out the energy of a γ-photon. Gamma-rays typically have frequencies greater than $10^{20}$ Hz. The energy of a γ-photon is therefore greater than

$$(6.63 \times 10^{-34} \times 10^{20}) \approx 10^{-13} \text{ J}$$

This is a very small amount of energy on the human scale, so we don't notice the effects of individual γ-photons. However, some astronauts have reported seeing flashes of light as individual cosmic rays, high-energy γ-photons, have passed through their eyeballs.

## Test yourself

To answer questions 1–7 you will need these values:

speed of light in a vacuum $c = 3.0 \times 10^8$ m s$^{-1}$

Planck constant $h = 6.63 \times 10^{-34}$ J s

1 Calculate the energy of a high-energy γ-photon, frequency $10^{26}$ Hz.

2 Visible light has wavelengths in the range 400 nm (violet) to 700 nm (red). Calculate the energy of a photon of red light and a photon of violet light.

3 Determine the wavelength of the electromagnetic waves for each photon below and hence use Figure **29.4** to identify the region of the electromagnetic spectrum to which each belongs.

The photon energy is:
a $10^{-12}$ J
b $10^{-15}$ J
c $10^{-18}$ J
d $10^{-20}$ J
e $10^{-25}$ J

4 A 1.0 mW laser produces red light of wavelength $6.48 \times 10^{-7}$ m. Calculate how many photons the laser produces per second.

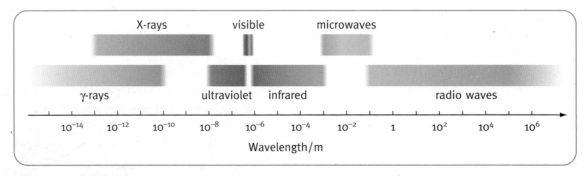

**Figure 29.4** Wavelengths of the electromagnetic spectrum. The boundaries between some regions are fuzzy.

## The electronvolt (eV)

The energy of a photon is extremely small and far less than a joule. Hence the joule is not a very convenient unit for measuring photon energies. Now we will define another energy unit, the **electronvolt**, which is useful for amounts of energy much smaller than a joule.

When an electron travels through a potential difference, energy is transferred. If an electron, which has a charge of magnitude $1.6 \times 10^{-19}$ C, travels through a potential difference of 1 V, its energy change $W$ is given by:

$$W = QV = 1.6 \times 10^{-19} \times 1 = 1.6 \times 10^{-19} \text{ J}$$

We can use this as the basis of the definition of the electronvolt:

One electronvolt (1 eV) is the energy transferred when an electron travels through a potential difference of one volt.

Therefore:

$$1 \text{ eV} = 1.6 \times 10^{-19} \text{ J}$$

So when an electron moves through 1 V, 1 eV of energy is transferred. When one electron moves through 2 V, 2 eV of energy are transferred. When five electrons move through 10 V, a total of 50 eV are transferred, and so on.

- To convert from eV to J, multiply by $1.6 \times 10^{-19}$.
- To convert from J to eV, divide by $1.6 \times 10^{-19}$.

### Test yourself

5 An electron travels through a cell of e.m.f. 1.2 V. How much energy is transferred to the electron? Give your answer in eV and in J.

6 Calculate the energy in eV of an X-ray photon of frequency $3.0 \times 10^{18}$ Hz.

7 To which region of the electromagnetic spectrum (Figure 29.4) does a photon of energy 10 eV belong?

When a charged particle is accelerated through a potential difference $V$, its kinetic energy increases. For an electron (charge $e$), accelerated from rest, we can write:

$$eV = \tfrac{1}{2}mv^2$$

We need to be careful when using this equation. It does not apply when a charged particle is accelerated through a large voltage to speeds approaching the speed of light $c$. For this, we would have to take account of relativistic effects. (The mass of a particle increases as its speed gets closer to $3.0 \times 10^8$ m s$^{-1}$.)

Rearranging the equation gives the electron's speed:

$$v = \sqrt{\frac{2ev}{m}}$$

This equation applies to any type of charged particle, including protons (charge $+e$) and ions.

### Test yourself

8 A proton (charge $= +1.6 \times 10^{-19}$ C, mass $= 1.7 \times 10^{-27}$ kg) is accelerated through a potential difference of 1500 V. Determine:
   a its final kinetic energy in joules (J)
   b its final speed.

## Estimating the Planck constant

You can obtain an estimate of the value of the Planck constant $h$ by means of a simple experiment. It makes use of light-emitting diodes (LEDs) of different colours (Figure 29.5). You may recall from Chapter 11 that an LED conducts in one direction only (the forward direction), and that it requires a minimum voltage, the **threshold voltage**, to be applied in this direction before it allows a current. This experiment makes use of the fact that LEDs of different colours require different threshold voltages before they conduct and emit light.

- A red LED emits photons that are of low energy. It requires a low threshold voltage to make it conduct.
- A blue LED emits higher-energy photons, and requires a higher threshold voltage to make it conduct.

Figure 29.5 Light-emitting diodes (LEDs) come in different colours. Blue (on the right) proved the trickiest to develop.

What is happening to produce photons of light when an LED conducts? The simplest way to think of this is to say that the electrical energy lost by a single electron passing through the diode reappears as the energy of a single photon.

Hence we can write:

energy lost by electron = energy of photon

$$eV = \frac{hc}{\lambda}$$

where $V$ is the threshold voltage for the LED. The values of $e$ and $c$ are known. Measurements of $V$ and $\lambda$ will allow you to calculate $h$. So the measurements required are:

- $V$ – the voltage across the LED when it begins to conduct (its threshold voltage). It is found using a circuit as shown in Figure **29.6a**;
- $\lambda$ – the wavelength of the light emitted by the LED. This is found by measurements using a diffraction grating or from the wavelength quoted by the manufacturer of the LED.

If several LEDs of different colours are available, $V$ and $\lambda$ can be determined for each and a graph of $V$ against $\frac{1}{\lambda}$ drawn (see Figure **29.6b**) The gradient of this graph will be $\frac{hc}{e}$ and hence $h$ can be estimated.

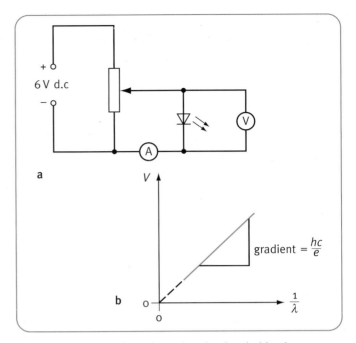

Figure 29.6 **a** A circuit to determine the threshold voltage required to make an LED conduct. An ammeter helps to show when this occurs. **b** The graph used to determine $h$ from this experiment.

## Test yourself

9 In an experiment to determine the Planck constant $h$, LEDs of different colours were used. The p.d. required to make each conduct was determined, and the wavelength of their light was taken from the manufacturer's catalogue. The results are shown in Table **29.3**. For each LED, calculate the experimental value for $h$ and hence determine an average value for the Planck constant.

| Colour of LED | Wavelength / $10^{-9}$ m | Threshold voltage / V |
|---|---|---|
| infrared | 910 | 1.35 |
| red | 670 | 1.70 |
| amber | 610 | 2.00 |
| green | 560 | 2.30 |

Table 29.3 Results from an experiment to determine $h$.

# The photoelectric effect

You can observe the photoelectric effect yourself by fixing a clean zinc plate to the top of a gold-leaf electroscope (Figure **29.7**). Give the electroscope a negative charge and the leaf deflects. Now shine electromagnetic radiation from a mercury discharge lamp on the zinc and the leaf gradually falls. (A mercury lamp strongly emits ultraviolet radiation.) Charging the electroscope gives it an excess of electrons. Somehow, the electromagnetic radiation from the mercury lamp helps the electrons to escape from the surface of the metal. The radiation causes electrons to be removed. The Greek word for light is **photo**, hence the word 'photoelectric'. The electrons removed from the metal plate in this manner are often known as photoelectrons.

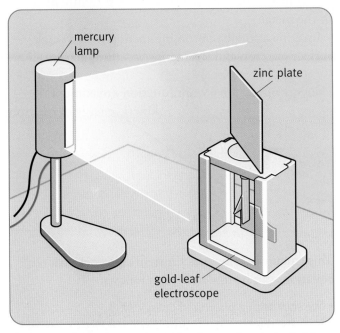

**Figure 29.7** A simple experiment to observe the photoelectric effect.

Placing the mercury lamp closer causes the leaf to fall more rapidly. This is not very surprising. However, if you insert a sheet of glass between the lamp and the zinc, the radiation from the lamp is no longer effective. The gold leaf does not fall. Glass absorbs **ultraviolet** radiation and it is this component of the radiation from the lamp that is effective.

If you try the experiment with a bright filament lamp, you will find it has no effect. It does not produce ultraviolet radiation. There is a minimum frequency that the incident radiation must have in order to release electrons from the metal. This is called the **threshold frequency**. The threshold frequency is a property of the metal plate being exposed to electromagnetic radiation.

> The threshold frequency is defined as the minimum frequency required to release electrons from the surface of a metal.

Physicists found it hard to explain why weak ultraviolet radiation could have an immediate effect on the electrons in the metal, but very bright light of lower frequency had no effect. They imagined light waves arriving at the metal, spread out over its surface, and they could not see how weak ultraviolet waves could be more effective than the intense visible waves. In 1905, Albert Einstein came up with an explanation based on the idea of photons.

Metals (such as zinc) have electrons that are not very tightly held within the metal. These are the conduction electrons and they are free to move about within the metal. When photons of electromagnetic radiation strike the metal, some electrons break free from the surface of the metal (Figure **29.8**). They only need a small amount of energy (about $10^{-19}$ J) to escape from the metal surface.

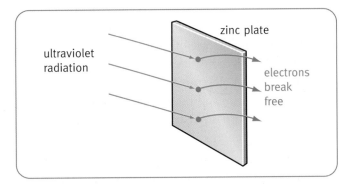

**Figure 29.8** The photoelectric effect. When a photon of ultraviolet radiation strikes the metal plate, its energy may be sufficient to release an electron.

We can picture the electrons as being trapped in an energy 'well' (Figure **29.9**). A single electron requires a minimum energy $\Phi$ (Greek letter phi) to escape the surface of the metal. The **work function energy**, or simply **work function**, of a metal is the minimum amount of energy required by an electron to escape its surface. (Energy is needed to release the surface electrons because they are attracted by the electrostatic forces due to the positive metal ions.)

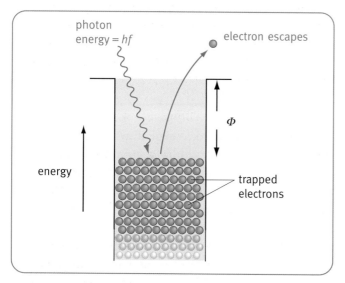

Figure 29.9 A single photon may interact with a single electron to release it.

Einstein did not picture electromagnetic waves interacting with all of the electrons in the metal. Instead, he suggested that a single photon could provide the energy needed by an individual electron to escape. The photon energy would need to be at least as great as $\Phi$. By this means, Einstein could explain the threshold frequency. A photon of visible light has energy less than $\Phi$, so it cannot release an electron from the surface of zinc.

When a photon arrives at the metal plate, it may be captured by an electron. The electron gains all of the photon's energy and the photon no longer exists. Some of the energy is needed for the electron to escape from the energy well; the rest is the electron's kinetic energy.

Now we can see that the photon model works because it models electromagnetic waves as concentrated 'packets' of energy, each one able to release an electron from the metal.

Here are some rules for the photoelectric effect:

- Electrons from the surface of the metal are removed.
- A single photon can only interact, and hence exchange its energy, with a single electron (one-to-one interaction).

- A surface electron is removed **instantaneously** from the metal surface when the energy of the incident photon is greater than, or equal to, the work function $\Phi$ of the metal. (The frequency of the incident radiation is greater than, or equal to, the threshold frequency of the metal.)
- Energy must be conserved when a photon interacts with an electron.
- Increasing the intensity of the incident radiation does not release a single electron when its frequency is less than the threshold frequency. The intensity of the incident radiation is proportional to the rate at which photons arrive at the plate. Each photon still has energy less than the work function.

Photoelectric experiments showed that the electrons released had a range of kinetic energies up to some maximum value, k.e.$_{max}$. These fastest-moving electrons are the ones which were least tightly held in the metal.

Imagine a single photon interacting with a single surface electron and freeing it. According to Einstein:

energy of photon = work function + maximum
kinetic energy of electron

$$hf = \Phi + \text{k.e.}_{max}$$

or

$$hf = \Phi + \frac{1}{2}mv_{max}^2$$

This equation, known as Einstein's photoelectric equation, can be understood as follows:

- We start with a photon of energy $hf$.
- It is absorbed by an electron.
- Some of the energy ($\Phi$) is used in escaping from the metal. The rest remains as kinetic energy of the electron.
- If the photon is absorbed by an electron that is lower in the energy well, the electron will have less kinetic energy than k.e.$_{max}$ (Figure 29.10).

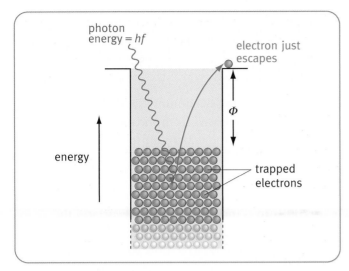

**Figure 29.10** A more tightly bound electron needs more energy to release it from the metal.

What happens when the incident radiation has a frequency equal to the threshold frequency $f_0$ of the metal?

The kinetic energy of the electrons is zero. Hence, according to Einstein's photoelectric equation:

$$hf_0 = \Phi$$

Hence, the threshold frequency $f_0$ is given by the expression:

$$f_0 = \frac{\Phi}{h}$$

What happens when the incident radiation has frequency less than the threshold frequency? A single photon can still give up its energy to a single electron, but this electron cannot escape from the attractive forces of the positive metal ions. The energy absorbed from the photons appears as kinetic energy of the electrons. These electrons lose their kinetic energy to the metal ions when they collide with them. This warms up the metal. This is why a metal plate placed in the vicinity of a table lamp gets hot.

Different metals have different threshold frequencies, and hence different work functions. For example, alkali metals such as sodium, potassium and rubidium have threshold frequencies in the visible region of the electromagnetic spectrum. The conduction electrons in zinc are more tightly bound within the metal and so its threshold frequency is in the ultraviolet region of the spectrum.

Table 29.4 summarises the observations of the photoelectric effect, the problems a wave model of light has in explaining them, and how a photon model is more successful.

| Observation | Wave model | Photon model |
|---|---|---|
| Emission of electrons happens as soon as light shines on metal | Very intense light should be needed to have immediate effect | A single photon is enough to release one electron |
| Even weak (low-intensity) light is effective | Weak light waves should have no effect | Low-intensity light means fewer photons, not lower-energy photons |
| Increasing intensity of light increases rate at which electrons leave metal | Greater intensity means more energy, so more electrons released | Greater intensity means more photons per second, so more electrons released per second |
| Increasing intensity has no effect on energies of electrons | Greater intensity should mean electrons have more energy | Greater intensity does not mean more energetic photons, so electrons cannot have more energy |
| A minimum threshold frequency of light is needed | Low-frequency light should work; electrons would be released more slowly | A photon in a low-frequency light beam has energy that is too small to release an electron |
| Increasing frequency of light increases maximum kinetic energy of electrons | It should be increasing intensity, not frequency, that increases energy of electrons | Higher frequency means more energetic photons; so electrons gain more energy and can move faster |

**Table 29.4** The success of the photon model in explaining the photoelectric effect.

You will need these values to answer questions **10–13**:

speed of light in a vacuum $c = 3.0 \times 10^8 \, \text{m s}^{-1}$

Planck constant $h = 6.63 \times 10^{-34} \, \text{J s}$

mass of electron $m_e = 9.1 \times 10^{-31} \, \text{kg}$

elementary charge $e = 1.6 \times 10^{-19} \, \text{C}$

**10** Photons of energies 1.0 eV, 2.0 eV and 3.0 eV strike a metal surface whose work function is 1.8 eV.
  **a** State which of these photons could cause the release of an electron from the metal.
  **b** Calculate the maximum kinetic energies of the electrons released in each case. Give your answers in eV and in J.

**11** Table **29.5** shows the work functions of several different metals.
  **a** Which metal requires the highest frequency of electromagnetic waves to release electrons?
  **b** Which metal will release electrons when the lowest frequency of electromagnetic waves is incident on it?
  **c** Calculate the threshold frequency for zinc.
  **d** What is the longest wavelength of electromagnetic waves that will release electrons from potassium?

| Metal | Work function $\Phi/\text{J}$ | Work function $\Phi/\text{eV}$ |
|---|---|---|
| caesium | $3.0 \times 10^{-19}$ | 1.9 |
| calcium | $4.3 \times 10^{-19}$ | 2.7 |
| gold | $7.8 \times 10^{-19}$ | 4.9 |
| potassium | $3.2 \times 10^{-19}$ | 2.0 |
| zinc | $6.9 \times 10^{-19}$ | 4.3 |

**Table 29.5** Work functions of several different metals.

*continued* ···⇴

**12** Electromagnetic waves of wavelength $2.4 \times 10^{-7} \, \text{m}$ are incident on the surface of a metal whose work function is $2.8 \times 10^{-19} \, \text{J}$.
  **a** Calculate the energy of a single photon.
  **b** Calculate the maximum kinetic energy of electrons released from the metal.
  **c** Determine the maximum speed of the emitted photoelectrons.

**13** When electromagnetic radiation of wavelength 2000 nm is incident on a metal surface, the maximum kinetic energy of the electrons released is found to be $4.0 \times 10^{-20} \, \text{J}$. Determine the work function of the metal in joules (J).

# Line spectra

We will now look at another phenomenon which we can explain in terms of light-as-photons. We rely a great deal on light to inform us about our surroundings. Using our eyes we can identify many different colours. Scientists take this further by analysing light, by breaking or splitting it up into a spectrum. (The technical term for the splitting of light into its components is **dispersion**.) You will be familiar with the ways in which this can be done, using a prism or a diffraction grating (Figure **29.11**). The spectrum of white light shows that it consists of a range of wavelengths, from about $4 \times 10^{-7} \, \text{m}$ (violet) to about $7 \times 10^{-7} \, \text{m}$ (red), as in Figure **29.12a**. This is a continuous spectrum.

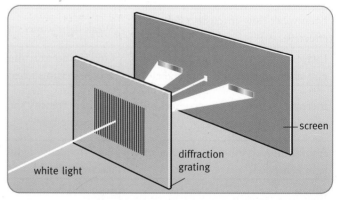

**Figure 29.11** White light is split up into a continuous spectrum when it passes through a diffraction grating.

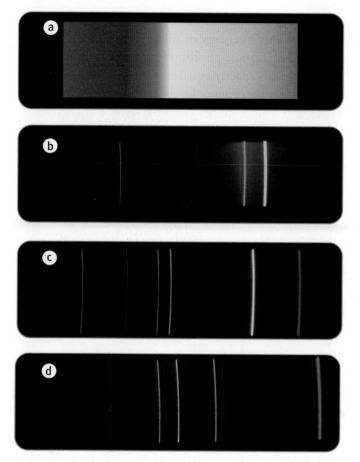

Figure 29.12 Spectra of a white light, and light from b mercury, c helium and d cadmium vapours.

Figure 29.13 An absorption line spectrum formed when white light is passed through cool mercury vapour.

It is more interesting to look at the spectrum from a hot gas. If you look at a lamp that contains a gas such as neon or sodium, you will see that only certain colours are present. Each colour has a unique wavelength. If the source is narrow and it is viewed through a diffraction grating, a **line spectrum** is seen.

Figures **29.12b** and **29.12c** show the line spectra of hot gases of the elements mercury and helium. Each element has a spectrum with a unique collection of wavelengths. Therefore line spectra can be used to identify elements. This is exactly what the British astronomer William Huggins did when he deduced which elements are the most common in the stars.

These line spectra, which show the composition of light emitted by hot gases, are called **emission line spectra**.

There is another kind of spectrum, called **absorption line spectra**, which are observed when white light is passed through cool gases. After the light has passed through a diffraction grating (Figure **29.13**), the continuous white light spectrum

is found to have black lines across it. Certain wavelengths have been absorbed as the white light passed through the cool gas.

Absorption line spectra are found when the light from stars is analysed. The interior of the star is very hot and emits white light of all wavelengths in the visible range. However, this light has to pass through the **cooler** outer layers of the star. As a result, certain wavelengths are absorbed. Figure **29.14** shows the spectrum for the Sun.

Figure 29.14 The Sun's spectrum shows dark lines. These dark lines arise when light of specific wavelengths coming from the Sun's hot interior is absorbed by its cooler atmosphere.

# Explaining the origin of line spectra

From the description above, we can see that the atoms of a given element (e.g. helium) can only emit or absorb light of certain wavelengths.

Different elements emit and absorb different wavelengths. How can this be? To understand this, we need to establish two points:

• First, as with the photoelectric effect, we are dealing with light (an electromagnetic wave) interacting with matter. Hence we need to consider light as consisting of photons. For light of a single wavelength $\lambda$ and frequency $f$, the energy $E$ of each photon is given by the equation:

$$E = hf \quad \text{or} \quad E = \frac{hc}{\lambda}$$

• Secondly, when light interacts with matter, it is the electrons that absorb the energy from the incoming photons. When the electrons lose energy, light is emitted by matter in the form of photons.

What does the appearance of the line spectra tell us about electrons in atoms? They can only absorb or emit photons of certain energies. From this we deduce that electrons in atoms can themselves only have certain fixed values of energy. This idea seemed very odd to scientists a hundred years ago. Figure **29.15** shows diagrammatically the permitted **energy levels** (or **energy states**) of the electron of a hydrogen atom. An electron in a hydrogen atom can have only one of these values of energy. It cannot have an energy that is between these energy levels. The energy levels of the electron are analogous to the rungs of a ladder. The energy levels have **negative** values because external energy has to be supplied to remove an electron from the atom. The negative energy shows that the electron is trapped within the atom by the attractive forces of the atomic nucleus. An electron with zero energy is free from the atom.

The electron makes a **transition** to a lower energy level. The loss of energy of the electron leads to the emission of a single photon of light. The energy of this photon is exactly equal to the energy difference between the two energy levels. If the electron makes a transition from a higher energy level, the energy loss of the electron is larger and this leads to the emission of a more energetic photon. The distinctive energy levels of an atom mean that the energy of the photons emitted, and hence the wavelengths emitted, will be unique to that atom. This explains why only certain wavelengths are present in the emission line spectrum of a hot gas.

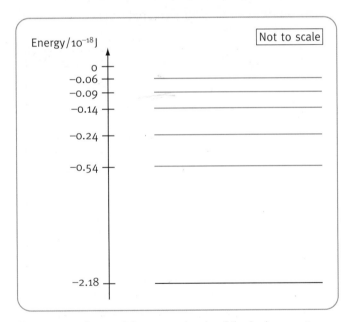

Figure **29.15** Some of the energy levels of the hydrogen atom.

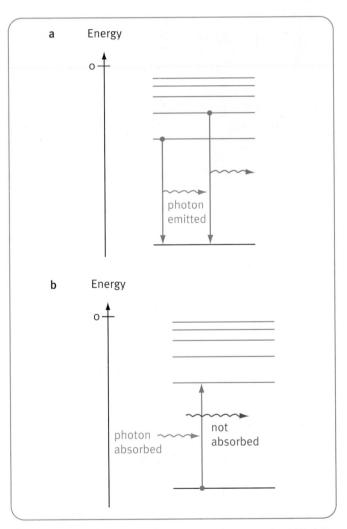

Figure **29.16** a When an electron drops to a lower energy level, it emits a single photon. b A photon must have just the right energy if it is to be absorbed by an electron.

The energy of the electron in the atom is said to be **quantised**. This is one of the most important statements of quantum physics.

Now we can explain what happens when an atom emits light. One of its electrons falls from a high energy level to a lower one (Figure **29.16a**).

Atoms of different elements have different line spectra because they have different spacings between their energy levels. It is not within the scope of this book to discuss why this is.

Similarly, we can explain the origin of absorption line spectra. White light consists of photons of many different energies. For a photon to be absorbed, it must have exactly the right energy to lift an electron from one energy level to another (Figure **29.16b**). If its energy is too little or too great, it will not be absorbed. This effect can also described as a form of resonance (Chapter **20**); the frequency of the photon must be such that its energy matches the gap between the two energy levels.

# Photon energies

When an electron changes its energy from one level $E_1$ to another $E_2$, it either emits or absorbs a **single** photon. The energy of the photon $hf$ is simply equal to the **difference** in energies between the two levels:

$$\text{photon energy} = \Delta E$$

$$hf = E_1 - E_2$$

or

$$\frac{hc}{\lambda} = E_1 - E_2$$

Referring back to the energy level diagram for hydrogen (Figure **29.15**), you can see that, if an electron falls from the second level to the lowest energy level (known as the **ground state**), it will emit a photon of energy:

$$\text{photon energy} = \Delta E$$

$$hf = [(-0.54) - (-2.18)] \times 10^{-18} \, \text{J}$$

$$hf = 1.64 \times 10^{-18} \, \text{J}$$

We can calculate the frequency $f$ and wavelength $\lambda$ of the emitted electromagnetic radiation.

The frequency is:

$$f = \frac{E}{h} = \frac{1.64 \times 10^{-18}}{6.63 \times 10^{-34}}$$

$$f = 2.47 \times 10^{15} \, \text{Hz}$$

The wavelength is:

$$\lambda = \frac{c}{f} = \frac{3.0 \times 10^8}{2.47 \times 10^{15}}$$

$$\lambda = 1.21 \times 10^{-7} \, \text{m} = 121 \, \text{nm}$$

This is a wavelength in the ultraviolet region of the electromagnetic spectrum.

## Test yourself

14 Figure **29.17** shows part of the energy level diagram of an imaginary atom. The arrows represent three transitions between the energy levels. For each of these transitions:
- calculate the energy of the photon
- calculate the frequency and wavelength of the electromagnetic radiation (emitted or absorbed)
- state whether the transition contributes to an emission or an absorption spectrum.

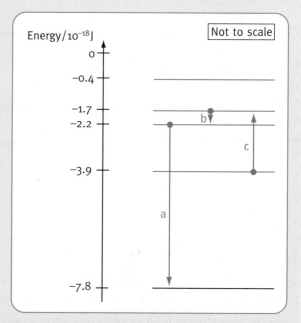

**Figure 29.17** An atomic energy level diagram, showing three electron transitions between levels – see Test yourself Q **14**.

15 Figure **29.18** shows another energy level diagram. In this case, energies are given in electronvolts

*continued* ···▸

(eV). From the list below, state which photon energies could be absorbed by such an atom:

**6.0 eV   9.0 eV   11 eV   20 eV   25 eV   34 eV   45 eV**

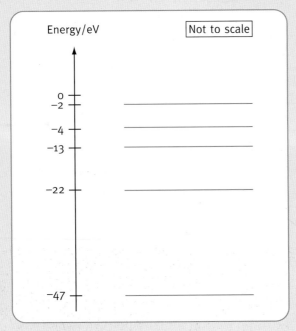

**Figure 29.18** An energy level diagram – see Test yourself Q **15**.

**16** The line spectrum for a particular type of atom is found to include the following wavelengths:

**83 nm   50 nm   25 nm**

  **a** Calculate the corresponding photon energies in eV.

  **b** Sketch the energy levels which could give rise to these photons. On the diagram indicate the corresponding electron transitions responsible for these three spectral lines.

# Isolated atoms

So far, we have only discussed the spectra of light from hot gases. In a gas, the atoms are relatively far apart, so they do not interact with one another very much. Gas atoms that exert negligible electrical forces on each other are known as **isolated atoms**. As a consequence, they give relatively simple line spectra. Similar spectra can be obtained from some gemstones and coloured glass. In these, the basic material is clear and colourless, but it gains its colour from impurity atoms, which are well separated from one another within the material.

In a solid or liquid, however, the atoms are close together. The electrons from one atom interact with those of neighbouring atoms. This has the effect of altering the energy level diagram, which becomes much more complicated, with a greater number of closely spaced energy levels. The corresponding spectra have many, many different frequencies present, so hot liquids and solids tend to produce continuous spectra.

# The nature of light – waves or particles?

It is clear that, in order to explain the photoelectric effect, we must use the idea of light (and all electromagnetic waves) as particles. Similarly, photons explain the appearance of line spectra. However, to explain diffraction, interference and polarisation of light, we must use the wave model. How can we sort out this dilemma?

We have to conclude that sometimes light shows wave-like behaviour; at other times it behaves as particles (photons). In particular, when light is absorbed by a metal surface, it behaves as particles. Individual photons are absorbed by individual electrons in the metal. In a similar way, when a Geiger counter detects γ-radiation, we hear individual γ-photons being absorbed in the tube.

So what is light? Is it a wave or a particle? Physicists have come to terms with the dual nature of light. This duality is referred to as the **wave–particle duality** of light. In simple terms:

- Light interacts with matter (e.g. electrons) as a particle – the photon. The evidence for this is provided by the photoelectric effect.
- Light travels through space as a wave. The evidence for this comes from the diffraction and interference of light using slits.

# Electron waves

Light has a dual nature. Is it possible that particles such as electrons also have a dual nature? This interesting question was first contemplated by Louis de Broglie (pronounced 'de Broy') in 1924 (Figure **29.19**).

**Figure 29.19** Louis de Broglie provided an alternative view of how particles behave.

De Broglie imagined that electrons would travel through space as a wave. He proposed that the wave-like property of a particle like the electron can be represented by its wavelength $\lambda$, which is related to its momentum $p$ by the equation:

$$\lambda = \frac{h}{p}$$

where $h$ is the Planck constant. The wavelength $\lambda$ is often referred to as the **de Broglie wavelength**. The waves associated with the electron are referred to as matter waves.

The momentum $p$ of a particle is the product of its mass m and its velocity $v$. Therefore, the de Broglie equation may be written as:

$$\lambda = \frac{h}{mv}$$

The Planck constant $h$ is the same constant that appears in the equation $E = hf$ for the energy of a photon. It is fascinating how the Planck constant $h$ is entwined with the behaviour of both matter as waves (e.g. electrons) and electromagnetic waves as 'particles' (photons).

The wave property of the electron was eventually confirmed in 1927 by researchers in America and in England. The Americans Clinton Davisson and Edmund Germer showed experimentally that electrons were diffracted by single crystals of nickel. The diffraction of electrons confirmed their wave-like property. In England, George Thomson fired electrons into thin sheets of metal in a vacuum tube. He too provided evidence that electrons were diffracted by the metal atoms.

Louis de Broglie received the 1929 Nobel Prize in Physics. Clinton Davisson and George Thomson shared the Nobel Prize in Physics in 1937.

## Electron diffraction

We can reproduce the same diffraction results in the laboratory using an electron diffraction tube, see Figure **29.20**.

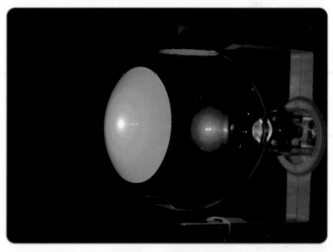

**Figure 29.20** When a beam of electrons passes through a graphite film, as in this vacuum tube, a diffraction pattern is produced on the phosphor screen.

In an electron diffraction tube, the electrons from the heated filament are accelerated to high speeds by the large potential difference between the negative heater (cathode) and the positive electrode (anode). A beam of electrons passes through a thin sample of polycrystalline graphite. It is made up of many tiny crystals, each of which consists of large numbers of carbon atoms arranged in uniform atomic layers. The electrons emerge from the graphite film and produce diffraction rings on the phosphor screen. The diffraction rings are similar to those produced by light (a wave) passing through a small circular hole.

The rings cannot be explained if electrons behaved as particles. Diffraction is a property of waves. Hence the rings can only be explained if the electrons pass through the graphite film as a wave. The electrons are diffracted by the carbon atoms and the spacing between the layers of carbon atoms. The atomic layers of carbon behave like a diffraction grating with many slits. The electrons show diffraction effects because their de Broglie wavelength $\lambda$ is similar to the spacing between the atomic layers.

This experiment shows that electrons appear to travel as waves. If we look a little more closely at the results of the experiment, we find something else even more surprising. The phosphor screen gives a flash of light for each electron that hits it. These flashes build up to give the diffraction pattern (Figure 29.21). But if we see flashes at particular points on the screen, are we not seeing individual electrons – in other words, are we not observing particles?

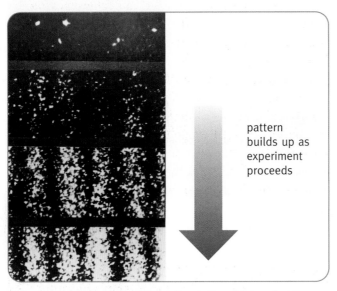

pattern builds up as experiment proceeds

Figure 29.21 The speckled diffraction pattern shows that it arises from many individual electrons striking the screen.

## Worked example

1   Calculate the de Broglie wavelength of an electron travelling through space at a speed of $10^7 \, \text{m s}^{-1}$. State whether or not these electrons can be diffracted by solid materials (atomic spacing in solid materials ~ $10^{-10} \, \text{m}$).

*continued ┄┄>*

**Step 1** According to the de Broglie equation, we have:

$$\lambda = \frac{h}{mv}$$

**Step 2** The mass of an electron is $9.1 \times 10^{-31}$ kg. Hence:

$$\lambda = \frac{6.63 \times 10^{-34}}{9.1 \times 10^{-31} \times 10^7} = 7.3 \times 10^{11} \, \text{m}$$

The electrons travelling at $10^7 \, \text{m s}^{-1}$ have a de Broglie wavelength of order of magnitude $10^{-10} \, \text{m}$. Hence they can be diffracted by matter.

## Investigating electron diffraction

If you have access to an electron diffraction tube (Figure 29.22), you can see for yourself how a beam of electrons is diffracted. The electron gun at one end of the tube produces a beam of electrons. By changing the voltage between the anode and the cathode, you can change the energy of the electrons, and hence their speed. The beam strikes a graphite target, and a diffraction pattern appears on the screen at the other end of the tube.

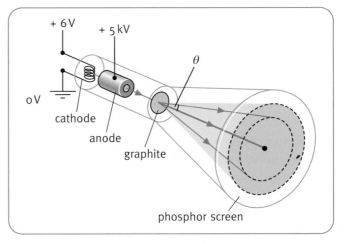

Figure 29.22 Electrons are accelerated from the cathode to the anode; they form a beam which is diffracted as it passes through the graphite film.

You can use an electron diffraction tube to investigate how the wavelength of the electrons depends on their speed. Qualitatively, you should find that increasing the anode–cathode voltage makes the pattern of diffraction rings shrink. The electrons have more kinetic energy (they are faster); the shrinking pattern shows that their wavelength has decreased. You can find the wavelength $\lambda$ of the electrons by measuring the angle $\theta$ at which they are diffracted:

$$\lambda = 2d \sin \theta$$

In the previous equation $d$ is the spacing of the atomic layers of graphite.

You can find the speed of the electrons from the anode–cathode voltage $V$:

$$\tfrac{1}{2}mv^2 = eV$$

## Test yourself

17 X-rays are used to find out about the spacings of atomic planes in crystalline materials.
   a Describe how beams of electrons could be used for the same purpose.
   b How might electron diffraction be used to identify a sample of a metal?

## People waves

The de Broglie equation applies to all matter; anything that has mass. It can also be applied to objects like golf balls and people!

Imagine a 65 kg person running at a speed of 3.0 m s$^{-1}$ through an opening of width 0.80 m. According to the de Broglie equation, the wavelength of this person is:

$$\lambda = \frac{h}{mv}$$

$$\lambda = \frac{6.63 \times 10^{-34}}{65 \times 3.0}$$

$$\lambda = 3.4 \times 10^{-36} \text{ m}$$

This wavelength is very small indeed compared with the size of the gap, hence no diffraction effects would be observed. People cannot be diffracted through everyday gaps. The de Broglie wavelength of this person is much smaller than any gap the person is likely to try to squeeze through! For this reason, we do not use the wave model to describe the behaviour of people; we get much better results by regarding people as large particles.

## Test yourself

18 A beam of electrons is accelerated from rest through a p.d. of 1.0 kV.
   a What is the energy (in eV) of each electron in the beam?
   b Calculate the speed, and hence the momentum ($mv$), of each electron.
   c Calculate the de Broglie wavelength of each electron.
   d Would you expect the beam to be significantly diffracted by a metal film in which the atoms are separated by a spacing of $0.25 \times 10^{-9}$ m?

## Probing matter

All moving particles have a de Broglie wavelength. The structure of matter can be investigated using the diffraction of particles. Diffraction of slow-moving neutrons (known as thermal neutrons) from nuclear reactors is used to study the arrangements of atoms in metals and other materials. The wavelength of these neutrons is about $10^{-10}$ m, which is roughly the separation between the atoms.

Diffraction of slow-moving electrons is used to explore the arrangements of atoms in metals (Figure 29.23) and the structures of complex molecules such as DNA (Figure 29.24). It is possible to accelerate electrons to the right speed so that their wavelength is similar to the spacing between atoms, around $10^{-10}$ m.

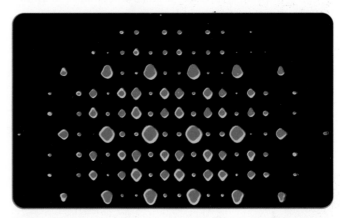

Figure 29.23 Electron diffraction pattern for an alloy of titanium and nickel. From this pattern, we can deduce the arrangement of the atoms and their separations.

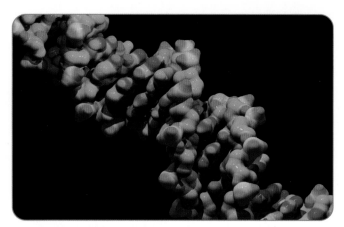

**Figure 29.24** The structure of the giant molecule DNA, deduced from electron diffraction.

High-speed electrons from particle accelerators have been used to determine the diameter of atomic nuclei. This is possible because high-speed electrons have shorter wavelengths of order of magnitude $10^{-15}$ m. This wavelength is similar to the size of atomic nuclei. Electrons travelling close to the speed of light are being used to investigate the internal structure of the nucleus. These electrons have to be accelerated by voltages up to $10^9$ V.

## The nature of the electron – wave or particle?

The electron has a dual nature, just like electromagnetic waves. This duality is referred to as the **wave–particle duality** of the electron. In simple terms:

- An electron interacts with matter as a particle. The evidence for this is provided by Newtonian mechanics.
- An electron travels through space as a wave. The evidence for this comes from the diffraction of electrons.

## Summary

☐ For electromagnetic waves of frequency $f$ and wavelength $\lambda$, each photon has energy $E$ given by:

$$E = hf \quad \text{or} \quad E = \frac{hc}{\lambda} \quad \text{where } h \text{ is the Planck constant.}$$

☐ One electronvolt is the energy transferred when an electron travels through a potential difference of 1 V.

$$1\,\text{eV} = 1.6 \times 10^{-19}\,\text{J}$$

☐ A particle of charge $e$ accelerated through a voltage $V$ has kinetic energy given by:

$$eV = \tfrac{1}{2}mv^2$$

☐ The photoelectric effect is an example of a phenomenon explained in terms of the particle-like (photon) behaviour of electromagnetic radiation.

☐ Einstein's photoelectric equation is:

$$hf = \Phi + \text{k.e.}_{max}$$

where $\Phi$ = work function = minimum energy required to release an electron from the metal surface.

☐ The threshold frequency is the minimum frequency of the incident electromagnetic radiation that will release an electron from the metal surface.

☐ Electron diffraction is an example of a phenomenon explained in terms of the wave-like behaviour of matter.

☐ The de Broglie wavelength $\lambda$ of a particle is related to its momentum ($mv$) by the de Broglie equation:

$$\lambda = \frac{h}{mv}$$

- Both electromagnetic radiation (light) and matter (electrons) exhibit wave–particle duality; that is, they show both wave-like and particle-like behaviours, depending on the circumstances. In wave–particle duality:
  - interaction is explained in terms of particles
  - travel through space is explained in terms of waves.
- Line spectra arise for isolated atoms (the electrical forces between such atoms is negligible).
- The energy of an electron in an isolated atom is quantised. The electron is allowed to exist in specific energy states known as energy levels.
- An electron loses energy when it makes a transition from a higher energy level to a lower energy level. A photon of electromagnetic radiation is emitted because of this energy loss. The result is an emission line spectrum.
- Absorption line spectra arise when electromagnetic radiation is absorbed by isolated atoms. An electron absorbs a photon of the correct energy to allow it to make a transition to a higher energy level.
- The frequency $f$ and the wavelength $\lambda$ of the emitted or absorbed radiation are related to the energy levels $E_1$ and $E_2$ by the equations:

$$hf = \Delta E = E_1 - E_2$$

and

$$\frac{hc}{\lambda} = \Delta E = E_1 - E_2$$

# End-of-chapter questions

1   Calculate the energy of a photon of frequency $4.0 \times 10^{18}$ Hz.

2   The microwave region of the electromagnetic spectrum is considered to have wavelengths ranging from 5 mm to 50 cm.

Calculate the range of energy of microwave photons.

3   In a microwave oven photons of energy $1.02 \times 10^{-5}$ eV are used to heat food.
    a   Express $1.02 \times 10^{-5}$ eV in joules.
    b   Calculate the frequency of the photons.
    c   Calculate the wavelength of the photons.

4   a   $\alpha$-particles of energy 5 MeV are emitted in the radioactive decay of radium. Express this energy in joules.
    b   Electrons in an cathode-ray tube are accelerated through a potential difference of 10 kV. State their energy **i** in electron volts **ii** in joules.
    c   In a nuclear reactor neutrons are slowed to energies of $6 \times 10^{-21}$ J. Express this in eV

5   A helium nucleus (charge $= +3.2 \times 10^{-19}$ C, mass $= 6.8 \times 10^{-27}$ kg) is accelerated through a potential difference of 7500 V.

Calculate:
a   its kinetic energy in electronvolts
b   its kinetic energy in joules
c   its speed.

6   Ultraviolet light of photon of energy $2.5 \times 10^{-18}$ J is shone onto a zinc plate. The work function of zinc is 4.3 eV.

Calculate the maximum energy with which an electron can be emitted from the zinc plate. Give your answer a in eV and b in J.

7   Calculate the minimum frequency of electromagnetic radiation that will cause the emission of photoelectrons from the surface of gold.

(Work function for gold $= 4.9$ eV.)

8   Figure 29.25 shows the energy levels in a helium ion.

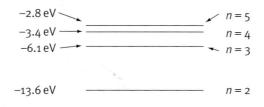

$-2.8$ eV      $n = 5$
$-3.4$ eV      $n = 4$
$-6.1$ eV      $n = 3$

$-13.6$ eV      $n = 2$

$-54.4$ eV      $n = 1$ (ground state)

**Figure 29.25**  For End-of-chapter Q **8**.

a   Calculate the energy, in joules, that is required to completely remove the remaining electron, originally in its ground state, from the helium nucleus.
b   Calculate the frequency of the radiation which is emitted when the electron drops from the level $n = 3$ to $n = 2$. State the region of the electromagnetic spectrum in which this radiation lies.
c   Without further calculation, describe qualitatively how the frequency of the radiation emitted when the electron drops from the level $n = 2$ to $n = 1$ compares with the energy of the radiation emitted when it drops from $n = 3$ to $n = 2$.

# Exam-style questions

1   The spectrum of sunlight has dark lines. These dark lines are due to the absorption of certain wavelengths by the cooler gases in the atmosphere of the Sun.

    **a** One particular dark spectral line has a wavelength of 590 nm. Calculate the energy of a photon with this wavelength.          **[3]**

    **b** The diagram below shows some of the energy levels of an isolated atom of helium.

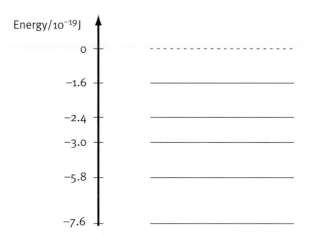

      **i** Explain the significance of the energy levels having negative values.     **[1]**

     **ii** Explain, with reference to the energy level diagram above, how a dark line in the spectrum may be due to the presence of helium in the atmosphere of the Sun.     **[2]**

    **iii** All the light absorbed by the atoms in the Sun's atmosphere is re-emitted. Suggest why a dark spectral line of wavelength of 590 nm is still observed from the Earth.     **[1]**

2   The diagram below shows the energy levels of an isolated hydrogen atom.

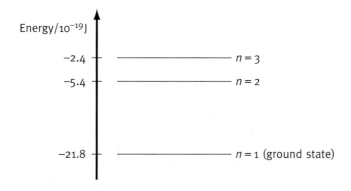

The lowest energy level of the atom is known as its **ground state**. Each energy level is assigned an integer number $n$, known as the principal quantum number. The ground state has $n = 1$.

**a** Explain what happens to an electron in the ground state when it absorbs the energy from a photon of energy $21.8 \times 10^{-19}$ J. [1]

**b i** Explain why a photon is emitted when an electron makes a transition between energy levels of $n = 3$ and $n = 2$. [2]

**ii** Calculate the wavelength of electromagnetic radiation emitted when an electron makes a jump between energy levels of $n = 3$ and $n = 2$. [3]

**iii** Use the energy level diagram above to show that the energy $E$ of an energy level is inversely proportional to $n^2$. [2]

**3 a i** Explain what is meant by the **wave–particle duality** of electromagnetic radiation. [2]

**ii** Explain how the photoelectric effect gives evidence for this phenomenon. [2]

The graph shows the maximum kinetic energy of the emitted photoelectrons as the frequency of the incident radiation on a sodium plate is varied.

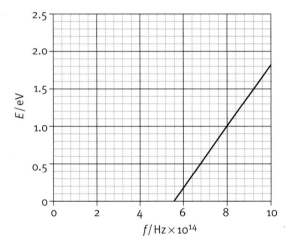

**b** Explain why there are no photoelectrons emitted when the frequency of the incident light is less than $5.6 \times 10^{14}$ Hz. [2]

**c** Calculate the work function for sodium. [3]

**d** Use the graph to calculate the value of the Planck constant in J s. [2]

**4 a** Explain what is meant by the de Broglie wavelength of an electron. [2]
   **b** The diagram shows the principles of an electron tube used to demonstrate electron diffraction.

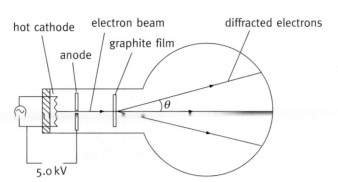

   **i** Calculate the kinetic energy (in joules) of the electrons incident on the graphite film. [1]
   **ii** Show that the momentum of the electrons is equal to $\sqrt{2E_k m}$ and hence calculate the momentum of the electrons. [3]
   **iii** Calculate the de Broglie wavelength of the electrons. [2]
   **c** Discuss how the wavelengths of neutrons and electrons moving with the same energy would compare. [3]

# 30 Nuclear physics

## Objectives

After studying this chapter, you should be able to:

- ☐ appreciate and use Einstein's mass-energy relationship $E = mc^2$
- ☐ relate nuclear binding energy to nuclear stability, fission and fusion
- ☐ solve problems involving activity and decay constant
- ☐ solve problems involving exponential decay and half-life

## Energy and the nucleus

Towards the end of the Second World War, two nuclear weapons were dropped on the Japanese cities of Hiroshima and Nagasaki. Nuclear explosions release so much energy that their size is often given in 'megatonnes' – that is, their equivalent in millions of tonnes of high explosive (Figure 30.1). A more peaceful use of nuclear materials is in nuclear power stations. Because materials such as uranium are such concentrated stores of energy, a nuclear power station requires only a small van-load of fuel each week, whereas a coal-fired power station may require a train-load every hour.

In this chapter, we will look at energy in the atomic nucleus and how this relates to nuclear stability; we will also look at how we can write equations to represent radioactive decay.

Figure 30.1 Our understanding of nuclear physics has proved to be a mixed blessing. Nuclear weapons dominated global politics for much of the 20th century.

## Mass and energy

In Chapter 17, we saw that energy is released when the nucleus of an unstable atom decays. How can we calculate the amount of energy released by radioactive decay? To find the answer to this, we need to think first about the masses of the particles involved.

We will start by considering a stable nucleus, $^{12}_{6}C$. This consists of six protons and six neutrons. Fortunately for us, because we have a lot of this form of carbon in our bodies, this is a very stable nuclide. This means that the nucleons are bound tightly together by the strong nuclear force. It takes a lot of energy to pull them apart.

Figure 30.2 shows the results of an imaginary experiment in which we have done just that. On the left-hand side of the balance is a single $^{12}_{6}C$ nucleus.

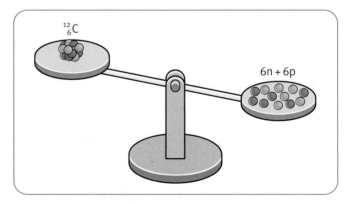

Figure 30.2 The mass of a nucleus is less than the total mass of its component protons and neutrons.

On the right-hand side are six protons and six neutrons, the result of dismantling the nucleus. The surprising thing is that the balance is tipped to the right. The separate nucleons have **more** mass than the nucleus itself. This means that the law of conservation of mass appears to have been broken. Have we violated what was thought to be a fundamental law of Nature, something that was held to be true for hundreds of years?

Notice that, in dismantling the $^{12}_{6}\text{C}$ nucleus, we have had to do work. The nucleons attract one another with nuclear forces and these are strong enough to make the nucleus very stable. So we have put energy into the nucleus to pull it apart, and this energy increases the potential energy of the individual nucleons. We can think of the nucleons within the nucleus as sitting in a deep potential well which results from the strong forces which hold the nucleus together. When we separate nucleons, we lift them out of this potential well, giving them more nuclear potential energy. This potential well is similar to that formed by the electric field around the nucleus; it is this well in which the atomic electrons sit, but it is much, much deeper. This explains why it is much easier to remove an electron from an atom than to remove a nucleon from the nucleus.

The problem of the appearing mass remains. To solve this problem, Einstein made the revolutionary hypothesis that energy has mass. This is not an easy idea. When bodies are in a higher energy state they have more mass than in a lower energy state. A bucket of water at the top of a hill will have more mass than when it is at the bottom because energy has been transferred to it in carrying it up the hill. A tennis ball travelling at $50\,\text{m s}^{-1}$ will have more mass than the same tennis ball when stationary. In everyday life the amount of extra mass is so small that it cannot be measured, but the large changes in energy which occur in nuclear physics and high-energy physics makes the changes in mass significant. Indeed, the increase in mass of particles, such as electrons, as they are accelerated to speeds near to the speed of light is a well-established experimental fact.

Another way to express this is to treat mass and energy as aspects of the same thing. Rather than having separate laws of conservation of mass and conservation of energy, we can combine these two. The total amount of mass and energy together in a system is constant. There may be conversions from one to the other, but the total amount of 'mass–energy' remains constant.

## Einstein's mass–energy equation

Albert Einstein produced his famous mass–energy equation, which links energy $E$ and mass $m$:

$$E = mc^2$$

where $c$ is the speed of light in free space. The value of $c$ is approximately $3.0 \times 10^8\,\text{m s}^{-1}$, but its precise value has been fixed as $c = 299\,792\,458\,\text{m s}^{-1}$.

Generally, we will be concerned with the changes in mass owing to changes in energy, when the equation becomes:

$$\Delta E = \Delta mc^2$$

According to Einstein's equation:

- the mass of a system **increases** when energy is supplied to it
- when energy is released from a system, its mass decreases.

Now, if we know the total mass of particles before a nuclear reaction and their total mass after the reaction, we can work out how much energy is released. Table 30.1 gives the mass in kilograms of each of the particles shown in Figure 30.2. Notice that this is described as the **rest mass** of the particle, that is, its mass when it is at rest (stationary); its mass is greater when it is moving because of its increase in energy. Nuclear masses are measured to a high degree of precision using mass spectrometers, often to seven or eight significant figures.

| Particle | Rest mass / $10^{-27}$ kg |
|---|---|
| $^{1}_{1}\text{P}$ | 1.672 623 |
| $^{1}_{0}\text{n}$ | 1.674 929 |
| $^{12}_{6}\text{C}$ nucleus | 19.926 483 |

Table 30.1 Rest masses of some particles. It is worth noting that the mass of the neutron is slightly greater than the proton (roughly 0.1% greater).

We can use the mass values to calculate the mass that is released as energy when nucleons combine to form a nucleus. So for our particles in Figure 30.2, we have:

$$\text{mass before} = (6 \times 1.672\,623 + 6 \times 1.674\,929) \times 10^{-27}\,\text{kg}$$
$$= 20.085\,312 \times 10^{-27}\,\text{kg}$$

mass after $= 19.926\,483 \times 10^{-27}\,\text{kg}$

mass difference $\Delta m = (20.085\,312 - 19.926\,483) \times 10^{-27}\,\text{kg}$
$= 0.158\,829 \times 10^{-27}\,\text{kg}$

When six protons and six neutrons combine to form the nucleus of carbon-12, there is a very small loss of mass $\Delta m$, known as the **mass defect**.

The mass defect of a nucleus is equal to the difference between the total mass of the individual, separate nucleons and the mass of the nucleus.

The loss in mass implies that energy is released in this process. The energy released $E$ is given by Einstein's mass–energy equation. Therefore:

$E = mc^2$
$= 0.158\,829 \times 10^{-27} \times (3.0 \times 10^8)^2$
$\approx 1.43 \times 10^{-11}\,\text{J}$

This may seem like a very small amount of energy, but it is a lot on the scale of an atom. For comparison, the amount of energy released in a chemical reaction involving a single carbon atom would typically be of the order of $10^{-18}\,\text{J}$, more than a million times smaller.

Now look at Worked example **1**.

### Worked example

**1** Use the data below to determine the minimum energy required to split a nucleus of oxygen-16 ($^{16}_{8}\text{O}$) into its separate nucleons. Give your answer in joules (J).

mass of proton $= 1.672\,623 \times 10^{-27}\,\text{kg}$

mass of neutron $= 1.674\,929 \times 10^{-27}\,\text{kg}$

mass of $^{16}_{8}\text{O}$ nucleus $= 26.551\,559 \times 10^{-27}\,\text{kg}$

speed of light $c = 3.0 \times 10^8\,\text{m s}^{-1}$

*continued* ⋯⟶

**Step 1** Find the difference $\Delta m$ in kg between the mass of the oxygen nucleus and the mass of the individual nucleons. The $^{16}_{8}\text{O}$ nucleus has 8 protons and 8 neutrons.

$\Delta m = \text{final mass} - \text{initial mass}$

$\Delta m = [(8 \times 1.672\,623 + 8 \times 1.674\,929)$
$\qquad\qquad - 26.551\,559] \times 10^{-27}\,\text{kg}$

$\approx 2.20 \times 10^{-28}\,\text{kg}$

There is an increase in the mass of this system because external energy is supplied.

**Step 2** Use Einstein's mass–energy equation to determine the energy supplied.

$\Delta E = \Delta mc^2$

$E = 2.20 \times 10^{-28} \times (3.0 \times 10^8)^2 \approx 1.98 \times 10^{-11}\,\text{J}$

## Mass–energy conservation

Einstein pointed out that his equation $\Delta E = \Delta mc^2$ applied to **all** energy changes, not just nuclear processes. So, for example, it applies to chemical changes, too. If we burn some carbon, we start off with carbon and oxygen. At the end, we have carbon dioxide and energy. If we measure the mass of the carbon dioxide, we find that it is very slightly less than the mass of the carbon and oxygen at the start of the experiment. The total potential energy of the system will be less than at the start of the experiment, hence the mass is less. In a chemical reaction such as this, the change in mass is very small, less than a microgram if we start with 1 kg of carbon and oxygen. Compare this with the change in mass that occurs during the fission of 1 kg of uranium, described later. The change in mass in a chemical reaction is a much, much smaller proportion of the original mass, which is why we don't notice it.

1 The Sun releases vast amounts of energy. Its power output is $4.0 \times 10^{26}$ W. Estimate by how much its mass decreases each second because of this energy loss.

2 a Calculate the energy released if a $^4_2$He nucleus is formed from separate protons and neutrons. The masses of the particles are given in Table 30.2.
   b Calculate also the energy released per nucleon.

| Particle | Mass / $10^{-27}$ kg |
|---|---|
| $^1_1$P | 1.672 623 |
| $^1_0$n | 1.674 929 |
| $^4_2$He | 6.644 661 |

**Table 30.2** Masses of some particles.

3 A golf ball has a mass of 150 g. Calculate its increase in mass when it is travelling at 50 m s$^{-1}$. What is this as a percentage of its rest mass?

# Energy released in radioactive decay

Unstable nuclei may emit $\alpha$- and $\beta$-particles with large amounts of kinetic energy. We can use Einstein's mass–energy equation $\Delta E = \Delta mc^2$ to explain the origin of this energy. Take, for example, the decay of a nucleus of uranium-238. It decays by emitting an $\alpha$-particle and changes into an isotope of thorium:

$$^{238}_{92}U \rightarrow {}^{234}_{90}Th + {}^4_2He$$

The uranium nucleus is in a high-energy, relatively unstable state. It emits the $\alpha$-particle and the remaining thorium nucleus is in a lower, more stable energy state. There is a decrease in the mass of the system. That is, the combined mass of the thorium nucleus and the $\alpha$-particle is less than the mass of the uranium nucleus. According to Einstein's mass–energy equation, this difference in mass $\Delta m$ is equivalent to the energy released as kinetic energy of the products. Using the most accurate values available:

mass of $^{238}_{92}U$ nucleus $= 3.952\ 83 \times 10^{-25}$ kg

total mass of $^{234}_{90}Th$ nucleus and $\alpha$-particle ($^4_2$He)
$$= 3.952\ 76 \times 10^{-25} \text{ kg}$$

change in mass $\Delta m = (3.952\ 76 - 3.952\ 83) \times 10^{-25}$ kg
$$= -7.0 \times 10^{-30} \text{ kg}$$

The minus sign shows a decrease in mass, hence, according to the equation $\Delta E = \Delta mc^2$, energy is released in the decay process:

energy released $\approx 7.0 \times 10^{-30} \times (3.0 \times 10^8)^2$
$$\approx 6.3 \times 10^{-13} \text{ J}$$

This is an enormous amount of energy for a single decay. One mole of uranium-238, which has $6.02 \times 10^{23}$ nuclei, has the potential to emit total energy equal to about $10^{11}$ J.

We can calculate the energy released in all decay reactions, including $\beta$ decay, using the same ideas as above.

4 A nucleus of beryllium $^{10}_4$Be decays into an isotope of boron by $\beta$-emission. The chemical symbol for boron is B.
   a Write a nuclear decay equation for the nucleus of beryllium-10.
   b Calculate the energy released in this decay and state its form.
   mass of $^{10}_4$Be nucleus $= 1.662\ 38 \times 10^{-26}$ kg
   mass of boron isotope $= 1.662\ 19 \times 10^{-26}$ kg
   mass of electron $= 9.109\ 56 \times 10^{-31}$ kg

# Binding energy and stability

We can now begin to see why some nuclei are more stable than others. If a nucleus is formed from separate nucleons, energy is released. In order to pull the nucleus apart, energy must be put in; in other words, work must be done against the strong nuclear force which holds the nucleons together. The more energy involved in this, the more stable is the nucleus.

> The minimum energy needed to pull a nucleus apart into its separate nucleons is known as the **binding energy** of the nucleus.

Take care: this is **not** energy stored in the nucleus; on the contrary, it is the energy that must be put in to the nucleus in order to pull it apart. In the example of $^{12}_{6}C$ discussed above, we calculated the binding energy from the mass difference between the mass of the $^{12}_{6}C$ nucleus and the masses of the separate protons and neutrons.

In order to compare the stability of different nuclides, we need to consider the binding energy per nucleon. We can determine the binding energy per nucleon for a nuclide as follows:

- Determine the mass defect for the nucleus.
- Use Einstein's mass–energy equation to determine the binding energy of the nucleus by multiplying the mass defect by $c^2$.
- Divide the binding energy of the nucleus by the number of nucleons to calculate the binding energy per nucleon.

Now look at Worked example **2**.

## Worked example

2   Calculate the binding energy per nucleon for the nuclide $^{56}_{26}Fe$.

$$\text{mass of neutron} = 1.675 \times 10^{-27}\,\text{kg}$$

$$\text{mass of proton} = 1.673 \times 10^{-27}\,\text{kg}$$

$$\text{mass of } ^{56}_{26}Fe \text{ nucleus} = 9.288 \times 10^{-26}\,\text{kg}$$

continued ⋯⟩

**Step 1** Determine the mass defect.

$$\text{number of neutrons} = 56 - 26 = 30$$

$$\begin{aligned}\text{mass defect} = (30 \times 1.675 \times 10^{-27} + 26 \times 1.673 \\ \times 10^{-27}) - 9.288 \times 10^{-26}\end{aligned}$$

$$= 8.680 \times 10^{-28}\,\text{kg}$$

**Step 2** Determine the binding energy of the nucleus.

$$\begin{aligned}\text{binding energy} &= \Delta m c^2 \\ &= 8.680 \times 10^{-28} \times (3.0 \times 10^8)^2 \\ &= 7.812 \times 10^{-11}\,\text{J}\end{aligned}$$

**Step 3** Determine the binding energy per nucleon.

$$\text{binding energy per nucleon} = \frac{7.812 \times 10^{-11}}{56}$$

$$\approx 14 \times 10^{-13}\,\text{J}$$

Figure **30.3** shows the binding energy per nucleon for stable nuclei, including the value for $^{56}_{26}Fe$ (shown as a red dot) from Worked example **2**. This is a graph plotted against the nucleon number $A$. The greater the value of the binding energy per nucleon, the more tightly bound are the nucleons that make up the nucleus.

If you examine this graph, you will see that the general trend is for light nuclei to have low binding energies per nucleon. Note, however, that helium has a much higher binding energy than its place in the periodic table might suggest. The high binding energy means that it is very stable. Other common stable nuclei include $^{12}_{6}C$ and $^{16}_{8}O$, which can be thought of as three and four α-particles bound together (Figure **30.4**).

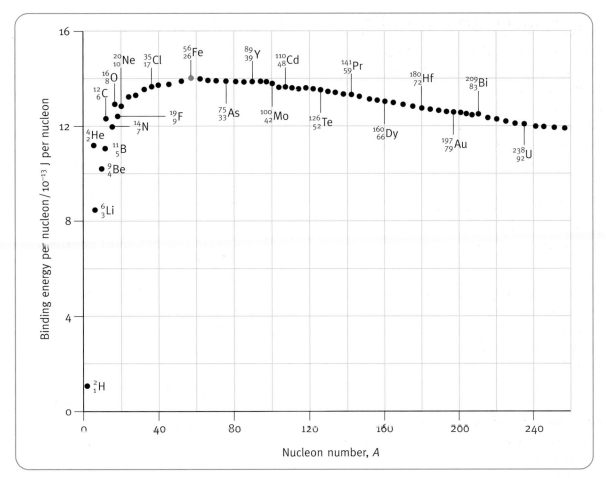

**Figure 30.3** This graph shows the binding energy per nucleon for a number of nuclei. The nucleus becomes more stable as binding energy per nucleon increases.

For nuclides with $A > 20$ approximately, there is not much variation in binding energy per nucleon. The greatest value of binding energy per nucleon is found for $^{56}_{26}$Fe This isotope of iron requires the most energy per nucleon to dismantle it into separate nucleons; hence iron-56 is the most stable isotope in nature.

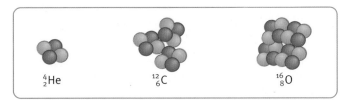

**Figure 30.4** More stable nuclei are formed when 'α-particles' are bound together. In $^{12}_{6}$C and $^{16}_{8}$O, the 'α-particles' do not remain separate, as shown here; rather, the protons and neutrons are tightly packed together.

**Test yourself**

5  Explain why hydrogen $^{1}_{1}$H does not appear on the graph shown in Figure **30.3**.

6  The mass of a $^{8}_{4}$Be nucleus is $1.33 \times 10^{-26}$ kg. A proton and a neutron have a mass of about $1.67 \times 10^{-27}$ kg. For the nucleus of $^{8}_{4}$Be determine:
   **a** the mass defect in kg
   **b** the binding energy
   **c** the binding energy per nucleon.

## Binding energy, fission and fusion

We can use the binding energy graph to help us decide which nuclear processes – fission, fusion, radioactive decay – are likely to occur (Figure **30.5**).

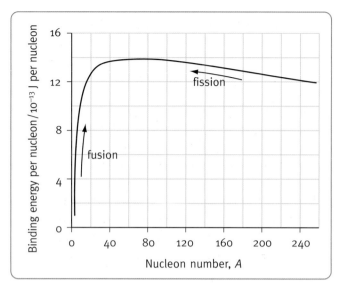

**Figure 30.5** Both fusion and fission are processes that tend to increase the binding energy per nucleon of the particles involved.

## Fission

Fission is the process in which a massive nucleus splits to form two smaller fragments (rather than simply emitting α- or β-radiation). For uranium, we have $A = 235$, and the typical fragments have $A = 140$ and 95. If we look at the binding energy curve, we see that these two fragments have greater binding energy (less potential energy) per nucleon than the original uranium nucleus. Hence, if the uranium nucleus splits in this way, energy will be released.

## Fusion

Fusion is the process by which two very light nuclei join together to form a heavier nucleus. (This is the process by which energy is released in the Sun, when hydrogen nuclei fuse to form helium nuclei.) If two light nuclei fuse, the final binding energy per nucleon will be greater than the original value. The high binding energy (low total energy) of the $^4_2\text{He}$ nuclide means that it is rare for these nuclei to fuse.

### Test yourself

7  Use the binding energy graph to suggest why fission is unlikely to occur with 'light nuclei' ($A < 20$), and why fusion is unlikely to occur for heavier nuclei ($A > 40$).

# The mathematics of radioactive decay

In Chapter **17**, we saw that radioactive decay is a random, spontaneous process. Because we cannot say when an individual nucleus will decay, we have to start thinking about very large numbers of nuclei. Even a tiny speck of radioactive material will contain more than $10^{15}$ nuclei. Then we can talk about the average number of nuclei that we expect to decay in a particular time interval; in other words, we can find out the **average** decay rate. Although we cannot make predictions for individual nuclei, we can say that certain types of nuclei are more likely to decay than others. For example, a nucleus of carbon-12 is stable; carbon-14 decays gradually over thousands of years; carbon-15 nuclei last, on average, a few seconds.

So, because of the spontaneous nature of radioactive decay, we have to make measurements on very large numbers of nuclei and then calculate averages. One quantity we can determine is the probability that an individual nucleus will decay in a particular time interval. For example, suppose we observe one million nuclei of a particular radioisotope. After one hour, 200 000 have decayed. Then the probability that an individual nucleus will decay in one hour is 0.2 or 20%, since 20% of the nuclei have decayed in this time. (Of course, this is only an approximate value, since we might repeat the experiment and find that only 199 000 decay because of the random nature of the decay. The more times we repeat the experiment, the more reliable our answer will be.)

We can now define the decay constant.

> The probability that an individual nucleus will decay per unit time interval is called the decay constant, $\lambda$.

For the example above, we have:

decay constant $\lambda = 0.20\,\text{h}^{-1}$

Note that, because we are measuring the probability of decay per unit time interval, $\lambda$ has units of $\text{h}^{-1}$ (or $\text{s}^{-1}$, $\text{day}^{-1}$, $\text{year}^{-1}$, etc.).

The **activity** of a source is defined as follows:

> The activity $A$ of a radioactive sample is the rate at which nuclei decay or disintegrate.

Activity is measured in decays per second (or $h^{-1}$, $day^{-1}$, etc.). An activity of one decay per second is one becquerel (1 Bq):

$$1\,Bq = 1\,s^{-1}$$

Clearly, the activity of a sample depends on the decay constant $\lambda$ of the isotope under consideration. The greater the decay constant (the probability that an individual nucleus decays per unit time interval), the greater is the activity of the sample. It also depends on the number of undecayed nuclei $N$ present in the sample. For a sample of $N$ undecayed nuclei, we have:

$$A = \lambda N$$

We can also think of the activity as the number of $\alpha$- or $\beta$-particles emitted from the source per unit time. Hence, we can also write the activity $A$ as:

$$A = \frac{\Delta N}{\Delta t}$$

where $\Delta N$ is equal to the number of emissions (or decays) in a small time interval of $\Delta t$.

Now look at Worked examples 3 and 4.

## Worked examples

3 A radioactive source emits $\beta$-particles. It has an activity of $2.8 \times 10^7$ Bq. Estimate the number of $\beta$-particles emitted in a time interval of 2.0 minutes. State one assumption made.

**Step 1** Write down the quantities given in SI units.

$$A = 2.8 \times 10^7\,Bq \qquad \Delta t = 120\,s$$

*continued ⋯→*

**Step 2** Determine the number of $\beta$-particles emitted.

$$A = \frac{\Delta N}{\Delta t} \qquad \Delta N = A\Delta t$$

$$\Delta N = 2.8 \times 10^7 \times 120 = 3.36 \times 10^9 \approx 3.4 \times 10^9$$

We have assumed that the activity remains constant over a period of 2.0 minutes.

4 A sample consists of 1000 undecayed nuclei of a nuclide whose decay constant is $0.20\,s^{-1}$. Determine the initial activity of the sample. Estimate the activity of the sample after 1.0 s.

**Step 1** Since activity $A = \lambda N$, we have:

$$A = 0.20 \times 1000 = 200\,s^{-1} = 200\,Bq$$

**Step 2** After 1.0 s, we might expect 800 nuclei to remain undecayed.

The activity of the sample would then be:

$$A = 0.2 \times 800 = 160\,s^{-1} = 160\,Bq$$

(In fact, it would be slightly higher than this. Since the rate of decay decreases with time all the time, less than 200 nuclei would decay during the first second.)

## Count rate

Although we are often interested in finding the activity of a sample of radioactive material, we cannot usually measure this directly. This is because we cannot easily detect **all** of the radiation emitted. Some will escape past our detectors, and some may be absorbed within the sample itself. A Geiger–Müller (GM) tube placed in front of a radioactive source therefore only detects a fraction of the activity. The farther it is from the source, the smaller the count rate. Therefore, our measurements give a received **count rate** $R$ that is significantly lower than the activity $A$. If we know how efficient our detecting system is, we can deduce $A$ from $R$. If the level of background radiation is significant, then it must be subtracted to give the **corrected** count rate.

8   A sample of carbon-15 initially contains 500 000 undecayed nuclei. The decay constant for this isotope of carbon is $0.30\,s^{-1}$. Determine the initial activity of the sample.

9   A small sample of radium gives a received count rate of 20 counts per minute in a detector. It is known that the counter detects only 10% of the decays from the sample. The sample contains $1.5 \times 10^9$ undecayed nuclei. Determine the decay constant of this form of radium.

10  A radioactive sample is known to emit α-, β- and γ-radiations. Suggest **four** reasons why the count rate measured by a Geiger counter placed next to this sample would be lower than the activity of the sample.

# Decay graphs and equations

The activity of a radioactive substance gradually diminishes as time goes by. The atomic nuclei emit radiation and become different substances. The pattern of radioactive decay is an example of a very important pattern found in many different situations, a pattern called **exponential decay**. Figure **30.6** shows the decay graphs for three different isotopes, each with a different rate of decay.

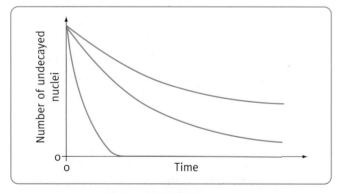

**Figure 30.6** Some radioactive materials decay faster than others.

Although the three graphs look different, they all have something in common – their shape. They are curved lines having a special property. If you know

what is meant by the **half-life** of a radioisotope, then you will understand what is special about the shape of these curves.

> The half-life $t_{1/2}$ of a radioisotope is the mean time taken for half of the active nuclei in a sample to decay.

In a time equal to one half-life, the activity of the sample will also halve. This is because activity is proportional to the number of undecayed nuclei ($A \propto N$). It takes the same amount of time again for half of the remainder of the nuclei to decay, and a third half-life for half of the new remainder to decay (Figure **30.7**).

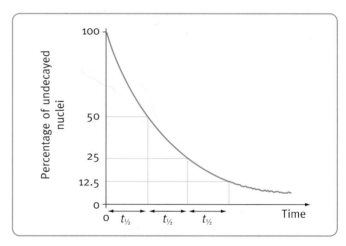

**Figure 30.7** All radioactive decay graphs have the same characteristic shape.

In principle, the graph never reaches zero; it just gets closer and closer. In practice, when only a few undecayed nuclei remain the graph will cease to be a smooth curve (because of the random nature of the decay) and it will eventually reach zero. We use the idea of half-life, because we cannot say when a sample will have completely decayed.

If you have already studied Chapter **24**, you will have met this form of graph before. It is an **exponential decay graph**, with the same pattern of decrease as the discharge of a capacitor in a $C$–$R$ circuit. We will shortly look at the exponential equations that we can use to calculate the activity of a decaying sample.

## Determining half-life

If you are to determine the half-life of a radioactive substance in the laboratory, you need to choose something that will not decay too quickly or

## Test yourself

14 Figure **30.10** shows the decay of a radioactive isotope of caesium, $^{134}_{55}$Cs. Use the graph to determine the half-life of this nuclide in years, and hence find the decay constant in year$^{-1}$.

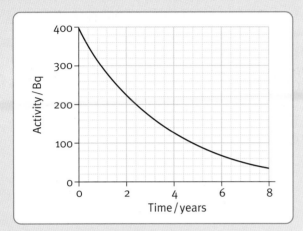

**Figure 30.10** Decay graph for a radioactive isotope of caesium – see Test yourself Q **14**.

15 The decay constant of a particular isotope is known to be $3.0 \times 10^{-4}\,\text{s}^{-1}$. Determine how long it will take

*continued* ⋯⫸

for the activity of a sample of this substance to decrease to one-eighth of its initial value.

16 The isotope $^{16}_{7}$N decays with a half-life of 7.4 s.
  a Calculate the decay constant for this nuclide.
  b A sample of $^{16}_{7}$N initially contains 5000 nuclei. Determine how many will remain after a time of:
  i  14.8 s
  ii 20.0 s

17 A sample contains an isotope of half-life $t_{\frac{1}{2}}$
  a Show that the fraction $f$ of the number of undecayed nuclei left in the sample after a time $t$ is given by the equation:

  $$f = \left(\tfrac{1}{2}\right)^n$$

  where $n = \dfrac{t}{t_{\frac{1}{2}}}$.

  b Calculate the fraction $f$ after each of the following times:
  i   $t_{\frac{1}{2}}$       iii 2.5$t_{\frac{1}{2}}$
  ii  2$t_{\frac{1}{2}}$      iv  8.3$t_{\frac{1}{2}}$

# Summary

- ☐ Einstein's mass–energy equation $\Delta E = \Delta mc^2$ relates mass changes to energy changes.
- ☐ The mass defect is equal to the difference between the mass of the separate nucleons and the nucleus.
- ☐ The binding energy of a nucleus is the minimum energy required to break up the nucleus into separate nucleons.
- ☐ The binding energy per nucleon indicates the relative stability of different nuclides.
- ☐ The variation of binding energy per nucleon shows that energy is released when light nuclei undergo fusion and when heavier nuclei undergo fission, because these processes increase the binding energy per nucleon and hence result in more stable nuclides.
- ☐ The half-life $t_{\frac{1}{2}}$ of a radioisotope is the mean time taken for half of the active nuclei in a sample to decay.
- ☐ The decay constant $\lambda$ is the probability that an individual nucleus will decay per unit time interval.
- ☐ The activity $A$ of a sample is related to the number of undecayed nuclei in the sample $N$ by $A = \lambda N$.
- ☐ The decay constant and half-life are related by the equation:

  $$\lambda t_{\frac{1}{2}} = \ln 2 \quad \text{or} \quad \lambda t_{\frac{1}{2}} = 0.693$$

- ☐ We can represent the exponential decrease of a quantity by an equation of the form:

  $$x = x_0\, e^{(-\lambda t)}$$

  where $x$ can be activity $A$, count rate $R$ or number of undecayed nuclei $N$.

# End-of-chapter questions

1   An antiproton is identical to a proton except that it has negative charge. If a proton and an antiproton collide they are annihilated and two photons are formed.
    a   Calculate the energy released in the reaction.
    b   Calculate the energy released if 1 mole of protons and 1 mole of antiprotons were annihilated by this process.
    (Mass of a proton = mass of an antiproton = $1.67 \times 10^{-27}$ kg.)

2   Calculate the mass that would be annihilated to release 1 J of energy.

3   In a nuclear reactor the mass of uranium and the fission fragments falls at a rate of $70\,\mu g\,s^{-1}$. Calculate the maximum power output from the reactor assuming that it is 100% efficient.

4   The equation shows the radioactive decay of Rn-222.

$$^{222}_{86}\text{Rn} \rightarrow \, ^{218}_{84}\text{Po} + \, ^{4}_{2}\alpha + \gamma$$

Calculate the total energy output from this decay and state what forms of energy are produced.

(Mass of $^{222}_{86}\text{Rn} = 221.970$ u, mass of $^{218}_{84}\text{Po} = 217.963$ u, mass of $^{4}_{2}\alpha = 4.002$ u; 1 u is the unified atomic mass unit = $1.660 \times 10^{-27}$ kg.)

(Hint: find the mass defect in u, then convert to kg.)

5   A carbon-12 atom consists of 6 protons, 6 neutrons and 6 electrons. The unified atomic mass unit (u) is defined as $\frac{1}{12}$ the mass of the carbon-12 atom.

Calculate:
    a   the mass defect in kilograms
    b   the binding energy
    c   the binding energy per nucleon.
    (Mass of a proton = 1.007 276 u, mass of a neutron = 1.008 665 u, mass of an electron = 0.000 548 u.)

6   The fusion reaction which holds most promise for the generation of electricity is the fusion of tritium $^{3}_{1}\text{H}$ and deuterium $^{2}_{1}\text{H}$. The equation below shows the process:

$$^{3}_{1}\text{H} + \, ^{2}_{1}\text{H} \rightarrow \, ^{4}_{2}\text{He} + \, ^{1}_{1}\text{H}$$

Calculate:
    a   the change in mass in the reaction
    b   the energy released in the reaction
    c   the energy released if one mole of deuterium were reacted with one mole of tritium.
    (Mass of $^{3}_{1}\text{H} = 3.015\,500$ u, mass of $^{2}_{1}\text{H} = 2.013\,553$ u, mass of $^{4}_{2}\text{He} = 4.001\,506$ u, mass of $^{1}_{1}\text{H} = 1.007\,276$ u.)

**7** The initial activity a sample of 1 mole of Rn-220 is $8.02 \times 10^{21} \, \text{s}^{-1}$. Calculate:
    **a** the decay constant for this isotope
    **b** the half-life of the isotope.

**8** Figure **30.11** Shows the count rate recorded when a sample of the isotope In-116 decays.

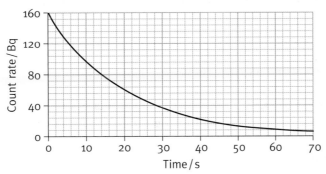

**Figure 30.11** For End-of-chapter Q **8**.

    **a** Use the graph to find the half-life of the isotope.
    **b** Calculate the decay constant.

**9** The proportions of different isotopes in rocks can be used to date the rocks. The half-life of uranium 238 is $4.9 \times 10^{9}$ years. A sample has 99.2% of the proportion of this isotope compared with newly formed rock.
    **a** Calculate the decay constant for this isotope of uranium.
    **b** Calculate the age of the rock.

**10** The table shows the received count rate when a sample of the isotope V-52 decays.

| Time / min | 0 | 1 | 2 | 3 | 4 | 5 | 6 | 7 | 8 |
|---|---|---|---|---|---|---|---|---|---|
| Count rate / Bq | 187 | 159 | 134 | 110 | 85 | 70 | 60 | 56 | 40 |

    **a** **i** Draw a graph of the count rate against the time.
        **ii** Comment on the scatter of the points.
    **b** From the graph, deduce the half-life of the isotope.
    **c** Describe the changes to the graph that you would expect if you were given a larger sample of the isotope.

# Exam-style questions

**1** This question is about the nucleus of uranium-235 ($^{235}_{92}\text{U}$), which has a mass of $3.89 \times 10^{-25} \, \text{kg}$.
    **a** State the number of protons and neutrons in this nucleus.         [1]
    **b** The radius $r$ of a nucleus is given by the equation:
        $r = 1.41 \times 10^{-15} A^{1/3}$

where $A$ is the nucleon number of the nucleus.

Determine the density of the $_{92}^{235}$U nucleus. [3]

c Explain why the total mass of the nucleons is different from the mass of the $_{92}^{235}$U nucleus. [2]

d Without calculations, explain how you can determine the binding energy per nucleon for the uranium-235 nucleus from its mass and the masses of a proton and a neutron. [4]

2 a Explain what is meant by **nuclear fusion** and explain why it only occurs at very high temperatures. [3]

b The main reactions which fuel the Sun are the fusion of hydrogen nuclides to form helium nuclides. However, other reactions do occur. In one such reaction, known as the triple alpha process, three helium nuclei collide and fuse to form a carbon-12 nucleus.

  i Explain why temperatures higher than those required for the fusion of hydrogen are needed for the triple alpha process. [1]

  ii Calculate the energy released in the triple alpha process. [3]

(Mass of a helium ($_{2}^{4}$He) nucleus = 4.001 506 u, mass of a carbon ($_{6}^{12}$C) nucleus = 12.000 000 u, 1 u = 1.660 × 10$^{-27}$ kg)

3 The radioactive isotope of polonium, $_{81}^{218}$Po, decays by the emission of an α-particle with a half-life of 183 s.

a In an accident at a reprocessing plant some of this isotope, in the form of dust, is released into the atmosphere.

Explain why a spillage in the form of a dust is very much more dangerous to health than a liquid spillage. [2]

b It is calculated that 2.4 g of the isotope is released into the atmosphere.

Calculate the initial activity of the released polonium. [4]

c It is felt that it would safe to re-enter the laboratory when the activity falls to background, about 10 Bq.

Calculate how many hours must pass before it is safe to re-enter the laboratory. [3]

4 A nuclear reactor is fuelled by fission of uranium. The output from the reactor is 200 MW. The equation below describes a typical fission reaction.

$$_{52}^{239}U + _{0}^{1}n \rightarrow _{62}^{239}U \rightarrow _{35}^{87}Br + _{57}^{146}La + 3_{0}^{1}n$$

a Suggest and explain into what form the majority of the energy released in the reaction is converted. [2]

b i Calculate the energy released in the reaction. The energy of the captured neutron is negligible. [2]

  ii Assume that the energy released in this fission is typical of all fissions of U-236. Calculate how many fissions occur each second. [1]

  iii Calculate the mass of uranium-235 that is required to run the reactor for 1 year. [3]

(Mass of $_{92}^{235}$U = 3.90 × 10$^{-25}$ kg, mass of $_{35}^{87}$Br = 1.44 × 10$^{-25}$ kg, mass of $_{57}^{146}$La = 2.42 × 10$^{-25}$ kg, mass of neutron = 1.67 × 10$^{-27}$ kg, 1 year = 3.15 × 10$^{7}$ s.)

# 31 Direct sensing

## Objectives

After studying this chapter, you should be able to:

- ☐ understand how electronic sensing devices are used to produce an output voltage
- ☐ describe the function of the following sensors: light-dependent resistor (LDR), negative temperature coefficient thermistor, piezo-electric transducer, metal-wire strain gauge
- ☐ recall the main properties of the ideal operational amplifier (op-amp)

- ☐ understand the use of an op-amp as a comparator, and as an inverting and non-inverting amplifier.
- ☐ recall the circuit diagrams and calculate the voltage gain of inverting and non-inverting amplifiers for a single signal input.
- ☐ understand output devices used in electronic circuits such as the light-emitting diode (LED), the relay and calibrated analogue and digital meters

## Sensing devices

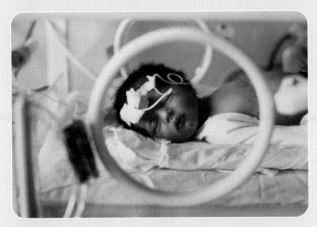

Figure 31.1 A newborn baby in an incubator. Sensors inside the incubator monitor and control the temperature, oxygen and humidity levels.

Sensing devices are widespread in the modern world. From birth to death, electronic sensors watch over and control many of our environments. The chances of survival of the newborn baby in Figure 31.1 are improved as a sensor inside the incubator measures the temperature of the air. The output of the sensor operates heating and cooling devices which keep the temperature as constant as possible. In this chapter, we will explore how some common sensing devices work.

## Sensor components

In its basic form, an electronic **sensor** may be represented as a sensing device, a processor that provides an output voltage, and an output device.

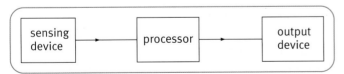

Figure 31.2 Block diagram of an electronic sensor

The sensing device is an electronic component with a property that changes when a physical quantity such as temperature or light intensity alters. In earlier chapters, we looked at such components as

the thermistor (Chapter 12) and the light-dependent resistor (LDR) (Chapter 13). The resistance of these components changes when the temperature or the light level alters. This change in resistance causes the processor to produce an output voltage that drives the output device. In this way the change in a physical quantity such as resistance can be used to trigger the output device. When the air in the incubator in Figure 31.1 becomes cold, the change in resistance of the sensor causes the processor to switch on the output device, a heater, to keep the baby warm. When it becomes too hot, the same sensing device and processor will switch the heater off.

It is important to note that we are not concerned with all the details of how a particular sensing device works or what there is inside the processor. We are only interested in knowing the output for various inputs and how the sensor can be used in a range of useful applications. Sensors make use of many basic ideas about electric circuits: resistance and current for example. A processor may contain many transistors, but it is not necessary to understand how a transistor works to appreciate the function of a processor. Some detail will be given, but if you wish to delve further into how these devices work, there are many useful websites that will help you to understand how physicists have used their knowledge and inspiration to good effect.

The sensing device is sometimes called a **transducer**. A transducer changes energy from one form into another. A microphone is an obvious example, as it changes sound into electrical energy. However even the thermistor used as the sensing device in the incubator in Figure **31.1** can be thought of as a transducer; a change in the internal energy of the air alters the electrical energy in the thermistor circuit.

## Piezo-electric transducers

Some crystals such as quartz produce an electric field when a force is applied and the shape of the crystal changes. This is known as the **piezo-electric effect**. A piezo-electric crystal is made of positive and negative ions in a regular arrangement. When the crystal is stressed, a small voltage is produced between the faces of the crystal. The crystal acts as a **transducer** since energy is changed from one form to another. There is more about piezo-electric transducers in Chapter **32** where their use in ultrasound scanning is described.

For use in a transducer, the piezo-electric crystal is made into a thin sheet with metal connections on opposite sides. When a sound wave hits one side of the sheet, the compressions and rarefactions cause the pressure to increase and decrease. The crystal changes shape in response to these pressure changes and a small voltage is formed across the connections. Figure **31.3** shows the symbol for a microphone.

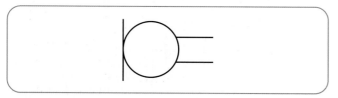

**Figure 31.3** The symbol for a microphone.

Acoustic guitars and other instruments often use a piezo-electric transducer to produce an electrical output. The microphone is stuck to the body of the guitar and the electrical output can be amplified and played back through loudspeakers.

## The light-dependent resistor (LDR)

An LDR is made of a high-resistance semiconductor. If light falling on the LDR is of high enough frequency, photons are absorbed by the semiconductor. As some photons are absorbed electrons are released from atoms in the semiconductor. The resulting free electrons conduct electricity and the resistance of the semiconductor is reduced.

The graph in Figure **31.4** shows the variation of the resistance of a typical LDR with light intensity. Only a narrow range of light intensity, measured in lux, is shown. A typical LDR will have a resistance of a few hundred ohms in sunlight, but in the dark, its resistance will be millions of ohms.

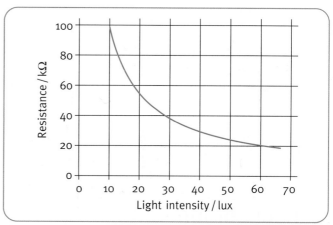

**Figure 31.4** Resistance plotted against light intensity for an LDR.

How is an LDR used as a sensing device? A voltage is needed to drive the output device yet the LDR only produces a change in resistance. The sensor must use this change in resistance to generate the change in voltage. The solution is to place the LDR in series with a fixed resistor, as shown in Figure **31.5**.

The voltage of the supply is shared between the two resistors in proportion to their resistance, so as the light level changes and the LDR's resistance changes, so does the voltage across each of the resistors. The two resistors form a potential divider, one of the practical circuits discussed in Chapter **13**.

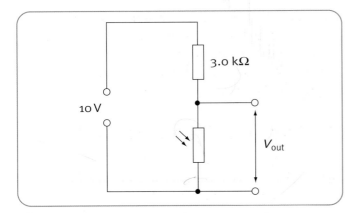

Figure 31.5 An LDR used in a sensor.

## Worked example

1   Using the graph in Figure **31.4**, calculate $V_{out}$ in Figure **31.5** when the light intensity is 60 lux.

**Step 1** Find the resistance of the LDR at 60 lux.

$$R_{LDR} = 20\,k\Omega$$

**Step 2** Divide the total voltage of 10 V in the ratio 3 : 20. The total number of parts is 23 so:

$$V_{out} = \frac{20}{23} \times 10 = 8.70\,V$$

The answer on your calculator might be 8.69565. When you give your answer to 3 significant figures do not write 8.69 – you must round correctly.

## Test yourself

1   What is the voltage across the 3.0 kΩ resistor in Figure **31.5** when the light intensity is 10 lux?

2   The circuit shown in Figure **31.5** produces a decreasing output voltage when the light intensity increases. How can the circuit be altered to produce an increasing output voltage as the light intensity increases?

## The thermistor

The thermistors that we deal with are known as **negative temperature coefficient** thermistors. This means that when the temperature rises, the resistance of the thermistor falls. This happens because the thermistor is made from a semiconductor material. One property of a semiconductor is that when the temperature rises the number of free electrons increases, and thus the resistance falls.

Figure **31.6** shows a graph of the resistance of a thermistor and the resistance of a metal wire plotted against temperature. You can see that the resistance of a metal wire increases with increase in temperature. A metal wire is not a negative temperature device, but it could be used as a sensing device. A thermistor is more useful than a metal wire because there is a much larger change in resistance with change in temperature. However, the change in resistance of a thermistor is not linear with temperature; indeed, it is likely to be an exponential decrease. This means that any device used to measure temperature electronically must be calibrated to take into account the resistance–temperature graph. The scale on an ordinary laboratory thermometer between 0 °C and 100 °C is divided up into 100 equal parts, each of which represents 1 °C. If the resistance of a thermistor were divided like this, the scale would be incorrect.

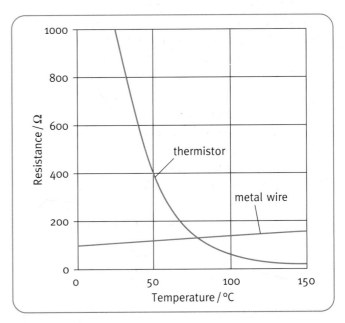

Figure 31.6 Variation of resistance with temperature.

The thermistor can be used as a sensing device in the same way as an LDR. Instead of sensing a change in light level, it senses a change in temperature.

## The metal-wire strain gauge

A **strain gauge** takes advantage of the change in resistance of a metal wire as its length and cross-sectional area change. When stretched, a metal wire becomes narrower and longer; both these changes increase the electrical resistance. When compressed, a metal wire becomes shorter and wider; as long as it does not buckle, these changes decrease its electrical resistance.

Figure 31.7 shows the structure of a strain gauge. A thin metal wire is placed between thin sheets of plastic. The metal wire zigzags up and down its plastic base so that the length of wire used is longer than the actual strain gauge.

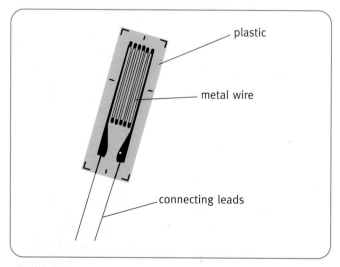

plastic

metal wire

connecting leads

**Figure 31.7** A metal-wire strain gauge.

Strain gauges are used in many situations. For example, an engineer may find a crack in a wall and want to know whether the crack is growing bigger. By sticking a strain gauge over the crack the engineer can measure the resistance many days or even years later and see if there has been any movement.

A gauge used in a dynamic experiment may measure the stress changes in an aircraft wing. A processor is used to produce a voltage output and show changes in length as they happen. This provides important information when testing an aircraft.

In Chapter **12**, we saw that a wire of length $L$, cross-sectional area $A$ and resistivity $\rho$ has a resistance $R$ given by:

$$R = \frac{\rho L}{A}$$

What happens to the resistance when the wire is stretched depends on the construction of the strain gauge. The simplest approximation is to assume that the cross-sectional area of the wire remains unchanged.

If the wire increases in length by a small amount $\delta L$ and the cross-sectional area $A$ is unchanged, then the resistance of the wire increases by $\delta R$, where:

$$R + \delta R = \frac{\rho(L + \delta L)}{A}$$

Subtracting the two equations gives:

$$\delta R = \frac{\rho \delta L}{A}$$

If the expression is divided by $R = \dfrac{\rho \delta L}{A}$, we get:

$$\frac{\delta R}{R} = \frac{\delta L}{L}$$

Usually the area $A$ decreases as the wire is stretched, which also increases the resistance change. It can be shown that if the volume of the wire remains constant, then the change in the area doubles the change in the resistance, so that for small changes:

$$\delta R = \frac{2\rho \delta L}{A} \quad \text{or} \quad \frac{\delta R}{R} = \frac{2\delta L}{L}$$

In both cases, the change in resistance is directly proportional to the increase in length, $\delta R \propto \delta L$.

The change in resistance is likely to be very small but with a suitable series resistor and a cell used as a sensor, the change in length can produce a measurable change in output voltage.

## Worked example

2  The wire in a strain gauge when unstretched has length 10.00 cm and resistance 120.0 Ω. When the wire is stretched by 0.10 cm, the resistance becomes 122.4 Ω. The strain gauge is connected in the circuit shown in Figure 31.8. What is the change in length of the wire in the strain gauge when the output voltage is 5.06 V?

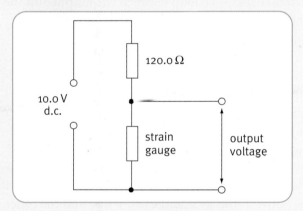

Figure 31.8 Circuit for Worked example 2.

**Step 1** Determine the resistance of the strain gauge $R_s$ by considering the two resistors as a potential divider. The 10 V supply is split in the ratio 5.06 V : 4.94 V and so:

$$R_s = \frac{5.06}{4.94} \times 120 = 122.9\,\Omega$$

Alternatively, apply the potential divider formula

$$V_{out} = \left(\frac{R_2}{R_1 + R_2}\right) \times V_{in}:$$

$$4.94 = \left(\frac{120}{120 + R_s}\right) \times 10.0$$

*continued ┈┈>*

It is easier to use 4.94 V, the voltage across the 120 Ω resistor. This gives a value for $R_s$ of 122.9 Ω.

**Step 2** The resistance of the wire has increased by 2.9 Ω. Since $\delta R \propto \delta L$, and an increase in length of 0.10 cm increases the resistance by 2.4 Ω, the length has increased by:

$$\frac{2.9}{2.4} \times 0.10 = 0.12\,\text{cm}$$

If the strain gauge is glued to a metal support, the strain in the metal support is the same as the strain in the gauge, in this case $\frac{0.12}{10} = 1.2\,\%$. Thus the strain gauge can easily measure strain.

## Test yourself

6  Using the data given in Worked example 2:
   a  calculate the increase in length of the wire when the output voltage is 5.1 V
   b  calculate the strain in the wire when the output voltage is 5.1 V
   c  calculate the output voltage when the wire is stretched by 0.05 cm.

# The operational amplifier (op-amp)

Operational amplifiers (op-amps) are among the most widely used electronic devices today, being used in a vast array of consumer, industrial and scientific devices. The amplifier is the basic building block of many electronic systems. The electrical output from the musicians in the concert shown in Figure 31.9 must be amplified before it can be passed to the loudspeakers and turned into sound.

An amplifier produces an output with more power and usually more voltage than the input. A perfect amplifier should produce an exact copy of the input. In particular, the different frequencies produced by the musicians and their instruments must be amplified by the same amount. If, for example, high-frequency notes are made louder than low-frequency notes then the whole performance will be altered. You may have

Figure 31.9 A concert – the loud music has been greatly amplified.

noticed that people sound different when talking on the telephone. This is often because some frequencies are not amplified as much as others.

The goal of producing an amplifier with a constant amplification or **gain** might seem simple, but it is hard to achieve. Unfortunately, electronic components, such as capacitors and transistors, amplify signals of different frequencies by different amounts.

One approach is to use an amplifier with a very high gain and then provide an external circuit which reduces the gain but ensures that the overall gain is the same for signals of a greater range of frequencies. Such a device is the **operational amplifier (op-amp)**.

Figure 31.10 shows an operational amplifier. Inside the plastic casing there are many transistors, resistors and other components. The op-amp has two inputs; one is marked (–) and is known as the **inverting input** and the other is marked (+) and is know as the **non-inverting input**. The one function of this device is to use the potential difference between the two inputs to

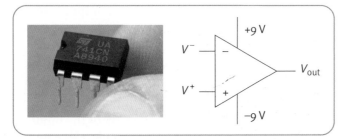

Figure 31.10 An operational amplifier and its symbol.

produce as large an output voltage $V_{out}$ as possible. $V^-$ is the potential at the inverting input (–) and $V^+$ is the potential at the non-inverting input (+).

The open-loop voltage gain $G_0$ is given by:

$$G_0 = \frac{\text{output voltage}}{\text{input voltage}}$$

For the op-amp in Figure **31.10** the open-loop voltage gain is given by:

$$G_0 = \frac{V_{out}}{(V^+ - V^-)}$$

It is called the open-loop gain because there is no loop of resistors or other components linking the output back to the input – it is just the operational amplifier alone. (As we shall see on page 477, an external circuit or loop between the output and the input can be used to provide **negative** feedback, which reduces the gain.)

The op-amp is not like a transformer. It does not transform the voltage or use the energy from the input signal to produce the output. The op-amp provides more voltage, current and power in the output than is present in the input. To do this it has two power supplies; these are shown in Figure **31.10** as the +9 V and –9 V connections to the op-amp. There is also a zero volt line, or earth. One power supply will be between the +9 V and the 0 V line and the other between the –9 V connection and the 0 V line.

The zero volt line, or earth, is very important as all voltages are measured relative to this potential. If the potential of the inverting input (–) is $V^-$ then the potential difference or voltage between that input and the zero volt line is also $V^-$.

The actual voltage used for the power supplies can vary in different circuits. The positive and negative supply voltages are of equal value and may be written as $+V_s$ and $-V_s$. The connections of the power supplies to the op-amp are often left out of a circuit diagram for clarity but they are always there. They provide the power for the op-amp.

The largest voltage that an op-amp can produce is a value close to the supply voltage. The op-amp in Figure **31.10** can only produce outputs between +9 V and –9 V. When the output voltage reaches either supply voltage, the largest value or smallest value that it can achieve, the amplifier is said to be **saturated**.

## The properties of an ideal op-amp

The ideal op-amp has the following properties.

### Infinite open-loop voltage gain

This means that when the op-amp is used on its own, with no feedback loop, then a small input signal will become an 'infinite' output signal. Clearly this is not possible (the output cannot exceed the supply voltage) and at its maximum output the amplifier is said to be saturated with output value $+V_s$ or $-V_s$. However, when a feedback loop is applied, the overall gain of the circuit is reduced to a sensible value. The infinite open-loop voltage gain makes sure that signals of a wide range of frequencies have the same gain when the feedback is applied. A typical op-amp has an open-loop gain of $10^5$ but this can be much higher.

### Infinite input resistance (or impedance)

The input to an op-amp is a voltage. If, for example, a piezo-electric microphone is connected to the op-amp, then the microphone is acting as the voltage supply. It acts just like an electrical battery but the voltage it produces changes with time. Any voltage supply has an internal resistance. You may remember that one of the effects of this is to reduce the terminal p.d. when a current is supplied. The infinite input resistance of an op-amp means that no current is drawn from the supply, there are no 'lost volts' and the input voltage to the op-amp is as large as possible. The resistance for an alternating voltage is known as impedance, so the ideal op-amp has infinite impedance and no current passes into the input terminals. The input impedance of an op-amp may be as high as $10^{12}\,\Omega$, but $10^6\,\Omega$ is typical.

### Zero output resistance (or impedance)

The output from an op-amp is a voltage. The op-amp is itself acting as a voltage supply to the next part of a circuit. If the op-amp has zero output resistance it is acting just like an electrical battery with zero internal resistance. This means that there will be no 'lost volts' when current is supplied by the op-amp. A typical op-amp has an output resistance of $75\,\Omega$.

### Infinite bandwidth

The bandwidth of an op-amp is the range of frequencies that are amplified by the same amount. The ideal op-amp will amplify signals of all frequencies and should have an infinite bandwidth. However, in some op-amps the bandwidth can be as low as a few kilohertz.

### Infinite slew rate

An ideal op-amp should change the output immediately the input is changed. The slew-rate measures the time delay between input and output and an infinite slew rate means that there is no time delay.

### Zero noise contribution

Any signal includes a small amount of noise. The ideal op-amp should not produce any noise itself, but it cannot help amplifying any noise that is present in its input.

## The op-amp as a comparator

The op-amp shown in Figure **31.11** is connected to two power supplies. One battery of 9 V is connected between the zero volt line and the $+9$ V positive supply terminal of the op-amp and the other between the zero volt line and the negative power supply terminal. These batteries are not shown.

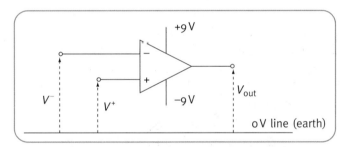

Figure **31.11** An op-amp used as a comparator.

The output voltage is given by $V_{out} = G_0 \times (V^+ - V^-)$ where $G_0$ is the open-loop voltage gain. Notice that all of these voltages are measured with reference to the zero volt line, which is often connected to earth.

Suppose that $G_0 = 10^5$ and that $V^+ = 0.15$ V and $V^- = 0.10$ V. The equation then gives:

$$V_{out} = 10^5 \times (0.15 - 0.10) = 5000\,\text{V}$$

Clearly this is impossible. The op-amp is therefore saturated and $V_{out}$ will be close to one of the power supply voltages, in this case $+9$ V because $V^+$ is bigger than $V^-$.

For a comparator:

- If $V^+$ is slightly bigger than $V^-$ then $V_{out}$ will be at the positive power supply voltage.
- If $V^+$ is slightly smaller than $V^-$ then $V_{out}$ will be at the negative power supply voltage.

The op-amp is comparing $V^+$ and $V^-$. If these two voltages are slightly different then the output voltage tells us which one is larger than the other. It is unlikely that the voltages will be exactly the same.

A comparator circuit can be used to compare two temperatures or two light levels. The circuit shown in Figure 31.12 is used to give a warning when the temperature sensed by thermistor T becomes smaller than a certain value.

To understand the action of this circuit you should notice that the positive power supply to the op-amp is also used to supply voltage and current to the thermistor T and a 10 kΩ resistor connected as a potential divider. There is also another potential divider circuit connected to the inverting input (–) of the op-amp. Note that there is no connection where the two connecting wires are shown crossing.

Worked example 3 explains how this circuit operates.

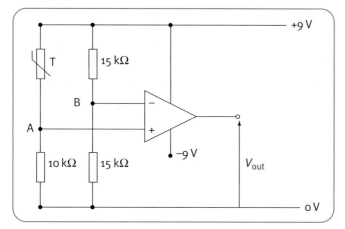

**Figure 31.12** An op-amp used as a comparator to monitor temperature.

## Worked example

3   For the circuit shown in Figure 31.12, the resistance of the thermistor T is 8 kΩ at a temperature of 15 °C. What are $V^-$ and $V^+$, the potentials at the inverting and non-inverting inputs? And what happens when the temperature falls so that the resistance of T rises above 10 kΩ?

**Step 1** $V^-$ and $V^+$ can be found by using the potential divider formula to find the potentials

at points A and B. The potential at A is the p.d. across the 10 kΩ resistor. So:

$$\text{potential at A} = 9 \times \frac{10}{18} = 5.0\,\text{V}$$

The potential at B is easier to find, as the two 15 kΩ resistors share the 9 V equally.

$$\text{potential at B} = \frac{9}{2} = 4.5\,\text{V}$$

The op-amp acts as a comparator and, since $V^+$ is larger than $V^-$, the output will be the highest voltage that the op-amp can produce, in this case +9 V.

**Step 2** The thermistor T is a negative temperature coefficient thermistor and so its resistance rises sharply and eventually becomes larger than 10 kΩ. Suppose it becomes 12 kΩ. Then:

$$\text{potential at A} = 9 \times \frac{10}{22} = 4.1\,\text{V}$$

Now $V^+$ is smaller than $V^-$ and the op-amp output voltage is the lowest it can provide, near the negative supply voltage, in this case –9 V.

This switch from +9 V to –9 V is quite sudden because of the large open-loop voltage gain. The value of the temperature when the output voltage switches from +9 V to –9 V can be altered by adjusting the resistance of the resistor in series with the thermistor.

## Test yourself

7   With an open-loop voltage gain $G_0 = 10^5$ and power supply voltages of +9 V and –9 V, what is the smallest difference between $V^+$ and $V^-$ for which the op-amp is not saturated?

8   What happens in the circuit shown in Figure 31.12 if the supply voltages are changed to +15 V and –15 V? Is the temperature at which

*continued* ⋯⟫

*continued* ⋯⟫

it switches over the same? Are the output voltages the same?

9 How can the circuit of Figure **31.12** be altered so that the output switches from –9 V when the temperature is hot to +9 V when the temperature is cold?

10 Calculate values of $V^+$, $V^-$ and $V_{out}$ in Figure **31.12** when the resistance of T is $3 \, k\Omega$.

# Negative feedback

What happens when the op-amp in Figure **31.12** is connected to a heater which warms the air around the thermistor? The op-amp senses when the room is cold and switches on the heater. The heater then warms the room and this information is fed back to the thermistor, which then senses that the room is now warm enough and switches off the heater. This process is known as **feedback** and keeps the room at a reasonably constant temperature.

The effect is shown in Figure **31.13**.

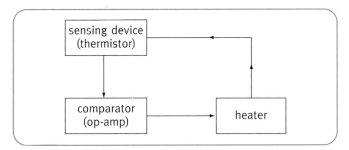

Figure **31.13** Feedback keeping temperature constant.

There are many examples of feedback. Your body temperature is remarkably constant because of a number of feedback mechanisms. When your skin senses that you are cold, a signal is sent via the nerves to your brain which closes down some of the blood vessels in your skin to reduce energy loss. If you are very cold the brain makes muscles contract and expand uncontrollably as you shiver. This will make the core of your body warm again and the effect is fed back to the brain, which switches off the shivering.

Electrical feedback is also very important. Consider the circuit shown In Figure **31.14**. In this circuit $V_{in}$, the input to the op-amp, is connected to the non-inverting input (+). The whole of the voltage output $V_{out}$ is fed back to the inverting input (–) of the op-amp. How does the op-amp behave with this feedback loop?

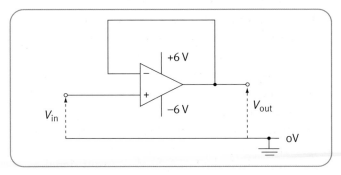

Figure **31.14** An op-amp with the output connected to the inverting input.

The potential $V^-$ at the inverting input (–) is always the same as $V_{out}$ because of the feedback loop.

Suppose the system starts with both $V_{in}$ and $V_{out}$ as 0 V and then the input voltage $V_{in}$ changes to +0.1 V. The op-amp multiplies the potential difference between $V^+$ and $V^-$ by the open-loop voltage gain to produce $V_{out}$. The gain is very high so $V_{out}$ increases quickly. What does $V_{out}$ become? We must consider that the output voltage is fed back to the inverting input.

We know that $V_{out} = G_0 \times (V^+ - V^-)$, where $G_0$ is the open-loop voltage gain.

Since $V_{out} = V^-$ and $V_{in} = V^+$ we have:

$$V_{out} = G_0(V_{in} - V_{out})$$

$$V_{out}(1 + G_0) = G_0 V_{in}$$

The closed-loop gain $G$ is given by:

$$G = \frac{V_{out}}{V_{in}} = \frac{G_0}{(1 + G_0)}$$

Because $G_0$ is very high, about $10^5$, there is little difference between $G_0$ and $(G_0 + 1)$, so the closed-loop gain is very nearly 1. Since the input voltage was +0.1 V the output voltage is also +0.1 V. This analysis is true as long as the output voltage is smaller than the supply voltage, in this case as long as $V_{out}$ is between –6 V and +6 V.

This may seem strange. We have taken an op-amp with a gain of $10^5$ and turned it into a device with a gain of 1, so the input voltage and output voltage are equal. This is hardly an amplifier, but it is useful.

The op-amp draws very little current from the input yet it can supply a reasonable current from its output. This circuit is often used as a buffer between electronic circuits. If something happens to one circuit it does not affect the other circuit.

A piezo-electric microphone has a high internal resistance and cannot supply much current. If it is connected to the input of the op-amp in Figure 31.12, the same voltage is output but the current can be larger.

Another advantage is that it does not matter whether the frequency of the input signal is high or low; the gain is the same. So the output signal is exactly the same as the input signal and there is no distortion. This is only true when the open-loop voltage gain is high. At very high frequencies the open-loop voltage gain falls and eventually the closed-loop gain falls. The **bandwidth**, the range of frequencies for which the gain is constant, is increased by using negative feedback.

To summarise, the benefits of using negative feedback to reduce the gain of an op-amp are:

- less distortion
- increased bandwidth
- the gain is more stable and not affected by changes in temperature, etc.
- the output resistance (impedance) can be low and the input resistance (impedance) high.

# The inverting amplifier

The **inverting amplifier** shown in Figure 31.15 uses negative feedback, but not all of the output voltage is fed back to the inverting input (–).

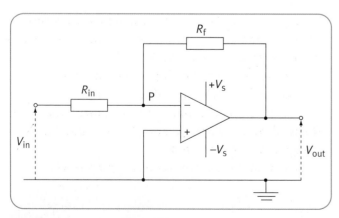

**Figure 31.15** An inverting amplifier.

When an op-amp is connected as an inverting amplifier :

- the non-inverting input (+) is connected to the 0 V line;
- part of the output voltage (or signal) is connected to the inverting input (–);
- the input voltage (or signal) is connected to the inverting input.

To understand how the inverting amplifier works, you need to understand the concept of the **virtual earth approximation**. In this approximation the potential at the inverting input (–) is very close to 0 V. Why is this true? There are two steps in the argument.

- The op-amp multiplies the difference in potential between the inverting and non-inverting inputs, $V^-$ and $V^+$, to produce the output voltage $V_{out}$. Because the open-loop voltage gain is very high, the difference between $V^-$ and $V^+$ must be almost zero.
- The non-inverting input (+) is connected to the zero volt line so $V^+ = 0$. Thus $V^-$ must be close to zero and the inverting input (–) is almost at earth potential.

Point P is known as a **virtual earth**. It cannot actually be 0 V but it is very close to 0 V. This approximation is true as long as the op-amp is not saturated and for frequencies where the open-loop voltage gain is high.

The virtual earth approximation can be used to find an expression for the gain of an inverting amplifier, as follows. If the current in the input resistor $R_{in}$ is $I_{in}$ and the current in the feedback resistor $R_f$ is $I_f$, then because point P is at 0 V:

$$I_{in} = \frac{V_{in}}{R_{in}}$$

and

$$I_f = \frac{V_{out}}{R_f}$$

The input resistance of the op-amp is very high and so virtually no current enters or leaves the inverting input (–) of the op-amp. This means that $I_{in}$ and $I_f$ must be equal in size.

If $V_{in}$ is a positive potential then the current in the two resistors flows from left to right. $V_{out}$ will be negative because the current flows from P, which is at 0 V, to the output connection, which must have a lower voltage than 0 V. Thus:

$$I_f = -I_{in}$$

and

$$\frac{V_{out}}{R_f} = -\frac{V_{in}}{R_{in}}$$

The gain of the inverting amplifier is thus given by:

$$G = \frac{V_{out}}{V_{in}} = -\frac{R_f}{R_{in}}$$

The negative sign shows that when the input voltage is positive then the output voltage is negative and when the input is positive the output is negative. If the input voltage is alternating then there will be a phase difference of 180° or $\pi$ rad between the input and the output voltages.

## Worked example

4 In the circuit shown in Figure **31.15** $R_{in} = 4\,k\Omega$ and $R_f = 20\,k\Omega$. Calculate:
   a the gain of the amplifier
   b the output voltage when the input voltage is 0.5 V
   c the maximum input voltage if the supply voltage is ±12 V
   d the input resistance of the amplifier.

The solutions can be found using the formula for gain $G$.

   a gain $G = -\dfrac{R_f}{R_{in}} = -\dfrac{20}{4} = -5$

   b $V_{out} = GV_{in} = -5 \times 0.5 = -2.5\,V$
   c The op-amp becomes saturated when $V_{out} = -12\,V$.

   $$V_{in} = \frac{V_{out}}{G} = \frac{12}{5} = 2.4\,V$$

   d The input resistance is just $R_{in} = 4\,k\Omega$, as point P is at 0 V.

## Test yourself

11 Draw the circuit diagram of an inverting amplifier with a gain of −100 and an input resistor $R_{in}$ of $10\,k\Omega$. Include the value of the feedback resistor $R_f$.

12 The supply voltage to an op-amp is +15 V. The op-amp is connected as an inverting amplifier of gain −20. Calculate the output voltage for the following input voltages:
   a +20 mV    b −400 mV    c +1.0 V

# The non-inverting amplifier

Figure **31.16** shows the circuit for a **non-inverting amplifier**. The input voltage is applied to the non-inverting input; part of the output voltage is fed back to the inverting input.

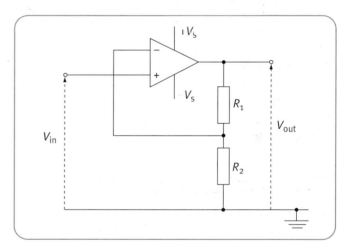

Figure 31.16 A non-inverting amplifier.

As long as the op-amp is not saturated, the potential difference between the inverting (−) and non-inverting inputs (+) is almost zero. So $V^- = V^+$.

Since the non-inverting input (+) is connected to the input voltage, $V^+ = V_{in}$. Thus $V^- = V_{in}$.

The two resistors $R_1$ and $R_2$ form a potential divider. The total voltage across $R_1$ and $R_2$ is $V_{out}$ and the voltage across $R_2$ alone is $V_{in}$.

The current in the two resistors can be written as:

$$\frac{V_{out}}{(R_1 + R_2)} = \frac{V_{in}}{R_2}$$

The gain is calculated from:

$$G = \frac{V_{out}}{V_{in}} = \frac{(R_1 + R_2)}{R_2} = 1 + \left(\frac{R_1}{R_2}\right)$$

Thus for a non-inverting amplifier the gain is given by:

$$G = 1 + \left(\frac{R_1}{R_2}\right)$$

For a non-inverting amplifier, the output is in phase with the input. When the input voltage is positive, so is the output voltage.

## Test yourself

13 The circuit shown in Figure 31.14 is also a non-inverting amplifier. What are the values of $R_1$ and $R_2$? Show that the gain of the amplifier is 1.

14 Draw the circuit of a non-inverting amplifier with a gain of 10. Explain whether the input resistance is very high or very low.

15 Suppose that the non-inverting amplifier in Figure 31.16 has $R_1 = 50\,k\Omega$, $R_2 = 5\,k\Omega$ and $V_s = 10\,V$.
   a Calculate the gain.
   b Calculate the output voltage when the input voltage is:
      i   −0.10 V          ii   +1.0 V.

# Output devices

The output voltage of an op-amp is used to operate some device according to the changing input voltage. We will now look at three types of output device.

## The relay

Although the output resistance of an op-amp is low, a typical op-amp can only provide a maximum output current of 25 mA. The maximum voltage output from an op-amp is also limited to the supply voltage, typically 15 V. To switch on larger currents and larger voltages the op-amp is connected to a relay.

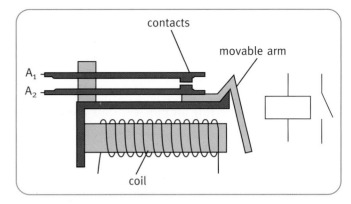

Figure 31.17 A relay and its circuit symbol

The **relay** is just an electromagnetic switch operated by a small current in the coil. Notice that there are two circuits, one to the coil and one involving the switch contacts $A_1$ and $A_2$. When a small current passes through the coil of the relay in Figure 31.17, the iron core attracts a movable arm and the contacts connected to $A_1$ and $A_2$ close, completing the second circuit.

The coil of the relay is the part connected to the output of an op-amp. The op-amp can easily provide the small current required for the coil. When the contacts $A_1$ and $A_2$ close they can switch large voltages or currents in another circuit.

There is, however, a problem using a relay connected to an op-amp. The current from the op-amp causes the coil to act as an electromagnet and creates a magnetic field. When this current is turned off there is a very rapid fall in the magnetic flux within the coil and a large e.m.f. is induced across the terminals of the coil, large enough to damage the op-amp. Switching off a relay can damage an op-amp.

To avoid this damage, a reverse-biased diode is placed across the relay coil. This is shown in Figure 31.18, where $D_1$ is the reverse-biased diode. When the op-amp switches off, the induced voltage in the coil causes the bottom of the coil to be more positive than the top of the coil. Diode $D_1$ is able to pass current round the coil without any damage to the op-amp.

The output of the op-amp can be negative as well as positive. Without diode $D_2$, the relay contacts close whether there is a negative output or a positive output from the op-amp because it does not matter which direction the current flows in the coil in Figure 31.17.

Diode $D_2$ ensures that current can only flow from the op-amp when the output of the op-amp is

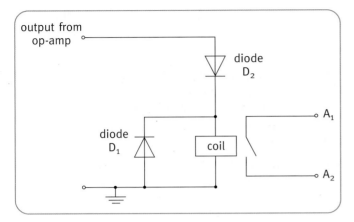

Figure 31.18 The output of an op-amp connected to a relay

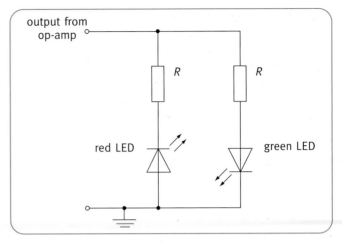

Figure 31.19 LEDs connected to the output of an op-amp

positive. Thus the relay contacts are closed only when the output of the op-amp is positive.

Since diode $D_1$ is reverse-biased, no current from the op-amp flows through $D_1$.

## The light-emitting diode (LED)

The light-emitting diode is a very convenient device to attach to the output of an op-amp. LEDs come in several different colours and only require a current of about 20 mA to produce a reasonable light output. When placed on the output of the op-amp they readily show the state of that output, whether it is positive, negative or zero.

In practice, an LED cannot be placed directly between the output of an op-amp and the zero-volt line. The current–voltage characteristic for an LED is shown in Chapter 12 (page 173). The LED starts to conduct when the voltage across it is greater than about 2 V, although this value depends on the type of LED used. Once the output of an op-amp is much bigger than 2 V, the current in the LED and the op-amp will be very high and will damage both of them. A series resistor is required to limit the current, as shown in Figure 31.19.

The value of the resistance of the series resistor $R$ can be calculated. If the current is to be 20 mA and the maximum voltage output from the op-amp is 12 V, then there will be just over 2 V across the LED and $12 - 2 = 10$ V across the series resistor $R$. The series resistor required is:

$$R = \frac{10}{0.02} = 500\,\Omega$$

In Figure **31.19**, when the output of the op-amp is sufficiently positive relative to earth the green LED will light. When the output is negative relative to earth, the red LED will light.

## The calibrated meter

An op-amp may be monitoring a physical quantity such as temperature or light intensity. It is helpful to display the value of that physical quantity directly on a meter and not to have to measure an output voltage and then calculate the physical quantity each time.

The output voltage of the op-amp is unlikely to be proportional to the physical quantity being measured, for example temperature. The numbers on a voltmeter connected to the output of an op-amp cannot simply be changed to read values of the physical quantity, but the voltmeter can still be calibrated in terms of the physical quantity.

Suppose that temperature is being measured and a digital voltmeter is connected to the output. Calibration can be achieved by placing the temperature sensor and a thermometer in a water bath and recording the voltmeter reading and the temperature of the water bath at a number of different temperatures. A calibration graph is then drawn, as shown in Figure 31.20.

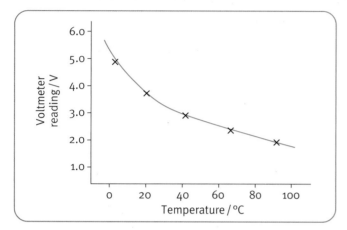

Figure 31.20 A calibration curve relates the output voltage of an op-amp to the variable it is being used to measure.

The calibration curve is used to change any other voltmeter reading into a value for the physical quantity, in this case temperature.

An analogue meter can be calibrated in the same way, but if the same meter is used all the time as the output, then the scale on the meter can be marked directly with values of the physical quantity. This means that the 'voltmeter' will measure temperature directly. Since the voltmeter reading is not proportional to the change in the physical quantity then the scale will not be linear. Figure 31.21 shows a meter with three scales. The bottom two scales are linear and might be the voltage recorded by a voltmeter. The top scale is non-linear and might be the value of the physical quantity being measured. Care is needed when reading a non-linear scale when the pointer is between the markings.

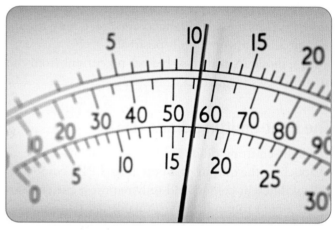

Figure 31.21 Linear and non-linear scales.

## Summary

- ☐ A sensor contains a sensing device and a processor to produce an output voltage.
- ☐ The resistance of an LDR decreases as the level of the light intensity increases.
- ☐ The resistance of a negative temperature coefficient thermistor falls as temperature rises.
- ☐ A piezo-electric transducer produces a variation in output voltage when a crystal is stressed, for example by pressure changes in sound.
- ☐ The change in resistance of a metal-wire strain gauge is proportional to extension.
- ☐ An operational amplifier used as a comparator produces either a high positive or a high negative voltage output, depending on which of two input voltage levels is larger.
- ☐ An operational amplifier can be used as an inverting or a non-inverting amplifier to amplify voltage signals.
- ☐ The gain of an inverting amplifier is $-\dfrac{R_f}{R_{in}}$
- ☐ The gain of a non-inverting amplifier is $1+\left(\dfrac{R_1}{R_2}\right)$
- ☐ Feedback reduces gain but increases bandwidth and stability and reduces distortion.
- ☐ Output devices which may be connected to an op-amp include relays, LDRs and calibrated meters.

# End-of-chapter questions

1 How can the circuit of Figure **31.12** be altered so that the op-amp switches from +9V to –9V when the temperature rises, instead of when it falls? Draw the circuit diagram.

2 Draw the circuit diagram of a comparator that switches the output voltage from positive to negative when the light intensity falling on an LDR decreases.

3 Explain what is meant by:
   a feedback
   b the virtual earth approximation.

4 In the inverting amplifier shown in Figure **31.15** $R_{in} = 10\,k\Omega$, $R_f = 200\,k\Omega$ and $V_s = 12\,V$. Calculate:
   a the gain of the amplifier
   b the input voltage when the output voltage is 8.0V
   c the maximum input voltage.

5 a Explain how an inverting amplifier can have a gain of –0.5.
   b Explain why the gain of a non-inverting amplifier cannot be less than 1.

6 The non-inverting amplifier in Figure **31.16** on page 479 has $R_1 = 15\,k\Omega$, $R_2 = 5\,k\Omega$ and $V_s = 10\,V$. An a.c. signal of amplitude 0.20V is applied to the input. Draw one sketch graph which shows both the input and the output voltage over two cycles of the input on the same axes.

7 Is the circuit shown in Figure **31.22** an inverting or non-inverting amplifier? Calculate its gain.

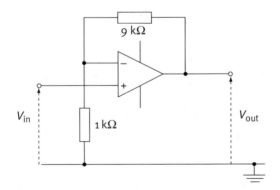

**Figure 31.22** For End-of-chapter Q 7.

# Exam-style questions

1 A light-dependent resistor is used with additional components to make a sensor. The voltage output increases as light intensity increases.
   **a** Sketch the diagram of a suitable circuit. [2]
   **b** Explain how your circuit works. [2]
   **c** State which parts of your circuit are the sensor, the processor and the output device. [2]

2 A strain gauge is used to measure the extension of a metal bar. The gauge is stuck to the bar and the change in resistance of the wire in the gauge enables the extension to be determined. The strain gauge is connected in the circuit shown.

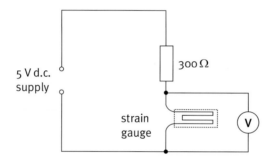

   **a** Explain why the resistance of the wire increases when it is stretched and show that the change in resistance is proportional to the extension, provided that the cross-sectional area is constant. [2]
   **b** The resistance of the strain gauge when unstretched is $150\,\Omega$. Calculate the reading on the voltmeter. [2]
   **c** State and explain the effect on the voltmeter reading when the strain gauge is stretched. [2]

3 In a fibre optic system, sound into a microphone is used to produce different intensities of light that are passed along the glass fibre.
   The microphone is connected to a non-inverting amplifier, the output of which is connected to an LED. An operational amplifier with dual 15 V power supplies is used as a non-inverting amplifier and the microphone produces a maximum output of +20 mV.
   **a i** Copy and complete the circuit to show the resistors necessary for a non-inverting amplifier. Make the necessary connection between the microphone and the amplifier. [2]
   **ii** Add to your diagram the necessary output components for the amplifier to work as described. [2]

**b** State **two** advantages of using negative feedback in the amplifier circuit. [2]

**c i** Calculate the maximum possible gain for the amplifier. [2]

**ii** The amplifier is used with the maximum possible gain. Suggest suitable values for the resistance of all the resistors drawn in **a i**. [2]

**d** Explain what happens in the system when the voltage output from the microphone rises. [2]

4 A student builds an electronic circuit to control a motor using two identical LDRs, P and Q. In a room with the same amount of light on each LDR, the resistance of each LDR is $500\,\Omega$. When the light from a torch shines on either LDR its resistance becomes $200\,\Omega$.

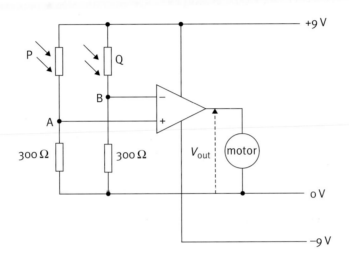

**a** State the value of the output voltage $V_{out}$ of the op-amp when:

**i** the potential at point A is greater than the potential at point B [1]

**ii** the potential at point B is greater than the potential at point A. [1]

**b** Calculate the potential at point A when a torch shines on P. [2]

**c i** Explain what happens in the circuit when a torch shines on P but not on Q. [1]

**ii** Explain what happens in the circuit when a torch shines on Q but not on P. [1]

**d** Explain why it is difficult to know what will happen if no torch shines on P or Q. [1]

5 **a** Explain what is meant by a **virtual earth** and use your explanation to show that the
gain of the inverting amplifier in the diagram is $-\dfrac{R_1}{R_2}$ . [5]

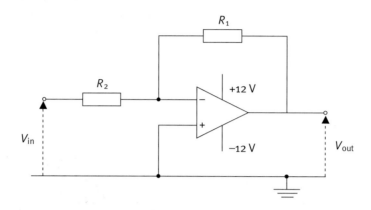

**b** The value of $R_1$ is $20\,k\Omega$ and the value of $R_2$ is $4\,k\Omega$. The value of $V_{in}$ is $0.50\,V$.
   **i**  Calculate the value of $V_{out}$. [2]
   **ii** A resistor of $4\,k\Omega$ is placed in parallel with $R_2$. Calculate the new value of $V_{out}$. [2]

# 32 Medical imaging

## Objectives

After studying this chapter, you should be able to:

- [ ] explain the need for non-invasive techniques of diagnosis in medicine
- [ ] explain how X-ray beams are produced and controlled
- [ ] describe how conventional and CT scan X-ray images are produced

- [ ] explain how ultrasound is produced and detected
- [ ] explain how ultrasound images are produced, revealing internal structures
- [ ] explain the principles of magnetic resonance imaging

## Medical diagnosis

When you are unwell, you may have external symptoms such as a rash or unusual skin colour which the doctor can use to diagnose your illness. Alternatively, you may be required to report on your internal symptoms – aches, pains and so on. The human body is opaque to light, so how can a doctor know what is going on inside you?

Although light does not penetrate the human body, other electromagnetic radiations do. The best known are X-rays, good for showing up bones (Figure 32.1) and the subject of the first part of this chapter. The sections that follow will look at the physics behind other medical diagnostic techniques, including the use of radioactive substances, magnetic resonance and ultrasound.

These techniques are often described as **non-invasive**. This is because they do not involve cutting the patient open to discover what is wrong. Nor do they involve inserting surgical

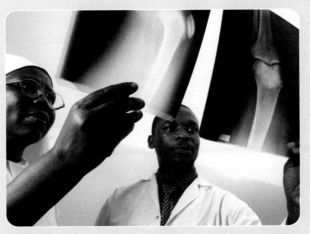

Figure 32.1 A radiographer and a doctor examine X-ray images of a patient's leg at a hospital in Uganda.

instruments into any of the body's orifices. Both of these are procedures that can allow infections to enter the body. Any damage to the body may take time to heal and can lead to permanent scarring.

## The nature and production of X-rays

X-rays are a form of electromagnetic radiation. They belong to the short-wavelength, high-frequency end of the electromagnetic spectrum, beyond ultraviolet radiation (Figure 32.2). They have wavelengths in the range $10^{-8}$ m to $10^{-13}$ m and are effectively the same as gamma-rays ($\gamma$-rays), the difference being in the way they are produced.

- X-rays are produced when fast-moving electrons are rapidly decelerated. As the electrons slow down,

their kinetic energy is transformed to photons of electromagnetic radiation.
- $\gamma$-rays are produced by radioactive decay. Following alpha ($\alpha$) or beta ($\beta$) emission, a gamma photon is often emitted by the decaying nucleus (see Chapter 17).

The X-rays used in medical applications are usually described as **soft X-rays**, because their energy is not very great, usually less than the energies of $\gamma$-rays produced by radioactive substances.

As with all electromagnetic radiation, we can think of X-rays either as waves or as photons (see Chapter 29). X-rays travel in straight lines through a uniform medium.

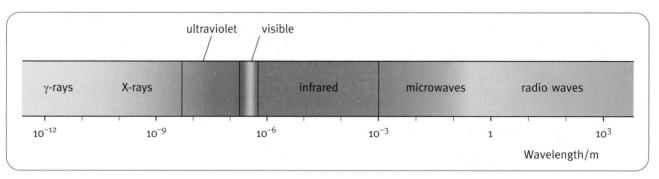

ultraviolet    visible

γ-rays    X-rays    infrared    microwaves    radio waves

$10^{-12}$    $10^{-9}$    $10^{-6}$    $10^{-3}$    1    $10^{3}$

Wavelength/m

**Figure 32.2** The electromagnetic spectrum; X-rays and γ-rays lie at the high-frequency, short-wavelength end of the spectrum.

## X-ray tube

Figure **32.3a** shows a patient undergoing a pelvic X-ray to check for bone degeneration. The X-ray machine is above the patient; it contains the **X-ray tube** that produces the X-rays which pass downwards through the patient's body. Below the patient is the detection system. In this case an electronic detector is being used, but often photographic film is used in the detection system. Figure **32.3b** shows the resulting image.

Figure **32.4** shows the principles of the modern X-ray tube. The tube itself is evacuated, and contains two electrodes.

- Cathode – the heated filament acts as the cathode (negative) from which electrons are emitted.
- Anode – the rotating anode (positive) is made of a hard metal such as tungsten. (The anode metal is often referred to as the 'target metal'.)

An external power supply produces a voltage of up to 200 kV between the two electrodes. This accelerates a beam of electrons across the gap between the cathode and the anode. The kinetic energy of an electron arriving at the anode is 200 keV. When the electrons strike the anode at high speed, they lose some of their kinetic energy in the form of X-ray photons which emerge in all directions. Part of the outer casing, the window, is thinner than the rest and allows X-rays to emerge into the space outside the tube. The width of the X-ray beam can be controlled using metal tubes beyond the window to absorb X-rays. This produces a parallel-sided beam called a **collimated beam**.

Only a small fraction, about 1%, of the kinetic energy of the electrons is converted to X-rays. Most of the incident energy is transferred to the anode, which becomes hot. This explains why the anode rotates; the region that is heated turns out of the beam so that it

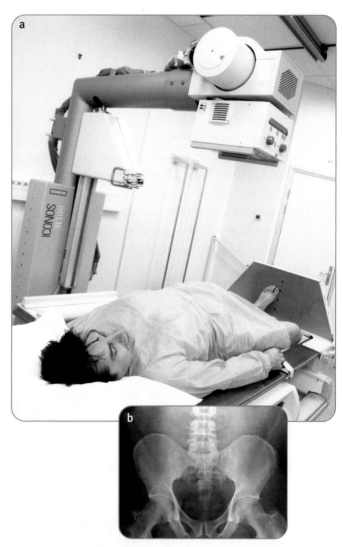

**Figure 32.3 a** A general-purpose X-ray system. **b** A typical X-ray image produced by such a machine, showing the region around the pelvis.

can cool down by radiating heat to its surroundings. Some X-ray tubes have water circulating through the anode to remove this excess heat.

**Step 2** Substitute in the equation for intensity and solve.

> Take care to calculate the exponent (the value of $-\mu x$) first.

$$I = I_0 e^{-\mu x}$$
$$= 20 \times e^{-(600 \times 0.04)} = 20 \times e^{-2.4}$$
$$= 1.8 \, \text{W m}^{-2}$$

So the intensity of the X-ray beam will have been reduced to about 10% of its initial value after passing through just 4.0 mm of bone.

## Half thickness

If we compare the graphs (or equations) for the attenuation of X-rays as they pass through a material with the decay of a radioactive nuclide we see that they are both exponential decays. From Chapter **30**, you should be familiar with the concept of the half-life of a radioactive isotope (the time taken for half the nuclei in any sample of the isotope to decay). In a similar manner we refer to the half-value thickness (or HVT) of an absorbing material. This is the thickness of material which will reduce the transmitted intensity of an X-ray beam of a particular frequency to half its original value.

### Test yourself

3  Use the equation $I = I_0 e^{-\mu x}$ to show that the half thickness $x_{1/2}$ is related to the attenuation coefficient $\mu$ by:

$$x_{1/2} = \frac{\ln 2}{\mu}$$

4  An X-ray beam transfers 400 J of energy through 5.0 cm$^2$ each second. Calculate its intensity in W m$^{-2}$.

5  An X-ray beam of initial intensity 50 W m$^{-2}$ is incident on soft tissue of attenuation coefficient 1.2 cm$^{-1}$. Calculate its intensity after it has passed through a 5.0 cm thickness of tissue.

# Improving X-ray images

The X-ray systems in use in hospitals and clinics today are highly developed pieces of technology. They do not simply show bones against a background of soft tissue. They can also show very fine detail in the soft tissue, including the arrangement of blood vessels.

Radiographers (the people in charge of X-ray systems) have three main aims:

- to reduce as much as possible the patient's exposure to harmful X-rays;
- to improve the **sharpness** of the images, so that finer details can be resolved;
- to improve the **contrast** of the image, so that the different tissues under investigation show up clearly in the image.

## Reducing dosage

X-rays, like all ionising radiation, can damage living tissue, causing mutations which can lead to the growth of cancerous tissue. It is therefore important that the dosage is kept to a minimum.

A radiographer may choose to record the X-ray image on film or digitally. X-rays are only weakly absorbed by photographic film, so, historically, patients had to be exposed to long and intense doses of X-rays. Today, **intensifier screens** are used. These are sheets of a material that contains phosphor, a substance that emits visible light when it absorbs X-ray photons. The film is sandwiched between two intensifier screens. Each X-ray photon absorbed results in several thousand light photons, which then blacken the film. This reduces the patient's exposure by a factor of 100–500.

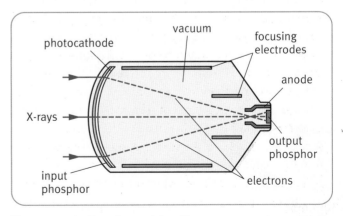

**Figure 32.7** An X-ray image intensifier.

In digital systems, **image intensifiers** are used (Figure **32.7**). The incoming X-rays strike a phosphor screen, producing visible light photons. These then release electrons (by the photoelectric effect) from the photocathode. The electrons are accelerated and focused by the positively charged anode so that they strike a screen, which then gives out visible light. The image on this screen can be viewed via a television camera. At the same time, the image can be stored electronically. Digital systems have the advantage that images can be easily stored, shared and viewed.

Image intensifiers are particularly useful in a technique called **fluoroscopy**. A continuous X-ray beam is passed through the patient onto a fluorescent screen where a real-time image is formed. Using an image intensifier ensures that the patient is not exposed to dangerous levels of X-rays over a long period.

## Improving sharpness

Figure **32.8** shows a remarkably sharp X-ray image of blood vessels in the human abdomen. The sharpness of the image is determined by the width of the X-ray beam. You will remember that the shadow of an object is much sharper if it is illuminated by a small lamp,

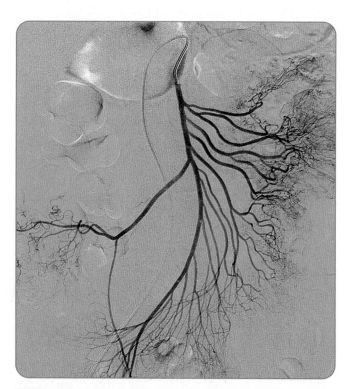

**Figure 32.8** An X-ray image of blood vessels branching out from an artery carrying oxygenated blood to the intestines.

rather than a large lamp (Figure **32.9**). So a good X-ray source must produce a **narrow** beam of **parallel** X-rays, as if they were coming from a distant point source.

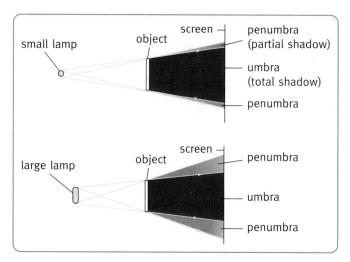

**Figure 32.9** The small lamp casts a smaller penumbra and this improves the sharpness of the shadow.

Three factors determine the width of the beam:

- the size of the anode – as shown in Figure **32.10**, the larger the anode, the wider the beam;
- the size of the aperture at the exit window – this can be reduced using adjustable lead plates (Figure **32.11**);
- collimation of the beam – the beam is passed through lead slits (Figure **32.12**), ensuring that it is parallel sided beam and does not fan out.

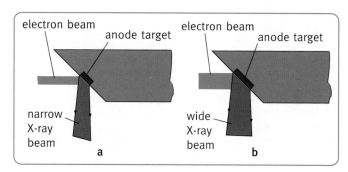

**Figure 32.10** A wide anode target results in a wide X-ray beam, giving fuzzy edges to the shadow image.

Inevitably some X-rays are scattered as they pass through the body. If these reach the detector they cause fogging and this reduces the sharpness of the image. Scattered X-rays approach the detector screen at an angle, and so an anti-scatter screen

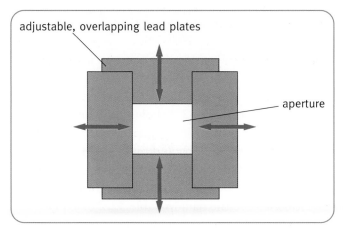

**Figure 32.11** The smaller the aperture the narrower the X-ray beam.

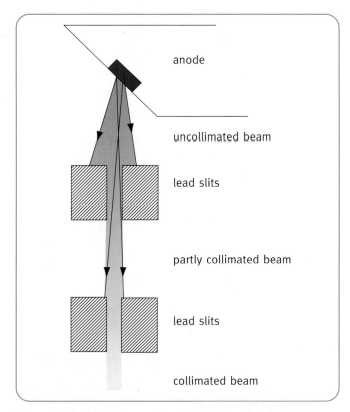

**Figure 32.12** Collimating an X-ray beam: The first set of slits produces a partly collimated beam but, due to the finite size of the anode target, there is still some spreading of the beam. The second set of slits reduces this spread further making the final beam almost parallel-sided.

(Figure 32.13) can be used to absorb them. This is made up of a series of plates which are made of a material (such as lead) opaque to X-rays, separated by plates made of a material (such as aluminium) transparent to X-rays. The plate is placed just above the screen, and the lead absorbs the scattered X-rays.

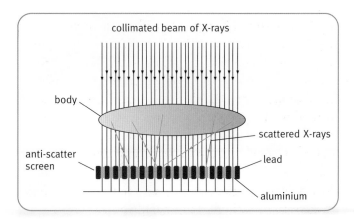

**Figure 32.13** An anti-scatter screen absorbs X-rays which arrive at an angle to the main beam.

## Improving contrast

Good contrast is said to be achieved if there is a clear difference in the blackening of the photographic film as the X-ray passes through different types of tissue. The contrast is largely determined by the hardness of the X-rays. Bone is a good absorber of the radiation. If the doctor is diagnosing a break in a bone he will use hard X-rays. In comparison, investigation of the tissue of the breast, where the tissue is a poor absorber, will require a longer exposure, using much softer (long-wavelength, low-frequency) X-rays.

As we have seen, different tissues show up differently in X-ray images. In particular, bone can readily be distinguished from soft tissue such as muscle because it is a good absorber of X-rays. However, it is often desirable to show up different soft tissues that absorb X-rays equally. In order to do this, **contrast media** are used.

A contrast medium is a substance such as iodine or barium which is a good absorber of X-rays. The patient may swallow a barium-containing liquid (a 'barium meal'), or have a similar liquid injected into the tissue of interest. This tissue is then a better absorber of X-rays and its edges show up more clearly on the final image.

Figure 32.14 shows an X-ray image of the intestine of a patient who has been given a barium meal. The large pale areas show where the barium has accumulated. Other parts of the intestine have become smeared with barium, and this means that the outline of the tissue shows up clearly.

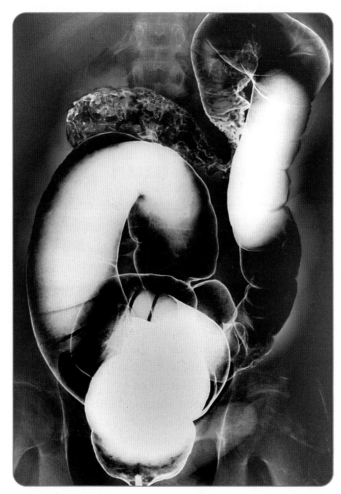

**Figure 32.14** X-ray image of a patient's intestine after taking a barium meal. Barium shows up as pale in this image, which has also been artificially coloured to highlight features of interest.

## Test yourself

**6** Outline the advantages of using an anti-scatter grid when taking an X-ray image.

**7** The data in Table **32.2** shows how the attenuation coefficient $\mu$ depends on the energy of the X-rays in bone and muscle. When making a diagnostic X-ray image, it is desirable that bone should be clearly distinguished from muscle. Use the data in Table **32.2** to explain why it would be best to use lower energy (50 keV) X-rays for this purpose.

| Maximum X-ray energy | Bone: $\mu/\text{cm}^{-1}$ | Muscle: $\mu/\text{cm}^{-1}$ |
|---|---|---|
| 4.0 MeV | 0.087 | 0.049 |
| 250 keV | 0.32 | 0.16 |
| 100 keV | 0.60 | 0.21 |
| 50 keV | 3.32 | 0.54 |

**Table 32.2** Data for Test yourself Q **7** and Q **8**.

**8** When low-energy X-rays are used, the attenuation coefficient $\mu$ is (roughly) proportional to the cube of the proton number $Z$ of the absorbing material. Use the data in Table **32.2** to show that bone absorbs X-rays eight times as strongly as muscle.

Contrast media are elements with high values of atomic number $Z$. This means that their atoms have many electrons with which the X-rays interact, so they are more absorbing. Soft tissues mostly consist of compounds of hydrogen, carbon and oxygen (low $Z$ values), while bone has the heavier elements calcium and phosphorus, and contrast media have even higher $Z$ values – see Table **32.1**.

| Substance | Elements ($Z$ values) | Average $Z$ |
|---|---|---|
| soft tissue | H (1), C (6), O (8) | 7 |
| bone | H (1), C (6), O (8), P (15), Ca (20) | 14 |
| contrast media | I (53), Ba (56) | 55 |

**Table 32.1** Proton (atomic) numbers of the constituents of different tissues, and of contrast media.

# Computerised axial tomography

A conventional X-ray image has an important limitation. Because an X-ray is essentially a two-dimensional shadow image, it shows the bones, organs, etc. at different depths within the body superimposed on each other. For example, in Figure **32.15**, it is difficult to distinguish the bones of the front and back of the ribcage. This can be overcome by taking several images at different angles. An experienced radiographer can then study these images and deduce what is going on inside the patient.

An ingenious technique for extending this approach was invented by Geoffrey Hounsfield and his colleagues at EMI in the UK in 1971. They developed the **computerised axial tomography** scanner (CAT

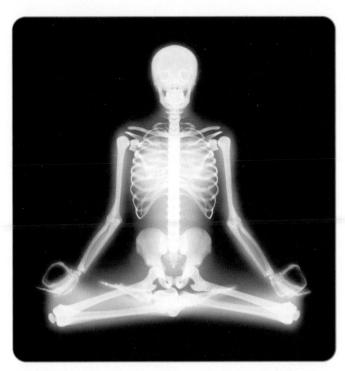

**Figure 32.15** Computer-generated X-ray image of a person in a yoga position. This shows the difficulty of distinguishing one bone from another when they overlap.

scanner or CT scanner). Figure **32.16** illustrates the principle of a modern scanner.

- The patient lies in a vertical ring of X-ray detectors.
- The X-ray tube rotates around the ring, exposing the patient to a fan-shaped beam of X-rays from all directions.
- Detectors opposite the tube send electronic records to a computer.
- The computer software builds up a three-dimensional image of the patient.
- The radiographer can view images of 'slices' through the patient on the computer screen.

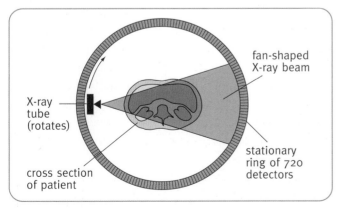

**Figure 32.16** Operation of a modern CAT scanner. The X-ray tube rotates around the patient while the detectors are stationary.

CAT scanners have undergone many developments since they were first invented. In a fifth-generation scanner, the patient's bed slides slowly through the ring of detectors as the X-ray tube rotates. The tube thus traces out a spiral path around the patient, allowing information to be gathered about the whole body.

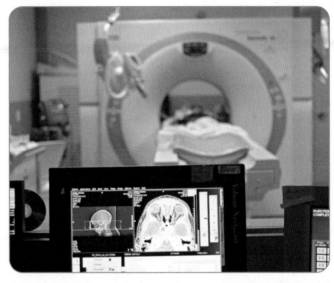

**Figure 32.17** A boy undergoes a CAT scan in an investigation of an eye condition.

Figure **32.17** shows a child undergoing a CAT scan. On the monitor you can see a cross-section of the patient's head.

This technique is called **computerised axial tomography** because it relies on a computer to control the scanning motion and to gather and manipulate the data to produce images; because the X-ray tube rotates around an axis; and because it produces images of slices through the patient – the Greek word **tomos** means **slice**.

## Building up the image

As the X-ray tube is rotated around the body hundreds of pieces of information are gathered and an image is built up. As shown in Figure **32.18**, we imagine the body as being divided up into a large number of tiny cubes called **voxels**. (This is the same as dividing a two-dimensional picture into a 2-D array of pixels, but a three-dimensional body must be divided into a 3-D array of voxels.)

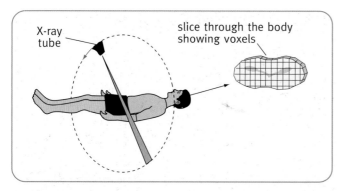

X-ray tube

slice through the body showing voxels

**Figure 32.18** In CAT scanning, we picture the body divided into an array of tiny cubic volumes called voxels.

To understand how the image is constructed from the data, we will simplify the procedure by considering a section made up of four voxels and imagine exposing this $2 \times 2$ grid to a beam of X-rays from four different directions. Different parts of the body have different 'densities'; that is, some are stronger absorbers of X-rays. We will represent this by labelling our four voxels with densities 5, 6, 2 and 8, as shown in Figure **32.19**. This diagram shows how the detectors read different values when the array is exposed to X-rays from different angles, and how we can then work back to the original densities.

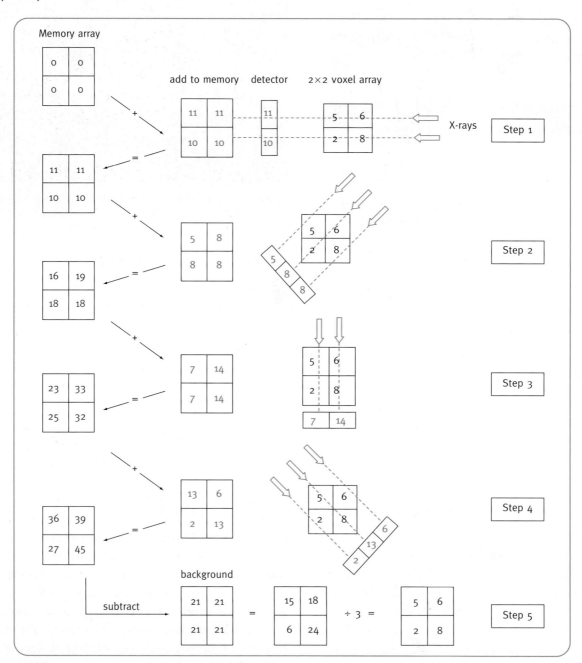

**Figure 32.19** Data is built up from a CT scan of a $2 \times 2$ voxel array, and then processed to deduce the original array.

## Step 1

The beam passes through the array from the side. The top part of the beam has passed through voxels with values 5 and 6, which makes 11. The value for the bottom part is $8 + 2 = 10$. This is recorded in a $2 \times 2$ memory grid as 11, 11 in the top row and 10, 10 below.

## Step 2

The beam is rotated through 45° so that it passes through the array diagonally. The top of the beam passes though just one voxel, of value 5. The central part passes through two voxels giving $6 + 2 = 8$. The lower part passes through one voxel of value 8. This gives a detected grid as shown, and this is added to the memory grid.

## Steps 3 and 4

The beam is rotated twice more through 45° and each time the detected values are added to the memory grid.

## Step 5

Now each voxel in the array has been exposed to X-rays from four different directions. How can we extract the original values from the final memory grid? Note that, in each step, the total density detected had a value of 21 ($10 + 11$ in Step 1, $5 + 8 + 8$ in Step 2, and so on). We subtract this background value from each square in the memory grid, and then divide by three. The final values in the memory grid are the same as in the original $2 \times 2$ array.

For a well-defined image in a CAT scan, we need the voxels to be small. Two things are needed to achieve this:

- The X-ray beam must be well-collimated so that it consists of parallel rays – the rays must not spread outwards.
- The detector must consist of a regular array of tiny detecting elements – the smaller each individual detector is, the better will be the resolution in the final image.

In practice, the body is exposed to X-rays from many directions, giving a large number of values from which a complex computer program can deduce the variation of X-ray absorption throughout the body. From this, an image of any section through the body can be constructed on a monitor screen. Figure **32.20** shows a sequence of sections through a child's head.

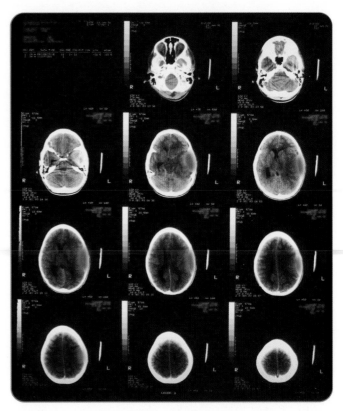

**Figure 32.20** Sections through the head of a 10-year-old boy. You can see the haematoma (bruising) arising from being struck on the side of the head; this causes pressure on his brain.

## Advantages of a CAT scan

Although single X-ray images still have many uses (and they can be made very quickly), CAT scans have a number of advantages:

- They produce images that show three-dimensional relationships between different tissues.
- They can distinguish tissues with quite similar densities (attenuation coefficients).

So, for example, a CAT scan can show up the precise position, shape and size of a tumour. This allows it to be precisely targeted in treatment with high-energy X-rays or γ-rays.

However, it is worth noting that a CAT scan involves using X-rays and any exposure to ionising radiation carries a risk for the patient. These risks are fairly small; it is estimated, with modern scanning equipment, that the radiation dose received is about one third the dose received from background radiation in a year, or is equivalent to the dose received on four long haul flights. Nevertheless, it is important to be aware of the dangers, particularly, if there are other underlying health problems or if a woman is pregnant.

# Using ultrasound in medicine

Ultrasound scanning is routinely used to check the condition of a baby in the womb (Figure 32.21). There do not seem to be any harmful side-effects associated with this procedure, and it can provide useful information on the baby's development. Indeed, for many children, their first appearance in the family photo album is in the form of an ante-natal (before birth) scan!

This technique has many other uses in medicine. It can be used to detect gallstones or kidney stones (two very painful complaints), so men as well as women may experience this type of scan.

The technique of ultrasound scanning is rather similar to the way in which sailors use echo sounding and echo location to detect the seabed and shoals of fish. Ultrasound waves are directed into the patient's

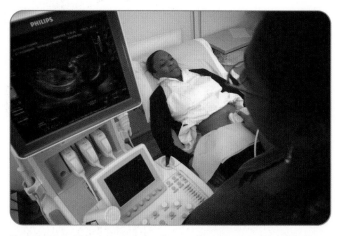

Figure 32.21 An expectant mother undergoes an ultrasound scan. The image of her baby is built up by computer and appears on the monitor.

body. These waves are partially reflected at the boundaries between different tissues and the reflected waves are detected and used to construct the image.

In this section, we will look at the principles of ultrasound scanning.

## Working with ultrasound

Ultrasound is any sound wave that has a frequency above the upper limit of human hearing. This is usually taken to imply frequencies above 20 kHz (20 000 Hz), although the limit of hearing decreases with age to well below this figure. In medical applications, the typical frequencies used are in the megahertz range.

Sound waves are longitudinal waves. They can only pass through a material medium; they cannot pass through a vacuum. The speed of sound (and hence of ultrasound) depends on the material. In air, it is approximately $330\,\text{m s}^{-1}$; it is higher in solid materials. A typical value for body tissue is $1500\,\text{m s}^{-1}$. Using the wave equation $v = f\lambda$, we can calculate the wavelength of 2.0 MHz ultrasound waves in tissue:

$$\lambda = \frac{v}{f} = \frac{1500}{2.0 \times 10^6}$$

$$\lambda = 7.5 \times 10^{-4}\,\text{m} \approx 1\,\text{mm}$$

This means that 2.0 MHz ultrasound waves will be able to distinguish detailed features whose dimensions are of the order of 1 mm. Higher-frequency waves have shorter wavelengths and these are used to detect smaller features inside the body.

## Producing ultrasound

Like audible sound, ultrasound is produced by a vibrating source. The frequency of the source is the same as the frequency of the waves it produces. In ultrasound scanning, ultrasonic waves are produced by a device in which a varying electrical voltage is used to generate ultrasound. The same device also acts as a detector. This device is known as a **transducer**; this is a general term used to describe any device that changes one form of energy into another.

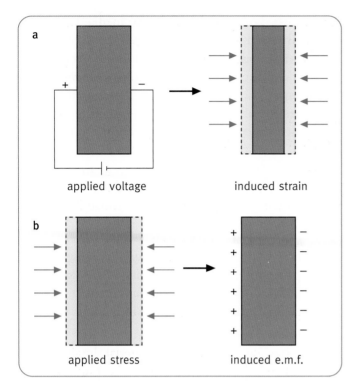

**Figure 32.22** The piezo-electric effect. **a** An applied voltage causes a piezo-electric crystal to contract or expand. **b** An applied stress causes an induced e.m.f. across the crystal.

At the heart of the transducer is a **piezo-electric crystal**, such as quartz. This type of crystal has a useful property: when a voltage is applied across it in one direction, it shrinks slightly – see Figure **32.22a**. When the voltage is reversed, it expands slightly. So an alternating voltage with frequency $f$ causes the crystal to contract and expand at the same frequency $f$. We say that the voltage induces a strain in the crystal. In the best piezo-electric substances, the maximum value of strain is about 0.1%; in other words, the crystal's width changes by about one part in a thousand.

In a piezo-electric transducer, an alternating voltage is applied across the crystal, which then acts as the vibrating source of ultrasound waves. A brief pulse of ultrasound waves is sent into the patient's body; the transducer then receives an extended pulse of reflected ultrasound waves.

## Detecting ultrasound

The transducer also acts as the detector of reflected ultrasound waves. It can do this because the piezo-electric effect works in reverse: a varying stress applied to the crystal produces a varying e.m.f. across the crystal – see Figure **32.22b**. To maximise the effect,

the frequency of the waves must match the resonant frequency of the crystal. The optimum size of the crystal is half the wavelength $(\frac{\lambda}{2})$ of the ultrasound waves.

Figure **32.23** shows the construction of a piezo-electric ultrasound transducer. Note the following features:

- The crystal is now usually made of polyvinylidene difluoride. Previously, quartz and lead zirconate titanate were used.
- The outer case supports and protects the crystal.
- At the base is the acoustic window made from a material that is a good transmitter of ultrasound.
- Behind the crystal is a large block of damping material (usually epoxy resin). This helps to stop the crystal vibrating when a pulse of ultrasound has been generated. This is necessary so that the crystal is not vibrating when the incoming, reflected ultrasound waves reach the transducer.

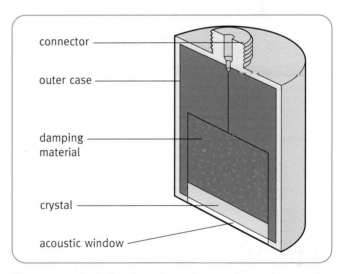

**Figure 32.23** A section through an ultrasound transducer.

## Test yourself

11 Quartz is an example of a piezo-electric material. The speed of sound in quartz is $5700\,\mathrm{m\,s^{-1}}$.
   **a** Calculate the wavelength of ultrasound waves of frequency 2.1 MHz in a quartz crystal.
   **b** If the crystal is to be used in an ultrasound transducer, its thickness must be half a wavelength. Calculate the thickness of the transducer.

*continued* ⋯⋗

12 Piezo-electric crystals have many applications other than in ultrasound scanning. For example, they are used:

    **a** in gas lighters (to produce a spark)

    **b** in inkjet printers (to break up the stream of ink into droplets)

    **c** in guitar pickups (to connect the guitar to an amplifier)

    **d** in the auto-focus mechanism of some cameras (to move the lens back and forth).

For each of these examples, state whether the piezo-electric effect is being used to convert energy in the vibrations of the crystal to electrical energy or the other way round.

# Echo sounding

The principle of an ultrasound scan is to direct ultrasound waves into the body. These pass through various tissues and are partially reflected at each boundary where the wave speed changes. The reflected waves are then detected and used to construct an internal image of the body.

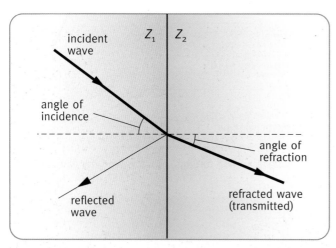

**Figure 32.24** An ultrasound wave is both refracted and reflected when it strikes the boundary between two different materials.

Figure **32.24** shows what happens when a beam of ultrasound reaches a boundary between two different media. The beam is partially refracted (so that the transmitted beam has changed direction) and partially reflected. This diagram should remind you of the way in which a ray of light is refracted and reflected when

it strikes the boundary between two media. It is the change in speed which causes the refraction of a wave.

For ultrasound, we are interested in the fraction of the incident intensity of ultrasound that is reflected at the boundary. This depends on the **acoustic impedance** $Z$ of each material. This quantity depends on the density $\rho$ and the speed of sound $c$ in the material. Acoustic impedance is defined as follows:

acoustic impedance = density × speed of sound

$$Z = \rho c$$

Since the unit of density is $kg\,m^{-3}$ and the unit of speed is $m\,s^{-1}$, the unit of acoustic impedance $Z$ is $kg\,m^{-2}\,s^{-1}$.

Table **32.3** shows values of $\rho$, $c$ and $Z$ for some materials that are important in medical ultrasonography.

| Material | Density / $kg\,m^{-3}$ | Speed of sound / $m\,s^{-1}$ | Acoustic impedance / $10^{6}\,kg\,m^{-2}\,s^{-1}$ |
|---|---|---|---|
| air | 1.3 | 330 | 0.0004 |
| water | 1000 | 1500 | 1.50 |
| **Biological** | | | |
| blood | 1060 | 1570 | 1.66 |
| fat | 925 | 1450 | 1.34 |
| soft tissue (average) | 1060 | 1540 | 1.63 |
| muscle | 1075 | 1590 | 1.71 |
| bone (average; adult) | 1600 | 4000 | 6.40 |
| **Transducers** | | | |
| barium titanate | 5600 | 5500 | 30.8 |
| lead zirconate titanate | 7650 | 3790 | 29.0 |
| quartz | 2650 | 5700 | 15.1 |
| polyvinylidene difluoride | 1780 | 2360 | 4.20 |

**Table 32.3** The density ($\rho$), speed of sound in air ($c$) and acoustic impedance ($Z$) of some materials important in medical scanning.

## Calculating reflected intensities

When an ultrasound beam reaches the boundary between two materials, the greater the **difference** in acoustic impedances, the greater the fraction of the ultrasound waves that is reflected. For normal incidence (i.e. angle of incidence $= 0°$) the ratio of the reflected intensity $I_r$ to the incident intensity $I_0$ is given by:

$$\frac{I_r}{I_0} = \frac{(Z_2 - Z_1)^2}{(Z_2 + Z_1)^2}$$

or

$$\frac{I_r}{I_0} = \left(\frac{Z_2 - Z_1}{Z_2 + Z_1}\right)^2$$

where $Z_1$ and $Z_2$ are the acoustic impedances of the two materials (see Figure 32.24). The ratio $I_r \backslash I_0$ indicates the fraction of the intensity of the beam that is reflected.

Now look at Worked example 2.

## Worked example

2  A beam of ultrasound is normally incident on the boundary between muscle and bone. Use Table 32.3 to determine the fraction of its intensity reflected.

**Step 1** Write down the values of $Z_1$ (for muscle) and $Z_2$ (for bone).

$$Z_1 = 1.71 \times 10^6 \, \text{kg m}^{-2} \, \text{s}^{-1}$$

$$Z_2 = 6.40 \times 10^6 \, \text{kg m}^{-2} \, \text{s}^{-1}$$

**Step 2** Substitute these values in the equation for $\frac{I_r}{I_0}$:

$$\frac{I_r}{I_0} = \frac{(Z_2 - Z_1)^2}{(Z_2 + Z_1)^2}$$

> We can use this equation because we know that the angle of incidence $= 0°$.

*continued* ⋯⟶

$$\frac{I_r}{I_0} = \frac{(6.40 - 1.71)^2}{(6.40 + 1.71)^2}$$

$$= 0.33$$

> We can ignore the factor of $10^6$ in the $Z$ values because this is a factor common to all the values, so they cancel out.

So 33% of the intensity of ultrasound will be reflected at the muscle–bone boundary.

## Comparing acoustic impedances

A big change in acoustic impedance gives a large fraction of reflected intensity. Inspection of Table 32.3 shows that:

- a very large fraction ($\frac{I_r}{I_0} \approx 99.95\%$) of the incident ultrasound will be reflected at an air–tissue boundary;
- a large fraction will be reflected at a tissue–bone boundary (as shown in Worked example 2);
- very little will be reflected at a boundary between soft tissues including fat and muscle.

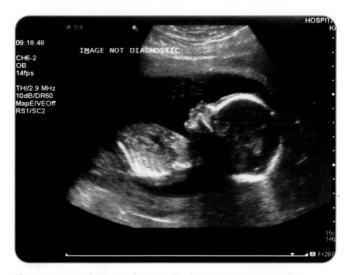

**Figure 32.25** Ultrasound scan of a fetus at 20 weeks; the baby's skin is clearly visible, as are its bony skull and ribs.

This means that bone shows up well in an ultrasound scan, but it is difficult to see different soft tissues (Figure 32.25). Another problem is that the patient's skin is in contact with air, and 99.95% of the ultrasound will be reflected before it has entered the body. To overcome this, the transducer must be 'coupled' to the skin using a gel whose impedance matches that of the skin. This process of **impedance matching** explains why the patient's skin is smeared with gel before a scan.

The acoustic impedance of the gel is typically $1.65 \times 10^6 \, \text{kg} \, \text{m}^{-2} \, \text{s}^{-1}$ and that of skin is $1.71 \times 10^6 \, \text{kg} \, \text{m}^{-2} \, \text{s}^{-1}$. With gel between the skin and the transducer, the percentage of the intensity reflected is 0.03%.

The poor match of impedance between air and tissue means that ultrasound cannot penetrate the lungs. The operator must take care to avoid any bubbles of gas in the intestines. Bones are also difficult to see through. For an ultrasound scan of the heart, the probe must be directed through the gap between two ribs.

As ultrasound waves pass through the body, they are gradually absorbed. Their absorption follows the same exponential pattern as we saw earlier for X-rays. The intensity $I$ decreases with distance $x$ according to the equation

$$I = I_0 e^{-\alpha x}$$

Here, $\alpha$ is the absorption coefficient, equivalent to the quantity $\mu$ in the absorption equation for X-rays; its value varies with the nature of the tissue through which the ultrasound is passing, and with the frequency of the ultrasound. In practice, absorption is not a serious problem when conducting an ultrasound scan as scanning relies on the reflection of ultrasound at the boundaries between different tissues.

## Test yourself

13 Calculate the acoustic impedance of brain tissue. (Density = $1025 \, \text{kg} \, \text{m}^{-3}$, speed of sound = $1540 \, \text{m} \, \text{s}^{-1}$.)

14 Determine the fraction of the intensity of an ultrasound beam that is reflected when a beam is incident normally on a boundary between water and fat. (Use values from Table **32.3**.)

15 The ultrasound image shown in Figure **32.25** clearly shows the baby's skin and some bones. Explain why these show up clearly while softer organs inside its body do not.

*continued* ···▸

16 Explain why ultrasound cannot readily be used to examine the brain. Suggest an alternative scanning technique(s) that can be used for this.

# Ultrasound scanning

There are several different types of ultrasound scan which are used in practice. To illustrate the basic principles, we will concentrate on the A-scan and the B-scan.

## A-scan

This is the simplest type of scan. A pulse of ultrasound is sent into the body and the reflected 'echoes' are detected and displayed on an oscilloscope or computer screen as a voltage–time graph.

A pulse generator controls the ultrasound transducer. It is also connected to the time base of the oscilloscope. Simultaneously, the pulse generator triggers a pulse of ultrasound which travels into the patient and starts a trace on the screen. Each partial reflection of the ultrasound is detected and appears as a spike on the screen (Figure **32.26**).

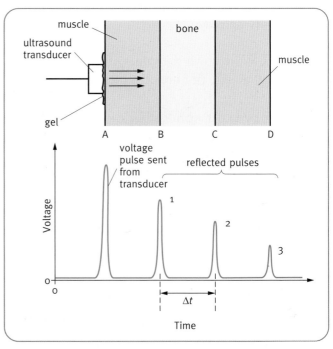

Figure 32.26 An A-scan. Information about the depth of reflecting tissues can be obtained from the positions of the spikes along the time axis; their relative amplitudes can indicate the nature of the reflecting surfaces.

In Figure **32.26**, the pulses 1, 2 and 3 are reflected at the various boundaries. Pulse 1 is the reflection at the muscle–bone boundary at B. Pulse 2 is the reflection at the bone–muscle boundary at C. The time $\Delta t$ is the time taken for the ultrasound to travel **twice** the thickness of the bone. Finally, pulse 3 is the reflection at the muscle–air boundary at D. The thickness of the bone can be determined from this A-scan.

time interval between pulses 1 and 2 $= \Delta t$

$$\frac{\text{distance travelled by ultrasound}}{2}$$

$$\text{thickness of bone} = \frac{c\Delta t}{2}$$

where $c$ is the speed of the ultrasound in the bone (see Worked example 3).

Because ultrasound waves are gradually attenuated as they pass through the body (their energy is absorbed so that their amplitude and intensity decrease), the echoes from tissues deeper in the body are weaker and must be amplified.

A-scans are used for some straightforward procedures such as measuring the thickness of the eye lens.

## Worked example

3  In a particular A-scan, similar to Figure **32.26**, the time interval between pulses 1 and 2 is 12 μs. The speed of ultrasound in bone is about 4000 m s$^{-1}$. Determine the thickness of the bone.

**Step 1** Determine the distance travelled by the ultrasound in the time interval of 12 μs.

distance = speed × time

distance $= 4000 \times 12 \times 10^{-6} = 4.8 \times 10^{-2}$ m

*continued* ⋯▷

**Step 2** Calculate the thickness of the bone.

The distance you have just calculated must be halved because the ultrasound has to travel through the bone twice.

$$\text{thickness of bone} = \frac{4.8 \times 10^{-2}}{2}$$

$$= 2.4 \times 10^{-2} \text{ m (2.4 cm)}$$

## B-scan

In a B-scan, a detailed image of a cross-section through the patient is built up from many A-scans. The ultrasound transducer is moved across the patient's body in the area of interest. Its position and orientation are determined by small sensors attached to it.

Each reflected pulse is analysed to determine the depth of the reflecting surface (from the time of echo) and the nature of the surface (from the amplitude of the reflected wave). A two-dimensional image is then built up on a screen by positioning dots to represent the position of the reflecting surfaces and with brightness determined by the intensity of the reflection, brighter dots indicating more reflected ultrasound (see Figure **32.27**).

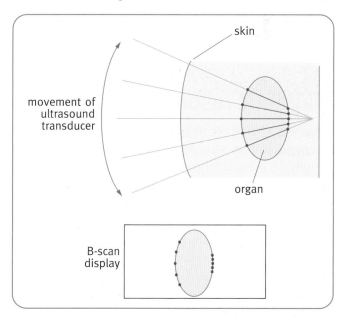

**Figure 32.27** In a B-scan, dots are produced on the screen rather than the pulses as in the A-scan. By moving the transducer, a series of dots on the screen trace out the shape of the organ being examined.

Figure **32.28** shows the result of a typical B-scan. Because it takes several seconds for the scanner to move across the body, problems can arise if the organs of interest are moving – this gives a blurred image.

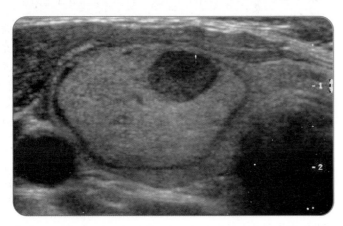

Figure **32.28** An ultrasonic B-scan of an abnormal thyroid gland.

# Magnetic resonance imaging

**Magnetic resonance imaging**, or MRI, is another technique from nuclear medicine. However, it does not rely on nuclides that are radioactive; rather, it relies on the fact that some atomic nuclei behave like tiny magnets in an external magnetic field.

(MRI was originally known as **nuclear magnetic resonance imaging**, but the word 'nuclear' was dropped because it was associated in patients' minds with bombs and power stations. To emphasise: MRI does not involve radioactive decay, fission or fusion.)

As in CAT scanning, MRI scanning involves electromagnetic radiation, in this case radio frequency (RF) electromagnetic waves. The patient lies on a bed in a strong magnetic field (Figure **32.29**), RF

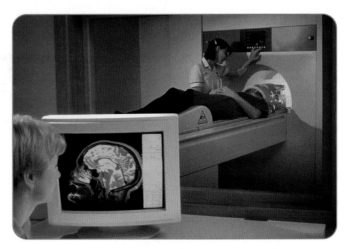

Figure **32.29** A patient undergoing an MRI scan of the brain. This is a form of tomography; the display shows different 'slices' through the patient's brain.

waves are sent into their body, and the RF waves that emerge are detected. From this, a picture of the patient's insides can be built up by computer. As we will see, MRI gives rather different information from that obtained by the other non-invasive techniques we have been looking at.

## Principles of nuclear magnetic resonance

The nuclei of certain atoms have a property called **spin**, and this causes them to behave as tiny magnets in a magnetic field. In MRI, it is usually the nuclei of hydrogen atoms that are studied, since hydrogen atoms are present in all tissues. A hydrogen nucleus is a proton, so we will consider protons from now on.

A proton has positive charge. Because it spins, it behaves like a tiny magnet with N and S poles. Figure **32.30a** shows a number of protons aligned randomly.

When a very strong external magnetic field is applied, the protons respond by lining up in the field (just as plotting compasses line up to show the direction of a magnetic field). Most line up with their N poles facing the S pole of the external field, a low energy state; a few line up the other way round, which is an unstable, higher energy state (Figure **32.30b**).

A proton does not align itself directly along the external field. In practice, its magnetic axis rotates around the direction of the external field (Figure **32.31**), just like the axis of a spinning top. This rotation or gyration action is known as **precession**.

The angular frequency of precession is called the **Larmor frequency** $\omega_0$, and depends on the individual

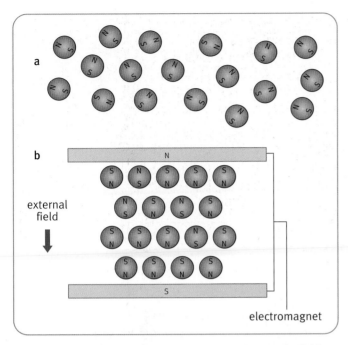

**Figure 32.30** How protons behave in a strong magnetic field.
**a** Protons are randomly directed when there is no external magnetic
field. **b** Because protons are magnetic, a strong external magnetic
field causes most of them to align themselves with the field.

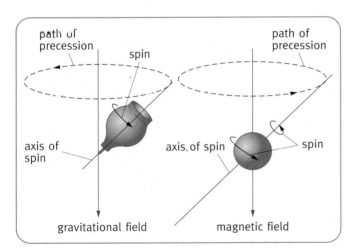

**Figure 32.31** A spinning top (left) rotates about its axis; at
the same time, its axis precesses about the vertical, which
is the direction of the gravitational field. In a similar way, a
proton (right) spins and its axis of rotation precesses about the
direction of the external magnetic field.

nucleus and the magnetic flux density $B_0$ of the
magnetic field:

$$\omega_0 = \gamma B_0$$

So, the stronger the external field, the faster the protons
precess about it. The quantity $\gamma$ is called the **gyromagnetic
ratio** for the nucleus in question and is a measure

of its magnetism. (Note that the Larmor frequency
is measured in radians per second. This means that,
strictly speaking, it is an angular velocity, not a
frequency.)

For protons, $\gamma$ has the approximate value
$2.68 \times 10^8 \, \text{rad s}^{-1} \, \text{T}^{-1}$. To determine the frequency $f_0$ of
the precessing nuclei, we can use the equation:

$$\omega_0 = 2\pi f_0$$

Therefore:

$$f_0 = \frac{\gamma B_0}{2\pi}$$

In an MRI scanner, the external magnetic field is
very strong, of the order of 1.5 T (thousands of times
the strength of the Earth's field). The precession
frequency $f_0$ is:

$$f_0 = \frac{2.68 \times 10^8 \times 1.5}{2\pi} = 6.4 \times 10^7 \, \text{Hz} = 64 \, \text{MHz}$$

This frequency lies in the radio frequency (RF) region
of the electromagnetic spectrum. You should recall
that **resonance** requires a system with a natural
frequency of vibration; when it is stimulated with
energy of the same frequency, it absorbs energy. In
MRI, protons precessing about the strong external
field are exposed to a burst or pulse of RF waves
whose frequency equals the frequency of precession.
Each proton absorbs a photon of RF energy and
flips up into the higher energy state; this is **nuclear
magnetic resonance** (Figure **32.32**).

Now we come to the useful bit. The RF waves are
switched off and the protons gradually relax into their
lower energy state. As they do so, they release their
excess energy in the form of RF waves. These can be
detected, and the rate of **relaxation** tells us something
about the environment of the protons.

In Figure **32.32**, you can see that the relaxation
of the protons follows an exponential decay
pattern. Curves like this are characterised by two
**relaxation times**:

• $T_1$, the spin–lattice relaxation time, where the energy
of the spinning nuclei is transferred to the surrounding
'lattice' of nearby atoms;
• $T_2$, the spin–spin relaxation time, where the energy is
transferred to other spinning nuclei.

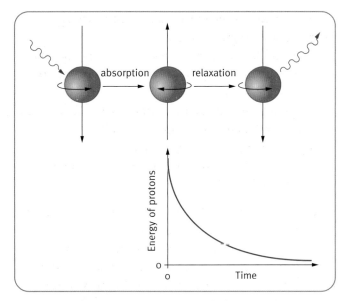

Figure 32.32 In nuclear magnetic resonance, a spinning nucleus is flipped into a higher energy state when it absorbs a photon of RF energy; then it relaxes back to its lower energy state.

These relaxation times depend on the environment of the nuclei. For biological materials, it depends on their water content:

- Water and watery tissues (e.g. cerebrospinal fluid) have relaxation times of several seconds.
- Fatty tissues (e.g. white matter in the brain) have shorter relaxation times, several hundred milliseconds.
- Cancerous tissues have intermediate relaxation times.

This means that different tissues can be distinguished by the different rates at which they release energy after they have been forced to resonate. That is the basis of medical applications of nuclear magnetic resonance.

## Test yourself

19 Protons precess at a frequency of 42.6 MHz in an external field of magnetic flux density 1.0 T.
   a Determine the frequency at which will they precess in a field of magnetic flux density 2.5 T.
   b State the frequency of RF radiation that will cause the protons to resonate in this stronger magnetic field.

20 Figure 32.33 shows how the amplitude of RF waves coming from watery tissue varies after

*continued* ⋯→

resonance. Copy the graph and add lines and labels to show the graphs you would expect to see for cancerous and fatty tissues.

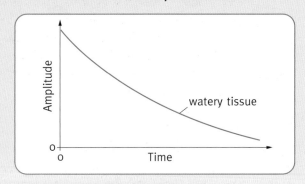

Figure 32.33 See Test yourself Q 20.

## MRI scanner

Figure 32.34 shows the main components of MRI scanner. The main features are:

- A large superconducting magnet which produces the external magnetic field (up to 2.0 T) needed to align the protons. Superconducting magnets are cooled to 4.2 K (−269 °C) using liquid helium.
- An RF coil that transmits RF pulses into the body.
- An RF coil that detects the signal emitted by the relaxing protons.
- A set of gradient coils. (For clarity, only one pair of gradient coils is shown in Figure 32.34.) These produce an additional external magnetic field that varies across the patient's body. These coils are arranged such that they alter the magnitude of the magnetic flux density across the length, depth and width of the patient.

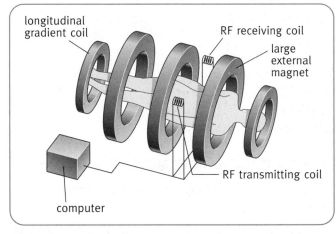

Figure 32.34 The main components of an MRI scanner.

This ensures that the Larmor frequency of the nuclei within the patient will be slightly different for each part of the body. This means that only a small volume of the body is at exactly the right field value for resonance and so the computer can precisely locate the source of the RF signal within the patient's body and construct an image.

- A computer that controls the gradient coils and RF pulses, and which stores and analyses the received data, producing and displaying images.

## Procedure

The patient lies on a bed which is moved into the bore of the electromagnet. The central imaging section is about 0.9 m long and 0.6 m in diameter. The magnetic field is very uniform, with variations smaller than 50 parts per million in its strength. The gradient field is superimposed on this fixed field. An RF pulse is then transmitted into the body, causing protons to flip (resonate). Then the receiving coils pick up the relaxation signal and pass it to the computer.

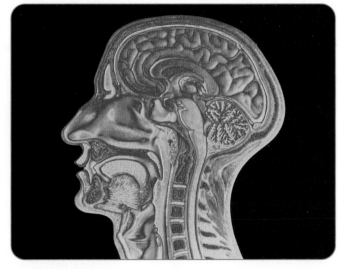

**Figure 32.35** MRI scan through a healthy human head. Different tissues, identified by their different relaxation times, are coloured differently.

The result is an image like the one shown in Figure 32.35. This image has been coloured to show up the different tissues, which are identified by their different relaxation times.

## Advantages and disadvantages of MRI

MRI has several advantages compared to other scanning techniques:

- It does not use ionising radiation which causes a hazard to patients and staff.

- There are no moving mechanisms, just changing currents and magnetic fields.
- The patient feels nothing during a scan (although the gradient coils are noisy as they are switched), and there are no after-effects.
- MRI gives better soft-tissue contrast than a CAT scan, although it does not show bone as clearly.
- Computer images can be generated showing any section through the volume scanned, or as a three-dimensional image.

One disadvantage of MRI is that any metallic objects in the patient, such as surgical pins, can become heated. Also, heart pacemakers can be affected, so patients with such items cannot undergo MRI scans. Loose steel objects must not be left in the room as these will be attracted to the magnet, and the room must be shielded from external radio fields.

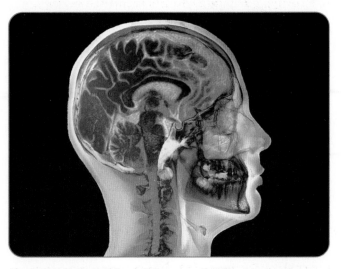

**Figure 32.36** A combined CAT scan and MRI scan, showing how the tissues revealed by MRI relate to the bone structure shown by X-rays.

Figure 32.36 shows how an MRI scan can be combined with a CAT scan to show detail of both bone and soft tissue, allowing medical staff to see how the two are related. Compare this with Figure 32.35.

### Test yourself

21 An MRI scan might be considered a safer procedure than a CAT scan.
 a Explain why it might be considered to be safer.
 b Why might a CAT scan be chosen in preference to an MRI scan?
 c Explain why MRI is described as **non-invasive**.

## Summary

☐ X-rays are short-wavelength, high-frequency electromagnetic radiation, produced when electrons are decelerated.

☐ The intensity of an X-ray beam is the power transmitted per unit cross-sectional area.

☐ The intensity of a collimated X-ray beam decreases exponentially according to the equation $I = I_0 e^{-\mu x}$, where $\mu$ is the attenuation coefficient of the medium. $\mu$ has units $m^{-1}$ (or $cm^{-1}$ or $mm^{-1}$).

☐ X-ray images can be improved using image intensifiers and contrast media (such as barium or iodine).

☐ Ultrasound is a longitudinal wave with a frequency greater than 20 kHz.

☐ Ultrasound transducers use the piezo-electric effect to generate and detect ultrasound waves.

☐ The acoustic impedance $Z$ of a material depends on its density $\rho$ and the speed $c$ of sound:

$$Z = \rho c$$

☐ The fraction of the intensity of an ultrasound wave reflected at a boundary is given by:

$$\frac{I_r}{I_0} = \frac{(Z_2 - Z_1)^2}{(Z_2 + Z_1)^2} \quad \text{or} \quad \frac{I_r}{I_0} = \left(\frac{Z_2 - Z_1}{Z_2 + Z_1}\right)^2$$

☐ To transfer a high proportion of the intensity of an ultrasound pulse into the patient's body, an impedance-matching gel must be used with acoustic impedance almost the same as that of the skin.

☐ In MRI scanning, spinning, precessing protons are forced to resonate using radio frequency pulses. RF radiation from relaxing protons is used to obtain diagnostic information about internal organs, particularly soft tissues.

☐ The main components of an MRI scanner are: superconducting magnet, RF transmitter coil, RF receiver coil, set of gradient coils and computer.

## End-of-chapter questions

1    a  Explain what is meant by **ionising radiation** and explain why it can be harmful to humans.
     b  Which of the following scans use ionising radiation?
        X-ray shadow imaging
        ultrasound A-scan
        ultrasound B-scan
        magnetic resonance imaging
        CAT scan

2    Calculate the minimum wavelength (in air) of X-rays produced when the accelerating potential across the source is 20 kV.

**3** Explain why a gel is used between the skin and the transducer when an ultrasound scan of a fetus is taken.

**4** The acoustic impedance of muscle, for ultrasound of frequency 3.5 MHz is $1.78 \times 10^6 \, \mathrm{kg \, m^{-2} \, s^{-1}}$ and that of soft tissue $1.63 \times 10^6 \, \mathrm{kg \, m^{-2} \, s^{-1}}$.
Calculate the percentage of the incident ultrasound reflected at a muscle–soft tissue boundary.

**5** A transducer produces ultrasonic waves of frequency 800 kHz. The speed of sound in the crystal is $5200 \, \mathrm{m \, s^{-1}}$.
Calculate the optimum thickness for the crystal.

**6** Explain what is meant by the **Larmor frequency** and state its units.

**7** State and explain **two** reasons why full-body CAT scans are not offered for regular checking of healthy patients.

# Exam-style questions

**1**  **a** Explain with the aid of a simple, labelled diagram how X-rays are produced.  [5]
  **b** Discuss the energy changes in the production of X-rays.  [3]

**2** The graph shows the spectrum of X-rays produced from an X-ray source.

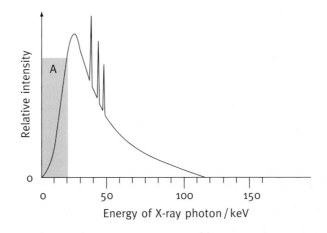

  **a** Describe the process by which:
  **i** the three sharp peaks of high-intensity X-rays are produced  [3]
  **ii** the broad band of X-rays is produced.  [1]
  **b** The X-rays in the shaded region, labelled A, are filtered out using an aluminium filter.
  Explain:
  **i** why it is advantageous to filter these X-rays out  [3]
  **ii** why aluminium is a suitable material to filter them out.  [1]
  **c** Calculate the maximum frequency of X-rays produced by this tube.  [3]

3    a   Explain what is meant by **acoustic impedance** and outline its role in the use of ultrasound scans. [3]

     b   Brain tissue has a density of $1.04 \times 10^3 \, \text{kg m}^{-3}$ and ultrasound travels at $1.58 \times 10^3 \, \text{m s}^{-1}$ through it.

       Calculate the acoustic impedance of brain tissue. [2]

     c   Figure **32.38** shows the trace screen of an oscilloscope, formed when ultrasound is reflected from the front and rear surfaces of the head of a fetus. The time-base of the oscilloscope is set at $10 \, \mu\text{s div}^{-1}$.

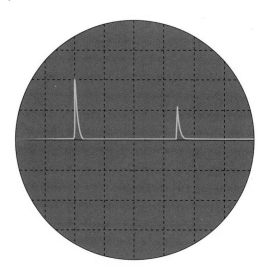

       i    Explain why the second peak is lower than the first. [1]

       ii   Calculate the diameter of the head of the fetus. [3]

4    a   With reference to nuclear magnetic resonance, explain what is meant by the **gyromagnetic ratio**. [1]

     b   A doctor is conducting an MRI scan on a patient there is a steady magnetic field of 1.8 T, superimposed on this is a much weaker field which oscillates at the RF frequency of 48 MHz.

       i     Assuming the RF frequency causes resonance of the protons, calculate the gyromagnetic ratio. [3]

       ii    Explain what **resonance** means in this application. [2]

       iii   Describe what happens when the RF field is removed and how this leads to information about the internal organs of the patient. [3]

5    a   Describe the main principles of how a CT scan image is produced and compare this with the formation of an X-ray shadow image. [7]

     b   A CT image is sometimes superimposed on an image from an MRI scan. Explain the advantages of using this dual approach. [2]

6   **a** An X-ray beam, containing X-rays with a variety of frequencies and which has
        an intensity of $4.0 \times 10^5$ W, is incident on an aluminium plate of thickness 5.0 cm.
        The average linear attenuation coefficient is 250 m$^{-1}$.
    **i**   Calculate the intensity of the transmitted beam.                                  [3]
    **ii**  Explain the advantages of passing the X-rays through this aluminium plate prior
            to their being incident on a patient.                                             [3]
    **b** Outline the use of an anti-scatter grid and explain its role in improving an X-ray
        shadow image.                                                                         [5]

## Objectives

After studying this chapter, you should be able to:

- [ ] understand amplitude and frequency modulation and comment on the relative advantages of AM and FM transmission
- [ ] describe digital transmission systems in terms of analogue-to-digital (ADC) and digital-to-analogue (DAC) conversion and sampling rate
- [ ] describe and compare different networks or channels of communication
- [ ] calculate signal attenuation in dB and dB per unit length
- [ ] explain the principal features of a mobile-phone system, including the mobile-phone handset

## Communications today

**Figure 33.1** A communications satellite.

The ability to communicate is an important feature of modern life. We can now speak directly to others right around the world and generate vast amounts of information every day. The invention of the mobile phone has increased our ability to talk to one another and to find out what is happening around us. This chapter looks briefly at how some communication systems work. Communication engineers have applied the principles of physics to change the present and shape the future.

## Radio waves

The person listening to the radio in Figure 33.2 is at the end of a communication system. The system starts with sound or music passing into a microphone. The sound signal is converted into a radio signal and at the end of the communication system the radio signal is converted back again into a sound signal.

Sound waves and radio waves are completely different types of wave; amongst other differences they have different frequencies, wavelengths and speeds.

A radio wave cannot be the same frequency and shape as the sound signal it carries. Audio frequencies cover the range from 50 Hz to 20 000 Hz. The aerial needed to receive radio waves at these frequencies would be so large it would not fit inside a radio receiver. More importantly, if more than one radio station transmitted waves of these frequencies your radio receiver would pick them all up at the same time. Imagine listening to a radio receiver where you hear every radio station at once!

Different radio signals must be separated in some way. This is achieved by giving each different radio signal a different **carrier wave** frequency. You can only hear one station at a time because when you tune a radio

**Figure 33.2** Part of a communication system.

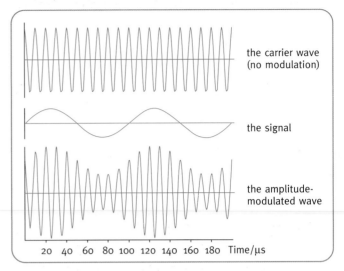

**Figure 33.3** Amplitude modulation.

receiver it only receives a carrier wave of one frequency. Carrier wave frequencies in the radio spectrum are much higher than the frequencies of sound signals.

The information, for example a sound signal, is carried by modulating or altering the carrier wave. **Modulation** is the variation of either the **amplitude** or the **frequency** of the carrier wave. The modulated wave is the actual wave transmitted. The signal is present in either the changing amplitude or the changing frequency of the modulated wave.

## Amplitude modulation

Figure **33.3** shows **amplitude modulation** (AM). The three diagrams show the carrier wave, the signal and the modulated wave. In each case, the horizontal axis represents time, shown on the axis at the bottom. The modulated wave is the carrier wave but its amplitude rises and falls to match the value of the signal at any instant. Look at the amplitude-modulated wave on its

own, and notice how the amplitude variation at top and bottom has the same pattern as the signal.

The amplitude of the signal must be less than half of the amplitude of the carrier wave; otherwise the variation in the amplitude at the top will be confused with the variation in amplitude at the bottom of the wave.

### Worked example

1  Calculate the frequencies of the carrier wave and signal shown in Figure **33.3**.

**Step 1** For the carrier wave, there are 10 complete waves in 100 μs. Hence:

time for one complete carrier wave,
$$T = 10\,\mu s = 1 \times 10^{-5}\,s$$

carrier wave frequency $f_c = \dfrac{1}{T} = 100\,000\,Hz$

**Step 2** For the signal, there is one complete wave in 100 μs. Hence:

$$\text{frequency of the signal } f_s = \frac{1}{(100 \times 10^{-6})}$$
$$= 10\,000\,Hz$$

A radio wave of 100 000 Hz is in the long-wavelength, low-frequency region of the radio electromagnetic spectrum. A sound frequency of 10 000 Hz is a very high frequency note but is audible.

If a radio station carries music, the wave transmitted by the radio station will differ from the wave shown in Figure **33.3**. There is only one signal frequency present in the signal in Figure **33.3**. Music consists of many, changing frequencies superimposed so that it has a more complex wave pattern. The amplitude of the carrier wave will change as the music pattern changes. The carrier wave frequency does not change but the amplitude of the trace will change with time.

In amplitude modulation (AM), the frequency of the modulated wave is constant. The amplitude of the modulated wave is proportional to, and in phase with, the signal.

## Test yourself

1 Imagine that all the numbers on the time axis in Figure **33.3** are doubled, so that 100 becomes 200 and 200 becomes 400. Calculate the frequency of the carrier wave and the frequency of the signal.

2 Draw an amplitude-modulated wave with a carrier wave of frequency 1.0 MHz and a signal frequency of 100 kHz. The time axis on your graph should be from 0 to 10 µs. On your graph, mark the time for one complete wave of the signal and for one complete wave of the carrier.

3 Explain how an amplitude-modulated wave changes when the input signal:
   **a** increases in loudness
   **b** increases in frequency.

## Frequency modulation

In **frequency modulation** (FM) the frequency of the modulated wave varies with time. Without any signal, the frequency of the modulated wave is equal to the frequency of the carrier wave. The size of the input signal at any instant causes the frequency of the modulated wave to change. When the input signal is positive, the frequency of the modulated wave is increased so that it is larger than the frequency of the carrier wave. The larger the signal, the greater is the increase in the frequency. When the signal is negative, the frequency of the modulated wave is less than the frequency of the carrier wave. Figure **33.4** shows frequency modulation.

In frequency modulation (FM), the modulated wave has a constant amplitude. It is the frequency of the modulated wave that changes as the signal changes.

The frequency deviation of the carrier wave may be given a value, for example, $25\,\text{kHz}\,\text{V}^{-1}$. This means that for every 1.0 V change in the voltage of the signal, the frequency of the carrier wave changes by 25 kHz. In some countries, the maximum allowed change in frequency during FM is set as 75 kHz, in order that the frequency of one station does not overlap the frequency of the next station. If the frequency deviation is $25\,\text{kHz}\,\text{V}^{-1}$ and the maximum change is 75 kHz, then the maximum signal producing the FM is 3.0 V.

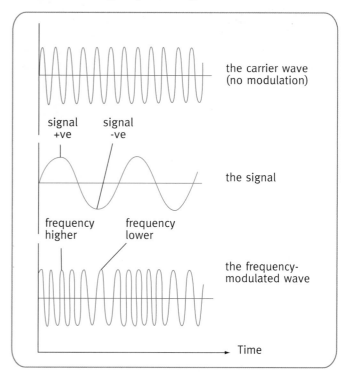

**Figure 33.4** Frequency modulation.

## Worked example

2 A carrier wave of frequency 300 kHz and amplitude 5.0 V is frequency modulated by a sinusoidal signal of frequency 6 kHz and amplitude 2.0 V. The frequency deviation of the carrier wave is $30\,\text{kHz}\,\text{V}^{-1}$. Describe the modulated carrier wave produced.

**Step 1** Consider the amplitude of the modulated signal. The amplitude of the carrier

*continued ···⟩*

wave is unchanged at 5.0 V during frequency modulation. The signal alters the frequency of the carrier wave, not its amplitude.

**Step 2** Now consider how the signal will modify the carrier frequency. The frequency shift produced by the signal is $\pm 2 \times 30 = \pm 60$ kHz, so the carrier wave varies in frequency between 240 and 360 kHz. This variation in frequency occurs 6000 times every second as the signal varies at this frequency.

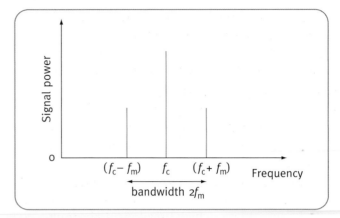

**Figure 33.5** The frequency spectrum of a carrier wave modulated in amplitude by a signal of one frequency.

## Test yourself

4 Explain how a frequency-modulated wave changes, when the input signal:
   **a** increases in loudness;
   **b** increases in frequency.

5 A signal of frequency 16 kHz and amplitude 3.0 V is used for frequency modulation of a carrier wave of frequency 500 kHz. The frequency deviation of the carrier wave is 8.0 kHz V$^{-1}$.
   **a** What is the maximum frequency shift produced?
   **b** What is the maximum frequency of the modulated carrier wave?
   **c** How many times per second does the modulated carrier wave increase and decrease in frequency?

## Sidebands and bandwidth

A carrier wave contains only one frequency, the carrier wave frequency $f_c$. When the carrier wave is modulated in amplitude by a single frequency $f_m$, then the carrier wave is found to contain two more frequencies, known as sideband frequencies, one at a frequency $(f_c - f_m)$ and the other at $(f_c + f_m)$. Figure **33.5** shows these frequencies.

When music or speech is transmitted, the carrier is modulated by a range of frequencies which change with time. Each frequency $f_m$ present in the signal gives rise to an extra pair of frequencies in the modulated wave. The result is a band of frequencies, called the **upper** and **lower sidebands** stretching above

and below the carrier frequency by the value of the highest modulating frequency.

Figure **33.6** shows the frequency spectrum for a carrier wave of frequency 1 MHz modulated with frequencies between 0 and $f_m = 15$ kHz $= 0.015$ MHz. The highest frequency present in the spectrum is $(f_c + f_m) = 1.015$ MHz and the lowest frequency is $(f_c - f_m) = 0.985$ MHz.

The actual shape of the sidebands in Figure **33.6** will vary at any instant as the signal changes. The maximum and minimum values are important, as these must not overlap the sidebands from any other radio station.

The value of $f_m$ needed depends on the quality required in the signal. High-quality music only needs frequencies up to 15 kHz, even though the ear can hear frequencies up to 20 kHz. Speech only needs frequencies up to 3.4 kHz for people to understand one another.

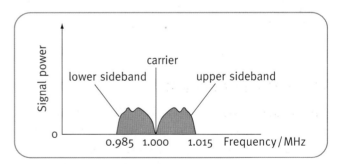

**Figure 33.6** The frequency spectrum for an amplitude-modulated wave.

You can see that the modulated carrier wave occupies a region of the spectrum from 0.985 MHz to 1.015 MHz. The **bandwidth** of a signal is the range of frequencies that the signal occupies. In other words, it is the difference between the highest-frequency signal component and the lowest-frequency signal component.

In Figure **33.6** the bandwidth is $1.015 - 0.985 = 0.030$ MHz. In Figure **33.5** the bandwidth is $(f_c + f_m) - (f_c - f_m) = 2f_m$.

The frequency spectrum of a frequency-modulated (FM) carrier wave is more complex. In particular, there are often more than two sideband frequencies for each signal frequency. This means that frequency modulation requires a greater bandwidth for each radio station.

## Worked example

3 Radio stations, which broadcast in the long-wave (LW) region of the electromagnetic spectrum, use a carrier frequency between 140 kHz and 280 kHz. The sidebands are within 4.5 kHz on either side of the carrier frequency. State the bandwidth of each radio station in the LW region of the spectrum and calculate the maximum number of radio stations which can transmit in the LW region.

**Step 1** The bandwidth of an individual station is twice the width of an individual sideband:

bandwidth $= 2 \times 4.5 = 9.0$ kHz

**Step 2** The LW region is divided into regions of width 9.0 kHz. Hence:

$$\text{number of stations} = \frac{\text{allowed frequency range}}{\text{bandwidth}}$$

$$= \frac{(280 - 140)}{9.0}$$

$$= 15.5 = 15 \text{ stations}$$

Suppose a country decides to increase the quality of music transmitted by each radio station. What happens to the bandwidth and the maximum number of stations in the LW region? Better sound quality requires an increase in the maximum frequency of the signal that modulates the carrier wave, and so the bandwidth needed increases. This decreases the number of available stations in the LW region of the spectrum.

## Comparing AM and FM transmissions

You may have noticed crackle on a radio when you switch lights in your house on and off or when there is a lightning strike nearby. The lightning strike or switching a current on or off creates a burst of radio waves. These radio waves produce unwanted electrical interference and change the amplitude of the radio wave received by a radio. Since the **amplitude** of the wave carries the signal, when amplitude modulation is used the output of the radio is affected. Most electrical interference does not affect the **frequency** of the radio wave received by a radio and thus electrical interference affects FM less than AM. FM radio was actually invented to overcome the electrical interference and noise problems of AM radio and this remains an important advantage today.

FM came later than AM and had to use higher frequencies than AM. Although there was extra cost in developing the electronics to work at these higher frequencies, it was still an advantage. The greater range of frequencies available means that each station can use a higher bandwidth (about 200 kHz, compared to 9 kHz for AM). FM signals typically contain frequencies of 15 kHz or higher and the quality of sound produced is much higher when using FM transmission.

However, AM transmission has a number of advantages.

- The bandwidth needed for each AM transmission is less than for FM transmission and this means that more stations can be included in any given frequency range of the electromagnetic spectrum.
- The actual receiver and transmitter used for AM are less complicated and cheaper than for FM transmission.
- AM transmissions use lower frequencies and have higher wavelengths than FM. This means that these radio waves can diffract some way around the Earth, whereas FM is line-of-sight only. Thus AM can cover a larger area than FM transmissions, for the same power output.

The relative advantages of FM and AM are summarised in Table **33.1**.

| Advantages of FM | Advantages of AM |
|---|---|
| less electrical interference and noise | greater area covered by one transmitter |
| greater bandwidth produces a better quality of sound | smaller bandwidth means more stations available in any frequency range |
| | cheaper radio sets |

Table **33.1** The relative advantages of FM and AM broadcasting.

6 Figure 33.7 shows the frequency spectrum of the signal from a radio transmitter. A carrier and two sideband frequencies are present.

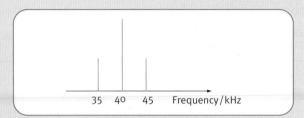

Figure 33.7 For Test yourself Q 6.

a What is the name of the type of modulation that produces two sideband frequencies?
b What is the carrier frequency?
c What is the frequency of the signal used to modulate the carrier wave?
d What is the bandwidth of the transmitted signal?

7 a Calculate the number of separate AM radio stations of bandwidth 9 kHz that are possible in the frequency spectrum available for AM between 530 and 1700 kHz.
  b Suggest why FM stations of bandwidth 200 kHz are not used for this range of frequencies.

8 Is the greater bandwidth available on FM an advantage or a disadvantage?

9 FM is used largely in towns and AM in rural settings. Suggest why.

# Analogue and digital signals

An analogue quantity is one that can have any value, for example the height of a person. A digital quantity has only a few values, usually just two; for example a person is either male or female.

So far, the signals we have dealt with in this book have been analogue signals. For example, the voltage signal generated by a microphone is an **analogue signal**; the output voltage from the microphone can have any value, within limits, and is an exact representation of the pressure variation in a sound wave.

A **digital signal** on the other hand looks completely different and consists of a series of zeros (0) and ones (1). A 1 in a digital signal is just the presence of a voltage pulse, usually a voltage value of a few volts. A 0 in a digital signal is the absence of a pulse and is a voltage close to 0 V. A typical digital electronic system will interpret any voltage below about 0.3 V as a 0 and any voltage above about 1.5 V as a 1. Small fluctuations in voltage will not be noticed.

Figure 33.8 shows an analogue and a digital signal. The digital signal is the number 0101001101, which is actually a pulse of 0 V followed by a pulse of 3 V and so on.

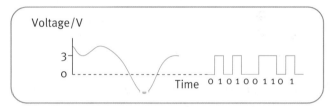

Figure 33.8 Analogue and digital signals.

## Advantages of digital signals

Most devices such as microphones or thermistors produce analogue voltage signals. However, digital signals have advantages and it is often worthwhile to change an analogue signal into a digital signal.

The major advantage is that digital signals can deal with 'noise' produced over long distances. All signals, both analogue and digital, become weaker as they travel and they pick up electrical noise. The decrease in strength is known as attenuation, and can be corrected by amplifying the signal at regular intervals during long-distance transmission.

Noise is electrical interference, caused in a number of different ways; by the spark from a car ignition, by induced voltages from the magnetic fields caused by currents around the home, by the radio signals emitted by a mobile phone nearby, and even by the random thermal motion of electrons in a wire or by vibrating atoms. You may have noticed a background hiss on telephone conversations. This also is an example of noise.

**Noise** is the random, unwanted signal that adds to and distorts a transmitted signal. Amplification of a signal amplifies the noise at the same time as the signal.

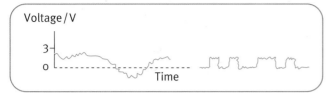

**Figure 33.9** Weakened and noisy signals.

Figure **33.9** shows the signals from Figure **33.8** after they have travelled a long distance. You will see that they are lower in amplitude and have unwanted variations, or noise.

There is little improvement possible for the analogue signal; amplification will not remove the noise. However, **regeneration** will remove the noise from a digital signal. The signal is 'cleaned' of the noise and returned to its initial shape.

At the end of a long-distance transmission, an electronic circuit, the regeneration amplifier, receives the digital signal. This electronic circuit expects to receive a pulse of a few volts or no pulse at all; any small variations added to the pulse or the 0 V make no difference. The regeneration amplifier can only give a 0 or a 1 as an output. As long as the noise does not completely change the shape of the signal, then the regeneration amplifier returns the digital signal shown in Figure **33.9** back into the perfect pulses shown in Figure **33.8**.

Other advantages of using digital signals are:

- digital signals are compatible with modern technology and can be stored and processed more easily, for example in a computer or on a compact disc (CD);
- digital electronic systems are, in general, more reliable and easier to design and build;
- digital signals build in safeguards so that if there is an error in reception it is noticed and parts of the signal can be sent again.

## Analogue to digital conversion

The key to the digital revolution has been the ability to change speech and music from analogue into digital form in **analogue-to-digital conversion (ADC)** and then convert them back again into analogue form in **digital-to-analogue conversion (DAC).**

In order to understand this process, you need to be able to count using binary numbers as well as ordinary decimal numbers. The decimal system has base 10 and the number of digits increases by one when going

from the number 9 to the number 10. The number 9 has only one digit whereas the number 10 has two digits. The binary number system has base 2 and the number of digits increases when going up from the number 1; so the next number above 1 is 10. The binary number 10 is not the same as the decimal number 10. Table **33.2** compares counting in the decimal system and in the binary system.

| Decimal number | Binary number | Decimal number | Binary number |
|---|---|---|---|
| 0 | 0 | 6 | 110 |
| 1 | 1 | 7 | 111 |
| 2 | 10 | 8 | 1000 |
| 3 | 11 | 9 | 1001 |
| 4 | 100 | 10 | 1010 |
| 5 | 101 | 11 | 1011 |

**Table 33.2** Binary and decimal numbers.

For example:

- in the decimal system, the number 243 is a combination of $2 \times 100$, $4 \times 10$ and $3 \times 1$;
- in the binary system, the number 111 is a combination of $1 \times 4$, $1 \times 2$ and $1 \times 1$.

Counting in the binary system is very similar to counting in the decimal system except that there are only the digits 0 and 1.

Each digit in the binary number is known as a **bit**. The bit on the left-hand side of a binary number is the most significant bit (MSB) and has the highest value. Large numbers require more bits. Table **33.2** shows numbers containing 4 bits, although 0011 is the correct way of writing a 4-bit number, rather than writing 11. A digital telephone system commonly transmits numbers containing 8 bits and there are $2^8 = 256$ different 8-bit binary numbers.

Changing an analogue signal into a digital signal involves sampling. In analogue-to digital conversion (ADC), **sampling** is the measurement of the analogue signal at regular time intervals.

The value of the sampled signal is used to produce a binary number. Each time that the signal is sampled the ADC produces a binary number of a certain number of bits. Since the sample is taken many times per second, many binary numbers are created, one after the other, and this series of 0s and 1s becomes the digital signal that is transmitted.

The process is illustrated in Figure **33.10** where 4-bit binary numbers are produced.

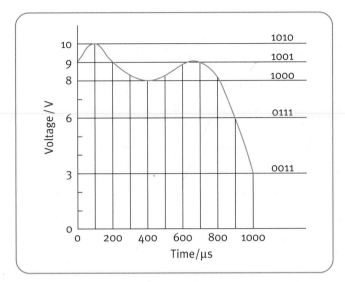

**Figure 33.10** Analogue to digital conversion.

When the time $t = 0$ the numerical value of the voltage signal is 9 as a decimal number. When converted into binary, this number is 1001. When $t = 100\,\mu s$ the voltage is 10 as a decimal number and 1010 as a binary number.

You will notice that at some values of $t$ the signal is not a whole number on the voltage axis. The nearest number is chosen.

When the output is sampled every $100\,\mu s$, a set of binary numbers is produced: (1001) then (1010) then (1001) then (1000) then (1000) and so on. These sets of 4-bit numbers are transmitted one after the other. If they are transmitted a long distance, a regeneration amplifier is used along the way to keep the same pattern of pulses. A digital-to-analogue converter changes the digital signal back into analogue form at the end of the transmission.

Figure **33.11** shows the result of this conversion back into analogue form. The blue circles show the values of the voltage, which are each a decimal number formed from a 4-bit binary number. The black line drawn through the circles is the output signal. Some electronic systems contain extra filter circuits that are able to smooth the output and they produce the blue line as the final output.

The black line, the output, is clearly not exactly the same as the original signal. There are two reasons for this.

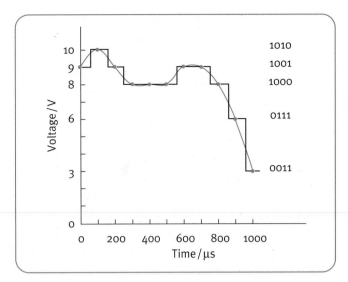

**Figure 33.11** Digital to analogue conversion.

Firstly, the sampled signal is not always a whole number. For example, in Figure **33.10** when $t = 300\,\mu s$ the actual voltage is 8.3 V but only the number 8 can be sent, not 8.3.

To improve the sampling, the voltage that corresponds to the difference between 0 and 1 must be decreased. In the above example, the difference between 0 and 1 in binary is 1 V and so the signal is 'accurate' to only 1 V. If the difference between 0 and 1 is made to be 0.1 V then 'accuracy' is improved. Adding an extra bit is similar to having an extra significant figure when measuring a voltage as 8.3 V rather than 8 V. Integers up to 10 need a 4-bit binary number. If the system handles numbers to within 0.1 then 10.0 requires an 8-bit number, which has 128 different possible levels.

The other problem is that the sampling rate is not high enough. The sampling rate is the number of samples made per second. In the example in Figure **33.10**, the sample is taken every $100\,\mu s$ and so the sampling rate is $\dfrac{1}{0.0001} = 10\,000$ times a second. If the signal changes between one sample and the next then no record is made of that change. Obviously the higher the sampling rate, the closer the final signal will be to the original signal. The maximum sampling rate required is only twice the highest frequency present in the signal (this is known as Nyquist's theorem). The human ear can hear up to 20 kHz and so the maximum sampling rate needed is 40 kHz for music. For every second of music on a compact disc storing eight-bit numbers sampled 40 000 times a second,

320 000 separate binary digits are stored. The sampling rate required for a telephone system will be less, since only frequencies up to about 3400 Hz are required for basic speech recognition. Many digital telephone systems sample the input signal 8000 times a second and so only transmit frequencies below 4 kHz.

## Test yourself

10 Convert the following decimal numbers into binary numbers:
   a 14     b 16

11 Convert the following binary numbers into decimal numbers:
   a 1111     b 0001011

12 The diagrams in Figure 33.12 show a digital signal at the start of a long cable and at the end of the cable. Both diagrams are drawn to the same horizontal scale (time) and vertical scale (voltage).

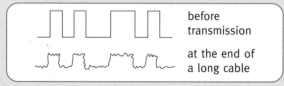

before transmission

at the end of a long cable

**Figure 33.12** For Test yourself Q **12.**

   a Explain what feature of the top diagram shows that the signal is digital.
   b State and explain **two** advantages of digital transmission rather than analogue transmission of data.
   c State and explain **two** reasons why the signal at the end of the long cable differs from the signal at the start.

# Channels of communication

The term **channel of communication** refers to the medium, the path or even the actual frequency range used to convey information from a transmitter to a receiver.

When you listen to a radio, the radio signal may have travelled through the air by a number of different routes. When you talk to someone on a telephone in a different country then the signal may have passed along a **wire-pair**, a **coaxial cable**, through the air by a **microwave link** or been converted into pulses of light and then transmitted down an **optic fibre**. These are all different channels of communication.

Before comparing the different channels you will need to understand another technical term, cross-linking, and be able to calculate signal attenuation.

You may have experienced cross-talk or **cross-linking** when using a radio or a telephone. If you tune your radio set to one radio station, sometimes you can also hear another station. When talking on the telephone you can suddenly find yourself listening to a completely different telephone conversation; the telephone network has connected your telephone to someone you have not dialled. Cross-linking occurs when a signal, transmitted on one circuit or channel, creates an undesired effect in another circuit or channel.

## Signal attenuation

Attenuation is the gradual decrease in the power of a signal the further it travels. The causes of energy loss depend on the type of signal.

- As an electrical signal passes along a wire, there is a voltage drop across the resistance of the wire itself. This reduces the voltage of the signal that arrives at the end of the wire. The energy loss in the wire causes electrical heating in the resistance of the wire ($I^2Rt$).
- A radio wave spreads out from a transmitter. On its own this spreading causes a decrease in intensity, but there is also a loss in signal strength because of the absorption of energy by the medium through which the wave travels.
- Light travelling through an optic fibre may be scattered or absorbed by irregularities in the glass structure.

The decrease in signal power from the transmitted value $P_1$ to that received $P_2$ can be very high. The ratio $P_2$ to $P_1$ is measured using a logarithmic scale rather than by the simple ratio of the two powers.

The logarithm to base 10 of the ratio gives us the number of bels (B). When multiplied by 10 we obtain the number of **decibel**s (dB). Your calculator may show logarithms to base 10 as $\log_{10}$. They are written here as lg and must not be confused with logarithms to base e, which are usually written as ln.

$$\text{number of B} = \lg\left(\frac{P_2}{P_1}\right)$$

$$\text{number of dB} = 10 \lg\left(\frac{P_2}{P_1}\right)$$

For example, suppose $P_2$ is a 1000 times greater than $P_1$:

$$\text{number of dB} = 10 \lg\left(\frac{1000}{1}\right) = 30$$

The number is positive because there is an increase in power – the signal is amplified. Attenuation produces a negative number of decibels; for example, an attenuation of $-30$ dB means that the received signal is 1000 times less than the signal transmitted.

You may be much more familiar with logarithms to base e than with logarithms to base 10. All logarithms obey the same rules; some, which you should know, are:

log of a product $\quad \log(ab) = \log(a) + \log(b)$

log of a ratio $\quad \log\left(\dfrac{a}{b}\right) = \log(a) - \log(b)$

log of a power $\quad \log(a^n) = n\log(a)$

## Worked example

4  A signal of power 18.0 mW passes along one cable, where the attenuation is 20 dB. It then passes along another cable, where the attenuation is 30 dB. What is the power at the end of the two cables?

**Step 1** Apply the decibel equation to each cable in turn.

In the first cable, if the input is $P_1$ and the output $P_2$, then:

$$20 = 10 \lg\left(\frac{P_1}{P_2}\right)$$

Notice that both sides of the equation produce a positive number since $P_1 > P_2$.

*continued ⋯*

In the second cable, the input is $P_2$, the output of the first channel. If the output is $P_3$, then:

$$30 = 10 \lg\left(\frac{P_2}{P_3}\right)$$

**Step 2** Add the two equations; this gives:

$$50 = 10\left[\lg\left(\frac{P_1}{P_2}\right) + \lg\left(\frac{P_2}{P_3}\right)\right]$$

Applying the 'log of a product rule' gives:

$$50 = 10 \lg\left(\frac{P_1}{P_2} \times \frac{P_2}{P_3}\right) = 10 \lg\left(\frac{P_1}{P_3}\right)$$

This shows that the total attenuation of the two cables is 50 dB, equal to the sum of the attenuations of the consecutive channels. Hence you can add attenuations to find the total attenuation (but be careful if a signal is being both amplified and attenuated).

**Step 3** We have $P_1 = 18$ mW and we need to find $P_3$. Substituting gives:

$$50 = 10 \lg\left(\frac{18}{P_3}\right)$$

so:

$$\lg\left(\frac{18}{P_3}\right) = \frac{50}{10} = 5$$

Taking inverse logs, or pressing the inverse lg button on your calculator, gives:

$$\left(\frac{18}{P_3}\right) = 10^5$$

$$P_3 = 1.8 \times 10^{-4} \text{ mW}$$

## Overcoming attenuation

In long-distance cables, the attenuation is given as attenuation per unit length, with units such as $dB\,km^{-1}$. The attenuation is found from the equation:

attenuation per unit length ($dB\,km^{-1}$)

$$= \frac{\text{attenuation (dB)}}{\text{length of cable (km)}}$$

When a signal travels along a cable, the level of the noise is important. The signal must be distinguishable above the level of the noise. The signal-to-noise ratio, measured in decibels, is given by the expression:

$$\text{signal-to-noise ratio} = 10\,\lg\left(\frac{\text{signal power}}{\text{noise power}}\right)$$

At regular intervals along a cable, **repeaters** amplify the signal. If the signal is analogue then repeaters also amplify the noise. Multiplying both signal and noise by the same amount keeps the signal-to-noise ratio the same. Regeneration of a digital signal at the same time as amplification removes most of the noise. This makes sure that the signal-to-noise ratio remains high.

### Worked example

5   The input signal to a cable has power $1.2 \times 10^{-3}\,W$. The signal attenuation per unit length in the cable is $14\,dB\,km^{-1}$ and the average noise level along the cable is constant at $1.0 \times 10^{-10}\,W$. An acceptable signal-to-noise ratio is at least $30\,dB$.

Calculate the minimum acceptable power for the signal and the maximum length of the cable that can be used without a repeater.

**Step 1** The signal-to-noise ratio must be at least $30\,dB$. Hence, using:

$$\text{signal-to-noise ratio} = 10\,\lg\left(\frac{\text{signal power}}{\text{noise power}}\right)$$

we have:

$$30 = 10\,\lg\left(\frac{P}{1 \times 10^{-10}}\right)$$

continued ⋯⟩

where $P$ is the minimum acceptable power. Solving for $P$ gives:

$$P = 1.0 \times 10^{-7}\,W$$

**Step 2** A repeater is needed to regenerate the signal when the signal-to-noise ratio falls to $30\,dB$, i.e. its power is $10^3$ times the noise level, and this is $1.0 \times 10^{-7}\,W$. We can calculate the attenuation needed to reduce the signal to this level:

$$\text{attenuation} = 10\,\lg\left(\frac{1.2 \times 10^{-3}}{1.0 \times 10^{-7}}\right)$$

$$= 41\,dB$$

Hence the length of cable is $\frac{41}{14} = 2.9\,km$.

If the cable is $10\,km$ in length, the total attenuation is:

$$14\,dB\,km^{-1} \times 10\,km = 140\,dB.$$

The signal of power $1.2 \times 10^{-3}\,W$ is attenuated to a power $P$ where:

$$140 = 10\,\lg\left(\frac{0.0012}{P}\right)$$

$$P = 12 \times 10^{-17}\,W$$

You can see that the power in the signal is much smaller than the minimum acceptable power – it is even smaller than the noise level. The signal-to-noise ratio is now $10\,\lg(12 \times 10^{-17}/\,1.0 \times 10^{-8}) = -79\,dB$, smaller than the acceptable $+30\,dB$. A repeater is needed well before the end of the $10\,km$ of cable.

### Test yourself

13 A signal has an input power $5.0\,mW$ and an output power of $0.000\,2\,mW$. What is the attenuation in dB?

14 The attenuation of a $6.0\,mW$ signal is $30\,dB$. What is the final power?

continued ⋯⟩

**15** What is the signal-to-noise ratio when the signal and the noise have equal power?

**16** A signal of 1.0 mW passes through an amplifier of gain 30 dB and then along a cable where the attenuation is 18 dB.
  **a** What is the overall gain of the signal in dB?
  **b** What is the output power at the end of the cable?

# Comparison of different channels

Each type of signal channel has its good points and its disadvantages, which we will now consider.

## Wire-pairs and coaxial cables

The earliest telephones used a pair of wires strung on either side of a pole (Figure **33.13**). As the use of electricity became more common, the amount of electrical interference increased, causing crackle and

Figure 33.13 An early telegraph pole.

hiss on the line. The potential difference between the two wires is the signal. Each wire acts as an aerial, picks up unwanted electromagnetic waves and distorts the signal.

When two wires are close together, each wire picks up the same amount of electrical interference. There is no additional potential difference between the two wires and so having the wires close together reduces the interference. Figure **33.14** shows a twisted wire-pair with the wires close together. The connection from your telephone to a socket nearby is likely to use two insulated copper wires placed close together or, more likely, a twisted pair of wires.

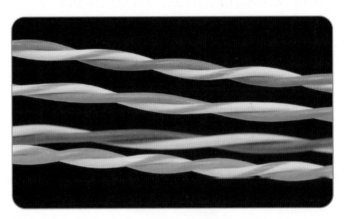

Figure 33.14 Twisted wire-pairs in a computer network.

A wire-pair is by far the cheapest transmission medium but it does have some disadvantages.

The changing currents in the wires themselves produce electromagnetic (EM) fields and this makes the wires act as aerials, radiating EM waves. The energy to emit these waves reduces the strength of the signal sent along the wire. As the frequency of the changing current increases, the emission of EM waves increases and so the bandwidth of wire-pairs is low. Energy is also lost in the wire due to electrical heating in the resistance of the wires.

Wire-pairs are often close together in a telephone system and EM waves pass from one wire-pair to another. This is the origin of some forms of cross-talk, where you can hear another telephone conversation.

Wire-pairs are easily 'tapped'. A connection made to each wire allows an unwanted person to hear a telephone conversation. The security of a wire-pair is low.

Coaxial cable, as shown in Figure 33.15, reduces the amount of cross-talk in wire-pairs when transmission occurs at high speed. The copper core and the finely woven copper wire or braid are the two conductors that transmit the signal. The braid is usually connected to earth, so, ideally, the potential of this wire does not change. Electromagnetic (EM) waves do not pass easily through metal and so the braid provides a screen or barrier that reduces the interference that reaches the copper core. An ideal coaxial cable also prevents any emission of EM waves at radio frequencies and has less attenuation than a wire-pair. Although coaxial cable is more expensive than a wire-pair, it can transmit data faster, over longer distances, and with less electrical interference. Coaxial cable often connects a radio transmitter to an aerial, as coaxial cable has a high bandwidth, which can exceed 100 MHz with a cable 30 m in length. It is also slightly more difficult to 'tap' into a coaxial cable than into a wire-pair.

Table 33.3 summarises the advantages and disadvantages of wire-pairs and coaxial cable.

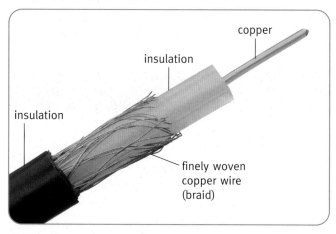

Figure 33.15 Coaxial cable.

| Wire-pairs | Coaxial cable |
|---|---|
| are cheap and convenient | is more expensive |
| strongly attenuate a signal | is less attenuating |
| have low bandwidth | has higher bandwidth |
| pick up some noise and interference | has less electrical interference and noise |
| suffer from cross-talk | has little cross-talk |
| have low security | is more secure |

Table 33.3 Comparison of wire-pairs and coaxial cable.

## Radio waves and microwave links

Radio waves can travel by a number of different paths from a transmitter to a receiver, as shown in Figure 33.16.

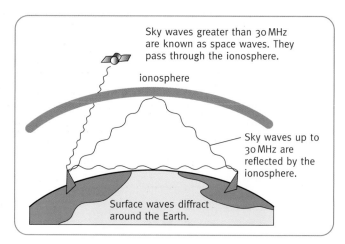

Figure 33.16 Radio wave transmissions.

Surface (ground) waves travel close to the surface of the Earth. Lower frequencies, up to 3 MHz, diffract around the surface of the Earth because of their long wavelengths; this gives them a long range of up to 1000 km. AM broadcasts in the medium-wave (MW) band and long-wave (LW) bands travel efficiently as surface waves.

Sky waves are waves above 3 MHz in frequency which are diffracted only a little by the Earth and travel almost in straight lines. Some waves at these frequencies travel for a short distance as surface waves, but they can only travel about 100 km in this way. Sky waves that travel in the atmosphere may be reflected from a layer of charged particles, known as the ionosphere. When these reflected waves reach the Earth's surface they may be reflected back to the ionosphere. Through multiple reflections by the ionosphere and the ground, sky waves can travel for large distances around the Earth. Because the density of charged particles in the ionosphere is constantly changing, the reflection of sky waves is not reliable. Short-wave (SW) radio uses frequencies in the high-frequency (HF) band that reflect from the ionosphere. Your radio set can receive distant SW radio stations at night, when the frequencies reflected by the ionosphere are not absorbed by other regions in the atmosphere.

Space waves are sky waves with a frequency greater than 30 MHz which pass through the ionosphere. The transmission is line-of-sight so, if the receiver and transmitter are on the Earth's surface, there must be a clear line between the receiver and the transmitter (not blocked by hills or mountains). Some police and emergency services, as well as television transmissions,

| | Frequency range | Communication method and waveband | Distance travelled |
|---|---|---|---|
| surface wave | up to 3 MHz | LW and MW radio in the LF band | up to 1000 km |
| sky wave | 3–30 MHz | SW radio in the HF band | worldwide by reflection |
| space wave | 30–300+MHz | FM radio in the VHF band, TV and mobile phones in the UHF band | line-of-sight |
| microwave | 1–300 GHz | microwave, satellite links and Wi-Fi in the super-high-frequency (SHF) and extra-high-frequency (EHF) bands. | line-of-sight except when retransmitted by satellite |

**Table 33.4** Data for radio and microwaves.

use space waves with frequencies above 30 MHz in the very-high-frequency (VHF) and ultra-high-frequency (UHF) bands. The boundary between radio waves and microwaves is not clearly defined, although frequencies above 1 GHz are generally described as microwaves. Microwaves are able to pass through the ionosphere to reach satellites in space. Bluetooth technology and Wi-Fi use microwaves for communication around the home. Using Wi-Fi, microwaves link your laptop to the main computer in your home.

Table **33.4** shows a summary of the frequencies used for the different radio transmissions and the distances travelled. The wavelength of any radio wave can be found using the formula $c = f\lambda$ where $c = 3.0 \times 10^8 \, \text{m s}^{-1}$, which is the speed of the radio wave and the speed of light. So, for example, a wave of frequency 1 GHz has a wavelength of:

$$\lambda = \frac{3.0 \times 10^8}{1 \times 10^9} = 0.3 \, \text{m}$$

The radio wave given out by a transmitting aerial travels in all directions. The atmosphere absorbs the wave, the amount of absorption depending on the radio frequency. The distance travelled by a radio wave therefore varies with its frequency. In some cases, the aerial focuses the radio waves towards the receiver by using an aerial shaped as a dish, as shown in Figure **33.17**. Without such a dish, the strength of the signal decreases strongly with distance.

The microwave tower shown in Figure **33.17** holds a number of parabolic reflectors or dishes. Each dish points towards a dish on another tower some miles away and they transmit microwaves back and forth between them. The transmission is line-of-sight and the height of the tower increases the distance of transmission.

The bandwidth available increases as the frequency of the wave increases. As microwaves have a high bandwidth, they can carry many telephone conversations at once. They are also very secure and difficult to tap into, as the beam of microwaves that travels between the two dishes is narrow and does not spread out. Until fibre optic cable was available, microwave links carried the majority of long-distance telephone conversations.

**Figure 33.17** A microwave tower.

To summarise, high-frequency radio waves and microwaves:

- have high bandwidth and can carry a large amount of information
- can be transmitted as narrow beams which are more secure
- are line-of-sight and often use a satellite or microwave link.

## Satellites and optical fibres

Transmissions on the LW and MW bands use a surface wave and do not travel further than about 1000 km. For long-distance communication, it is possible to transmit using a sky wave or using a space wave and a satellite.

Figures **33.1** and **33.18** both show a communications satellite in space. The satellite receives a space wave from a transmitter on Earth, the uplink, with a carrier frequency in the microwave region. Because the satellite can only reflect a tiny fraction of the signal sent from Earth, the reflected signal received back on Earth would be far too small. Instead, the satellite re-transmits the signal it receives as the downlink back to Earth, on another frequency and with more power than it received. If the downlink and uplink frequencies were the same, then the much larger signal sent from Earth would swamp the signal sent from the satellite, so different frequencies are used. The satellite transmits the signal back to an individual satellite dish back on Earth or to many dishes, over a wide area, particularly when broadcasting television programmes.

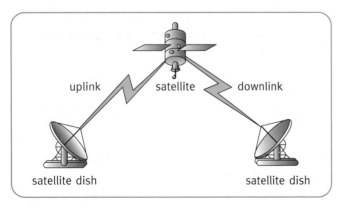

**Figure 33.18** A satellite system.

The first communications satellites used a frequency of 6 GHz for the uplink and 4 GHz for the downlink, but now even higher frequencies are used.

Here are some advantages of communication by satellite rather than by sky wave:

- The concentration of ions in the ionosphere is constantly changing and reflection of the sky wave is not always possible; sometimes layers in the ionosphere even absorb radio frequencies.
- The satellite boosts the signal for its return to Earth and provides a stronger signal than is obtained by reflection from the ionosphere.
- Satellite communication uses higher frequencies, which have higher bandwidth and can carry more information per second.
- Only a few frequencies in the MW and SW bands are available. More frequencies are available for communicating if a satellite uses higher frequencies.

In order to obtain a constant link between the satellite and the satellite dish on Earth, it is essential that the satellite dish always points towards the satellite. If the satellite moves across the sky, the dish must move to track the movement of the satellite. To avoid this problem many communications satellites rotate around the Earth in a geostationary orbit. They orbit the Earth in the same direction as the Earth rotates, at a height of 36 000 km above the Earth's surface. At this height, each satellite has a period of rotation of 24 hours. This means that each satellite naturally takes 1 day to orbit the Earth, exactly the time that it takes a point on the surface of the Earth to make one complete rotation. A geostationary satellite is also in orbit above the equator and it never appears to move when viewed from any point on the Earth. The satellite does not rotate with the same **speed** as a point on the Earth because its orbit is far larger than the circumference of the Earth.

There are many other satellites around the Earth. Some of these are in polar orbit. These satellites commonly travel above the North and South Poles in a time much shorter than a day. They are usually closer to the Earth than geostationary satellites and are used for surface observation and as weather satellites. At a commonly used height of 1000 km above the Earth's surface, the period of rotation around the Earth is only 100 minutes. Being closer to the Earth, polar-orbit satellites can see smaller detail when used for observation and espionage. As they orbit from the North to the South Pole, the Earth rotates underneath them and so they pass over the whole Earth in a 24-hour period.

There is always a delay in sending a message to a satellite because the satellite is high above the Earth. This delay can be annoying when talking by telephone. For example, if the satellite is directly overhead and the signal travels a distance of 72 000 km up to the satellite and then down to the other person, the time delay is 0.24 s. The reply from the other person also takes 0.24 s and so there always seems to be a delay of at least 0.48 s in the conversation.

Geostationary satellites used for communication can transmit to each other around the world but they cannot always receive from regions close to the poles, as the curvature of the Earth blocks the signal. The delay when communicating with a polar satellite is much smaller but you may have to wait until the satellite is overhead to transmit or receive.

The features of a geostationary satellite are:

- the satellite rotates with the same period as the Earth;
- the satellite is in orbit above the equator with a period of 1 day;
- the satellite appears to remain fixed in position above a point on the equator and so satellite dishes do not need to be moved.

Compared to a geostationary satellite, a satellite in polar orbit:

- travels from pole to pole, with an shorter period of orbit;
- is at a smaller height above the Earth and can detect objects of smaller detail;
- is not always in the same position relative to the Earth and so dishes must be moved;
- has smaller delay times.

An alternative for long-distance communications is the optic fibre, a very thin glass or plastic fibre that carries light or infrared. Optic fibres use glass and infrared for long distances, rather than plastic or light, as the glass can be very pure and does not absorb or scatter infrared. As optic fibres have very low signal attenuation, the distance between repeater amplifiers can be high.

Figure 33.19 shows a photograph of a number of optic fibres and the internal structure of one fibre. The three rays of light are totally internally reflected from one end of the fibre to the other.

When used for communication, an electrical signal causes a laser or a light-emitting diode (LED) to emit pulses of light or infrared, with a frequency of the order of $2 \times 10^{14}$ Hz or $2 \times 10^8$ MHz. Because the frequency is so high, the potential bandwidth available is also very high. The pulses of light or infrared provide the digital signal that passes along the fibre. With a cable containing more than a hundred fibres and each fibre carrying a large number of pulses per second, the whole cable can carry ten million telephone conversations at the same time.

**Figure 33.19** An optic fibre passing through the eye of a needle, and its internal structure.

optic fibre    cladding

Fibre optic cables have replaced the use of satellites for long-distance transmission. Just a few fibre optic cables running across the oceans and from city to city link almost the whole world and make the internet possible, the 'information superhighway'. The delay between transmission and reception is less than with a satellite as the distances travelled round the world by the signal are less than up to a satellite and back down again. The disadvantages of optic fibre are that an electrical signal must first be converted to pulses of light and the optic fibres are difficult to connect to one another as two fibres cannot just be glued together.

Compared to a metal cable, a fibre optic cable:

- has much greater bandwidth and can carry more information per second;
- has less signal attenuation, so repeater and regeneration amplifiers can be further apart;
- is impossible to tap, making the data it carries more secure;
- does not suffer from electrical interference and cross-talk;
- weighs less and so large lengths can be handled more easily;
- is immune to lightning and the effects of nearby power lines;
- can be used in flammable situations as no sparks are produced;
- is cheaper than the same length of copper wire.

## The public switched telephone network (PSTN)

The first telephones had no network but were just connected together in pairs. Without a network, you would need a different telephone in your house for every person that you call.

Nowadays each telephone connects to a network of other telephones, which cover cities, countries, and whole continents and make up the **public switched telephone network** (PSTN). Each telephone has a 'fixed' line connected to a local exchange and, if the call is not local, the exchange switches the connection to a trunk exchange. High-speed electronic circuits enable the actual switching. When the connection is to a telephone in another country, an international

gateway exchange makes the connection. The cable to the local exchange is usually a wire-pair but connections to trunk exchanges and international gateways are more likely to use fibre optic cable, because of the increased bandwidth.

Figure **33.20** illustrates the system.

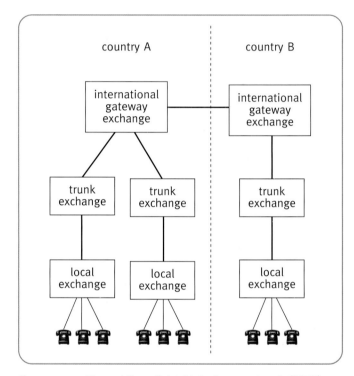

**Figure 33.20** The public switched telephone network (PSTN).

## The mobile or cell phone network

A **mobile phone** (or cell phone) contains a low-powered radio transmitter and receiver with a range of no more than 10 km. The system works with a network of small 'cells' covering the country, each containing a **base station**, somewhere near the centre of the cell, as shown in Figure **33.21**. Each base station can contact any mobile phone within its own cell on a number of frequencies. The mobile phone uses different frequencies to transmit a signal to the base station and to receive a signal back from the base station. This allows you to talk and listen at the same time when using a mobile phone. The number of frequencies is limited and this limits the number of different calls one base station can handle at any time. The size of each cell varies according to the geography of the area, as buildings and hills may block the signal, and according to the expected number of users.

Suppose that 700 different frequencies are available for a city. The actual number of frequencies used can be much larger if digital technology and high frequencies are used. Without a mobile-phone network, only 700 mobile phones can connect at once, a very small number. However, mobile phones in cells that are far from each other can share the same frequencies.

Each cell in a hexagonal array has six adjacent cells, so if the 700 frequencies are shared between seven different cells, each cell has $\frac{700}{7}$ = 100 frequencies available. As the base station transmits on one frequency and the mobile phone on another, the number of different calls possible within one cell is $\frac{100}{2}$ = 50. The power used in transmission is low and the radio wave does not travel far outside a cell, particularly as UHF and microwave frequencies are used. This means that frequencies used in one cell can be used in other cells, as long as the cells sharing the same frequencies are not adjacent. In Figure 33.21, cells of the same colour can use the same frequencies. In the system shown there are only four different colours and so all the available frequencies can be shared between four different cells. A large city can have thousands of cells and connect many mobile phones, although each base station only handles a small proportion of the calls at one time.

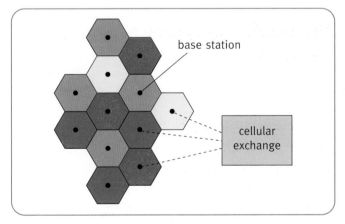

Figure 33.21 The cellular network.

Figure 33.21 shows the connection between a few base stations and the **cellular exchange.** In reality, every base station connects directly to the cellular exchange. Computers in the cellular exchange handle the allocation of frequencies and know all the mobile phones switched on at one time and which base station is nearest to each phone.

When you first switch a mobile phone on, the mobile phone sends an identifying signal and continues to do so at regular intervals. The cellular exchange selects the base station with the strongest signal and allocates a pair of frequencies for the mobile phone to transmit and receive using that base station. Each base station monitors the strength of signals from within its cell and adjacent cells. When a mobile phone moves into another cell, the cellular exchange recognises that the base station in the next cell is receiving a stronger signal and switches the connection to the next cell.

When a mobile phone starts to make a call to another mobile phone, the cellular exchange not only allocates the pair of frequencies that are used but also provides the link between the two base stations involved. Thus a connection is made from one mobile to its base station to the cellular exchange to the other base station and finally to the other mobile.

A connection also links the cellular exchange and the PSTN. When a mobile phone calls a telephone on a fixed line, the cellular exchange just connects the call directly to the PSTN.

Modern mobile phones use digital technology. The analogue voltage produced by the microphone passes through the stages shown in the block diagram in Figure 33.22.

The audio amplifier amplifies the signal and passes it to an analogue-to-digital converter. The analogue-to-digital converter samples the signal at regular intervals and, for each sample, produces an 8-bit binary number. The parallel-to-series, or parallel-to-serial, converter takes the 8 bits from one sample and places them after the 8 bits from the previous sample to produce a continuous series of binary digits. An oscillator provides the carrier wave at a frequency selected by the cellular exchange from the available frequencies at the base station. The digital signal modulates the carrier wave and the final signal passes to the aerial through the switch.

Reception of the signal is the reverse process, except that a tuning circuit selects only the one frequency

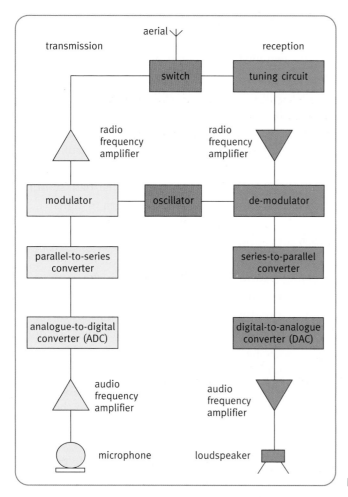

allocated by the cellular exchange for that mobile phone. The radio-frequency amplifier provides the amplification before demodulation produces a series of bits, which represent the signal in binary form. The series-to-parallel converter and digital-to-analogue converter produce an analogue signal. Amplification of the audio signal occurs and the final signal passes to a loudspeaker to produce sound.

**Figure 33.22** Block diagram of a mobile-phone handset.

## Test yourself

18 Explain why it is better to use a low-power transmitter in a mobile phone than a high-power transmitter that can reach all the cells in the mobile-phone network.

19 Describe the process of connecting one mobile phone to another.

# Summary

☐ Modulation varies either the amplitude or frequency of a carrier wave to carry information in the signal.

☐ Bandwidth is the range of frequencies present in a broadcast signal.

☐ FM broadcasts have higher bandwidth and sound quality.

☐ Analogue and digital signals transmit information.

☐ Analogue-to-digital conversion (ADC) turns analogue signals into digital signals and digital-to-analogue conversion (DAC) turns them back again.

☐ Regeneration removes noise and interference from digital signals.

☐ For good reproduction of a signal, the sampling rate and number of bits should be high.

☐ Wire-pairs, coaxial cables, radio waves, microwaves and optic fibres transmit signals.

☐ Attenuation of a signal is measured in dB, where number of $dB = 10 \lg \left( \dfrac{P_1}{P_2} \right)$.

☐ Satellites for communication are often in geostationary or polar orbits.

☐ The public switched telephone network (PSTN) connects fixed telephones and the cellular exchange of the mobile-phone network.

☐ A mobile-phone network divides an area into cells, each having a base station.

☐ The cellular exchange selects frequencies for use by the base station and mobile phone.

# End-of-chapter questions

1  **a** Draw a sketch graph of an AM wave and use your graph to explain how the AM wave has been formed from the carrier wave and a signal. Refer to the frequencies involved.
   **b** Draw a sketch graph of an FM wave and use your graph to explain how the FM wave has been formed from a carrier wave and a signal. Refer to the frequencies involved.

2  The output of a microphone is an **analogue** signal with a **bandwidth** of 3.4 kHz.
   **a** Explain what is meant by **i** analogue; **ii** bandwidth.
   **b** Compare the bandwidth of the microphone with the typical range of frequencies that can be heard by the human ear. Comment on the difference between the two values.

3  An LED provides input power of 1.26 mW to an optic fibre of length 60 m. The output at the other end of the fibre is 1.12 mW.
   **a** Calculate the attenuation in the optic fibre.
   **b** Calculate the attenuation per unit length in the optic fibre.

4  The signal attenuation per unit length of an optic fibre is 0.30 dB km$^{-1}$. An input signal to the optic fibre is 100 dB above the noise level. The level of the noise remains constant along the optic fibre at 6.0 pW.

   Calculate:
   **a** the power of the input signal to the optic fibre
   **b** the maximum length of the optic fibre used, if the signal at the end of the fibre is to remain at least 30 dB above the noise level.

5  **a** Describe the orbit of a geostationary satellite.
   **b** State a typical wavelength for communication between the Earth's surface and a geostationary satellite.
   **c** State **one** advantage and **one** disadvantage of the use of a geostationary satellite rather than a satellite in polar orbit for telephone communication.

6  Figure **33.15** shows a coaxial cable.
   **a** State and explain the purpose of the fine woven copper wire or braid.
   **b** Optical fibre has a larger bandwidth than a coaxial cable. Explain why increased bandwidth has reduced the cost of telephone calls to distant countries.
   **c** **i** Explain what is meant by electrical noise.
      **ii** State **two** causes of the noise in a copper cable.

7  Radio signals may transmit by surface (ground) waves, by space waves and by sky waves. State a typical value for the frequency and the maximum distance of transmission for each type of wave.

8  Whilst making a call using a mobile phone, the person making the call moves from one cell to the next. Explain how the cellular exchange enables continuous reception of signals to and from the mobile phone.

9  Why does a mobile-phone handset have a tuning circuit for reception but not for transmission?

# Exam-style questions

**1** The graph shows an amplitude-modulated radio wave carrying a signal.

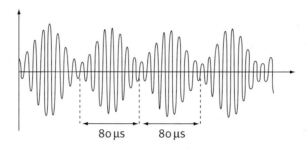

80 µs    80 µs

   **a** Determine the radio frequency of the carrier wave. [2]
   **b** Calculate the frequency of the signal. [2]
   **c** Draw the frequency spectrum of the modulated radio wave [3]

**2** The diagram shows the variation with time of a signal voltage, $V$, over a 5-hour period.

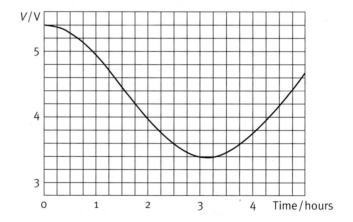

   **a** State the name of the type of signal shown in the diagram. [1]
   **b** The signal is turned into a digital signal with 4-bit binary numbers. The value of $V$ is (0000) when $V$ is 3 V and each subsequent binary unit represents an extra 0.2 V. Copy and fill in the table to give the value of $V$ as a decimal and a binary number for times of 0, 2 and 4 hours. [3]

| Time / hours | $V$/V (decimal) | $V$/V (binary) |
|---|---|---|
| 0 | | |
| 2 | | |
| 4 | | |

**c** The digital signal that is produced cannot be used to produce a perfect reproduction of the original signal.

    **i** Explain why this is the case. [2]

    **ii** Explain how the sampling process can be improved. [2]

**3** A cable of length 20 km signal transmits a signal from one end to the other. The attenuation per unit length of the cable is 10 dB km$^{-1}$. Four repeater amplifiers along the cable, each have a gain of 40 dB.

  **a** Calculate:

    **i** the total attenuation caused by the cable [1]

    **ii** the total gain caused by the amplifiers. [1]

  **b** The input signal has power 200 mW. Calculate the output power of the signal from the cable. [2]

  **c** Calculate the power output of the signal from the cable if repeater amplifiers are not used. [1]

**4** A communication satellite in geostationary orbit receives an uplink signal at a frequency of 14 GHz and transmits a downlink signal back to Earth at a frequency of 11 GHz.

  **a** Describe the key features of a **geostationary** satellite. [2]

  **b** Suggest a reason why different frequencies are used for the uplink and the downlink. [1]

  **c** The uplink signal has a power of 2 kW and the downlink signal 20 W. Suggest why the power in the two signals is so different. [1]

**5** **a** Suggest and explain why the mobile-phone network divides the country into a number of cells. [2]

  **b** Describe the role of the base station and the cellular exchange when a mobile-phone handset is first switched on, without a call being made. [3]

  **c** The block diagram of a mobile-phone handset during transmission contains a number of components. State the name of the two components which are connected to the parallel-to-series converter and explain their functions. [4]

  **d** Suggest why the radio-frequency connection from a mobile phone to a base station is a space wave on the UHF band or at microwave frequencies, rather than a ground wave. [2]

## Practical work in physics

Throughout your A level physics course you will develop your skills in practical work, and they will be assessed at both AS and A level. This appendix outlines the skills you will develop in the first year of the course; it includes some questions to test your understanding as you go along.

The sciences differ from most other subjects in that they involve not only theory but also practical work. The very essence of science is that theory can be tested by practical experiment. So the ability to carry out practical exercises in a logical and scientific manner is essential.

## Using apparatus and following instructions

You need to familiarise yourself with the use of simple measuring instruments such as metre rules, balances, protractors, stopwatches, ammeters and voltmeters.

When using measuring instruments like these you need to ensure that you are fully aware of what each division on a scale represents. If you look at Figure **A1.1** you will see that, on the first ruler each division is 1 mm and on the second each division is 2 mm. If you use instruments incorrectly, you may introduce errors into your readings. For example, when taking

a reading you should always look perpendicularly towards the scale and the object you are measuring, otherwise you will introduce a parallax error; this is shown in Figure **A1.2**. Looking from point A the length of the rod appears to be 21 mm, from point C, 25 mm and from point B, the correct position, the length is 23 mm.

We will look at errors and uncertainties in more detail later.

It is also important that you become familiar with setting up apparatus. Simple instructions will be given and the only way to be become confident with this aspect is through practice. You may be given a variety of tasks from setting up a pendulum system to measuring the angle at which a tilted bottle falls.

You must also learn to set up simple circuits from circuit diagrams. The most common error in building circuits comes where components need to be connected in parallel. A good piece of advice here is to build the main circuit first and then add the components which need to be connected in parallel. This is shown in Figure **A1.3**.

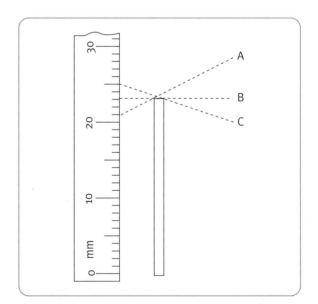

Figure A1.2

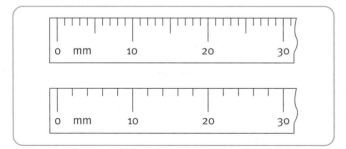

Figure A1.1

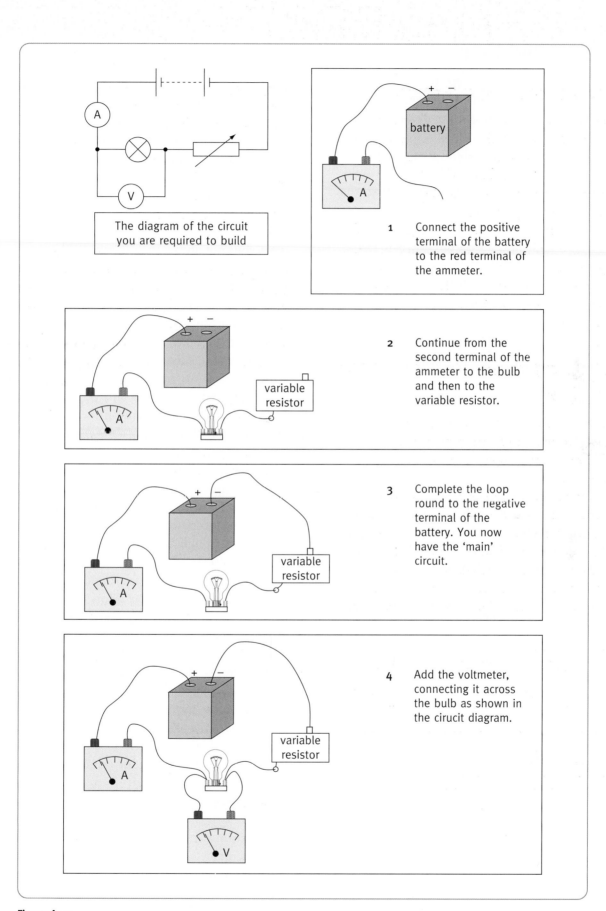

The diagram of the circuit you are required to build

1  Connect the positive terminal of the battery to the red terminal of the ammeter.

2  Continue from the second terminal of the ammeter to the bulb and then to the variable resistor.

3  Complete the loop round to the negative terminal of the battery. You now have the 'main' circuit.

4  Add the voltmeter, connecting it across the bulb as shown in the cirucit diagram.

Figure A1.3

# Gathering evidence

When gathering evidence you need to take into account the range of results that you are going to take. If you are investigating the extension of a spring with load, for loads of between 0 N and 20 N, you must take a fair spread of readings throughout that range. For instance, six readings between 12 N and 20 N would not be sensible because you are not investigating what happens with smaller loads. Equally, three readings below 5 N and three more between 15 N and 20 N omits testing what happens with intermediate loads.

A sensible set of readings might be at 0 N, 4 N, 8 N, 12 N, 16 N and 20 N. This covers the whole range in roughly equal steps.

## Test yourself

1 You are told to investigate how the current through a resistor depends on its resistance when connected in a circuit. You are given resistors of the following values:

50 Ω, 100 Ω, 150 Ω, 200 Ω, 250 Ω, 300 Ω, 350 Ω, 400 Ω, 450 Ω, 500 Ω

You are asked to take measurements with just six of these resistors. Which six resistors would you choose?

# Precision, accuracy, errors and uncertainties

No measurement can ever be perfect; there will always be a degree of uncertainty. It is important to think about this aspect of your measurements, and to reflect it in the way you present your findings.

We will first consider **precision**. If you make several measurements of quantity and they are all very similar, they will all be closely clustered around the average. The level of precision is high. However, if your measurements are spread widely around the average, they are less precise. This can arise because of practical difficulties in making the measurements.

Precision is reflected in how the results are recorded. If a distance is quoted as 15 m then it implies that it was only measured to the nearest metre, whereas if it is quoted as 15.0 m then it suggests that it was measured to the nearest 0.1 m.

Take care not to confuse precision with **accuracy**. A result is described as 'accurate' if it is close to the true value of the quantity being measured. You could make very precise measurements of, say, the diameter of a wire using a micrometer screw gauge (which measures to the nearest 0.01 mm), but the result could be inaccurate if the gauge has been incorrectly calibrated.

Whenever you make a measurement you should be aware of the uncertainty in the measurement. It will often, but not always, be determined by the smallest division on the measuring instrument. On a metre ruler which is graduated in millimetres we should be able to read to the nearest half millimetre, but beware! If we are measuring the length of a rod there are two readings to be taken, one at each end of the rod. Each of these readings has an uncertainty of 0.5 mm, giving a total uncertainty of 1 mm.

The uncertainty will not only depend on the precision of the calibrations on the instrument you are using, but also on your ability to observe and on **errors** introduced by less than perfect equipment or poor technique in taking the observations. Here are some examples of where uncertainties might arise.

• **Systematic error** – A spring on a forcemeter might, over time, become weaker so that the forcemeter reads consistently high. Similarly the magnet in an ammeter might, over the years, become weaker and the needle may not move quite as far round the scale as might be expected. The parallax errors described earlier are another example of a systematic error. In principle, systematic errors can be corrected for by recalibrating the instrument or by correcting the technique being used.

• **Zero error** – The zero on a ruler might not be at the very beginning of the ruler. This will introduce a fixed error into any reading unless it is allowed for. This is a type of systematic error.

Even with good equipment and good technique, so that the uncertainties introduced are negligible, difficulties and judgements in making observations will limit the precision of your measurements. Here are two examples of how the challenges in observation will determine the uncertainty in your measurement.

**Random uncertainties** occur when judgements have to be made by the observer. Look at the two examples below.

## Example 1

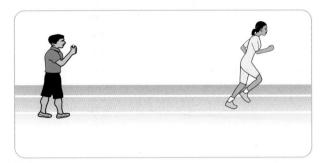

**Figure A1.5**

Tambo has a digital stopwatch which measures to the nearest one hundredth of a second. He is timing Nana in a hundred metre race (Figure **A1.5**). He shows her the stopwatch which reads 11.87 s. She records in her notebook the time 11.9 s. She explains to Tambo that he cannot possibly measure to the nearest one hundredth of a second as he has to judge both when the starting pistol was fired and the exact moment at which she crossed the finishing line. To do this to any closer than the nearest one tenth of a second is impossible.

## Example 2

Fatima is asked to measure the maximum displacement of a pendulum bob as it oscillates, as shown in Figure **A1.6**. She uses a ruler calibrated in millimetres. She argues that she can measure the displacement to the nearest millimetre. Joanne, however, correctly argues that she can only measure it to the nearest two millimetres, as not only is there the uncertainty at either end (0.5 mm) but she also has to judge precisely the point at which the bob is at its greatest displacement, which adds an extra millimetre to the uncertainty.

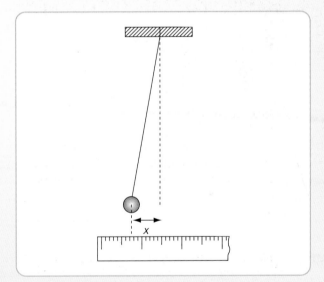

**Figure A1.6**

## Test yourself

2  Figure **A1.4** shows a lever-arm balance, initially with no mass in the pan and then with a standard 200 g mass in the pan.

Explain what types of errors might arise in using this equipment.

*continued* ⋯⟩

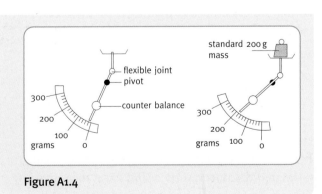

**Figure A1.4**

3 Estimate the uncertainty when a student measures the length of a room using a steel tape measure calibrated in millimetres.

4 Estimate the uncertainty when a girl measures the temperature of a bath of water using the thermometer in Figure **A1.7**.

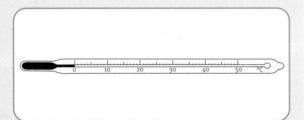

**Figure A1.7**

5 A student is asked to measure the wavelength of waves on a ripple tank using a metre rule which is graduated in millimetres. Estimate the uncertainty in his measurement.

6 Estimate the uncertainty when a student attempts to measure the time for a single swing of a pendulum.

## Percentage uncertainty

We have seen how to assess the uncertainty in a measurement. Percentage uncertainty expresses this as a fraction of the measured value and is found by taking the uncertainty, dividing it by the measured value and multiplying by 100%.

$$\text{percentage uncertainty} = \frac{\text{uncertainty}}{\text{measured value}} \times 100\%$$

For example, in Test yourself Q **6** you may have estimated the uncertainty as 0.2 s and measured the time as 1.4 s.

$$\text{percentage uncertainty} = \frac{\text{uncertainty}}{\text{measured value}} \times 100\%$$

$$= \frac{0.2}{1.4} \times 100\% = 14.3\%$$

This gives a percentage uncertainty of nearly 15%, which is very high. This could be reduced by measuring the time for 20 swings. In doing so the uncertainty remains 0.2 s (it is the uncertainty in starting and stopping the stopwatch which is the important thing here, not the accuracy of the stopwatch itself), but the total time recorded might now be 28.4 s.

$$\text{percentage uncertainty} = \frac{0.2}{28.4} \times 100\% = 0.70\%$$

So measuring 20 oscillations rather than just one reduces the percentage uncertainty to less than 1%. If the time for one swing is now calculated by dividing the total time by 20, the percentage uncertainty remains at 0.70%.

7 The depth of water in a bottle is measured as 24.3 cm, with an uncertainty of 0.2 cm. (This could be written as 24.3 ± 0.2 cm.) Calculate the percentage uncertainty in this measurement.

8 The angular amplitude of a pendulum is measured as 35 ± 2°.
   a Calculate the percentage uncertainty in the measurement of this angle.
   b The protractor used in this measurement was calibrated in degrees. Suggest why the user only feels confident to give the reading to within 2°.

9 A student measures the potential difference across a battery as 12.4 V and states that his measurement has a percentage uncertainty of 2%. Calculate the absolute uncertainty in his measurement.

# Recording results

It is important that you develop the skill of recording results in a clear and concise manner.

Generally, numerical results will be recorded in a table. The table should be neatly drawn using a ruler and each heading in the table should include both the quantity being measured and the unit it is measured in.

Table **A1.1** shows how a table may be laid out. The measured quantities are the length of the wire and the current though it; both have their units included. Similarly the calculated quantity, $\frac{1}{\text{current}}$, is included and this too has a unit, $A^{-1}$.

When recording your results, you need to think once more about the precision to which the quantities are measured. In the example in Table **A1.1**, the length of the wire might be measured to the nearest millimetre and the current might be measured to the nearest milliampere.

Note how '.0' is included in the second result for the length of the wire, to show that the measurement is to the nearest millimetre, not the nearest centimetre. Similarly the zero after the 0.35 shows that it is measured to the nearest milliampere or 1/1000 th of an ampere.

The third column is calculated and should show the same number of significant figures, or one more than the quantity (or quantities) it is calculated from. In this example the current is measured to three significant figures so the inverse of the current is calculated to three significant figures.

| Length of wire / cm | Current / A | $\frac{1}{\text{current}}$ /A⁻¹ |
|---|---|---|
| 10.3 | 0.682 | 1.47 |
| 19.0 | 0.350 | 2.86 |
| | | |

**Table A1.1** A typical results table.

## Test yourself

**10** A ball is allowed to roll down a ramp from different starting points. Figure **A1.8** shows the apparatus used. The ramp is placed at a fixed height above the floor. You are asked to

continued ⋯⟩

measure the vertical height $h$ of the starting point above the bottom of the ramp and the horizontal distance $d$ the ball travels after it leaves the ramp.

You are also told to include the square of the horizontal distance the ball travels after it leaves the ramp.

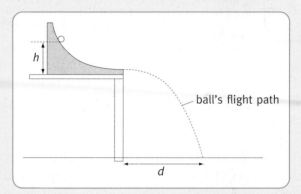

**Figure A1.8**

Table **A1.2** shows the raw results for the experiment. Copy and complete the table.

| $h$ / cm | $d$ / cm | $d^2$ / |
|---|---|---|
| 1.0 | 18.0 | |
| 2.5 | 28.4 | |
| 4.0 | 35.8 | |
| 5.5 | 41.6 | |
| 7.0 | 47.3 | |
| 9.0 | 53.6 | |

**Table A1.2**

# Analysing results

When you have obtained your results the next thing to do is to analyse them. Very often this will be done by plotting a graph.

When plotting a graph you may be told what to plot; however, the general rule is that the variable you control (the **independent variable**) is plotted on the $x$-axis and the variable which that changes as a result (the **dependent variable**) is plotted on the $y$-axis.

In the example in Table **A1.1**, the length of the wire would be plotted on the $x$-axis and the current (or 1/current) would be plotted on the $y$-axis.

You must label your axes with both the quantities you are using and their units. You must then choose your scales to use as much of the graph paper as possible. However, you also need to keep the scales simple. Never choose scales which are multiples of 3, 7, 11 or 13. Try and stick to scales which are simple multiples of 1, 2 or 5.

Plot your points carefully using small crosses; dots tend to disappear into the page and larger dots become blobs, the centre of which is difficult to ascertain.

Many, but not all, graphs you meet will be straight lines. The points may not all lie exactly on the straight line and it is your job to choose the **best fit line**. Choosing this line is a skill which you will develop through the experience of doing practical work.

Generally, there should be equal points either side of the line (but not three on one side at one end and three on the other at the other end). Sometimes all the points bar one lie on the line. This point, which is often referred to as an anomalous point, should be checked if possible. If it still appears to be off the line it might be best to ignore it and use the remaining points to give the best line.

In Figure **A1.9**, the line chosen on the first graph is too shallow. By swinging it round so that it is steeper, it goes closer to more points and they are more evenly distributed above and below the line.

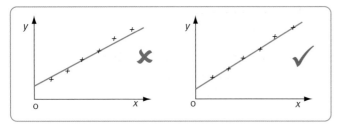

Figure A1.9

## Deductions from graphs

There are two major points of information that can be obtained from straight-line graphs: the gradient and the intercept with the $y$-axis. When measuring the gradient a triangle should drawn, as in Figure **A1.10**, using at least half of the line that has been drawn.

$$\text{gradient} = \frac{\text{the change in } y}{\text{change in } x} = \frac{\Delta y}{\Delta x}$$

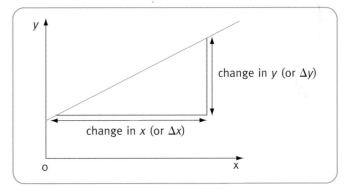

Figure A1.10

In the mathematical equation $y = mx + c$, $m$ is equal to the gradient of the graph and $c$ is the intercept with the $y$-axis. If $c$ is equal to zero, the graph passes through the origin, the equation becomes $y = mx$ and we can say that $y$ is proportional to $x$.

## Test yourself

**11 a** Use your results from Test yourself Q **10** to plot a graph of the height $h$ from which the ball is released against the square of the horizontal distance it travels before it hits the ground $d^2$. Draw the best fit line.

 **b** Determine the gradient of the line on your graph and the intercept with the $y$-axis. Remember, both the gradient and the intercept have units; these must be included in your answer.

## Curves and tangents

You also need to develop the skill of drawing smooth curves through a set of points, and drawing tangents to those points. When drawing curves you need to draw a single smooth curve, without any jerks or feathering. As with a straight line, not every point will lie precisely on the curve, and there should be a balance of points on either side.

In the first graph of Figure **A1.11**, the student has joined each of the points using a series of straight lines. This should never be done. The second graph is much better, although there is some feathering at the left-hand side. The third graph shows the sort of curve which is required.

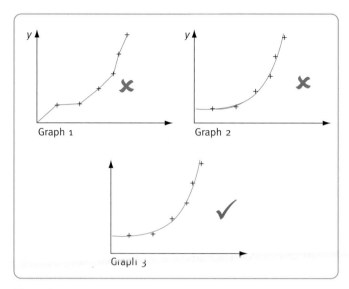

**Figure A1.11**

# Evaluating conclusions

No experiment is perfect and the ability to see weaknesses in the experimental setup and the techniques used is an important skill. Part of this is to be able to make sensible estimates of uncertainties and to recognise that the minimum uncertainty in the final results will be determined by the raw measurement which has the greatest percentage uncertainty. You should also take the opportunity to think of ways to improve the experimental technique, thereby reducing the overall percentage uncertainty. The following example illustrates this.

A student is asked to investigate the depth $D$ of a crater made when ball-bearings of different diameters $d$ are dropped into sand. He drops two ball bearings from the same height and measures the depth of the crater using a 30 cm ruler. The results are shown in Table A1.3.

| Diameter of ball bearing $d$/ mm | Depth of the crater $D$/ mm | $D/d$ |
|---|---|---|
| 5.42 ± 0.01 | 36 ± 2 | 6.64 |
| 3.39 ± 0.01 | 21 ± 2 | 6.19 |

**Table A1.3**

It is suggested that the depth $D$ of the crater is directly proportional to the diameter $d$ of the ball-bearing; in other words, the ratio $\dfrac{D}{d}$ is constant. Do the readings support this hypothesis?

The third column in Table **A1.3** shows calculated values of this ratio. The values are similar. They differ by 0.45, which is:

$$\frac{0.45}{6.19} \times 100\% = 7.2\%$$

So the measurements differ by 7.2% of the smaller value.

The uncertainty in the smaller measurement of the crater depth can be calculated as:

$$\text{uncertainty in } D = \frac{2}{21} \times 100\% = 9.5\ \%$$

The percentage uncertainty in the experimental results is greater than in the ratios. Therefore the experiment is consistent with the hypothesis, but we cannot say for sure that the hypothesis is correct. To do that we would need to greatly reduce the percentage uncertainties.

## Worked example

1  A student obtains data shown in Table **A1.4**.

| $x$/ cm | $d$/ cm |
|---|---|
| 2.0 | 3.0 |
| 3.5 | 5.0 |

**Table A1.4**

The first reading of was found to have an uncertainty of ± 0.1. Do the results show that $d$ is proportional to $x$?

**Step 1** Calculate the ratio of $\dfrac{d}{x}$ in both cases:

$$\left(\frac{d}{x}\right)_1 = 1.50$$

$$\left(\frac{d}{x}\right)_2 = 1.43$$

**Step 2** Calculate how close to each other the two constants are.

$$1.50 - 1.43 = 0.07$$

*continued* ⋯⇢

So the two values of $\left(\dfrac{d}{x}\right)$ are $\dfrac{0.07}{1.43} = 5\%$ different.

**Step 3** Compare the values and write a conclusion.

The uncertainty in $x$ is 5% so the difference in the two values of $\dfrac{d}{x}$ (5%) is just within the uncertainty of the experiment and so the relationship is supported.

## Test yourself

**12** A candidate obtains the following data between two variables $t$ and $r$ (Table **A1.5**).

| $r$ / cm | $t$ / s |
|---|---|
| 6.2 | 4.6 |
| 12.0 | 6.0 |

**Table A1.5** Data for Test yourself Q **12**.

The first value of $r$ has an uncertainty of $\pm 0.2$ cm, which is much greater than the percentage uncertainty in $t$. Do the results show that $t^2$ is proportional to $r$?

## Identifying limitations in procedures and suggesting improvements

The ability to criticise experimental procedures and then to suggest improvements is one that develops with experience. Table **A1.6** shows problems in the previous experiment, together with suggested improvements to the method.

| Suggestion | Problem | Improvement |
|---|---|---|
| 1 | Two results are not enough to draw a valid conclusion. | Take more results and plot a graph of $D$ against $d$. |
| 2 | The ruler is too wide to measure the depth of the crater. | Use a knitting needle and mark the sand level on the needle and then measure with a ruler. |
| 3 | There may be a parallax error when measuring the top level of the crater. | Keep the eye parallel to the horizontal level of the sand, or use a stiff card. |
| 4 | It is difficult to release the ball bearing without giving it a sideways velocity, leading to a distorted crater. | Use an electromagnet to release ball. |
| 5 | The crater lip is of varying height. | Always measure to the highest point. |

**Table A1.6**

It is worth making some points regarding these suggestions.

1  This is a simple idea but it is important to explain how the extra results are to be used. In this case a graph is suggested – alternatively the ratio $\dfrac{D}{d}$ could be calculated for each set of readings.

2  The problem is clearly explained. It is not enough to just say that the depth is difficult to measure.

3  It is not enough to just say parallax errors. We need to be specific as to where they might occur. Likewise, make sure you make it clear where you look from when you suggest a cure.

4  There is no evidence that this will affect the crater depth, but it might and is a point worthy of consideration.

5  An interesting point: does the crater depth include the lip or is it just to the horizontal sand surface? Consistency in measurement is what is required here.

# Summary question

This question is designed to illustrate some of the factors that are being looked for in the AS practical papers. It is not a formal practical question, but it is designed to simulate one and to take you through some of the steps.

The experiment explores the relationship between the period of a vibrating spring and the mass in a pan holder.

The candidate is instructed to set up the apparatus as in Figure **A1.12a**, with a mass of 200 g in the pan. The candidate is then told to move the pan downwards by approximately 1 cm and to release it so that it vibrates in a vertical direction.

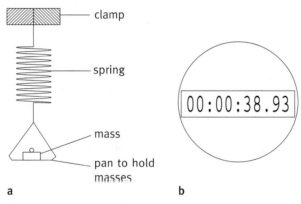

Figure A1.12

a   Record the time taken for 20 vibrations of the spring.
   The candidate is now required to repeat the procedure, using masses of between 20 g and 200 g until he has six sets of readings. To be included in the table are $\sqrt{m}$ and $T$, the period of the pendulum.
b   Suggest suitable values of $m$ to use in the experiment.
c   What points need to be considered when the table is drawn and completed?
   Table **A1.7** shows the table, as completed by a student.

| Mass / g | $\sqrt{m}$ / $g^{\frac{1}{2}}$ | Time for 20 oscillations / s | Period |
|---|---|---|---|
| 20 | | 12.2 | 0.61 |
| 50 | | 15.0 | 0.75 |
| 100 | | 18.7 | 0.94 |
| 150 | | 21.8 | 1.09 |
| 200 | | 24.5 | 1.23 |
| 190 | | 24.0 | 1.20 |

Table A1.7

**d** Copy the table and fill in the values for $\sqrt{m}$.

**e** List any mistakes the student has made in recording the results.

**f** Draw a graph of $\sqrt{m}$ (*x-axis*) against the time period (*y-axis*).

**g** Discuss your reasoning in choosing the scales for the graph.

**h** Comment on the errors the student has made when drawing the graph (Figure **A1.13**).

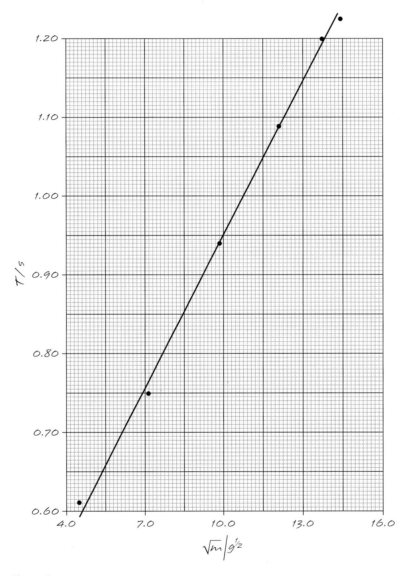

Figure A1.13

The student is now asked to calculate the gradient and to find the $y$-intercept. The calculation below shows how he found the gradient.

$$\text{gradient} = \frac{\text{change in } y}{\text{change in } x}$$

$$= \frac{(1.135 - 0.945)}{(13.0 - 10.0)} = 0.633$$

i  What must the student do to complete this answer?

j  Comment on the student's determination of the gradient.

k  The $y$-intercept is not on the graph. Suggest how this value could be found.

It is suggested that the relationship between the period and the value of $m$ is of the form:

$$T = C + k\sqrt{m}$$

l  Find the values of the two constants $C$ and $k$.

The practical work in the second year of your A level course builds on what you have covered in the first year. The examination will test you on two areas: planning experiments, and analysis and evaluation of your results.

# Planning

Although you should be thinking of experimental procedures from as soon as you embark on an A level course, if not before, by the time you complete the course you should be competent in planning experimental procedures.

There are different stages in planning an experiment.

## Defining the problem

It may seem obvious, but the first thing is to identify the problem. To do that you must identify:

• the **independent variable** in the experiment
• the **dependent variable** in the experiment
• the variables that are to be controlled.

For instance you may be investigating the response time of a thermocouple when it is used to measure changing temperatures, as shown in Figure **A2.1**. What are the variables here?

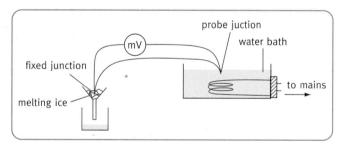

**Figure A2.1** Investigating the response time of a thermocouple thermometer.

The independent variable would be the temperature which is to be measured.

The dependent variable would be the time it takes for the reading on the thermocouple meter to reach a steady value.

There maybe several other variables that could affect the result. One might be the starting temperature of the thermostat 'probe junction', another is the

(fixed) temperature of the second junction of the thermocouple.

## Data collection

The next task is to think about how you are going to carry the experiment out. Once you have a method in mind you need to:

• Describe the method to be used to vary the independent variable.
• Describe how the independent variable is to be measured.
• Describe how the dependent variable is to be measured.
• Describe how other variables are to be controlled.
• Describe, with the aid of a clear, labelled diagram, the arrangement of apparatus for the experiment and the procedures to be followed.

In the experiment to investigate the response time of a thermocouple you may decide that the simplest way of varying the independent variable is to have a water bath and to vary its temperature. When the temperature has reached the required level, plunge the 'probe junction' into the water.

The procedure would be:

1 Measure the temperature of the water with a laboratory thermometer.
2 The reading from the thermocouple will be displayed on a millivoltmeter and the dependent variable, the time taken for the reading to reach its steady value, measured with a stop watch.
3 There are several different variables that need to be controlled. In practice you will only need to consider one or two.

    • The second junction of the thermocouple should be kept at a constant temperature by keeping it in contact with melting ice.
    • The probe junction should be cooled to the same temperature each time, again by holding it in the melting ice.

Your description of the experiment should be clear and concise. It sometimes helps to give the description in the form of bullet points or a numbered list. A labelled diagram will always clarify your description. In the experiment described here, the diagram shown in Figure **A2.1** would be sufficient.

# Method of analysis

This requires that you describe how the data should be used in order to reach a conclusion, including details of derived quantities to be calculated. In our example, we could plot a graph of the temperature of the water bath (*x*-axis) against the response time (*y*-axis).

How would we use the graph? If the graph gives a straight line through the origin, then we see that the response time is linear across the temperature range tested.

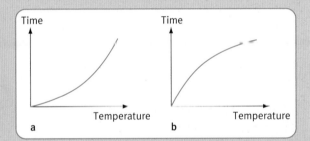
## Safety

You need to assess the risks of the experiment and describe precautions that should be taken to keep risks to a minimum.

In our example it is sufficient to mention simple ideas such as wearing goggles to protect the eyes when heating liquids, or ensuring that the water bath is stable and cannot be easily knocked over. The use of tongs to put the thermocouple junction into the bath is another example.

## Additional details

This tests your experience of doing practical work. Have you had sufficient experience to see things which will improve the experiment?

Here are some ideas that might be incorporated in the general description of the experiment:

- Stir the water in the bath so that it all reaches a uniform temperature.
- Use an oil bath to give a wider range of temperatures.
- Replace the water bath with different substances at their melting or boiling points so that the temperatures are more repeatable.
- Check the reading on the thermocouple voltmeter at the melting or boiling points of the different substances before carrying out the main experiment.
- Use a digital voltmeter so that it is easy to spot when the thermocouple reaches the steady temperature.

## Mathematical analysis of data

In Appendix **A1**, we saw how to rearrange simple equations into the form $y = mx + c$ and how to use a straight-line graph to find the constants $m$ and $c$. However, you also need to be able to deal with quantities related by equations of the form $y = ax^n$ and $y = ae^{kx}$. For these, you need to be able to use logarithms (logs).

In handling data, our aim is usually to process the data to obtain a straight line graph. Then we can deduce quantities from the gradient and the intercepts. Table **A2.1** shows the graph which should be plotted in each case, and the quantities which can be deduced from the graph.

| Relationship | Graph | Gradient | Intercept on *y*-axis | because … |
|---|---|---|---|---|
| $y = mx + c$ | $y$ against $x$ | $m$ | $c$ | |
| $y = ax^n$ | $\ln y$ against $\ln x$ | $n$ | $\ln a$ | $\ln y = n\ln x + \ln a$ |
| $y = ae^{kx}$ | $\ln y$ against $x$ | $k$ | $\ln a$ | $\ln y = kx + \ln a$ |

**Table A2.1** Choice of axes for straight-line graphs.

# A relationship of the form $y = ax^n$

A ball falls under gravity in the absence of air resistance. It falls a distance $s$ in time $t$. The results are given in the first two columns of Table **A2.2**. Notice that the unit for the logarithm is written as $\ln(s/m)$ and not $\ln(s)/m$ or $\ln(s)/\ln(m)$.

| Time $t/s$ | Distance fallen $s/m$ | $\ln(t/s)$ | $\ln(s/m)$ |
|---|---|---|---|
| 0.20 | 0.20 | −1.61 | −1.61 |
| 0.40 | 0.78 | −0.92 | −0.25 |
| 0.60 | 1.76 | −0.51 | 0.57 |
| 0.80 | 3.14 | −0.22 | 1.14 |
| 1.00 | 4.90 | 0.00 | 1.59 |
| 1.20 | 7.05 | 0.18 | 1.95 |

**Table A2.2** Results for Example 1.

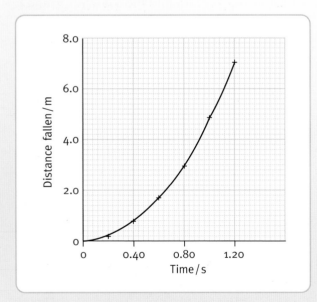

**Figure A2.3** A distance–time graph plotted using the data in Table **A2.2**.

A graph of the distance fallen against time gives the curve shown in Figure **A2.3**. This, being a curve, tells us little about the relationship between the variables. If, however, we suspect that the relationship is of the form $y = ax^n$, we can test this idea by plotting a graph of $\ln s$ against $\ln t$ (a 'log–log plot'). Table **A2.2** shows the values for $\ln s$ and $\ln t$, and the resulting graph is shown in Figure **A2.4**. (Notice that here we are using 'natural logs', but we could equally well use logs to base 10, written as 'lg'.)

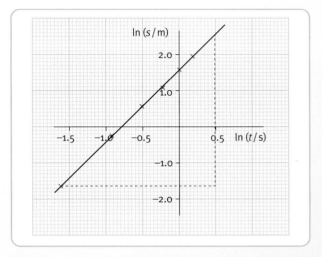

**Figure A2.4** A log–log plot for the data shown in Table **A2.2**.

From this graph the gradient is equal to the value of $n$, the power of $t$.

$$n = \text{gradient} = \frac{(-1.55 - 0.5)}{(-1.50 - 2.55)}$$

$$= 1.98 \approx 2.0$$

So the equation is of the form $s = at^2$. The intercept on the $y$-axis is equal to $\ln a$, so:

$$\ln a = 1.6$$

By taking the antilogarithm we get:

$$a = 4.95\,\text{m s}^{-2} \approx 5.0\,\text{m s}^{-2}$$

If we think of the equation for free fall $s = \frac{1}{2}gt^2$, the constant $a = \frac{1}{2}g$. But $g = 9.8\,\text{m s}^{-2}$ which is consistent with the value we get for our constant.

## A relationship of the form $y = ae^{kx}$

A current flows from a charged capacitor when it is connected in a circuit with a resistor. The current decreases exponentially with time (the same pattern we see in radioactive decay).

Figure A2.5 shows the circuit and Table A2.3 shows typical values of current $I$ and time $t$ from such an experiment.

| Current $I$/mA | Time $t$/s | $\ln(I/\text{mA})$ |
|---|---|---|
| 10.00 | 0.00 | 2.303 |
| 6.70 | 0.20 | 1.902 |
| 4.49 | 0.40 | 1.502 |
| 3.01 | 0.60 | 1.102 |
| 2.02 | 0.80 | 0.703 |
| 1.35 | 1.00 | 0.300 |

**Table A2.3** Results from a capacitor discharge experiment.

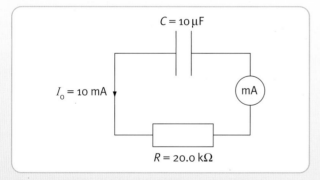

**Figure A2.5** A circuit for investigating the discharge of a capacitor.

The graph obtained from these results (Figure A2.6) shows a typical decay curve, but we cannot be sure that it is exponential. To show that the curve is of the form $I = I_0\,e^{kt}$, we plot $\ln I$ against $t$ (a 'log-linear plot'). Values of $\ln I$ are included in Table A2.3. (Here, we must use logs to base e rather than to base 10.)

The graph of $\ln I$ against $t$ is a straight line (Figure A2.7), confirming that the decrease in current follows an exponential pattern. The negative gradient showing exponential decay, rather than growth.

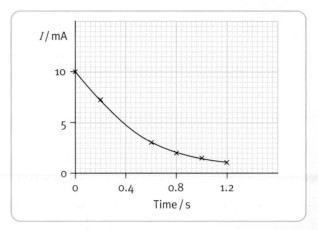

**Figure A2.6**

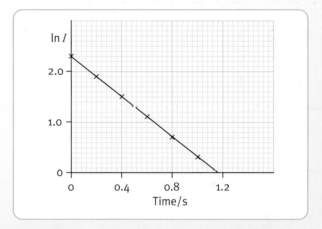

**Figure A2.7**

The gradient of the graph gives us the value of the constant $k$.

$$k = \text{gradient} = \frac{(0 - 1.16)}{(2.30 - 0)} = -0.504\,\text{s}^{-1} \approx -0.50\,\text{s}^{-1}$$

From the graph, we can also see that the intercept on the $y$-axis has the value 2.30 and hence (taking the inverse log) we have $I_0 = 9.97 \approx 10.0$ mA. Hence we can write an equation to represent the decreasing current as follows:

$$I = 10.0\,e^{-0.50t}$$

We could use this equation to calculate the current at any time $t$.

2 In the expressions that follow $x$ and $y$ are variables in an experiment. All the other quantities in the expressions are constants.

In each case, state the graph you would plot to produce a straight line. Give the gradient of each line in terms of the constants in the expression.

**a** $y = kx^{3/2}$

**b** $y = cx^q$

**c** $m = \dfrac{8x}{By^2}$

**d** $y = y_0 e^{kx}$

**e** $R = \dfrac{(y - y_0)}{x^2}$

3 The period of oscillation $T$ of a small spherical mass supported by a length $l$ of thread is given by the expression

$$T = 2\pi \sqrt{\frac{l}{g}}$$

where $g$ is the acceleration due to gravity.

Design a laboratory experiment using this expression to determine the acceleration due to gravity. You should draw a diagram showing the arrangement of your equipment. In your account, you should pay particular attention to:

**a** the procedure to be followed

**b** the measurements to be taken

**c** how to analyse the data to determine $g$

**d** any safety precautions that you would take.

# Treatment of uncertainties

All results should include an estimate of the absolute uncertainty. For example, when measuring the time for a runner to complete the 100 m you may express this as $12.1 \pm 0.2$ s. This can also be expressed as a percentage uncertainty (see Appendix A1); the percentage uncertainty is equal to $\dfrac{0.2}{12.1} \times 100\% = 1.65\%$. so we write the value as $12.1$ s $\pm 1.7\%$.

## Combining uncertainties

When quantities are added or subtracted, their absolute uncertainties are added. A simple example is that when measuring the length of a stick using a millimetre scale there is likely to be an uncertainty of 0.5 mm at both ends, giving a total uncertainty of 1.0 mm.

To combine uncertainties when quantities are multiplied or divided is a little more complex. You can only add or subtract quantities if they are in the same units; you cannot subtract current from voltage! However, you can multiply or divide them. To find the combined uncertainty in a case like this we add the percentage uncertainties.

1 The potential difference across a resistor is measured as $6.0 \pm 0.2$ V, whilst the current is measured as $2.4 \pm 0.1$ A.

Calculate the resistance of the resistor and the absolute uncertainty in its measurement.

**Step 1** Find the percentage uncertainty in each of the quantities:

$$\text{percentage uncertainty in p.d.} = \frac{0.2}{6.0} \times 100\%$$
$$= 3.3\%$$

percentage uncertainty in current

$$= \frac{0.1}{2.4} \times 100\% = 4.2\%$$

**Step 2** Add the percentage uncertainties
$$= (3.3 + 4.2)\% = 7.5\%$$

**Step 3** Calculate the resistance value and find the absolute uncertainty

$$R = \frac{V}{I} = \frac{6.0}{2.4} = 2.5\,\Omega$$

$$7.5\% \text{ of } 2.5 = 0.1875 \approx 0.2\,\Omega$$

The resistance of the resistor is $2.5 \pm 0.2\,\Omega$.

When you calculate the uncertainty in the square of a quantity then, since this is an example of multiplication you should double the percentage uncertainty. For example if $A = 2.0 + 0.2$ cm then $A$ has a percentage uncertainty of 10% so $A^2 = 4.0$ m$^2 \pm 20\%$; or using the absolute uncertainty $A^2 = 4.0 \pm 0.8$ cm$^2$.

## Uncertainties and logarithms

When a log graph is used and we need to include error bars (see uncertainties and graphs) we must find the logarithm of the measured value and either the logarithm of the largest or smallest possible value. The uncertainty will be the difference between the two.

## Uncertainties and graphs

We can use error bars to show uncertainties on graphs. Table **A2.4** shows results for an experiment on stretching a spring.

| Load / N | Length of spring / cm | Extension / cm |
|---|---|---|
| 0 | $12.4 \pm 0.2$ | 0.0 |
| 1.0 | $14.0 \pm 0.2$ | $1.6 \pm 0.4$ |
| 2.0 | $15.8 \pm 0.2$ | $3.4 \pm 0.4$ |
| 3.0 | $17.6 \pm 0.2$ | $5.2 \pm 0.4$ |
| 4.0 | $18.8 \pm 0.2$ | $6.4 \pm 0.4$ |
| 5.0 | $20.4 \pm 0.2$ | $8.0 \pm 0.4$ |

**Table A2.4** Results from an experiment on stretching a spring.

When plotting the graph the points are plotted as usual, and then they are extended to show the extreme values, as shown in Figure **A2.8**. Then the best fit line is drawn.

To estimate the error in the gradient we draw not only the best fit line but also the 'worst acceptable line'. This line is the worst line which goes through all the error bars, and is shown in Figure **A2.9**.

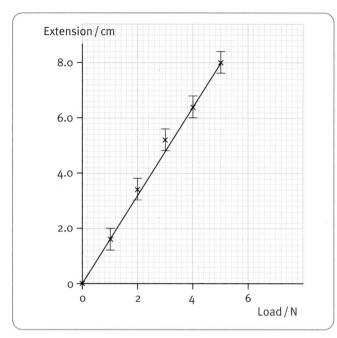

Figure A2.8 A graph representing the data in Table A2.4, with error bars and a line of best fit drawn.

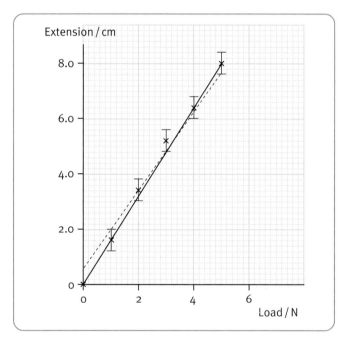

Figure A2.9 The same graph as in Figure A2.8, with a 'worst acceptable' line drawn (dashed).

The gradients for both best fit and worst fit lines are calculated and the error is the difference in their gradients:

error = (gradient of best fit line) – (gradient of worst acceptable line)

In our experiment, the gradients are:

line of best fit: gradient $= \left( \dfrac{8.2 - 0}{5.0 - 0} \right) \text{cm N}^{-1}$

$= 1.58 \, \text{cm N}^{-1} \approx 1.6 \, \text{N cm N}^{-1}$

line of worst fit: gradient $= \left( \dfrac{8.4 - 0}{5.0 - 0} \right) \text{cm N}^{-1}$

$= 1.4 \, \text{cm N}^{-1}$

So the uncertainty in the gradient $= 1.6 - 1.7$
$= \pm 0.1 \, \text{cm N}^{-1}$

The gradient is therefore: $1.6 \pm 0.1 \, \text{cm N}^{-1}$.

## Test yourself

6 Suggest why there are no uncertainties included in the measurements of the load.

7 It is suggested that $R$ and $r$ are related by the equation:

$R = ar^b$    where $a$ and $b$ are constants.

a A graph is plotted with $\ln R$ on the $y$-axis and $\ln r$ on the $x$-axis. Express the gradient and $y$-intercept in terms of $a$ and $b$.

b Values of $R$ and $r$ are given in Table A2.5.

| $r$ / mm | $R$ / $\Omega$ |
|---|---|
| $2.0 \pm 0.1$ | 175.0 |
| $3.0 \pm 0.1$ | 77.8 |
| $4.0 \pm 0.1$ | 43.8 |
| $5.0 \pm 0.1$ | 28.0 |
| $6.0 \pm 0.1$ | 19.4 |

Table A2.5 Results for Test yourself Q 7.

Calculate and record values of $\ln (R / \Omega)$ and $\ln (r / \text{mm})$ in the table and include the absolute uncertainties in $\ln (r / \text{mm})$.

c Plot a graph of $\ln (R / \Omega)$ and $\ln (r / \text{mm})$. Include error bars for $\ln (r / \text{mm})$.

continued ⋯⟶

d Draw the line of best fit and a worst acceptable straight line on your graph.

e Determine the gradient of the line of best fit. Include the uncertainty in your answer.

f Using your answer to **e**, determine the value of $b$.

g Determine the value of **a** and its uncertainty.

# Conclusions and evaluation of results

In the previous experiment we can conclude that the extension/load for the spring in this example is $1.6 \pm 0.2\,\text{cm N}^{-1}$. If a hypothesis is made that the extension is proportional to the load then there is enough evidence here for the conclusion to be supported, as a straight line can be drawn from the origin through all the error bars. If this is not possible then the hypothesis is not validated.

Now, suppose that the hypothesis is that the spring obeys Hooke's law and stretches by 5.8 cm when a load of 3.5 N is applied. The first part is validated for the reasons given above. However, an extension of 5.0 cm for a load of 2.5 N gives a value of $2.0\,\text{cm N}^{-1}$ for the gradient. This is clearly outside the range allowed for by the uncertainty in our measurements, and therefore the hypothesis is not supported.

# B  Physical quantities and units

Physical quantities have a numerical value and a unit. In physics, it is essential to give the units of physical quantities. For example, mass is measured in kilograms. Hence you might write the mass of the trolley as:

mass of trolley = 0.76 kg

It would be a serious error to omit the unit kg at the end of the numerical value.

The scientific system of units is called the Système Internationale d'Unités (or SI system). The seven **base units** of this system are listed in Table **B1**. Each of the units is carefully defined, but the definitions need not concern us here.

All other units can be derived from the seven base units. For example:
- volume is measured in cubic metres ($m^3$)
- velocity is measured in metres per second ($m\,s^{-1}$)
- density is measured in kilograms per cubic metre ($kg\,m^{-3}$).

| Physical quantity | Unit |
|---|---|
| mass | kilogram, kg |
| length | metre, m |
| time | second, s |
| temperature | kelvin, K |
| electric current | ampere, A |
| amount of substance | mole, mol |
| luminous intensity | candela, cd |

**Table B1** The seven base units of the SI system. (Note that you are not required to use the candela.)

## Prefixes

In physics, you will have to cope with very small and very large numbers. Numbers are written using powers of 10 to make them less awkward. This is known as **scientific notation**. Prefixes are used as an abbreviation for some of the powers of 10. For example, the height of a 5400 m high mountain may be written as either $5.4 \times 10^3$ m or 5.4 km. The prefixes needed for the CIE A level physics specification are shown in Table **B2**.

## Estimation

When you carry out an experiment or a calculation, it is sensible to look at the answer that you get (and the results of intermediate calculations) to see if they seem reasonable. The only way you can know if an answer is absurd is if you have an awareness of some benchmarks. Some suggestions are given below. Try to add to this list as you go through your physics course.

| | |
|---|---|
| mass of a person | 70 kg |
| height of a person | 1.5 m |
| walking speed | $1\,m\,s^{-1}$ |
| speed of a car on the motorway | $30\,m\,s^{-1}$ |
| volume of a can of drink | $300\,cm^3$ |
| density of water | $1000\,kg\,m^{-3}$ |
| weight of an apple | 1 N |
| typical current in domestic appliance | 13 A |
| e.m.f. of a car battery | 12 V |

| Prefix | pico | nano | micro | milli | centi | kilo | mega | giga | tera |
|---|---|---|---|---|---|---|---|---|---|
| Symbol | p | n | μ | m | c | k | M | G | T |
| Value | $10^{-12}$ | $10^{-9}$ | $10^{-6}$ | $10^{-3}$ | $10^{-2}$ | $10^3$ | $10^6$ | $10^9$ | $10^{12}$ |

**Table B2** Some of the prefixes used in the SI system.

## Data

Values are given to three significant figures, except where more significant figures are useful.

| | | |
|---|---|---|
| speed of light in a vacuum | $c$ | $3.00 \times 10^8 \, \text{m s}^{-1}$ |
| permeability of free space | $\mu_0$ | $4\pi \times 10^{-7} \, \text{H m}^{-1}$ |
| permittivity of free space | $\varepsilon_0$ | $8.85 \times 10^{-12} \, \text{C}^2 \text{N}^{-1} \text{m}^{-2} (\text{F m}^{-1})$ |
| elementary charge | $e$ | $1.60 \times 10^{-19} \, \text{C}$ |
| Planck constant | $h$ | $6.63 \times 10^{-34} \, \text{J s}$ |
| unified atomic mass constant | $u$ | $1.66 \times 10^{-27} \, \text{kg}$ |
| gravitational constant | $G$ | $6.67 \times 10^{-11} \, \text{N m}^2 \text{kg}^{-2}$ |
| Avogadro constant | $N_A$ | $6.02 \times 10^{23} \, \text{mol}^{-1}$ |
| molar gas constant | $R$ | $8.31 \, \text{J mol}^{-1} \text{K}^{-1}$ |
| Boltzmann constant | $k$ | $1.38 \times 10^{-23} \, \text{J K}^{-1}$ |
| electron rest mass | $m_e$ | $9.11 \times 10^{-31} \, \text{kg}$ |
| proton rest mass | $m_p$ | $1.67 \times 10^{-27} \, \text{kg}$ |
| neutron rest mass | $m_n$ | $1.675 \times 10^{-27} \, \text{kg}$ |
| $\alpha$-particle rest mass | $m_\alpha$ | $6.646 \times 10^{-27} \, \text{kg}$ |
| acceleration of free fall* | $g$ | $9.81 \, \text{m s}^{-2}$ |

*Note that this is the value of $g$ which you should use in examinations; $g$ varies significantly over the Earth's surface, with values ranging from $9.78 \, \text{m s}^{-2}$ at the equator to $9.83 \, \text{m s}^{-2}$ at the poles.

## Conversion factors

| | |
|---|---|
| unified atomic mass unit | $1 \, \text{u} = 1.661 \times 10^{-27} \, \text{kg}$ |
| electronvolt | $1 \, \text{eV} = 1.60 \times 10^{-19} \, \text{J}$ |
| | $1 \, \text{day} = 8.64 \times 10^4 \, \text{s}$ |
| | $1 \, \text{year} \approx 3.16 \times 10^7 \, \text{s}$ |
| | $1 \, \text{light year} \approx 9.5 \times 10^{15} \, \text{m}$ |

## Mathematical equations

arc length $= r\theta$

circumference of circle $= 2\pi r$

area of circle $= \pi r^2$

curved surface area of cylinder $= 2\pi rh$

volume of cylinder $= \pi r^2 h$

surface area of a sphere $= 4\pi r^2$

volume of sphere $= \frac{4}{3}\pi r^3$

Pythagoras' theorem: $a^2 = b^2 + c^2$

cosine rule: $a^2 = b^2 + c^2 - 2bc \cos A$

sine rule: $\dfrac{a}{\sin A} = \dfrac{b}{\sin B} = \dfrac{c}{\sin C}$

for small angle $\theta$: $\sin \theta \approx \tan \theta \approx \theta$ and $\cos \theta \approx 1$

$\lg(AB) = \lg(A) + \lg(B)$

$\lg(\frac{A}{B}) = \lg(A) - \lg(B)$

$\ln(x^n) = n \ln(x)$

$\ln(e^{kx}) = kx$

# Formulae and relationships

| | |
|---|---|
| uniformly accelerated motion | $v = u + at$ |
| | $s = \frac{1}{2}(u + v)t$ |
| | $s = ut + \frac{1}{2}at^2$ |
| | $v^2 = u^2 + 2as$ |
| simple harmonic motion | $a = -\omega^2 x$ |
| | $v = v_0 \cos \omega t$ |
| | $v = \pm w \sqrt{(x_0^2 - x^2)}$ |
| work done on or by a gas | $W = p\Delta V$ |
| pressure of an ideal gas | $p = \frac{1}{3}\frac{Nm}{V}<c^2>$ |
| hydrostatic pressure | $p = h\rho g$ |
| gravitational potential | $\varphi = \frac{-Gm}{r}$ |
| resistors in series | $R = R_1 + R_2 + \cdots$ |
| resistors in parallel | $\frac{1}{R} = \frac{1}{R_1} + \frac{1}{R_1} + \cdots$ |
| electric potential | $V = \frac{Q}{4\pi\varepsilon_0 r}$ |
| capacitors in series | $\frac{1}{C} = \frac{1}{C_1} + \frac{1}{C_2} + \cdots$ |
| capacitors in parallel | $C = C_1 + C_2 + \cdots$ |
| energy of charged capacitor | $W = \frac{1}{2}QV$ |
| alternating current or voltage | $x = x_0 \sin \omega t$ |
| radioactive decay | $x = x_0 \exp(-\lambda t)$ or $x = x_0 e^{-\lambda t}$ |
| decay constant | $\lambda t_{1/2} = 0.693$ |

**Key**

atomic symbol
name
atomic (proton) number

| Group 1 | Group 2 | | | | | | | | | | | | Group 3 | Group 4 | Group 5 | Group 6 | Group 7 | Group 0 |
|---|---|---|---|---|---|---|---|---|---|---|---|---|---|---|---|---|---|---|
| H hydrogen 1 | | | | | | | | | | | | | | | | | | He helium 2 |
| Li lithium 3 | Be beryllium 4 | | | | | | | | | | | | B boron 5 | C carbon 6 | N nitrogen 7 | O oxygen 8 | F fluorine 9 | Ne neon 10 |
| Na sodium 11 | Mg magnesium 12 | | | | | | | | | | | | Al aluminium 13 | Si silicon 14 | P phosphorus 15 | S sulfur 16 | Cl chlorine 17 | Ar argon 18 |
| K potassium 19 | Ca calcium 20 | Sc scandium 21 | Ti titanium 22 | V vanadium 23 | Cr chromium 24 | Mn manganese 25 | Fe iron 26 | Co cobalt 27 | Ni nickel 28 | Cu copper 29 | Zn zinc 30 | Ga gallium 31 | Ge germanium 32 | As arsenic 33 | Se selenium 34 | Br bromine 35 | Kr krypton 36 |
| Rb rubidium 37 | Sr strontium 38 | Y yttrium 39 | Zr zirconium 40 | Nb niobium 41 | Mo molybdenum 42 | Tc technetium 43 | Ru ruthenium 44 | Rh rhodium 45 | Pd palladium 46 | Ag silver 47 | Cd cadmium 48 | In indium 49 | Sn tin 50 | Sb antimony 51 | Te tellurium 52 | I iodine 53 | Xe xenon 54 |
| Cs caesium 55 | Ba barium 56 | La lanthanum 57 | Hf hafnium 72 | Ta tantalum 73 | W tungsten 74 | Re rhenium 75 | Os osmium 76 | Ir iridium 77 | Pt platinum 78 | Au gold 79 | Hg mercury 80 | Tl thallium 81 | Pb lead 82 | Bi bismuth 83 | Po polonium 84 | At astatine 85 | Rn radon 86 |
| Fr francium 87 | Ra radium 88 | Ac actinium 89 | Rf rutherfordium 104 | Db dubnium 105 | Sg seaborgium 106 | Bh bohrium 107 | Hs hassium 108 | Mt meitnerium 109 | Ds darmstadtium 110 | Rg roentgenium 111 | | | | | | | |

Elements with atomic numbers 112–118 have been observed but are currently unnamed

| | | | | | | | | | | | | | |
|---|---|---|---|---|---|---|---|---|---|---|---|---|---|
| Ce cerium 58 | Pr praseodymium 59 | Nd neodymium 60 | Pm promethium 61 | Sm samarium 62 | Eu europium 63 | Gd gadolinium 64 | Tb terbium 65 | Dy dysprosium 66 | Ho holmium 67 | Er erbium 68 | Tm thulium 69 | Yb ytterbium 70 | Lu lutetium 71 |
| Th thorium 90 | Pa protactinium 91 | U uranium 92 | Np neptunium 93 | Pu plutonium 94 | Am americium 95 | Cm curium 96 | Bk berkelium 97 | Cf californium 98 | Es einsteinium 99 | Fm fermium 100 | Md mendelevium 101 | No nobelium 102 | Lr lawrencium 103 |

# Answers to Test yourself questions

## Chapter 1

1  $\dfrac{10\,000}{1577.53} = 6.34\,\mathrm{m\,s^{-1}}$

2  **a** $\mathrm{mm\,s^{-1}}$
   **b** mph
   **c** $\mathrm{km\,s^{-1}}$
   **d** $\mathrm{m\,s^{-1}}$
   **e** $\mathrm{km\,h^{-1}}$

3  $2.0\,\mathrm{mm\,s^{-1}}$

4  $0.125\,\mathrm{m\,s^{-1}} \approx 0.13\,\mathrm{m\,s^{-1}}$

5  **a** Constant speed.
   **b** Increasing speed (accelerating).

6  For example, attach a card to a weight and drop it through a light gate. Alternatively, attach ticker-tape to the falling mass.

7  **a** Displacement
   **b** Speed
   **c** Velocity
   **d** Distance

8  $300\,\mathrm{m}$

9  The Earth's speed is $29.9\,\mathrm{km\,s^{-1}} \approx 30\,\mathrm{km\,s^{-1}}$. As the Earth orbits the Sun, its direction of motion keeps changing. Hence its velocity keeps changing. In the course of one year, its displacement is zero so its average velocity is zero.

10  Sloping sections: bus moving; horizontal sections: bus stationary (e.g. at bus stops).

11  OA: constant speed; AB: stationary; BC: reduced constant speed; CD: running back to gate.

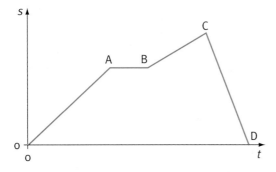

12  **a** $85\,\mathrm{m\,s^{-1}}$
    **b** Graph is a straight line through the origin, with gradient $= 85\,\mathrm{m\,s^{-1}}$.

13  **a** Graph is a straight line for the first 3 h; then less steep for the last hour.
    **b** $23\,\mathrm{km\,h^{-1}}$
    **c** $21\,\mathrm{km\,h^{-1}}$

14  **a** $7.0\,\mathrm{km}$
    **b, c** $5.0\,\mathrm{km}$; $53°\,\mathrm{E}$ of N (or $37°\,\mathrm{N}$ of E)

15  **a, b** $8.5\,\mathrm{km}$; $48°\,\mathrm{W}$ of S

16  $2.154\,\mathrm{m\,s^{-1}} \approx 2.2\,\mathrm{m\,s^{-1}}$ at $68°$ to the river bank

17  **a, b** $17.3\,\mathrm{m\,s^{-1}} \approx 17\,\mathrm{m\,s^{-1}}$
    **c** $43.9° \approx 44°$ to the vertical

## Chapter 2

1  $3.0\,\mathrm{m\,s^{-2}}$

2  $a = -0.60\,\mathrm{m\,s^{-2}}$

   The magnitude of the deceleration is $0.60\,\mathrm{m\,s^{-2}}$.

3  **a** $9.81 \approx 9.8\,\mathrm{m\,s^{-1}}$
   **b** $29.4\,\mathrm{m\,s^{-1}} \approx 29\,\mathrm{m\,s^{-1}}$

4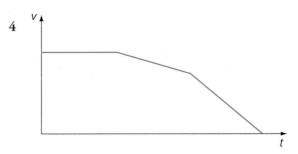

5  **a**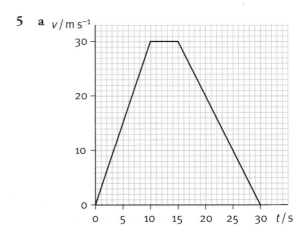
   **b, c** $3.0\,\mathrm{m\,s^{-2}}$
   **d** $-2.0\,\mathrm{m\,s^{-2}}$
   **e** From area under graph: $525\,\mathrm{m}$

**6** Dots evenly spaced, then getting steadily closer together.

**7** $u = 0.25\,\mathrm{m\,s^{-1}}$; $v = 1.0\,\mathrm{m\,s^{-1}}$; $\Delta t = 0.30\,\mathrm{s}$; $a = 2.5\,\mathrm{m\,s^{-2}}$

**8** $u = 1.0\,\mathrm{m\,s^{-1}}$; $v = 1.6\,\mathrm{m\,s^{-1}}$; $\Delta t = 0.10\,\mathrm{s}$; $a = 6.0\,\mathrm{m\,s^{-2}}$

**9**
 **a** $20\,\mathrm{m\,s^{-1}}$
 **b** $100\,\mathrm{m}$
 **c** $12\,\mathrm{s}$

**10**
 **a** $0.16\,\mathrm{m\,s^{-2}}$
 **b** $12\,\mathrm{m\,s^{-1}}$
 **c** $1200\,\mathrm{m}$

**11** $10\,\mathrm{m\,s^{-1}}$

**12** $64.3\,\mathrm{m} \approx 64\,\mathrm{m}$

**13** Speed $25.5\,\mathrm{m\,s^{-1}}$; just over the speed limit.

**14**
 **a** $t = 7.5\,\mathrm{s}$; $v = 220\,\mathrm{m\,s^{-1}}$
 **b** Approximately $20\,\mathrm{m\,s^{-2}}$

**15**
 **a** The car is slowing down with constant (uniform) deceleration.
 **b** $20\,\mathrm{m\,s^{-1}}$; $8\,\mathrm{m\,s^{-1}}$
 **c** $-0.40\,\mathrm{m\,s^{-2}}$
 **d** $420\,\mathrm{m}$
 **e** $420\,\mathrm{m}$

**16**
 **a**

| Time / s | 0 | 1.0 | 2.0 | 3.0 | 4.0 |
|---|---|---|---|---|---|
| Displacement / m | 0 | 4.9 | 19.6 | 44.1 | 78.5 |

 **b** Graph is a parabola through the origin.
 **c** $30.6\,\mathrm{m} \approx 31\,\mathrm{m}$
 **d** $2.86\,\mathrm{s} \approx 2.9\,\mathrm{s}$ (Check using $s = ut + \frac{1}{2}at^2$.)

**17**
 **a** $0.40\,\mathrm{s}$
 **b** $3.96 \approx 4.0\,\mathrm{m\,s^{-1}}$

**18**
 **a** $9.36\,\mathrm{m\,s^{-2}} \approx 9.4\,\mathrm{m\,s^{-2}}$
 **b** Air resistance; delay in release of ball.

**19**
 **a**

*h / m graph plotted against $t^2 / s^2$, a straight line through the origin.*

**b** $1.6\,\mathrm{m\,s^{-2}}$ (approx.)
 **c** This object is not falling on the Earth; perhaps on the Moon.

**20** Drop an object towards the sensor, but take care not to break it. A better method is to use a sloping ramp with a trolley; gradually increase the angle of slope. Deduce the value of the acceleration when the ramp is vertical.

**21**
 **a** $F_x = 17.3\,\mathrm{N} \approx 17\,\mathrm{N}$; $F_y = 10\,\mathrm{N}$
 **b** $v_x = 1.7\,\mathrm{m\,s^{-1}}$; $v_y = -4.7\,\mathrm{m\,s^{-1}}$
 **c** $a_x = -5.2\,\mathrm{m\,s^{-2}}$; $a_y = -3.0\,\mathrm{m\,s^{-2}}$
 **d** $F_x = 77.3\,\mathrm{N} \approx 77\,\mathrm{N}$; $F_y = 20.7\,\mathrm{N} \approx 21\,\mathrm{N}$

**22** $5\,\mathrm{s}$ (i.e. 1 s more).

In solving the quadratic equation, you will have found a second solution, $t = -1\,\mathrm{s}$. Obviously, the stone could not take a negative time to reach the foot of the cliff. However, this solution does have a meaning: it tells us that, if the stone had been thrown upwards from the foot of the cliff at the correct speed, it would have been travelling upwards at $20\,\mathrm{m\,s^{-1}}$ as it passed the top of the cliff at $t = 0\,\mathrm{s}$.

**23**
 **a**

| Velocity / m s⁻¹ | 30 | 20.19 | 10.38 | 0.57 | −9.24 | −19.05 |
|---|---|---|---|---|---|---|
| Time / s | 0 | 1.0 | 2.0 | 3.0 | 4.0 | 5.0 |

 **b**

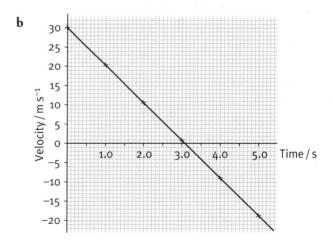

 **c** $3.1\,\mathrm{s}$

**24**
 **a** $3.0\,\mathrm{m\,s^{-1}}$
 **b** $78.5\,\mathrm{m}$

**25** a $5.14 \approx 5.1 \, \text{ms}^{-1}$

  b $0$

  c $0.524 \approx 0.52 \, \text{s}$

  d $6.13 \approx 6.1 \, \text{m s}^{-1}$

  e $3.21 \approx 3.2 \, \text{m}$

**26** $163 \approx 160 \, \text{m}$

# Chapter 3

**1** $1600 \, \text{N}$

**2** $40 \, \text{m s}^{-2}$

**3** $a = 2 \, \text{m s}^{-2}$

  $v = 10 \, \text{m s}^{-1}$

**4** Apples vary in mass; the acceleration due to gravity varies from place to place.

**5** a $\text{kg m}^{-1} \text{s}^{-2}$

  b $\text{kg m}^{2} \text{s}^{-2}$

  c $\text{kg m}^{-3}$

**6** a Base unit of pressure = $\text{kg m}^{-1} \text{s}^{-2}$

  Base unit of $\rho g h = (\text{kg m}^{-3}) \times (\text{m s}^{-2}) \times (\text{m}) = \text{kg m}^{-1} \text{s}^{-2}$

  Since the base units are the same, the equation is homogeneous.

  b Base unit of speed × time = $(\text{m s}^{-1}) \times (\text{s}) = \text{m}$

  Base unit of $\frac{1}{2}at^2 = (\text{m s}^{-2}) \times (\text{s}^2) = \text{m}$

  Since both terms have base unit m, the base unit of distance, the equation is homogeneous.

**7** Sides are 27.5 cm and 21.8 cm

  Area = $27.5 \times 21.8 = 599.5 \approx 600 \, \text{cm}^2$ to 3 sig. fig.
  = $0.0600 \, \text{m}^2$ to 3 sig. fig.

**8** a $6 \times 10^{-8} \, \text{A}$

  b $5 \times 10^{8} \, \text{W}$

  c $20 = 2 \times 10^{1} \, \text{m}$

**9** Estimated masses are shown in brackets.

  a (1.0 kg) 10 N

  b (1.0 kg) 10 N

  c (60 kg) 600 N

  d (0.025 kg) 0.25 N

  e 400 000 N

**10** The greater the mass of the car, the greater the force needed to slow it down with a given deceleration. For large cars, it is less demanding on the driver if the engine supplies some of the force needed to brake the car.

**11** Due to inertia, the driver continues to move forward although the car stops. A seat belt provides the force needed to overcome this inertia.

**12** The large one; its weight is greater, so it reaches a greater speed before air resistance is sufficient to equal its weight.

**13** a Lubricate the skis to reduce friction.

  b Wear tight-fitting, smooth clothing to reduce air resistance.

  c Develop powerful muscles to provide a large forward force.

  d The steeper the slope the better, to maximise the force of gravity.

**14** a The lighter one; lower terminal velocity.

  b Turn head-first and pull in his arms and legs to produce a streamlined shape.

**15** a Upthrust

  b Friction

  c Weight

  d Contact force (normal reaction)

  e Tension

  f Drag

**16**

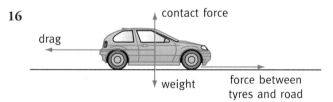

**17** a Going up    b Going down

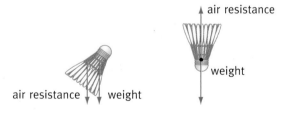

**18** a Force up on your foot and down on the foot that you tread on. Both forces are contact forces (normal reactions).

  b Force backwards on the car and forwards on the wall. Both forces are contact forces (normal reactions).

**c** Backwards force on car and forwards force **on ground**. Both forces are frictional forces.

**d** Upwards force on ball and downwards force on your hand. Both forces are contact forces (normal reactions).

# Chapter 4

**1 a**

force of parachute = 2000 N

direction of travel

weight of parachutist = 1000 N

**b** 1000 N upwards

**c** She will accelerate upwards (i.e. decelerate).

**2 a** Yes, constant velocity (not accelerating).

**b** 1000 kN

**c** 50 kN

**3 a** 2.5 N at 37° to vertical.

**b** No.

**4** With rope horizontal, the force pulling the box is $F$. With the rope at an angle $\theta$ to the horizontal, the horizontal component (= $F\cos\theta$) is less, since $\cos\theta$ is less than 1.

**5 a**

contact force

60°

30°

500 N

**b** 250 N

**c** It's at 90°.

**d** Friction; up the slope.

**6 a** $4.1\,\mathrm{m\,s^{-2}}$

**b** $2.1\,\mathrm{m\,s^{-2}}$

**7 a** 67 N

**b** 160 N

**8 a** 173 g

**b** By this method, weighing could be carried out with a limited selection of relatively small masses.

**9 a, b** $F_1$, 0 N m; $F_2$, 2.5 N m clockwise; $F_3$, 2.5 N m clockwise; $F_4$, 5 N m anticlockwise.

**c** Yes, the moments are balanced.

**10** $761\,\mathrm{N} \approx 760\,\mathrm{N}$

# Chapter 5

**1 a** Yes, work done against friction.

**b** Yes, gravity does work in making you go faster.

**c** No, because the stone remains at constant distance from the centre of the circle.

**d** No, because the force does not move.

**2** $1720 \approx 1700\,\mathrm{J}$

**3 a** 2500 J

**b** 2500 J (ignoring work done against air resistance)

**4** 20 kJ

**5** Work done by force up slope = 50 J; work done by contact force = 0 J; work done by force down slope = –15 J; work done by gravity = 35 J.

**6** 200 J

**7** $1275\,\mathrm{J} \approx 1300\,\mathrm{J}$

**8** 5400 kJ or 5.4 MJ

**9 a** Elastic potential energy

**b** Work is done on the magnets in pulling them apart. The potential energy in the magnets has come from chemical energy in the student.

**10** The motorcycle has more k.e.

**11** 10 J

**12** The result is unchanged for any value of mass.

**13** $7.1 \times 10^9\,\mathrm{J}$. This energy becomes increased energy of the air – its temperature rises.

**14** $14\,\mathrm{m\,s^{-1}}$

**15 a** 0.92 (92%)

**b** Converted to heat (because work is done against air resistance).

**16** $3.0 \times 10^6\,\mathrm{J}$ (or 3.0 MJ)

**17** 70 kW

**18 a** 28 000 J (28 kJ)

**b** 28 kW

**19** 560 W

# Chapter 6

**1 a** B

**b** B

**2 a** $10\,\text{kg}\,\text{m}\,\text{s}^{-1}$

**b** $5.0 \times 10^5\,\text{kg}\,\text{m}\,\text{s}^{-1}$

**c** $1.82 \times 10^{-23} \approx 1.8 \times 10^{-23}\,\text{kg}\,\text{m}\,\text{s}^{-1}$

**3** Momentum before = momentum after = $-0.5\,\text{kg}\,\text{m}\,\text{s}^{-1}$ (i.e. to the left).

**4**

| Type of collision | Momentum | Kinetic energy | Total energy |
|---|---|---|---|
| perfectly elastic | conserved | conserved | conserved |
| inelastic | conserved | not conserved | conserved |

**5 a** $+10\,\text{kg}\,\text{m}\,\text{s}^{-1}$; $-6\,\text{kg}\,\text{m}\,\text{s}^{-1}$

**b** $-6\,\text{kg}\,\text{m}\,\text{s}^{-1}$; $+10\,\text{kg}\,\text{m}\,\text{s}^{-1}$

**c** Yes.

**d** k.e. before = k.e. after = 4.5 J + 12.5 J = 17 J

**e** Relative speed before = relative speed after = $4.0\,\text{m}\,\text{s}^{-1}$

**6 a**

**b** $0.40\,\text{m}\,\text{s}^{-1}$, in reverse direction.

**7 a** If you consider the star to be stationary before exploding, the star has zero momentum. After the explosion, matter flies off in all directions – equal amounts of momentum are created in all directions, so their (vector) sum is zero. Momentum is conserved.

**b** You give downward momentum to the Earth; as you slow down, so does the Earth; as you start to fall back down, the Earth starts to 'fall' back up towards you. At all times, your momentum is equal and opposite to that of the Earth, so combined momentum is zero, i.e. conserved.

**8** Change in momentum of ball = $1.08\,\text{kg}\,\text{m}\,\text{s}^{-1}$; Change in k.e. = $-0.162\,\text{J}$. The wall has gained momentum. The ball has lost energy to internal energy (thermal energy) of the ball and air.

**9 a** change in momentum = $1.4 \times 10^4\,\text{kg}\,\text{m}\,\text{s}^{-1}$

**b** $933\,\text{N} \approx 930\,\text{N}$

**10 a** $60\,\text{kg}\,\text{m}\,\text{s}^{-1}$ (or 60 N s)

**b** In the direction of the kicking force.

**11** 50 N (bouncing: greater force because of greater change in momentum).

**12** $1.77 \times 10^3\,\text{N} \approx 1.8\,\text{kN}$

# Chapter 7

**1** $8.89\,\text{g}\,\text{cm}^{-3} = 8890\,\text{kg}\,\text{m}^{-3}$

**2** 111 kg

**3** 20 kPa

**4** Taking weight = 600 N, area of feet = $500\,\text{cm}^2 = 0.05\,\text{m}^2$, pressure = 12 kPa.

**5** The pressure due to the water varies between $7.85 \times 10^3\,\text{Pa}$ and $2.35 \times 10^4\,\text{Pa}$. The total maximum pressure = $1.25 \times 10^5\,\text{Pa}$.

**6** 7900 m. This figure is too small because it assumes the density of the air is constant. In fact density decreases with height.

**7** **Solid:** small spacing, well ordered in a lattice structure, no motion except lattice vibrations.

**Liquid:** small spacing but some gaps, less well ordered, motion fairly slow.

**Gas:** large spacing, no order, faster and random motion.

**8** The distance between the atoms increases on expansion. Each atom is likely to stay the same in volume.

**9** $\frac{1}{2}MV^2 = \frac{1}{2}mv^2$

$$\frac{v}{V} = \sqrt{\frac{M}{m}}$$

Since $M \gg m$, it follows that $v \gg V$.

**10** Different numbers of molecules hit one side than the other; the number of molecules striking any area per second will vary; the speed of the molecules hitting will vary; the angle that the molecules hit the smoke particle will vary.

**11** The small dots of light (smoke particles) move faster and more erratically. At higher temperature the molecules of air are moving faster and on impact cause a greater change in momentum of the smoke particle.

**12** Pressure increases because more molecules are hitting unit area of the tyre per second. The molecules have the same speed and each collision causes the same impulse or change in momentum. Since more molecules hit per second the rate of change of momentum, i.e. the force, increases.

**13** At higher temperatures the molecules have higher internal energy and move faster. The number of collisions per second increases and the change in momentum of each collision also increases. For both these reasons the rate of change of momentum of the molecules increases. The force on the wall is equal and opposite to the rate of change of momentum of the molecules. As the force increases the pressure inside the can may cause it to explode.

**14** Kinetic energy of the solid atoms increases. This increases their vibration in the lattice. Eventually they vibrate fast enough to break free from neighbouring atoms.

**15** It requires energy to break free from the force between neighbouring molecules. Only those molecules with enough energy can escape.

**16** The average kinetic energy of molecules increases with temperature. At higher temperatures more molecules have enough energy to escape.

# Chapter 8

**1**　**a** D
　　**b** A
　　**c** C

**2** Metals from most stiff to least stiff:

| | Metal | Young modulus / GPa |
|---|---|---|
| Most stiff | steel | 210 |
| | iron (wrought) | 200 |
| | copper | 130 |
| | brass | 90–110 |
| | aluminium | 70 |
| | tin | 50 |
| Least stiff | lead | 18 |

**3** Stiffest non-metal is glass (Young modulus = 70–80 GPa).

**4** A, 15 GPa; B, 5.0 GPa

**5** $1.0 \times 10^8$ Pa, $5.0 \times 10^{-4}$ (0.05%), $2.0 \times 10^{11}$ Pa

**6** $9.79 \times 10^{-5}$ m $\approx 9.8 \times 10^{-5}$ m

**7** Stress = $8.0 \times 10^6$ Pa; strain = $1.25 \times 10^{-3}$ (at most); Young modulus = $6.4 \times 10^9$ Pa (but could be more, because extension may be less than 1 mm).

**8**　**a** Small loads, iron bath is elastic. Large loads, the cast iron is brittle and breaks.
　　**b** At high pressure (load) the aluminium undergoes plastic deformation: it is ductile.

**9**　**a** 50 GPa, 150 MPa
　　**b** 100 GPa, 130 MPa
　　**c** 25 GPa, 100 MPa

**10** 1.08 J $\approx$ 1.1 J

The rubber band is assumed to obey Hooke's law; hence the answer is an estimate.

**11** $9.6 \times 10^{-3}$ J

**12**　**a** A has greater stiffness (less extension per unit force).
　　**b** A requires greater force to break (line continues to higher force value).
　　**c** B requires greater amount of work done to break (larger area under graph).

# Chapter 9

**1**　**a** Diagram **i** shows positive charges repelling.
　　**b** Diagram **iii** shows negative charges repelling.
　　**c** Diagram **ii** shows opposite charges attracting.

**2**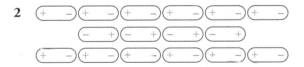

**3** The field strength is greatest at the top/pointed part of the building. The electric field lines are closest together here.

**4**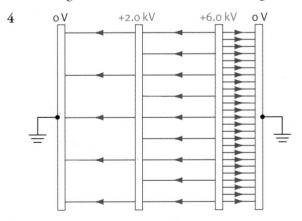

**5** $7500\,\text{N}\,\text{C}^{-1}$ downwards

**6** $2500\,\text{V}\,\text{m}^{-1} = 2500\,\text{N}\,\text{C}^{-1}$

**7** $5000\,\text{V}\,\text{m}^{-1}$ or $\text{N}\,\text{C}^{-1}$

**8**  **a** $160\,000\,\text{V}$
    **b** $0.08\,\text{mm}$
    **c** $400\,\text{MV}$

**9**  **a**

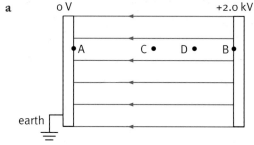

    **b** $2.0\,\text{kV}$
    **c** $8.0\,\text{kV}\,\text{m}^{-1}$ at both.
    **d** $0.04\,\text{N}$ to the left.

**10** $5.0 \times 10^4\,\text{V}\,\text{m}^{-1}$ or $\text{N}\,\text{C}^{-1}$; $0.10\,\text{N}$

**11** $8.8 \times 10^{17}\,\text{m}\,\text{s}^{-2}$

**12**  **a**

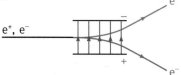

    **b**

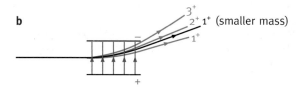

Ions with a greater mass will show smaller deflection.
Ions with greater charge will have greater deflection.

# Chapter 10

**1** To the right

**2**

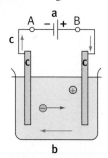

**3** $6.0\,\text{C}$

**4** $5\,\text{A}$

**5** $2.5\,\text{A}$

**6**  **a** $15$ minutes
    **b** $180\,000\,\text{C}$

**7** $6.25 \times 10^{18}$ protons

**8** $0.33\,\text{A}$

**9** $60\,\text{W}$ lamp. It allows less current through for the same potential difference (power is current $\times$ potential difference so, applying Ohm's law $P = \dfrac{V^2}{R}$, so power is inversely proportional to resistance).

**10**  **a** $50\,\text{V}$
    **b** $100\,\text{V}$

**11** $575\,\Omega$

**12** $2.5\,\Omega$

**13** $0.26\,\text{A}$

**14** $1.0 \times 10^9\,\text{W}$ ($1000\,\text{MW}$ or $1\,\text{GW}$)

**15**  **a** $43\,\text{A}$
    **b** $45$ to $50\,\text{A}$

**16** $0.45\,\text{mW}$

**17**  **a** $0.065\,\text{A}$
    **b** $3500\,\Omega$

**18** $540\,\Omega$

**19** $2\,160\,000\,\text{J}$ or $2.16\,\text{MJ}$

**20**  **a** $200\,\text{C}$
    **b** $2.0\,\text{J}\,\text{C}^{-1}$
    **c** $2.0\,\text{V}$

# Chapter 11

**1** $4.5\,\text{A}$

**2** $1.5\,\text{A}$ towards P

**3** $\Sigma I_{\text{in}} = 6.5\,\text{A}$, $\Sigma I_{\text{out}} = 6.5\,\text{A}$; yes Kirchhoff's law is satisfied.

**4** $I_x = -2.0\,\text{A}$, which means the current is towards P.

**5** $8.0\,\text{V}$; $80\,\Omega$

**6**  **a** The loop containing the $5\,\text{V}$ cell at the top, the $10\,\Omega$ resistor with current $I$, and the central $5\,\text{V}$ cell, as the only current involved is $I$.
    **b** $1.0\,\text{A}$

**7** $18\,\Omega$

**8** In series the 1 C charge passes through both batteries and gains or loses 6 J in both. If they are connected back to front it gains energy in one cell but lose it in the other. In parallel, half the charge flows through one battery and half through the other so the total energy gained is 6 J.

**9** $A_1 = 0.50\,A$, $A_2 = 0.25\,A$, $A_3 = 0.25\,A$.

**10** $20\,\Omega$

**11** $0.8\,V$

**12 a** All five in series.
   **b** All five in parallel OR three in series, then two facing in the opposite direction.
   **c** Four in series then one facing in the opposite direction, OR two in parallel to two more in parallel in series with first pair, then single cell in series with the two sets in parallel.

**13** $2.5\,\Omega$

**14 a** $300\,\Omega$
   **b** $67\,\Omega$
   **c** $120\,\Omega$

**15 a** $0.024\,A$
   **b** $0.008\,A$
   **c** $0.036\,A$

**16** Total resistances possible are: $40\,\Omega$, $50\,\Omega$, $67\,\Omega$, $75\,\Omega$, $100\,\Omega$ (two ways), $167\,\Omega$, $200\,\Omega$, $250\,\Omega$, $300\,\Omega$ and $400\,\Omega$

**17** $10\,\Omega$

**18** $0.50\,A$

**19** $0.95\,A$

**20** $20\,\Omega$

**21** Two in series, connected with two in parallel.

**22** A, $6.0\,A$; B, $6.0\,A$; C, $1.0\,A$; D, $5.0\,A$; E, $6.0\,A$

**23 a** $0.10\,A$
   **b** $0.095\,A$

# Chapter 12

**1 a** *I* / A

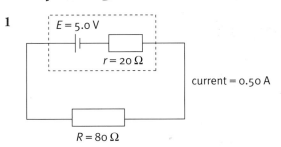

**b** All except point at 7.9; ignore this one.
   **c** $48\,\Omega$
   **d** Yes

**2** At $2.0\,V$, $R = 200\,\Omega$; at $8.0\,V$, $R = 133\,\Omega$. No, it does not obey Ohm's law.

**3 a** $\theta_1$, $12.5\,\Omega$; $\theta_2$, $10\,\Omega$.
   **b** $\theta_1$ is the higher temperature.

**4 a** Filament lamp is A, steel wire is B.
   **b** $8.0\,V$
   **c** $2.4\,\Omega$

**5 a i** $3.1\,k\Omega$
   **ii** $1.5\,k\Omega$
   **b i** $5\,°C$
   **ii** $36\,°C$

**6** The lamp will become brighter because the resistance of the thermistor decreases. This reduces the total resistance in the circuit and therefore the current increases.

**7 a** A thermistor's resistance changes more per degree of temperature change than a metal wire.
   **b** A Metal wire will work over a much wider range than a thermistor.

**8 a** $0.45\,m$
   **b** $2.2\,m$
   **c** $4.5\,m$

**9** $0.11\,\Omega$

**10 a** $2.5\,\Omega$
   **b** $2.0\,\Omega$

**11** $40\,\Omega$. The resistance increases by a factor of four (because cross-sectional area has halved and length doubled).

# Chapter 13

**1**

$E = 5.0\,V$

$r = 20\,\Omega$

current $= 0.50\,A$

$R = 80\,\Omega$

**2 a** $0.125\,A$, $0.5\,V$, $2.5\,V$
   **b** $0.33\,A$, $1.33\,V$, $1.67\,V$

**3** $2.5\,A$

**4** $0.71\,\Omega$

**5** $1.5\,V$, $0.5\,\Omega$

**6  a** $8\,V$
    **b** $4\,\Omega$
    **c** $16\,W$

**7** $0$ to $8\,V$

**8** $20\,°C$, $9.5\,V$; $60\,°C$, $0.91\,V$

**9** The resistance of the LDR decreases so the output voltage decreases.

**10** $6\,V$ in full sunlight; $12\,V$ (just under) in darkness.

**11**

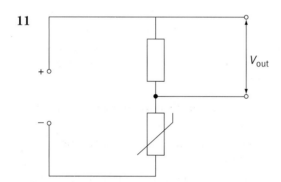

**12  a** $0.04\,V$, $25\,cm$
    **b** $1.48\,V$, the driver cell will have internal resistance and it is supplying current to the potentiometer wire. Therefore the p.d. across its terminals, and the wire will be slightly less than the e.m.f. ($4.0\,V$) of the cell.
    **c** $1.459\,V \approx 1.46\,V$

# Chapter 14

**1  a** $15\,cm$, $4.0\,cm$
    **b** $20\,cm$, $2.0\,cm$

**2** $80\,Hz$

**3**

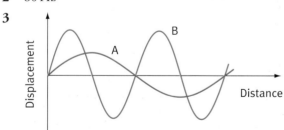

**4  a** $7.96\,W\,m^{-2} \approx 8.0\,W\,m^{-2}$
    **b** $1.99\,W\,m^{-2} \approx 2.0\,W\,m^{-2}$

**5  a** $1600\,W\,m^{-2}$
    **b** $2.5\,cm$

**6** $20\,240\,Hz \approx 20\,kHz$

**7** $89.6\,m\,s^{-1} \approx 90\,m\,s^{-1}$

**8  a** $5.0\,cm$
    **b** $30\,Hz$
    **c** $1.5\,m\,s^{-1}$

**9**

| Station | Wavelength / m | Frequency / MHz |
|---|---|---|
| Radio A (FM) | 3.07 | 97.6 |
| Radio B (FM) | 3.17 | 94.6 |
| Radio B (LW) | 1515 | 0.198 |
| Radio C (MW) | 693 | 0.433 |

**10  a** $4.3 \times 10^{14}\,Hz$
    **b** $4.3 \times 10^{14}\,Hz$; $470\,nm$

**11**

| Radiation | Wavelength range / m | Frequency / Hz |
|---|---|---|
| radio waves | >$10^6$ to $10^{-1}$ | 300 to $3 \times 10^9$ |
| microwaves | $10^{-1}$ to $10^{-3}$ | $3 \times 10^9$ to $3 \times 10^{11}$ |
| infrared | $10^{-3}$ to $7 \times 10^{-7}$ | $3 \times 10^{11}$ to $4.3 \times 10^{14}$ |
| visible | $7 \times 10^{-7}$ (red) to $4 \times 10^{-7}$ (ultraviolet) | $4.3 \times 10^{14}$ to $7.5 \times 10^{14}$ |
| ultraviolet | $4 \times 10^{-7}$ to $10^{-8}$ | $7.5 \times 10^{14}$ to $3 \times 10^{16}$ |
| X-rays | $10^{-8}$ to $10^{-13}$ | $3 \times 10^{16}$ to $3 \times 10^{21}$ |
| $\gamma$-rays | $10^{-10}$ to $10^{-16}$ | $3 \times 10^{18}$ to $3 \times 10^{24}$ |

**12  a** Visible
    **b** Ultraviolet
    **c** $1–100\,mm$
    **d** $400–700\,nm$
    **e** $4.3 \times 10^{14}\,Hz$ to $7.5 \times 10^{14}\,Hz$

**13  a** Radio waves, **b** microwaves, **c** infrared, **d** visible light, **e** ultraviolet, **f** X-rays or $\gamma$-rays.

**14  a** Radio waves, **b** radio waves, **c** visible light, **d** X-rays or $\gamma$-rays.

# Chapter 15

**1**

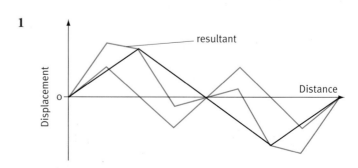

**2** The grid spacing is much smaller than the wavelength of the microwaves, so the waves do not pass through. However, the wavelength of light is much smaller, so it can pass through unaffected.

**3** Two loudspeakers with slightly different frequencies might start off in step, but they would soon go out of step. The interference at a particular point might be constructive at first, but would become destructive.

**4** The intensity would increase.

**5**

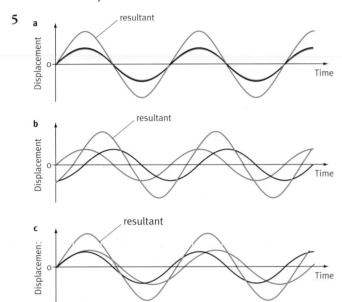

**6** D: dark fringe, because rays from slits 1 and 2 differ in path length by one-and-a-half wavelengths ($1\frac{1}{2}\lambda$).

E: bright fringe, because the path difference is $2\lambda$.

**7** 3.0 mm

**8** **a** $x = \dfrac{\lambda D}{a}$. Therefore $x \propto \dfrac{1}{a}$, so decreasing $a$ gives increased $x$.

**b** Blue light has shorter wavelength, so $x$ is less ($x \propto \lambda$).

**c** For larger $D$, $x$ is greater, so there is greater precision in $x$ ($x \propto D$).

**9** 3.5 mm

**10** $D$ and $a$ are fixed. So:

$$\frac{\lambda_1}{x_1} = \frac{\lambda_2}{x_2}$$

and so:

$$x_2 = \frac{4.5 \times 10^{-7} \times 2.4 \times 10^{-3}}{6.0 \times 10^{-7}}$$

$$= 1.8 \times 10^{-3}\,\text{m} = 1.8\,\text{mm}$$

(Or, wavelength is $\frac{3}{4}$ of previous value, so spacing of fringes is $\frac{3}{4}$ of previous value.)

**11** For the second-order maximum, rays from adjacent slits have a path difference of $2\lambda$, so they are in phase.

**12** **a** 20.4°

**b** Maxima at 31.5°, 44.2°, 60.6°. You cannot have $\sin\theta > 1$. There are 11 maxima.

**13** **a** $\theta$ increases, so the maxima are more spread out and there may be fewer of them. (Note: $\sin\theta \propto \lambda$)

**b** $d$ decreases, so again $\theta$ increases, the maxima are more spread out and there may be fewer of them. (Note: $\sin\theta \propto \dfrac{1}{d}$)

**14** **a** **Calculation** gives a total width of 8.7 mm, but with a ruler the student will **measure** 9 mm.

**b** **Calculation** gives an angle of 19.12°, but the student will **measure** 19.1°.

**c** For the double-slit experiment, a measured width of 9 mm for ten fringes will give an answer for the wavelength of 562 nm. For the diffraction grating experiment, the measured second-order angle of 19.1° will give an answer of 545 nm. Hence the diffraction grating method is more accurate. In practice, it is also much more precise because the fringes are bright and sharp (well-defined).

**15** **a** $\theta_{red} = 20.5°$; $\theta_{violet} = 11.5°$; angular separation = 9.0°.

**b** The third-order maximum for violet light is deflected through a smaller angle than the second-order maximum for red light.

# Chapter 16

**1** **a** 50 cm

**b** 12.5 cm

**2** **a** 60 cm; 30 cm

**b**

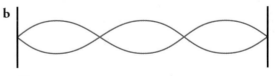

**c** 40 cm

**3  a**

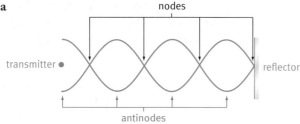

**b**  28 mm, $1.07 \times 10^{10}$ Hz $\approx 11$ GHz

**4**  In both cases, waves are reflected (by the metal sheet or by the water). The outgoing and reflected waves combine to produce a stationary wave pattern.

**5  a**  Much easier to detect where sound falls to zero than where sound is a maximum.

**b**  Increased accuracy – if the wavelength is short it is difficult to measure just one wavelength.

**6  a**  13.3 cm $\approx$ 13 cm

**b**  330 m s$^{-1}$

**7  a**  52.4 cm $\approx$ 52 cm

**b**  0.50 cm

**c**  330 m s$^{-1}$

# Chapter 17

**1**  If there were air molecules in the container, the $\alpha$-particles would scatter off them as well and distort the results. The $\alpha$-particles may also be absorbed by 6 cm of air.

**2  a**  More back-scattered, because greater chance of close approach to gold nucleus.

**b**  Fewer back-scattered, because their inertia would tend to carry them forward.

**c**  Fewer back-scattered, because the repulsive force would be less. (Note: gold and silver atoms occupy roughly the same volume.)

**3**  Volume = $1.6 \times 10^{-29}$ m$^3$; radius $\sim 2 \times 10^{-15}$ m (assuming little empty space between atoms).

**4  a**  7

**b**  44

**c**  60

**d**  118

**e**  122

**5  a**  $+e$

**b**  No charge.

**c**  $+Ze$, where $Z$ is the proton number.

**d**  No charge.

**e**  $+2e$

**6**  143 and 146 neutrons.

**7  a**  Proton number 80 for all.
Neutron numbers 116, 118, 119, 120, 121, 122, 124.

**b**  200.6

**8**  They are grouped into isotopes as follows: A and E; C; D, F and G; B and H.

| | | |
|---|---|---|
| A = $^{44}_{20}$Ca | isotope of calcium |
| B = $^{50}_{23}$V | isotope of vanadium |
| C = $^{46}_{21}$Sc | isotope of scandium |
| D = $^{46}_{22}$Ti | isotope of titanium |
| E = $^{46}_{20}$Ca | isotope of calcium |
| F = $^{48}_{22}$Ti | isotope of titanium |
| G = $^{50}_{22}$Ti | isotope of titanium |
| H = $^{51}_{23}$V | isotope of vanadium |

**9  a**  $^{220}_{86}$Rn $\rightarrow$ $^{216}_{84}$Po + $^{4}_{2}$He

**b**  $^{25}_{11}$Na $\rightarrow$ $^{25}_{12}$Mg + $^{0}_{-1}$e

**10**  $^{41}_{18}$Ar $\rightarrow$ $^{41}_{19}$K + $^{0}_{-1}$e

**11  a**  A $\beta$-particle has less charge, is smaller and travels faster.

**b**  Air is much less dense and so less ionisation is caused per unit distance travelled.

**12  a, b**

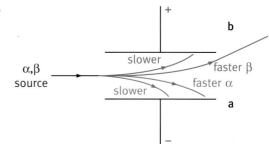

The $\alpha$-particles are deflected much less than the $\beta$-particles.

**13**  Most strongly ionising implies many more collisions occur, so there is greater loss of momentum and therefore less penetration.

**14**  The $\alpha$-particles pass between two plates connected to an electric power supply. The $\alpha$-particles cause ionisation in the air between the plates and a small current flows. When smoke enters the device, the $\alpha$-particles are absorbed and there is less ionisation of the air and thus less current in the external circuit. The circuit then switches on the alarm. Alpha-radiation is most suitable because it is the most strongly ionising. It causes a greater current to flow and also $\alpha$-particles are more likely to be absorbed by smoke. Also the range of the $\alpha$-particles is so small that they are unlikely to constitute a hazard to the user.

# Chapter 18

1   **a** 30°
    **b i** 180°
       **ii** $\dfrac{3.5}{12} \times 360° = 105°$

2   **a** 0.52 rad, 1.57 rad, 1.83 rad
    **b** 28.6°, 43.0°, 180°, 90°
    **c** $\dfrac{\pi}{6}$ rad, $\dfrac{2\pi}{3}$ rad, $\dfrac{3\pi}{2}$ rad, $4\pi$ rad

3   The magnitude of the velocity remains the same. (The speed is constant.)

4   **a** $0\,\text{m s}^{-1}$
    **b** $0.4\,\text{m s}^{-1}$

5   Second hand turns through 360° in 1 minute or $2\pi$ rad in one minute.

    $\dfrac{2\pi}{60}$ rad in 1 second

    $\omega = \dfrac{2\pi}{60} = 0.105\,\text{rad s}^{-1}$

6   **a** $20\,\text{rev s}^{-1}$
    **b** $40\pi\,\text{rad s}^{-1} = 130\,\text{rad s}^{-1}$

7   $0.19\,\text{cm s}^{-1}$

8   **a** $0.105\,\text{rad s}^{-1}$
    **b** $5.2\,\text{m s}^{-1}$

9   $1.1 \times 10^{-3}\,\text{rad s}^{-1}$

10  **a** The gravitational pull of the Earth on the Moon.
    **b** The frictional force of the road on the wheels.
    **c** Tension in the string supporting the pendulum.

11  There will be no frictional force between the road and the wheels. If the driver turns the steering wheel the car will continue in a straight line.

12  Speed and kinetic energy are scalar quantities, the others are vectors. Speed is constant; velocity has a constant magnitude but continuously changing direction (the direction is tangential to the circle); kinetic energy is constant; momentum has a constant magnitude but continuously changing direction (the direction is tangential to the circle); the centripetal

force has a constant magnitude but continuously changing direction (the direction is always towards the centre of the circle); the centripetal acceleration behaves in the same way as the centripetal force.

13  $a = \dfrac{v^2}{r}$

    $v = \omega r$

    $a = \dfrac{(\omega r)^2}{r}$

    $a = \omega^2 r$

14  $5.08 \times 10^3\,\text{s}$ (84.6 min)

15  $3.46\,\text{m s}^{-1} \approx 3.5\,\text{m s}^{-1}$

16  **a** $3.1 \times 10^6\,\text{N}$
    **b** $7.7 \times 10^3\,\text{m s}^{-1}$
    **c** $5.50 \times 10^3\,\text{s} \approx 1.5\,\text{h}$
    **d** 15.7 times

17  **a** $9.42\,\text{m s}^{-1} \approx 9.4\,\text{m s}^{-1}$
    **b** $178\,\text{m s}^{-2} \approx 180\,\text{m s}^{-2}$
    **c** $71\,\text{N}$

18  **a** $2.43 \times 10^4\,\text{m s}^{-1} \approx 24\,\text{km s}^{-1}$
    **b** $2.57 \times 10^{-3}\,\text{m s}^{-2}$
    **c** $1.64 \times 10^{21}\,\text{N}$

19  The tension in the string must have a vertical component to balance the weight of the bung.

20  In level flight, lift balances the weight. During banking the vertical component of the lift is less than the weight, so the aeroplane loses height unless the speed can be increased to provide more lift.

21  The normal contact force of the wallof the slide has a horizontal component, which provides the centripetal force. If you are going fast, you need a bigger force, so the horizontal component must be greater. This happens as you move up the curved wall of the slide.

# Chapter 19

1   **a** $6.67 \times 10^{-9}\,\text{N}$
    **b** $1.0 \times 10^{-8}\,\text{N}$
    **c** $1.2 \times 10^5\,\text{N}$

2   About $10^{-6}\,\text{N}$. Weight is greater by a factor of approximately $10^9$.

3   Approximately $3\,\text{N}$. This would be just about detectable, although other factors such as dehydration would be more significant.

**4 a i** $1.6\,\mathrm{N\,kg^{-1}}$

   **ii** $270\,\mathrm{N\,kg^{-1}}$

  **b** Gravitational field strength is very weak on the Moon so gas molecules will have enough energy to escape from the Moon, whereas the Sun has a very high field strength and therefore pulls gas molecules very close together.

**5 a** $2.8 \times 10^{-3}\,\mathrm{N\,kg^{-1}}$
  **b** $2.1 \times 10^{20}\,\mathrm{N}$, $2.8 \times 10^{-3}\,\mathrm{m\,s^{-2}}$

**6** $25\,\mathrm{N\,kg^{-1}}$

**7** Gravitational field strength due to the Sun is $5.9 \times 10^{-3}\,\mathrm{N\,kg^{-1}}$.

  Gravitational field strength due to the Moon is $3.4 \times 10^{-5}\,\mathrm{N\,kg^{-1}}$.

  So the Sun has a greater pull on each kilogram of the seawater.

**8 a** $1.7 \times 10^{-8}\,\mathrm{N}$
  **b** $8.3 \times 10^{-8}\,\mathrm{N}$

**9** Closer to the Moon. The point will be $3.4 \times 10^{5}\,\mathrm{km}$ from the Earth.

**10 a** $-6.3 \times 10^{7}\,\mathrm{J\,kg^{-1}}$
  **b** $-2.8 \times 10^{6}\,\mathrm{J\,kg^{-1}}$
  **c**

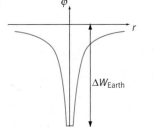

Potential well for Earth    Potential well for Moon

  **d** $\Delta W_{\mathrm{Earth}}$ is the energy needed for each kilogram, initially on the Earth's surface, to escape from the Earth's field which can be seen to be much greater than $\Delta W_{\mathrm{Moon}}$, the energy needed for each kilogram, initially on the moon's surface, to escape from its field. So the rocket does not need to carry so much fuel.

**11** $7.8\,\mathrm{km\,s^{-1}}$

**12** Diagram showing the satellite spiralling in towards Earth. The satellite needs to fire small thruster rockets to maintain its speed and orbit.

**13** $20\,600\,\mathrm{km}$

**14** Time delay $= 0.24\,\mathrm{s}$, signals travel 30% slower in cables but the distance is much shorter.

# Chapter 20

**1 a** Forced
  **b** Free
  **c** Free
  **d** Forced

**2** Curved (Figure 20.6a)

**3** Amplitude $= 10\,\mathrm{cm}$, period $= 120\,\mathrm{ms}$ $(0.12\,\mathrm{s})$, frequency $= 8.3\,\mathrm{Hz}$

**4 a** $\frac{1}{2}$ an oscillation
  **b** The waves have different frequencies so the phase difference is continuously changing.

**5** The trolley is the mass; the central position of the trolley is the equilibrium position; the resultant restoring force of the springs is the force.

**6** The restoring force is not proportional to the distance from the equilibrium point, when the person is not in contact with the trampoline the restoring force is equal to the person's weight which is constant.

**7 a** Amplitude $= 0.02\,\mathrm{m}$
  **b** Time period $= 0.40\,\mathrm{s}$
  **c** Maximum velocity $= 0.31\,\mathrm{m\,s^{-1}}$
  **d** Maximum acceleration $= 5.0\,\mathrm{m\,s^{-2}}$

**8** At the extreme left of the oscillation (i.e. maximum negative displacement), the acceleration is positive (towards the right).

**9** Gradient $= 0$, velocity $= 0$

**10 a** $0\,\mathrm{cm\,s^{-1}}$
  **b** $47\,\mathrm{cm\,s^{-1}}$
  **c** $0\,\mathrm{cm\,s^{-2}}$

**11 a** $0.5\,\mathrm{s}$
  **b** $2\,\mathrm{Hz}$
  **c** $4\pi\,\mathrm{rad\,s^{-1}}$

**12 a** $0.20\,\mathrm{m}$
  **b** $0.4\,\mathrm{s}$
  **c** $2.5\,\mathrm{Hz}$
  **d** $5\pi\,\mathrm{rad\,s^{-1}}$
  **e** $-0.1\,\mathrm{m}$
  **f** $0\,\mathrm{m\,s^{-1}}$
  **g** $3.1\,\mathrm{m\,s^{-1}}$

**13 a**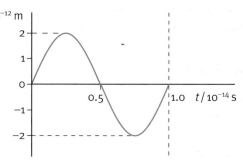

**b** Gradient at steepest point giving approximately $1.3 \times 10^3 \, \text{m s}^{-1}$.

**14 a** $3 \times 10^{-4} \, \text{m} \, (0.3 \, \text{mm})$

**b** $120 \, \text{Hz}$

**c** $8.3 \times 10^{-3} \, \text{s}$

**15 a** $x = 0.15 \cos (\pi t)$

**b**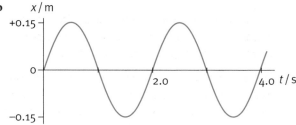

**16 a** $a = 77.4x$

**b** $3.9 \, \text{m s}^{-2}$

**17** $2.76 \, \text{Hz} \approx 2.8 \, \text{Hz}$

**18 a** $2.0 \, \text{s}$

**b** $0.5 \, \text{Hz}$

**c** $\pi \, \text{rad s}^{-1}$ or $3.14 \, \text{rad s}^{-1}$

**d** $a = -9.87x$ or $a = -\pi^2 x$

**e** $37.6 \, \text{cm s}^{-1} \approx 38 \, \text{cm s}^{-1}$

**f** $32.6 \, \text{cm s}^{-1} \approx 33 \, \text{cm s}^{-1}$

**19 a** The restoring force $= kx$ (from Hooke's law), $a \propto F$ therefore $a \propto x$, the force acts in the opposite direction to the displacement.

**b** $a = -\dfrac{F}{m} = -\dfrac{kx}{m} = -\omega^2 x$

$\omega^2 = \dfrac{kx}{m}$

$\omega = \sqrt{\dfrac{k}{m}}$

$f = \dfrac{\omega}{2\pi} = \dfrac{1}{2\pi} \sqrt{\dfrac{k}{m}}$

$T = \dfrac{1}{f} = 2\pi \sqrt{\dfrac{m}{k}}$

**20 a** Gravitational potential energy

**b** Gravitational potential energy is transferred to kinetic energy which reaches a maximum when the bob passes through the lowest point; then k.e. is converted to g.p.e. once more.

**21**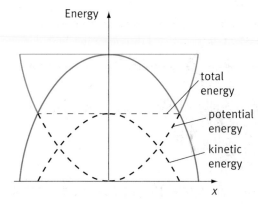

**22 a** $0.35 \, \text{m s}^{-1}$

**b** $0.12 \, \text{J}$

**c** $0.12 \, \text{J}$

**d** $0.17 \, \text{m s}^{-2}$

**e** $3.4 \, \text{N}$

**23 a**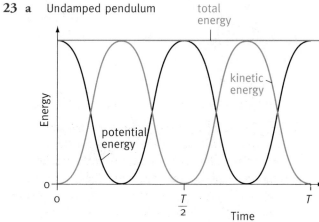

**b** The total energy of the pendulum will decrease gradually and hence the maximum values of k.e. and p.e. will also decrease.

**24**

| Example | Useful/problem? | What is resonating? |
|---|---|---|
| Buildings in earthquake | Problem | Mechanical structure forced by energy from waves of earthquake. |
| Components in engines | Problem | At certain rates of rotation, parts of an engine may resonate mechanically; the resonance is driven by the energy output of the engine. This can lead to components cracking or disintegrating, with dangerous consequences. |
| Positive feedback in amplification systems (gives high-pitched squealing sound) | Problem | Microphone held too close to loudspeaker that is emitting waves of the same frequency as the microphone is tuned to, so the waves from the loudspeaker force the amplifier to resonate. |
| Tuned radio | Useful | Electric signal in circuit forced by incoming radio waves. |
| Microwave cooker | Useful | Water molecules forced by microwaves. |
| Magnetic resonance in atoms | Useful | Nuclei in atoms behave as magnets; they can be made to resonate by electromagnetic waves. Each nucleus resonates at a different frequency, so the structures of molecules can be determined. |

# Chapter 21

1   Bonds are still relatively strong (stronger than gas but weaker than a solid) and the molecules are free to move through the body of the liquid.

2   a  Energy has to be supplied to convert the liquid into vapour – this takes time.

    b  When converting ice to liquid water only a few intermolecular bonds are broken whereas when liquid is converted to vapour all the molecules are totally separated. This requires more energy.

    c  Dogs do not sweat through their skin like humans, instead they sweat from their tongues. The sweat evaporates and cools the dog. The panting blows air across the tongue increasing the rate of evaporation.

3   a  +750 kJ
    b  50 kJ

4   a  273 K, 293 K, 393 K, 773 K, 250 K, 73 K
    b  273 °C, 253 °C, 173 °C, 27 °C, 100 °C, 227 °C

5

| Temperature / °C | Resistance / Ω | Temperature / K |
|---|---|---|
| 10 | 3120 | 283 |
| 50 | 3900 | 348 |
| 100 | 4200 | 373 |
| 150 | 4800 | 423 |
| 220 | 5640 | 493 |
| 260 | 6120 | 533 |

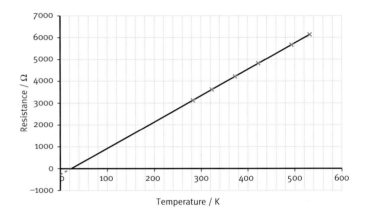

6   a  Calibration
    b  Range
    c  Linearity
    d  Sensitivity

7   1.67 MJ ≈ 1.7 MJ

8   Copper just (7600 J compared with 7560 J).

9   435 J kg$^{-1}$ K$^{-1}$ ≈ 440 J kg$^{-1}$ K$^{-1}$

10  At higher temperatures the greater the rate of energy loss to the surroundings, therefore the slower the temperature rise.

11  Systematic – it can (theoretically) be removed by perfect insulation.

12  5700 J kg$^{-1}$ K$^{-1}$. Biggest source of error will be energy loss due to poor insulation. There will also be an error because we have ignored the specific heat capacity of the beaker.

13  a  AB, solid; BC, solid + liquid; CD, liquid.
    b  Internal energy increases in all three sections.

**c** Greater when it was a solid; the gradient is greater when liquid, so it takes less time to raise the temperature the same amount and therefore less energy.

14 660 J. When a solid melts, only about one bond per atom/molecule is broken. On boiling, several remaining bonds are broken, requiring more energy.

15 $1.4 \times 10^4 \, \text{J kg}^{-1}$.

# Chapter 22

1 $4000 \, \text{s}^{-1}$

2 **a** $6.02 \times 10^{23}$
**b** 4.5, $27.1 \times 10^{23}$
**c** $5.0 \times 10^{25}$

3 **a** $3.90 \times 10^{-22} \, \text{g}$
**b i** $8.51 \times 10^{-5} \approx 8.5 \times 10^{-5}$
**ii** $5.12 \times 10^{19} \approx 5.1 \times 10^{19}$

4 Typical relative atomic mass = 10, so 1 kg contains 100 moles = $6 \times 10^{25} \sim 10^{26}$ molecules. Note for heavier elements, e.g. iron, $A_r \sim 60$ and number of atoms $\sim 10^{25}$.

5 $1.92 \times 10^5 \, \text{Pa} \approx 1.9 \times 10^5 \, \text{Pa}$

6 1200 K

7 **a** 3.5 / mol
**b** $0.086 \, \text{m}^3$ or $86 \, \text{dm}^3$

8 $0.020 \, \text{m}^3$

9 $0.104 \, \text{m}^3 \approx 0.1 \, \text{m}^3$

10 385 K

11 **a** $166 \, \text{g} \approx 170 \, \text{g}$
**b** $2.65 \, \text{kg} \approx 2.7 \, \text{kg}$

12 Both sides $\text{kg m}^{-1} \text{s}^{-2}$

13 **a** $2.3 \times 10^5 \, \text{m}^2 \, \text{s}^{-2}$
**b** $480 \, \text{m s}^{-1}$, which is 50% greater than the speed of sound in air.

14 **a** $R = 8.31 \, \text{J K}^{-1}$, $N_A = 6.02 \times 10^{23}$

$$\frac{8.31 \, \text{J K}^{-1}}{6.02} \times 10^{23} = 1.38 \times 10^{-23} \, \text{J K}^{-1}$$

**b** $E = \frac{3}{2} kT$

15 $6.2 \times 10^{-21} \, \text{J}$

16 242 K, $-31 \, °\text{C}$

17 Temperature is proportional to the (average speed)². So, if the speed doubles the temperature increases by a factor of $2^2 = 4$.

18 **a** Halved
**b** Remains the same

19 Mean k.e. = $6.1 \times 10^{21}$ J; average speed of oxygen molecule = $480 \, \text{m s}^{-1}$; average speed of nitrogen molecule = $510 \, \text{m s}^{-1}$

20 Internal energy = $E = N_A \left(\frac{3}{2} kT\right) = \frac{3}{2} RT$

Change per kelvin = $\frac{3}{2} R$

# Chapter 23

1 **a** $2.9 \times 10^5 \, \text{V m}^{-1}$ (or $\text{N C}^{-1}$)
**b** 0.072 N
**c** $4.32 \, \text{V m}^{-1}$ (or $\text{N C}^{-1}$) (towards the negative sphere)

2 $1.8 \times 10^{-5} \, \text{C}$

3 **a** A 0 J, B 2 kJ, C 1 kJ, D 1.5 kJ
**b** A 0 J, B 4 kJ, C 2 kJ, D 3 kJ

4 $1.1 \times 10^{-6} \, \text{C}$, 50 kV

5 **a** E → H, 5 kJ; E → F, 2.5 kJ; F → G, 0 J; H → E, −5 kJ
**b i** E → H, −5 kJ; E → F, −2.5 kJ; F → G, 0 J; H → E, +5 kJ
**ii** E → H, 10 kJ; E → F, 5 kJ; F → G, 0 J; H → E, −10 kJ

6 Electrostatic force 230 N; gravitational force $1.9 \times 10^{-34}$ N. This answer tells us that the gravitational attraction is nowhere near enough to balance the electric repulsion. Some other force must hold the protons together. (In fact, it is the **strong nuclear force**.)

# Chapter 24

1 $3300 \, \mu\text{C}$, $3.3 \times 10^{-3} \, \text{C}$

2 $2.0 \times 10^{-6} \, \text{F}$, $2.0 \, \mu\text{F}$, $2.0 \times 10^6 \, \text{pF}$

3 $0.050 \, \text{A}$ (50 mA)

**4**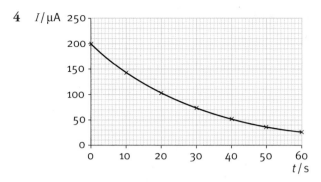

Charge = area under graph ≈ 5.1 mC

Capacitance ≈ $6.0 \times 10^{-4}$ F (600 μF)

**5** Gradient = $\dfrac{V}{Q} = \dfrac{1}{C}$

**6** **a** $1.0 \times 10^{-3}$ F (1 mF)

**b**

| $Q$/mC | $V$/V | Area of strip $\Delta W$/mJ | Sum of areas $W$/mJ |
|--------|-------|------------------------------|----------------------|
| 1.0 | 1.0 | 0.5 | 0.5 |
| 2.0 | 2.0 | 1.5 | 2.0 |
| 3.0 | 3.0 | 2.5 | 4.5 |
| 4.0 | 4.0 | 3.5 | 8.0 |

**c** The graph is a parabola.

**7** **a** $6.25 \times 10^{-2}$ J ≈ $6.3 \times 10^{-2}$ J

**b** $6.3 \times 10^{-8}$ J

**c** 5.29 J ≈ 5.3 J

**8** Charge is the same for both capacitors ($2.0 \times 10^{-2}$ C). Energy stored is greater in the 100 μF capacitor (2.0 J compared to 1.0 J).

**9** **a** 0.72 J

**b** 0.02 s

**10** **a** 1.8 C, 8.1 J

**b** 810 W

**c** 180 A

**d** 0.025 Ω

**11** **a** 200 μF

**b** $4.0 \times 10^{-3}$ C (4000 μC)

**12** Two 20 μF and one 10 μF connected in parallel; or five 10 μF connected in parallel.

**13** 100 μF

**14** **a** $C_{\text{total}} = \dfrac{C}{2}$

**b** $C_{\text{total}} = \dfrac{C}{n}$

**c** $C_{\text{total}} = 2C$

**d** $C_{\text{total}} = nC$

**15** **a** $\dfrac{1}{G_{\text{total}}} = \dfrac{1}{G_1} + \dfrac{1}{G_2}$

**b** $G_{\text{total}} = G_1 + G_2$

**16** **a** 33.3 μF

**b** 300 μF

**c** 66.7 μF

**d** 150 μF

**17** **a** Four in parallel.

**b** Four in series.

**c** Two in series with two in parallel.

**18** Maximum: in parallel, 900 pF.

Minimum: in series, 60 pF.

**19** 4.0 μF

**20** **a** 40 μF

**b** 0.40 C

**c** $2.0 \times 10^3$ J

**21** **a** 25 μF

**b** $4.0 \times 10^{-3}$ C (4000 μC)

**c** 160 V

**d** $8.0 \times 10^{-2}$ J (80 mJ)

**22** 0.000 71 F ≈ 700 μF

# Chapter 25

**1** current flowing into page       current flowing out of page, strength doubled

**2**

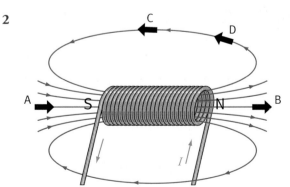

**3** Pair **a** will repel, pair **b** will attract.

4   a  No force.
    b  Force into the plane of the paper.
    c  Force down the page.

5   0.030 N

6   0.050 T

7   a  0.16 A
    b  $4.0 \times 10^{-4}$ N (0.40 mN)

8   a  Section of wire in field tilts down.
    b  Tilts down.
    c  Will try to move horizontally, **into** horseshoe.
    d  No movement.

9   $7.8 \times 10^{-3}$ T

10  $6.0 \times 10^{-3}$ N (6.0 mN)

11  a  2.0 N
    b  Pivoted along a line parallel to one edge with the magnetic field in the same plane as the coil.
    c  Greater torque provided by: increasing current, increasing number of turns in coil, increasing length of side in field, pivoting by centre of coil and have magnets either side, having magnets all round the circle through which the coil turns, increasing field strength.

12  a  $0.375$ N $\approx 0.38$ N
    b  $0.265$ N $\approx 0.27$ N
    c  0 N.

    Both **a** and **b** are into the plane of the paper.

13  They attract; if you consider each flat coil as a small electromagnet then unlike poles are facing one another. If you think of the currents in the wires, these are parallel (rather than anti-parallel) and the coils attract. When the current is reversed, it is reversed in both coils and they still attract.

# Chapter 26

1
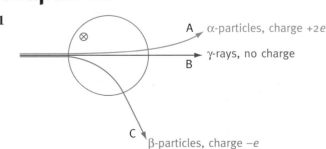

A  α-particles, charge +2e

B  γ-rays, no charge

C  β-particles, charge −e

2   a  $8.0 \times 10^{-14}$ N
    b  $5.66 \times 10^{-14}$ N $\approx 5.7 \times 10^{-14}$ N

3   Since the particles have opposite charges, they experience a force in opposite directions.

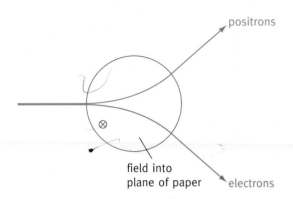

positrons

field into
plane of paper   electrons

4   Out of the plane of the photograph.

5   All have same mass, charge and speed. (There is more about this when you study how J. J. Thomson discovered the electron on page **393**.)

6   a  Circular path will have smaller radius.
    b  Electrons will circle in the opposite direction.
    c  Circular path will have smaller radius.
    d  Electrons will spiral around field lines because they will have a constant component of velocity in the direction of the field lines.

7   a  The magnetic force is upwards, towards the positive plate and the electric force is downwards, towards the negative plate.
    b  $5.0 \times 10^{3}$ m s$^{-1}$
    c  Magnetic force > electric force; the ion travels in an upward **curved** path (towards the positive plate) and hence misses the slit S.

8   $9.09 \times 10^{-31}$ kg

9   a  Charge on droplet must be negative.
    b  180 V cm$^{-1}$ or $1.8 \times 10^{4}$ V m$^{-1}$
    c  $5.79 \times 10^{-15}$ N
    d  $5.79 \times 10^{-15}$ N
    e  $-3.2 \times 10^{-19}$ C. This is two electrons' worth of charge and means that the drop contains an excess of two electrons.
    f  β-radiation must be adding negative charge to the droplet. (You could argue that it is somehow reducing the mass, but this is less plausible and is not the correct interpretation.)
    g  120 V

# Chapter 27

1. The rotating magnet changes the magnetic flux linking the coil, hence an e.m.f. is induced. The induced current in the coil will light the lamp connected to the generator.

2. Current flows from A to B and from C to D. Y is positive so that current flows from Y to X in the external circuit to make it flow from A to B inside the coil.

3. Left wingtip positive. It is negative in the southern hemisphere because the field direction is reversed.

4. Magnetic flux = $BA$. A stronger magnet means greater flux linking the coil and hence a greater induced e.m.f.

   Faster movement means more flux cut/linked per second and more current generated, or larger e.m.f.

5. The wire is moved parallel to the field, hence only small components cut due to slight curvature at edges of field.

6. Frequency is determined by speed of rotation (so to keep constant, must be geared). E.m.f. is affected by magnet strength, number of turns in coil, size of coil. The e.m.f. is normally affected by the speed of rotation, but in this case this has to be fixed as the frequency is fixed.

7. $2.25 \times 10^{-5}\,\text{Wb} \approx 2.3 \times 10^{-5}\,\text{Wb}$

8. $7.9 \times 10^{-6}\,\text{Wb}$

9. $0.54\,\text{Wb}$

10. Rate of change in area = $lv$; rate of change of flux = $B \times (lv) = Blv$.

11. $6.0\,\text{mV}$

12. $0.33\,\text{T}$

13. a. Stop pushing implies no change in flux linkage, so no current is generated. Therefore, no magnetic poles are formed and no work is done; there is no movement.
    b. Pull away implies that flux is decreased in the flux linkage, but end of solenoid near to magnet becomes a south pole, so the poles attract each other, and work has to be done to pull magnet and coil apart.

14. 
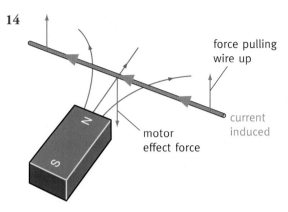

15. a. There is a sudden **increase** in the flux linkage for the coil, so there is an induced e.m.f.
    b. There is no change in the flux linking the coil. The motion is parallel to the field.
    c. Magnet leaves coil, there is a **decrease** in the flux linking the coil and hence the e.m.f. is in reverse (negative) direction. The induced current is the opposite direction (Lenz's law). Peak e.m.f. is greater because magnet moving faster (acceleration due to gravity), the rate of change of flux linkage is greater.

16. You have to do work against the motor effect force from an induced current when the lights are on. When the lights are off there is no induced current (although there is still an induced e.m.f.) and so no motor effect force.

17. 
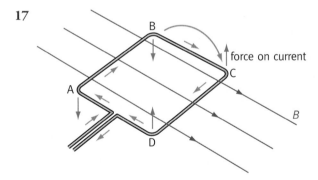

18. Alternating current. Usually, a bar magnet rotates inside a fixed coil. As the north pole passes one side of the coil, the current flows one way. Then the south pole passes, and the current reverses.

19. $B$ greater means greater flux, hence $\dfrac{\Delta(N\Phi)}{\Delta t}$ is greater; therefore $E \propto B$.

    $A$ greater means greater flux, hence $\dfrac{\Delta(N\Phi)}{\Delta t}$ is greater; therefore $E \propto A$.

$N$ greater means greater flux linkage, hence $\frac{\Delta(N\Phi)}{\Delta t}$ is greater; therefore $E \propto N$.

$f$ greater means rate of change of flux linkage is greater, hence $\frac{\Delta(N\Phi)}{\Delta t}$ is greater; therefore $E \propto f$.

**20** For d.c. supply, the flux linkage is constant – there is no change in the flux, and hence no induced e.m.f.

# Chapter 28

**1  a** 2 A, positive
   **b** 15 ms
   **c** 20 ms
   **d** 50 Hz

**2  a** 2 A, $100\pi$ rad s$^{-1}$
   **b** $I = 2\sin(100\pi t)$

**3  a** 5 A, $120\pi$ rad s$^{-1}$, 60 Hz, 17 ms
   **b**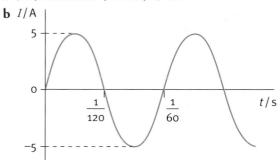

**4  a** 300 V, $100\pi$ rad s$^{-1}$, 50 Hz
   **b** 176 V
   **c**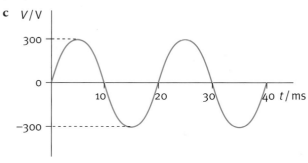

**5**  10 V, 40 ms, 25 Hz

**6**  The exact starting point on the graph below may be different, but the trace has an amplitude of 1 cm and one complete wave is 1 cm horizontally.

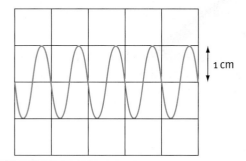

**7**  1.8 A

**8**  325 V

**9**  450 W

**10 a** 230 V
   **b** 0.23 A
   **c** 53 W

**11 a** Step-up: $15:5 = 3$, or $16:6 = 2.7$
   **b** Step-down: $4:8 = 0.5$, or $5:9 = 0.56$
   **c** Step-up: 30 V or 27 V; step-down: 5.0 V or 5.6 V

**12** 32 000 turns

**13 a** 200 V, 5 mA
   **b** 19%

**14**

| Transformer | $N_p$ | $N_s$ | $V_p$/V | $V_s$/V | $I_p$/A | $I_s$/A | $P$/W |
|---|---|---|---|---|---|---|---|
| A | 100 | 500 | 230 | 1150 | 1.0 | 0.2 | 230 |
| B | 500 | 100 | 230 | 46 | 1.0 | 5.0 | 230 |
| C | 100 | 2000 | 12 | 240 | 0.2 | 0.01 | 2.4 |

**15** Diode 3 is pointing the wrong way, so the current flows through diode 4, through $R$ and then through diode 1.

a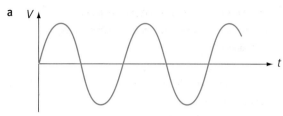

b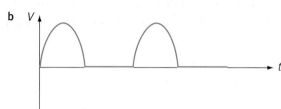

**16**

c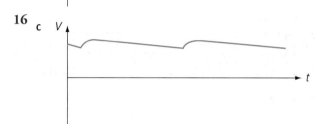

d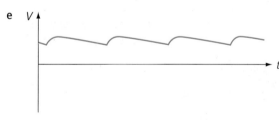

e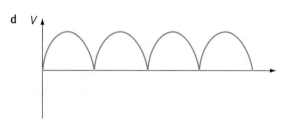

**17** The voltage will be half-wave rectified. Current can flow through diode 2 when terminal A is positive; when terminal B is positive, current cannot flow because there is no complete path to terminal A.

**18** **a** Less pronounced ripple.
   **b** More pronounced ripple.

# Chapter 29

**1** $6.63 \times 10^{-8}\,\text{J} \approx 6.6 \times 10^{-8}\,\text{J}$

**2** $2.8 \times 10^{-19}\,\text{J}$, $5.0 \times 10^{-19}\,\text{J}$

**3** **a** $\gamma$-ray
   **b** X-ray
   **c** Ultraviolet
   **d** Infrared
   **e** Radio wave

**4** $3.26 \times 10^{15}\,\text{s}^{-1} \approx 3.3 \times 10^{15}\,\text{s}^{-1}$

**5** $1.2\,\text{eV}$, $1.92 \times 10^{-19}\,\text{J} \approx 1.9 \times 10^{-19}\,\text{J}$

**6** $12\,400\,\text{eV} \approx 12\,\text{keV}$

**7** Ultraviolet (wavelength $\approx 1.24 \times 10^{-7}\,\text{m}$)

**8** **a** $2.4 \times 10^{-16}\,\text{J}$
   **b** $5.31 \times 10^{5}\,\text{m s}^{-1} \approx 5.3 \times 10^{5}\,\text{m s}^{-1}$

**9** $\sim 6.5 \times 10^{-34}\,\text{J s}$

**10** **a** $2.0\,\text{eV}$, $3.0\,\text{eV}$
   **b** $0.2\,\text{eV}$ and $1.2\,\text{eV}$; $3.2 \times 10^{-20}\,\text{J}$ and $1.9 \times 10^{-19}\,\text{J}$

**11** **a** Gold
   **b** Caesium
   **c** $1.04 \times 10^{15}\,\text{Hz}$
   **d** $620\,\text{nm}$

**12** **a** $8.3 \times 10^{-19}\,\text{J}$
   **b** $5.5 \times 10^{-19}\,\text{J}$
   **c** $1.1 \times 10^{6}\,\text{m s}^{-1}$

**13** $5.9 \times 10^{-20}\,\text{J}$

**14** **a** $5.6 \times 10^{-18}\,\text{J}$, $8.4 \times 10^{15}\,\text{Hz}$, $3.6 \times 10^{-8}\,\text{m}$ (emission)
   **b** $5.0 \times 10^{-19}\,\text{J}$, $7.5 \times 10^{14}\,\text{Hz}$, $4.0 \times 10^{-7}\,\text{m}$ (emission)
   **c** $2.2 \times 10^{-18}\,\text{J}$, $3.3 \times 10^{15}\,\text{Hz}$, $9.0 \times 10^{-8}\,\text{m}$ (absorption)

**15** $9.0\,\text{eV}$, $11\,\text{eV}$, $25\,\text{eV}$, $34\,\text{eV}$ and $45\,\text{eV}$ correspond to differences between energy levels, so they can all be absorbed. $6.0\,\text{eV}$ and $20\,\text{eV}$ do not correspond to differences between energy levels and so cannot be absorbed.

**16** **a** $15.0\,\text{eV}$, $24.9\,\text{eV}$, $49.7\,\text{eV}$
   **b** See figure for one possible solution.

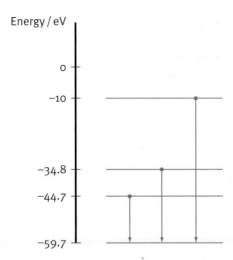

**17 a** Electrons can behave as waves so they can be diffracted by spaces between atoms.
  **b** Each metal has a different lattice structure, so each will produce a different diffraction pattern.

**18 a** $1.0\,\text{keV}$
  **b** $1.9 \times 10^7\,\text{m s}^{-1}$; $1.7 \times 10^{-23}\,\text{kg m s}^{-1}$
  **c** $3.9 \times 10^{-11}\,\text{m}$
  **d** The wavelength is much smaller than the spacing, so there will only be a small amount of diffraction.

# Chapter 30

**1** $4.4 \times 10^9\,\text{kg}$

**2 a** $4.5 \times 10^{-12}\,\text{J}$
  **b** $1.1 \times 10^{-12}\,\text{J}$

**3** $2.1 \times 10^{-12}\,\text{J}$, $1.4 \times 10^{-12}\,\%$

**4 a** $^{10}_{4}\text{Be} \rightarrow {}^{10}_{5}\text{B} + {}^{0}_{+1}\text{e}$
  **b** $8.9 \times 10^{-14}\,\text{J}$; the energy is released as kinetic energy of the products.

**5** It is a single nucleon and hence does not have binding energy.

**6 a** $6.00 \times 10^{-29}\,\text{kg}$
  **b** $5.40 \times 10^{-12}\,\text{J}$, $3.38 \times 10^7\,\text{eV}$
  **c** $6.75 \times 10^{-13}\,\text{J}$, $4.22 \times 10^6\,\text{eV}$

**7** Fission for $A < 20$ is unlikely because the products would have a smaller binding energy per nucleon. The reaction would require an input of external energy. Similarly, fusion for $A > 40$ is unlikely for the same reason.

**8** $150\,000\,\text{s}^{-1}$, or $150\,000\,\text{Bq}$

**9** $2.2 \times 10^{-9}\,\text{s}^{-1}$

**10** Count rate is less than activity because:
  **i** Gamma-rays are not always detected (weakly ionising).
  **ii** The counter is inefficient.
  **iii** Some radiation is absorbed within the sample before reaching the detector.
  **iv** The detector is directional, so some radiation will move away from the detector rather than towards it.

**11 a** $N = N_0 e^{-\lambda t}$
  **b** $4.0 \times 10^{10}$, $2.0 \times 10^{10}$
  **c** $7.0 \times 10^{10}$

**12 a** $3.37 \times 10^7 \approx 3.4 \times 10^7$
  **b** $3.4 \times 10^6\,\text{Bq}$

**13**

| $t/s$ | 0 | 20 | 40 | 60 | 80 | 100 | 120 | 140 |
|-------|-----|-----|-----|-----|-----|-----|-----|-----|
| $N$ | 400 | 330 | 272 | 224 | 185 | 153 | 126 | 104 |

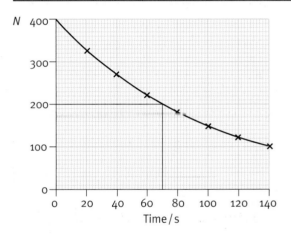

Half-life is about $70\,\text{s}$.

**14** $2.4$ years, $0.29\,\text{year}^{-1}$

**15** $6.93 \times 10^3 \approx 6900\,\text{s}$

**16 a** $0.094\,\text{s}^{-1}$
  **b i** 1250
   **ii** 768 (approximately)

**17 a** $N = N_0 e^{-\lambda t}$; $\dfrac{N}{N_0} = f = e^{-\left(\frac{\ln 2}{t_{1/2}}\right)t} = e^{-\ln 2\left(\frac{t}{t_{1/2}}\right)}$;
  $f = \left(e^{-0.693}\right)^{\frac{t}{t_{1/2}}}$ ; $f = \left(\dfrac{1}{2}\right)^{\frac{t}{t_{1/2}}}$

  **b i** 0.50
   **ii** 0.25
   **iii** $0.177 \approx 0.18$
   **iv** 0.0032

# Chapter 31

**1** $\dfrac{3}{103} \times 10 = 0.29$ V. There are 9.7 V across the LDR.

**2** The easiest way is to swap the $3\,\text{k}\Omega$ and the LDR resistor. Alternatively you can take the output as the voltage across the $3\,\text{k}\Omega$ resistor. You can also use an inverting amplifier which is covered later in the chapter.

**3** If the thermistor is in series with a fixed resistor and a battery, a changing temperature will cause a changing voltage across the thermistor.

**4** Both are made from semiconductor material. Both have a decreasing resistance when, for an LDR the light intensity increases and for the thermistor the temperature increases. Both have a non-linear change in resistance with light intensity or temperature.

**5**

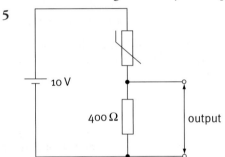

The output voltage is shown across the $400\,\Omega$ resistor. When the temperature rises, the resistance of the thermistor decreases and so the p.d. across the thermistor decreases and the p.d. across the $400\,\Omega$ resistor increases. You can also have the output voltage across the thermistor and then when temperature rises, the output voltage falls.

**6 a** $5.1 = \dfrac{R}{120} + R \times 10$

   $R = 124.9\,\Omega$

   $\Delta l = \dfrac{4.9}{2.4} \times 0.1 = 0.204 = 0.20\,\text{cm}$

   **b** Strain $= \dfrac{0.204}{10} = 0.0204 \approx 2.0\%$

   **c** $R$ becomes $121.2\,\Omega$

   $V = 5.0249 \approx 5.0\,\text{V}$

**7** About $9 \times 10^{-5}\,\text{V}$

**8** The op-amp switches at the same temperature. The output voltages become $+15\,\text{V}$ or $-15\,\text{V}$.

**9** Swap T and the $10\,\text{k}\Omega$ resistor; swap the connections to the $V^+$ and $V^-$ terminals of the op-amp.

**10** $V^+ = +6.9\,\text{V}$, $V^- = +4.5\,\text{V}$, $V_{\text{out}} = +9\,\text{V}$

**11**

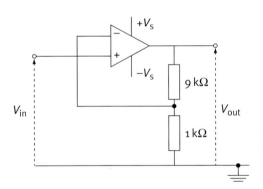

**12 a** $-0.40\,\text{V}$

   **b** $+8.0\,\text{V}$

   **c** $-15\,\text{V}$

**13** $R_1 = 0$, $R_2 = \infty$, gain $= 1 + \dfrac{R_1}{R_2} = 1 + \dfrac{0}{\infty} = 1$

**14** Any top resistor in the diagram must be 9 times larger than the bottom resistor. You cannot choose very small resistors , e.g. $9\,\Omega$ and $1\,\Omega$, because the op-amp cannot provide large enough currents into such small resistances. The input resistance is very high because of the very high input resistance to the op-amp and because there are no other resistors connected to the input.

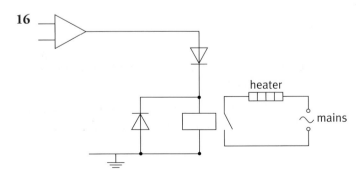

**15 a** Gain $= 11$

   **b i** $-1.1\,\text{V}$

   **ii** $+10\,\text{V}$

**16**

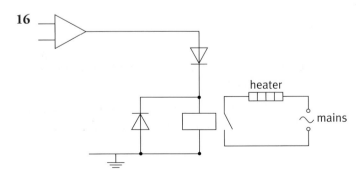

**17** When the op-amp switches off the coil in the relay, there is a large induced e.m.f. because of the change in magnetic flux in the coil. The reverse-biased diode prevents any induced current reaching the op-amp. There is no induced e.m.f. in an LED and so the reverse-biased diode is not needed.

# Chapter 32

**1** **a** Electrical energy from supply transferred to energy of electron beam (100%).

Energy of electron beam transferred to internal energy of anode (~99%) and energy of X-ray photons (~1%).

**b** 80 keV, $1.28 \times 10^{-14}$ J $\approx 1.3 \times 10^{-14}$ J, $1.68 \times 10^{8}$ m s$^{-1}$ $\approx 1.7 \times 10^{8}$ m s$^{-1}$

**2** Photon energy $E = \dfrac{hc}{\lambda} = V \times e$

Wavelength $\lambda = 1.04 \times 10^{-11}$ m $\approx 1.0 \times 10^{-11}$ m

**3** When $x = x_{\frac{1}{2}}$ the intensity had dropped to half its initial value. Hence $I = I_0 e^{-\mu x}$ becomes $\dfrac{I}{2} = I_0 e^{-\mu x_{\frac{1}{2}}}$. Taking logs of both sides gives $\ln\left(\tfrac{1}{2}\right) = -\mu x_{\frac{1}{2}}$ or $\ln 2 = \mu x_{\frac{1}{2}}$. Rearranging gives $x_{\frac{1}{2}} = \ln\dfrac{2}{\mu}$

**4** $8.0 \times 10^{5}$ W m$^{-2}$

**5** $0.12$ W m$^{-2}$

**6** The grid absorbs scattered X-rays, which would otherwise cloud the image.

**7** Consider the ratio of attenuation coefficients bone : muscle. This is approximately 6 for 50 keV X-rays, so bone is a much better absorber at this energy than is muscle. At 4.0 MeV, the ratio is less than 2, so bone and muscle will not appear very different on the image. (You could also calculate the fraction of X-rays absorbed by, say, 1 cm of tissue. At 4.0 MeV, only a small fraction is absorbed, so the X-ray image will be flooded with unabsorbed X-rays.)

**8** The ratio $\dfrac{Z_{\text{bone}}}{Z_{\text{soft issue}}} \approx 2$. Since attenuation coefficient $\mu \propto Z^3$, the ratio $\dfrac{m_{\text{bone}}}{m_{\text{soft issue}}} = 2^3 = 8$.

**9** Breathing causes movement of the body so that organs or bones of interest may move in the X-ray beam as the image is processed.

**10** The skull has bone all round. In a conventional X-ray, the beam must pass through both sides of the skull and this makes it difficult to see the inner tissue. In a CAT scan, the inner tissue shows up more clearly and any damage to the skull bones can be pinpointed accurately.

**11** **a** $2.7 \times 10^{-3}$ m (2.7 mm)

**b** $1.35 \times 10^{-3}$ m $\approx 1.4$ mm

**12** **a** Mechanical to electrical.

**b** Electrical to mechanical.

**c** Mechanical to electrical.

**d** Electrical to mechanical.

**13** $1.58 \times 10^{6}$ kg m$^{-2}$ s$^{-1}$ $\approx 1.6 \times 10^{6}$ kg m$^{-2}$ s$^{-1}$

**14** $3.2 \times 10^{-3}$ (0.32%)

**15** There is a big change in acoustic impedance when ultrasound passes from fluid into skin, and from tissue into bone. These surfaces therefore give strong reflections. Other soft tissues have similar values of acoustic impedance and so reflections are very weak.

**16** The brain is surrounded by solid bone which reflects ultrasound. Little penetrates the brain and hence the signal is very weak. An alternative is the CT scan.

**17** $0.026$ m (26 mm)

**18** X-rays are ionising radiation and hence are damaging to the fetus. Ultrasound carries very little risk because it is not a form of ionising radiation. (The intensity used must not cause heating of the baby's tissues.)

**19** **a** 106.5 MHz

**b** This is also their resonant frequency (106.5 MHz).

**20**

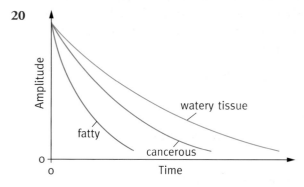

**21** **a** MRI uses non-ionising RF electromagnetic radiation, whereas CAT scanning uses X-rays, which are a form of ionising radiation.

**b** CAT scans show up bone, which is poorly imaged by MRI.

**c** The patient's body does not have to be cut open; nor do any instruments have to be inserted into the body.

# Chapter 33

1  $f_c = 50\,\text{kHz}$, $f_s = 5\,\text{kHz}$

2
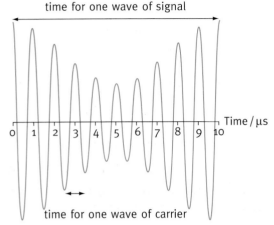

3  **a** The difference in amplitude of the carrier wave increases, i.e. the peaks of the waveform fall and rise more in height.
   **b** The time interval decreases between successive instances when the signal waveform is at its very highest.

4  **a** The maximum difference in frequency between the signal and the carrier wave increases, i.e. the signal has higher and lower frequencies.
   **b** The signal increases and decreases in frequency more times per second.

5  **a** 24 kHz
   **b** 524 kHz
   **c** 16 000 times a second

6  **a** Amplitude modulation
   **b** 40 kHz
   **c** 5 kHz
   **d** 10 kHz

7  **a** 130
   **b** Very few FM stations are possible (only five).

8  If you are concerned about the quality of the signal that you are listening to then FM is better. If you want more stations and are not in line of sight with the transmitter then AM is better.

9  AM covers a larger area than FM. FM can reach all the inhabitants of a town but the expense of aerials and transmitters means this is not possible in rural areas.

10 **a** 1110
   **b** 10 000

11 **a** 15
   **b** 11

12 **a** The value on the vertical axis (the voltage) has only one of two values, 0 or 1.
   **b** Digital signals can be more easily regenerated, can be stored and processed more easily, errors in transmission can be detected and digital electronic systems are more reliable.
   **c** Noise is introduced; for example, by random thermal motion of electrons. The signal is attenuated due to energy loss ($I^2Rt$) in the wires.

13 An attenuation of 44 dB or a gain of −44 dB.

14 $6.0 \times 10^{-3}\,\text{mW}$

15 1.0

16 **a** 12 dB
   **b** $15.8\,\text{mW} \approx 16\,\text{mW}$

17 **a** **Coaxial cable** contains a central copper core surrounded by an insulator and a mesh, or braid, made of copper wires made into a tube.
   An **analogue signal** can have any value, within limits, and is not restricted to just a few values.
   A **space wave** is an electromagnetic wave above 30 MHz which is not reflected or refracted back to Earth by the ionosphere and may be received by a satellite in space or be detected by line-of-sight within the Earth's atmosphere.
   A **sky wave** is an electromagnetic wave which is reflected or refracted back to the Earth by the ionosphere.
   **b** Space wave frequency greater than 30 MHz, wavelength less than 10 m
   Sky wave frequency between 3 and 30 MHz, wavelength between 10 and 100 m

   **c**

| Method | Advantage | Disadvantage |
|---|---|---|
| coaxial | less attenuation, noise, interference than wire-pair | more expensive than wire-pair |
| analogue signal | no ADC and DAC conversion required | more noise, interference than digital |
| space wave | can be received by satellite | satellite use expensive |
| sky wave | worldwide reception possible with multiple reflections | reflection by the ionosphere is not reliable |

Other answers are possible.

**18** More mobile phones can be connected because a frequency available in one cell can be used at the same time by another phone in a different cell.

**19** Mobile phone 1 starts a call. The cellular exchange allocates frequencies for connection of mobile phone 1 and base station. The cellular exchange finds the base station of mobile phone 2 and provides frequencies for connection to this other base station. Provided mobile phone 2 is switched on, connection is then made.

# Appendix A1

**1** Probably: $50\,\Omega$, $100\,\Omega$, $200\,\Omega$, $300\,\Omega$, $400\,\Omega$, $500\,\Omega$

**2** Pointer doesn't indicate zero when load = 0; scale incorrectly calibrated.

**3** 1 mm at either end = ± 2 mm; but if several measurements are required end-to-end and the tape measure is not long enough, this will increase the uncertainty.

**4** $\pm 0.5\,°C$ or $\pm 1.0\,°C$

**5** Between ±0.2 cm and ±1 cm.

**6** Between ±0.2 s and ±0.5 s.

**7** ± 0.8%

**8** **a** ± 5.7%
**b** The pendulum is moving during measurement.

**9** ± 0.25 V

**10**

| $h$ / cm | $d$ / cm | $d^2$ / cm² |
|---|---|---|
| 1.0 | 18.0 | 324 |
| 2.5 | 28.4 | 807 |
| 4.0 | 35.8 | 1280 |
| 5.5 | 41.6 | 1730 |
| 7.0 | 47.3 | 2240 |
| 9.0 | 53.6 | 2870 |

**11 a**

**b** Gradient = 320 cm; $y$-intercept = 0 cm² approx.

**12** Even if $r$ has its greatest possible value (6.4 cm), the values of $\frac{t^2}{r}$ differ significantly, suggesting that the results are not consistent with $t^2 \propto r$.

$\frac{t^2}{r} = 3.41$ and 3.00. These values differ by 14%. The error in $r$ is 3%, which is much less than the error in the two values of $\frac{t^2}{r}$ and so the relationship is not verified.

# Appendix A2

**1** Left-hand graph: response time increases more and more rapidly as the temperature rises.

Right-hand graph: response time increases rapidly at first, then more and more slowly.

**2** **a** $y^2$ against $x^3$ has gradient $k^2$; $y$ against $x^{3/2}$ has gradient $k$; $\ln y$ against $\ln x$ has gradient $\frac{3}{2}$ and intercept $\ln k$.
**b** $\ln y$ against $\ln x$ has gradient $q$.
**c** $y^2$ against $x$ has gradient $\frac{8}{mB}$; $\ln y$ against $\ln x$, $k = \frac{1}{2}$, intercept $= \frac{8}{Bm}$.
**d** $\ln y$ against $x$ has gradient $k$ and intercept $\ln y_0$.
**e** $y$ against $x^2$ has gradient $R$ and intercept $y_0$.

**3** Defining the problem:
- Vary $l$ or $l$ is the independent variable.
- Determine the period $T$ or $T$ is the dependent variable.

Methods of data collection:
- Diagram showing the simple pendulum attached, e.g. retort stand and clamp
- Many oscillations repeated to determine average $T$ ($n \geq 10$ or $t \geq 10\,s$ for stopwatch).
- Measure $l$ using metre rule/ruler.
- Measure to centre (of gravity) of mass.
- Use of vernier caliper/micrometer to measure the diameter of the bob and hence the centre of mass.
- At least five different values of $l$ chosen.
- Range of values of $l$ at least 50 cm.

Method of analysis:
- Appropriate graph plotted, e.g. $T^2$ against $l$; or $\ln T$ against $\ln l$.
- Gradient $= \dfrac{4\pi^2}{g}$ (if $T^2$ against $l$) or intercept of $\ln T - \ln l$ graph is $\ln\left(\dfrac{2\pi}{\sqrt{g}}\right)$.
- Calculation of $g$ from gradient.

Safety considerations:
- Relevant safety precaution related to the use of masses, e.g. avoid fast-moving mass, keep feet away, keep distance from experiment, use clamp stand to avoid toppling.

Additional detail – relevant points might include:
- Discussion of use of motion sensor, e.g. light gates with detail.
- Use small amplitude or small angle oscillations (to ensure equation is valid).
- Method of securing string to clamp, e.g. use bulldog clip.
- Discussion of magnitude of mass: large enough so that air resistance does reduce amplitude significantly.
- Use of fiducial marker.
- Time from the middle of the swing.

4 **a** $3.0 \pm 0.6\,m$
 **b** $1.0 \pm 0.6\,m$
 **c** $0.40 \pm 0.12\,m$ ($\pm 30\%$)
 **d** $10.05 \pm 1.5\,m\,s^{-1}$ ($\pm 15\%$)
 **e** $1.0 \pm 0.8\,m^2$ ($\pm 80\%$)
 **f** $2.0 \pm 0.4\,m$ ($\pm 40\%$)
 **g** $1.41 \pm 0.25\,m^2$ ($\pm 17.5\%$)

5 $150 \pm 15\,m\,s^{-1}$

6 Standard masses are used for the load. The uncertainties in these are much smaller than any others in the experiment, so they are negligible.

7 **a** Gradient $= b$, $y$-intercept $= \ln a$

 **b**

| $r/\,mm$ | $R/\,\Omega$ | $\ln(r/\,mm)$ | $\ln(R/\,\Omega)$ |
|---|---|---|---|
| $2.0 \pm 0.1$ | 175.0 | $0.69 \pm 0.05$ | 5.16 |
| $3.0 \pm 0.1$ | 77.8 | $1.10 \pm 0.03$ | 4.35 |
| $4.0 \pm 0.1$ | 43.8 | $1.39 \pm 0.03$ | 3.78 |
| $5.0 \pm 0.1$ | 28.0 | $1.61 \pm 0.02$ | 3.36 |
| $6.0 \pm 0.1$ | 19.4 | $1.79 \pm 0.02$ | 2.97 |

 **e** Gradient $= -2.00 \pm 0.07$
 **f** $-2.00 \pm 0.07$
 **g** $\ln a = 6.5$, $a = 670 \pm 120\,\Omega\,mm^2$

# Glossary

**absolute scale of temperature** *see* thermodynamic scale

**absolute zero** The temperature at which a system has minimum internal energy; equivalent to −273.15 °C.

**absorption line spectrum** A dark line of a unique wavelength seen in a continuous spectrum.

**acceleration** The rate of change of an object's velocity:

$$a = \frac{\Delta v}{\Delta t}$$

Unit: $m\,s^{-2}$.

**accuracy** An accurate value of a measured quantity is one which is close to the true value of the quantity.

**acoustic impedance** Acoustic impedance $Z$ is the product of the density $\rho$ of a substance and the speed $c$ of sound in that substance ($Z = \rho c$). Unit: $kg\,m^{-2}\,s^{-1}$.

**activity** The rate of decay or disintegration of nuclei in a radioactive sample.

**amorphous** Describes a material whose particles are arranged in a disordered way.

**ampere** The SI unit of electric current.

**amplitude modulation** A form of modulation where the signal causes variations in the amplitude of a carrier wave.

**amplitude** The maximum displacement of a particle from its equilibrium position.

**analogue signal** A signal that is continuously variable, having a continuum of possible values.

**analogue-to-digital conversion (ADC)** Conversion of a continuous analogue signal to discrete digital numbers.

**angular displacement** The angle through which an object moves in a circle.

**angular frequency** The rate of change of angle expressed in radian per second:

$$\text{angular frequency } \omega = \frac{2\pi}{T}$$

**angular velocity** The rate of change of the angular position of an object as it moves along a curved path.

**antinode** A point on a stationary wave with maximum amplitude.

**antiphase** Describes two waves or oscillations that are 180° out of phase.

**astronomical unit** The average distance of the Earth from the Sun.

**attenuation** The gradual loss in strength or intensity of a signal.

**average speed** The total distance travelled by an object divided by the total time taken.

**Avogadro constant** The number of particles in one mole of any substance ($6.02 \times 10^{23}$ $mol^{-1}$), denoted $N_A$.

**bandwidth (communications)** A measure of the width of a range of frequencies being transmitted.

**base station** A receiver and transmitter used to maintain contact with a number of mobile phones (cell phones) in a local area.

**best fit line** A line drawn through the points plotted on a graph so that it passes through as many points as possible, taking into consideration a balance between the number of points above and below the line.

**binding energy** The minimum external energy required to separate all the neutrons and protons of a nucleus.

**bit** A basic unit of information storage. The amount of information stored by a device that exists in only two distinct states, usually given as the binary digits 0 and 1.

**Boyle's law** The pressure exerted by a fixed mass of gas is inversely proportional to its volume, provided the temperature of the gas remains constant.

**braking radiation** X-rays produced when electrons are decelerated (also called Bremsstrahlung radiation).

**brittle** Describes a material that shows no plastic deformation and breaks just beyond its elastic limit.

**Brownian motion** The random movement of small particles caused by bombardment of invisible molecules.

**capacitance** The ratio of charge stored by a capacitor to the potential difference across it.

**carbon-dating** A technique used to date relics using the carbon-14 isotope.

**carrier wave** a waveform (usually sinusoidal) that is modulated with an input signal to carry information.

**cellular exchange** A switching centre connecting all the base stations in an area.

**centre of gravity** The point where the entire weight of an object appears to act.

**centripetal force** The net force acting on an object moving in a circle; it is always directed towards the centre of the circle.

**chain reaction** An exponential growth of a fission reaction caused by the increasing flux of neutrons causing fission.

**characteristic radiation** Very intense X-rays produced in an X-ray tube having specific wavelengths that depend on the target metal.

**charge carrier** Any charged particles, such as electrons, responsible for a current.

**Charles's law** The volume occupied by a gas at constant pressure is directly proportional to its thermodynamic (absolute) temperature.

**closed system** A system of interacting objects where there are no external forces.

**coaxial cable** An electrical cable with an inner conductor surrounded by a tubular insulating layer and an outside conducting layer.

**coherent** Two sources are coherent when they emit waves with a constant phase difference.

**collimated beam** A parallel-sided beam of radiation.

**collimator** A device for producing a parallel beam of radiation.

**components (of a vector)** The magnitudes of a vector quantity in two perpendicular directions.

**compression** A region in a sound wave where the air pressure is greater than its mean value.

**compressive** Describes a force that squeezes an object.

**computerised axial tomography** A technique where X-rays are used to image slices of the body in order to produce a computerised 3-D image.

**conservation of momentum** In a closed system, when bodies interact, the total momentum in any specified direction remains constant.

**constructive interference** When two waves reinforce to give increased amplitude.

**contact force** The force an object exerts on another with which it is in contact.

**contrast media** Materials such as barium that easily absorb X-rays. A contrast medium is used to reveal the outlines or edges of soft tissues in an X-ray image.

**contrast** In a high-contrast image, there is a big difference in brightness between bright and dark areas.

**control rods** Rods of a neutron-absorbing material used to reduce the rate of a nuclear chain reaction.

**coolant** A substance used to transfer thermal energy from the core of a nuclear reactor.

**coulomb** The SI unit of electrical charge. A charge of $1\,C$ passes a point when a current of $1\,A$ flows for $1\,s$. $1\,C = 1\,A\,s$

**Coulomb's law** Any two point charges exert an electrical force on each other that is proportional to the product of their charges and inversely proportional to the square of the distance between them.

**count rate** The number of particles (beta or alpha) or gamma-ray photons detected per unit time by a Geiger–Müller tube. Count rate is always a fraction of the activity of a sample.

**cross-linking (cross-talk)** A signal transmitted in one circuit or channel picked up, undesirably, in another circuit or channel.

**crystalline** Describes a material whose particles are arranged in an ordered way.

**damped** Describes an oscillatory motion where the amplitude decreases with time due to energy losses.

**de Broglie wavelength** The wavelength associated with a moving electron given by the equation:

$$\lambda = \frac{h}{mv}$$

**decay constant** The constant $\lambda$ for an isotope that appears in the equation $A = \lambda N$. It is equal to the probability of an isotope decaying per unit time interval.

**decibel** A logarithmic unit of measurement that expresses the relative sizes of two powers using the formula $10\lg\left(\dfrac{P_1}{P_2}\right)$.

**density** The mass per unit volume of a material:

$$\rho = \frac{m}{V}$$

Unit: $kg\,m^{-3}$.

**dependent variable** The variable in an experiment which is controlled by the experimenter.

**destructive interference** When two waves cancel to give reduced amplitude.

**diffraction** The spreading of a wave when it passes through a gap or past the edge of an object.

**digital signal** A signal that has only a few possible values, often only two.

**digital-to-analogue conversion (DAC)** Conversion of a series of digital numbers into a continuous analogue signal.

**dispersion** The splitting of light into its different wavelengths.

**displacement** The distance moved by an object in a particular direction (measured from a fixed starting point).

**drag** A force that resists movement of a body through a fluid.

**ductile** Describes a material that can easily be drawn into wires (e.g. copper).

**dynamics** A study of motion involving force and mass.

**e.m.f.** The total work done when unit charge moves round a complete circuit. Unit: $J\,C^{-1}$ or volt (V).

**efficiency** The ratio of useful output energy to the total input energy for a device, expressed as a percentage:

$$\text{efficiency} = \frac{\text{useful output energy}}{\text{total input energy}} \times 100\%$$

**Einstein relation** This refers to the equation for the energy of a photon – that is:

$$E = hf \quad \text{or} \quad E = \frac{hc}{\lambda}$$

**elastic** Describes a material which will return to its original shape when the forces acting on it are removed.

**elastic hysteresis** This occurs when the extension of an elastic material is different in loading and unloading.

**elastic limit** The value of stress beyond which an object will not return to its original dimensions.

**elastic potential energy** Energy stored in an extended or compressed material.

**electric charge** A property of many particles which gives rise to a force between them.

**electric field** A region in which a charged body experiences a force.

**electric field strength** The force per unit positive charge at a point. Unit: $V\,m^{-1}$ or $N\,C^{-1}$.

**electric potential** The energy per unit charge due to a charged body's position in an electric field.

**electrical resistance** The ratio of potential difference to current. Unit: ohm ($\Omega$).

**electrolyte** An electrically conducting solution. The conduction is due to positive and negative ions in the solution.

**electromagnetic spectrum** A family of waves that travel through a vacuum at a speed of $3.0 \times 10^8\,m\,s^{-1}$.

**electronvolt** The energy gained by an electron travelling through a p.d. of 1 volt. $1\,eV = 1.6 \times 10^{-19}\,J$.

**elementary charge** The smallest unit of charge that a particle or an object can have. It has a magnitude of $1.6 \times 10^{-19}\,C$.

**emission line spectrum** A sharp and bright line of a unique wavelength seen in a spectrum.

**energy level** The quantised energy states of an electron in an atom.

**equation of state** Equation for an ideal gas:

$$pV = nRT \quad \text{or} \quad pV = NkT$$

(Also known as the ideal gas equation.)

**equations of motion** Four equations that can be used to determine quantities such as displacement, initial velocity, final velocity and acceleration.

**equilibrium** An object in equilibrium is either at rest or travelling with a constant velocity because the net force on it is zero.

**errors** Inaccuracies when taking measurements.

**evaporation** The process by which a liquid becomes a gas at a temperature below its boiling point.

**exponential decay graph** A decaying graph that has a constant-ratio property for a given interval of time.

**exponential decay** A quantity that has a 'constant-ratio property' with respect to time.

**extension** The change in the length of a material from its original length.

**farad** The unit of capacitance. $1\,F = 1\,C\,V^{-1}$.

**Faraday's law of electromagnetic induction** The induced e.m.f. is proportional to the rate of change of magnetic flux linkage.

**field lines** Lines drawn to represent the strength and direction of a field of force.

**field of force** A region of space where an object feels a force; the force may be gravitational, electric, magnetic, etc.

**First law of thermodynamics** The increase in internal energy of a body is equal to the thermal energy transferred to it by heating plus the mechanical work done on it.

**Fleming's left-hand (motor) rule** This rule is used to predict the force experienced by a current-carrying conductor placed in an external magnetic field: thu<u>mb</u> → <u>m</u>otion, <u>first</u> finger → magnetic <u>field</u> and se<u>c</u>ond finger → conventional <u>c</u>urrent.

**Fleming's right-hand (generator) rule** This rule is used to predict the direction of the induced current or e.m.f. in a conductor moved at right angles to a magnetic field: thu<u>mb</u> → <u>m</u>otion, <u>first</u> finger → magnetic <u>field</u> and se<u>c</u>ond finger → induced conventional <u>c</u>urrent.

**force constant** The ratio of force to extension for a spring or a wire. Unit: $N\,m^{-1}$.

**forced oscillation** An oscillation caused by an external driving force whose frequency is equal to that of the driving force.

**free oscillation** An oscillation whose frequency is the natural frequency of the oscillator.

**frequency** The number of oscillations of a particle per unit time. Unit: hertz (Hz).

**frequency modulation** A form of modulation where the signal causes variations in the frequency of a carrier wave.

**fundamental frequency** The lowest-frequency stationary wave for a particular system.

**gain** The voltage gain of an amplifier is the ratio of the output voltage to the input voltage.

**geostationary orbit** The orbit of an artificial satellite which has a period equal to one day so that the satellite remains above the same point on the Earth's equator. From Earth the satellite appears to be stationary.

**gravitational field** A region where any object with mass experiences a force.

**gravitational field strength** The gravitational force experienced by an object per unit mass:

$$g = \frac{F}{m}$$

**gravitational potential** The gravitational potential energy per unit mass at a point in a gravitational field.

**gravitational potential energy** The energy a body has due to its position in a gravitational field.

**ground state** The lowest energy state that can be occupied by an electron in an atom.

**half-life** The mean time taken for half the number of active nuclei in a radioactive sample to decay.

**harmonic** A wave of frequency $n$ times the fundamental frequency, where $n$ is an integer.

**Hooke's law** The extension produced in an object is proportional to the force producing it, provided the elastic limit is not exceeded.

**hydrogen burning** A sequence of nuclear reactions in which four protons fuse together to produce a helium nucleus:

$$4\,{}^{1}_{1}H \rightarrow {}^{4}_{2}He + 2\,{}^{0}_{+1}e$$

**ideal gas equation** Equation for an ideal gas:

$$pV = nRT \quad \text{or} \quad pV = NkT$$

(Also known as the equation of state.)

**ideal gas** A gas that behaves according to the equations $pV = nRT$ and $pV = NkT$.

**image intensifier** A device used to change a low-intensity X-ray image into a bright visual image.

**impedance matching** The reduction in intensity of reflected ultrasound at the boundary between two substances, achieved when the two substances have similar acoustic impedances.

**impulse** The product of the force $F$ and the time $\Delta t$ for which it acts:

$$\text{impulse} = F\Delta t$$

**independent variable** The variable which changes when the dependent variable changes.

**induced nuclear fission** A fission reaction started when a neutron is absorbed by a nucleus.

**inelastic** A collision is inelastic when the kinetic energy is not conserved; some is transferred to other forms such as heat. Momentum and total energy are always conserved.

**inertia** A measure of the mass of an object. A massive object has a large inertia.

**instantaneous speed** The speed of an object measured over a very short period of time.

**intensity** The power transmitted normally through a surface per unit area:

$$\text{intensity} = \frac{\text{power}}{\text{cross-sectional area}}$$

Unit: $W\,m^{-2}$.

**interference** The formation of points of cancellation and reinforcement where two coherent waves pass through each other.

**internal energy** The sum of the random distribution of kinetic and potential energies of the atoms or molecules in a system.

**internal resistance** The resistance of an e.m.f. source. The internal resistance of a battery is due to its chemicals.

**inverting amplifier** A circuit, involving the use of an amplifier, where the output is 180° out of phase with the input.

**ion** An atom with a net positive or negative charge.

**isotopes** Nuclei of the same element with a different number of neutrons but the same number of protons.

**I–V characteristic** A graph of current against voltage for a particular component. You can identify a component from its I–V graph.

**kilowatt-hour** The energy transferred by a 1 kW device in a time of 1 hour. 1 kW h = 3.6 MJ.

**kinematics** A study of motion using quantities such as time, distance, displacement, speed, velocity and acceleration.

**kinetic energy** Energy of an object due to its motion.

**kinetic theory of gases** A model based on the microscopic motion of atoms or molecules of a gas.

**Kirchhoff's first law** The sum of the currents entering any point (or junction) in a circuit is equal to the sum of the currents leaving that same point. This law conveys the conservation of charge.

**Kirchhoff's second law** The sum of the e.m.f.s round a closed loop in a circuit is equal to the sum of p.d.s in that same loop.

**Larmor frequency** The frequency of precession of nuclei in an external magnetic field.

**Lenz's law** The induced current or e.m.f. is in a direction so as to produce effects which oppose the change producing it.

**light-dependent resistor (LDR)** A resistor whose resistance decreases as the intensity of light falling on it increases.

**light-emitting diode (LED)** A semiconductor component that emits light when it conducts.

**linear momentum** The product of an object's mass and its velocity, $p = mv$. Momentum is a vector quantity.

**longitudinal wave** A wave in which particles oscillate along the direction in which the wave travels.

**lost volts** The difference between the e.m.f. and the terminal p.d. It is also equal to the voltage across the internal resistance.

**macroscopic** Visible to the naked eye.

**magnetic field** A force field in which a magnet, a wire carrying a current, or a moving charge experiences a force.

**magnetic flux density** The strength of a magnetic field. Magnetic flux density $B$ is defined as:

$$B = \frac{F}{Il}$$

where $F$ is the force experienced by a conductor in the magnetic field, $I$ is the current in the conductor and $l$ is the length of the conductor in the magnetic field. (The conductor is at right angles to the field.)

**magnetic flux linkage** The product of magnetic flux and the number of turns. Unit: weber (Wb).

**magnetic flux** The product of magnetic flux density normal to a circuit and the cross-sectional area of the circuit. Unit: weber (Wb).

**magnetic resonance imaging (MRI)** a medical imaging technique which uses nuclear magnetic resonance.

**mass** A measure of the amount of matter within an object. Unit: kilogram (kg).

**mass defect** The difference between the total mass of the individual, separate nucleons and the mass of the nucleus.

**mean drift velocity** The average speed of charged particles along the length of a conductor.

**microscopic** Too small to be viewed with the naked eye.

**microwave link** A communications system that uses a beam of radio waves in the microwave frequency range to transmit audio, data or video information.

**mobile phone (cell phone)** An electronic device used for mobile communication by connecting to a cellular network of base stations.

**moderator** A material used in a nuclear reactor to slow down fast-moving neutrons so that they have a greater chance of interacting with the fissile nuclei.

**modulation** The process of using one waveform to alter the frequency, amplitude or phase of another waveform.

**mole** The amount of matter which contains $6.02 \times 10^{23}$ particles.

**moment** The moment of a force about a point is the magnitude of the force, multiplied by the perpendicular distance of the point from the line of the force. Unit: N m.

**natural frequency** The unforced frequency of oscillation of a freely oscillating object.

**negative feedback** The output of a system acts to oppose changes to the input of the system, with the result that the changes are reduced.

**neutron number** The number of neutrons in the nucleus of an atom.

**newton** The force that will give a 1 kg mass an acceleration of $1\,\mathrm{m\,s^{-2}}$ in the direction of the force. $1\,\mathrm{N} = 1\,\mathrm{kg\,m\,s^{-2}}$.

**Newton's first law of motion** An object will remain at rest or keep travelling at constant velocity unless it is acted on by an external force.

**Newton's law of gravitation** Any two point masses attract each other with a force that is directly proportional to the product of their masses and inversely proportional to the square of their separation.

**Newton's second law of motion** The net force acting on an object is equal to the rate of change of its momentum. The net force and the change in momentum are in the same direction.

**Newton's third law of motion** When two bodies interact, the forces they exert on each other are equal and opposite.

**node** A point on a stationary wave with zero amplitude.

**noise** An unwanted random addition to a transmitted signal.

**non-inverting amplifier** A circuit, involving the use of an amplifier, where the output is in phase with the input.

**nuclear fission** The splitting of a nucleus (e.g. $^{235}_{92}\mathrm{U}$) into two large fragments and a small number of neutrons.

**nuclear fusion** A nuclear reaction where two light nuclei (e.g. $^{2}_{1}\mathrm{H}$) join together to form a heavier but more stable nucleus.

**nuclear magnetic resonance** A process in which radio waves are absorbed or emitted by nuclei spinning in a magnetic field.

**nuclear model of the atom** A model of the atom in which negative charges (electrons) are distributed outside a tiny nucleus of positive charge.

**nucleon number** The number of neutrons and protons in the nucleus of an atom (also called mass number).

**nucleon** A particle found in an atomic nucleus, i.e. a neutron or a proton.

**nucleus** The tiny central region of the atom that contains most of the mass of the atom and all of its positive charge.

**nuclide** A specific combination of protons and neutrons in a nucleus.

**Ohm's law** The current in a metallic conductor is directly proportional to the potential difference across its ends, provided its temperature remains constant.

**operational amplifier (op-amp)** A high-gain electronic d.c. voltage amplifier with differential inputs and, usually, a single output.

**optic fibre** A glass or plastic fibre that carries light along its length.

**oscillates** Another term for 'vibrates'.

**oscillation** A repetitive back-and-forth or up-and-down motion.

**parallel** A term used when components are connected across each other in a circuit.

**path difference** The difference in the distances travelled by two waves from coherent sources at a particular point.

**perfectly elastic** A collision is perfectly elastic when kinetic energy is conserved. Momentum and total energy are always conserved.

**period** The time taken by an object (e.g. a planet) to complete one orbit. The period is also the time taken for one complete oscillation of a vibrating object. Unit: second (s).

**phase difference** The fraction of an oscillation between the vibrations of two oscillating particles, expressed in degrees or radians.

**phase** Describes the point that an oscillating mass has reached in a complete cycle.

**photoelectric effect** An interaction between a photon and an electron in which the electron is removed from the atom.

**photomultiplier tubes** Devices used in a gamma camera to change the energy of an incident γ-ray photon into an electrical pulse.

**photon** A quantum of electromagnetic energy.

**piezo-electric crystal** A material that produces an e.m.f. when it is compressed. Also, when a voltage is applied across it in one direction, it shrinks slightly.

**piezo-electric effect** The production of an e.m.f. across the faces of a crystal when the crystal is compressed.

**Planck constant** The constant which links the energy of a photon and its frequency, given by the equation:

$$E = hf$$

**plane polarised** Describes transverse waves that oscillate in only one plane.

**plastic deformation** The deformation of a material beyond the elastic limit.

**plum pudding model** A model of the atom in which negative charges are distributed throughout a sphere of positive charge.

**point mass** An object with mass that is represented as a point (dot) because its size is extremely small compared with the separation between objects.

**polymer** A material containing large molecules composed of repeating structural units.

**positron** A positively charged particle with mass equal to that of an electron.

**potential difference (p.d.)** The energy lost per unit charge by charges passing through a component. Unit: $J\,C^{-1}$ or volt (V).

**potential divider** A circuit in which two or more components are connected in series to a supply. The output voltage from the circuit is taken across one of the components.

**potentiometer** A circuit which allows the measurement of an e.m.f. by comparison with a known e.m.f.

**power** The rate at which energy is transferred or the rate at which work is done. Unit: watt (W).

**precession** The movement of the axis of a spinning object (proton) around another axis.

**precision** The smallest change in value that can be measured by an instrument or an operator. A precise measurement is one obtained several times and achieving the same, or very similar, values.

**pressure** The force acting normally per unit area of a surface:

$$p = \frac{F}{A}$$

Unit: $N\,m^{-2}$ or Pa.

**principle of moments** The sum of clockwise moments about a point is equal to the sum of anticlockwise moments about the same point for a body in equilibrium.

**principle of superposition** When two or more waves meet at a point, the resultant displacement is the sum of the displacements of the individual waves.

**progressive wave** A wave that carries energy from one place to another.

**projectile** Any object thrown in the Earth's gravitational field.

**proton number** The number of protons in the nucleus of an atom (also called atomic number).

**public switched telephone network** The network which connects public telephones throughout the world.

**radian** An alternative unit for measuring angles. $2\pi$ radians = 360° or $\pi$ radians = 180°.

**range** The horizontal distance covered by an object.

**rarefaction** A region in a sound wave where the air pressure is less than its mean value.

**rectification** The process of converting alternating current (a.c.) into direct current (d.c.).

**reflection** The bouncing back of a wave from a surface.

**refraction** The change in direction of a wave as it crosses an interface between two materials where its speed changes.

**regeneration** Restoring a signal to its original form, usually removing or reducing noise and increasing signal strength.

**relative speed** The magnitude of the difference in velocities between two objects.

**relaxation time** The time taken for the nuclei to fall back to their lower energy state.

**relay** An electrically operated switch, caused to open and close by current in a coil.

**repeater** An electronic device that receives a signal and retransmits it.

**resistivity** The property of a material defined by:

$$\text{resistivity} = \frac{\text{resistance} \times \text{cross-sectional area}}{\text{length}}$$

$$\rho = \frac{RA}{L}$$

Unit: $\Omega\,\text{m}$.

**resistor** An electrical component whose resistance in a circuit remains constant. Its resistance is independent of current or potential difference.

**resonance** The forced motion of an oscillator characterised by maximum amplitude when the forcing frequency matches the oscillator's natural frequency. A system absorbs maximum energy from a source when the source frequency is equal to the natural frequency of the system.

**rest mass** The mass of a an isolated stationary particle.

**resultant force** The net force acting on an object.

**resultant** Total or net.

**right-hand grip rule** A rule for finding the direction of the magnetic field inside a solenoid. If the right hand grips the solenoid with the fingers following the direction of the current around the solenoid, then the thumb points in the direction of the magnetic field.

**sampling** Taking the value of a continuous signal at regular intervals.

**scalar quantity** A scalar quantity has magnitude but no direction.

**semiconductor diode** An electrical component made from a semiconductor material (e.g. silicon) that only conducts in one direction. A diode in 'reverse bias' has an infinite resistance.

**sensor** A device that produces an output (usually a voltage) in response to an input.

**series** A term used when components are connected end-to-end in a circuit.

**sharpness** The degree of resolution in an image, which determines the smallest item that can be identified.

**sidebands** A band of frequencies above or below the carrier frequency produced as a result of modulation.

**simple harmonic motion** Motion of an oscillator where its acceleration is directly proportional to its displacement from its equilibrium position and is directed towards that position.

**solenoid** A long current-carrying coil used to generate a uniform magnetic field within its core.

**specific heat capacity** The energy required per unit mass of a substance to raise its temperature by $1\,\text{K}$ (or $1\,°\text{C}$). Unit: $\text{J}\,\text{kg}^{-1}\,\text{K}^{-1}$.

**specific latent heat of fusion** The energy required per kilogram of a substance to change it from solid to liquid without a change in temperature. Unit: $\text{J}\,\text{kg}^{-1}$.

**specific latent heat of vaporisation** The energy required per kilogram of a substance to change it from liquid to gas without a change in temperature. Unit: $\text{J}\,\text{kg}^{-1}$.

**speed** The rate of change of the distance moved by an object:

$$\text{speed} = \frac{\text{distance}}{\text{time}}$$

Unit: $\text{m}\,\text{s}^{-1}$.

**speed** The rate of change of the distance moved by an object:

**spin** A fundamental property of subatomic particles which is conserved during atomic and nuclear reactions.

**stationary wave** A wave pattern produced when two progressive waves of the same frequency travelling in opposite directions combine. It is characterised by nodes and antinodes. Also known as a standing wave.

**strain energy** The potential energy stored in an object when it is deformed elastically.

**strain gauge** A device that contains a fine wire sealed in plastic. Its electrical resistance changes when the object to which it is attached changes shape.

**strain** The extension per unit length produced by tensile or compressive forces:

$$\text{strain} = \frac{\text{extension}}{\text{original length}}$$

**stress** The force acting per unit cross-sectional area:

$$\text{strain} = \frac{\text{force}}{\text{cross-sectional area}}$$

**systematic error** An error in readings which is repeated through out an experiment, either producing a constant absolute error or a constant percentage error.

**tensile** A term used to denote tension or pull.

**terminal p.d.** The potential difference across the external resistor connected to an e.m.f. source.

**terminal velocity** The constant velocity of an object travelling through a fluid. The net force on the object is zero.

**tesla** The SI unit for magnetic flux density. Unit: tesla (T). $1\,T = 1\,N\,A^{-1}\,m^{-1}$.

**thermal energy** Energy transferred from one object to another because of a temperature difference; another term for heat energy.

**thermal equilibrium** A condition when two or more objects in contact have the same temperature so that there is no net flow of energy between them.

**thermistor** A device whose electrical resistance changes when its temperature changes.

**thermocouple** A device consisting of wires of two different metals across which an e.m.f. is produced when the two junctions of the wires are at different temperatures

**thermodynamic scale** A temperature scale where temperature is measured in kelvin (K).

**threshold frequency** The minimum frequency of the electromagnetic radiation that will eject electrons from the surface of a metal.

**threshold voltage** The minimum forward bias voltage across a light-emitting diode (LED) when it starts to conduct and emit light.

**time constant** The time taken for the current, charge stored or p.d. to fall to 1/e (about 37%) when a capacitor discharges through a resistor. It is also equal to the product of capacitance and resistance.

**torque** The product of one of the forces of a couple and the perpendicular distance between them. Unit: N m.

**tracers** Radioactive substances used to investigate the function of organs of the body.

**transducer** A general term used for any device that changes one form of energy into another.

**transition** When an electron makes a 'jump' between two energy levels.

**transverse wave** A wave in which the oscillation is at right angles to the direction in which the wave travels.

**triangle of forces** A closed triangle drawn for an object in equilibrium. The sides of the triangle represent the forces in both magnitude and direction.

**turns-ratio equation** An equation relating the ratio of voltages to the ratio of numbers of turns on the two coils of a transformer:

$$\frac{V_s}{V_p} = \frac{n_s}{n_p}$$

**ultimate tensile stress (UTS)** The maximum stress that a material can withstand.

$$UTS = \frac{maximum\ force}{cross\text{-}sectional\ area}$$

**unified atomic mass unit** A convenient unit used for the mass of atomic and nuclear particles (1 u is equal to $\frac{1}{12}$ the mass of a $^{12}_{6}C$ carbon atom). $1\,u = 1.66 \times 10^{-27}\,kg$.

**uniform acceleration** Acceleration that remains constant.

**uniform motion** Motion of an object travelling with a constant acceleration.

**upthrust** The upward force that a liquid exerts on a body floating or immersed in a liquid.

**vector addition** Using a drawing, often to scale, to find the resultant vector.

**vector quantity** A vector quantity has both magnitude and direction.

**vector triangle** A triangle drawn to determine the resultant of two vectors.

**velocity** The rate of change of the displacement of an object:

$$velocity = \frac{change\ in\ displacement}{time}$$

Unit: $m\,s^{-1}$. (You can think of velocity as 'speed in a certain direction'.)

**virtual earth approximation** An approximation where the two inputs of an op-amp are taken to be at the same potential.

**viscous forces** Forces that act on a body moving through a fluid that are caused by the resistance of the fluid.

**voxel** A small cube in a three dimensional picture, the equivalent of a pixel in a two-dimensional picture.

**wave** A periodic disturbance travelling through space, characterised by vibrating particles.

**wavelength** The distance between two adjacent peaks or troughs.

**weight** The force on an object caused by a gravitational field acting on its mass:

$$weight = mass \times acceleration\ of\ free\ fall$$

Unit: newton (N).

**wire-pair** A form of wiring in which the two conductors needed to carry a signal are placed close together.

**work done** The product of the force and the distance moved by the force in the direction of travel.

**work function** The minimum energy required by a single electron to escape the metal surface.

**X-ray tube** A device that produces X-rays when accelerated electrons hit a target metal.

**Young modulus** The ratio of stress to strain for a given material, resulting from tensile forces, provided Hooke's law is obeyed:

$$\text{Young modulus} = \frac{\text{stress}}{\text{strain}}$$

Unit: Pa (or MPa, GPa).

**zero error** A systematic error in an instrument that gives a non-zero reading when the true value of a quantity is zero.

# Index

absolute zero, 317, 318
absorption line spectra, 441
acceleration, 15–23, 26–8, 40–2, 263–5, 293–4, 296–7
acoustic impedance, 500–2
air columns, 235, 237
air resistance, 45, 49
alpha-decay, 249
alpha-particles, 242–4, 249, 250, 251, 252
alpha radiation, 249, 251, 252–3
alternating currents, 416–27
alternating voltages, 417
ammeters, 165–6
amorphous polymers, 110
ampere, 147
amplitude, 196, 199, 289–90
amplitude modulation (AM), 513–14
AM transmission, 516
analogue signals, 517, 518, 528, 530
analogue-to-digital conversion (ADC), 518
angles in radians, 259
angular displacement, 258, 259, 267
angular frequency, 294, 297, 417, 504
angular momentum, 94
angular velocity, 261, 262, 265, 267, 505
antinodes, 232, 233, 234, 235, 236, 238
atomic structure, 110, 245, 432
atoms, 111, 242, 243, 251, 444
attraction, 132–3

balanced forces, 48, 64–7
bandwidth, 515–16
Barton's pendulums, 302, 303
base stations, 528
base units, 42, 381
beta-decay, 249, 250
beta-particles, 249, 250, 251
beta-radiation, 249, 253
binding energy, 458, 459
Boyle's law, 332, 336, 338
braking radiation, 489
breaking point, 124
Bremsstrahlung radiation, 489
bridge rectifiers, 425–6
brittle, 124, 125
Brownian motion, 111–12, 341

calibrated meters, 481–2
capacitance, 356–66
capacitors, 356–9, 361–3, 364, 426
carrier waves, 512–17, 529
cast iron, 124
cathode-ray oscilloscopes (c.r.o.), 418–19
cell phone network, 528–30
cellular exchange, 529
centre of gravity, 44, 62–3
centripetal acceleration, 263, 264, 265
centripetal forces, 262, 266–7, 390

changes of state, 107, 113–14, 312
channels of communication, 520–3
charge carriers, 146, 148
charged particles, 146, 148, 171, 202, 344, 387–95, 435, 524
charge of electron, 393–4
charge storage, 357
charge-to-mass ratio of electron, 390–1
Charles's law, 333, 334, 336
circuit design, 157
circuit symbols and diagrams, 144–5
circular motion, 258–67, 294
climbing bars, 82–4
clocks, 258–9
closed systems, 85, 94, 103, 250
coaxial cables, 520, 523–4
coherence, 219–20
collimated beam, 488, 490, 493
collisions, 92, 93, 95–6, 330
combining displacements, 9–10
combining forces, 57–9
combining velocities, 10–11
combining waves, 212–26
compressive forces, 119–20, 316
computer-aided design (CAD), 157
computerised axial tomography (CAT), 494–8
conduction, 146, 177, 178, 437
conservation of charge, 158
conservation of energy, 162
conservation of momentum, 94
constant phase difference, 219, 226
constructive interference, 217, 218, 224, 226
contact force, 51–3, 57, 60–2, 108, 266, 267
contrast media, 493, 494
conventional current, 146, 387, 388, 402, 407
copper, 124
Coulomb's law, 343–52
count rate, 461
crash-landings, 98–9
crosslinking, 520
crystalline materials, 110
curved trajectory, 30–1

damped oscillations, 300–1
damping, 302, 304
de Broglie wavelength, 445
decay constant, 461, 463, 464
decay graphs and equations, 462
deformation, 124
density, 107–8
derived units, 42, 381, 382
destructive interference, 217, 218, 226
dielectrics, 356, 357, 358
diffraction, 213–15
diffraction gratings, 223–4, 225
digital signals, 517–18
digital-to-analogue conversion (DAC), 518

direct current, 419–20
dispersion, 225
displacement, 4, 7–8, 9–10, 18–19, 195, 196, 213, 289, 290, 293, 296–7
distance, 4
drag, 49, 51
driver cells, 189, 190
ductile metals, 124, 125

Earth, 99, 139, 265, 273, 278, 280
echo sounding, 498, 500–1
eddy currents, 410, 412
Einstein relation, 434
Einstein's mass–energy equation, 455–6
elastic hysteresis, 125
elastic limit, 120, 124–8
elastic potential energy, 126–7, 299
electrical cells, 183
electrical components, 144, 145, 151, 174
electrical forces, 53
electrical power, 151, 419–20, 424
electrical resistance, 149–50, 152
electric charges, 132, 147, 365
electric currents, 145–6, 147, 378–80, 424
electric fields, 134–5, 136, 251–2, 343, 345, 349, 350–1, 391–2
electricity, 145, 421
electric potential, 346, 348, 349
electric potential energy, 79, 346–7
electrolytes, 146, 147
electromagnetic force, 134, 202
electromagnetic induction, 399–412, 417
electromagnetic radiation, 199, 202, 203, 249, 437, 487, 504
electromagnetic spectrum, 202, 204, 433
electromagnetic waves, 202–3, 204, 434, 438, 445
electromagnets, 371
electromotive force (e.m.f.), 149, 161, 185, 190, 402, 407, 409, 410
electron beams, 388, 391
electron beam tubes, 387
electron diffraction, 445–7
electronic sensors, 469
electronic timers, 28
electrons, 390–1, 393–4, 445–7, 448
electronvolt, 435
electron waves, 444–5
electrostatic forces, 244, 351, 438
electrostatic repulsion, 244
elementary charge, 148
emission line spectra, 441, 442, 449
energy, 73–4, 153, 277, 299, 302, 348, 454, 457
energy changes, 313, 320, 347
energy conservation, 83, 84–5
energy graphs, 299–300
energy levels, 442
energy storage, 358–9, 360
energy transfers, 74, 75, 80–1, 82–4, 148, 153
energy transformation, 81
energy units, 75
errors, 238–9, 322, 536

evaporation, 114, 314, 315
explosions, 98–9, 454
exponential decay, 462

Faraday's law of electromagnetic induction, 405
field of force, 134
first law of thermodynamics, 316
Fleming's left-hand (motor) rule, 374
Fleming's right-hand (generator) rule, 401
fluid resistance, 49–50
fluids theory, 133
fluoroscopy, 492
FM transmission, 516
forced oscillations, 287–8
forces, 41–2, 50–1, 57–9, 76, 120, 125, 138–9, 264–5, 380, 387–8
free electrons, 146
free fall, 48–9
free oscillations, 287–8
frequency, 196, 197, 294
frequency modulation (FM), 514–15
friction, 51, 133
fringe separation, 221
fundamental frequency, 236, 237
fundamental mode of vibration, 236
fuses, 151

gain, 474
gamma-emission, 249
gamma radiation, 249, 251, 253, 433
gas atoms, 111
gases, 77, 316, 330–2
Geiger–Müller (GM) tube, 252, 253, 254, 461
generators, 410–11
geostationary orbit, 280, 281, 526
glass, 110, 124
gold, 124
graphs (acceleration against time), 293–4
graphs (displacement against distance), 196
graphs (displacement against time), 7–8, 213, 289, 290, 293
graphs (force against extension), 125
graphs (stress against strain), 123, 124
graphs (velocity against time), 17, 18, 25, 293
gravitational fields, 45, 272, 273, 275–6, 277, 278, 350–1
gravitational forces, 53, 99, 139, 262, 265
gravitational potential, 277–8
gravitational potential energy (GPE), 78, 79, 80–1
gravitational pull, 44–5
gravity, 26–30, 272–82
ground state, 443
gyromagnetic ratio, 505

half-life, 462–3, 464
Hall probe, 376, 377
heating ice, 313–14
Helmholtz coils, 391–2
high-speed trains, 371
Hooke's law, 120, 124, 127
horizontal polarisation, 205
human power, 87

*I–V* characteristic, 172
ice, 313–14
ideal gases, 330–40
image intensifiers, 492
impedance matching, 502, 508
inelastic collision, 96–7
inertia, 41, 46–7, 390
instantaneous speed, 1
intensifier screens, 491
intensity, 199
interference, 216–18, 218, 219, 220
interference fringes, 220, 222
internal energy, 83, 315–16
internal resistance, 184–5, 186
inverting amplifiers, 478–9
ionisation, 251
ions, 247
isolated atoms, 444
isotopes, 246–8

joules, 75

Kelvin scale, 317–18, 331
kinetic energy, 79–81, 251, 299, 300, 316, 338–9
kinetic model of a gas, 336
kinetic model of matter, 110
kinetic theory of gases, 336
Kirchhoff's first law, 157–8, 160–2
Kirchhoff's second law, 159–60, 161
Kundt's dust tube, 237

Larmor frequency, 504, 505, 507
Lenz's law, 405, 407, 409, 410
light beams, 203, 214–15, 218, 431, 433, 444
light-dependent resistors (LDR), 187, 469, 470
light-emitting diodes (LED), 173, 357, 425, 435–6, 481
light gates, 3, 19, 29–30
linear momentum, 94, 96, 101
line spectra, 440–3
liquid-crystal displays, 207
longitudinal waves, 198, 204, 205, 235, 236, 498
lost volts, 185, 190, 191, 475
loudspeakers, 216–19, 289, 473

magnetic fields, 202, 251–2, 371–3, 391–2, 400–2, 408
magnetic flux, 401, 403, 407
magnetic flux density, 375–7, 403
magnetic flux linkage, 403, 411
magnetic forces, 374–5, 389
magnetic levitation, 371
magnetic resonance imaging (MRI), 304–5, 504–6
magnets, 371, 399–400
magnitude, 203
mass, 41–2, 45–6, 250, 331–2, 454–5
mass defect, 456, 458, 459
mass–energy conservation, 456
mass–energy relationship, 250, 454
mass–spring system, 288, 289, 299, 303
mathematical decay, 463
matter, 107

maximum current, 151, 186
mechanical waves, 196, 199, 201
medical diagnosis, 487
medical imaging, 487–508
Melde's experiment, 233, 234
metallic conductors, 150, 172, 173, 179, 180
metal-wire strain gauge, 472–3
metric units, 75
micro-mechanical acceleration sensors, 19
microwave links, 520, 524–6
microwaves, 215, 219, 234
microwave transmitters, 205, 206, 219, 234
Millikan's oil-drop experiment, 393
mobile phones, 528–30
molecular energy, 316
molecules, 112, 245, 330–1, 337, 338–9
moments of forces, 63–4
momentum, 92, 97, 100
monochromatic light, 223, 224
Moon, 45–6, 272, 280
motion in two dimensions, 30
motion sensors, 4, 20–1, 292, 293
MRI scanners, 506–7
musical instruments, 236–7

natural frequency, 287, 288, 302–4, 505
negative feedback, 474, 477–8
negative temperature coefficient (NTC) thermistors, 187
neutron number, 246, 249
neutrons, 249
newtons, 42, 75
Newton's first law of motion, 47, 100, 262
Newton's law of gravitation, 273–5, 344
Newton's second law of motion, 41, 101–2, 265
Newton's third law of motion, 53, 102–3, 273
non-inverting amplifiers, 479–80
non-uniform acceleration, 25–6
nuclear density, 245–6
nuclear fission, 460
nuclear fusion, 460
nuclear model of atoms, 243
nuclei, 242–4, 245
nucleon number, 246, 247
nucleons, 246

ohm, 149
ohmic components, 173
Ohm's law, 173–4
open-ended air columns, 235–6
operational amplifiers (op-amps), 473–6
optic fibres, 520, 526–8
orbital speed, 265
orbiting charges, 389–90
orbits, 278–80
order of atoms, 110
oscillations, 287–306
oscilloscopes, 388, 418–19

particle models, 107, 110, 431–2, 433
pendulums, 287, 288, 291, 292, 302, 303

people waves, 447
perfectly elastic collision, 96
period, 196, 279–80, 289–90
periodic table, 557
permanent magnets, 375
permittivity of free space, 344
Perspex, 124
phase, 198–9, 290
phase difference, 198–9, 218, 219, 290
photoelectric effect, 433–4, 437–9, 441
photons, 249, 254, 433–4, 438, 443
piezo-electric crystals, 499
piezo-electric effects, 470
piezo-electric transducers, 470
Planck constant, 434, 435, 445
plane polarised light, 205, 207
plastic deformation, 124
plum pudding model, 242, 244
point charges, 135, 344, 345, 352
point masses, 273, 274, 277, 345
polarisation, 204–5
polarised light, 205–6
Polaroid sunglasses, 206
polymers, 110
polythene, 124
potential difference, 149, 172, 190, 346
potential dividers, 186–8, 190, 470, 476
potential energy, 78, 79, 278, 299, 300, 313, 316
potentiometer circuits, 189–90
potentiometers, 189
power, 85, 86–7, 152
power lines, 421, 422
prefixes, 44
pressure, 108–9, 112–13, 331
Principle of Conservation of Energy, 85
principle of moments, 64–6
principle of superposition, 213, 216
progressive waves, 195, 231
projectiles, 30–4
proton number, 246, 247
protons, 245, 249
public switched telephone network (PSTN), 528
pull of gravity, 44–5
pushes and pulls, 51

quantisation of charge, 394
quantum physics, 431–49

radar guns, 2
radiation from radioactive substances, 249
radiation penetration, 252
radioactive decay, 249, 254, 457, 460–1
radioactivity, 242–55
radioisotopes, 460, 462, 465
radio telescopes, 195
radio waves, 215, 512–13, 524–6
real gases, 334
rectification, 424–5
rectifiers, 425–6
relays, 480–1

repeaters, 522, 527, 528, 533
repulsion, 132–3
resistance, 174, 176–7
resistivity, 177–8
resistors, 162–4, 172, 363
resonance, 235, 302–5
resonance tubes, 235
rest mass, 455
resultant forces, 48, 52, 57, 58, 59, 266, 293
resultant velocity, 11
right-hand grip rule, 373
ripples in water, 213–14
ripple tanks, 217–18
road traffic accidents, 25
root-mean-square (r.m.s.), 420–1
rubber, 125

scalar quantity, 4
semiconductor diodes, 145, 173, 179
sensor components, 469–70
sensors, 469
shock waves, 200, 304
sidebands, 515–16
signal attenuation, 520–3, 527, 528, 531
signal noises, 517–18
sign conventions, 58
simple harmonic motion (s.h.m.), 291–3, 299
sinusoidal currents, 416
SI units, 42, 43, 381–2, 554
slit separation, 221, 225
slit-to-screen distance, 221
solenoids, 371, 372, 373, 409
sound waves, 214–15, 216, 236, 238, 512
specific heat capacity, 320–1
specific latent heat, 323–4
speed, 1, 3–4, 5–6, 203, 237–8, 260
speed cameras, 2, 42
spontaneous decay, 254–5
springs, 121, 302
spring–trolley systems, 292
springy collisions, 93
stationary waves, 231–9
steady speed, 16, 27, 46, 47, 49, 79, 139, 197, 260, 262, 263
step-down transformers, 422–3
step-up transformers, 422–3
sticky collisions, 93
strain, 121–2
strain energy, 126
strain gauges, 469, 472–3, 482, 484
strength of materials, 125
stress, 121–2, 123, 124, 207
stretched strings, 233–4
stretching materials, 121–3
superconductivity, 171
superconductors, 171
superposition of waves, 212–13

temperature, 174, 178, 317, 331, 333–4, 338–9
tensile forces, 119–20
tension, 51

terminal velocity, 48, 49, 394
tesla, 375
thermal energy, 83, 317, 412
thermal equilibrium, 317
thermistors, 175, 469, 471–2
thermocouples, 319
thermodynamic scale, 317–18
thermometers, 318–19
threshold frequency, 437, 438, 439
threshold voltage, 173, 435, 436
ticker-timers, 3–4, 20, 29
top speed, 16, 47–8
torque, 67, 68
transducers, 469, 470, 482, 498–500, 502
transformers, 410, 412, 422–4, 474
transverse waves, 198, 200, 202, 205, 207, 212, 231, 235, 236
triangle of forces, 58–9
turning forces, 63, 67–8
turns-ratio equation for transformer, 423

ultimate tensile stress (UTS), 125
ultrasound scanning, 498–500, 502–4
ultraviolet radiation, 437, 487
unbalanced forces, 48, 59, 64–7, 262
uniform acceleration, 25–6
uniform field, 136–7
uniform motion, 47, 54, 262
units, 2, 6–7, 16–17, 75, 86
upthrust, 51, 52, 330

vapour, 114, 314
variable resistances, 187
vector addition, 9
vector components, 31, 59–61

vector diagrams, 263
vector quantity, 4
velocity, 5–6, 8, 10–11, 15, 19–21, 260, 261, 292, 297
velocity against time graphs, 17, 18, 25, 293
velocity selectors, 392
vertical polarisation, 205
virtual earth approximation, 478
viscous forces, 49
voltage, 148–9, 331, 424
voltmeters, 165–6
volume, 331

watt, 86
wave energy, 199
wave equation, 200–1
wavelength, 196, 204, 221–2, 224, 237–8
wave models, 432, 433, 439, 444, 447
wave–particle duality, 444, 448, 449
waves, 195–6
wave speed, 200
weight, 44, 45–6, 51
white light, 173, 222, 225–6, 440, 441, 443
wire-pair, 520, 523–4
work done, 74–5, 77, 127
work function, 437, 438

X-ray attenuation, 490–1
X-ray images, 491–4
X-rays, 249, 433, 487, 490, 493
X-ray spectrum, 489
X-ray tubes, 488, 489, 495

Young double-slit experiment, 220–1, 225
Young modulus, 119, 122–3, 124